Fodor's

MONTANA & WYOMING

4th Edition

**Where to Stay and Eat
for All Budgets**

**Must-See Sights
and Local Secrets**

Ratings You Can Trust

Fodor's Travel Publications   New York, Toronto, London, Sydney, Auckland
www.fodors.com

FODOR'S MONTANA & WYOMING

Editor: Matthew Lombardi

Editorial Contributors: Linda Cabasin, Carolyn Galgano, Debbie Harmsen, Michael Nalepa

Writers: Joyce Dalton, Dustin Floyd, Jessica Gray, Amy Grisak, Tom Griffith, Brian Kevin, Andrew McKean, Debbie Olson, Ray Sikorski, Shauna Stephenson

Production Editor: Carrie Parker
Maps & Illustrations: Mark Stroud and Henry Colomb, Moon Street Cartography; David Lindroth, Ed Jacobus, *cartographers;* Bob Blake, Rebecca Baer, *map editors;* William Wu, *information graphics*
Design: Fabrizio La Rocca, *creative director;* Guido Caroti, Siobhan O'Hare, *art directors;* Tina Malaney, Chie Ushio, Ann McBride, Jessica Walsh, *designers;* Melanie Marin, *senior picture editor*
Cover Photo: (Glacier National Park, Montana): Tom Bol
Production Manager: Angela L. McLean

4th Edition

ISBN 978-1-4000-0431-7

ISSN 1559-0801

SPECIAL SALES

This book is available at special discounts for bulk purchases for sales promotions or premiums. Special editions, including personalized covers, excerpts of existing books, and corporate imprints, can be created in large quantities for special needs. For more information, write to Special Markets/Premium Sales, 1745 Broadway, MD 6-2, New York, New York 10019, or e-mail specialmarkets@randomhouse.com.

AN IMPORTANT TIP & AN INVITATION

Although all prices, opening times, and other details in this book are based on information supplied to us at press time, changes occur all the time in the travel world, and Fodor's cannot accept responsibility for facts that become outdated or for inadvertent errors or omissions. So **always confirm information when it matters,** especially if you're making a detour to visit a specific place. Your experiences—positive and negative—matter to us. If we have missed or misstated something, **please write to us.** We follow up on all suggestions. Contact the Montana and Wyoming editor at editors@fodors.com or c/o Fodor's at 1745 Broadway, New York, NY 10019.

PRINTED IN THE UNITED STATES OF AMERICA

10 9 8 7 6 5 4 3 2 1

Be a Fodor's Correspondent

Your opinion matters. It matters to us. It matters to your fellow Fodor's travelers, too. And we'd like to hear it. In fact, we need to hear it.

When you share your experiences and opinions, you become an active member of the Fodor's community. That means we'll not only use your feedback to make our books better, but we'll publish your names and comments whenever possible. Throughout our guides, look for "Word of Mouth," excerpts of your unvarnished feedback.

Here's how you can help improve Fodor's for all of us.

Tell us when we're right. We rely on local writers to give you an insider's perspective. But our writers and staff editors—who are the best in the business—depend on you. Your positive feedback is a vote to renew our recommendations for the next edition.

Tell us when we're wrong. We're proud that we update most of our guides every year. But we're not perfect. Things change. Hotels cut services. Museums change hours. Charming cafés lose charm. If our writer didn't quite capture the essence of a place, tell us how you'd do it differently. If any of our descriptions are inaccurate or inadequate, we'll incorporate your changes in the next edition and will correct factual errors at fodors.com immediately.

Tell us what to include. You probably have had fantastic travel experiences that aren't yet in Fodor's. Why not share them with a community of like-minded travelers? Maybe you chanced upon a beach or bistro or B&B that you don't want to keep to yourself. Tell us why we should include it. And share your discoveries and experiences with everyone directly at fodors.com. Your input may lead us to add a new listing or highlight a place we cover with a "Highly Recommended" star or with our highest rating, "Fodor's Choice."

Give us your opinion instantly at our feedback center at www.fodors.com/feedback. You may also e-mail editors@fodors.com with the subject line "Montana and Wyoming Editor." Or send your nominations, comments, and complaints by mail to Montana and Wyoming Editor, Fodor's, 1745 Broadway, New York, NY 10019.

You and travelers like you are the heart of the Fodor's community. Make our community richer by sharing your experiences. Be a Fodor's correspondent.

Happy Trails!

Tim Jarrell, Publisher

CONTENTS

MAPS

ABOUT THIS BOOK

Our Ratings

Sometimes you find terrific travel experiences and sometimes they just find you. But usually the burden is on you to select the right combination of experiences. That's where our ratings come in.

As travelers we've all discovered a place so wonderful that its worthiness is obvious. And sometimes that place is so unique that superlatives don't do it justice: you just have to be there to know. These sights, properties, and experiences get our highest rating, **Fodor's Choice,** indicated by orange stars throughout this book. Black stars highlight sights and properties we deem **Highly Recommended,** places that our writers, editors, and readers praise again and again for consistency and excellence.

By default, there's another category: any place we include in this book is by definition worth your time, unless we say otherwise. And we will.

Disagree with any of our choices? Care to nominate a place or suggest that we rate one more highly? Visit our feedback center at www.fodors.com/feedback.

Budget Well

Hotel and restaurant price categories from ¢ to $$$$ are defined in the opening pages of each chapter. For attractions, we always give standard adult admission fees; reductions are usually available for children, students, and senior citizens. Want to pay with plastic? **AE, D, DC, MC, V** following restaurant and hotel listings indicate whether American Express, Discover, Diners Club, MasterCard, and Visa are accepted.

Restaurants

Unless we state otherwise, restaurants are open for lunch and dinner daily. We mention dress only when there's a specific requirement and reservations only when they're essential or not accepted—it's always best to book ahead.

Hotels

Hotels have private bath, phone, TV, and air-conditioning and operate on the European Plan, meaning without meals, unless we specify that they use the Continental Plan (CP, with a Continental breakfast), Breakfast Plan (BP, with a full breakfast), or Modified American Plan (MAP, with breakfast and dinner), or are all-inclusive (including all meals and most activities). We always list

facilities but not whether you'll be charged an extra fee to use them, so when pricing accommodations, find out what's included.

Many Listings	
★	Fodor's Choice
★	Highly recommended
⊠	Physical address
✛	Directions or Map coordinates
⌂	Mailing address
☎	Telephone
🖷	Fax
⊕	On the Web
✉	E-mail
💷	Admission fee
☉	Open/closed times
Ⓜ	Metro stations
▭	Credit cards
Hotels & Restaurants	
🏨	Hotel
⇌	Number of rooms
⚲	Facilities
⊺⊙⊺	Meal plans
✕	Restaurant
⚳	Reservations
🏛	Dress code
↘	Smoking
⚇	BYOB
Outdoors	
⚶	Golf
⟁	Camping
Other	
♺	Family-friendly
⇨	See also
⊠	Branch address
☞	Take note

1

Experience Montana and Wyoming

WORD OF MOUTH

"The time I spent in Yellowstone is one of the best experiences I have ever had . . . Be prepared to stop and animal watch for an hour at any point in your trip. If you see cars parked a the side of a road, pull over and see what kind of animal they are watching."

—spirobulldog

"We took a three-week vacation to Grand Teton, Yellowstone, and Glacier, with our 15-year-old daughter—you know this kind of teenager, lost without cellphone, internet, or TV. After two "hard days," she began to discover nature, views, wildlife . . . and her parents. At the end of the trip, she wanted to go back next year."

—monpetit

www.fodors.com/community

WHAT'S WHERE

2 **Yellowstone National Park.** When mountain men like John Colter and Jim Bridger first saw the geyser basins of what would become Yellowstone National Park, they knew it was a wondrous place. Today Yellowstone remains just as alluring, and despite the millions of people who visit annually, you can still find solitude and listen to the sounds of nature: bubbling mudpots, steaming geysers, and the wind in the pines.

3 **Grand Teton National Park.** You might think Grand Teton would suffer in comparison to Yellowstone, but when you see the peaks rising out of Jackson Hole, you realize the park is its own spectacular destination. A trip along the backcountry's 200 mi of trails reveals the majesty of what the Shoshone tribes called *Teewinot* (Many Pinnacles).

4 **Northwest Wyoming.** Here you need to keep one thing straight: there's Jackson— the town that's the region's cultural center; then there's Jackson Hole—the area surrounding the town, home to world-class skiing (and called a hole because it's encircled by mountains). To the south is the Wind River range, where you can learn about Native American traditions on the Wind River Reservation.

5 **Southwest Montana.** Larger copper deposits found in the late 19th century make this region central to Montana's long mining history. Today the region's treasures are its untamed national forests and blue-ribbon trout streams. Three of Yellowstone National Park's five entrances are here, as are the incredible Beartooth Highway, the Absaroka-Beartooth Wilderness, and the nation's longest free-flowing river.

6 **Glacier National Park.** The rugged mountains of Glacier draw 2 million visitors each year to hike its 730 mi of trails and take in the blues and emerald greens of its lakes and streams. Going-to-the-Sun Road, running through the center of the park, is one of America's great drives.

7 **Northwest Montana.** Crowned by Glacier National Park, flanked by the Bob Marshall Wilderness Area, and watered by the lakes of the Seeley Valley, northwest Montana is a wild realm of nearly 3 million acres. The National Bison Range, Jewel Basin Hiking Area, Flathead River, and Flathead Lake—the largest body of fresh water in the West—provide some of Montana's finest scenery. The region's largest city, Missoula, is home to the state's liveliest arts community.

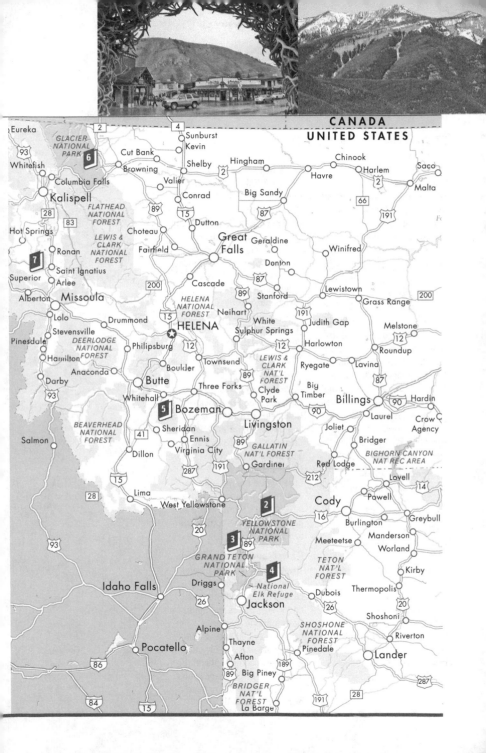

WHAT'S WHERE

8 The Montana Plains. East of the Rocky Mountains are the high plains of Montana, vast expanses of grassy prairie where cattle often outnumber people. Though much of the land has a lonesome, empty look to it, it's rich with the history of America's last frontier.

9 Northern Wyoming. Northern Wyoming is divided almost exactly in half by the Big Horn Mountains. The wide-open plains of the Powder River Basin lie to the east, extending for 150 mi to the Black Hills that straddle the Wyoming–South Dakota border. To the west is the Big Horn Basin, which is nearly as arid as a desert. The storied settlement of Cody sits on its western edge near Yellowstone National Park.

10 Southern Wyoming. Southern Wyoming spans the wheat fields of the southeast, the lush meadows of the Platte River and Bridger valleys, and the wide-open sagebrush lands of the southwest. Cheyenne, Wyoming's state capital, anchors the southeast, and there are major services in Laramie, Rawlins, Rock Springs, Green River, and Evanston, towns that got their start because of the Union Pacific Railroad.

11 The South Dakota Black Hills. A few hundred miles east of the Rockies sit the Black Hills, an ancient mountain range that crosses the Wyoming–South Dakota border. Western legends such as Deadwood Dick and the Sundance Kid once roamed its canyons and prairies; today you can see their legacy in Deadwood, site of one of the country's largest ongoing historic preservation projects. The biggest draw is Mount Rushmore National Memorial, with its unblinking granite faces of four iconic presidents.

12 Wind Cave National Park. Bounded by Black Hills National Forest to the west and prairie to the east, Wind Cave comprises 28,295 acres and two distinct ecosystems—mountain forest and mixed-grass prairie—plus a 125-mi-long cave, one of the largest in the world. There's great hiking here, both above and below ground.

13 Badlands National Park. The eroded buttes and spires of Badlands National Park cast amazing shades of red and yellow across the South Dakota prairie. Badlands occupies 244,000 acres about 80 mi east of Rapid City, but it feels like another planet. In addition to the scenery, it has some of the world's richest mammal fossil beds.

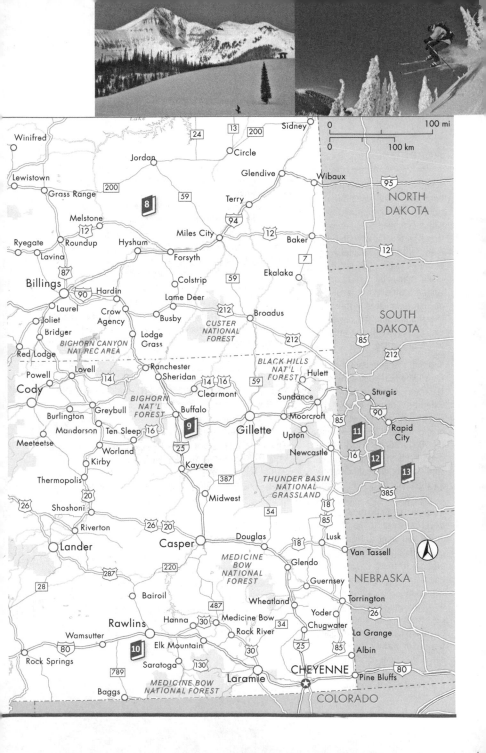

MONTANA AND WYOMING PLANNER

Living with Animals

Whether they're wrangling a herd of cattle, waiting for a trout to bite, or sharing a trail with a mountain goat, people in these parts interact with other members of the animal kingdom to a degree you just don't find in many other places in the United States. What results is an unromanticized respect for the animals and the places in which they live. It's an attitude worth emulating.

Spotting the abundant, beautiful wildlife that populates Montana and Wyoming is a thrill, whether you're driving the Grand Loop in Yellowstone or hiking through the backcountry. The locals get a kick out of it, too—but they know to tread softly and keep a safe distance, for the animals' benefit as well as their own. In the wilderness, give all animals their space, never attempt to feed them, and if you want to take photographs, bring a long lens—don't attempt to sneak in close for a good shot. To avoid encounters with dangerous animals such as bears and mountain lions, be conspicuous when you're on the hiking trail by making noise. For further information, see "The Bear Essentials" in Chapter 4 and the "Safety" in the Travel Smart section.

Eating Well, Western Style

You're in the land of the unrepentant carnivore here: fine dining first and foremost means steaks grilled to perfection. It's also prime hunting and fishing territory. Antelope, elk, venison, and grouse make regular appearances on menus, and you often have a choice of rainbow trout, salmon, and bass pulled from someone's favorite fishing spot. You can find adventurous chefs doing creative things in the kitchen, but nothing that smacks of "highfalutin'." No matter where you go, your server is likely to greet you with a smile, and blue jeans are always okay.

Microbreweries are another noteworthy phenomenon— you'll find local operations all over. And the fruits are exceptional: huckleberries are used in everything from muffins to ice cream, and apples, peaches, and pears from roadside stands are full of tree-ripened goodness.

Rodeos, Rendezvous, and Powwows

The Western tradition of working hard and then cutting loose is alive and well—look no further than Cheyenne Frontier Days, the rodeo extravaganza that's known simply as "The Daddy of 'Em All." It's the biggest event on the calendar, but it's hardly alone. In July and August a weekend doesn't go by without some sort of celebration: there are rodeos, Native American powwows, and rendezvous (events commemorating 19th-century trappers and traders—the Green River Rendezvous in Pinedale, Wyoming, is one of the best).

Winter begins with torchlight ski parades and traditional Christmas celebrations, but as the season wears on, things turn wacky: in Whitefish, Montana, contestants race down the slopes in their favorite furniture, and it's golf on ice at the Wild West Winter Carnival in Riverton, Wyoming.

Driving in Big Sky Country

When to Go

With some effort, you can get from point to point in Montana and Wyoming by bus, train, or plane. (For information, see "Getting Here and Around" at the start of chapters and the Travel Smart section at the end of this book.) Most travelers, though, will explore this part of the country in a car, whether it's their own or a rental. No matter where you're starting from or where you're going, it's inevitable in these immense spaces that you'll spend significant time behind the wheel.

In the Rockies you'll encounter soaring summits and spectacular vistas, along with the challenges of mountain driving. You won't be bored, and if you're a driving enthusiast, you may be thrilled. The plains that dominate the eastern part of the region have their own "big sky" beauty, but the vastness of the land can feel overwhelming. The horizon heads off toward infinity in every direction, a few high clouds drift by overhead, and the only sign of civilization is the road beneath your feet.

The interstate system and state highways are well maintained, so road conditions are seldom a problem. Because of the great distances, you should always begin your journey with a full tank of gas, as there can be long stretches with no opportunity to fill up. Be prepared to see lots of wildlife and, in some areas, few other people.

Summer in the area begins in late June or early July. Days are warm, with highs often in the 80s, but nighttime temperatures at higher elevations fall to the 40s and 50s. Afternoon thunderstorms are common over the higher peaks. Fall begins in September, often with a week of unsettled weather around mid-month, followed by four to six gorgeous weeks of Indian Summer. Winter creeps in during November, and deep snows arrive by December. Temperatures can reach as high as freezing by day in the mountain sun, but drop considerably overnight, to as low as -20°F. Winter tapers off in March, though snow lingers into April in valleys bottoms and July on mountain passes. The Rockies have a reputation for extreme weather, but no condition ever lasts for long.

Hotels in tourist destinations book up early, especially in July and August, and hikers spread into the backcountry from June through Labor Day. Ski resorts buzz from December to early April, especially during Christmas and Presidents' Day holiday weeks.

Spring is a good time for fishing, rafting, birding, and wildlife viewing, but keep in mind that snow usually blocks the high country well into June. In fall, aspens splash the mountainsides with gold, and wildlife comes down to lower elevations. The fish are spawning, and the angling is excellent.

DISTANCES BETWEEN CITIES

	Miles	Typical Driving Time
Billings–Helena	239	3 hr 30 min
Helena–Missoula	113	1 hr 45 min
Missoula–Kalispell	122	2 hr 15 min
Missoula–West Yellowstone	280	4 hr 15 min
Old Faithful–Jackson	98	2 hr 30 min
Jackson–Cody	175	4 hr 30 min
Cody–Casper	215	3 hr 30 min
Casper–Cheyenne	180	2 hr 45 min
Cheyenne–Rapid City	310	4 hr 45 min
Rapid City–Billings	325	5 hr

MONTANA AND WYOMING TOP ATTRACTIONS

The National Parks

(A) Yellowstone is the most famous, but all of the national parks in this part of the country—Yellowstone and Grand Teton in Wyoming, Glacier in Montana, Wind Cave and Badlands in South Dakota—are natural wonderlands, each uniquely, spectacularly beautiful. They aren't the only reason to visit here, but they're definitely main draws—places well worth planning your trip around.

Yellowstone, Wind Cave, and Badlands are striking, each in its own way, for their geological novelties, probably unlike anything you've ever seen before. It's Glacier and Grand Teton, though, that you're more likely to return to year after year for the combination of beauty and tranquility. In this book we devote a separate chapter to each park.

National Bison Range

(B) Flathead Indian Reservation, Montana. The 19-mi loop road of the range gives you unparalleled views of elk, pronghorn, deer, mountain sheep, and a 400-head bison herd. (⇨ *Chapter 7*)

C. M. Russell Museum Complex

(C) Great Falls, Montana. Through an extensive collection of art and artifacts, this museum commemorates not only the life of Charlie Russell, one of the most famous Western artists, but also the passing of frontier culture and the coming of civilization. (⇨ *Chapter 8*)

Pryor Mountain Wild Horse Range

(D) Bighorn Canyon, Montana. Set between the thousand-foot cliffs of the Bighorn River and the towering peaks of the Pryor Mountains, this isolated refuge is home to the wild descendants of horses first brought to this continent by the Spanish in the 16th century. (⇨ *Chapter 8*)

Buffalo Bill Historical Center

(E) Cody, Wyoming. This complex is one of the finest cultural institutions of the West, with five major museums related to Plains Indians, Western art, firearms, natural history, and, of course, Buffalo Bill. (⇨ *Chapter 9*)

Cheyenne Frontier Days

(F) Cheyenne, Wyoming. The premier event in the Cowboy State has been held the last full week of July every year since 1897. You'll see the world's top rodeo cowboys and cowgirls, parades featuring dozens of horse-drawn carriages, and nightly shows by top entertainers. (⇨ *Chapter 10*)

Grand Encampment Museum

(G) Encampment, Wyoming. Beyond doubt the best small-town museum in Wyoming, this volunteer-run pioneer town has relics from the mining, ranching, and timbering heritage of the area, including everything from a stage station to a two-story outhouse. (⇨ *Chapter 10*)

Deadwood

(H) Black Hills, South Dakota. This famous Wild West town, once the epicenter of America's last gold rush, is still filled with brick-paved streets and Victorian buildings. (⇨ *Chapter 11*)

Mount Rushmore National Memorial

(I) Black Hills, South Dakota. America's "Shrine of Democracy," depicting George Washington, Thomas Jefferson, Theodore Roosevelt, and Abraham Lincoln on a massive scale, is one of the nation's most enduring icons. (⇨ *Chapter 11*)

Crazy Horse Memorial

(J) Black Hills, North Dakota. When completed, this mountain monument to Native American leaders will be the largest sculpture in the world; until then, you can watch the carving in progress—perhaps including a few dynamite blasts. (⇨ *Chapter 11*)

OUTDOOR ADVENTURES

Horseback Riding

Horseback riding in Montana and Wyoming can mean anything from a quick trot around a ring to a weeklong stay at a working dude ranch where guests rise at dawn and herd cattle.

Horse-pack trips are a great way to visit the backcountry, since horses can travel distances and carry supplies that would be impossible for hikers. Northwest Montana's Bob Marshall Wilderness Area is the perfect example: in the state's largest stretch of roadless wilderness, a horse-pack trip is just about the only way to travel the huge expanses. Although horsemanship isn't required for most trips, it's helpful, and even an experienced rider can expect to be a little sore for the first few days. June through August is the peak period for horse-pack trips; before signing up with an outfitter, ask what skills are expected.

Dude ranches fall roughly into two categories: working ranches and guest ranches. Working ranches, where you participate in such activities as roundups and cattle movements, sometimes require experienced horsemanship. Guest ranches offer a wide range of activities in addition to horseback riding, including fishing, four-wheeling, spa services, and cooking classes. At a typical dude ranch you stay in log cabins and are served meals family-style in a lodge or ranch house; some ranches now have upscale restaurants on-site, too. For winter, many ranches have added such snow-oriented amenities as sleigh rides, snowshoeing, and cross-country skiing.

The ranches are equipped to handle guests arriving with no gear, although all offer lists of what to bring for travelers who want to use their own. Jeans and cowboy boots are still the preferred attire for horseback, although hiking boots and Gore-Tex have long since become fashionable, especially in colder months and at higher altitudes. Long pants are a must either way. Layering is key; plan to have some kind of fleece or heavier outer layer no matter the time of year, since the mountains will be cooler the higher you go.

When choosing a ranch, consider whether the place is family-oriented or adults-only, and check on the length-of-stay requirements. Working ranches plan around the needs of the business, and thus often require full-week stays for a fixed price, whereas guest ranches operate more like hotels.

Gunsel Horse Adventures, Yellowstone. To get a taste of Yellowstone far from the traffic jams, pack up and head into the backcountry on trips ranging from 4 to 10 days.

Paradise Guest Ranch, Buffalo, Northern Wyoming. For a hundred years this ranch has been putting guests on horseback. You can take rodeo training, hit the trail for a multiday pack trip, and get out of the saddle for barbecues and square dances.

Seven Lazy P Guest Ranch, Bob Marshall Wilderness Area, Northwest Montana. From this comfortable all-inclusive ranch you can take rides into "the Bob," where the terrain has changed little since the days of Lewis and Clark.

Skiing and Snowboarding

The champagne powder of the Rocky Mountains can be a revelation for skiers and snowboarders familiar only with the slopes of other regions.

Forget treacherous sheets of rock-hard ice, single-note hills where the bottom can be seen from the top, and mountains that offer only one kind of terrain from every angle. In the Rockies the snow builds up quickly, leaving a solid base that hangs tough all ski season, only to be layered upon by thick, fluffy powder that holds an edge, ready to be groomed into rippling corduroy or left in giddy stashes along the sides and through the trees. Volkswagen-size moguls and half-pipe–studded terrain parks are the norm, not the special attractions.

Skiing the Rockies means preparing for all kinds of weather, sometimes on the same day, because the high altitudes can start a day off sunny and bright but kick in a blizzard by afternoon. Layers help, as well as plenty of polypropylene to wick away sweat in the sun, and a water-resistant outer layer to keep off the powdery wetness that's sure to accumulate—especially if you're a beginner snowboarder certain to spend time on the ground. Must-haves: plenty of sunscreen, because the sun is closer than you think, and a helmet, because the trees are, too.

The added bonus of Rocky Mountain terrain is that so many of the areas have a wide variety of easier (green circle), intermediate (blue square), advanced (black diamond), and expert (double black diamond) slopes—often in the same ski resort. Turn yourself over to the rental shops, which are specialized enough at each resort to offer experts to help you plan your day and the types of equipment you'll need. Renting is also a great chance for experienced skiers and snowboarders to try out the latest technology before investing in a purchase.

Shop around for lift tickets before you leave home. Look for package deals, multiple-day passes, and online discounts. Call the resort and ask if there are any off-site locations (such as local supermarkets) where discount tickets can be purchased. The traditional ski season usually runs from mid-December until early April, with Christmas, New Year's, and the month of March being the busiest times at the resorts.

Big Mountain, Whitefish, Northwest Montana. The highlight here is the long high-speed quad, the Glacier Chaser. The scene isn't as glamorous as Jackson Hole or Aspen, and skiers here think that's just fine.

Big Sky, Southwest Montana. An easygoing atmosphere combined with the second-greatest vertical drop in the United States makes for a first-rate ski destination.

Jackson Hole, Northwest Wyoming. The steep descents draw America's best skiers, but with thousands of ways to get down the mountain, this is a world-class experience no matter what your skill level.

Lone Mountain Ranch, Southwest Montana. If cross-country skiing is your thing, this is the place to go. The 50 mi of groomed trails are beautiful and wonderfully varied.

OUTDOOR ADVENTURES

Hiking

Hiking is easily the least expensive and most accessible recreational pursuit. Sure, you could spend a few hundred dollars on high-tech hiking boots, a so-called "personal hydration system," and a collapsible walking staff made of space-age materials, but there's no need for such expenditure. All that's really essential are sturdy athletic shoes, water, and the desire to see the landscape under your own power.

Hiking in the Rockies is a three-season sport that basically lasts as long as you're willing to tromp through snow. (You could look at snowshoeing as winter hiking—the trails are often the same.) One of the greatest aspects of this region is the wide range of hiking terrain, from high-alpine scrambles that require stamina to flowered meadows that invite a relaxed pace, to confining slot canyons where flash floods are a real danger and can be fatal to the unwary adventurer.

There are few real hazards to hiking, but a little preparedness goes a long way. Know your limits, and make sure the terrain you are about to embark on does not exceed your abilities. It's a good idea to check the elevation change on a trail before you set out—a 1-mi trail might sound easy, until you realize how steep it is—and be careful not to get caught on exposed trails at elevation during afternoon thunderstorms in summer. Dress appropriately by bringing layers to address changing weather conditions, and always carry enough drinking water. Also make sure someone knows where you're going and when to expect your return.

There are literally thousands of miles of hiking trails in Montana and Wyoming. The national parks have particularly well-marked and well-maintained trails, and admission to all trails is free. In fact, hiking is sometimes the only way to get close to certain highlights on protected land. Primarily for safety reasons, overnight hikers are usually expected to register with park or forest rangers. Also keep in mind that run-ins with bears and mountain lions are increasingly common.

Clear Creek Trail, Buffalo, Northern Wyoming. An easy 11-mi path goes through the historic town of Buffalo and out into nature, with good spots to stop for fishing and photography.

The Highline Trail, Glacier National Park. This gorgeous 7-mi hike leads from Logan Pass to Granite Chalet, a rustic National Landmark lodge where you can bed down for the night.

Jewel Basin Hiking Area, Flathead Lake, Northwest Montana. Thirty-five miles of well-maintained trails run past 27 trout-filled alpine lakes.

Yellowstone Association Institute, Yellowstone National Park. This is the group to contact for guided hikes through the park, from day trips to overnight backpacking in the backcountry.

Bicycling

The Rockies are a favorite destination for bikers. Wide-open roads with great gains and losses in elevation test and form road cyclists' stamina, although riders who prefer pedaling fat tires have plenty of mountain and desert trails on which to test their skills. Unmatched views often make it difficult to keep your eyes on the road.

Thanks to the popularity of the sport here, it's usually easy to find a place that rents bicycles if you'd prefer to leave yours at home. Shops often rent a variety of bikes from entry level to high end, though the latter come at a premium, and if you're in the market for a used bike, good deals can often be found when shops unload one season's rentals to make room for next year's models. Bike shops are also a good bet for information on local rides and group tours.

Mountain biking has a huge following—it's more popular in the region than touring on paved roads. The Montana-based Adventure Cycling Association ⊕ *www.adventurecycling.org* has mapped interconnecting back roads, logging and Forest Service roads, and trails stretching from Canada to Mexico. Few people ride the whole route, which covers close to 2,500 mi, but it's easy to pick a segment to suit any rider's stamina. Although the route does follow, very approximately, the Continental Divide, the riding is not all big-mountain climbing and descending. Portions of the trip are negotiable by children as young as 10. The Adventure Cycling Association leads tours and can provide maps (complete with lodging and camping options), information, and advice for self-guided trips.

The rules of the road are the same here as elsewhere, though some areas are less biker-friendly than others. On the road, watch for trucks and stay as close as possible to the side of the road, in single file. On the trail, ride within your limits and keep your eyes peeled for hikers and horses (both have the right of way), as well as dogs. Always wear a helmet and carry plenty of water.

Adventure Cycling, Missoula, Southwest Montana. This organization is the first stop for mountain bikers looking for routes, maps, advice, and guided tours.

Mickelson Trail, Deadwood, South Dakota. More than 100 mi of former railroad line run the length of the Black Hills.

Railroad-Daly Loop, Darby, Northwest Montana. Sixteen miles of mountainous terrain provide lots of opportunities for spotting moose, deer, and elk.

Rimrocks, Billings, Montana Plains. Trails to suit every level of mountain biker are within easy reach in the terrain surrounding Billings.

OUTDOOR ADVENTURES

Rafting

Rafting brings on emotions varying from the calm induced by flat waters surrounded with stunning scenery, backcountry, and wildlife, to the thrill and excitement of charging a raging torrent of foam.

For the inexperienced, the young, and the aged, dozens of tour companies offer relatively tame floats ranging from one hour to one day starting at $20, which are ideal for anyone from 4 years old to 90. Others fulfill the needs of adventure tourists content only with chills, potential spills, and the occasional wall of water striking them smack-dab in the chest. Beginners and novices should use guides, but experienced rafters may rent watercraft.

Seasoned outfitters know their routes and their waters as well as you know the road between home and work. Many guides offer multiday trips in which they do everything, including searing your steak in a beach barbecue, setting up your tent, and rolling out your sleeping bag. Select an outfitter based on recommendations from the local chamber, experience, and word of mouth.

The International Scale of River Difficulty is a widely accepted rating system that ranks waters from Class I (the easiest) to Class VI (the most difficult—think Niagara Falls). Ask your guide about the rating on your route before you book. Remember, ratings can vary greatly throughout the season because of runoff and weather events.

Wear a swimsuit or shorts and sandals and bring along sunscreen and sunglasses. Outfitters are required to supply a life jacket for each passenger, although most states don't require that it be worn. Midsummer is the ideal time to raft in the West, but many outfitters will stretch the season, particularly on calmer routes.

Numerous outfitters and guide services offer rafting trips in Wyoming and Montana, and the journey can vary from relaxing family outings to white-knuckle runs through raging waters. In all cases you'll discover scenery, wildlife, and an off-the-road experience that you'll never get looking through a windshield.

Alberton Gorge near Missoula, Northwest Montana. This canyon section of the Clark Fork River is perfect for a hot summer day.

North Platte River, near Casper, Northern Wyoming. Outfitters offer trips ranging from one hour to a full day on this tranquil stretch of water, ideal for the whole family.

Snake River Canyon, south of Jackson, Northwest Wyoming. Some of the wildest white water in the Rockies is in this winding stretch lined with trees, steep granite walls, alpine meadows, and abundant wildlife.

Upper middle fork of the Flathead River, Northwest Montana. A white-water rafting adventure takes you into the 286,700-acre Great Bear Wilderness.

Yellowstone River near Gardiner, Southwest Montana. Raft through Yankee Jim Canyon and experience Boxcar, Big Rock, and Revenge rapids.

Fishing

Trout do not live in ugly places.

And so it is in Montana and Wyoming, where you'll discover unbridled beauty, towering pines, rippling mountain streams, and bottomless pools. It's here that blue-ribbon trout streams remain much as they were when Native American tribes, French fur trappers, and a few thousand faceless miners, mule skinners, and sod busters first placed a muddy footprint along their banks.

Those early-day settlers had one advantage that you won't—time. To make the best use of that limited resource, consider the following advice.

Hire a guide. You could spend days locating a great fishing spot, learning the water currents and fish behavior, and determining what flies, lures, or bait the fish are following. A good guide will cut through the options, get you into fish, and turn your excursion into an adventure complete with a full creel.

If you're comfortable with your fishing gear, bring it along, though most guides lend or rent equipment. Bring a rod and reel, waders, vest, hat, sunglasses, net, tackle, hemostats, and sunscreen. Always buy a fishing license.

If you're not inclined to fork over the $250-plus that most high-quality guides charge per day for two anglers and a boat, your best bet is a stop at a reputable fly shop. They'll shorten your learning curve, tell you where the fish are, what they're biting on, and whether you should be "skittering" your dry-fly on top of the water or "dead-drifting" a nymph.

Famed fisherman Lee Wolff wrote that "catching fish is a sport. Eating fish is not a sport." Most anglers practice "catch and release" in an effort to maintain productive fisheries and to protect native species.

Season is always a consideration. Spring runoffs can cloud the waters, summer droughts may reduce stream flows, and fall weather can be unpredictable. But, as many fishing guides will attest, the best time to come and wet a line is whenever you can make it.

Black Feet Reservation, near Browning, Northwest Montana. Twenty-some stocked reservoirs regularly yield lunker lake trout from 2 to 8 pounds.

Flaming Gorge Reservoir, Southern Wyoming. Home to state records for smallmouth bass, kokanee salmon, brown trout, channel catfish, Utah chub, and lake trout.

Gallatin Canyon, south of Bozeman, Southwest Montana. The clarity and variety of water is outstanding; the scenery incredible.

North Fork of Shoshone River, west of Cody, Northern Wyoming. The river drops roughly 3,000 feet in 70 mi from the Silvertip Basin to Buffalo Bill Reservoir.

Platte River, near Casper, Northern Wyoming. With depths ranging from 1 to 15 feet, this blue-ribbon water attracts fishermen from all over the world.

Yellowstone National Park. Simply a tremendous fishing destination.

Yellowstone River through Paradise Valley, Southwest Montana. Fish surrounded by snowcapped peaks, free-roaming wildlife, and soaring hawks and eagles.

GLACIER TO GRAND TETON DRIVING TOUR

GLACIER NATIONAL PARK AND MONTANA SCENIC BYWAYS

Day 1

After visiting **Glacier National Park ❶**, with its 1,500 square mi of exquisite ice-carved terrain, plan to spend half a day (or more, depending on stops) driving on a scenic, 160-mi route through western Montana. Start off going southwest on U.S. 2 to **Kalispell ❷**, then south on Highway 206 and Highway 83, through the Seeley–Swan Valley, where you'll have a view of the Mission Range to the west and the Swan Range to the east. South of **Seeley Lake ❸** turn east on Route 200, and then take Route 141 to the small town of **Avon ❹**, about 36 mi west of Helena. From here, turn west on U.S. 12 to connect with I–90. Continue southeast 10 mi to **Deer Lodge ❺**, and 41 mi to the century-old mining town of **Butte ❻**, where the lavish Copper King Mansion reveals what you could buy with an unlimited household budget back in the 1880s, when it was built. From Butte, follow I–90 to **Bozeman ❼** or **Livingston ❽**. Either town is a good place to spend the night and get a good night's sleep before exploring Yellowstone.

YELLOWSTONE NATIONAL PARK

Days 2 and 3

Dedicate the next two days to **Yellowstone National Park ❾**. From Bozeman, you can reach **West Yellowstone ❿** by following I–90 west 8 mi to U.S. 287, then driving south 106 mi. (From Livingston, enter the park from the north by driving south 57 mi on U.S. 89 through the Paradise Valley.) Spend the rest of your first day

THE PLAN

Distance: 850–1,000 mi

Time: 5 days

Breaks: Overnight in Glacier National Park, and Bozeman or Livingston, MT; and Yellowstone National Park, Grand Teton National Park, and Jackson, WY.

on the park's 142-mi Grand Loop Road. It passes nearly every major Yellowstone attraction, and you'll discover interpretive displays, overlooks, and short trails along the way. On your second day in the park, hike the trails, visit the geyser basins, or watch the wildlife. For your accommodations, you really can't go wrong with a stay at Old Faithful Inn, with its lodgepole-pine walls and ceiling beams, an immense volcanic rock fireplace, and green-tinted, etched windows.

GRAND TETON NATIONAL PARK

Days 4 and 5

On the final two days of your tour, experience Wyoming's other national treasure, **Grand Teton National Park ⓫**. Its northern boundary is 7 mi from Yellowstone's south entrance. The sheer ruggedness of the Tetons makes them seem imposing and unapproachable, but a drive on Teton Park Road, with frequent stops at scenic turnouts, will get you up close and personal with the peaks. Overnight in one of the park lodges and spend your final day in the park hiking, horseback riding, or taking a river float trip before continuing south to **Jackson ⓬**, with its landmark elk-antler arches in the town square, fine dining, art galleries, museums, and eclectic shopping.

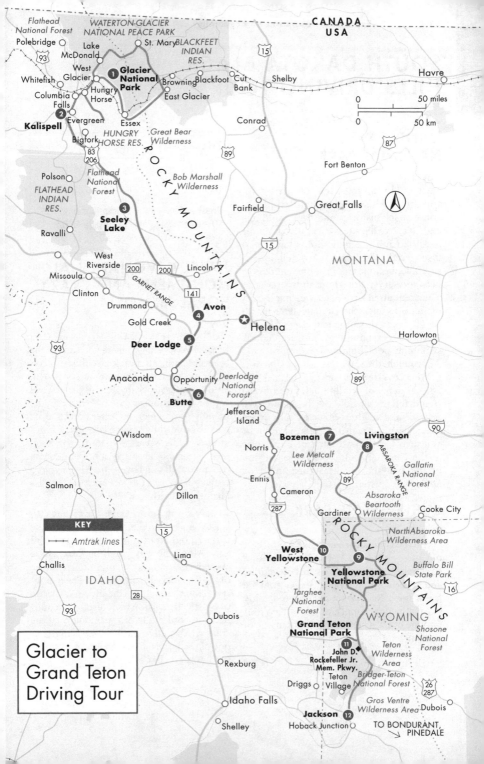

SOUTH DAKOTA BLACK HILLS DRIVING TOUR

WIND CAVE NATIONAL PARK

Day 1

Start in Hot Springs, the southern gateway to Wind Cave National Park. Here you can see historic sandstone buildings and an active dig site where the remains of fossilized full-size mammoths have been discovered. The mammoths fell into a sinkhole, became trapped, died, and have been preserved for thousands of years. They remain in situ. After viewing the 55 mammoths unearthed to date at **Mammoth Site ❶**, take a dip into **Evans Plunge ❷**—the world's largest natural warm-water indoor swimming pool, holding 1 million gallons. After lunch, drive 6 mi north on U.S. 385 to **Wind Cave National Park ❸**. The park has 28,000 acres of wildlife habitat aboveground and the world's fourth-longest cave below. Take an afternoon cave tour and a short drive through the park. Overnight at nearby Custer State Park, or stay in one of the Custer Resort Lodges—or in one of the bed-and-breakfasts around Hot Springs or Custer.

CUSTER STATE PARK

Day 2

Spend today at **Custer State Park ❹**, 5 mi east of Custer on U.S. 16A. The 110-square-mi park has exceptional drives, lots of wildlife, and fingerlike granite spires rising from the forest floor. Relax on a hayride and enjoy a chuck-wagon supper, or take a Jeep tour into the buffalo herds. Overnight in one of four enchanting mountain lodges.

THE PLAN

Distance: 120 mi

Time: 5 days

Breaks: Overnight in Hot Springs or Custer, SD; Custer State Park, SD; Keystone, SD; Rapid City, SD; Deadwood, SD.

JEWEL CAVE NATIONAL MONUMENT AND CRAZY HORSE MEMORIAL

Day 3

Today, venture down U.S. 16 to **Jewel Cave National Monument ❺**, where you can see the beautiful nailhead and dogtooth spar crystals lining its 145 mi of passageways. As you head from Custer State Park to Jewel Cave National Monument, you pass through the friendly community of Custer on U.S. 385. It's surrounded by some of the Black Hills' most striking scenery—picture towering rock formations spearing out of ponderosa pine forests. If you have extra time, explore Cathedral Spires, Harney Peak, and Needles Highway (Highway 87).

After visiting Jewel Cave, head back to Custer and take U.S. 16/385 toward the former gold and tin mining town of Hill City. Along the way you'll hit **Crazy Horse Memorial ❻**, the colossal mountain carving of the legendary Lakota leader. The memorial's complex includes the Indian Museum of North America, which displays beautiful bead- and quillwork from many of the continent's native nations. Overnight at one of the hotels in and around Keystone, such as the K Bar S Lodge.

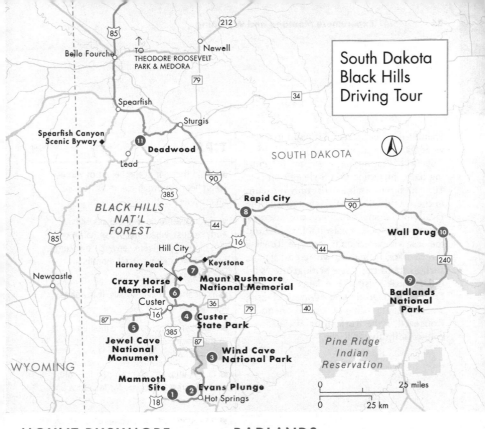

MOUNT RUSHMORE NATIONAL MEMORIAL

Day 4

This morning, travel 3 mi from Keystone (10 from Hill City) on Route 244 (the Gutzon Borglum Memorial Highway) to **Mount Rushmore National Memorial 7**, where you can view the huge, carved renderings of Washington, Jefferson, Roosevelt, and Lincoln and have breakfast with the presidents. Afterward, head northwest on U.S. 16 to **Rapid City 8**, western South Dakota's largest city and the eastern gateway to the Black Hills. Overnight here.

BADLANDS NATIONAL PARK

Day 5

Begin your day early and drive 55 mi on Route 44 to the North Unit of **Badlands National Park 9**. Badlands Loop Road wiggles through this moonlike landscape for 32 mi. When you've had enough of this 380-square-mi geologic wonderland, head back to the hills. Exit onto Route 240 at the northeast entrance to catch I–90. For a fun excursion, take a little detour east to Wall for its world-famous **Wall Drug 10**. Founded on the premise that free ice water would attract road-weary travelers, the emporium carries all manner of Westernalia.

Spend this afternoon and tonight in **Deadwood** ⑪, reached via U.S. 14 and 14A. This Old West mining town has 80 gaming halls, including Old Style Saloon No. 10, which bills itself as "the only museum in the world with a bar." Upstairs, at the Deadwood Social Club, you can discover outstanding food at reasonable prices and the best wine selection in the state. To view rare artifacts from the town's colorful past, such as items that once belonged to Wild Bill Hickok, visit the Adams Museum. Overnight in Deadwood's Franklin Hotel, where past guests have included Theodore Roosevelt, Babe Ruth, John Wayne, and country duo Big & Rich.

TIPS

■ Avoid the tour at the height of winter, when heavy snowfall can make roads impassable.

■ If you plan to be in the Black Hills in early August, when more than half a million motorcycle riders converge on Sturgis, make reservations several months in advance.

■ You cannot collect fossils. It is against federal law.

■ You *can* collect rocks in small amounts in the Black Hills National Forest, but no digging is allowed.

■ In certain areas you can pan for gold; contact forest personnel for locations and rules.

■ It's a good idea to pick up a Forest Service map if you plan to venture off the beaten path when in the Black Hills. The Black Hills National Forest intermixes with private property, so you'll want to know where you are at all times.

Pack appropriately; hot summer days can reach temperatures over 100 degrees and nights can be chilly with temperatures into the 40s and 50s.

Yellowstone National Park

WORD OF MOUTH

"Rarely do you find in one place the geological wonders and diversity Yellowstone has to offer. Add to that the diversity of the wildlife, and you've got almost the perfect picture of the totality of nature's collective handiwork in one location, and all in peaceful co-existence."

—dfr4848

WELCOME TO YELLOWSTONE

TOP REASONS TO GO

★ **Hot spots:** Thinner-than-normal crust depth and a huge magma chamber beneath the park explain Yellowstone's abundant geysers, steaming pools, hissing fumaroles, and bubbling mudpots.

★ **Bison:** They're just one of many species that roam freely here. Seemingly docile, the bison make your heart race if you catch them stampeding across Lamar Valley.

★ **Hiking:** Yellowstone has more than 1,000 mi of trails, along which you can summit a 10,000-foot peak, follow a trout-filled creek, or descend into the Grand Canyon of the Yellowstone.

★ **Yellowstone Lake:** Here you can fish, boat, kayak, stargaze, and bird-watch on black obsidian beaches—just don't stray too far into the frigid water.

★ **Canyon:** The Colorado River runs through the park, creating a deep yellow-colored canyon with two impressive waterfalls.

1 **Grant Village/West Thumb.** Named for President Ulysses S. Grant, Grant Village is on the western edge of Yellowstone Lake.

2 **Old Faithful area.** Famous for its regularity and awesome power, Old Faithful erupts every 94 minutes or so. The most important geyser site in the world is a full-service area with inns, restaurants, campsites, cabins, a visitor center, and general stores.

3 **Madison.** Here the Madison River is formed by the joining of the Gibbon and Firehole rivers. Fly fishermen will find healthy stocks of brown and rainbow trout and mountain whitefish.

4 **Norris.** The Norris area is the hottest and most changeable part of Yellowstone National Park. There are campsites here and a small information center.

5 **Mammoth Hot Springs.** This full-service fortlike area has an inn, restaurants, campsites, a visitor center, and general stores.

6 **Tower-Roosevelt.** This least-visited area of the park is the place to go for solitude, horseback riding, and animal sightings. There are a lodge, restaurant, and campsites here.

7 Canyon area. The Yellowstone River runs through here, and the yellow walls of the canyon lend the park its name. Two massive waterfalls highlight "downtown" Yellowstone, where cars, services and natural beauty all converge.

8 Lake area. The largest body of water within the park, Yellowstone Lake is believed to have once been 200 feet higher than it presently is. This is a full-service area with a hotel, lodge, restaurants, campsites, cabins, and general stores.

GETTING ORIENTED

At more than 2.2 million acres, Yellowstone National Park is considered one of America's most scenic and diverse national parks. The park has five entrances, each with its own attractions: the South has the Lewis River canyon; the East, Sylvan Pass; the West, the Madison River valley; the North, the beautiful Paradise Valley; and the Northeast, the spectacular Beartooth Pass.

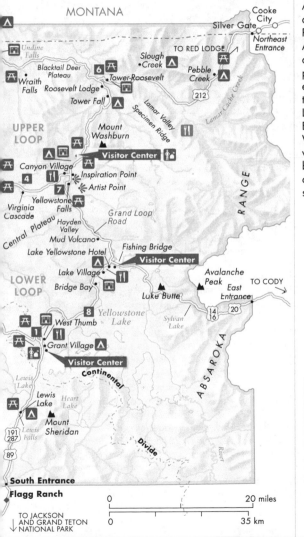

KEY	
👫	Ranger Station
⛺	Campground
🏕	Picnic Area
🍴	Restaurant
🏞	Lodge
🚶	Trailhead
🚻	Restrooms
⇝	Scenic Viewpoint
·····	Walking/Hiking Trails
······	Bicycle Path

YELLOWSTONE PLANNER

When to Go

There are two major seasons in Yellowstone: summer (May–October), the only time when most of the park's roads are open to cars; and winter (mid-December–February), when over-snow travel (snowmobiles, snow coaches, and skis) takes a fraction of the number of visitors to a frigid, bucolic sanctuary. Except for services at park headquarters at Mammoth Hot Springs, the park closes from October to mid-December and from March to late April or early May.

You'll find big crowds from mid-July to mid-August. There are fewer people in the park the month or two before and after this peak season, but there are also fewer facilities open. There's also more rain, especially at lower elevations. Except for holiday weekends, there are few visitors in winter. Snow is possible year-round at high elevations.

Flora and Fauna

Eighty percent of Yellowstone is forest, and the great majority of it is lodgepole pine. Miles and miles of the "telephone pole" pines burned in the massive 1988 fire that burned more than 35% of the park. The fire's heat created the ideal condition for the lodgepole pine's serotinous cones to release their seeds—which now provides a stark juxtaposition between 20-year-old and 100-year-old trees.

Yellowstone's scenery astonishes any time of day, though the play of light and shadow makes the park most appealing in early morning and late afternoon. That's exactly when you should be looking for wildlife, as most are active around dawn and dusk, moving out of the forest in search of food and water. May and June are the best months for seeing baby bison, moose, and other young arrivals. Look for glacier lilies among the spring wildflowers and goldenrod amidst the changing foliage of fall. Winter visitors see the park at its most magical, with steam billowing from geyser basins to wreath trees in ice, and elk foraging close to roads transformed into ski trails.

Bison, elk, and coyotes populate virtually all areas; elk and bison particularly like river valleys and the geyser basins. Moose like marshy areas along Yellowstone Lake and in the northeast corner of the park. Wolves are most common in the Lamar Valley and areas south of Mammoth; bears are most visible in the Pelican Valley–Fishing Bridge area, near Dunraven Pass, and near Mammoth. Watch for trumpeter swans along the Yellowstone River and for sandhill cranes near the Firehole River and in Madison Valley.

AVG. HIGH/LOW TEMPS

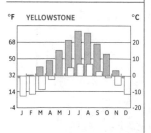

°F   YELLOWSTONE   °C

Getting Here and Around

Yellowstone National Park is served by airports in nearby communities, including Cody, Wyoming, one hour east; Jackson, Wyoming, one hour south; Bozeman, Montana, 90 minutes north; and West Yellowstone, Montana, just outside the park's west gate, which has only summer service. The best places to rent cars in the region are at airports in Cody, Jackson, Bozeman, and West Yellowstone. There is no commercial bus service to Yellowstone.

Yellowstone is well away from the interstates, so drivers make their way here on two-lane highways that are long on miles and scenery. From Interstate 80, take U.S. 191 north from Rock Springs; it's about 177 mi to Jackson, then another 60 mi north to Yellowstone. From Interstate 90, head south at Livingston, Montana, 80 mi to Gardiner and the park's North Entrance. From Bozeman, travel south 90 mi to West Yellowstone.

Yellowstone has five primary entrances. Many visitors arrive through the South Entrance, north of Grand Teton National Park and Jackson, Wyoming. Other entrances are the East Entrance, with a main point of origin in Cody, Wyoming; the West Entrance at West Yellowstone, Montana, and the North Entrance at Gardiner, Montana (these are the only two entrances open in winter); and the Northeast Entrance at Cooke City, Montana, which can be reached from either Cody, Wyoming, via the Chief Joseph Scenic Highway, or from Red Lodge, Montana, over the Beartooth Pass.

■TIP→ **The best way to keep your bearings in Yellowstone is to remember that the major roads form a figure eight, known as the Grand Loop, which all entrance roads feed into.** It doesn't matter at which point you begin, as you can hit most of the major sights if you follow the entire route.

The 370 mi of public roads in the park used to be riddled with potholes and had narrow shoulders—a bit tight when a motor home was pulled over to the side to capture wildlife or scenery on film. But because of the park's efforts to upgrade its roads, most of them are now wide and smooth. Roadwork is likely every summer in some portion of the park—check the Yellowstone Today newspaper or ask a ranger. On holiday weekends road construction usually halts, so there are no construction delays for travelers. Remember, snow is possible any time of year in almost all areas of the park.

Where to Stay

There are a couple of factors to consider when deciding on which community to stay overnight in at the park. Some of these include deciding whether you want to camp or want a hotel. But just as important is assessing your overnight accommodations based on the length of your trip. If you're only going to spend a day or two in the park, choose one location in the area that is most important for you to visit.

If you've never been to the park before and you only have a day or two, you'll probably want to choose Old Faithful, so you're near Yellowstone's most famous geyser. But if you're more interested in seeing the wildlife, you may want to choose the Canyon or Lake area so you're near Hayden and Pelican valleys.

On the other hand, if you're going to spend five days to a week or more in the park, you'll benefit from splitting your time between two or more regions of this huge park (such as Old Faithful and Canyon) so you aren't spending all of your time driving to the various communities. ⇨ *Where to Stay toward the back of the chapter for lodging reviews.*

Updated by
Steve Pastorino

A trip to Yellowstone has been a rich part of the American experience for five generations now. Though it's remote, we come, 3,000,000 strong year after year. When we arrive, we gasp at the incomparable combination of natural beauty, rugged wilderness, majestic peaks, and abundant wildlife. Indescribable geysers, mudpots, fumaroles, and hot springs make this magma-filled pressure cooker of a park unlike any place else on earth. If you're not here for the geysers, chances are that you've come to spot some of the teeming wildlife, from grazing bison to cruising trumpeter swans.

PARK ESSENTIALS

ACCESSIBILITY

Yellowstone has long been a National Park Service leader in providing for people with disabilities. Restrooms with sinks and flush toilets designed for those in wheelchairs are in all developed areas except Norris and West Thumb, where more rustic facilities are available. Accessible campsites and restrooms are at Bridge Bay, Canyon, Madison, Mammoth Hot Springs, and Grant Village campgrounds, while accessible campsites are found at both Lewis Lake and Slough Creek campgrounds. Ice Lake has an accessible backcountry campsite. An accessible fishing platform is about 3½ mi west of Madison at Mt. Haynes Overlook.

If you need a sign-language interpreter for NPS interpretive programs, arrange for it by calling ☎ 307/344–2251 three weeks in advance. For details, contact the accessibility coordinator at ☎ 307/344–2018 or pick up a free copy of *Visitor Guide to Accessible Features in Yellowstone National Park*.

ADMISSION FEES AND PERMITS

Entrance fees of $25 per car, $20 per motorcycle, and $12 per visitor (16 and older) arriving on a bus, motorcycle, or snowmobile provide visitors with access for seven days to both Yellowstone and Grand Teton. An annual pass to the two parks costs $50.

Fishing permits (available at ranger stations, visitor centers, and Yellowstone general stores) are required if you want to take advantage of Yellowstone's abundant lakes and streams. Live bait is not allowed, and for all native species of fish a catch-and-release policy stands. Anglers 16 and older must purchase a $15 three-day permit, a $20 seven-day permit, or a $35 season permit; those 12 to 15 need a free permit or must fish under the direct supervision of an adult with a permit; those 11 and under do not need a permit but must be supervised by an adult.

All camping outside of designated campgrounds requires a free back-country permit. Horseback riding also requires a free permit. All boats, motorized or nonmotorized, including float tubes, require a permit, which are $20 (annual) or $10 (seven days) for motorized boats and $10 (annual) or $5 (seven days) for nonmotorized vessels. Permits from Grand Teton National Park are valid in Yellowstone, but owners must register their vessel in Yellowstone.

ADMISSION HOURS

Depending on the weather, Yellowstone is generally open late April to November and mid-December to early March. In winter, only one road, going from the Northeast Entrance at Cooke City to the North Entrance at Gardiner, is open to wheeled vehicles; other roads are used by over-snow vehicles. The park is in the mountain time zone.

CELL-PHONE RECEPTION

A comprehensive cell-phone coverage plan is in process, but currently reception in the park is hit or miss, and generally confined to developed areas like Old Faithful and Canyon. In general, don't count on it. Public telephones are near visitor centers and major park attractions. ■ TIP→ Try to use inside phones rather than outside ones, so your conversation doesn't distract you from being alert to wildlife that might approach you while you're on the phone.

RELIGIOUS SERVICES

Religious services are held at several park locations during the summer and on religious holidays. For times and locations of park services, check at visitor centers or lodging front desks.

SHOPS AND GROCERS

A dozen Yellowstone general stores are located throughout the park. Each offers basic souvenirs and snacks, but several are destinations unto themselves. The 1950s-inspired Canyon General Store, the 100-year-old "Hamilton's Store" at Old Faithful, and the Fishing Bridge store are three of the largest, combining architectural significance with a broad variety of groceries, books, apparel, outdoor needs, and soda-fountain-style food service.

Hours vary seasonally, but most stores are open 7:30 AM to 9:30 PM from late May to September; all except Mammoth General Store close for winter. All accept credit cards.

PARK CONTACT INFORMATION

Yellowstone National Park ⌂ *P.O. Box 168, Mammoth, WY 82190-0168* ☎ *307/344-7381* ⊕ *www.nps.gov/yell.*

SCENIC DRIVES

Firehole Canyon Drive. The 2-mi narrow asphalt road twists through a deep canyon and passes the 40-foot Firehole Falls. In summer look for a sign marking a pullout and swimming hole. This is one of only two places in the park (Boiling River on the North Entrance Road is the other) where you can safely and legally swim in the park's thermally heated waters. Look carefully for osprey and other raptors. ⊠ *1 mi south of Madison junction off Grand Loop Rd.*

YELLOWSTONE IN ONE DAY

If you plan to spend just one full day in the park, your best approach would be to concentrate on one or two of the park's major areas, such as the two biggest attractions: the famous Old Faithful geyser and the Grand Canyon of the Yellowstone. En route between these attractions, you can see geothermal activity and most likely some wildlife.

Plan on at least two hours for Old Faithful, one of the most iconic landmarks in America. Eruptions are approximately 90 minutes apart, though they can be as close as 60 minutes apart. Before and after an eruption you can explore the surrounding geyser basin and Old Faithful Inn. To the north of Old Faithful, make Grand Prismatic Spring your can't-miss geothermal stop; farther north, near Madison, veer off the road to the west to do the short Firehole Canyon Drive to see the Firehole River cut a small canyon and waterfall (Firehole Falls).

If you're arriving from the east, start with sunrise at **Lake Butte, Fishing Bridge, and the wildlife-rich Hayden Valley** as you cross the park counter-clockwise to **Old Faithful.** To try and see wolves or bears, call ahead and ask when/if rangers will be stationed at roadside turnouts with spotting scopes. Alternatively, hike any trail in the park at least 2 mi—and remember that you're entering the domain of wild and sometimes dangerous animals, so be alert and don't hike alone.

If you're entering through the North or Northeast entrance, begin at dawn looking for wolves and other animals in Lamar Valley, then head to **Tower-Roosevelt** and take a horseback ride into the surrounding forest. After your ride, continue west to **Mammoth Hot Springs,** where you can hike the **Lower Terrace Interpretive Trail** past Liberty Cap and other strange, brightly colored limestone formations. If you drive 1½ mi south of the visitor center, you will reach the **Upper Terrace Drive,** for close-ups of hot springs. In the late afternoon, drive south, keeping an eye out for wildlife as you go—you're almost certain to see elk, buffalo, and possibly even a bear. Alternatively, from Tower-Roosevelt you can head south to go through **Canyon Village** to see the north or south rim of the **Grand Canyon of the Yellowstone** and its waterfalls, and then head west through Norris and Madison.

When you reach **Old Faithful,** you can place the famous geyser into context by walking the 1½-mi **Geyser Hill Loop.** Watch the next eruption from the deck of the **Old Faithful Inn.**

Firehole Lake Drive. This one-way, 3-mi-long road takes you past **Great Fountain Geyser,** which shoots out jets of water reaching as high as 200 feet about twice a day. Rangers' predictions have a two-hour window of opportunity. Should you witness it, however, you'll be rewarded with a view of waves of water cascading down the terraces that form the edges of the geyser. Watch for bison, particularly in the winter. ⊠ *Firehole Lake Dr., 8 mi north of Old Faithful.*

Hayden Valley on Grand Loop Road. Bison, bears, coyotes, wolves, and birds of prey all call Hayden Valley home almost year-round. Once part of Yellowstone Lake, the broad valley now features peaceful meadows, rolling hills, and the placid Yellowstone River. There are multiple turnouts and picnic areas on the 16-mi drive, many with views of the river and valley. Ask a ranger about "Grizzly Overlook," an unofficial site where wildlife watchers, including NPS rangers with spotting scopes for the public to use, congregate in the summer. It's three turnouts north of Mud Volcano—there's no sign, so look for the timber railings. ⊠ *Between Canyon and Fishing Bridge on Grand Loop Rd.*

Fodor's Choice
★
Northeast Entrance Road and Lamar Valley. The 29-mi road features the richest diversity of landscape of the five entrance roads. Just after you enter the park, you cut between 10,928-foot Abiathar Peak and the 10,404-foot Barronette Peak. You pass the extinct geothermal cone called Soda Butte as well as the two nicest campgrounds in the park, Pebble Creek and Slough Creek. Lamar Valley is the melancholy home to hundreds of bison, while the rugged peaks and ridges adjacent to it are home to some of the park's most famous wolf packs (reintroduced in 1995). The main wolf-watching activities in the park occur here during early-morning and late-evening hours year-round. As you exit Lamar Valley, the road crosses the Yellowstone River before leading you to the rustic Roosevelt Lodge. ⊠ *From Northeast Entrance near Cooke City to junction with Grand Loop Rd. at Roosevelt Lodge.*

Northeastern Grand Loop. A 19-mi segment of Grand Loop Road climbs to nearly 9,000 feet as it passes some of the park's finest scenery, twisting beneath a series of leaning basalt towers 40 to 50 feet high. That behemoth to the east is 10,243-foot Mt. Washburn. ⊠ *Between Canyon Village and Roosevelt Falls.*

Upper Terrace Drive. Limber pines as old as 500 years line this 1½-mi loop near Mammoth Hot Springs, where a variety of mosses grow through white travertine, composed of lime deposited by the area's hot springs. ⊠ *Approximately 2 mi by car from Mammoth Hot Springs Hotel on Grand Loop Rd. Reachable on foot from Lower Terrace Dr.*

WHAT TO SEE

Along the park's main drive—the Grand Loop (also referred to as Yellowstone's Figure Eight)—are eight primary "communities," or developed areas. On the Western Yellowstone map are five of those communities—Grant Village, Old Faithful, Madison, Norris, and Mammoth Hot Springs—with their respective sights, while the East Yellowstone map shows the remaining three—Tower-Roosevelt, Canyon, and Lake (for Yellowstone Lake area)—with their respective sights.

GRANT VILLAGE AND WEST THUMB

Along the western edge of Yellowstone Lake (called the West Thumb), Grant Village is the first community you encounter from the South Entrance. It has basic lodging and dining facilities.

SCENIC STOPS

☾ **West Thumb Geyser Basin.** The primary Yellowstone caldera was created by one volcanic eruption, while West Thumb came about as the result of another, later volcanic eruption. This unique geyser basin is the only place to see active geothermal features in Yellowstone Lake. Two boardwalk loops are offered; take the longer one to see features like Fishing Cone, where fishermen used to catch fish, pivot, and drop their fish straight into boiling water for cooking without ever taking it off the hook. This area is particularly popular for winter visitors, who take advantage of the nearby warming hut and a stroll around the geyser basin before continuing their trip via snow coach or snowmobile. ⊠ *Grand Loop Rd., 22 mi north of South Entrance, West Thumb.*

VISITOR CENTER

Grant Village Visitor Center. Each visitor center in the park tells a small piece of the park's history. This one tells the story of fire in the park. A seminal moment in Yellowstone's historical record, the 1988 fire burned 36% of the total acreage of the park and forced multiple federal agencies to reevaluate their fire-control policies. Watch an informative video, purchase maps or books, and learn more about the 25,000 firefighters from across America who fought the 1988 fire. After a 2008 remodeling, bathrooms and a backcountry office are now housed here as well. ⊠ *Grant Village* ☎ *307/242–2650* ☉ *Late May–Sept. 30, daily 8–7.*

West Thumb Information Station. This historic log cabin houses a Yellowstone Association bookstore and doubles as a warming hut in the winter. There are restrooms in the parking area. Check for informal ranger-led discussions beneath the old sequoia tree in the summer. ⊠ *West Thumb* ☉ *Late May–late Sept., daily 9–5.*

OLD FAITHFUL

★ The world's most famous geyser is the centerpiece of this area, which has extensive boardwalks through the Upper Geyser Basin and equally extensive visitor services, including several choices in lodging and dining. In winter you can dine and stay in this area and cross-country ski or snowshoe through the Geyser Basin.

HISTORICAL SITES

Ⓒ **Old Faithful Inn.** It's hard to imagine how any work could be accom-
Fodor's Choice plished when snow and ice blanket the region, but this historic hotel
★ was constructed over the course of a single winter in 1903. Serving as a lodging establishment since 1904, this massive log structure is an attraction in its own right. Even if you don't spend a night at the Old Faithful Inn, walk through or take the free 45-minute guided tour to admire its massive open-beam lobby and rock fireplace (where tours begin). There are antique writing desks on the second-floor balcony, and during evening hours a pianist plays there as well. You can watch Old Faithful geyser from two second-floor outdoor decks. ⊠ *Old Faithful Bypass Rd., Old Faithful* ☎ *307/344–7901* ☉ *May–mid-Oct.; tours daily, times vary.*

SCENIC STOPS

Biscuit Basin. North of Old Faithful, this basin is also the trailhead for the Mystic Falls Trail. The namesake "biscuit" formations were reduced to crumbs when Sapphire Pool erupted after the 1959 Hebgen Lake earthquake. Now, Sapphire is a calm, beautiful blue pool again, but that could change at any moment. ⊠ *3 mi north of Old Faithful on Grand Loop Rd., Old Faithful.*

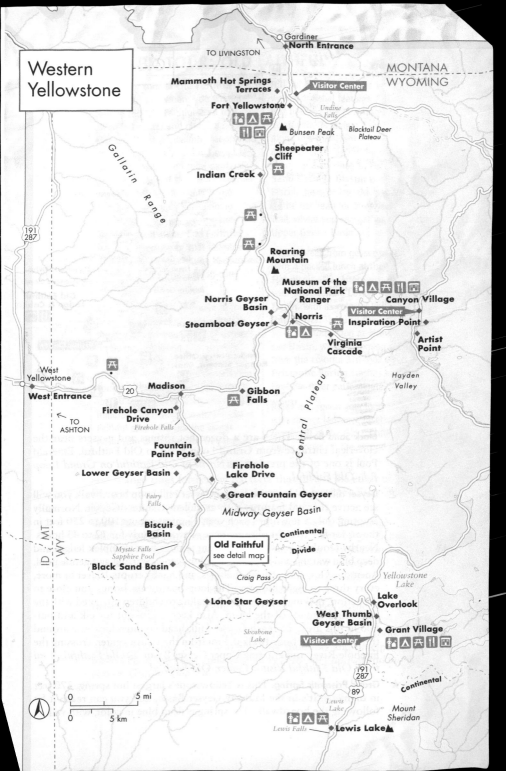

Basin. With Old Faithful as its central attraction, this asin contains about 140 different geysers—one-fifth of ysers in the world. It's an excellent place to spend a day ring. You will find a complex system of boardwalks and of them used as bicycle trails—that take you to the basin's tions. ⊠ *Old Faithful.*

lmost every visitor includes the world's most famous geyer itinerary. Yellowstone's most predictable big geyser— its largest or most regular—sometimes reaches 180 feet, s 130 feet. Sometimes it doesn't shoot as high, but in those tions usually last longer. The mysterious plumbing of Yellengthened Old Faithful's cycle somewhat in recent years, minutes or so. To find out when Old Faithful is likely to at the visitor center or at any of the lodging properties in can view the eruption from a bench just yards away, from om at the lodge cafeteria, or the second-floor balcony of Inn. The 1-mi hike to Observation Point yields yet another above—of the geyser and its surrounding basin. ⊠ *South- , Grand Loop Rd.*

er Basin. Called "Hell's Half Acre" by writer Rudyard Kipling, ser Basin is a more interesting stop than Lower Geyser Basin. oardwalks wind their way to the Excelsior Geyser, which 00 gallons of vivid blue water per minute into the Firehole ove Excelsior is Yellowstone's largest hot spring, Grand Pris. Measuring 370 feet in diameter, it's deep blue in color with orange rings formed by bacteria that give it the effect of a tween Old Faithful and Madison on Grand Loop Rd.

ry Pool. Shaped somewhat like a morning-glory flower, this was a deep blue, but tourists dropping coins and other debris ged the plumbing vent. As a result, the color is no longer as o reach the pool, follow the boardwalk past Geyser Hill Loop y Castle Geyser, which has the biggest cone in Yellowstone. It ry 10 to 12 hours, to heights of 90 feet, for as much as an hour . From Morning Glory Pool it's about 2 mi back to the Old Faith- r center. Morning Glory is the inspiration for popular children's an Brett's story *Hedgie Blasts Off*, in which a hedgehog goes to planet to unclog a geyser damaged by space tourists' debris. ⊠ *At th end of Upper Geyser Basin at Old Faithful.*

R CENTER

ithful Visitor Center. A new LEED-certified visitor center is sched- o open here by August 2010, and plans indicate that it will be one e jewels of the entire national park system. This is the best place quire about geyser eruption predictions. Backcountry and fishing its are handled out of the ranger station adjacent to the Old Faith- now Lodge. ⊠ *Old Faithful Bypass Rd.* ☎ *307/545-2750* ☉ *Late y–late Sept., daily 8–7; late Dec.–early Mar., daily 9–6.*

MADISON

The area around the junction of the West Entrance Road and the Lower Loop is a good place to take a break as you travel through the park, because you will almost always see bison grazing along the Madison River, and often elk are in the area as well. Limited visitor services are here, including no dining facilities.

SCENIC STOPS

Gibbon Falls. Water rushes over the caldera rim in this 84-foot waterfall on the Gibbon River. You can see it on your right from the road as you're driving east from Madison to Canyon. ⊠ *4 mi east of Madison on Grand Loop Rd.*

VISITOR CENTER

Madison Information Center. In this National Historic Landmark the ranger shares the space with a Yellowstone Association bookstore, which features high-quality books, guides, music, and learning aids. You may find spotting scopes set up for wildlife viewing out the rear window; if this is the case, look for eagles, swans, bison, elk, and more. Rangers will answer questions about the park, provide basic hiking information and maps, and issue permits for backcountry camping and fishing. Picnic tables, toilets, and an amphitheater for summer-evening ranger programs are shared with the nearby Madison campground. The park encourages Junior Rangers to start here. ⊠ *Grand Loop Rd. at West Entrance Rd.* ☎ *307/344–2821* ☉ *Late May–late Sept., daily 9–6.*

NORRIS

The area at the western junction of the Upper and Lower Loops has the most active geyser basin in the park. The underground plumbing occasionally reaches such high temperatures—the ground itself has heated up in areas to nearly 200°F—that a portion of the basin is periodically closed for safety reasons. There are limited visitor services: two museums, a bookstore, and a picnic area. ■TIP→ Ask rangers at the Norris Geyser Basin Museum when different geysers are expected to erupt and to plan your walk accordingly.

SCENIC STOPS

Back Basin. The trail through Back Basin is a 1½-mi loop guiding you past dozens of features highlighted by Steamboat Geyser. When it erupts fully (most recently in 1985), it's the world's largest, climbing 400 feet above the basin. More often, Steamboat growls and spits constantly, sending clouds of steam high above the basin. Kids will love the Puff 'n' Stuff Geyser and the mysterious cave-like Green Dragon Spring. Ask the Norris ranger for an anticipated schedule of geyser eruptions—you might catch the Echinus Geyser, which erupts almost hourly. ⊠ *Grand Loop Rd. at Norris junction.*

Norris Geyser Basin. From the Norris Ranger Station, choose either Porcelain Basin or Back Basin, or both. These volatile thermal features are constantly changing, although you can expect to find a variety of geysers and springs here at any time. The area is accessible via an extensive system of boardwalks, some of them suitable for people with disabilities. The famous Steamboat Geyser is here. ⊠ *Grand Loop Rd. at Norris.*

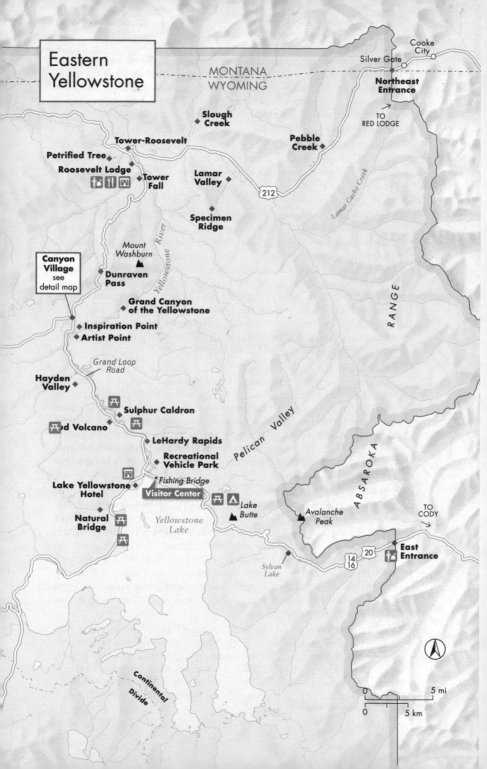

2

Porcelain Basin. In the eastern portion of the Norris Geyser Basin, this thermal area is reached by a ¾-mi, partially boardwalked loop from the Norris Geyser Basin Museum. In this geothermal field of whitish geyserite stone, the earth bulges and belches from the underground pressure. You'll find bubbling pools, some milky white and others ringed in orange because of the minerals in the water, as well as small geysers such as extremely active Whirligig. ⊠ *Grand Loop Rd.*

MAMMOTH HOT SPRINGS

This northern community in the park is known for its massive natural terraces, where mineral water flows continuously, building an ever-changing display. (Note, however, that water levels can fluctuate, so if it's late in a particularly dry summer, you won't see the terraces in all their glory.) You will often see elk grazing here. In the early days of the park it was the site of Fort Yellowstone, and the brick buildings constructed during that era are still used for various park activities.

HISTORICAL SITES

Fort Yellowstone. The oldest buildings at Mammoth Hot Springs served as Fort Yellowstone from 1886 to 1916, the period when the U.S. Army managed the park. The redbrick buildings cluster around an open area reminiscent of a frontier-era fort parade ground. You can pick up a self-guided tour map of the area to make your way around the historic fort structures. ⊠ *Mammoth Hot Springs.*

SCENIC STOPS

ⓒ **Mammoth Hot Springs Terraces.** Multicolor travertine terraces formed by
★ slowly escaping hot mineral water mark this unusual geological formation. It constantly changes as a result of shifts in water flow. You can explore the terraces via an elaborate network of boardwalks. The best is the Lower Terrace Interpretive Trail. If you start at Liberty Cap, at the area's north end, and head uphill on the boardwalks, you'll pass bright and ornately terraced Minerva Spring. It's about an hour's walk. Along the way you may spy elk, as they graze nearby. Alternatively, you can drive up to the Lower Terrace Overlook on Upper Terrace Drive and take the boardwalks down past New Blue Springs to the Lower Terrace. This route, which also takes an hour, works especially well if you can park a second vehicle at the foot of Lower Terrace. ■TIP→ There are lots of steps on the lower terrace boardwalks, so plan to take your time there. ⊠ *Northwest corner of Grand Loop Rd.*

VISITOR CENTER

ⓒ **Albright Visitor Center.** Serving as bachelor quarters for cavalry officers from 1886 to 1918, this red-roof building now holds a museum with exhibits on the early inhabitants of the region and a theater showing films about the history of the park. There are original Thomas Moran paintings of the park on display here as well. Kids and taxidermists will love extensive displays of park wildlife, including bears and wolves. ⊠ *Mammoth Hot Springs* ☎ *307/344–2263* ☉ *Late May–Sept., daily 8–7; Oct.–late May, daily 9–6.*

TOWER-ROOSEVELT

The northeast region of Yellowstone is the least-visited part of the park, making it a great place to explore without running into as many people. Packs of wolves may be spotted in the Lamar Valley.

SCENIC STOPS

Petrified Tree. If you enjoy seeing bears in zoo pens, you'll get the same level of satisfaction as you look at this geological landmark surrounded on all four sides by high wrought-iron gates. Unfortunately, a century of vandalism has forced park officials to completely enclose this 45-million-year-old redwood tree—utterly ruining the experience. ⊠ *Grand Loop Rd., 1 mi west of Tower-Roosevelt.*

↻ **Tower Fall.** This is one of the easiest waterfalls to see from the roadside (follow signs to the lookout point); you can also view volcanic pinnacles here. Tower Creek plunges 132 feet at this waterfall to join the Yellowstone River. A trail runs to the base of the falls, but it is closed at this writing (and for the foreseeable future) because of erosion several hundred yards above the bottom of the canyon; thus, there is no access to the base of Tower Fall from this trail at present. ⊠ *2 mi south of Roosevelt on Grand Loop Rd.*

CANYON

The Yellowstone River's source is in the Absaroka Mountains in the southeast corner of the park. It winds its way through the heart of the park, entering Yellowstone Lake then heading northward under Fishing Ridge through Hayden Valley. When it cuts through the multicolored Grand Canyon of the Yellowstone, it creates one of the most spectacular gorges in the world, enticing visitors with its steep canyon walls and waterfalls. All types of visitors' services are here, as well as lots of hiking opportunities.

SCENIC STOPS

★ **Artist Point.** An impressive view of the Lower Falls of the Yellowstone River is seen from this point, which has two different viewing levels, one of which is accessible to wheelchairs. The South Rim Trail goes right past this point, and there is a nearby parking area open in both summer and winter. ⊠ *East end of South Rim Rd.*

Fodor's Choice **Grand Canyon of the Yellowstone.** This stunning canyon is 23 mi long, but
★ there is only one trail from rim to base. As a result, a majority of park visitors clog the north and south rims to see Upper and Lower Falls. The North Rim Road was rebuilt and widened in 2008, and its new one-way (south to north) traffic pattern enhances visitor flow and enjoyment. Unless you're up for the six-hour strenuous hike called Seven Mile Hole, you have no choice but to join the crowds on the rims to see this natural wonder. The red-and-ochre canyon walls are topped with emerald-green forest. It's a feast of color. Also look for ospreys, which nest in the canyon's spires and precarious trees. ⊠ *Canyon.*

Lookout Point. Midway on the North Rim Trail—or accessible via the one-way North Rim Drive—Lookout Point gives you a view of the Grand Canyon of the Yellowstone from above the falls. Follow the right-hand fork in the path to descend a steep trail (approximately 500-foot elevation change) for an "eye-to-eye" view of the falls from a half mile downstream.

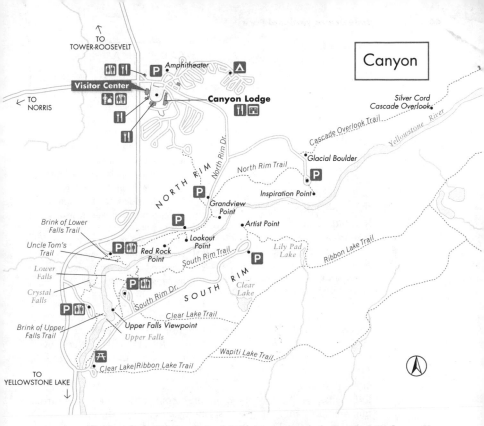

The best time to hike the trail is early morning, when sunlight reflects off the mist from the falls to create a rainbow. ⊠ *Off North Rim Dr.*

Upper Falls View. A spur road off Grand Loop Road south of Canyon gives you access to the west end of the North Rim Trail and takes you down a fairly steep trail for a view of Upper Falls from almost directly above. ⊠ *Off Grand Loop Rd., ¾ mi south of Canyon.*

VISITOR CENTER

Canyon Visitor Center. This gleaming visitor center is the pride of the Park Service, with elaborate interactive exhibits for adults and kids. The focus here is volcanoes and earthquakes, but there are also exhibits on Native Americans and park wildlife, including bison and wolves. The video titled *Land to Life* is a riveting look at the geo- and hydrothermal basis for the park. As at all visitor centers, you can obtain park information, backcountry camping permits, etc. The adjacent bookstore, operated by the Yellowstone Association, is the best in the park, with guidebooks, trail maps, gifts, and hundreds of books on the park, its history, and the science surrounding it. ⊠ *Canyon Village* ☎ *307/242-2552* ⊙ *Late May–late Sept., daily 8–8; early–mid-May, daily 9–5.*

LAKE AREA

In the park's southeastern segment, the area is permeated by the tranquillity of massive Yellowstone Lake. Near Fishing Bridge you might see grizzly bears. They like to hunt for fish spawning or swimming near the lake's outlet to the Yellowstone River. Visitor centers include Lake Yellowstone Hotel, Fishing Bridge RV Park (for hard-sided vehicles only), and Bridge Bay Campground, the park's largest, with 432 sites.

HISTORICAL SITES

★ **Lake Yellowstone Hotel.** Completed in 1891, this structure on the National Register of Historic Places is the oldest lodging in any national park. Spiffed up for its centennial in 1991, it now feels fresh and new. Casual daytime visitors can lounge in white wicker chairs in the sunroom and watch the waters of Yellowstone Lake through massive windows. Robert Reamer, the architect of the Old Faithful Inn, added its columned entrance in 1903 to enhance the original facade. ⊠ *Lake Village Rd., Lake Village* ☎ *307/344–7901* ⊙ *Mid-May–early Oct.*

> **CAUTION: A WILD PLACE**
>
> As you explore the park, keep this thought in mind: Yellowstone is not an amusement park. It is a wild place. The animals may seem docile or tame, but they are wild, and every year careless visitors are injured, sometimes even killed, when they venture too close. Particularly dangerous are female animals with their young, and bison, which can turn and charge in an instant. (Watch their tails: when they are standing up or crooked like a question mark, the bison is agitated.)

SCENIC STOPS

LeHardy Rapids. Witness one of nature's epic battles as cutthroat trout migrate upstream to spawn in spring by catapulting themselves out of the water to get by, over, and around rocks and rapids here on the Yellowstone River. The quarter-mile forested loop takes you to the river's edge. Also keep an eye out for waterfowl and bears, which feed on the trout. ⊠ *3 mi north of Fishing Bridge, Fishing Bridge.*

↻ **Mud Volcano.** Gasses hiss from parking-lot vents, underscoring the volatile nature of this area's geothermal features. The ¾-mi round-trip Mud Volcano Interpretive Trail loops gently around seething, sulfuric mudpots with names such as Black Dragon's Cauldron (which makes a noise like a dragon) and Sizzling Basin before making its way around Mud Volcano itself, a boiling pot of brown goo. ⊠ *10 mi south of Canyon; 4 mi north of Fishing Bridge on Grand Loop Rd., Fishing Bridge.*

Sulphur Caldron. You can smell the sulfur before you even leave your vehicle to walk to the overlook of Sulphur Caldron, where hissing steam escapes from a moonscape-like surface as superheated bubbling mud. ⊠ *9½ mi south of Canyon; 4½ mi north of Fishing Bridge on Grand Loop Rd., Fishing Bridge.*

↻ **Yellowstone Lake.** One of the world's largest alpine lakes, encompassing **Fodor's Choice** 132 square mi, Yellowstone Lake was formed when glaciers that once ★ covered the region melted into a caldera—a crater formed by a volcano. The lake has 141 mi of shoreline, less than one-third of it followed by the East Entrance Road and Grand Loop Road, along which you will often see

2

moose, elk, waterfowl, and other wildlife. In winter you can sometimes see otters and coyotes stepping gingerly onto the ice at the lake's edge. Many visitors head here for the excellent fishing—streams flowing into the lake give it an abundant supply of trout. ⊠ *Intersection of East Entrance Rd. and Grand Loop Rd., between Fishing Bridge and Grant Village.*

VISITOR CENTER

☺ **Fishing Bridge Visitor Center.** This distinctive stone-and-log building, which was built in 1931, has been designated a National Historic Landmark. If you can't distinguish between a Clark's nut hatch and an ermine (note: one's a bird, the other a rodent), check out the extensive exhibits on park birds and other smaller wildlife. Step out the back door to find yourself on one of the beautiful black obsidian beaches of Yellowstone Lake. Adjacent is one of the park's larger amphitheaters. It features ranger presentations nightly in the summer. The Yellowstone Association bookstore here features books, guides, and other educational materials, but you can't buy coffee. ⊠ *East Entrance Rd., 1 mi from Grand Loop Rd.* ☎ *307/242–2450* ☉ *Memorial Day–late Sept., daily 8–7.*

SPORTS AND THE OUTDOORS

BOATING

Motorized boats are allowed only on Lewis Lake and Yellowstone Lake. Kayaking or canoeing is allowed on all park lakes except Sylvan Lake, Eleanor Lake, Twin Lakes, and Beach Springs Lagoon; however, most lakes are inaccessible by car, so accessing the park's lakes requires long portages. Boating is not allowed on any park river, except for the Lewis River between Lewis Lake and Shoshone Lake, where nonmotorized boats are permitted.

You must purchase a seven-day, $5 permit for boats and floatables, or a $10 permit for motorized boats at Bridge Bay Ranger Station, South Entrance Ranger Station, Grant Village Backcountry Office, or Lewis Lake Ranger Station (at the campground). Nonmotorized permits are available at the Northeast entrance, West Yellowstone Information Center; backcountry offices at Mammoth, Old Faithful, and Canyon; Bechler Ranger Station; and locations where motorized boats are sold. Annual permits are also available for $20.

Boat permits issued in Grand Teton National Park are honored in Yellowstone, but owners must register their vessel in Yellowstone and obtain a no-charge Yellowstone validation sticker from a permit issuing station.

OUTFITTERS
AND
EXPEDITIONS
☺
★
Watercraft, from rowboats to powerboats, are available for trips on Yellowstone Lake at **Bridge Bay Marina** (⊠ *Grand Loop Rd., 2 mi south of Lake Village, Lake area* ☎ *307/344–7311* ☎ *$76–$96/hr for guided cruisers for fishing or sightseeing; $9.75/hr for rowboat; $47/hr for small boat with outboard motor* ☉ *Late May–early Sept., daily 8:30–8:30*). You also can rent 22- and 34-foot cabin cruisers with a guide. Daily rentals must be returned by 7 PM. Run by Xanterra Parks & Resorts, **Yellowstone Lake Scenic Cruises** (⊠ *Bridge Bay Marina, Lake area* ☎ *307/242–3876* ☎ *Cruises $14.25* ☉ *Late May–mid-Sept., daily 8:30 AM–8:30 PM*), take visitors on one-hour cruises aboard the *Lake Queen II* throughout

the day. The vessel makes its way from Bridge Bay to Stevenson Island and back. Reservations are strongly recommended.

FISHING

Anglers flock to Yellowstone beginning the Saturday of Memorial Day weekend, when fishing season begins. By the time the season ends in November, thousands have found a favorite spot along the park's rivers and streams. Native cutthroat trout are one of the prize catches, but four other varieties—brown, brook, lake, and rainbow—along with grayling and mountain whitefish, inhabit Yellowstone's waters. Popular sportfishing opportunities include the Gardner and Yellowstone rivers, as well as Soda Butte Creek, but the top fishing area in the region is Madison River, known to fly fishermen throughout the country.

Yellowstone fishing permits are required for anglers over age 16. Montana and Wyoming fishing permits are not valid in the park. Yellowstone fishing permits cost $15 for a three-day permit, $20 for a seven-day permit, or $35 for a season permit. Anglers ages 12 to 15 must have a (nonfee) permit or fish under direct supervision of an adult with a permit. Anglers younger than 12 don't need a permit but must be with an adult who knows the regulations. Permits are available at all ranger stations, visitor centers, and Yellowstone general stores.

HIKING

OLD FAITHFUL

Fountain Paint Pots Nature Trail. Take the easy ½-mi loop boardwalk of Fountain Paint Pot Nature Trail to see fumaroles (steam vents), blue pools, pink mudpots, and mini-geysers in this thermal area. It's popular in both summer and winter because it's right next to Grand Loop Road. ⊠ *Trailhead at Lower Geyser Basin, between Old Faithful and Madison.*

Ⓒ **Old Faithful Geyser Loop.** Old Faithful and its environs in the Upper Geyser Basin are rich in short-walk options, starting with three connected

Fodor's Choice
★ loops that depart from Old Faithful visitor center. The 0.75-mi loop simply circles the benches around Old Faithful, filled nearly all day long in summer with tourists. Currently erupting approximately every 94 minutes, Yellowstone's most frequently erupting big geyser—although not its largest or most regular—reaches heights of 100 to 180 feet, averaging 130 feet. ⊠ *Trailhead at Old Faithful Village, Old Faithful.*

MODERATE **Mystic Falls Trail.** From the Biscuit Basin boardwalk's west end, this trail
★ gently climbs 1 mi (3½ mi round-trip from Biscuit Basin parking area) through heavily burned forest to the lava-rock base of 70-foot Mystic Falls. It then switchbacks up Madison Plateau to a lookout with the park's least-crowded view of Old Faithful and the Upper Geyser Basin. ⊠ *Trailhead 3 mi north of Old Faithful Village off Grand Loop Rd., Old Faithful.*

MAMMOTH HOT SPRINGS

MODERATE **Bunsen Peak Trail.** Past the entrance to Bunsen Peak Road, the moderately difficult trail is a 4-mi, three-hour round-trip that climbs 1,300 feet to Bunsen Peak for a panoramic view of Blacktail Plateau, Swan Lake Flats, the Gallatin Mountains, and the Yellowstone River valley. (Use a topographical map to find these landmarks.) ⊠ *Trailhead at Grand Loop Rd., 1½ mi south of Mammoth Hot Springs.*

TOWER-ROOSEVELT

MODERATE

Fodor'sChoice

★

Slough Creek Trail. Starting at Slough Creek Campground, this trail climbs steeply along a historic wagon trail for the first 1½ mi before reaching expansive meadows and prime fishing spots, where moose are common and grizzlies occasionally wander. From this point the trail, now mostly level, meanders another 9½ mi to the park's northern boundary. Anglers absolutely rave about this trail. ✉ *Trailhead 7 mi east of Tower-Roosevelt off Northeast Entrance Rd.*

2

CANYON

MODERATE

★

Brink of the Lower Falls Trail. Especially scenic, this trail branches off of the North Rim Trail at the Brink of the Upper Falls parking area. The steep ½-mi one-way trail switchbacks 600 feet down to within a few yards of the top of the Yellowstone River's Lower Falls. ✉ *Trailhead 300 yards east of Grand Loop Rd. on entrance to North Rim Drive, 1 mi south of Canyon.*

★ **North Rim Trail.** Offering great views of the Grand Canyon of the Yellowstone, the 3-mi North Rim Trail runs from Inspiration Point to Chittenden Bridge. You can wander along small sections of the trail or combine it with the South Rim Trail. Especially scenic is the 0.5-mi section of the North Rim Trail from the Brink of the Upper Falls parking area to Chittenden Bridge that hugs the rushing Yellowstone River as it approaches the canyon. This trail is paved and fully accessible between Lookout Point and Grand View. ✉ *Trailhead 1 mi south of Canyon.*

South Rim Trail. Partly paved and fairly flat, this 1¾-mi trail along the south rim of the Grand Canyon of the Yellowstone affords impressive views and photo opportunities of the canyon and falls of the Yellowstone River. It starts at Chittenden Bridge and ends at Artist Point. Along the way you can take a break for a snack or a picnic, but you'll need to sit on the ground, as there are no picnic tables. Beyond Artist Point the trail gives way to a high plateau and high mountain meadows. Although popular with day hikers, technically, this is backcountry, and there were bear sightings in 2009, so prepare accordingly. ✉ *Trailhead at Chittenden Bridge, off South Rim Dr., Canyon.*

DIFFICULT

Uncle Tom's Trail. Accessed by the South Rim Drive, the spectacular and strenuous 700-step trail ½ mi east of Chittenden Bridge descends 500 feet from the parking area to the roaring base of the Lower Falls of the Yellowstone. Much of this walk is on steel sheeting, which can have a film of ice on early summer mornings or anytime in spring and fall. ✉ *Trailhead at South Rim Drive, 1 mi. east of Chittenden Bridge, 3 mi south of Canyon.*

LAKE

EASY **Storm Point Trail.** Well marked and
☺ mostly flat, this 1½-mi loop leaves
★ the south side of the road for a perfect beginner's hike out to Yellowstone Lake. The trail rounds the
western edge of Indian Pond, then
passes moose habitat on its way to
Yellowstone Lake's Storm Point,
named for its frequent afternoon
windstorms and crashing waves.

FAMILY PICKS
■ Old Faithful
■ Grand Canyon of the Yellowstone
■ Historic Yellow Bus Tours
■ Roosevelt Old West Cookout

Heading west along the shore, you're likely to hear the shrill chirping
of yellow-bellied marmots, rodents that grow as long as 2 feet. Also look
for ducks, pelicans, and trumpeter swans. You will pass several small
beaches where kids can explore on warm summer mornings. ⊠ *Trailhead
3 mi east of Lake Junction on East Entrance Rd., Fishing Bridge.*

DIFFICULT **Avalanche Peak Trail.** On a busy day in summer, maybe six parties will
Fodor's Choice fill out the trail register at the Avalanche Peak trailhead, so you won't
★ have a lot of company on this hike. Yet many say it's one of the best-
kept secrets in the park. Starting across from a parking area on the East
Entrance Road, the difficult 4-mi, four-hour round-trip climbs 2,150
feet to the peak's 10,566-foot summit, from which you'll see the rugged
Absaroka Mountains running north and south. Some of these peaks
have patches of snow year-round. Look around the talus and tundra
near the top of Avalanche Peak for alpine wildflowers and butterflies.
Don't try this trail before late June or after early September—it may be
covered in deep snow. Also, rangers discourage hikers from attempt-
ing this hike in September or October because of bear activity. Whenever you decide to go, carry a jacket: the winds at the top are strong.
⊠ *Trailhead 2 mi east of Sylvan Lake on north side of East Entrance
Rd., Fishing Bridge.*

HORSEBACK RIDING

Xanterra Parks & Resorts offers horseback rides of one and two hours
in length at Mammoth, Tower-Roosevelt, and Canyon. Advance reservations are recommended. Guides (and horses) catered to beginning
riders (they estimate 90% of riders have not been on a horse in at least
10 years), but let them know if you're an experienced rider and would
like a more challenging pace or ride.

Private stock can be brought into the park. Horses are not allowed in
front-country campgrounds but are permitted in certain backcountry
campsites. For information on planning a backcountry trip with stock,
call the Backcountry Office (☎ *307/344–2160*).

OUTFITTER One- and two-hour horseback trail rides run by **Xanterra Parks & Resorts**
AND (☎ *307/344–7311* ⊕ *www.travelyellowstone.com* ⊠ *$37–$56*) leave
EXPEDITIONS from three sites in the park: Mammoth Hot Springs, Roosevelt Lodge,
☺ and Canyon Village. Children must be at least 8 years old and 48 inches
tall; kids ages 8 to 11 must be accompanied by someone age 16 or older.
In order not to spook horses or wildlife, guests are prohibited from
bringing cameras or cell phones. Exclusively dedicated to trips inside

CLOSE UP

Yellowstone in Winter

To see a spectacularly different Yellowstone than that experienced by 90% of the park's visitors, come in winter. Rocky outcroppings are smoothed over. Waterfalls are transformed into jagged sheets of ice.

The best reason for a visit to Yellowstone between December and March is the opportunity to experience the park without the crowds. The first thing that strikes you during this season is the quiet. The gargantuan snowpack—as many as 200 inches annually at low elevation—seems to muffle the sounds of bison foraging in the geyser basins and of hot springs simmering. Yet even in the depths of a deep freeze, the park is never totally still: the mudpots bubble, geysers shoot skyward, and wind rustles the snow-covered pine trees. Above these sounds, the cry of a hawk, the yip of a coyote, or even on rare occasions the howl of a wolf may pierce the air.

Animals in Yellowstone head *down* when the thermometer falls. Herbivores like elk and bison head to the warmer, less snowy valleys to find vegetation; predators like wolves and cougars follow them. As a result, you're more likely to see these animals in the front country in winter. The snow also makes it easier to pick out animal tracks.

Snowmobiling is popular, but is also controversial (critics cite noise and pollution). At the time of this writing, guided trips with capped speed limits are offered in both Yellowstone and Grand Teton national parks. There are also the options of cross-country skiing and snowshoeing through geyser basins and along the canyon, both excellent ways to see the park. Dogsledding isn't permitted in the park, but outfitters in Jackson lead trips in the nearby national forests.

—Brian Kevin, excerpted from *Fodor's Compass American Guides Yellowstone and Grand Teton National Parks*

2

Yellowstone National Park, **Yellowstone Wilderness Outfitters** (📠 *406/223–3300* ⊕ *www.yellowstone.ws* ✉ *From $110 for half-day trips to $2,700 for multiday trips*) employs musically inclined Jett Hitt as its multi-talented guide. Trips range from half- and full-day family rides to three- to 10-day pack trips in every area of the park. Trips may feature wildlife biologists and lecturers.

SKIING, SNOWSHOEING, AND SNOWMOBILING

Yellowstone can be the coldest place in the continental United States in winter, with temperatures of -30°F not uncommon. Still, winter-sports enthusiasts flock here when the park opens for its winter season the last week of December. Until early March, the park's roads teem with over-snow vehicles like snowmobiles and snow coaches. Its trails bristle with cross-country skiers and snowshoers.

Snowmobiling is an exhilarating way to experience Yellowstone. It's also controversial: there's heated debate about the pollution and disruption to animal habitats. The number of riders per day is limited, and you must have a reservation, a guide, and a four-stroke engine (which is less polluting than the more common two-stroke variety). About a dozen companies have been authorized to lead snowmobile excursions into the park from the North, West, South, and East entrances. Prices vary, as do itineraries and inclusions—be sure to ask about insurance, guides, taxes, park entrance fees, clothing, helmets, and meals. Regulations are subject to change.

At Mammoth Hot Springs Hotel and Old Faithful Snow Lodge, **Xanterra Parks & Resorts** (☎ *307/344–7901* ⊕ *www.travelyellowstone.com*) rents skis, snowmobiles, and snowshoes. Ski rentals (including skis, poles, gloves, and gaiters) are $12 per half day, $18.50 per full day. Snowshoes rentals are $10 per half day, $15 per full day. Shuttle service is $14.50 from Snow Lodge, $15.50 from Mammoth. Group and private lessons are available. Skier shuttles run from Mammoth Hotel to Indian Creek and from Old Faithful Snow Lodge to Fairy Falls. Guided tours on snowmobiles start at $198/person. Guided snow-coach tours are available for $52.50 to $68. Both types of tours run from late December through early March. The **Yellowstone Association Institute** (☎ *307/344–2293* ⊕ *www.yellowstoneassociation.org*) offers everything from day-long cross-country skiing excursions to multiday Lodging and Learning trips geared around hiking, skiing, and snowshoeing treks. Expect to pay $200 to $500 for excursions; $500 to $1,000 or more for Lodging and Learning trips.

EDUCATIONAL OFFERINGS

CLASSES AND SEMINARS

Expedition: Yellowstone! Since 1985, this four- to five-day residential program for grades four through eight has taught kids about the natural and cultural history of Yellowstone, as well as the issues affecting its ecosystem. The curriculum includes hikes, discussions, journal keeping, and presentations. ⊠ *Lamar Buffalo Ranch facilities* ☎ *307/344–2658* ☯ *Sept.–May.*

Yellowstone Institute. Stay in a log cabin in Lamar Valley while taking a course about the park's ecology, history, or wildlife. Search with a historian for the trail the Nez Perce Indians took in their flight a century ago from the U.S. Army, or get the perfect shot with tips from professional photographers. Facilities are fairly primitive—guests do their own cooking and camp during some of the courses—but prices are reasonable. Some programs are specifically designed for young people and families. ⊠ *North Park Rd., between Tower-Roosevelt and Northeast Entrance* ☎ *307/344–2294* ⊕ *www.yellowstoneassociation.org/institute* ☯ *Year-round, programs vary with season.*

RANGER PROGRAMS

Yellowstone offers a busy schedule of guided hikes, talks, and campfire programs. For dates and times, check the park's *Yellowstone Today* newsletter, available at all entrances and visitor centers.

☾ ★ **Evening Programs.** Gather around to hear tales about Yellowstone's fascinating history, with hour-long programs on topics ranging from the return of the bison to 19th-century photographers. Every major area hosts programs, but check visitor centers or campground bulletin

GOOD READS

■ *The Yellowstone Story,* by Aubrey L. Haines, is a classic.

■ *Yellowstone Place Names,* by Lee Whittlesey, tells the stories behind the names of many park destinations.

■ *Yellowstone: The Official Guide to Touring America's First National Park,* published by Yellowstone Association, is a magazine-sized, full-color, glossy 80-page "yearbook."

■ *Decade of the Wolf,* by Douglas Smith, is the most comprehensive and gripping account of the reintroduction of wolves into the park in the 1990s.

■ *Yellowstone Trails, A Hiking Guide,* by Mark C. Marschall, will help you navigate the shortest and longest trails in the park.

■ *Lost In My Own Backyard,* by Tim Cahill, is a hilarious account of one person's experience in the park.

■ Explaining the park's geological processes are William R. Keefer's *The Geologic Story of Yellowstone National Park* and Robert B. Smith and Lee J. Siegel's *Windows into the Earth: The Geologic Story of Yellowstone and Grand Teton National Parks.*

■ Alston Chase's controversial *Playing God in Yellowstone* chronicles a century of government mismanagement.

boards for updates. Most programs begin at 9 or 9:30 PM, though there are earlier programs at Norris, Fishing Bridge, and Old Faithful. ⊗ *June–Aug., nightly at 9 and 9:30.*

☾ **Daytime Walks and Talks.** Ranger-led programs run during both the winter and summer seasons. Ranger Adventure Hikes are more strenuous and must be reserved in advance (the number of participants is limited), but anyone can join the regular ranger talks and ranger walks. Winter programs are held at West Yellowstone, Old Faithful, and Mammoth.

☾ **Junior Ranger Program.** Children ages 5 to 12 are eligible to earn patches and become Junior Rangers. Pick up the Junior Ranger Newspaper at Madison, Canyon, or Old Faithful for $3 and start the fun, self-guided curriculum.

TOURS

Old Yellow Bus Tour. The historic 14-passenger yellow buses are originals built in 1937. Restored and reintroduced in 2007, the White Motors' vehicles are the most elegant way to learn about the park. Your driver, who narrates the trip, will roll back the soft-top convertible for you to bask under the sun (and look up to take in the sights!) if it's warm enough and not raining. More than a dozen itineraries range from one hour to all day, and will likely include wildlife sightings, photo opportunities, and some of the park's favorite landmarks. Yellow buses depart from various locations, including the Grey Wolf Inn in West Yellowstone and Canyon Lodge in Canyon. ☎ *866/439–7375* ⊕ *www. travelyellowstone.com* ✉ *$14.50–$92* ⊗ *June–Sept.*

Park Ranger Mary Wilson

For Yellowstone National Park Ranger Mary Wilson, every day is an adventure, and even after two decades of working in some of the nation's most pristine preserves, she never tires of assisting visitors who have come to explore America's natural treasures.

"Almost every day, I am approached by visitors who, in awe of the wonderful and exciting things they have experienced in the parks, tell me that these places are the most beautiful and inspiring places they have ever seen or been," she says. "Somehow, these places help foster memories and feelings that last a lifetime."

Wilson's passion for animals, combined with a love for the outdoors and helping people, turned her professional interests toward the National Park Service. "Serving as a park ranger was a way to achieve a little of all of those worlds," says Wilson, who grew up in Muncie, IN, and earned her bachelor's and master's degrees from Purdue University.

After serving stints as a student volunteer in South Dakota's Custer State Park and Montana's Glacier National Park, working side by side with rangers, Wilson was hired by the National Park Service in Glacier. Since then, she's taken assignments at Rocky Mountain, Grand Canyon, and Sequoia/Kings Canyon national parks, and Montezuma Castle National Monument. At her job at Yellowstone she supervises other rangers as well as assists visitors.

RANGER WILSON'S TOP 10 TIPS

1. Before your trip, go online to get information from the park's official Web site, ⊕ *www.nps.gov/yell.*

2. Upon arrival at the park, stop at the nearest visitor center for information and updates.

3. Pack for all types of weather no matter what time of year.

4. Avoid the crowds by getting an early start to your day.

5. Stay at least 75 feet away from wildlife (300 feet for bears).

6. Stay on geyser basin boardwalks to prevent serious thermal burns.

7. Drive defensively, and allow more time than you think you need.

8. Try to be at your destination before dark to avoid hitting wildlife on park roads.

9. Take a friend when you go hiking; it's safer and a lot more fun!

10. Don't try to see and do everything. You need two to three days just to visit the park highlights.

WHAT'S NEARBY

Because of its airport and its proximity to both Grand Teton and Yellowstone national parks, **Jackson,** the closest town to Yellowstone's South Entrance, is the region's busiest community in the summer and has the widest selection of dining and lodging options. Meanwhile, the least well-known gateway, the little town of **Dubois**, southeast of the park, is far from the madding crowds and a good place to stop on the way in or out of the park if you want to visit the National Bighorn Sheep Interpretive Center.

The most popular gateway from Montana, particularly in winter, is **West Yellowstone,** near the park's West Entrance. This is where the open plains of southwestern Montana and northeastern Idaho come together along the Madison River Valley. Affectionately known among winter recreationists as the "snowmobile capital of the world," this town of 1,000 is also a good place to go for fishing, horseback riding, and downhill skiing. There's also plenty of culture, as this is where you'll find the Museum of the Yellowstone. There is also a small airport here.

As the only entrance to Yellowstone that's open the entire year, **Gardiner,** in Montana, is always bustling. The town's Roosevelt Arch has marked the park's North Entrance since 1903, when President Theodore Roosevelt dedicated it. The Yellowstone River slices through town, beckoning fishermen and rafters. The town of 800 has quaint shops and good restaurants. North of Gardiner, along Interstate 90, is **Livingston,** a town of 7,500 known for its charming historic district.

With both Yellowstone and the Absaroka-Beartooth Wilderness at its back door, the Montana village of **Cooke City,** at the park's Northeast Entrance, is a good place for hiking, horseback riding, mountain climbing, and other outdoor activities. Some 50 mi to the east of Cooke City and 60 mi southeast of Billings via U.S. 212 is the small resort town of **Red Lodge.** Nestled against the foot of the pine-draped Absaroka-Beartooth Wilderness and edged by the Limestone Palisades, Red Lodge has a ski area, trout fishing, a golf course, horseback riding, and more options for dining and lodging than Cooke City. Driving along the Beartooth Scenic Byway between Red Lodge and Cooke City, you'll cross the southern tip of the Beartooth range, literally in the ramparts of the Rockies. From Cooke City, the drive into Yellowstone through the Lamar Valley is one of the prettiest routes in the park.

Named for Pony Express rider, army scout, and entertainer William F. "Buffalo Bill" Cody, the town of **Cody,** in Wyoming, sits near the park's East Entrance. It is a good base for hiking trips, horseback riding excursions, and white-water rafting on the North Fork of the Shoshone or the Clark Fork of the Yellowstone. It also is home to dude ranches and, in season, the nightly rodeo.

WHERE TO EAT AND STAY

ABOUT THE RESTAURANTS

When traveling in Yellowstone it's always a good idea to bring along a cooler—that way you can carry some snacks and lunch items for a picnic or break and not have to worry about making it to one of the more developed areas of the park, where all restaurants and cafeterias are managed by two competing companies (Xanterra and Delaware North). Generally, you'll find burgers and sandwiches at cafeterias and full meals (as well as a kid's menu) at restaurants. There is a good selection of entrées, such as free-range beef and chicken; game meats such as elk, venison, and trout; plus organic vegetables. At the several delis and general stores in the park you can purchase picnic items, snacks, sandwiches, and desserts like fudge and ice cream. Considering that you are in one of the most remote outposts of the United States, selection and quality are above average—but expect to pay more as well. Note that reservations are often needed for dinner at the dining rooms during the busy summer season.

ABOUT THE HOTELS

Park lodgings range from two of the national park system's magnificent old hotels to simple cabins to bland modern motels. Make reservations at least a year in advance for July and August for all park lodgings. Old Faithful Snow Lodge and Mammoth Hot Springs Hotel are the only accommodations open in winter; rates are the same as in summer. Ask about the size of beds, bathrooms, thickness of walls, and room location when you book, especially in the older hotels, where accommodations vary and upgrades are ongoing. Telephones have been put in some rooms, but there are no TVs. All park lodging is no-smoking. There are no roll-away beds available.

ABOUT THE CAMPGROUNDS

Yellowstone has a dozen front-country campgrounds scattered around the park, in addition to more than 200 backcountry sites. Most campgrounds have flush toilets; some have coin-operated showers and laundry facilities. ■TIP→ **Fishing Bridge RV Park is the only campground offering water, sewer, and electrical hookups, and it is for hard-sided vehicles only (no tents or tent-trailers are allowed).**

The seven small campgrounds operated by the National Park Service—Norris, Lewis Lake, Mammoth, Indian Creek, Tower Fall, Slough Creek, and Pebble Creek—are available on a first-come, first-served basis. Choice sites like those at Slough Creek fill up by 10 AM each day in the summer. To get a site in an NPS campground, arrive in the morning, pick out your site, pay (cash only, no change available) at a drop box near the campground host (look for a sign near the entrance to the campground), and leave your receipt and an inexpensive item (empty cooler, water jug, etc.) at the campsite. NPS limits campers to 14 days maximum at any one location in the summer.

The campgrounds run by Xanterra Parks & Resorts—Bridge Bay, Canyon, Fishing Bridge, Grant Village, and Madison—accept bookings in advance, although you'll pay about a $5 premium over the National Park Service campsites. These campgrounds are in great settings, but they are large—more than 250 sites each—and can feel very crowded. Tents and RVs coexist, although Xanterra designates certain areas as "tent only." Larger groups can reserve space in Bridge Bay, Grant, and Madison from late May through September. To reserve, call ☎ 307/344-7311.

If you're prepared to carry your own water and other necessities, you could also consider a backcountry campsite. There are more than 300 backcountry sites in the park, located as little as 2 mi from parking lots and trailheads. Check availability and obtain the required (though free) permit at any ranger station, visitor center, or backcountry office; you may also pay $20 to reserve one of these sites in advance (the reservations open on April 1 each year). Talk to the park's accessibility coordinator about ADA-accessible backcountry sites. All backcountry campsites have restrictions on group size and length of stay. Boating is prohibited throughout the backcountry, and pit fires are prohibited at certain campsites.

WHAT IT COSTS					
	¢	$	$$	$$$	$$$$
Restaurants	under $8	$8–$12	$13–$20	$21–$30	over $30
Hotels	under $70	$70–$100	$101–$150	$151–$200	over $200
Campgrounds	under $10	$10–$17	$18–$35	$36–$49	over $50

Restaurant prices are per person for a main course at dinner. Hotel prices are per night for two people in a standard double room in high season, excluding taxes and service charges. Camping prices are for a standard (no hookups, pit toilets, fire grates, picnic tables) campsite per night.

WHERE TO EAT

¢–$
FAST FOOD
✕**Bear Paw Deli.** You can grab a quick bite and not miss a geyser eruption at this snack shop located off the lobby in the Old Faithful Inn. Burgers, chicken sandwiches, and chili typify your choices for hot meals. If you're staying at the inn, this is also a good place to fill up your water bottles with cold water from the soda fountain. This is strictly a grab-and-go place, with no tables or bar seating. ⊠ *Old Faithful Village, Old Faithful* ☎ *307/344–7311* ⊟ *AE, D, DC, MC, V* ⊘ *Closed early Oct.–late May.*

¢–$$
AMERICAN
✕**Canyon Lodge Cafeteria.** This busy lunch spot serves such traditional and simple American fare as country-fried steak and hot turkey sandwiches. Grab a tray and get in line. It stays open for late diners and is open for early risers, too, with a full breakfast menu. ⊠ *Canyon Village* ☎ *307/344–7311* ⊟ *AE, D, DC, MC, V* ⊘ *Closed mid-Sept.–early June.*

¢–$
FAST FOOD
☾
✕**Geyser Grill.** Location drives this busy grill, where burgers, chicken nuggets, and hot dogs highlight the kids' menu and Mom and Dad can squeak by on a sparse assortment of soup, salads, and sandwiches. Remember you're here for the geyser, not the grub. ⊠ *Inside Old Faithful Lodge at the south end of Old Faithful Village* ☎ *307/344–7311* ⊟ *AE, D, DC, MC, V* ⊘ *Closed Nov.–mid-Dec. and early Jan.–mid-Apr. Closes at 5 PM in winter.*

$–$$$
AMERICAN
✕**Grant Village Dining Room.** The floor-to-ceiling windows of this lakeshore restaurant provide views of Yellowstone Lake through the thick stand of pines. The most contemporary of the park's restaurants, it makes you feel at home with pine-beam ceilings and cedar-shake walls. You'll find dishes ranging from pasta to wild salmon to bison meatloaf; in late season you'll find a sandwich buffet on Sundays. ⊠ *About 2 mi south of West Thumb junction in Grant Village* ☎ *307/344–7311* ⚠ *Reservations essential* ⊟ *AE, D, DC, MC, V* ⊘ *Closed late Sept.–late May.*

¢–$$
AMERICAN
☾
✕**Lake Lodge Cafeteria.** One of the park's most inspiring views overlooking the lake does not make up for this casual eatery's dreary cafeteria menu. Roast turkey breast, Stroganoff, and pot roast are typical fare. On the plus side, portions are hearty. It also has a full breakfast menu. ⊠ *At the end of Lake Village Rd., about 1 mi south of Fishing Bridge junction* ☎ *307/344–7311* ⊟ *AE, D, DC, MC, V* ⊘ *Closed mid-Sept.–early June.*

$$-$$$$
AMERICAN
Fodor's Choice
★

✕ **Lake Yellowstone Hotel Dining Room.** Opened in 1893 and renovated by Robert Reamer beginning in 1903, this double-colonnaded dining room off the hotel lobby is the most elegant dining experience in the park. It is an upgrade from Old Faithful Inn in every way—service, china, view, menu sophistication, and even the quality of the crisp salads. Arrive early and enjoy a beverage in the airy Reamer Lounge. The dinner menu includes attractive starters like an artisanal cheese plate and organic salads. Main courses feature elk, buffalo, steak, and at least one imaginative pasta, vegetarian, and fish entrée. The wine list focuses on wines from California, Oregon, and Washington—with prices as high as $125 for a bottle of Mondavi Reserve Cabernet. Reservations are not needed for breakfast or lunch, but are essential for dinner; you can make them up to a year in advance with your hotel room reservations; or 60 days in advance without a hotel reservation. ✉ *Approximately 1 mi south of Fishing Bridge Junction at Lake Village Rd., Lake Village* ☎ *307/344–7311* ⚲ *Reservations essential* ▭ *AE, D, DC, MC, V* ⊙ *Closed early Oct.–mid-May.*

$-$$$
AMERICAN

✕ **Mammoth Hot Springs Dining Room.** A wall of windows overlooks an expanse of green that was once a military parade and drill field at Mammoth Hot Springs. The art-deco-style restaurant, decorated in shades of gray, green, and burgundy, has an airy feel with its bentwood chairs. Montana beef, bison, and fish are featured, and there is always at least one pasta and vegetarian dish. ✉ *5 mi south of North Entrance in village of Mammoth Hot Springs* ☎ *307/344–7311* ⚲ *Reservations essential* ▭ *AE, D, DC, MC, V* ⊙ *Closed mid-Oct.–mid-Dec. and mid-Mar.–mid-May.*

¢-$
FAST FOOD

✕ **Mammoth Terrace Grill.** Although the exterior looks rather elegant, this restaurant in Mammoth Hot Springs serves only fast food, ranging from biscuits and gravy for breakfast to hamburgers and veggie burgers for lunch and dinner. ✉ *Mammoth Springs Hotel, Mammoth Hot Springs, 5 mi south of North Entrance* ☎ *307/344–7311* ▭ *AE, D, DC, MC, V* ⊙ *Closed late Sept.–mid-May.*

$$-$$$$
STEAK
Fodor's Choice
★

✕ **Obsidian Dining Room.** From the wood-and-leather chairs etched with figures of park animals to the intricate lighting fixtures that resemble snowcapped trees, there's ample Western atmosphere at this smaller dining room (capacity: 106 guests) inside the Old Faithful Snow Lodge. The huge windows give you a view of the Old Faithful area, and you can sometimes see the famous geyser as it erupts. Aside from Mammoth Hot Springs Dining Room, this is the only place in the park where you can enjoy a full dinner in winter. The French onion soup will warm you up on a chilly afternoon; among the main courses, look for prime rib, elk, beef, or salmon. ✉ *Old Faithful Snow Lodge, south end of Old Faithful Village* ☎ *307/344–7311* ▭ *AE, D, DC, MC, V* ⊙ *Closed mid-Oct.–mid-Dec. and mid-Mar.–early May. No lunch.*

$$-$$$
AMERICAN

✕ **Old Faithful Inn Dining Room.** Just behind the lobby, the original dining room designed by Robert Reamer in 1903—and expanded by him in 1927—has lodgepole-pine walls and ceiling beams and a giant volcanic-rock fireplace graced with a contemporary painting of Old Faithful by the late Paco Young. Note the etched glass panels featuring partying cartoon animals that separates the dining room from the Bear Pit Lounge. These are reproductions of oak panels commissioned by Reamer in

1933 to celebrate the end of Prohibition. A buffet offers quantity over quality: bison, chicken, shrimp, two salads, two soups, and a dessert. You're better off choosing from nearly a dozen entrées on the à la carte menu, including grilled salmon, baked chicken, prime rib, and bison rib eye. Expect at least one vegetarian entrée in addition to a choice of salads and soups (e.g., roasted red pepper and Gouda). Save room for a signature dessert such as the Caldera, a chocolate truffle torte with a molten middle. The most extensive wine list in the park offers more than 50 (all American) choices, including sparkling and nonalcoholic varieties (from $20 to $70 per bottle). For breakfast, there's a buffet as well as individual entrées. ⊠ *Take first left off Old Faithful Bypass Road for the hotel parking lot; Old Faithful Village* 🕾 *307/344–7311* ♣ *Reservations essential* 🖃 *AE, D, DC, MC, V* ⊗ *Closed late Oct.–early May.*

¢–$$ ✕ **Old Faithful Lodge Cafeteria.** As you navigate this noisy family-oriented
AMERICAN eatery, remember that you came for the park, not the services. This caf-
☾ eteria serves kid-friendly fare such as pizza and hamburgers. Its redeeming feature is that it has some of the best views of Old Faithful, so you can watch it erupt while you eat. It is not open for breakfast, but the snack shop just outside is, offering a small selection of baked goods and cereal. ⊠ *At the end of Old Faithful Bypass Rd., less than 300 yards east of Old Faithful* 🕾 *307/344–7311* 🖃 *AE, D, DC, MC, V* ⊗ *Closed mid-Sept.–mid-May.*

$$–$$$ ✕ **Roosevelt Lodge Dining Room.** At this rustic log cabin in a pine forest, the
AMERICAN menu ranges from barbecued ribs and baked beans to hamburgers and
☾ fries. Don't miss the killer cornbread muffins. Arrive early and watch horses and stagecoaches come and go from the front porch. For a real Western adventure, call ahead to join the popular chuck-wagon cookout ($55; reservations essential) that includes an hour-long trail ride or a stagecoach ride. ⊠ *Tower-Roosevelt, immediately south of the junction of Northeast Entrance Rd. and Grand Loop Rd.* 🕾 *307/344–7311* 🖃 *AE, D, DC, MC, V* ⊗ *Closed early Sept.–early June.*

PICNIC AREAS The 49 picnic areas in the park range from secluded spots with a couple of tables to more popular stops with a dozen or more tables and several amenities. Only nine areas—Snake River, Grant Village, Spring Creek, Nez Perce, Old Faithful East, Bridge Bay, Cascade Lake Trail, Norris Meadows, and Yellowstone River—have fire grates. Only gas stoves may be used in the other areas. None have running water; all but a few have pit toilets. You can stock up your cooler at any of the park's general stores. It is also possible to purchase box lunches that include drinks, snacks, sandwiches, and fruit, or vegetarian or cheese-and-crackers selections from some park restaurants.

■ TIP➔ **Keep an eye out for wildlife;** you never know when a herd of bison might decide to march through (if that happens, it's best to leave your food and move a safe distance away from them).

☾ **Firehole River.** The Firehole River rolls past and you might see elk grazing along its banks. This picnic area has 12 tables and one pit toilet. ⊠ *Grand Loop Rd., 3 mi south of Madison.*

Gibbon Meadows. You are likely to see elk or buffalo along the Gibbon River from one of nine tables at this area, which has a wheelchair-accessible pit toilet. ⊠ *Grand Loop Rd., 3 mi south of Norris.*

Sedge Bay. On the northern end of this volcanic beach, look carefully for the large rock slabs pushed out of the lake bottom. Nearby trees offer shade and a table, or hop onto the level rocks for an ideal lakeside picnic. You may see bubbles rising from the clear water around the rocks—these indicate an active underwater thermal feature. The only company you may have here could be crickets, birds, and bison. ⊠ *East Entrance Rd., 8 mi east of Fishing Bridge Junction.*

WHERE TO STAY

CANYON

$–$$ **Canyon Cabins.** Unattractive and unassuming, these pine-frame cabins are mostly in clusters of four, six, and eight units. Thanks to an upgrade, they all now have private bathrooms, and higher-end cabins also have knotty-pine bed frames, hand sinks, and coffeemakers. Their popularity is based primarily on their location—you're in the heart of the park less than 30 minutes away from Lamar Valley, Hayden Valley, and Yellowstone Lake; Old Faithful is less than 45 minutes away. You also can park close to the door, so you don't have to schlep your luggage far. From the cabins there's a trail you can take down to the Grand View overlook of the canyon—it's through bear country, so make a lot of noise as you walk. Three restaurants and a bar are nearby. **Pros:** affordability; location; private baths. **Cons:** too much asphalt; too many neighbors; no central lodge/lobby area for hanging out. ⊠ *North Rim Dr. at Grand Loop Rd., Canyon Village* ☎ *307/344–7901* ⊕ *www.travelyellowstone. com* ⇱ *428 cabins* ⚹ *In-room: no a/c, no phone, no TV* ⊟ *AE, D, DC, MC, V* ☯ *Closed mid-Sept.–late May.*

$$$ **Cascade Lodge.** Pine wainscoting and brown carpets set the tone in this lodge built in 1992 in the trees above the Grand Canyon of the Yellowstone. The location is at the farthest edge of the Canyon Village, which means it's quite a hike to the nearest dining facilities—and you have to pass through rows upon rows of cabins, parking lots, and roads to get anywhere; the payoff is a quiet environment, because it's away from the major traffic. **Pros:** the Canyon location is central; indoor lounge and outdoor patio can be a great place for a family card game. **Cons:** you'll mostly likely want to drive to restaurants. ⊠ *North Rim Dr. at Grand Loop Rd., Canyon Village* ☎ *307/344–7901* ⊕ *www.travelyellowstone. com* ⇱ *40 rooms* ⚹ *In-room: no a/c, no TV. In-hotel: bar* ⊟ *AE, D, DC, MC, V* ☯ *Closed mid-Sept.–late May.*

$$$ **Dunraven Lodge.** This dorm-style lodge is in the pine trees at the edge of the Grand Canyon of the Yellowstone, adjacent to the essentially identical Cascade Lodge. It's at the farthest edge of the Canyon Village, so it's a hike to the nearest dining facilities. **Pros:** canyon location. **Cons:** far from dining and other services; with children you'll need to drive to restaurants. ⊠ *North Rim Dr., at Grand Loop Rd., Canyon Village* ☎ *307/344–7901* ⊕ *www.travelyellowstone.com* ⇱ *41 rooms* ⚹ *In-room: no a/c, no TV. In-hotel: bar* ⊟ *AE, D, DC, MC, V* ☯ *Closed mid-Sept.–late May.*

CAMPING   **Canyon.** A massive campground with 250-plus sites, the Canyon
$$ campground accommodates everyone from hiker/biker tent campers to
☙   large RVs. The campground is accessible to Canyon's many short trails. Nearby Canyon Village offers every service—stores, laundry, ranger

station, ice, etc.—which makes this campground a hit with families. The location is near laundry facilities and the visitor center. Generators are allowed from 8 AM to 8 PM. **Pros:** a great base in the middle of the park; all services close by. **Cons:** tents and RVs may share close quarters; not a very quiet campground; highest elevation (and therefore the coldest!) campground in the park. ⊠ *North Rim Dr., ¼ mi east of Grand Loop Rd., Canyon Village* ☎ *307/344–7311* ⊕ *www.travelyellowstone.com* ⚏ *Flush toilets, drinking water, guest laundry, showers, bear boxes, fire pits, picnic tables, public telephone, ranger station* ⚏ *272 sites* ⊟ *AE, D, DC, MC, V* ☉ *Early June–early Sept.*

GRANT VILLAGE

CAMPING ⚏ **Grant Village.** The park's second-largest campground, Grant Village
$$ has some sites with great views of Yellowstone Lake. Some of the sites are wheelchair accessible. The campground has a boat launch but no dock. Generators are allowed from 8 AM to 8 PM. **Pros:** group sites available; ease of access to Grand Teton National Park. **Cons:** huge campground means lots of engine noise, generators, and kid chatter in the evening; a long, long way from Mammoth Hot Springs and the wildlife-rich Lamar Valley. ⊠ *South Entrance Rd., 2 mi south of West Thumb* ☎ *307/344–7311* ⊕ *www.travelyellowstone.com* ⚏ *Flush toilets, dump station, drinking water, guest laundry, showers, bear boxes, picnic tables, public telephone, ranger station* ⚏ *425 sites* ⊟ *AE, D, DC, MC, V* ☉ *Late June–late Sept.*

MADISON

CAMPING ⚏ **Madison.** The largest National Park Service–operated campground,
$$ where no advance reservations are accepted, Madison has eight loops and nearly 300 sites. The outermost loop backs up to the Madison River, but other sites feel a bit claustrophobic. You can't beat the location, though, halfway between the Old Faithful village and the West Entrance, so you're minutes from five different geyser basins, Old Faithful, and three picturesque rivers (the Firehole, Madison, and Gibbon). The campground can accommodate trailers up to 45 feet. Generators are allowed from 8 AM to 8 PM. **Pros:** location; rivers; nearby geysers. **Cons:** no store for last-minute purchases; it's a busy junction (for both cars and buffalo). ⊠ *Grand Loop Rd., Madison* ☎ *307/344–7311* ⊕ *www.travelyellowstone.com* ⚏ *Flush toilets, dump station, drinking water, bear boxes, fire pits, picnic tables, public telephone, ranger station* ⚏ *277 tent/RV sites* ⊟ *AE, D, DC, MC, V* ☉ *Closed late Sept.–early May.*

MAMMOTH HOT SPRINGS

$–$$ 🏨 **Mammoth Hot Springs Hotel and Cabins.** Built in 1937, this hotel has a spacious art-deco lobby, where you'll find an espresso cart after 4 PM. The rooms are smaller and less elegant than those at the park's other two historic hotels, but the Mammoth Hot Springs Hotel is less expensive and usually less crowded. In summer the rooms can get hot, but you can open the windows, and there are fans. More than half the rooms do not have their own bathrooms; shared baths are down the hall. The cabins, set amid lush lawns, are the nicest inside the park, but most do not have private bathrooms, and only two very expensive suites have TVs. This is one of only two lodging facilities open in winter.

Some cabins have hot tubs, a nice amenity after a day of cross-country skiing or snowshoeing. **Pros:** great rates for a historic property; terrific place to watch elk in the fall. **Cons:** those elk grazing on the lawn can create traffic jams; many hotel rooms and cabins are without private bathrooms; rooms can get hot during the day. ⊠ *Mammoth Hot Springs* ☎ *307/344–7901* ⊕ *www.travelyellowstone.com* ⤺ *97 rooms, 67 with bath; 2 suites; 115 cabins, 76 with bath* ⟡ *In-room: no a/c, no phones (some), no TV. In-hotel: restaurant, bar* ⊟ *AE, D, DC, MC, V* ⊘ *Closed early Oct.–late-Dec. and mid-Mar.–early May.*

CAMPING   △ **Indian Creek.** In a picturesque setting next to a creek, this campground
$ is in the middle of a prime wildlife-viewing area. There are some combination sites that can accommodate trailers up to 40 feet. **Pros:** tree-covered creek-side sites are some of the park's most tranquil places to rest; nice spot to watch wildlife. **Cons:** pit toilets only. ⊠ *8 mi south of Mammoth Hot Springs on Grand Loop Rd.* ☎ *no phone* ⟡ *Pit toilets, bear boxes, fire pits, picnic tables* △ *75 tent/RV sites* ⊟ *No credit cards* ⊘ *Closed mid-Sept.–mid-June.*

NORRIS

CAMPING   △ **Norris.** Straddling the Gibbon River, this is a quiet, popular camp-
$ ground. A few of its "walk-in" sites are among the best in the park. Anglers love catching brook trout and grayling here. The campground can accommodate trailers up to 45 feet. Generators are allowed from 8 AM to 8 PM. **Pros:** a fisherman's dream; some sites are especially secluded. **Cons:** the secret is out—this campsite fills up quickly. ⊠ *Grand Loop Rd., Norris* ☎ *307/344–2177* ⟡ *Flush toilets, drinking water, bear boxes, fire pits, picnic tables, ranger station* △ *116 tent/RV sites* ⊟ *No credit cards* ⊘ *Closed late Sept.–mid-May.*

OLD FAITHFUL AREA

$$$–$$$$ 🏨 **Old Faithful Inn.** This Robert Reamer signature building is deserving
♺   of its National Historic Landmark status—and has been a favorite of
Fodor'sChoice   five generations of park visitors. The so-called Old House was originally
★   built in 1904, and is worth a visit regardless of whether or not you are staying the night. The lobby has a 76-foot-high, eight-sided fireplace, bright red iron-clad doors, and two balconies as well as a fantasy-like "tree house" of platforms, ladders, and dormer windows high above the foyer. You can stay in 1904-era rooms with thick wood timber walls and ceilings for less than $100 if you are willing to forsake a private bathroom. Rooms with bathrooms in either the Old House or the "modern" wings (built in 1913 and 1927) rent for as high as $200-plus. There's no insulation, so it's closed in the winter. **Pros:** a one-of-a-kind property, Old House rooms are truly memorable with pine-pine walls and ceilings. **Cons:** thin walls; waves of tourists in the lobby; shared baths make you recall college dorm days. ⊠ *Old Faithful Village* ⊹ *Take the first left off of the Bypass Road to the hotel parking lot and miss the busy geyser parking area, Old Faithful* ☎ *307/344–7901* ⊕ *www.travelyellowstone. com* ⤺ *324 rooms, 246 with bath; 6 suites* ⟡ *In-room: no a/c, no phone (some), no TV. In-hotel: restaurant, bar* ⊟ *AE, D, DC, MC, V* ⊘ *Closed mid-Oct.–early May.*

2

¢–$$ Old Faithful Lodge Cabins. There are no rooms inside the Old Faithful Lodge, though there are 97 cabins sitting at the northeast end of the village. Typical of cabins throughout the park, these are very basic—lacking most amenities (including bathrooms in about one-third of the cabins), views, or character. However, the location can't be beat—cabins are almost as close to the geyser as Old Faithful Inn. If you plan to spend a day or three exploring the geyser basins or the central area of the park, this is a great budget-conscious place to lay down your head, since you'll be out and about most of the time anyway. **Pros:** considering its location, price can't be beat; a stone's throw from Old Faithful geyser, all area services are within walking distance. **Cons:** some cabins lack private bathrooms; pretty basic. ⊠ *South end of Old Faithful Bypass Rd.* ☎ *307/344–7901* ⊕ *www.travelyellowstone.com* ⤹ *96 cabins, 60 with bath* ⚿ *In-room: no a/c, no phone, no TV. In-hotel: restaurant* ☱ *AE, D, DC, MC, V* ☉ *Closed mid-Sept.–mid-May.*

$$$ Old Faithful Snow Lodge. Built in 1998, this massive structure brings back the grand tradition of park lodges by making good use of heavy timber beams and wrought-iron accents in a distinctive facade. Inside, you'll find soaring ceilings, natural lighting, and a spacious lobby with a stone fireplace. Nearby is a long sitting room, where writing desks and overstuffed chairs invite you to linger. Guest rooms combine traditional style with modern amenities. This is one of only two lodging facilities in the park that are open in winter, when the only way to get here is on over-snow vehicles. **Pros:** the most modern hotel in the park; the lobby and adjacent breezeway are great for relaxing; the only property on the interior of the park open in winter. **Cons:** pricey, but you're paying for location and some modern conveniences. ⊠ *Far end of Old Faithful Bypass Rd., Old Faithful* ☎ *307/344–7901* ⊕ *www.travelyellowstone.com* ⤹ *100 rooms* ⚿ *In-room: no a/c, no TV. In-hotel: restaurant, bicycles* ☱ *AE, D, DC, MC, V* ☉ *Closed mid-Oct.–mid-Dec. and mid-Mar.–early May.*

$–$$ Old Faithful Snow Lodge Cabins. The massive 1988 fires claimed some of the cabins just yards from Old Faithful, but like the park's foliage, new ones have sprung up. Western cabins feature brighter interiors, newer furnishings, and modern motel ambience. Frontier cabins resemble barracks, but the simple pine structures offer a roof, warmth, and shelter during cool summer nights. **Pros:** price and proximity to America's iconic geyser. **Cons:** expect no amenities beyond the basics of a bathroom, double beds, a roof, and a radiator. ⊠ *Far end of Old Faithful Bypass Rd., Old Faithful* ☎ *307/344–7901* ⊕ *www.travelyellowstone. com* ⤹ *100 rooms* ⚿ *In-room: no a/c, no TV. In-hotel: restaurant, bicycles* ☱ *AE, D, DC, MC, V* ☉ *Closed mid-Oct.–early May.*

TOWER-ROOSEVELT

¢–$$ Roosevelt Lodge Cabins. Near the beautiful Lamar Valley in the park's northeast corner, this simple lodge dating from the 1920s surpasses some of the more expensive options. All lodging is in rustic cabins set amid a pine forest. Some cabins have bathrooms, but most do not, though there is a bathhouse nearby. Roughrider cabins may have woodstoves as the only heating system. You can make arrangements here for horseback and stagecoach rides. **Pros:** closest cabins to Lamar Valley and its world-famous wildlife; authentic Western ranch feel; Roughrider cabins are the most inexpensive in the park. **Cons:** cabins are very close together; many lack private bathrooms; you may have to draw straws to stoke the fire at 3 AM if your Roughrider cabin has only a woodstove for heat. ⊠ *Tower-Roosevelt Junction on Grand Loop Rd., Tower-Roosevelt* ☎ *307/344–7901* ⊕ *www.travelyellowstone.com* ⌁ *80 cabins, 14 with bath* ⌂ *In-room: no a/c, no TV. In-hotel: restaurant* ⊟ *AE, D, DC, MC, V* ⊘ *Closed early Sept.–early June.*

CAMPING △ **Pebble Creek.** Beneath multiple 10,000-foot peaks (Thunderer, Bar-
$ ronnette Peak, and Mt. Norris) this easternmost campground in the park
★ is set creek-side in a forested canopy. Pebble Creek is a babbling stream here, but hike a few yards north of the canyon to see the small canyon the river has carved. Great fishing, hikes, and wildlife abound in the vicinity. Along with nearby Slough Creek, this is the best campground in the park. Because of its small size, it fills up by 10 AM on busy days. It's also smaller than most, which means it tends to be a little quieter. Sites can accommodate trailers up to 45 feet. Charming campground hosts Ray and Darlene Rathmell have been here for more than a decade. **Pros:** a small wilderness camping experience in one of the busiest national parks in the world; unparalleled setting. **Cons:** no services for miles. ⊠ *Northeast Entrance Rd., 22 mi east of Tower-Roosevelt Junction* ☎ *No phone* ⌂ *Pit toilets, bear boxes, fire pits, picnic tables* △ *32 tent/RV sites* ⊟ *No credit cards* ⊘ *Closed late Sept.–mid-June.*

$ △ **Slough Creek.** Down the most rewarding 2 mi of dirt road in the park,
★ Slough Creek is a gem. Nearly every site is adjacent to the creek, which is prized by anglers. The campground sits at the edge of the wildlife-rich Lamar Valley, and one of the famous wolf packs introduced in 1995 has taken up residence several miles up the river and bears the name Slough Creek Pack. Listen carefully for grunting bison, howling wolves, and bugling elk. If you want to stay here in the summer, make this your first stop in the morning— on many days it fills up by 10 AM. **Pros:** one of the last campgrounds to close annually; lower elevation often means warmer temps. **Cons:** there are fewer than three-dozen sites here, so you'll be hard-pressed to get a site in the summer if you're not here first thing in the morning to grab your spot. ⊠ *Northeast Entrance Rd., 10 mi east of Tower-Roosevelt Junction* ☎ *No phone* ⌂ *Pit toilets, bear boxes, fire pits, picnic tables* △ *29 tent/RV sites* ⊟ *No credit cards* ⊘ *Closed late Oct.–late May.*

$ △ **Tower Fall.** It's within hiking distance of the roaring waterfall, so this modest-size campground gets a lot of foot traffic. It can accommodate shorter trailers. Hot water and flush toilets are at Tower Store restrooms nearby. **Pros:** can't beat the price for a spot so close to the waterfall; easy to navigate; you can go for the ice cream at nearby Tower store. **Cons:** feels cramped and crowded. ⊠ *3 mi southeast of Tower-Roosevelt on Grand Loop Rd.* ☎ *No phone* △ *32 tent/RV sites* ⌂ *Pit toilets, bear boxes, fire pits, picnic tables* ⊟ *No credit cards* ⊘ *Closed late Sept.–mid-May.*

YELLOWSTONE LAKE AREA

$$–$$$$ ▥ **Lake Yellowstone Hotel.** More Kennebunkport than Western, this dis-
★ tinguished hotel is the park's oldest. Dating from 1891, the white-and-pastel-color hotel has maintained an air of refinement that Old Faithful Inn can't because of its constant tour buses full of visitors. Just off the lobby, a spacious sunroom offers priceless views of Yellowstone Lake at

sunrise or sunset. It's also a great place to play cards, catch up on a newspaper from the gift shop, or just soak in the grandeur of a 117-year-old National Historic Landmark. Note the tile-mantel fireplace, the etched windows of the gift shop, and the beautiful bay windows. Rooms have white wicker furnishings, which give them a light, airy feeling; some have views of the water. There is one two-room suite with lake views that has been used as accommodations for U.S. presidents. The least expensive rooms are in an annex, not the original building. **Pros:** an oasis of elegance in the park, with the best views of any park lodging. **Cons:** the most expensive property in the park; restaurant is expensive; not particularly kid-friendly. ⊠ *Lake Village Rd., Lake Village, about 1 mi south of Fishing Bridge* ☎ *307/344–7901* ⊕ *www.travelyellowstone. com* ☞ *194 rooms* ⚹ *In-room: no a/c, no TV. In-hotel: restaurant, bar* ⊟ *AE, D, DC, MC, V* ☉ *Closed early Oct.–mid-May.*

¢–$$ 🏠 **Lake Lodge Cabins.** Just beyond the Lake Yellowstone Hotel lies one
☺ of the park's hidden treasures: Lake Lodge, built in 1920. The 140-foot lobby and porch offer one of the best views of sunrise in the park. The lodge itself no longer offers rooms. Rather, check in at the lobby (make a note to return to enjoy the two fireplaces, a visiting speaker, or a meal), and then head for your cabin, which is just north of the lodge. The accommodations are basic Yellowstone no-frills style—clean, with one to three beds, and a sink (some also have a shower/tub). There are views of the lake from the lodge but not from the rooms. **Pros:** the best front porch at a Yellowstone lodge and a great lobby; affordability; good for families. **Cons:** no frills of any kind; sound of dribbling basketballs in the employee gym can ruin the lobby atmosphere. ⊠ *Lake Village Rd., Lake Village, about 1 mi south of Fishing Bridge* ☎ *307/344–7901* ⊕ *www.travelyellowstone.com* ☞ *186 rooms, 100 with bath* ⚹ *In-room: no a/c, no phones, no TV. In-hotel: restaurant, bar* ⊟ *AE, D, DC, MC, V* ☉ *Closed mid-Sept.–early June.*

CAMPING △ **Bridge Bay.** The park's largest campground, Bridge Bay rests in a
$$ wooded grove above Yellowstone Lake and adjacent to the park's major
★ marina. Ask for one of the few sites with a lake view. Xanterra tries to keep tent and RV campers separate—make sure to ask if you have a preference. If you end up on one of the inner loops, you may find yourself surrounded. You can rent boats at the nearby marina, take guided walks, or listen to rangers lecture about the history of the park. Don't expect solitude, as there are more than 400 campsites. Generators are allowed from 8 AM to 8 PM. Hot showers and laundry are 4 mi north at Fishing Bridge. **Pros:** the best spot for boaters to wake up, rev their outboard motor, and head out on the lake. **Cons:** the campground's size prevents this from being a wilderness camping experience. ⊠ *3 mi southwest of Lake Village on Grand Loop Rd., Bridge Bay* ☎ *307/344–7311* ⊕ *www.travelyellowstone.com* ⚹ *Flush toilets, dump station, drinking water, showers, bear boxes, fire pits, picnic tables, public telephone, ranger station* △ *432 tent/ RV sites* ⊟ *AE, D, DC, MC, V* ☉ *Closed mid-Sept.–late May.*

$$ △ **Fishing Bridge RV Park.** Fishing Bridge is the only facility in the park that caters exclusively to recreational vehicles. It's more of a parking lot than a campground, but RV services like tank filling/emptying and plug-ins are available. Because of bear activity in the area, only hard-sided

campers are allowed. Liquid propane is available. Generators are allowed from 8 AM to 8 PM. No boat access here (put in at Bridge Bay Marina, 4 mi away). Note that the nearby Fishing Bridge service station offers RV-specific services, including engine, mechanical, and "living space" repairs, as well as diesel gasoline and parts. **Pros:** Fishing Bridge general store has ample supplies and groceries. **Cons:** this is active bear country, so safeguard your food, children, and pets. ✉ *East Entrance Rd. at Grand Loop Rd.* ☎ *307/344–7311* 🌐 *www.travelyellowstone.com* ⛺ *344 RV sites* 👍 *Flush toilets, full hookups, dump station, drinking water, guest laundry, showers, bear boxes, picnic tables, public telephone, ranger station* 💳 *AE, D, DC, MC, V* ⏰ *Closed late Sept.–mid-May.*

Grand Teton National Park

WORD OF MOUTH

"The scenery in Grand Teton is breathtaking! I literally gasped as we drove up Hwy. 89 in Jackson, came around the curve and we got our first glimpse of the Teton Range!"

—luv2globetrot

WELCOME TO GRAND TETON

TOP REASONS TO GO

★ **Heavenward hikes:** Trek where grizzled frontiersmen roamed. Jackson Hole got its name from mountain man David Jackson; now there are dozens of trails for you to explore.

★ **Wildlife big and small:** Keep an eye out for little fellows like short-tailed weasels and beaver, as well as bison, elk, wolves, and both black and grizzly bears.

★ **Waves to make:** Float the Snake River or take a canoe onto Jackson Lake or Jenny Lake.

★ **Homesteader history:** Visit the 1890s barns and ranch buildings of Mormon Row or Menor's Ferry.

★ **Rare bird-watching:** Raise the binoculars—or just your head—to see more than 300 species of birds, including trumpeter swans, bald eagles, and osprey.

★ **Trout trophies:** Grab your rod and slither over to the Snake River, where cutthroat trout are an angler's delight.

1 Antelope Flats. Buffalo and antelope frequently roam across this sagebrush-covered area of the park northeast of Moose, and it is also where homesteader barns along Mormon Row dot the landscape. It's a popular place for wildflower viewing and bicycle rides.

2 Jenny Lake. In this developed area you can go to the visitor center, purchase supplies, or talk to a ranger—plus ride a boat across the lake, hike around it, have a picnic, or camp nearby.

3 Moose. Just north of Craig Thomas Discovery and Visitor Center, this historical area is home to the Chapel of the Transfiguration, and was once the stomping grounds of early settlers at Menor's Ferry.

4 Oxbow Bend. At this famously scenic spot the Snake River, its inhabitants, and the Tetons all converge, especially in early morning or near dusk. You're likely to see moose feeding in willows, elk grazing in aspen stands, and birds such as bald eagles, osprey, sandhill cranes, ducks, and American white pelicans.

GETTING ORIENTED

Grand Teton's immense peaks jut dramatically up from the Jackson Hole valley floor. Without any foothills to soften the blow, the sight of these glacier-scoured crags is truly striking. Several alpine lakes reflect the mountains, and the winding Snake River cuts south along the eastern side of the park. The northern portion of the park is outstanding wildlife-watching territory—you can see everything from rare birds to lumbering moose to the big predators (mountain lions and black and grizzly bears). Two main roads run through the 310,000-acre park; Highway 26/89/191 curves along the eastern or outer side and Teton Park Road (also called the inner park road, which is closed during winter) runs closer to the mountain range.

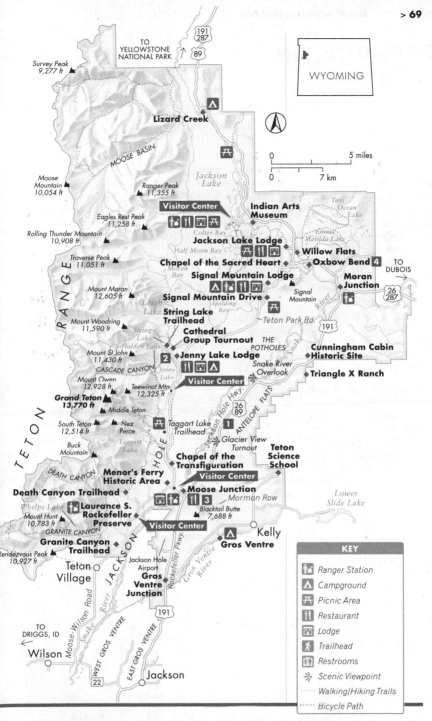

WYOMING

Survey Peak
9,277 ft

TO
YELLOWSTONE
NATIONAL PARK

3

MOOSE BASIN

Lizard Creek

Moose
Mountain
10,054 ft

Ranger Peak
11,355 ft

*Jackson
Lake*

0   5 miles

0   7 km

Eagles Rest Peak
11,258 ft

Visitor Center

Rolling Thunder Mountain
10,908 ft

Colter Bay

**Indian Arts
Museum**

Two
Ocean
Lake

Traverse Peak
11,051 ft

Jackson Lake Lodge
Half Moon Bay

Willow Flats

Emma
Matilda Lake

Chapel of the Sacred Heart   **Oxbow Bend**

TO
DUBOIS

Moran
Bay

Signal Mountain Lodge

**Moran
Junction**

Mount Moran
12,605 ft

Signal Mountain Drive

Signal
Mountain

26
287

Leigh
Lake

Spalding
Bay

Mount Woodring
11,590 ft

**String Lake
Trailhead**

String
Lake

Hidden Falls

Teton Park Rd.

Snake River

**Cathedral
Group Tournout**

THE
POTHOLES

191

**Cunningham Cabin
Historic Site**

Mount St John
11,430 ft

Jenny Lake Lodge

Snake River
Overlook

CASCADE CANYON

Jenny
Lake

Triangle X Ranch

Mount Owen
12,928 ft

Teewinot Mtn
12,325 ft

Visitor Center

**Grand Teton
13,770 ft**

Middle Teton

South Teton
12,514 ft

Nez
Perce

ANTELOPE FLATS

26
89

JACKSON HOLE Hwy

Buck
Mountain

Taggart
Lake

**Taggart Lake
Trailhead**

Glacier View
Turnout

**Teton
Science
School**

DEATH CANYON

**Chapel of the
Transfiguration**

**Menor's Ferry
Historic Area**

Death Canyon Trailhead

Phelps Lake

Visitor Center

Mount Hunt
10,783 ft

**Laurance S.
Rockefeller
Preserve**

Moose Junction

Mormon Row

GRANITE CANYON

Blacktail Butte
7,688 ft

Lower
Slide Lake

**Granite Canyon
Trailhead**

Visitor Center

Rendezvous Peak
10,927 ft

JACKSON HOLE

Jackson Hole
Airport

**Gros
Ventre
Junction**

Kelly

Gros Ventre

Teton
Village

Rockefeller Pkwy.

Gros Ventre River

191

TO
DRIGGS, ID

Moose-Wilson Road

Snake River

WEST GROS VENTRE

EAST GROS VENTRE

Wilson

22

Jackson

KEY	
🏚	*Ranger Station*
⛺	*Campground*
🌲	*Picnic Area*
🍴	*Restaurant*
🖼	*Lodge*
🥾	*Trailhead*
🚻	*Restrooms*
✦	*Scenic Viewpoint*
----	*Walking/Hiking Trails*
····	*Bicycle Path*

GRAND TETON PLANNER

When to Go

In July and August all the roads, trails, and visitor centers are open, and the Snake River's float season is in full swing. **To have access to most services without the crowds, plan a trip between May and June or in September.** Lower rates and smaller crowds can be found in spring and fall, but some services and roads are limited. Grand Teton Lodge Company, the park's major outfitter, winds down its activities in September, and most of Teton Park Road closes from late October through early May.

Towns outside the park rev up in winter. Teton Village and Jackson both buzz with the energy of Snow King Resort and Jackson Hole Mountain Resort, the former conveniently in town, the latter an international skiing hot spot deep in the valley. (Prices rise for the peak winter season.) Because of the many skiers, U.S. Highway 26/191/89 stays open all winter.

AVG. HIGH/LOW TEMPS.

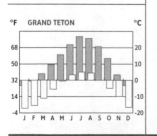

Flora and Fauna

Grand Teton's short growing season and arid climate create a complex ecosystem and hardy plant species. The dominant elements are big sagebrush, which gives a gray-green cast to the valley, lodgepole pine trees, quaking aspen, and ground-covering wildflowers such as bluish-purple alpine forget-me-nots. In spring and early summer you will see the vibrant yellow arrowleaf balsamroot and the delicate blue camas, a plant prized by American Indians for its nutritional value. The growing season in Jackson Hole is short, but gives rise to spectacular though short-lived displays of wildflowers. The best time to see these natural displays are mid-June to early July, although the changing of the aspen and cottonwood leaves in early fall can be equally spectacular.

On almost any trip to Grand Teton, you will see bison, antelopes, and moose. More rarely you will see a black or grizzly bear or a mountain lion or wolf. Watch for elk along the forest edge, and, in the summer, on Teton Park Road. Oxbow Bend and Willow Flats are good places to look for moose, beavers, and otters any time of year. Pronghorn antelope and bison appear in summer along Jackson Hole Highway and Antelope Flats Road. If animals are crossing the road, they have the right-of-way.

The park's smaller animals—yellow-bellied marmots and golden-mantled ground squirrels, as well as a variety of birds and waterfowl—are commonly seen along park trails and waterways. Seek out the water sources—the Snake River, the alpine lakes, and marshy areas—to see birds such as bald eagles, ospreys, ducks, and trumpeter swans. Your best chance to see wildlife is at dawn or dusk.

Getting Here and Around

The best way to see Grand Teton National Park is by car. Unlike Yellowstone's Grand Loop, Grand Teton's road system doesn't allow for easy tour-bus access to the major sights. Only a car will get you close to Jenny Lake, into the remote east Jackson Hole hills, and to the top of Signal Mountain. You can stop at many points along the roads within the park for a hike or a view. Be extremely cautious in winter when whiteouts and ice are not uncommon. There are adequate road signs throughout the park, but a good road map is handy to have in the vehicle.

Jackson Hole Highway (U.S. 89/191) runs the entire length of the park, from Jackson to Yellowstone National Park's south entrance. (This highway is also called Route 26 south of Moran Junction and U.S. 287 north of Moran Junction.) This road is open all year from Jackson to Moran Junction and north to Flagg Ranch, 2 mi south of Yellowstone. Depending on traffic, the southern (Moose) entrance to Grand Teton is about 15 minutes from downtown Jackson via Jackson Hole Highway. Coming from the opposite direction on the same road, the northern boundary of the park is about 15 minutes south of Yellowstone National Park. Also open year-round, U.S. 26/287 runs east from Dubois over Togwotee Pass to the Moran entrance station, a drive of about one hour.

Two back-road entrances to Grand Teton require high-clearance vehicles. Both are closed by snow from November through mid-May and are heavily rutted through June. Moose-Wilson Road (Route 390) starts at Route 22 in Wilson (west of Jackson) and travels 12 mi north past Teton Village, then turns into an unpaved road for 3 mi leading to the Moose entrance. It's closed to large trucks, trailers, and RVs. Even rougher is 60-mi Grassy Lake Road, which heads east from Route 32 in Ashton, Idaho, through Targhee National Forest. It connects with U.S. 89/287 in the John D. Rockefeller Jr. Memorial Parkway, sandwiched between Grand Teton and Yellowstone.

Festivals and Events

YEAR-ROUND **Grand Teton Music Festival** presents monthly concerts featuring solo performers as well as duos and groups at Walk Festival Hall in Teton Village. Tickets range from $25 to $50, but there are also many free events throughout the year. ☎ *307/733–1128* ⊕ *www.gtmf. org.*

MARCH The **Pole-Pedal-Paddle** is a mini-marathon, ski-cycle-canoe relay race held every year in March or April, starting at Jackson Hole Ski Resort and finishing down the Snake River. ☎ *307/733–6433* ⊕ *www.polepedalpaddle.com.*

MAY Jackson's **Old West Days** include a rodeo, American Indian dancers, a Western swing-dance contest, Mountain Man Rendezvous, and cowboy poetry readings. ☎ *307/733–3316.*

MAY–SEPTEMBER Gunslingers stage **The Shootout** in the summer at 6:15 PM daily (except Sunday) on the southeast corner of the Jackson Town Square. Don't worry, the bullets aren't real. ☎ *307/733–3316.*

3

Updated by
Brian Kevin

Your jaw will probably drop the first time you see the Teton Range jabbing up from the Jackson Hole valley floor. With no foothills to get in the way, you'll have a close-up, unimpeded view of magnificent, jagged, snowcapped peaks. This massif is long on natural beauty. Before your eyes, mountain glaciers creep imperceptibly down 12,605-foot Mt. Moran. Large and small lakes gleam along the range's base. Many of the West's iconic animals (elk, bears, bald eagles) call this park home.

PARK ESSENTIALS

ACCESSIBILITY
The front-country portions of Grand Teton are largely accessible to people using wheelchairs. There's designated parking at most sites, and some interpretive trails are easily accessible. There are accessible restrooms at visitor centers. For the *Accessibility* brochure, a guide to accessible trails and facilities, stop by any visitor center.

ADMISSION FEES AND PERMITS
Park entrance fees are $25 per car, truck, or RV; $20 per motorcycle; and $12 per person on foot or bicycle, good for seven days in both Grand Teton and Yellowstone parks. Annual park passes are $40. A winter day-use fee is $5.

Backcountry permits, which must be retrieved in person at the Craig Thomas Visitor Center, Colter Bay Visitor Center, or Jenny Lake Ranger Station, are $25 to reserve in advance or free to pick up one day before your hike. Permits are required for all overnight stays outside designated campgrounds. Seven-day boat permits, available year-round at Craig Thomas Discovery and Visitor Center and in summer at Colter Bay and Signal Mountain ranger stations, cost $20 for motorized craft and $10 for nonmotorized craft and are good for seven days. Annual permits are $40 for motorized craft and $20 for nonmotorized craft.

ADMISSION HOURS
The park is open 24/7 year-round. It's in the mountain time zone.

ATMS/BANKS
In the park, ATMs are at Colter Bay Grocery and General Store, Dornan's, Jackson Lake Lodge, and Signal Mountain Lodge. You can also find ATMs at Flagg Ranch Resort, which is north of the park before the southern entrance to Yellowstone. The nearest full-service banks are in Jackson and Dubois.

CELL-PHONE RECEPTION

Cell phones work in most developed areas and occasionally on trails. Public phones are at Moose, Dornan's, south Jenny Lake, Signal Mountain Lodge, Moran Entrance Station, Jackson Lake Lodge, Colter Bay Village, Leeks Marina, and Flagg Ranch.

RELIGIOUS SERVICES

Late spring through early autumn, Christian services are held on weekends at the park's two chapels (⇨ *Scenic Stops under What to See*).

PARK CONTACT INFORMATION

Grand Teton National Park ⌂ *P.O. Box 170, Moose, WY 83012* ☎ *307/739–3300* ⊕ *www.nps.gov/grte.*

SCENIC DRIVES

☾ **Antelope Flats Road.** Off U.S. 191/89/26, about 2 mi north of Moose Junction, this narrow road wanders eastward over rolling plains, rising buttes, and sagebrush flats. The road intersects Mormon Row, where you can turn off to see abandoned homesteaders' barns and houses from the turn of the 20th century. Less than 2 mi past Mormon Row is a four-way intersection where you can turn right to loop around past the town of Kelly and Gros Ventre campground and rejoin U.S. 191/26/89 at Gros Ventre Junction. Keep an eye out for pronghorn, bison, moose, and mountain bikers.

Fodor'sChoice **Jenny Lake Scenic Drive.** This 4-mi, one-way loop provides the park's
★ best roadside close-ups of the Tetons as it winds south through groves of lodgepole pine and open meadows. Roughly 1.5 mi off Teton Park Road, the Cathedral Group Turnout faces 13,770-foot Grand Teton (the range's highest peak), flanked by 12,928-foot Mt. Owen and 12,325-foot Mt. Teewinot. ⊠ *Jenny Lake.*

☾ **Signal Mountain Road.** This exciting drive climbs Signal Mountain's
Fodor'sChoice 1,040-foot prominence along a 4-mi stretch of switchbacks. As you
★ travel through forest you can catch glimpses of Jackson Lake and Mt. Moran. At the top of the winding road you can park and follow the well-marked dirt path to be treated to one of the best panoramic views in the park. From 7,720 feet above sea level your gaze can sweep over all of Jackson Hole and the 40-mi Teton Range. The views are particularly dramatic at sunset. The road is not appropriate for long trailers and is closed in winter. ⊠ *Off Teton Park Rd., south of Jackson Lake Junction and near Chapel of the Sacred Heart.*

WHAT TO SEE

HISTORIC AND CULTURAL SITES

☾ **Indian Arts Museum.** This collection's standout exhibits include Plains Indian weapons and clothing. You will see Crow blanket strips with elegant beadwork, sashes from both the Shawnee and Hopi tribes, as well as weapons, games, toys, flutes, drums, and a large collection of moccasins from many tribes. From June through early September, watch crafts demonstrations, take guided museum tours, and listen to a 45-minute program on American Indian culture. ⊠ *Colter Bay*

GRAND TETON IN ONE DAY

Begin the day by packing a picnic lunch or picking one up at a Jackson eatery. Arrive at **Craig Thomas Discovery and Visitor Center** in time for a 9 AM, two-hour, guided Snake River float trip (make reservations in advance with one of the dozen or so outfitters that offer the trip). When you're back on dry ground, drive north on Teton Park Road, stopping at scenic turnouts—don't miss Teton Glacier—until you reach Jenny Lake Road, which is one-way headed south.

After a brief stop at **Cathedral Group Turnout,** park at the Jenny Lake ranger station and take the 20-minute boat ride to **Cascade Canyon** trailhead for a short hike. Return to your car by mid-afternoon, drive back to Teton Park Road, and head north to Signal Mountain Road

to catch a top-of-the-park view of the Tetons. In late afternoon descend the mountain and continue north on Teton Park Road.

At Jackson Lake Junction, you can go east to **Oxbow Bend** or north to **Willow Flats,** both excellent spots for wildlife viewing before you head to **Jackson Lake Lodge** for dinner and an evening watching the sun set over the Tetons. Or if you'd like to get back on the water, drive to **Colter Bay Marina,** where you can board a 1½-hour sunset cruise across Jackson Lake to Waterfalls Canyon. You can reverse this route if you're heading south from Yellowstone: start the day with a 7:30 AM breakfast cruise from Colter Bay and end it with a sunset float down the Snake River.

Visitor Center, 2 mi off U.S. 89/191/287, 5 mi north of Jackson Lake Junction ☎ *307/739–3594* ✉ *Free* ☉ *June–early Sept., daily 8–7; early Sept.–mid-Oct., daily 8–5.*

★ **Menor's Ferry Historic Area.** Down a path from the Chapel of the Transfiguration, the ferry on display here is not the original, but it's an accurate re-creation of the double-pontoon craft built by Bill Menor in 1894. It demonstrates how people crossed the Snake River before bridges were built. In the cluster of turn-of-the-20th-century buildings there are historical displays, including a collection of photos taken in the area; one building has been turned into a small general store. Pick up a pamphlet for a self-guided tour, and check out the nearby general supplies store, where candy and pop are sold in the summer. The ferry typically runs after spring runoff, between June and August, and only when a park ranger is available to operate it. ⊠ *½ mi off Teton Park Rd., 1 mi north of Moose Junction* ☉ *Daily dawn–dusk.*

Mormon Row Historic Area. Settled by homesteaders between 1896 and 1907, this area received its name because many of them were members of the Church of Jesus Christ of Latter-day Saints, otherwise known as the Mormons. The remaining barns, homes, and outbuildings are representative of early homesteading in the West. You can wander among the buildings, hike the row, and take photographs. ⊠ *Just off Antelope Flats Rd., 2 mi north of Moose Junction* ☉ *Daily.*

SCENIC STOPS

Chapel of the Sacred Heart. This small log chapel sits in the pine forest with a view of Jackson Lake. It's open only for services, but you can enjoy the view anytime. ⊠ *½ mi north of Signal Mountain Lodge, off Teton Park Rd.* ☎ *307/733–2516* ☉ *Services June–Sept., Sat. at 5:30* PM *and Sun. at 5* PM.

Fodor's Choice ★ **Chapel of the Transfiguration.** This tiny chapel built in 1925 on land donated by Maud Noble is still a functioning Episcopal church. Couples come here to exchange vows with the Tetons as a backdrop, and tourists come to take photos of the small church with its awe-inspiring view. ⊠ *½ mi off Teton Park Rd., 1.1 mi north of Moose Junction, 2 mi north of Moose* ✛ *Turn off Teton Park Rd. onto Chapel of the Transfiguration Rd.* ☎ *307/733–2603* ☉ *Late May–late Sept., Sun., Eucharist at 8* AM, *service at 10* AM.

Fodor's Choice ★ **Jackson Lake.** The biggest of Grand Teton's glacier-carved lakes, this body of water in the northern reaches of the park was enlarged by construction of the Jackson Lake Dam in 1906. You can fish, sail, and windsurf here. Three marinas (Colter Bay, Leeks, and Signal Mountain) provide access for boaters, and several picnic areas, campgrounds, and lodges overlook the lake. ⊠ *U.S. 89/191/287 from Lizard Creek to Jackson Lake Junction, and Teton Park Rd. from Jackson Lake Junction to Signal Mountain Lodge, Oxbow Bend.*

★ **Jenny Lake.** Named for the wife of mountain man Beaver Dick Leigh, this alpine lake south of Jackson Lake draws paddle-sports enthusiasts to its pristine waters and hikers to its tree-shaded trails. ⊠ *Off Teton Park Rd. midway between Moose and Jackson Lake.*

Fodor's Choice ★ **Oxbow Bend.** This peaceful and much-admired spot overlooks a quiet backwater left by the Snake River when it cut a new southern channel. White pelicans stop here on their spring migration (many stay on through summer), sandhill cranes and trumpeter swans visit frequently, and great blue herons nest amid the cottonwoods along the river. Use binoculars to search for bald eagles, ospreys, moose, beavers, and otters. The Oxbow is known for the reflection of Mt. Moran that marks its calm waters in early morning. ⊠ *U.S. 89/191/287, 2.5 mi east of Jackson Lake Junction.*

★ **Willow Flats.** You will almost always see moose grazing in the marshy area here, in parts because of its good growth of willow trees, where moose both eat and hide. This is also a good place to see birds and waterfowl. ⊠ *U.S. 89/191/287, 1 mi north of Jackson Lake Junction, Oxbow Bend.*

VISITOR CENTERS

If you plan to do any hiking or exploring on your own, it is important to stop at a visitor center to get up-to-date information about weather conditions. Rangers also will know if any trails are temporarily closed due to wildlife activity. Before beginning any backcountry explorations, you must obtain permits, which you can get at visitor centers.

Colter Bay Visitor Center. The auditorium here hosts several free daily programs about American Indian culture and natural history. Also, at 11 and 3 daily, a 30-minute "Teton Highlights" ranger lecture provides tips on park activities. ⊠ *Colter Bay, ½ mi west of Colter Bay Junction on*

GOOD READS

■ *Teewinot: Climbing and Contemplating the Teton Range,* by Jack Turner. A trained philosopher turned climbing guide, Turner reflects on mountain ecology and mountain culture in essays both poetic and precise.

■ *A Naturalist's Guide to Grand Teton and Yellowstone National Parks,* by Frank Craighead. An accessible homage to greater Yellowstone, Craighead's text reveals natural patterns and concordances in the Tetons, week to week and season to season.

■ *Windows into the Earth: The Geologic Story of Yellowstone and Grand Teton National Parks,* by Robert B. Smith and Lee J. Siegel. The graphics-heavy text is handily the best book on the market for non-specialists hoping to grasp Teton and Yellowstone geology.

Hwy. 89/191/287, Oxbow Bend ☎ *307/739–3594* ☉ *June–early Sept., daily 8–7; early Sept.–mid-Oct., daily 8–5.*

Craig Thomas Discovery and Visitor Center. Completed in August 2007, this center has interactive and interpretive exhibits dedicated to themes of preservation, mountaineering, and local wildlife. There's also a 3-D map of the park and streaming video along a footpath showing the area's intricate natural features. ⊠ *½ mi west of Moose Junction, Moose* ☎ *307/739–3399* ☉ *Early June–early Sept., daily 8–7; early Sept.–early June, daily 8–5.*

Jenny Lake Visitor Center. Geology exhibits, including a relief model of the Teton Range, are on display here. ⊠ *S. Jenny Lake Junction, 8 mi north of Moose Junction on Teton Park Rd., Jenny Lake* ☎ *307/739–3392* ☉ *June–early Sept., daily 8–7; early Sept.–late Sept., daily 8–5.*

★ **Laurance S. Rockefeller Preserve Interpretive Center.** The park's newest and eco-friendliest visitor center opened its doors in 2008, a modern, wood-and-steel structure that feels more like an art gallery than an interpretive facility. The elegant, LEED-certified building is more than just eye candy—you can experience the sounds of the park in a cylindrical audio chamber, and laminated maps in the reading room are great for trip planning. ⊠ *East side of Moose-Wilson Rd., about 4 mi south of Moose and 3 mi north of Granite Canyon Entrance Station* ☎ *307/739–3654* ☉ *Late May–early Sept., daily 8–6; early-Sept.–late Sept., daily 8–5.*

SPORTS AND THE OUTDOORS

BICYCLING

Teton Park Road and Jackson Hole Highway are generally flat with long, gradual inclines, and have well-marked shoulders. Cyclists should be very careful when sharing the road with vehicles, especially RVs and trailers. The first phase of a paved bike path along Teton Park Road was completed in 2008, and runs between Moose and the visitor center at Jenny Lake. A bike lane allows for northbound bike traffic along the one-way Jenny Lake Loop Road, a one-hour ride. The River Road, 4 mi north of Moose, is an easy four-hour mountain-bike ride along a ridge above the Snake River on a gravel road. Bicycles are not allowed on trails or in the backcountry.

In Jackson, ride the Snow King trails system that begins at Snow King resort. The Cache Creek to Game Creek loop is a 25-mi ride on dirt roads and trails. The two trails systems also link together. In addition, the surrounding Bridger-Teton National Forest has abundant mountain-biking trails and roads.

OUTFITTERS AND EXPEDITIONS Jackson's hub for cycling culture, **Fitzgerald's Bicycles** (⊠ 245 W. Hansen St., Jackson ☎ 307/734–6886) offers mountain- and road-bike rentals, sales, accessories, and repairs.

BIRD-WATCHING

With over 300 species of birds in the park, the Tetons make for excellent bird-watching country. Here you might spot both the calliope hummingbird (the smallest North American hummingbird) and the trumpeter swan (the world's largest waterfowl). The two riparian habitats described below draw lots of attention, but there are many other bird-busy areas as well. Birds of prey circle around Antelope Flats Road, for instance—the surrounding fields are good hunting turf for red-tailed hawks and prairie falcons. At Taggart Lake you'll see woodpeckers, bluebirds, and hummingbirds. Look for songbirds, such as pine and evening grosbeaks and Cassin's finches, in surrounding open pine and aspen forests.

Oxbow Bend. Some seriously impressive birds tend to congregate at this quiet spot (⇨ Scenic Stops). In spring white pelicans stop by during their northerly migration; in summer bald eagles, great blue herons, and osprey nest nearby. Year-round, you'll have a good chance of seeing trumpeter swans. Nearby Willow Flats has similar bird life, plus sandhill cranes. ⊠ U.S. 89/191/287, 2 mi east of Jackson Lake Junction.

Phelps Lake. The moderate 1.8-mi round-trip Phelps Lake Overlook Trail takes you from the Death Canyon trailhead up conifer- and aspen-lined glacial moraine to a view that's accessible only by trail. Expect abundant bird life: Western tanagers, northern flickers, and ruby-crowned kinglets thrive in the bordering woods, and hummingbirds feed on scarlet gilia beneath the overlook. Don't neglect the newly opened Phelps Lake Trail, which circles the lake and is accessible from either Death Canyon or the Rockefeller Preserve. ⊠ Moose-Wilson Rd., about 3 mi off Teton Park Rd.

BOATING AND WATER SPORTS

Water sports in Grand Teton are diverse. You can float the Snake River, which runs high and fast early in the season (May and June) and more slowly during the latter part of the summer. Canoes and kayaks dominate the smaller lakes and share the water with motorboats on the impressively large Jackson Lake. Motorboats are allowed on Jenny, Jackson, and Phelps lakes. On Jenny Lake there's an engine limit of 10 horsepower. You can launch your boat at Colter Bay, Leek's Marina, Signal Mountain, and Spalding Bay.

If you're floating the Snake River on your own, you are required to purchase a permit ($20 per raft for the entire season, or $10 per raft for seven days). Permits are available year-round at Craig Thomas Discovery and Visitor Center and at Colter Bay, Signal Mountain, and Buffalo (near the Moran entrance) ranger stations in summer. Before you set out, check with park rangers for current conditions.

You may prefer to take one of the many guided float trips through calm-water sections of the Snake; outfitters pick you up at the float-trip parking area near Craig Thomas Discovery and Visitor Center for a 10- to 20-minute drive to upriver launch sites. Ponchos and life preservers are provided. Early-morning and evening floats are your best bets for wildlife viewing, but be sure to carry a jacket or sweater. Float season runs mid-April to December.

MARINAS

Colter Bay Marina. All types of services are available to boaters, including free parking for boat trailers and vehicles, free mooring, boat rentals, guided fishing trips, and fuel. ⊠ *On Jackson Lake* ☎ *307/543–3100, 307/543–2811, or 800/628–9988.*

Leek's Marina. Both day and short-term parking for boat trailers and vehicles are available for up to three nights maximum. There are no boat rentals, but you can get fuel, and there's free short-term docking plus a pizza restaurant. This marina is operated by park concessionaire Signal Mountain Lodge. ⊠ *U.S. 89/191/287, 6 mi north of Jackson Lake Junction* ☎ *307/543–2831* ☉ *Mid-May–late Sept.*

Signal Mountain Lodge Marina. The marina rents pontoon boats, deck cruisers, motorboats, kayaks, and canoes by the hour or for full-day cruising; rates range from $12 an hour for a kayak to $62 an hour for a pontoon boat. ⊠ *Teton Park Rd., 3 mi south of Jackson Lake Junction* ☎ *307/543–2831* ☉ *Mid-May–late Sept.*

OUTFITTERS AND EXPEDITIONS Travel the peaceful parts of the Snake River looking for wildlife as knowledgeable guides on **Barker-Ewing Float Trips** (☎ *307/733–1800 or 800/365–1800* ⊕ *www.barkerewing.com* ☒ *$55* ☉ *May–Sept.*) talk about area history, plants, and animals. Rent motorboats, kayaks, and canoes at **Colter Bay Marina** from **Grand Teton Lodge Company** (☎ *307/543–3100, 307/543–2811, or 800/628–9988* ⊕ *www.gtlc.com* ☒ *Motorboats $30/hr, canoes $14/hr, kayaks $13–$15/hr* ☉ *Late May–late Sept.*). On **Grand Teton Lodge Company Snake River Float Trips** (☎ *307/543–3100 or 800/628–9988* ⊕ *www.gtlc.com* ☒ *Scenic float $53, lunch float $64, steak-fry float $70* ☉ *June–Aug.*) choose from a scenic float trip with or without lunch, or an evening trip with a steak-fry dinner. Make reservations at the activities desk at Colter Bay Village or Jackson Lake Lodge. **Mad River Boat Trips** (☎ *307/733–6203 or 800/458–7238* ⊕ *www.mad-river.com* ☒ *$59–$92* ☉ *Mid-May–Sept.*) leads a variety of white-water and scenic float trips, some combined with breakfast, lunch, or dinner. Obtain some instruction in the fine art of paddling with **Snake River Kayak and Canoe** (☎ *307/733–9999 or 800/529–2501* ⊕ *www.snakeriverkayak.com* ☒ *Raft trips $45–$125, 1-day clinics $200–$300, multiday instruction $275–$1,400* ☉ *Apr.–Oct.*), then test yourself on the river. **Triangle X Float Trips** (☎ *307/733–5500 or 888/860–0005* ⊕ *www.trianglex.com* ☒ *$60–$75* ☉ *Mid-May–late Sept.*) offers subdued river trips in Grand Teton National Park, including a sunset supper float.

CLIMBING

The Teton Range has some of the nation's most diverse general mountaineering. Excellent rock, snow, and ice routes abound for climbers of all experience levels. Unless you're already a pro, it's recommended that you take a course from one of the area's climbing schools before tackling the tough terrain.

OUTFITTERS AND EXPEDITIONS **Exum Mountain Guides** (☎ *307/733–2297* ⊕ *www.exumguides.com* ✉ *1-day climbs $295–$395, climbing schools $135–$165*) leads a variety of climbing experiences, including one-day mountain climbs and back-country adventures on skis and snowboards. **Jackson Hole Mountain Guides** (☎ *307/733–4979 or 800/239–7642* ⊕ *www.jhmg.com* ✉ *1-day guided climbs $250–$400, climbing classes $140–$375*) instructs beginning to advanced climbers.

FISHING

Rainbow, brook, lake, and native cutthroat trout inhabit the park's waters. The Snake's 75 mi of river and tributary are world-renowned for their fishing. To fish in Grand Teton National Park you need a Wyoming fishing license. A day permit for nonresidents is $10, and an annual permit is $65 plus a $10 conservation stamp; for state residents a license costs $15 per season plus $10 for a conservation stamp. Children under age 14 can fish free with an adult who has a license.

Buy a fishing license at Colter Bay Marina, Moose Village Store, Signal Mountain Lodge, and at area sporting-goods stores, where you also can get solid information on good fishing spots and the best flies or lures to use. Or obtain a license from the **Wyoming Game and Fish Department** (⊠ *420 N. Cache St., Jackson* ☎ *307/733–2321* ⊕ *gf.state.wy.us*).

OUTFITTERS AND EXPEDITIONS The park's major concessionaire, **Grand Teton Lodge Company** (⊠ *Colter Bay Marina or Jackson Lake Lodge* ☎ *307/543–3100 or 800/628–9988* ⊕ *www.gtlc.com* ✉ *$150–$450 and up* ۞ *June–Sept.*) operates guided fishing trips on Jackson Lake that include boat and tackle, and guided fly-fishing trips on the Snake River. Make reservations at the activities desks at Colter Bay Village or Jackson Lake Lodge, where trips originate. Hourly and half-day Jackson Lake fishing trips with a guide leave from the marina at **Signal Mountain Lodge** (⊠ *Teton Park Rd., 3 mi south of Jackson Lake Junction* ☎ *307/543–2831* ⊕ *www.signalmountainlodge.com* ✉ *$80/hr* ۞ *Mid-May–late Sept.*). Equipment and tackle are included in the price.

HIKING

Most of Grand Teton's trails are unpaved, with just a few short paved sections in the vicinity of developed areas. You can get trail maps and information about hiking conditions from rangers at the park visitor centers at Moose, Jenny Lake, or Colter Bay, where you will also find bathrooms or outhouses; there are no facilities along the trails themselves. Of the more than 250 mi of maintained trails, the most popular are those around Jenny Lake, the Leigh and String lakes area, and Taggart Lake Trail, with views of Avalanche Canyon.

Front country or backcountry, you may see moose and bears, but keep your distance. Pets are not permitted on trails or in the backcountry, but you can take them on paved front-country trails so long as they are on a leash no more than 6 feet long. Always sign in at trailheads, let someone know where you are going and when you expect to return, and carry plenty of water, snacks, and a cell phone.

EASY

🐾 **Cascade Canyon Trail.** Take the 20-minute boat ride from the Jenny Lake dock to the start of a gentle, ½-mi climb to 200-foot Hidden Falls, the park's most popular and crowded trail destination. With the boat ride, plan on a couple of hours to experience this trail. Listen here for the distinctive bleating of the rabbitlike pikas among the glacial boulders and pines. The trail continues ½ mi to Inspiration Point over a rocky path that is moderately steep. There are two points on the climb that afford good views of Jenny Lake and the surrounding area, but keep climbing; after passing a rock wall you'll finally reach the true Inspiration Point, with the best views. To avoid crowds, try to make your way to Inspiration Point in early morning or late afternoon. To reach the Cascade Canyon trailhead, go to the Jenny Lake Visitor Center to catch a ride across Jenny Lake with **Jenny Lake Boating** (☎ *307/734–9227* ☎ *$5–$7* ⊙ *June–early Sept.*). ⊠ *Access trailhead from Jenny Lake Visitor Center, Jenny Lake, 2 mi off Teton Park Rd., 8 mi north of Moose Junction.*

Colter Bay Nature Trail Loop. This very easy, 1¾-mi round-trip excursion treats you to views of Jackson Lake and the Tetons. As you follow the level trail from Colter Bay Visitor Center and along the forest's edge, you may see moose and bald eagles. Allow yourself two hours to complete the walk. ⊠ *Trailhead at Colter Bay Visitor Center, 2 mi off U.S. 89/191/287, 5 mi north of Jackson Lake Junction.*

Lunchtree Hill Trail. One of the park's easiest trails begins at Jackson Lake Lodge and leads ½ mi to the top of a hill above Willow Flats. The area's willow thickets, beaver ponds, and wet, grassy meadows make it a birder's paradise. Look for sandhill cranes, hummingbirds, and the many types of songbirds described in the free bird guide available at visitor centers. You might also see moose. The round-trip walk takes no more than half an hour. ⊠ *Trailhead at Jackson Lake Lodge, U.S. 89/191/287, ½ mi north of Jackson Lake Junction.*

MODERATE

🐾 **Jenny Lake Trail.** You can walk to Hidden Falls from Jenny Lake ranger
★ station by following the mostly level trail around the south shore of the lake to Cascade Canyon Trail. Jenny Lake Trail continues around the lake for 6½ mi. It's an easy trail—classed here as moderate because of its length—that will take you two to three hours. You'll walk through a lodgepole-pine forest, have expansive views of the lake and the land to the east, and hug the shoulder of the massive Teton range itself. Along the way you are likely to see elk, pikas, golden mantle ground squirrels, a variety of ducks and water birds, plus you may hear elk bugling, birdsong, and the chatter of squirrels. ⊠ *Trailhead at Jenny Lake Visitor Center, S. Jenny Lake Junction, ½ mi off Teton Park Rd., 8 mi north of Moose Junction.*

Leigh Lake Trail. The flat trail follows String Lake's northeastern shore to Leigh Lake's south shore, covering 2 mi in a round-trip of about an hour. You can extend your hike into a moderate 7½-mi, four-hour round-trip

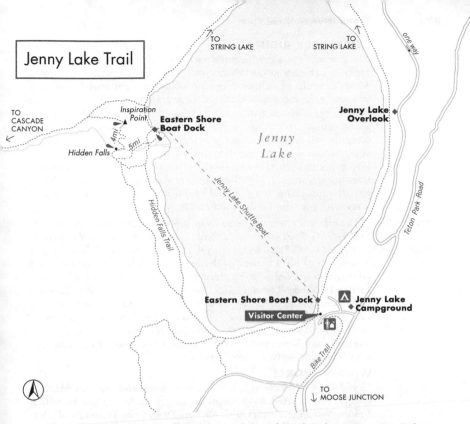

Jenny Lake Trail

TO STRING LAKE

TO STRING LAKE

one way

TO CASCADE CANYON

Inspiration Point

.4 mi

.5 mi

Hidden Falls

Eastern Shore Boat Dock

Jenny Lake Overlook

Jenny Lake

Hidden Falls Trail

Jenny Lake Shuttle Boat

Teton Park Road

Eastern Shore Boat Dock

Visitor Center

Jenny Lake Campground

Bike Trail

TO MOOSE JUNCTION

by following the forested east shore of Leigh Lake to Bearpaw Lake. Along the way you'll have views of Mt. Moran across the lake, and you may be lucky enough to spot a moose. ⊠ *Leigh Lake Trailhead, northwest corner of String Lake Picnic Area, ½ mi west of Jenny Lake Rd., 2 mi off Teton Park Rd., 12 mi north of Moose Junction.*

String Lake Trail. This moderate 3½-mi, three-hour loop around String Lake lies in the shadows of 11,144-foot Rockchuck Peak and 11,430-foot Mt. Saint John. This is also a good place to see moose, hear songbirds, and view wildflowers. This trail is a bit more difficult than other mid-length trails in the park, which means it is also less crowded. ⊠ *String Lake Trailhead, ¼ mi west of Jenny Lake Rd., 2 mi off Teton Park Rd., 12 mi north of Moose Junction.*

DIFFICULT

Death Canyon Trail. This 7.6-mi trail is a strenuous hike with lots of hills to traverse, ending with a climb up into Death Canyon. Plan to spend most of the day on this steep trail. ⊠ *Death Canyon Trailhead, off Moose-Wilson Rd., 4 mi south of Moose Junction.*

HORSEBACK RIDING

You can arrange a guided horseback tour at Colter Bay Village and Jackson Lake Lodge corrals or with a number of private outfitters. Most offer rides of an hour or two up to all-day excursions. If you want to spend even more time riding in Grand Teton and the surrounding mountains, consider a stay at a dude ranch. Shorter rides are almost all appropriate for novice riders, while more experienced cowboys and cowgirls will enjoy the longer journeys where the terrain gets steeper and you may wind through deep forests. For any ride be sure to wear long pants and boots (cowboy boots or hiking boots). Because you may ride through trees, a long-sleeve shirt is also a good idea and a hat is always appropriate, but it should have a stampede string to make sure it stays on your head if the wind comes up.

OUTFITTERS AND EXPEDITIONS
One- and two-hour rides leave **Colter Bay Village Corral** (⊠ *2 mi off U.S. 89/191/287, 5 mi north of Jackson Lake Junction* ☎ *307/543–3100 or 800/628–9988* ⊕ *www.gtlc.com* ✉ *1-hr rides $36, 2-hr rides $54* ⊙ *June–Aug.*) for a variety of destinations, while half-day trips—for advanced riders only—go to Hermitage Point. One-hour trail rides at **Jackson Lake Lodge Corral** (⊠ *U.S. 89/191/287, ½ mi north of Jackson Lake Junction* ☎ *307/543–3100 or 800/628–9988* ⊕ *www.gtlc.com* ✉ *1-hr rides $36, 2-hr rides $54* ⊙ *June–Aug.*) give an overview of the Jackson Lake Lodge area; two-hour rides go to Emma Matilda Lake, Oxbow Bend, and Christian Pond. Experienced riders can take a half-day ride to Two Ocean Lake.

WINTER SPORTS

Grand Teton has some of North America's finest and most varied cross-country skiing. (And don't forget the nearby Jackson Hole Mountain Resort; ⇨ *chapter 4*.) Ski the gentle 3-mi Swan Lake–Heron Pond Loop near Colter Bay Visitor Center, the mostly level 10-mi Jenny Lake Trail, or the moderate 4-mi Taggart Lake–Beaver Creek Loop and 5-mi Phelps Lake Overlook Trail. Advanced skiers should head for the Teton Crest Trail. In winter, overnight backcountry travelers must register or make a reservation at the Craig Thomas Discovery and Visitor Center. The Jackson Hole Mountain Resort aerial tram from Teton Village deposits riders at the mountains' crest of the range, from where they can access backcountry on both sides of the range.

Snowmobiling is permitted on Jackson Lake. Since snowmobiles must be towed into the park, sledders pay only the regular park entrance fees. Snowmobilers wishing to proceed north from Flagg Ranch into Yellowstone National Park must be with a commercial tour guide. The speed limit for snowmobiles on Jackson Lake is 45 MPH. The Flagg Ranch Information Station closed beginning with the 2007–08 winter season, and consequently ski and snowshoe trails went unmarked (in fact, any references in brochures or maps to signed or maintained trails should be disregarded until further notice). For a ranger-guided snowshoe walk, call the Craig Thomas Visitor Center (⇨ *Visitor Centers*).

OUTFITTERS AND EXPEDITIONS **Jack Dennis Outdoor Shop** (⊠ *50 E. Broadway Ave., Jackson* ☎ *307/733–3270 Jackson, 307/733–6838 Teton Village* ⊕ *www.jackdennis.com* ✉ *Ski rental $27–$49, snowboard and boot rental $27–$36*) stocks skis and snowboards for sale and rent, and outdoor gear for any season. In Teton Village you can buy or rent skis or snowboards at **Pepi Stiegler Sports** (⊠ *Teton Village* ☎ *307/733–4505* ⊕ *www.jackdennis.com/pepis* ✉ *Ski or snowboard rental $27–$49* ☉ *Nov.–Apr.*), conveniently located at the base of the Jackson Hole ski mountain. Rent a snowmobile at **Togwotee Mountain Lodge** (⊠ *U.S. 26/287, Moran* ☎ *307/543–2847 or 866/278–4245* ⊕ *www.togwoteelodge.com* ✉ *Snowmobile rentals $149–$210 per day* ☉ *Nov.–Apr.*) and then ride it on an extensive trail network along the Continental Divide.

EDUCATIONAL OFFERINGS

CLASSES AND SEMINARS

Teton Science School. Adults and families can join one of the school's single- or multiday wildlife expeditions in Grand Teton, Yellowstone, and surrounding forests to see and learn about wolves, bears, mountain sheep, and other animals. Junior-high and high-school students can take multiweek field ecology courses while living at the school, backpacking, and camping out. Weekdays, kids in grades one through six can join Young Naturalists programs that don't involve sleepovers. ⊠ *700 Coyote Canyon Rd., Jackson* ☎ *307/733–1313* ⊕ *www.tetonscience.org* ✉ *Wildlife expeditions $69–$1,995, youth programs $200–$3,600*

PROGRAMS AND TOURS

Grand Teton Lodge Company Bus Tours. Half-day tours depart from Jackson Lake Lodge and include visits to scenic viewpoints, visitor centers, and other park sites. Interpretive guides provide information about the park geology, history, wildlife, and ecosystems. Buy tickets in advance at Colter Bay or Jackson Lake Lodge activities desks. Tours include Grand Teton, Yellowstone, or a combination of the two parks. ⊠ *Jackson Lake Lodge* ☎ *307/543–2811 or 800/628–9988* ⊕ *www.gtlc.com* ✉ *$36–$66* ☉ *Mid-May–early Oct., Mon.–Sat.*

Gray Line Bus Tours. Full-day bus tours provide an overview of Grand Teton National Park. They depart from Jackson and you will learn about the park's geology, history, birds, plants, and wildlife. ⊠ *1580 W. Martin La., Jackson* ☎ *307/733–4325 or 800/443–6133* ⊕ *www.graylinejh.com* ✉ *$100 plus $12 park entrance fee* ☉ *Memorial Day–Sept., Mon., Wed., and Sat.*

Jackson Lake Cruises. Grand Teton Lodge Company runs 1½-hour Jackson Lake scenic cruises from Colter Bay Marina throughout the day as well as breakfast cruises and sunset steak-fry cruises. Interpretive guides explain how forest fires and glaciers have shaped the Grand Teton landscape. ⊠ *2 mi off U.S. 89/191/287, 5 mi north of Jackson Lake Junction* ☎ *307/543–3100, 307/543–2811, or 800/628–9988* ⊕ *www.gtlc.com* ⊠ *Scenic cruise $24, breakfast cruise $36, steak-fry cruise $57* ☉ *Late May–mid-Sept.*

RANGER PROGRAMS

Campfire Programs. Park rangers lead free nightly slide shows from June through September at the Colter Bay, Gros Ventre, and Signal Mountain amphitheaters. For schedules of topics check the park newspaper, *Teewinot,* or at visitor centers. ⊠ *Colter Bay Amphitheater, 2 mi off U.S. 89/191/287, 5 mi north of Jackson Lake Junction* ⊠ *Gros Ventre Amphitheater, 4 mi off U.S. 26/89/191 and 2½ mi west of Kelly on Gros Ventre River Rd., 6 mi south of Moose Junction* ⊠ *Signal Mountain Amphitheater, Teton Park Rd., 4 mi south of Jackson Lake Junction* ☎ *307/739–3399 or 307/739–3594* ☉ *June and July, nightly at 9:30; Aug. and Sept., nightly at 9.*

Jackson Lake Lodge Ranger Talks. Visit the Wapiti Room to hear a slide-illustrated ranger presentation on topics such as area plants and animals, geology, and natural history. Also, you can chat with the ranger on the back deck of the lodge 6:30 PM–8 PM daily, early June through early September. ⊠ *U.S. 89/191/287, ½ mi north of Jackson Lake Junction* ☎ *307/739–3300* ☉ *Late June–mid-Aug., nightly at 8:30.*

Ⓒ **Ranger Walks.** Rangers lead free walks throughout the park in summer, from a one-hour lakeside stroll at Colter Bay to a three-hour hike from Jenny Lake. The talks focus on a variety of subjects, from wildlife to birds and flower species to geology. Call for itineraries, times, and reservations. ☎ *307/739–3300* ☉ *Early June–early Sept.*

Ⓒ **Junior Rangers Program.** Children ages 8–12 learn about the natural world of the park as they take an easy 2-mi hike with a ranger. Kids should wear old clothes and bring water, rain gear, and insect repellent. The hike, which takes place at Moose, Jenny Lake, or Colter Bay, is 1½ hours long and is limited to 12 children. ⊠ *Moose: meet at fireplace in Craig Thomas Discovery and Visitor Center; Jenny Lake: meet at the flagpole in front of the visitor center; Colter Bay: meet at the visitor center* ☎ *307/739–3399 or 307/739–3594* ☉ *Mid-June–mid-Aug., daily 1:30.*

Ⓒ **Nature Explorer's Backpack Program.** Rangers lend a nature journal and a backpack full of activities to children ages 6 through 12 before sending them out along the trails at the Rockefeller Preserve. ⊠ *Laurance S. Rockefeller Preserve Interpretive Center, on east side of Moose-Wilson Rd., about 4 mi south of Moose and 3 mi north of Granite Canyon Entrance Station* ☎ *307/739–3654* ☉ *June–early Sept., backpacks available daily 8–6.*

WHAT'S NEARBY

The major gateway to Grand Teton National Park is **Jackson**—but don't confuse this with Jackson Hole. Jackson Hole is the mountain-ringed valley that houses Jackson and much of Grand Teton National Park. The town of Jackson, located south of the park, is a small community (roughly 7,000 residents) that gets flooded with more than 3 million visitors annually. Expensive homes and fashionable shops have sprung up all over, but Jackson manages to maintain at least part of its true western character. With its raised wooden sidewalks and old-fashioned storefronts, the town center still looks a bit like a Western movie set. There's a lot to do here, both downtown and in the surrounding countryside.

If it's skiing you're after, **Snow King Resort** is the oldest resort in the valley, and its 7,808-foot mountain overlooks the town of Jackson and the National Elk Refuge. It's at the end of Snow King Avenue. **Teton Village,** on the southwestern side of the park, is a cluster of businesses centered around the facilities of the Jackson Hole Mountain Resort—a ski and snowboard area with an aerial tram, gondola, and various other lifts. There are plenty of places to eat, stay, and shop here.

On the "back side of the Tetons," as eastern Idaho is known, is **Driggs,** the western gateway to Yellowstone and Grand Teton. Easygoing and rural, Driggs resembles the Jackson of a few decades ago. To reach the park from here you have to cross a major mountain pass that is sometimes closed in winter by avalanches. **Dubois,** about 85 mi east of Jackson, is the least known of the gateway communities to Grand Teton and Yellowstone, but this town of 1,000 has all the services of the bigger towns. You can still get a room for the night here during the peak summer travel period without making a reservation weeks or months in advance (though it's a good idea to call a week or so before you intend to arrive).

About an hour to the south is **Pinedale,** another small Wyoming town with lodging, restaurants, and attractions. Energy development has made the area a hopping place these days, so be sure to plan ahead if you want to stay in town.

For more information about nearby towns and attractions, see chapter 4.

WHERE TO EAT AND STAY

ABOUT THE RESTAURANTS

Though the park itself has some excellent restaurants, don't miss dining in Jackson, where restaurants combine game, fowl, and fish with the enticing spices and sauces of European cuisine and the lean ingredients, vegetarian entrées, and meat cuts that reflect the desires of health-conscious diners. Steaks are usually cut from grass-fed Wyoming beef, but you'll also find buffalo and elk on the menu; poultry and pasta are offered by most restaurants, and you'll find fresh salads and fish (trout, tilapia, and salmon are most common). Just about everywhere, you can order a burger or a bowl of homemade soup. Casual is the word for most dining both within and outside the park. An exception is Jenny Lake Lodge, where jackets and ties are recommended for dinner. Breakfast is big: steak and eggs, pancakes, biscuits and gravy; lunches are lighter, often taken in a sack to enjoy on the trail.

ABOUT THE HOTELS

The choice of lodging properties within the park is as diverse as the landscape itself. Here you'll find simple campgrounds, cabins, and basic motel rooms. You can also settle into a homey bed-and-breakfast, or a luxurious suite in a full-service resort. Between June and August, room rates go up, and rooms are harder to get without advanced reservations. Nonetheless, if you're looking to stay in a national park that's tailored to individual pursuits, this is it. Although this park is becoming more popular and crowded each year, it still resembles the haven its founders envisioned in 1929 and again in 1950, a place where man can contemplate and interact with nature.

ABOUT THE CAMPGROUNDS

You'll find a variety of campgrounds, from small areas where only tents are allowed to full RV parks with all services. If you don't have a tent, but want to bring your sleeping bags, you can take advantage of the tent cabins at Colter Bay, where you have a hard floor, cots, and canvas walls for shelter. Standard campsites include a place to pitch your tent or park your trailer/camper, a fire pit for cooking, and a picnic table. All developed campgrounds have toilets and water; plan to bring your own firewood. Check in at National Park Service campsites as early as possible—sites are assigned on a first-come, first-served basis.

You can camp in the park's backcountry year-round, provided you have the requisite permit and are able to gain access to your site. Between June 1 and September 15, backcountry campers in the park are limited to one stay of up to 10 days. Campfires are prohibited in the backcountry except at designated lakeshore campsites. You can reserve a backcountry campsite between January 1 and May 15 for a $25 nonrefundable fee (Social Security numbers must be included on all checks) using the online reservation system, by fax, or in writing to **GTNP-Backcountry Permits** (⊙ *P.O. Box 170, Moose, WY 83012* 🖷 *307/739–3438* ⊕ *www.nps.gov/grte*). You can also take a chance that the site you want will be open when you arrive in the park, in which case you pay no fee at all, but a trip to Craig Thomas Visitor and Discovery Center or Jenny Lake Ranger Station is still required for a permit and mandatory bear-proof canister. Campfires are prohibited in the backcountry except at designated lakeshore campsites. Jackson Hole Mountain Resort tram provides access to the park's backcountry, which can also be reached on foot.

■ TIP→ Because bears and lions live in the park, campers should store food in bear containers and never in the tent.

WHAT IT COSTS					
	¢	$	$$	$$$	$$$$
Restaurants	under $8	$8–$12	$13–$20	$21–$30	over $30
Hotels	under $70	$70–$100	$101–$150	$151–$200	over $200
Campgrounds	under $10	$10–$17	$18–$35	$36–$49	over $50

Restaurant prices are per person for a main course at dinner. Hotel prices are per night for two people in a standard double room in high season, excluding taxes and service charges. Camping prices are for a standard (no hookups, pit toilets, fire grates, picnic tables) campsite per night.

3

WHERE TO EAT

$$–$$$ ✗ **Dornan's Chuck Wagon.** Hearty portions of beef, beans, potatoes, short
BARBECUE   ribs, stew, and lemonade or hot coffee are the dinner standbys at Dor-
☺   nan's. Locals know this spot for the barbecue cooked over wood fires.
★   At breakfast, count on old-fashioned staples such as sourdough pancakes or biscuits and gravy. You can eat your chuck-wagon meal inside
one of the restaurant's teepees if it happens to be raining or windy; otherwise, sit at outdoor picnic tables with views of the Snake River and
the Tetons. The quick service and inexpensive prices make this a good
choice for families. Weekly "Hootenanny" open-mike nights attract
family tourists as well as rowdy young Jacksonians. A pizza parlor
(⇨ Dornan's Restaurant) serves lunch year-round. ⊠ 10 Moose Rd., off
Teton Park Rd. at Moose Junction ☎ 307/733–2415 ⊕ www.dornans.
com ⊟ AE, D, MC, V ☺ Closed early Sept.–mid-June.

$$ ✗ **Dornan's Restaurant.** Tasty pizzas and pastas are the main standbys at
PIZZA   Dornan's, located at Moose on a longtime family inholding, but you'll
also find generous margaritas, a surprisingly diverse wine list, and occa-
sional live music. Place your order at the front counter, and your food
is brought out to you—either at a picnic table facing the Tetons, inside
one of the huge teepees (ideal in rainy weather, or for those traveling
with kids), or upstairs on the roof with stunning mountain views, the
perfect place to unwind with a margarita after a strenuous day's hike.
The extremely popular eatery serves both steak and pasta and has an
extensive salad bar. There's also a long inside bar with stellar views
and friendly barkeeps. Check Dornan's schedule for live music and be
sure to explore the wine shop next door: it's one of the most varied
and well stocked in the valley. It's where local resident and movie star
Harrison Ford has been seen buying his *vino.* ⊠ 10 Moose Rd., off
Teton Park Rd. at Moose Junction ☎ 307/733–2415 ⊕ www.dornans.
com ⊟ AE, D, MC, V.

$$–$$$$ ✗ **Jackson Lake Lodge Mural Room.** The ultimate park dining experience
AMERICAN   is found in this large room that gets its name from a 700-square-foot
Fodor's Choice   mural painted by western artist Carl Roters. The mural details an 1837
★   Wyoming mountain-man rendezvous and covers two walls of the dining
room. Select from a menu that includes trout, elk, beef, and chicken. The
plantain-crusted trout is a great choice, or try the bison prime rib. The
tables face tall windows affording a panoramic view of Willow Flats and

Jackson Lake to the northern Tetons. ⊠ *U.S. 89/191/287, ½ mi north of Jackson Lake Junction* ☎ *307/543–3463 or 800/628–9988* ⊕ *www. gtlc.com* ⊟ *AE, MC, V* ⊙ *Closed mid-Oct.–late May.*

$–$$$
AMERICAN–
CASUAL

✗**Jackson Lake Lodge Pioneer Grill.** With an old-fashioned soda fountain, friendly service, and seats along a winding counter, this eatery recalls a 1950s-era luncheonette. Tuck into burgers, sundaes, and other classic American fare here. ⊠ *U.S. 89/191/287, ½ mi north of Jackson Lake Junction* ☎ *307/543–2811* ⊕ *www.gtlc.com* ⊟ *AE, MC, V* ⊙ *Closed early Oct.–late May.*

$$$$
AMERICAN
★

✗**Jenny Lake Lodge Dining Room.** Elegant yet rustic, this is Grand Teton National Park's finest dining establishment, with easily the most ambitious menu in any national park. The menu is ever-changing and offers ambitious items like tempura squash blossoms and pinot-glazed veal cheeks; the wine list is extensive. Dinner is prix-fixe, and though lunch is à la carte, the inventive soups and *panini* are no less decadent. Jackets are encouraged for men at dinner. ⊠ *Jenny Lake Rd., 2 mi off Teton Park Rd., 12 mi north of Moose Junction* ☎ *307/733–4647 or 800/628– 9988* ⊕ *www.gtlc.com* ⚐ *Reservations essential* ⊟ *AE, MC, V* ⊙ *Closed early Oct.–late May.*

¢–$
MEXICAN

✗**John Colter Cafe Court.** At this Colter Bay Village spot you can buy tacos and burritos, plus a few American faves like burgers and hot dogs. The Southwestern theme extends to the cafeteria's decor. ⊠ *5 mi north of Jackson Lake Lodge* ☎ *307/543–2811* ⊕ *www.gtlc.com* ⊟ *AE, MC, V* ⊙ *Closed early Sept.–early June.*

$$$–$$$$
AMERICAN

✗**The Peaks.** Part of Signal Mountain Lodge, this casual room has exposed ceiling beams and big square windows overlooking southern Jackson Lake and the Tetons. The emphasis here is on fish: Rocky Mountain trout is marinated, lightly floured, and grilled, or simply grilled and topped with lemon-parsley butter. ⊠ *Teton Park Rd., 4 mi south of Jackson Lake Junction* ☎ *307/543–2831* ⊕ *www.signalmountainlodge.com* ⊟ *AE, D, MC, V* ⊙ *Closed mid-Oct.–mid-May.*

$–$$$
AMERICAN

✗**Ranch House at Colter Bay Village.** New in 2009, the Ranch House delivers quick service and inexpensive prices, making it a good choice for families or travelers on a budget. Dinner entrées skew Western: thick steaks, barbecued ribs, chicken with chili sauce. The kitchen will also prep your day's catch if you deliver it by 4 PM. ⊠ *2 mi off U.S. 89/191/287, 5 mi north of Jackson Lake Junction, Colter Bay* ☎ *307/543–2811* ⊕ *www. gtlc.com* ⊟ *AE, MC, V* ⊙ *Closed late Sept.–late May.*

PICNIC AREAS

The park has 11 designated picnic areas, each with tables and grills, and most with pit toilets and water pumps or faucets. In addition to those listed here you can find picnic areas at Colter Bay Village Campground, Cottonwood Creek, the east shore of Jackson Lake, and South Jenny Lake and String Lake trailhead.

Chapel of the Sacred Heart. From this intimate lakeside picnic area you can look across southern Jackson Lake to Mt. Moran. ⊠ *¼ mi east of Signal Mountain Lodge, off Teton Park Rd..*

Colter Bay Visitor Center. This big picnic area, spectacularly located right on the beach at Jackson Lake, gets crowded in July and August. It's conveniently close to flush toilets and stores. ⊠ *2 mi off U.S. 89/191/287, 5 mi north of Jackson Lake Junction.*

Hidden Falls. Adjacent to the Jenny Lake shuttle-boat dock is this shaded, pine-scented picnic site. An easy ½-mi hike takes you to the falls. Take the shuttle boat across Jenny Lake to reach the Cascade Canyon trailhead. ⊠ *At the Cascade Canyon trailhead.*

WHERE TO STAY

$$ ⛺ **Colter Bay Village.** Near Jackson Lake, this complex of Western-style cabins—some with one room, others with two or more rooms—is within walking distance of the lake. The property has splendid views and an excellent marina and beach for the windsurfing crowd (you'll need a wet suit because of the cold). There are also camping options: a 112-space RV park as well as tent cabins (⇨ *Camping, below*), which share communal baths. **Pros:** prices are good for what you get; many nearby facilities. **Cons:** little sense of privacy; not all cabins have bathrooms. ⊠ *2 mi off U.S. 89/191/287, 10 mi north of Jackson Lake Junction, Colter Bay* ☎ *307/543–3100 or 800/628–9988* ⊕ *www.gtlc.com* ⏍ *166 cabins (9 with shared baths), 66 tent cabins* ⚒ *In-room: no a/c, no phone, no TV. In-hotel: 2 restaurants, bar, laundry facilities, some pets allowed, Wi-Fi* ⊟ *AE, MC, V* ⊗ *Closed late Sept.–late May (shorter season for tent cabins).*

$$$–$$$$ ⛺ **Dornan's Spur Ranch Cabins.** Part of Dornan's all-in-one shopping–dining–recreation development at Moose, these one- and two-bedroom cabins have great views of the Tetons and the Snake River. Each cabin has a full kitchen, with electric stove, toaster, pots, pans, dishes, coffeemaker, and utensils as well as a generously sized living-dining room and a furnished porch with a Weber grill in summer. However, there's only one microwave on-site, so you'll want to request it early. **Pros:** cabins are simple but clean; full kitchens allow you to make your own meals to save money. **Cons:** proximity of cabins means not much privacy, cabins have little atmosphere and no fireplaces. ⊠ *10 Moose Rd., off Teton Park Rd. at Moose Junction, Moose* ☎ *307/733–2522* ⊕ *www.dornans.com* ⏍ *8 1-bedroom cabins, 4 2-bedroom cabins* ⚒ *In-room: no a/c, kitchen, no TV. In-hotel: 2 restaurants, bar* ⊟ *AE, D, MC, V.*

$$$$ ⛺ **Jackson Lake Lodge.** This large, full-service resort stands on a bluff with spectacular views across Jackson Lake to the Tetons. (And we do mean full service: there's everything from live music in the bar to in-house religious services.) The upper lobby has 60-foot picture windows and a collection of American Indian artifacts and Western art. Many guest rooms have spectacular lake and mountain views, while others have little or no view, so ask when you book. A top-down renovation in late 2008 freshened up rooms with refurbished oak furniture, new upholstery, and some cool photos from the lodge's early days. **Pros:** central location for visiting both Grand Teton and Yellowstone; heated outdoor pool; on-site medical clinic. **Cons:** rooms without views are pricey for what you get; the hotel hosts a lot of large meetings. ⊠ *U.S. 89/191/287, ½ mi north of Jackson Lake Junction* ☎ *307/543–3100 or 800/628–9988* ⊕ *www.gtlc.com* ⏍ *385 rooms* ⚒ *In-room: no a/c, refrigerator (some), no TV. In-hotel: 2 restaurants, bar, pool, some pets allowed, Wi-Fi* ⊟ *AE, MC, V* ⊗ *Closed early Oct.–mid-May.*

$$$$ 🏨 **Jenny Lake Lodge.** This lodge (the most expensive in any U.S. national park) has been serving tourists, sportspeople, and travelers since the 1920s. Nestled off the scenic one-way Jenny Lake Loop Road, bordering a wildflower meadow, its guest cabins are well spaced in lodgepole-pine groves. Cabin interiors, with sturdy pine beds and handmade quilts and electric blankets, live up to the elegant rustic theme, and cabin suites have fireplaces. Bathroom renovations in 2008 added new stonework and rain-dome showerheads. Breakfast, bicycle use, horseback riding, and dinner are always included the price. Room telephones are provided only on request. **Pros:** maximum comfort in a pristine setting; perhaps the best hotel in the national park system. **Cons:** very expensive; not suitable for families with kids under 17; pretty formal for a national-park property. ⊠ *Jenny Lake Rd., 2 mi off Teton Park Rd., 12 mi north of Moose Junction* ☎ *307/733–4647 or 800/628–9988* ⊕ *www.gtlc.com* ⟳ *37 cabins* ⅋ *In-room: no a/c, no TV. In-hotel: restaurant, bicycles, Wi-Fi* ▤ *AE, MC, V* ☻ *Closed early Oct.–late May* ⦿ *MAP.*

$–$$$ 🏨 **Moulton Ranch Cabins.** Along Mormon Row, these cabins stand a
Fodor's Choice few dozen yards south of the famous Moulton Barn, which you see
★ on brochures, jigsaw puzzles, and photographs of the park. The land was once part of the T. A. Moulton homestead, and the cabins are still owned by the Moulton family. The quiet property has views of the Teton and the Gros Ventre ranges, and the owners can regale you with stories about early homesteaders. There's a dance hall in the barn, making this an ideal place for family and small group reunions. Smoking is not permitted on the premises. There's no Sunday check-in. **Pros:** quiet and secluded; as picturesque as any lodging in the park. **Cons:** fairly basic accommodations; little nightlife nearby. ⊠ *Off Antelope Flats Rd., off U.S. 26/89/191, 2 mi north of Moose Junction* ☎ *307/733–3749 or 208/529–2354* ⊕ *www.moultonranchcabins. com* ⟳ *5 cabins* ⅋ *In-room: no a/c, kitchen (some), no TV* ▤ *MC, V* ☻ *Closed Oct.–May.*

$$–$$$ 🏨 **Signal Mountain Lodge.** These relaxed, pine-shaded cabins sit on Jackson Lake's southern shoreline. The main building has a cozy lounge and a grand pine deck overlooking the lake. Some cabins are equipped with sleek kitchens and pine tables. The smaller log cabins are in shaded areas, and eight of them have a fireplace. Rooms 151–178 have lake views, and there are a handful of suite and bungalow options as well. **Pros:** restaurants and bar are popular hot spots; on-site gas station; general store sells ice. **Cons:** rooms are pretty motel-basic; fireplaces are gas. ⊠ *Teton Park Rd., 3 mi south of Jackson Lake Junction* ☎ *307/543–2831* ⊕ *www.signalmountainlodge.com* ⟳ *47 rooms, 32 cabins* ⅋ *In-room: no a/c, kitchen (some), refrigerator (some), no TV. In-hotel: 2 restaurants, bar, Wi-Fi* ▤ *AE, D, MC, V* ☻ *Closed mid-Oct.–mid-May.*

CAMPING ⛺ **Colter Bay Campground.** Busy, noisy, and filled by noon, this camp-
$$ ground has both tent and trailer or RV sites—and one great advantage:
★ it's centrally located. Try to get a site as far from the nearby cabin road as possible. This campground also has hot showers at the nearby Colter Bay launderette. The maximum stay is 14 days. Reservations are not

accepted. **Pros:** most amenities of any campground in the park; lake access; flush toilets. **Cons:** very crowded in peak season; fills up early. ⊠ *2 mi off U.S. 89/191/287, 5 mi north of Jackson Lake Junction, Colter Bay* ☎ *307/543–3100 or 800/628–9988* ⊕ *www.gtlc.com* ⚏ *350 tent/ RV sites* ⚒ *Flush toilets, dump station, drinking water, guest laundry, showers, bear boxes, fire grates, picnic tables* ⊟ *AE, MC, V* ☉ *Late May–late Sept.*

$$$–$$$$ ⚏ **Colter Bay Tent Village and RV Park.** Adjacent to the Colter Bay campground, this slightly more developed area is the only RV park in Grand Teton Park. You'll find showers nearby, too. **Pros:** water, sewer, and electric hookups available; five-minute walk to Jackson Lake. **Cons:** no open fires in RV park; no bedding provided in tent village. ⊠ *2 mi off U.S. 89/191/287, 5 mi north of Jackson Lake Junction, Colter Bay* ☎ *307/543–3100 or 800/628–9988* ⊕ *www.gtlc.com* ⚏ *66 tent cabins, 112 RV sites* ⚒ *Flush toilets, full hookups, drinking water, guest laundry, showers, bear boxes, fire grates, picnic tables* ⊟ *AE, MC, V* ☉ *June–Sept.*

$$ ⚏ **Gros Ventre.** The park's biggest campground is set in an open, grassy area on the bank of the Gros Ventre River, away from the mountains and 2 mi southwest of Kelly, WY. Try to get a site close to the river. The campground usually doesn't fill until nightfall, if at all. There's a maximum stay of 14 days. Reservations are not accepted. **Pros:** low traffic on Gros Ventre Rd.; many wooded sites; often doesn't fill. **Cons:** crowded in peak season; no showers; nearest general store in Kelly. ⊠ *4½ mi off U.S. 26/89/191, 2½ mi west of Kelly on Gros Ventre Rd., 6 mi south of Moose Junction* ☎ *307/543–3100 or 800/628–9988* ⚏ *350 tent/RV sites, 5 group sites* ⚒ *Flush toilets, dump station, drinking water, bear boxes, fire grates, picnic tables* ⊟ *AE, MC, V* ☉ *May–mid-Oct.*

¢–$$ ⚏ **Jenny Lake.** Wooded sites and Teton views make this the most desir-
★ able campground in the park, and it fills early. The small, quiet facility allows tents only, and there's a maximum of one vehicle (no longer than 14 feet) per campsite. Reservations are not accepted. **Pros:** no loud RVs; stunning views; central location. **Cons:** no showers. ⊠ *Jenny Lake, ½ mi off Teton Park Rd., 8 mi north of Moose Junction, Jenny Lake* ☎ *307/543–3100 or 800/628–9988* ⚏ *49 tent sites (10 walk-in)* ⚒ *Flush toilets, drinking water, bear boxes, fire grates, picnic tables* ⊟ *No credit cards* ☉ *Mid-May–late Sept.*

¢–$$ ⚏ **Lizard Creek.** Views of Jackson Lake, wooded sites, and the relative isolation of this campground make it a relaxing choice. No vehicles over 30 feet are allowed, and there's a 14-day limit. Reservations are not accepted. **Pros:** no crowds; well-spaced sites. **Cons:** no staffed amenities; low lake levels sometimes lead to mudflat views. ⊠ *U.S. 89/191/287, 13 mi north of Jackson Lake Junction* ☎ *307/543–2831 or 800/672–6012* ⚏ *61 tent/RV sites* ⚒ *Flush toilets, drinking water, bear boxes, fire grates, picnic tables* ⊟ *No credit cards* ☉ *Early June–late Aug.*

$$ ⚏ **Signal Mountain.** This campground in a hilly setting on Jackson Lake has boat access to the lake. Many campsites offer spectacular views of the Tetons across the lake. No vehicles or trailers over 30 feet are allowed, and there's a maximum stay of 14 days. Reservations are not accepted. **Pros:** nightly ranger programs at the amphitheater; walking

3

distance to Signal Mountain Lodge amenities. **Cons:** high noise level in peak season; many sites close to road. ⊠ *Teton Park Rd., 3 mi south of Jackson Lake Junction* ☎ *307/543–2831 or 800/672–6012* ⚠ *81 tent/ RV sites* ⚹ *Flush toilets, dump station, drinking water, fire grates, picnic tables* ▭ *AE, D, MC, V* ⊙ *Early May–mid-Oct.*

Northwest Wyoming

WITH JACKSON AND THE WIND RIVER RANGE

WORD OF MOUTH

"Jackson is well worth a day's visit. The business district has some historic buildings which can be visited via a tour that leaves from the Town Square. The shops, galleries, bars, and restaurants provide a good couple hours of pleasant wandering and noshing time. The National Museum of Wildlife Art just north of town has a surprisingly very good moderate-sized collection. And there's a fun home-grown feel to the local rodeo, which happens in the summer on Wednesday and Saturday evenings."

—bachslunch

Updated by
Brian Kevin

Northwest Wyoming is mountain country, where high peaks—some of which remain snowcapped year-round—tower above deep, glacier-carved valleys. In addition to the tallest, most spectacular peaks in the state, there's a diverse wildlife population that includes wolves, grizzly bears, Rocky Mountain bighorn sheep, and antelope. Here you can hike through mountain meadows, challenge white water, explore Native American culture, and trace the history of westbound 19th-century emigrants.

From skiing, to hiking, kayaking, and parasailing, name an outdoor activity and you can probably do it here. You can hike or ride a horse along one of the backcountry trails near Grand Teton National Park, Dubois, or Lander; scale mountain peaks in the Wind River or Grand Teton ranges; or fish or float the Snake River near Jackson. Come winter, take a sleigh ride through the National Elk Refuge, snowmobile on hundreds of miles of trails, cross-country ski throughout the region, or hit the slopes at Snow King Mountain, Grand Targhee, or Jackson Hole Mountain Resort, one of the greatest skiing destinations in the country.

Wildlife watching in northwest Wyoming ranks among the best in the state: look for Rocky Mountain bighorn sheep at Whiskey Mountain near Dubois; buffalo, elk, and even wolves in Jackson Hole; and moose near Pinedale or north of Dubois. One of the best ways to admire the landscape—mountain flowers, alpine lakes, and wildlife ranging from fat little pikas to grizzly bears—is to pursue an outdoor activity.

There's more to northwest Wyoming than the great outdoors. A handful of museums, well worth a few hours of your trip, offer a window on the history of the American West. The Jackson Hole Museum concentrates on the early settlement of Jackson Hole, and the Museum of the Mountain Man in Pinedale takes an informative look at the trapper heritage.

ORIENTATION AND PLANNING

GETTING ORIENTED

Jackson Hole, the valley to the east of the Tetons, is a world-class ski destination, with literally thousands of ways to get down the slopes. In the valley the town of Jackson works to maintain its small-town charm while serving as the area's cultural center. In the Wind River Mountains the Oregon-California-Mormon trail sites near South Pass merit a visit, and you can learn about Native American traditions on the Wind River Indian Reservation.

You will need a car to tour northwest Wyoming; to reach the really spectacular backcountry a four-wheel-drive vehicle is best. Major routes through the area include U.S. 191, which runs north–south through Jackson, on the western edge of the state, and U.S. 26/287, which runs east of Grand Teton National Park (also on the western edge of the state, within the Jackson Hole valley) toward Dubois. Much of the driving you do here will take you through the mountains—including the Absaroka and Wind River ranges that dominate the region.

TOP REASONS TO GO

■ The Grand Teton range and sweeping Snake River: They're simply breathtaking.

■ Wildlife: Moose, bald eagles, elk, grizzlies, mountain lions...this is home turf for an abundance of awe-inspiring wild animals.

■ Restaurants: Some of the best food in the region, not just Western fare, is available here.

■ People: Jacksonites are friendly, and are knowledgeable, if slightly prideful, about their beautiful town.

4

PLANNING

WHEN TO GO

Most people visit northwest Wyoming in summer, although winter draws skiing enthusiasts (the ski season generally lasts December through March). The months between Memorial Day and Labor Day are the busiest, with all attractions operating at peak capacity. If you don't mind a few limitations on what you can do and where you can stay and eat, the best times to visit the region are in late spring (May) and early fall (September and October). Not only will you find fewer people on the roads and at the sights, but you also will have some of the best weather (although springtime can be wet, and it can and does snow here every month of the year). In general, spring is the best time to see wildlife, particularly young animals. Fall brings a rich blaze of colors, painting the aspen and cottonwood trees with a palette of red, gold, and orange. The days are warm, reaching into the 60s and 70s, and the nights are cool in fall. There are also fewer thunderstorms than in midsummer, plus fewer biting insects (such as mosquitoes) to bother you.

PLANNING YOUR TIME

Any tour of northwest Wyoming should include a day or two, at minimum, in Jackson Hole, where you can explore Grand Teton National Park (⇨ *Chapter 3*). Also in Jackson Hole is the small but bustling town of Jackson, with its one-of-a-kind town square entered through elk-antler arches and a stagecoach that gives rides throughout the day in summer. In winter, action is concentrated at nearby Teton Village, where you'll find unparalleled winter sports offerings at the Jackson Hole Mountain Resort. You're likely to share the slopes with Olympic champion skiers and snowboarders.

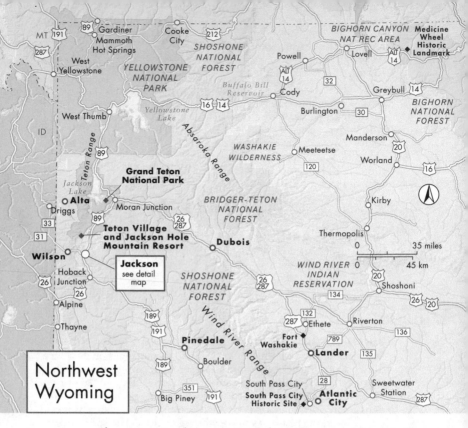

Northwest
Wyoming

If you can extend your stay, travel over Togwotee Mountain Pass to little Dubois, where you can stay at a guest ranch, ride horses in the Bridger-Teton National Forest, learn about local history at the Wind River Historical Center, and glimpse the region's wildlife at the National Bighorn Sheep Interpretive Center. After Dubois and environs, head south onto the Wind River Indian Reservation to find exceptional shops filled with arts and crafts locally made by Northern Arapaho and Eastern Shoshone tribal members.

Spend some time in Lander and explore the Wind River Mountains before heading south and then west to South Pass City State Historic Site, near Atlantic City. From here, follow the emigrant trail corridor west and then northwest to Pinedale and its excellent Museum of the Mountain Man.

GETTING HERE AND AROUND
AIR TRAVEL

American, Delta, SkyWest, and United Airlines/United Express provide multiple flights to Jackson daily, with connections in Chicago, Denver, and Salt Lake City. Scheduled jet service increases during the ski season. United and Great Lakes Airlines fly between Denver and Riverton.

The major airports in the region are Jackson Hole Airport, about 10 mi north of Jackson in Grand Teton National Park and nearly 50 mi south of Yellowstone National Park, and Riverton Regional Airport in Riverton, which is 30 mi northeast of Lander and about 76 mi southeast of Dubois.

Many lodgings have free shuttle-bus service to and from Jackson Hole Airport. Alltrans is the primary shuttle serving the Jackson Hole Airport, in addition to several taxi companies. If you're coming into the area from the Salt Lake City airport, you can travel to Jackson and back on a Jackson Hole Express shuttle for about $150 round-trip —even less from the airport in Pocatello or Idaho Falls.

AirlinesAmerican Airlines (☎ 800/433-7300 ⊕ www.aa.com). Delta (☎ 800/221-1212 ⊕ www.delta.com). Great Lakes Airlines (☎ 307/587-7683 or 800/554-5111 ⊕ www.greatlakesav.com). United Airlines/United Express (☎ 800/241-6522 ⊕ www.united.com).

AirportsJackson Hole Airport (✉ 1250 E. Airport Rd., Jackson Hole ☎ 307/733-7682). Riverton Regional Airport (✉ 4800 Airport Rd., Riverton ☎ 307/856-1307 ⊕ www.flyriverton.com).

Transfers Alltrans (☎ 307/733-3135 or 800/443-6133). Jackson Hole Express (☎ 307/733-1719 or 800/652-9510). Superior Ride (☎ 307/690-8005).

BUS TRAVEL

During the ski season, START buses shuttle people between Jackson and the Jackson Hole Mountain Resort as well as Star Valley to the south. The fare is free around town, $3 one-way to Teton Village, and $1 along the Teton Village Road. Buses operate from 6 AM to 11 PM. In summer START buses operate from 5:45 AM to 10:30 PM. They stop at more than 45 locations in Jackson. People with mobility-related disabilities must make reservations 48 hours in advance for START buses. The Targhee Express runs between Jackson and the Grand Targhee Ski and Summer Resort, with pickups at various lodging properties in Jackson and Teton Village. The cost is $44 per day, or you can buy a combination shuttle/Grand Targhee lift ticket for $84. Advance reservations are required.

Bus Information START (☎ 307/733-4521). Targhee Express (☎ 307/733-9754 or 800/443-6133).

CAR TRAVEL

If you didn't drive to Wyoming, rent a car once you arrive. The airports have major car-rental agencies, which offer four-wheel-drive vehicles and ski racks.

Northwest Wyoming is well away from the interstates, so drivers make their way here on two-lane highways that are long on miles and scenery. To get to Jackson from I–80, take U.S. 191/189 north from Rock Springs for about 177 mi. From I–90, drive west from Sheridan on U.S. 14 or Alternate U.S. 14 to Cody. U.S. 14 continues west to Yellowstone National Park, and you can also hook up with U.S. 191, which leads south to Jackson.

Be extremely cautious when driving in winter; game crossings, whiteouts, and ice on the roads are not uncommon. Contact the Wyoming

Department of Transportation for road and travel reports. For emergency situations, dial 911 or contact the Wyoming Highway Patrol.

Contacts **Grand Teton Park Road Conditions** (☎ 307/739-3682). **Wyoming Department of Transportation** (☎ 307/777-4375 from outside Wyoming for road conditions, 888/996-7623 or log on to ⊕ www.wyoroad.info). **Wyoming Highway Patrol** (☎ 307/777-4301, 800/442-9090 for emergencies, #4357 [#HELP] from a cell phone for emergencies).

RESTAURANTS

Northwest Wyoming has many restaurants. Anyplace you go you'll find basic Western fare such as steaks, chicken, and burgers; in Jackson there's a wider selection, with menus listing everything from Chinese and Thai dishes to trout, buffalo, and elk. There are also a few fine-dining establishments in the region. Arguably the best steaks in all of Wyoming are prepared at Svilars', a steak house in the tiny community of Hudson, east of Lander.

HOTELS

No other part of Wyoming has such a variety of lodging properties that appeal to all budgets. Lodging options in the area include elegant and expensive properties such as the Amangani resort in Jackson Hole, guest ranches in the Dubois and Jackson areas, historic inns, simple cabins, and dozens of chain motels.

It's a good idea to reserve well ahead for lodging in the town of Jackson in July and August. You should also reserve lodgings at Teton Village well in advance for skiing at Jackson Hole Mountain Resort.

WHAT IT COSTS					
	¢	$	$$	$$$	$$$$
Restaurants	under $8	$8–$12	$13–$20	$21–$30	over $30
Hotels	under $70	$70–$100	$101–$150	$151–$200	over $200

Restaurant prices are for a main course at dinner, excluding sales tax of 4%–7%. Hotel prices are for two people in a standard double room in high season, excluding service charges and 5%–10% tax.

CAMPING

There are numerous campgrounds within Grand Teton National Park and Bridger-Teton, Shoshone, and Caribou-Targhee national forests. (Caribou-Targhee National Forest borders Grand Teton National Park on the west; most of the forest lies within Idaho.) Few of these campgrounds accept reservations. Campgrounds in the national forests tend to fill up more slowly than those in Grand Teton.

Reservations can be made for a small number of national-forest campgrounds near Jackson through U.S. Forest Reservations.

Contacts **Bridger-Teton National Forest** (☎ 307/739-5500). **Caribou-Targhee National Forest** (☎ 208/524-7500). **Grand Teton National Park** (☎ 307/739-3300). **U.S. Forest Service Recreation Reservations** (☎ 877/444-6777).

JACKSON

Most visitors to northwest Wyoming come to Jackson, which remains a small but booming Western town that's "howdy" in the daytime and hopping in the evening. For active types, it's a good place to stock up on supplies before heading for outdoor adventures in Grand Teton National Park, Yellowstone, and the surrounding Jackson Hole area. It's also a great place to kick back and rest your feet while taking in the wealth of galleries, Western-wear shops, varied cuisines, a $35 million arts center, and active nightlife centering on bars and music.

Unfortunately, Jackson's charm and popularity have put it at risk. On busy summer days traffic often slows to a crawl on the highway that dog-legs through downtown. Proposals for new motels and condominiums sprout like the purple asters in the spring as developers vie for a share of the upscale vacation market. Old-timers suggest that the town—in fact, the entire Jackson Hole—has already lost some of its dusty charm from when horses stood at hitching rails around Town Square. However, with national parks and forests and state lands occupying some of the most beautiful real estate in the country, there's only 3%–4% in unprotected ground on which to build. These limitations, along with the cautious approach of locals, may yet keep Jackson on a human scale.

GETTING HERE AND AROUND

Coming from Yellowstone or Grand Teton national parks, you enter Jackson from the north on U.S. 191, passing the sagebrush flats of the National Elk Refuge. West of town, Hwy. 22 comes in from Idaho, over 8,431-foot Teton Pass; those entering Jackson from the "back side" of the Tetons should expect snowy conditions as late as June. Reach Jackson from the south via U.S. 191 from Pinedale or U.S. 89 from the Star Valley. The two routes merge 13 mi south of town at Hoback Junction. Driving in Jackson can be frustrating, particularly in the pedestrian-heavy and traffic-clogged downtown area. Best to hoof it, ride the free and frequent START buses, or rent a bike from a local outfitter—a fleet cyclist can cross town end-to-end in fifteen minutes.

VISITOR INFORMATION

Jackson Hole Chamber of Commerce (✉ *990 W. Broadway, Box 550, Jackson* ☎ *307/733-3316* 🖷 *307/733-5585* 🌐 *www.jacksonholechamber.com*).

EXPLORING JACKSON

Numbers correspond to the Jackson map.

TOP ATTRACTIONS

⑤ **National Elk Refuge.** Wildlife abounds on this 25,000-acre refuge year-round at the foot of Sleeping Indian mountain. But from around late November through March the real highlight is the more than 7,500 elk, many with enormous antler racks, that winter here. There are also buffalo, and limited hunts, depending on population size, to cull the herds. The Refuge Road entrance lies about 1 mi from the Town Square, just past St. John's hospital on East Broadway. Elk can also be observed from various pull-outs along U.S. 191 or up close by slowly driving your car

Fodor'sChoice
★

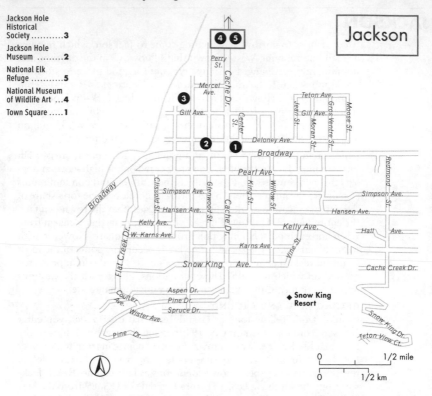

Jackson

on the refuge's winding, unpaved roads. There's also a horse-drawn sleigh ride, giving visitors the chance to see the elk stand or eat calmly as sleighs loaded with families and supplied with alfalfa pellets move in their midst. Among the other animals that make their home here are buffalos, coyotes, mountain sheep, trumpeter swans, and other waterfowl. Arrange for sleigh rides through the Jackson Hole & Greater Yellowstone Visitor Center at 532 N. Cache (⊕ www.fws.gov/nationalelkrefuge) in Jackson; wear warm clothing, including hats, gloves, boots, long johns, and coats. ⊠ 532 N. Cache Dr. ☎ 307/733–5771 ☞ Sleigh rides $18 ⊙ Year-round; sleigh rides mid-Dec.–Mar.

❹ **National Museum of Wildlife Art.** Among the paintings and sculptures of
★ bighorn sheep, elk, and other animals of the West you'll find fine-art representations and photographs of wildlife by such artists as John J. Audubon, Frederick Remington, George Catlin, Tucker Smith, and Charles M. Russell. The collection includes works in various mediums and styles, the earliest pieces dating to 2000 BC. A deck here affords views across the National Elk Refuge, where, particularly in winter, you can see wildlife in a natural habitat. ⊠ 2820 Rungius Rd., 3 mi north of Jackson ☎ 307/733–5771 ⊕ www.wildlifeart.org ☞ $10 ⊙ Mid-May–mid-Oct., daily 9–5; mid-Oct.–mid-May, Mon.–Sat. 9–5, Sun. 1–5.

A GOOD TOUR OF JACKSON

If you don't plan to shop on Town Square, you can easily do this tour in a few hours. But if you want to hit the stores, budget a full day. Note that the Jackson Hole Museum is closed from October through May.

Start your visit at the corner of Cache and Broadway at **Town Square ❶**, easily identifiable by its elk-antler arches and bustle of activity. Stroll around the square and visit the many shops and galleries here. Walk one block west to Glenwood Street and the **Jackson Hole Museum ❷** for a lesson on local history, a collection of artifacts from Native American and early frontier life, and a compilation of Hollywood movie memorabilia from Westerns shot on location here. For $4 you can also pick up a self-guided walking tour. Once you've done the town, hop into your car and drive 3 mi north on Cache Drive to the **National Wildlife Art Museum ❹**, with its wonderful collection of timeless Western talents like Charles Russell and Frederic Remington. The museum is devoted to the fine art of depicting wildlife in all its natural splendor. From a deck at the museum, between November and March, you can see the real thing: thousands of elk, plus waterfowl, mountain sheep, and coyotes wintering at the elk refuge below. The museum also hosts periodic lectures covering international wildlife issues and cultural events. Those who want to see the animals up close can drive down to the **National Elk Refuge ❺** in the valley below. In winter you can take a sleigh ride to the refuge.

❶ **Town Square.** You can spend an entire day wandering around Jackson's always-bustling Town Square, a parklike area crisscrossed with walking paths and bedecked with arches woven from hundreds of elk antlers. Various shops and restaurants surround the square, and there's often entertainment going on in the square itself, including a rip-roaring "shoot-out" most summer evenings at approximately 6:30. At the southwest corner of the square you can board a stagecoach for a ride around the area; it costs about $6 per adult.

WORTH NOTING

❸ **Jackson Hole Historical Society.** Displays at this log cabin illuminate local history. In addition to historic artifacts and photographs, the society houses manuscripts, maps, and an oral-history collection. ⊠ *105 Mercill Ave.* ☎ *307/733–9605* ⊕ *www.jacksonholehistory.org.*

❷ **Jackson Hole Museum.** For some local history, visit this museum, where you can get acquainted with the early settlers and find out how Dead Man's Bar got its name. You'll also learn how Jackson elected the first all-female town government, not to mention a lady sheriff who claimed to have killed three men before hanging up her spurs. Kids can try on vintage clothes and hats and see what they'd look like as homesteaders. Among the exhibits are Native American, ranching, and cowboy artifacts. ⊠ *Glenwood St. and Deloney Ave.* ☎ *307/733–2414* ⊕ *www.jacksonholehistory.org* ⤳ *$3* ⊙ *Memorial Day–Sept., Mon.–Sat. 9:30–6, Sun. 10–5.*

OFF THE
BEATEN
PATH

Granite Hot Springs. Soothing thermal baths in pristine outback country await in the heart of the Bridger-Teton National Forest, just a short drive south of Jackson. Concerted local and federal efforts have preserved the wild lands in this hunter's and fisherman's paradise where ranches dot the Teton Valley floor. The Snake River turns west and the contours sheer into steep vertical faces. By Hoback Junction there's white-water excitement. The drive south along U.S. 191 provides good views of the river's bends and turns and the life-jacketed rafters and kayakers who float through the Hoback canyon. At Hoback Junction, about 11 mi south of Jackson, head east (toward Pinedale) on U.S. Highway 189/191 and follow the Hoback River east through its beautiful canyon. A tributary canyon 10 mi east of the junction is followed by a well-maintained and marked gravel road to Granite Hot Springs, in the Bridger-Teton National Forest. Drive 9 mi off U.S. 189/191 (northeast) on Granite Creek Road to reach the hot springs. People also come for the shady, creek-side campground and moderate hikes up Granite Canyon to passes with panoramic views. You'll want to drive with some caution, as there are elevated turns, the possibility of a felled tree, and wandering livestock that can own the road ahead on blind curves. In winter there's a popular snowmobile and dogsled trail from the highway. The 93°F to 112°F thermal bath at the end of the road is pure physical therapy, but it's closed from November through mid-December. There's also an admission price of $6 per person.

SPORTS AND THE OUTDOORS

For more listings of sports outfitters serving the Jackson area, see Outfitters and Expeditions information in Chapter 3.

BICYCLING

The trip up to **Lower Slide Lake,** north of town, is a favorite of cyclists. Turn east off U.S. 26/89/191 to Kelly, and then follow Slide Lake Road. Cyclists ride the **Spring Gulch Road,** part pavement, part dirt, off Route 22, along the base of Gros Ventre Butte, rejoining U.S. 26/89/191 near the Gros Ventre River.

Bike rentals for all skill levels and age groups are available at **Edge Sports** (✉ 490 W. Broadway ☎ 307/734-3916); the company also does on-site repairs. You can rent a mountain bike to explore on your own or take a tour at **Hoback Sports** (✉ 520 W. Broadway ☎ 307/733-5335). General tours are geared to intermediate and advanced riders, but Hoback can also custom-design a tour to suit your abilities and interests. The store also sells bike, ski, skate, and snowboard apparel and equipment. Mountain bikers of all skill levels can take guided half-, full-, or multiday tours with **Teton Mountain Bike Tours** (✆ Box 7027, 83002 ☎ 307/733-0712 or 800/733-0788 ⊕ www.wybike.com) into both Grand Teton and Yellowstone national parks, as well as to the Bridger-Teton and Caribou-Targhee national forests and throughout Jackson Hole.

CANOEING, KAYAKING, AND RAFTING

South of Jackson, where the Hoback joins the Snake River and the canyon walls become steep, there are lively white-water sections. But the upper Snake, whose rating is Class I and II, is a river for those who value scenery over white-water thrills. For the most part, floating rather than taking on rapids is the theme of running the Snake. As such, it's a good choice for families with children. What makes the trip special is the Teton Range, looming as high as 8,000 feet above the river. This float trip can also be combined with two or more days of kayaking on Jackson Lake. Raft trips take place between June and September. Experienced paddlers run the Hoback, too.

The Snake River's western Idaho portion has earned a strange footnote in history. It's the river that Evel Knievel tried (and failed miserably) to jump over on a rocket-powered motorcycle in the mid-1970s.

Rendezvous River Sports (✉ *945 W. Broadway* ☎ *307/733–2471 or 800/ 733–2471* ⊕ *www.jacksonholekayak.com*) is the premiere paddle-sports outfitter in the region, offering expert instruction so you can test yourself on western Wyoming's ancient rivers and lakes. The company also schedules more relaxed and scenic trips, including guided tours of Slide, Lewis, and Yellowstone lakes, and rapid-shooting rides on the Hoback River down Granite Creek to the Snake River while you marvel at south Jackson's majestic canyons. Raft and canoe rentals are also available.

DOGSLEDDING

Dogsledding excursions are available through **Iditarod Sled Dog Tours** (✉ *11 Granite Creek Rd.* ☎ *307/733–7388 or 800/554–7388* ⊕ *www. jhsleddog.com*). Veteran Iditarod racer Frank Teasley leads half-day introductory trips and full-day trips to Granite Hot Springs. It's a great way to see wintering native wildlife such as moose, elk, bighorn sheep, deer, and bald eagles in the Bridger-Teton National Forest. Sled trips are offered only in season, which can begin as early as November and run as late as April.

HIKING

Bridger-Teton National Forest (⌂ *340 N. Cache St., Box 1888, 83001* ☎ *307/739–5500* ⊕ *www.fs.fed.us/btnf*) covers hundreds of thousands of acres of western Wyoming and shelters abundant wildlife. Permits for backcountry use of the forest are necessary only for groups and commercial operators such as outfitters. Contact the forest office for more information.

The guides at **the Hole Hiking Experience** (⌂ *Box 7779, 83002* ☎ *866/733– 4453 or 307/690–4453* ⊕ *www.holehike.com*) will take you to mountain meadows or to the tops of the peaks on half- or full-day tours. Some outings are suitable for the very experienced, others for any well-conditioned adult, and still others for families.

SKIING

☾ **Snow King Resort** (✉ *400 E. Snow King Ave.* ☎ *307/733–5200 or 800/522–5464* ⊕ *www.snowkingmountain.com*), at the western edge of Jackson, has 400 acres of ski runs for daytime use and 110 acres suitable for night skiing, plus an extensive snowmaking system on Snow King Mountain. You'll also find a snow-tubing park. In summer there's a 2,500-foot alpine slide and miles of biking and hiking paths, all the way to the mountaintop. For $12 and under a person, you can also ride the scenic chairlift to the top and back. Or you can stop off at the summit, which is 7,808 feet above sea level, for a picnic and feast on the stunning 50-mi view of Jackson. From up here, on a clear day, you can see over the neighboring buttes and count the clouds passing around the Tetons. **Spring Creek Ranch** (⊠ *1800 Spirit Dance Rd.* ☎ *307/733–8833 or 800/443–6139*) offers lessons and use of its groomed cross-country trails for a fee.

SLEIGH RIDES

☾ Sleigh rides into the National Elk Refuge last about 45 minutes and depart from in front of the **Jackson Hole & Greater Yellowstone Visitor Center** (⊠ *532 N. Cache Dr.* ☎ *307/733–3316*) daily in winter, 10 to 4, about every 20 minutes. Dinner sleigh rides are available through **Spring Creek Ranch** (⊠ *1800 Spirit Dance Rd.* ☎ *307/733–8833 or 800/443–6139*), with dinner at its Granary restaurant.

SNOWMOBILING

Numerous companies in the Jackson area rent snowmobiles. **Rocky Mountain Snowmobile Tours** (⊠ *1050 S. U.S. 89* ☎ *307/733–2237 or 800/647–2561* ⊕ *www.rockymountainsnow.com*) guides one- to five-day trips, beginning at $210 per day, to such areas as Granite Hot Springs, Togwotee Pass, Gros Ventre Mountains, Grey's River near Alpine, and Yellowstone National Park.

WHERE TO EAT

$

AMERICAN–
CASUAL

✕ **Billy's Giant Hamburgers & Cadillac Grille.** True to its name, Billy's serves big—really big—burgers and waffle fries that are really, really good, albeit greasy. Not to be outdone, there are also hot dogs and several deli-style sandwiches that you can munch around a 1950s-style lunch counter with clear views of the Town Square. The portions in general are huge. Service is quick and unpretentious. Billy's shares space with the more refined but equally fun Cadillac Grille, where you can enjoy a casual atmosphere of a few booths and tables or grab a stool—if you can find one—around its usually jam-packed circular bar. ⊠ *55 N. Cache Dr.* ☎ *307/733–3279* ⊕ *www.cadillac-grille.com* ⊟ *AE, MC, V.*

$$$

CONTINENTAL

✕ **The Blue Lion.** For 30 years consistently excellent, distinctive fare has been the rule at this white-and-blue clapboard house two blocks from Town Square. The sophisticated offerings range from Dijon-mustard-rubbed rack of lamb to grilled elk with port wine sauce to fresh fish dishes, including rainbow trout. There's patio dining in summer and a wine list. Early-bird specials (6–6:30 PM) are a great value in an otherwise pricey restaurant. This is a no-smoking establishment. ⊠ *160 N. Millward St.* ☎ *307/733–3912* ⊕ *www.bluelionrestaurant.com* ⊟ *AE, D, MC, V* ☾ *Closed Tues. in Oct. and Mar. No lunch.*

$$

SOUTHERN

✕ **Bubba's Barbecue Restaurant.** Succulent baby back ribs and mouthwatering spareribs are the specialties at this busy barbecue joint, which evokes the Old West with its large wooden porch, wooden booths, Western paintings, and antique signs. Sandwiches and a huge salad bar with plenty of nonmeat choices are also available. This is also one of the most affordable breakfast options in Jackson, but whenever you go there can be long waits. The desserts include homemade pies of the chocolate-buttermilk and fudge-pecan variety. ⊠ *525 W. Broadway* ☎ *307/733–2288* ▭ *AE, D, MC, V.*

$ ✕ **The Bunnery.** Lunch is served year-round and dinner is served in summer at the Bunnery, but it's the breakfasts of omelets and home-baked pastries that are irresistible; the coffee is also very good. All the breads are made on the premises, most from OSM flour (oats, sunflower, millet). It's elbow to elbow inside, so you may have to wait to be seated on busy mornings, but any inconvenience is well worth it. There's also a decent vegetarian selection here. Try a giant almond stick, a sticky bun, or a piece of Very Berry Pie made from raspberries, strawberries, and blueberries. In summer there's outdoor seating. On-street parking can be hard to find here. ⊠ *Hole-in-the-Wall Mall, 130 N. Cache Dr.* ☎ *307/734–0075* ⊕ *www.bunnery.com*▭ *AE, D, MC, V* ⊗ *No dinner Sept.–May.*

AMERICAN
Fodor'sChoice
★

$$$ ✕ **Burke's Chop House.** Offering fine dining in casual elegance, Burke's is considered by many to be Jackson's best steak house. The menu ranges from a variety of game dishes—venison, elk, and buffalo—to haute cuisine such as beef tournedos with truffles and foie gras. The wine list is extensive. The food and service here are first-rate, but the restaurant is usually crowded and can be noisy. A kids' menu is available, and this is a completely no-smoking restaurant. Its semiprivate dining room seats up to 25. ⊠ *72 S. Glenwood* ☎ *307/733–8575* ⊕ *www. burkeschophousejacksonhole.com*▭ *AE, D, MC, V* ⊗ *Closed Nov. and May. No lunch.*

STEAK
★

$$$ ✕ **The Gun Barrel Steak & Game House.** At Jackson's legendary game and steak lodge, all dishes are slow-cooked over an open river-rock mesquite grill. The dining atmosphere is rustic and fun, with an Old West collection of mounted game, wildlife, and memorabilia. Service is always friendly. The menu offers a wide variety of unique dishes, but some, such as velvet elk, may be too rich for those unaccustomed to game. The bar has an ample list of bourbons, scotches, and wines to sample if you just want a drink. ⊠ *862 W. Broadway, approximately 1 mi from Town Square in Grand Teton Plaza* ☎ *307/733–3287* ⊕ *www.gunbarrel.com*▭ *AE, D, MC, V* ⊗ *Closed Nov. and Apr. No lunch.*

STEAK

$ ✕ **Jedediah's House of Sourdough.** Friendly, noisy, and elbow knocking, this restaurant a block east of Town Square—which also has a branch at the airport—makes breakfast and lunch for those with big appetites. There are plenty of excellent "sourjacks" (sourdough flapjacks) and biscuits and gravy. Burgers are mountain-man size. The airport location tends to be more expensive than the restaurant downtown, but it's open later. ⊠ *135 E. Broadway* ☎ *307/733–5671* ⊠ *1250 Airport Rd.* ☎ *307/733–6063* ▭ *AE, D, DC, MC, V* ⊗ *No dinner.*

AMERICAN

$ ✕ **Merry Piglets.** No pork is served here (hence the name). But otherwise, you'll get more than generous portions of Mexican fare, over a mesquite grill if you like, with a range of homemade sauces from mild to spicy. Favorites include sizzling fajitas, carne asada, shrimp mango wraps, and a Tex-Mex–style seafood chimichanga. It's usually noisy and jam-packed, but there's a full-service bar whipping up frozen strawberry margaritas that you can sip in the festive atmosphere while waiting for your table. ⊠ *160 N. Cache Dr., near Teton Theatre* ☎ *307/733–2966* ⌂ *Reservations not accepted* ▭ *AE, D, MC, V.*

MEXICAN
★

4

$$$ ✕ **Snake River Grill.** Dine in Western fireside elegance, with white table-
AMERICAN cloths and an excellent wine list aimed at true oenophiles. Those looking
for a brew may find the beer list lacking. Choose from fresh fish, free-
range meats, and organic produce at this second-floor restaurant over-
looking the Town Square and Snow King Mountain. Buffalo cowboy
steaks, vegetarian pasta with mushrooms and artichokes, and grilled
elk chops are among the standout entrées, but some may find the prices
on the high side. A room for private parties right off the bar seats up to
16. Kids are welcome; however, there are no high chairs and there's no
children's menu. ⊠ *84 E. Broadway* ☎ *307/733–0557* ⊕ *www.snakeriv-
ergrill.com* ⊟ *AE, D, MC, V* ☉ *Closed Apr. and Nov. No lunch.*

$$$ ✕ **Sweetwater Restaurant.** Imaginative takes on salmon, pork tenderloin,
AMERICAN buffalo, and pot roast are on the dinner menu in this historic log build-
ing built in 1915 with antique oak furnishings. The atmosphere is rustic,
homey, and comforting. There's a great dessert menu, too. Try lemon
raspberry cake with extra homemade whipped cream if they have it.
For lunch, you can have a wrap, salad, or sandwich in the outdoor dining area (weather permitting), though even there the views aren't great.
Reservations are essential in busy seasons. ⊠ *85 S. King St.* ☎ *307/733–
3553* ⊟ *AE, D, MC, V.*

$ ✕ **Teton Thai.** For the best Thai this side of San Francisco—and maybe
THAI the entire inner-mountain West—this family-owned local favorite tops
Fodor's Choice the list of everyone in Jackson. Just one block off Town Square—across
★ from the Teton Theatre and next to Gaslight Alley—it's always packed.
In winter there's takeout or counter seating right in the kitchen, but in
summer you can sit on the patio outside, where the atmosphere can
become boisterous with big crowds and nightly DJs. Service can sometimes be slow, but the *tom kha gai* (coconut milk, lemongrass, and
chicken soup) and tofu curry dishes are always worth the wait. ⊠ *135
N. Cache Dr.* ☎ *307/733–0022* ⊕ *www.tetonthai.com* ⊟ *No credit
cards* ☉ *Closed Sun. and Nov. No lunch weekends.*

WHERE TO STAY

There are three reservations services for Jackson Hole. You can make
reservations for most lodgings in Jackson through **Jackson Hole Central
Reservations** (☎ *888/838–6606* ⊕ *www.jacksonholewy.com*). Properties
managed by **Jackson Hole Resort Lodging** (☎ *800/443–8613* ⊕ *www.jhrl.
com*) include rooms, condominiums, and vacation homes at Teton Village, Teton Pines, and the Jackson Hole Racquet Club. **Mountain Property
Management** (⌖ *250 Veronica La., Box 2228, 83001* ☎ *800/992–9948*
⊕ *www.mpmjh.com*) offers condominium, cabin, and luxury-home
rentals throughout Jackson Hole.

$$$$ ▦ **Amangani.** This exclusive resort built of sandstone and redwood melds
★ into the landscape of Gros Ventre Butte, affording beautiful views of
Spring Creek Valley from its cliff-top location. The warm hospitality is
Western, but the setting is that of Eastern (as in Asian) simplicity, with tall
ceilings, clean lines, and rooms with platform beds, large soaking tubs,
and plenty of space. The amenities here are the best in Jackson Hole,
and include horseback riding, tennis, and nearby cross-country skiing

and sleigh rides in winter. **Pros:** extremely luxurious; impeccable service; excellent views of the Tetons. **Cons:** very expensive; too detached from the mundane world below (even by Jackson standards); decor seems a bit too exotic for western Wyoming. ⊠ *1535 N.E. Butte Rd.* ☎ *307/734–7333 or 877/734–7333* ⊕ *www.amangani.com* ⤳ *40 suites* ⚼ *In-room: safe, refrigerator, DVD, Wi-Fi. In-hotel: restaurant, room service, bar, tennis courts, pool, spa, laundry service, no-smoking rooms* ☰ *AE, D, DC, MC, V* ▯❀▯ *EP.*

WORD OF MOUTH

"One word of caution about your final day and flight. If you are catching an early flight out of Jackson and are in the middle of YNP the night before, allow plenty of time to get to the airport. Those same animals that are incredible to photograph and view on earlier days have a way of wandering in front of your car when you are trying to catch a flight."

                                        –gail

¢–$$$ ▣ **Antler Inn.** Perhaps no motel in Jackson has a better location than the Antler, one block south of Town Square. Some rooms have fireplaces and two have Jacuzzis, but otherwise they're standard motel rooms. In winter there's a complimentary ski shuttle. **Pros:** restaurants nearby; family-run operation with owner on premises; good prices in the off-season. **Cons:** frequently booked in summer; can get rowdy during Hill Climb, a snowmobile festival in March at nearby Snow King. ⊠ *43 W. Pearl St.* ☎ *307/733–2535 or 800/483–8667* ⤳ *110 rooms* ⚼ *In-hotel: some pets allowed, no-smoking rooms* ☰ *AE, D, DC, MC, V* ▯❀▯ *EP.*

$$–$$$ ▣ **Cowboy Village Resort.** Stay in your own small log cabin with covered decks and barbecue grills. There is a ski-waxing room, and both the START bus and Targhee Express buses that serve the ski areas stop here. **Pros:** near town; late-night dinner option next door; grills available for cooking outside. **Cons:** crowded in summer; few amenities; more like a motel with cabins than a true resort. ⊠ *120 S. Flat Creek Dr.* ☎ *307/733–3121 or 800/962–4988* ⊕ *www.cowboyvillage.com* ⤳ *82 cabins, 2 hotel rooms* ⚼ *In-room: kitchen (some). In-hotel: gym, laundry facilities, no-smoking rooms* ☰ *AE, D, DC, MC, V* ▯❀▯ *EP.*

$$$$ ▣ **Parkway Inn.** From the moment you enter its ground floor "salon,"
★   a vintage ambience soothes the soul in period furniture and black-and-white photographs, showing the rise of east Jackson. Each room has a distinctive look—with oak or wicker furniture—and each is filled with antiques from the 19th century onward. The overall effect is homey and delightful, especially if you plan to stay a few days or longer. Continental breakfast is served in an antiques-filled lounge. This quiet property is three blocks from Town Square. **Pros:** convenient location; boutique atmosphere. **Cons:** not a full-service hotel; no restaurant on premises. ⊠ *125 N. Jackson St.* ☎ *307/733–3143 or 800/247–8390* ⊕ *www.parkwayinn.com* ⤳ *33 rooms, 12 suites* ⚼ *In-hotel: pool, gym, Internet terminal, Wi-Fi, no-smoking rooms* ☰ *AE, D, MC, V* ▯❀▯ *CP.*

$$$$ ▣ **Rusty Parrot.** An imposing river-rock fireplace in the cathedral lounge lends warmth to this timber inn near the center of Jackson. You can walk the four blocks to shops, galleries, and restaurants on Town Square. Handcrafted wooden furnishings fill the rooms, some of which have

fireplaces and oversize whirlpool tubs. With body wraps, massages, and facials, the spa is a nice extra. Have dinner at the Wild Sage Restaurant ($$$$), which serves duck, pork, halibut, and Montana Legend Beef. **Pros:** in town yet off the beaten path; fine dining in the charming restaurant; good off-season deals. **Cons:** not geared toward families; limited views. ⊠ *175 N. Jackson St.* ☎ *307/733–2000 or 800/458–2004* ⊕ *www.rustyparrot.com* ⤴ *31 rooms* ♿ *In-room: refrigerator (some), DVD, Wi-Fi. In-hotel: restaurant, room service, spa, Wi-Fi, no-smoking rooms* ⊟ *AE, D, MC, V* ⊠⊘ *CP.*

$$$$ 🖵 **Trapper Inn.** This motel is within walking distance of Town Square and has some of the best-appointed rooms in Jackson for people with disabilities. It's also undergone a major renovation geared toward turning it into an executive-stay hotel. Downstairs you'll find an open reception desk with friendly and helpful staff, free coffee, plenty of tall windows, ample sitting space, free Wi-Fi, a stone fireplace, and vintage trapper gear big enough to snare a grizzly. **Pros:** walking distance to town; small pool and Jacuzzi. **Cons:** limited views; must drive to mountains. ⊠ *285 N. Cache St.* ☎ *307/733–2648 or 888/771–2648* ⊕ *www.trapperinn. com* ⤴ *89 rooms, 53 suites* ♿ *In-room: kitchen (some), refrigerator, Wi-Fi. In-hotel: pool, laundry facilities, Internet terminal, no-smoking rooms* ⊟ *AE, MC, V* ⊠⊘ *BP.*

$$$$ 🖵 **The Wort Hotel.** This brick Victorian hotel near Town Square, built
Fodor's Choice   in 1941, seems to have been around as long as the Tetons, but it feels
★   fresh inside (where there's property-wide Wi-Fi). A fireplace warms the lobby, and a sitting area is just up the stairs. Locally made Western-style furnishings of lodgepole-pine beds, pine dressers, carpets, drapes, and bed coverings are in warm, muted blues and mauves. You can sip a drink in the Silver Dollar Bar & Grill ($$$)—aptly named for the 2,032 silver dollars embedded on top of the bar—or amble through swinging doors into the restaurant for a fine meal. **Pros:** charming old building with lots of history; convenient location in town; some good-value packages offered. **Cons:** limited views; must drive to parks and mountains. ⊠ *50 N. Glenwood St.* ☎ *307/733–2190 or 800/322–2727* ⊕ *www.worthotel.com* ⤴ *59 rooms, 5 suites* ♿ *In-room: refrigerator (some), Wi-Fi. In-hotel: restaurant, room service, bar, gym, no-smoking rooms* ⊠⊘ *BP* ⊟ *AE, D, MC, V.*

CAMPING

🏕 **Curtis Canyon.** Numerous trees surround this simple campground northeast of Jackson Hole. Part of Bridger-Teton National Forest, the campground is near a popular mountain-biking area and sits at an elevation of 6,600 feet. No trailers longer than 30 feet. Ten-day limit. **Pros:** ideal for budget-conscious campers; isolated and quiet. **Cons:** no staffed amenities; rough road for cars without four-wheel drive; not suitable for large RVs. ♿ *Pit toilets, drinking water, fire pits, picnic tables* ⤴ *11 sites* ⊠ *From Elk Refuge Headquarters in Jackson, take Flat Creek Road northeast 7 mi* ☎ *307/739–5400 or 307/543–2386* ⊕ *www.fs.fed.us/btnf* ⚠ *Reservations not accepted* ⊟ *No credit cards* ⊘ *June–Sept.*

🏕 **Granite Creek.** Part of Bridger-Teton National Forest, this wooded, 52-site campground is a sprawling place convenient to hiking and mountain-biking trails. An added bonus is the thermally heated pool of Granite Hot Springs. The elevation is 7,100 feet, and there are wheel-chair-accessible sites. **Pros:** hot springs just up the road; rarely fills up; abundant wildlife. **Cons:** no staffed amenities; rough road for cars without four-wheel drive; not suitable for large RVs. ⚿ *Flush toilets, pit toilets, drinking water, fire pits, picnic tables* ⟿ *52 sites* ✉ *Granite Creek Rd. off U.S. 189/191, 35 mi southeast of Jackson* ☎ *307/739–5400 or 307/543–2386* ⊕ *www.fs.fed.us/btnf* ⚠ *Reservations not accepted* ▬ *No credit cards* ☽ *Late May–Sept.*

NIGHTLIFE AND THE ARTS

NIGHTLIFE

There's never a shortage of live music in Jackson, where local performers play country, rock, and folk. Some of the most popular bars are on Town Square. At the **Million Dollar Cowboy Bar** (✉ *25 N. Cache St.* ☎ *307/733–2207*) everyone dresses up in cowboy garb, two-steps into the Old West, or moseys over to the bar and slides into authentic horse-saddle seats. There are plenty of pool tables, and there's good pub grub and live country music most nights but Sunday, not to mention free country-western dance lessons on Thursday. Downstairs is a popular restaurant serving certified Black Angus steaks. **43 North** (✉ *645 S. Cache Dr.* ☎ *307/733–0043*), at the base of Snow King Mountain, serves continental cuisine for both lunch and dinner, with outdoor seating (weather permitting) and a stellar view of the mountain in summer. You can also curl up inside by the stone fireplace at this locals' hangout and grab a drink at a table or the antique bar. There's lots of free parking and frequent live music; call for a schedule of events. Locals head to happy hour at **Snake River Brewing** (✉ *265 S. Millward St.* ☎ *307/733–2792*) for cold pints and pub fare. Avoid the loud chatter levels by nabbing a sought-after seat on the picnic-table patio.

THE ARTS

Center for the Arts (✉ *240 S. Glenwood* ☎ *307/734–8956* ⊕ *www.jhcenterforthearts.org*) is Jackson's $35 million center dedicated to supporting the fine and performing arts, including theater, film, and dance. It also hosts lectures on global issues, rotating exhibits, and showcases of star talent from Hollywood to Broadway. Classes for adults are included in the center's mission.

Artists who work in a variety of mediums show and sell their work at the **Jackson Hole Fall Arts Festival** (☎ *307/733–3316*), with special events highlighting art, poetry, and dance. Festival events take place throughout town in September, and many art galleries in Jackson have special programs and exhibits.

For those seeking a contemporary theater experience, **Off-Square Theatre** (✉ *Center for the Arts, 240 S. Glenwood* ☎ *307/733–3021* ⊕ *www.off-square.org*) is a space for children and adults where theater professionals and nonprofessionals strut their stuff and sometimes go outside the box. The company is one of the leading theater companies in the region.

SHOPPING

Jackson's peaceful Town Square is surrounded by storefronts with a mixture of specialty and outlet shops—most of them small scale—with moderate to expensive prices. North of Jackson's center, on Cache Street, is a small cluster of fine shops on Gaslight Alley.

BOOKS

One of Gaslight Alley's best shops is **Valley Bookstore** (⊠ *125 N. Cache St.* ☎ *307/733–4533*). It ranks among the top bookstores in the region, with a big selection of regional history, guidebooks on flora and fauna, and fiction by Wyoming and regional authors.

CLOTHING

Fodor's Choice
★ **Hide Out Leather** (⊠ *40 N. Center St.* ☎ *307/733–2422*) carries many local designs and has a diverse selection of men's and women's coats, vests, and accessories such as pillows and throws. At **Jackson Hole Clothiers** (⊠ *45 E. Deloney Ave.* ☎ *307/733–7211*) there's a large selection of Western wear, belts, purses, and leather jackets for women.

CRAFT AND ART GALLERIES

★ Jackson's art galleries serve a range of tastes. Fine nature photography by Tom Mangelson from around the globe is displayed and sold at his **Images of Nature Gallery** (⊠ *170 N. Cache St.* ☎ *307/733–9752*). **JH Muse Gallery** (⊠ *62 S. Glenwood St.* ☎ *307/733–0555*) is Jackson's hot spot for contemporary work, abandoning wildlife and landscape art in favor of hip and often playful painting, sculpture, and jewelry. It's a bit of SoHo nestled in the Rockies. **Trailside Galleries** (⊠ *130 E. Broadway* ☎ *307/733–3186*) sells traditional Western art and jewelry. The photography of Abi Garaman is highlighted at **Under the Willow Photo Gallery** (⊠ *50 S. Cache St.* ☎ *307/733–6633*). He has been photographing Jackson Hole for decades, and has produced a wide selection of images of wildlife, mountains, barns, and both summer and winter scenes. **Wilcox Gallery** (⊠ *1975 N. U.S. 89* ☎ *307/733–6450*) showcases wildlife and landscape paintings, sculpture, pottery, and other works by contemporary artists. At **Wild by Nature Gallery** (⊠ *95 W. Deloney Ave.* ☎ *307/733–8877*) 95% of the images are of local wildlife and landscape photography by Henry W. Holdsworth; there's also a selection of books and note cards.

SPORTING GOODS

Jackson's premier sports shop, **Jack Dennis Sports** (⊠ *50 E. Broadway* ☎ *307/733–3270*) is well stocked with the best in outdoor equipment for winter and summer activities. It also has a store at Teton Village. **Skinny Skis** (⊠ *65 W. Deloney Ave.* ☎ *307/733–6094*) offers everything a cross-country skier might need. **Teton Mountaineering** (⊠ *170 N. Cache St.* ☎ *307/733–3595*) specializes in Nordic-skiing, climbing, and hiking equipment and clothing. **Westbank Anglers** (⊠ *3670 N. Moose–Wilson Rd.* ☎ *307/733–6483*) can provide all the equipment necessary for fly-fishing.

AROUND JACKSON HOLE

Although you might headquarter in Jackson, most of the outdoor activities in the region are found in Jackson Hole and "The Valley." The valley has a world-class ski mountain and hiking and biking trails, and the Snake River, ideal for fishing or floating, runs right through the middle of it.

TETON VILLAGE AND JACKSON HOLE MOUNTAIN RESORT

11 mi northwest of Jackson via Hwy. 22 and Teton Village Rd.

Teton Village resounds with the clomping of ski boots in winter and with the sounds of violins, horns, and other instruments at the Grand Teton Music Festival in summer. The village mostly consists of the restaurants, lodging properties, and shops built to serve the skiers who flock to Jackson Hole Mountain Resort. This is possibly the best ski resort area in the United States, and the expanse and variety of terrain are incredible. In summer folks come here to hike, ride the tram, and attend high-caliber concerts. Because "the Vill" is small, with winding and sometimes unnamed streets, street addresses are often superfluous.

GETTING HERE AND AROUND

Scenic but mostly gravel Moose–Wilson Road is a direct route to Teton Village from the park entrance station at Moose. Be prepared to marvel at moose- and elk-sightings while simultaneously cursing your shocks. From Jackson, follow Highway 22 west for 6 mi, then head 7 mi north past resorts and trophy homes on Highway 390, commonly known as Teton Village Road. The city's START buses make the trip hourly for $3. Streets in the village are winding and far apart, and sometimes turn abruptly into parking lots—this is an area primarily designed for pedestrians.

VISITOR INFORMATION

Jackson Hole Mountain Resort (⌖ *Box 290, Teton Village 83025* ☎ *307/733–2292 or 800/333–7766* ☎ *307/733–2660* ⊕ *www.jacksonhole.com*).

EXPLORING

As it travels to the summit of Rendezvous Peak, the **Aerial Tramway** has always afforded spectacular panoramas of Jackson Hole. There are several hiking trails at the top of the mountain. A newer, sleeker tram was unveiled to much fanfare in 2008, and the updated "Big Red Box" remains a popular attraction even outside of ski season. Tram rides are first-come, first-served and run $24 in midsummer, $19 during the first and last three weeks of the season. ⊠ *Teton Village* ☎ *307/733–2292 or 800/333–7766* ⊕ *www.jacksonhole.com* ☉ *Closed late Sept.–late May.*

DOWNHILL SKIING AND SNOWBOARDING

Fodor's Choice
★

A place to appreciate both as a skier and as a voyeur, **Jackson Hole Mountain Resort** (⌖ *Box 290, Teton Village 83025* ☎ *307/733–2292 or 800/333–7766* ⊕ *www.jacksonhole.com*) is truly one of the great skiing experiences in America. There are literally thousands of ways of getting from top to bottom, and not all of them are hellishly steep, despite Jackson's reputation. First-rate racers such as Olympic champion skier Tommy Moe and snowboarders Julie Zell, A. J. Cargill, and Rob Kingwill regularly train here. As Kingwill has put it, "Nothing really compares to Jackson Hole . . . This place has the most consistently steep terrain. You can spend years and years here and never cross your trail."

On the resort map, about 111 squiggly lines designate named trails, but this doesn't even begin to suggest the thousands of different skiable routes. The resort claims 2,500 skiable acres, a figure that seems unduly conservative. And although Jackson is best known for its advanced to extreme skiing, it is also a place where imaginative intermediates can go exploring and have the time of their lives. It is not, however, a good place for novices.

⚠ **High snowfall some winters can lead to extreme avalanche danger in spite of efforts by the Ski Patrol to make the area as safe as possible.** Before venturing from known trails and routes, check with the Ski Patrol for conditions. Ski with a friend, and always carry an emergency locator device. Ski passes range from $55 for adults in early season to $91 come late December.

BACKCOUNTRY SKIING — Few areas in North America can compete with Jackson Hole when it comes to the breadth, beauty, and variety of backcountry opportunities. For touring skiers, one of the easier areas (because of flatter routes) is along the base of the Tetons toward Jenny and Jackson lakes. Telemark skiers (or even skiers on alpine gear) can find numerous downhill routes by skiing in from Teton Pass, snow stability permitting. A guide isn't required for tours to the national park lakes, but might be helpful for those unfamiliar with the lay of the land; trails and trail markers set in summer can become obscured by winter snows. When you are touring elsewhere, a guide familiar with the area and avalanche danger is a virtual necessity. The Tetons are big country, and the risks are commensurately large as well.

Jackson Hole Alpine Guides (✉ *Teton Village* ☎ *307/739–2663*) leads half-day and full-day backcountry tours into the national parks and other areas near the resort for more downhill-minded skiers. Arrangements can also be made through the Jackson Hole Mountain Sports School. **Jackson Hole Mountain Guides** (✉ *165 N. Glenwood St., Jackson* ☎ *307/733–4979* ⊕ *www.jhmg.com*) leads strenuous backcountry tours. The **Jackson Hole Nordic Center** (✉ *Teton Village* ☎ *307/739–2629 or 800/450–0477*) has cross-country, telemark, and snowshoe rentals and track and telemark lessons. The center also leads naturalist tours into the backcountry. Rental packages begin at $30 and lessons start at $85, including rental equipment and a $14 trail pass. Forest Service rangers lead free snowshoe tours; the Nordic Center also runs private snowshoe tours, starting from $85. Sled-dog tours are available (call to inquire about prices).

FACILITIES — 4,139-foot vertical drop; 2,500 skiable acres; 10% beginner, 40% intermediate, 50% expert; 1 gondola, 6 quad chairs, 2 triple chairs, 1 double chair, 1 magic carpet.

HELI-SKIING   In general, heli-skiing is best done when there has been relatively little recent snowfall. For two or three days after a storm, good powder skiing can usually be found within the ski area. Daily trips can be arranged through **High Mountain Heli-Skiing** (⊠ *Jackson Hole Mountain Resort base area, Teton Village* ☎ *307/733–3274* ⊕ *www.heliskijackson.com*).

LESSONS AND PROGRAMS   Half-day group lessons at the **Jackson Hole Mountain Sports School** (⊠ *Teton Village* ☎ *307/733–2292 or 800/450–0477*) start at $100. There are extensive children's programs, including lessons for kids 6 to 13 years old, and day care is available for children from 6 months to 2 years old. Nordic-skiing lessons start at $85. For expert skiers, the **Jackson Hole Ski Camps** (⊠ *Teton Village* ☎ *307/739–2779 or 800/450–0477*), headed by such skiers as Tommy Moe, the 1994 Olympic gold medalist, and top snowboarders like Julie Zell, A.J. Cargill, and Jessica Baker, run for four or five days, teaching everything from big-mountain freeskiing to racing techniques. The cost is $675–$900 per person, not including lift tickets.

LIFT TICKETS   Lift tickets cost $58 to $91. You can save about 10% to 20% if you buy a 5- to 15-day ticket.

RENTALS   Equipment can be rented at ski shops in Jackson and Teton Village. **Jackson Hole Sports** (⊠ *Teton Village* ☎ *307/739–2687*), at the Bridger Center at the ski area, offers ski- and snowboard-rental packages starting at $22 a day. You can buy or rent skis or snowboards at **Pepi Stiegler Sports Shop** (⊠ *3395 W. McCollister Dr., Teton Village* ☎ *307/733–4505* ⊕ *www.pepistieglersports.com*), which is run by the famous Stiegler family. Daughter Resi, who calls Jackson Hole home, competed in the 2006 Olympics in Turin, Italy. Pepi, her father, is a native of Austria who won a bronze in the giant slalom at the 1964 Innsbruck games. Ski rentals cost between $28 and $49; snowboard rentals are $36. The store is at the base of Rendezvous Peak.

TRACK SKIING   The **Jackson Hole Nordic Center** (⊠ *Teton Village* ☎ *307/739–2629 or 800/450–0477* ⊕ *www.jacksonhole.com*) is at the ski-resort base. The scenic 17 km (10½ mi) of groomed track is relatively flat. Because the Nordic Center and the downhill ski area are under the same management, downhill skiers with multiday passes can switch over to Nordic skiing in the afternoon for no extra charge. Otherwise the cost is $14 for a day pass. Rentals and lessons are available; alpine lift tickets are also good at the Nordic Center.

WHERE TO EAT

$$$$
AMERICAN
Fodor'sChoice
★   ✗ **Couloir.** The gondola at Teton Village provides access to this stylish dining room at 9,095 feet, where diners can look out over Jackson Hole while lingering over signature cocktails and a smart, contemporary prix-fixe dinner menu. Entrée options might include house-smoked bison cuts or fork-tender Kurobuta pork, along with clever sides like chickpea pancakes and fried green "Wyomatoes." Fake cowhide upholstery, exposed ductwork, and a towering back bar give the room a fun, modern feel. Foodies buzzed when Couloir opened in 2007, and the clamor hasn't died down much since. Days and hours can change with the seasons, so call for reservations. ⊠ *Atop the gondola at Teton Village* ☎ *307/739–*

2675 ⚐ *Reservations essential* ▭ *AE, D, MC, V* ⊘ *Closed Mon. and Tues., and late Sept.–late Nov. and Apr.–mid-June. No lunch.*

$$$ ✗ **Mangy Moose.** Folks pour in off the ski slopes for a lot of food and talk
AMERICAN at this two-level restaurant with a bar and an outdoor deck. There's a high noise level but decent food consisting of halibut, buffalo meat loaf, and fish and pasta dishes. The place is adorned with antiques, including a full-size stuffed moose and sleigh suspended from the ceiling. The bar is a popular nightspot, with live music and frequent concerts by top bands. ✉ *3295 Village Dr., Teton Village* ☎ *307/733–4913* ⊕ *www. mangymoose.net* ▭ *AE, MC, V.*

WHERE TO STAY

In the winter ski season it can be cheaper to stay in Jackson, about 20 minutes away; in summer it's generally cheaper to stay at Teton Village.

$$–$$$$ 🛏 **Alpenhof Lodge.** This small Austrian-style hotel is in the heart of Jackson Hole Mountain Resort, next to the tram. Hand-carved Bavarian furniture fills the rooms. All the deluxe rooms have balconies, and some have fireplaces and bathtub jets. Standard rooms are smaller and don't have balconies. Entrées such as wild-game loaf, Wiener schnitzel, and fondue are served in the dining room, and a relatively quiet bistro/nightclub offers casual dining. **Pros:** quaint; Old World feel; cozy surroundings; spa treatments available. **Cons:** some rooms are small rahter than cozy, especially for the price. ✉ *Teton Village* ☎ *307/733–3242 or 800/732–3244* ⊕ *www.alpenhoflodge.com* ⤶ *42 rooms* ♿ *In-room: refrigerator (some), Wi-Fi. In-hotel: 2 restaurants, bar, pool, spa, laundry facilities, some pets allowed, no-smoking rooms* ▭ *AE, D, DC, MC, V* ⊘ *Closed mid-Oct.–Dec. 1 and early Apr.–May 1* ⎮◎⎮ *BP.*

¢–$$ 🛏 **The Hostel.** Although the classic hostel accommodations at this lodge-style inn are basic, you can't get any closer to Jackson Hole Mountain Resort for a better price. It's popular with young, budget-conscious people. Rooms, some of which have twins, bunks, and king beds, sleep from two to four people; rooms with shared bunks are also available. Comfy common areas include a lounge with a fireplace, a game room, a movie room, a library, and a ski-waxing room. Rates vary wildly with the seasons, at times changing from week to week—check the Web for specifics. **Pros:** superb deal for the upscale locale; truly convivial and communal atmosphere. **Cons:** not family-friendly; little privacy; no matter how you slice it, this is still a hostel. ✉ *3315 McCollister Dr., Teton Village* ☎ *307/733–3415* ⊕ *www.thehostel.us* ⤶ *55 rooms* ♿ *In-room: no a/c, no phone, no TV, Wi-Fi. In-hotel: laundry facilities, some pets allowed, no-smoking rooms* ▭ *MC, V*

$$$$ 🛏 **Hotel Terra.** Other properties talk the eco-talk, but Hotel Terra takes green hospitality to the next level. From café seatbacks made of recycled seat belts to custom-made, non-chemical mattresses, from bottle-free water stations to the building's abundance of natural light, there's a true conservation mind-set at the heart of this hotel. It's also luxe to the core, with a hip, urban feel and all the amenities the price tag suggests. Il Villaggio Osteria ($$$–$$$$), the on-site restaurant, is a sexy space with a top-notch wine list. **Pros:** greenest hotel ever; expert staff; organic spa. **Cons:** not for the budget-conscious; in a crowded corner of Teton Village. ✉ *Teton Village* ☎ *307/379–4000 or 800/631–6281* 🌐 *www.hotelterrajacksonhole.com* ⇨ *132 rooms* ⚐ *In-room: kitchen (some), refrigerator, Wi-Fi. In-hotel: 2 restaurants, room service, bar, pool, spa, no-smoking rooms* ▭ *AE, D, MC, V* |◎| *EP.*

$$$–$$$$ **R Lazy S Ranch.** Jackson Hole, with the spectacle of the Tetons in the background, is true dude-ranch country, and the R Lazy S is one of the largest dude ranches in the area. Horseback riding and instruction are the main attraction, with a secondary emphasis on fishing in private waters on the ranch. Kids' activities counselors keep young'uns busy through late August—after that it's adults-only. Guests stay in log-cabin cottages and gather for meals in the large main lodge. **Pros:** authentic dude-ranch experience; very popular with older kids and preteens; absolutely beautiful setting. **Cons:** few modern trappings; not for the high-maintenance traveler. ✉ *1 mi north of Teton Village on outskirts of Grand Teton National Park* ☎ *307/733–2655* 🌐 *www.rlazys.com* ⇨ *14 cabins* ⚐ *In-room: no a/c, no TV. In-hotel: Wi-Fi, no kids under 7, no-smoking rooms* ▭ *No credit cards* ⊙ *Closed Oct.–mid-June* |◎| *FAP* ☞ *1-wk minimum; rates based on double occupancy.*

WILSON

6 mi south of Teton Village on Teton Village Rd., 4 mi west of Jackson on Hwy. 22.

If you want to avoid the hustle and bustle of Jackson, Wilson makes a good alternative base for exploring Grand Teton National Park or skiing at Jackson Hole Mountain Resort. This small town takes its name from Nick Wilson, one of the first homesteaders in the area, a man who spent part of his childhood living with the Shoshone Indians.

GETTING HERE AND AROUND

It's hard to get lost in Wilson, as 90% of it is clustered along a few blocks of Highway 22, a short drive west of Jackson. Travelers from the east will find the town right at the foot of the pass. Since summer bike traffic can be high on Highway 22, both drivers and cyclists should use caution.

WHERE TO EAT

$$$ AMERICAN Fodor's Choice ★ ✕ **Bar J Chuckwagon.** At the best bargain in the Jackson Hole area, you'll get a true ranch-style meal in a long hall along with some of the liveliest Western entertainment you'll find in the region. The food, served on a tin plate, includes barbecued roast beef, chicken, or rib-eye steak, plus potatoes, beans, biscuits, applesauce, spice cake, and ranch coffee or lemonade. The multitalented Bar J Wranglers sing, play instruments, share cowboy stories and poetry, and even yodel. "Lap-size" children eat free. The doors open at 5:30, so you can explore the Bar J's Western village—including a saloon and several shops—before the dinner bell rings at 7:30. The dining area is covered, so no need to worry if the sun isn't shining. Reservations are strongly suggested. ✉ *Off Moose–Wilson Rd., 1 mi north of Hwy. 22* ☎ *307/733–3370* 🌐 *www.barjchuckwagon.com* ▭ *D, MC, V* ⊙ *Closed Oct.–Memorial Day.*

The Bear Essentials

The northern Rockies are bear country—grizzlies and black bears are a presence throughout the region. Seeing one across a valley, through a pair of binoculars, is fun, but meeting one at closer range isn't. There have been few fatal encounters, but almost every summer there are incidents involving bears.

Wherever you venture in Wyoming and Montana, keep in mind these tips for travel in bear country:

PRACTICAL PRECAUTIONS
Avoid sudden encounters. Whenever possible, travel in open country, during daylight hours, and in groups. Make noise—talking or singing is preferable to carrying "bear bells"—and leave your dog at home. Most attacks occur when a bear is surprised at close quarters or feels threatened.

Stay alert. Look for signs of bears, such as fresh tracks, scat, matted vegetation, or partially consumed salmon.

Choose your tent site carefully. Pitch the tent away from trails, streams with spawning salmon, and berry patches. Avoid areas that have a rotten smell or where scavengers have gathered; these may indicate the presence of a nearby bear cache, and bears aggressively defend their food supplies.

Keep food away from campsites. Cook meals at least 100 feet from tents, and store food and other items that give off odors (including personal products such as soap, shampoo, lotions, and even toothpaste) away from campsites. Hang food between trees where possible, or store your food in bear-resistant food containers. Avoid strong-smelling foods, and clean up after cooking and eating.

Store garbage in airtight containers or burn it and pack up the remains.

IF YOU ENCOUNTER A BEAR
Identify yourself. Talk to the bear, to identify yourself as a human. Don't yell. And don't run. Running will trigger a bear's predatory instincts, and a bear can easily outrun you. Back away slowly, and give the bear an escape route. Don't ever get between a mother and her cubs.

Bigger is better. Bears are less likely to attack a larger target. Therefore, increase your apparent size. Raise your arms above your head to appear larger and wave them slowly, to better identify yourself as a human. With two or more people, it helps to stand side by side. In a forested area it may be appropriate to climb a tree, but remember that black bears and young grizzlies are agile tree climbers.

As a last resort, play dead. If a bear charges and makes contact with you, fall to the ground, lie flat on your stomach or curl into a ball, hands behind your neck, and remain passive. If you are wearing a pack, leave it on. Once a bear no longer feels threatened, it will usually end its attack. Wait for the bear to leave before you move. The exception to this rule is when a bear displays predatory behavior. Instead of simply charging, a bear hunting for prey will show intense interest while approaching at a walk or run and it may circle, as if stalking you. But remember that such circumstances are exceedingly rare and most often involve black bears, which are much smaller and less aggressive than grizzlies (and can be driven off more easily).

$$$ ✕ **Nora's Fish Creek Inn.** Nora's is one of those inimitable Western places
AMERICAN that have earned their keep as local treasures among their many loyal
Fodor's Choice customers. Look for the giant trout on the roof outside. It's a great spot
★ to catch a hearty weekend breakfast of pancakes or huevos rancheros
that barely fit on your plate and dinner among the talkative locals.
Among the imaginative dishes served at this casual log inn are honey-
hickory baby back ribs, prime rib, elk tenderloin with blackberry-
wine sauce, and nut-crusted trout, plus nightly specials. Soups such as pump-
kin warm your bones, and there's wine by the glass and a kids' menu.
You can dine in one of two large rooms or sit at the counter for quick
service. Breakfast, but not lunch, is served on weekends. ✉ *5600 Hwy.
22, 6 mi outside Jackson at base of pass* ☎ *307/733–8288* ☲ *AE, D,
MC, V* ☉ *Closed Nov. and Apr. No lunch weekends.*

4

WHERE TO STAY

$$$$ ⬚ **Teton Tree House.** On a steep hillside and surrounded by trees, this is
a real retreat. Ninety-five steps lead to this cozy lodgepole-pine bed-
and-breakfast tucked away in the forest. Decks abound, rooms are
full of wood furniture and warm Southwestern colors, and an invit-
ing common area has a two-story old-fashioned adobe fireplace. **Pros:**
scenic locale; good breakfast; knowledgeable hosts. **Cons:** not open in
winter; must drive to town; small climb up to the B&B. ✉ *6175 Heck
of a Hill Rd.* ☎ *307/733–3233* ⬦ *6 rooms* ♿ *In-room: no a/c, no TV,
Wi-Fi. In-hotel: no kids under 5, no-smoking rooms* ☲ *D, MC, V* ◑ *BP*
☉ *Closed Oct.–Apr.*

$$$$ ⬚ **The Wildflower Inn.** This log country inn built in 1989 is cozy, clean,
and comfortable, and serves gourmet breakfasts. Just down the road
from Jackson Hole Mountain Resort and Teton Village, the inn is sur-
rounded by 3 acres of aspen and pine trees frequented by moose, deer,
and other native wildlife. Each room has a private deck and bathroom,
handcrafted log bed piled high with comforters, and its own alpine
theme. There's also a plant-filled solarium, hot tub, and sunlit dining
room. **Pros:** excellent views; frequent wildlife sightings just outside;
plenty of loaner gear available. **Cons:** books far in advance; 12 mi from
Jackson itself. ✉ *3725 Moose–Wilson Rd.,* ☎ *307/733–4710* ⊕ *www.
jacksonholewildflower.com* ⬦ *5 rooms* ♿ *In-room: refrigerator (some),
Wi-Fi. In-hotel: bicycles, no-smoking rooms* ☲ *MC, V* ◑ *BP.*

NIGHTLIFE

The **Stagecoach Bar** (✉ *5575 W. Hwy. 22* ☎ *307/733–4407*) fills to burst-
ing when local bands play. Disco Night is on Thursday and attracts a
packed house of swingers. "The Coach" is a good place to enjoy a drink
and conversation at other times, and there's an adjacent Mexican café
and kitchen where you can grab a quick bite.

ALTA

27 mi northwest of Wilson via Hwy. 22 to Hwy. 33 (in Idaho) to Alta cutoff (back to Wyoming).

Alta is the site of the Grand Targhee Ski and Summer Resort, famed for its deep powder and family atmosphere. The slopes never feel crowded, but to experience complete solitude, try a day of Sno-Cat skiing in untracked powder.

GETTING HERE AND AROUND

The Targhee Express (☎ 307/733–9754 or 800/443–6133 ⊕ www.jacksonholealltrans.com) will bring you from Jackson to Alta by appointment for $46. By car, head 20 mi west from Jackson on Highway 22, over the Teton Pass and onto Idaho's Highway 33. From Victor, Idaho, it's another 8 mi north to Ski Hill Road in Driggs; follow that 5 mi west to Alta and Grand Targhee, then park and navigate the tiny ski town's few streets on foot.

SPORTS AND THE OUTDOORS

An average of 500 inches of powdery "white gold" attracts skiers to **Grand Targhee Ski and Summer Resort** (⊠ 3300 E. Ski Hill Rd. ☎ 307/353–2300 or 800/827–4433 ⊕ www.grandtarghee.com), with 3,000 acres, 1,000 of which are dedicated to powder Sno-Cat skiing and 15 km (9 mi) to cross-country trails. 'Boarders have two trick terrain parks and lots of freestyle areas with rails and mailboxes to tear it up. There are four lifts and one rope tow, and the vertical drop is 2,419 feet. Lift tickets are about $70 per day; Nordic trail permits are $10. Classes by expert instructors are also available. Lifts operate 9–4 daily.

WHERE TO STAY

$$–$$$$ **Grand Targhee Ski and Summer Resort.** Lodging at this hidden gem ski resort on the west side of the Tetons has a handsome, natural-wood look and the atmosphere of an alpine village. Choose from dorm-style quads, motel rooms, and high-end suites available across three different facilities. Budget options are simply furnished with Western furniture and centered on common areas with fireplaces; the high-end condominium rooms are brighter and more spacious. The Branding Iron Bar and Grille ($$$) is the resort's flagship restaurant. The Trap Bar and Grille and Wild Bill's Grille serve quicker, less expensive meals, and Snorkel's has bakery items, espresso, and deli sandwiches. **Pros:** a cozy and laid-back alternative to the glitz of Jackson Hole; excellent lift access. **Cons:** Wi-Fi can be spotty; fewer après options than in Jackson Hole. ⊠ 3300 E. Ski Hill Rd. ☎ 307/353–2300 or 800/827–4433 ⊕ www.grandtarghee.com ↝ 96 rooms, 32 suites ⚴ In-room: Wi-Fi. In-hotel: 4 restaurants, pool, spa ➡ AE, D, MC, V ⧪ BP.

THE WIND RIVER RANGE

Rising to the east and southeast of Jackson Hole is the Wind River Range, which remains snowcapped year-round and still holds small glaciers. Much of this range is rugged wilderness, ideal for backcountry hiking and horseback riding. Several towns here make good bases for exploring the area, including Pinedale on the west side of the range; Atlantic City, within the range itself; and Lander, Fort Washakie, and Dubois on the east side of the range.

PINEDALE

77 mi southeast of Jackson on Hwy. 191.

A southern gateway to Jackson Hole, Pinedale has much to offer on its own, for the spirit of the mountain man lives on here. Fur trappers found the icy streams of the Green River watershed to be among the best places to capture beaver. In the mid-1800s they gathered on the river near what is now Pinedale for seven annual rendezvous. Now the Museum of the Mountain Man preserves their heritage, and modern-day buckskinners continue to meet in the area each summer.

GETTING HERE AND AROUND

U.S. 191 reaches Pinedale from Jackson to the northwest and Farson and the South Pass area to the south. In town, the highway becomes the main thoroughfare of Pine Street. You can park on the street for free and do downtown on foot, but you'll need wheels to head northwest of town on Fremont Road, a paved route accessing Half Moon Lake, Fremont Lake, and the breathtaking Skyline Drive scenic route through the Winds.

VISITOR INFORMATION

Pinedale Chamber of Commerce (✉ *32 E. Pine St., Box 176, Pinedale* ☎ *307/367-2242* 🖶 *307/367-6830* ⊕ *www.pinedalechamber.com*).

EXPLORING

To the east are millions of acres of Bridger-Teton National Forest, much of it off-limits to all but foot and horse traffic. The peaks reach higher than 13,000 feet, and the area is liberally sprinkled with more than a thousand high-mountain lakes where fishing is generally excellent.

Contact the **Bridger-Teton National Forest, Pinedale Ranger District** (✉ *29 E. Fremont Lake Rd., Box 220* ☎ *307/367-4326* ⊕ *www.fs.fed.us/r4/ btnf*) for more information. Although outdoor activities still beckon in the forest, an oil and gas boom in the area keeps motel rooms full year-round and restaurants often busy.

♻ ★ The **Museum of the Mountain Man** depicts the trapper heritage of the area with displays of 19th-century guns, traps, clothing, and beaver pelts. There's also an interpretive exhibit devoted to the pioneer and ranch history of Sublette County as well as an overview of the Western fur trade. In summer the museum hosts living-history demonstrations, children's events, a reenactment of the 19th-century Green River Rendezvous, and lectures. ✉ *700 E. Hennick Rd.* ☎ *307/367-4101 or 877/686-6266* ⊕ *www.museumofthemountain-man.com* 🎫 *$5* ⊙ *May–Sept., daily 9–5; Oct., daily 9–4.*

> **WORD OF MOUTH**
>
> "If you are in Pinedale spend a few hours at the Museum of the Mountain Man."
>
> –RedRock

THE ALLURES OF THE WIND RIVER RANGE

History: From ancient Native American settlements to early pioneer trails, towns, and red rock canyons and mountains…nearly anywhere you look out here, man and nature have left their indelible marks.

Space: The drive westward and from the southeast never fails to enchant newcomers with one of America's least-populated frontiers.

Sights: As you approach Dubois from the flatlands of Riverton and enter the ascending Wind River

Range, keep an eye peeled for mule deer and robust wildlife.

Sounds: Park the car at any scenic overlook, or camp out at the right time of year, and you'll understand why "The Wind River" area resounds with timeless music.

Colors: Yellowed, tawny prairies in late summer and early fall; ochre-stained geology around Dubois; and lazy sunsets that paint the skies indigo and red cast a spell on unhurried visitors.

SPORTS AND THE OUTDOORS

Encompassing parts of the Wind River Range, the **Bridger-Teton National Forest, Pinedale Ranger District** (⊠ *Forest office, 29 E. Fremont Lake Rd., Box 220* ☎ *307/367–4326* ⊕ *www.fs.fed.us/r4/btnf*) holds hundreds of thousands of acres to explore. The fishing is good in the numerous mountain lakes, and you can also hike, horseback ride, snowmobile, camp, and picnic here.

Cabins at secluded **Half Moon Lake** are available from **Lakeside Lodge** (☎ *307/367–2221* ⊕ *www.lakesidelodge.com*), on nearby Fremont Lake. The modern lakefront cabins have both electricity and phones. Pastimes at this jewel of the Wind River Range include boating, fishing, camping, and hiking. Trout, whitefish, and mackinaw await anglers and ice fishers, too. There are also guided horseback rides, a boat launch, and a campground with picnic tables, trailer pull-throughs, vault toilets, fire grates, and refuse containers. The lake has a beach where children can build sand castles and bigger kids can enjoy canoeing, waterskiing, and inner tubing. The resort area is open May–mid-September. It's about 10 mi northeast of Pinedale. Take Fremont Lake Road north out of Pinedale; the turnoff for Half Moon Lake is about 8 mi from town along a narrow, winding gravel road.

WHERE TO EAT

$ ✕ **China Gourmet.** Serving full-fare, Cantonese-style "Western" Chinese
CHINESE   food, this might be the only joint in America where you'll find a Budweiser sign over the door, Asian decor on the walls, large-screen TVs playing all the big games, and ketchup on a table beside a bowl of eggdrop soup. It's good for families with picky eaters, as the menu carries more than 100 items—from lo mein and mu shu shrimp to hamburgers, pork chops, and fried chicken. Many dishes also come with mushrooms and barbecue sauce; some even have spaghetti. ⊠ *44 W. Pine St.* ☎ *307/367–4788* ▭ *AE, D, MC, V.*

$ ✕**Rock Rabbit.** Easily Pinedale's most subversive coffeehouse-bakery–
AMERICAN head shop–restaurant, this downtown café takes its interior design cues
★ from Jimmy Buffet and Jerry Garcia. Locals and tourists alike stop in
for massive burritos and a dinner menu of American-style tapas. The
tapestries and Grateful Dead records on the wall are a fitting backdrop
for Tuesday open-mike nights and weekend concerts. ⊠ *23 W. Pine St.*
☎ *307/367–2448* ⊕ *www.rockrabbit.com* ⊟ *AE, MC, V.*

$$ ✕ **Stockman's Restaurant.** The salad bar is shaped like a tepee and there's
AMERICAN a 1903 map of the United States at this locals' hangout since 1933.
On the menu are burgers, salads, prime rib, steaks, and seafood. It's
a good stop for dessert and coffee (try the thick, crumbly cheesecake
served warm). Early risers can grab breakfast here before 6 AM flanked
by mineral-field workers. The restaurant serves lunch, too. Smoking is
allowed, so it can get hazy at times. You can sit in the no-smoking sec-
tion, but there's no wall separating it from the rest of the room. After
eating you can get a drink, shoot a game of pool, or relax in the roomy,
low-lighted lounge. There's also a beer and package store for those on
the run. ⊠ *117 W. Pine St.* ☎ *307/367–4562 bar, or 307/367–4563
restaurant* ⊟ *AE, D, MC, V.*

$ ✕ **Wind River Brewing Co.** This microbrewery and grill serves award-
AMERICAN winning grog and high-quality pub grub, from steaks and sandwiches to
daily specials. ⊠ *402 W. Pine St.* ☎ *307/367–2337* ⊟ *AE, D, MC, V.*

WHERE TO STAY

$$ ⌂ **Best Western Pinedale Inn.** On the north side of town, this motel is within
five blocks of downtown shopping and restaurants. The rooms aren't
large, but they have contemporary furniture. **Pros:** swimming pool; continental breakfast; good location. **Cons:** check cancellation policy (reportedly locked by computer); prices not always best around. ⊠ *864 W. Pine
St.* ☎ *307/367–6869* 🖷 *307/367–6897* ⊕ *www.bestwesternwyoming.com*
↩ *84 rooms* ⌂ *In-room: refrigerator, Wi-Fi. In-hotel: pool, some pets
allowed, no-smoking rooms* ⊟ *AE, D, DC, MC, V* ⑩ *CP.*

$–$$ ⌂ **Chambers House B&B.** Huge pine trees surround this 1933 log home
★ filled with the owner's family antiques. Downstairs there's a sitting room
where you can relax with a book or chat with other guests. The master
bedroom, with a fireplace, private bathroom, and private entrance, is
also on the ground floor. Two of the upstairs bedrooms share bathroom
facilities; the other two have private bathrooms, and one has a fireplace.
Pros: charming old house; solid breakfast; recently renovated. **Cons:** limited reading materials and games; some rooms share bathroom. ⊠ *111
W. Magnolia St.* ☎ *307/367–2168 or 800/567–2168* ⊕ *www.cham-
bershouse.com* ↩ *5 rooms, 3 with bath* ⌂ *In-room: no a/c, no phone
(some), Wi-Fi. In-hotel: no-smoking rooms* ⊟ *AE, D, MC, V* ⑩ *BP.*

$–$$ ⌂ **The Lodge at Pinedale.** This three-story motel is across a parking lot
from the town's movie theater and bowling alley. Green carpeting and
bed coverings decorate the rooms. **Pros:** Jacuzzi; pool; complimentary evening cookies. **Cons:** some guests have mentioned maintenance
problems; doesn't offer a classic, rustic experience. ⊠ *1054 W. Pine St.*
☎ *307/367–8800 or 866/995–6343* 🖷 *307/367–8812* ⊕ *www.lodgeat-
pinedale.com* ↩ *41 rooms, 2 suites* ⌂ *In-room: refrigerator, Wi-Fi. In-*

4

hotel: pool, Internet terminal, some pets allowed, no-smoking rooms
✉ *AE, D, DC, MC, V* ⍥ *CP.*

SHOPPING

The Cowboy Shop (✉ *129 W. Pine St.* ☎ *877/567–6336* ⊕ *www.cowboy-shop.com*) stocks Western and cowpoke clothing for all ages, including hats and boots, and also sells leather goods and regional books.

▌ EN
   ROUTE
As you drive south of Pinedale along U.S. 191, the mountains of the Wind River Range seem to fade to a low point. This is **South Pass,** the area through which some 500,000 emigrants traveled over the Oregon, Mormon, and California trails between 1843 and 1870.

ATLANTIC CITY

81 mi southeast of Pinedale via U.S. 191 to Farson, then Hwy. 28.

A near ghost town amid the real ghost towns of Miner's Delight and South Pass City, this bygone gold rush–era settlement still has a few residents, a couple of tourist-oriented businesses, dirt streets, late-19th-century buildings, and a whole lot of character. Formed in 1868 when gold rushers flocked to the area seeking their fortunes and known for its red-light district, Atlantic City was where Wyoming Territory's first brewery opened in the late 1860s. Once the gold boom went bust less than a decade later, however, residents deserted the town. Atlantic City had a few more smaller rushes over the years, but none ever matched its early days.

GETTING HERE AND AROUND

From Highway 28 look for green sign "Atlantic City" and take wide dirt road for about 4 mi. More than likely, you'll need four-wheel drive in snow season. Both Atlantic City and South Pass City are literally one-road towns, so getting around is a snap. Park in front of one of the local businesses, and then hit the town on foot.

EXPLORING

South Pass City, 2 mi west of Atlantic City, was established in 1867 after gold was discovered in a creek called Sweetwater in 1842. In its heyday, by various accounts, before the gold thinned out in the 1870s, there were between 1,500 and 4,000 residents. After Sioux and Cheyenne raids, over settlers hunting indigenous game herds and miners poisoning their drinking water, the town still boomed until going bust and dropping to double digits by 1872. Its well-preserved remains
Fodor's Choice   are now the **South Pass City State Historic Site.** You can tour many of the
   ★   original surviving buildings that have been restored, and you can even try your hand at gold panning. With artifacts and photographs of the town at its peak, the small museum here gives an overview of the South Pass gold district.

South Pass City has another claim to fame. Julia Bright and Esther Hobart Morris are two of the women from the community who firmly believed that women should have the right to vote. It is suspected that they encouraged Bright's husband, Representative William Bright, to introduce a bill for women's suffrage in the Wyoming Territorial Legislature. He did so, the bill was ratified, and South Pass went down in history as the birthplace of women's suffrage in Wyoming. In 1870 Morris became the first female justice of the peace in the nation, serving South Pass City. ⊠ *South Pass City Rd., off Hwy. 28, South Pass* ☎ *307/332–3684* ⊕ *wyoparks.state.wy.us* ⊠ *$4* ⊙ *Mid-May–Sept., daily 9–6.*

WHERE TO EAT AND STAY

$$
AMERICAN
★
✕ **Atlantic City Mercantile.** The town's oldest saloon, known as the "Merc," serves refreshments in a room that has seen its share of gold miners, perhaps an outlaw or two, and certainly some ruffians. When you step through the doors of this 1893 building with tin ceilings, a massive back bar, and an assortment of mismatched oak tables and chairs, you may feel as though you've walked directly into an episode of *Gunsmoke*. At times a honky-tonk piano player is on hand. The menu includes steak, chicken, and seafood, plus sandwiches and big burgers. ⊠ *100 E. Main St.* ☎ *307/332–5143* ⊙ *Closed Tues.* ⊟ *AE, D, MC, V.*

¢
AMERICAN
✕ **Miner's Grub Stake.** Drop in for pancakes, French toast, omelets, and coffee for breakfast; or a buffalo burger, tuna salad, or Reuben sandwich for lunch. You can also warm your bones with beef vegetable soup, chili, and hot cider before stocking up on paper goods, groceries, sunscreen, soft drinks, two-cycle motor oil, pet food, and other supplies. Daily specials include meat loaf on Friday—a locals' favorite. Dinner ends at 8 PM so as not to compete with the neighboring Mercantile. ⊠ *150 W. Main St.* ☎ *307/332–0915* ⊙ *Closed Nov.* ⊟ *D, MC, V.*

$
★
▦ **Miner's Delight Inn & B&B.** Live like the prospectors did in the olden days and stay in one of the authentic, rustic cabins. Each has a small washstand with a bowl and a pitcher of water, and it's a short walk to the main house's bathroom and shower. Rooms in the lodge, built in 1904 as the town's hotel, are larger, have private bathrooms, cost a couple of bucks more, and share a kitchen downstairs. There are patchwork curtains and ample bed coverings. The red velvet wallpaper was reportedly hung by a pair of chic New Yorkers who ran the place in the 1960s, allegedly prompting a "Jazz Age" revival in the ghost town, replete with gourmet dinners and Paris gowns. Current innkeepers Barbara and Bob Townsend are gracious raconteurs whose breakfast salon doubles as a gallery featuring local artists. The inn borrows its name from the real, nearby ghost town of Miner's Delight. Writers are encouraged to finish and hawk their works here. The "two bit" Cowboy Saloon by the downstairs fireplace has not only a beautiful hand-carved bar, but also the state's best selection of single-malt scotch—aficionados drive miles for periodic tasting events. **Pros:** true West ghost town charm; gracious hosts; late-night saloon and fireplace. **Cons:** remote location; no Internet/TV; some rooms share bath. ⊠ *290 Atlantic City Rd.* ☎ *307/332–0248 or 888/292–0248* ⊕ *www.minersdelightinn.com* ↪ *3 lodge rooms, 5 cabins without bath* ♨ *In-room: no a/c, no phone, no TV. In-hotel: nosmoking rooms* ⊟ *MC, V* ⊙| *BP.*

SHOPPING

South Pass Mercantile (⊠ *50 South Pass Main* ☎ *307/332–9935 or 307/332–8120*) sells Wyoming-made products ranging from clothing to the largest selection of books in the area by regional authors, plus gold mining and prospecting supplies.

LANDER

About 31 mi northeast of Atlantic City via Hwy. 28/U.S. 287.

At the southwestern edge of the Wind River Indian Reservation and in the heart of country held dear by Chief Washakie (circa 1804–1900), one of the greatest chiefs of the Shoshone tribe, and his people, Lander has always had a strong tie to the Native American community. East of the Wind River Range, Lander makes a good base for pursuing mountain sports and activities ranging from backcountry hiking to horse-packing trips.

GETTING HERE AND AROUND

Lander stretches out along U.S. 287 (Main Street, in town) with a few blocks of pedestrian-friendly downtown and a handful of other restaurants, shops, and attractions best reached by car on the north edge of the city. The **Wind River Transportation Authority** (☎ 800/439–7118 ⊕ *www.wrtabuslines.com*) runs weekday buses between and around Lander, Riverton, and Fort Washakie for a $1 fare. You can also call about shuttles from Jackson to Lander, which run on a somewhat arbitrary schedule throughout the year. Coming from Jackson or Pinedale involves going over South Pass, which may have snow into early summer.

VISITOR INFORMATION

Lander Chamber of Commerce (✉ 160 N. 1st St., Lander ☎ 307/332–3892 or 800/433–0662 🖷 307/332–3893 ⊕ www.landerchamber.org).

EXPLORING

At **Sinks Canyon State Park,** the Popo Agie (pronounced pa-*po*-sha, meaning "Tall Grass River" to the Crow Indians) flows into a limestone cavern. The crashing water "sinks" into fissures only to resurface ½ mi downstream in the "rise," where it reemerges and huge fish (mainly rainbow and brown trout) swim in the calm pool. Wildflowers, Rocky Mountain bighorn sheep, black bears, golden eagles, moose, mule deer, marmots, and other wildlife wander the grounds. The park is ideal for hiking, camping, and picnicking. No fishing is allowed, but visitors can toss fish food to the trout from the observation deck. ✉ 3079 Sinks Canyon Rd., 6 mi south of Lander on Hwy. 131 ☎ 307/332–3077 ⊕ wyoparks.state.wy.us 🖾 Park free, camping $11 for nonresidents ☉ Park daily, sunrise–10; visitor center Memorial Day–Labor Day, daily 9–6.

SPORTS AND THE OUTDOORS

For more than 35 years, adventurers and students have been exploring the remote Wind River Range to learn all aspects of mountaineering—from low-impact camping and horse packing to rock climbing and fly-fishing—by taking a course from the **National Outdoor Leadership School** (✉ 284 Lincoln St. ☎ 307/332–5300 ⊕ www.nols.edu).

FISHING There's great fishing on the Wind River Indian Reservation, but you must first obtain a tribal license; contact **Shoshone and Arapaho Tribes** (✉ Fish and Game Dept., Box 217, Fort Washakie ☎ 307/332–7207 ⊕ www.wrfishandgame.com) for more information. At **Sweetwater Fishing Expeditions,** (☎ 307/332–3986 ⊕ www.sweetwaterfishing.com) George Hunker, a former Orvis guide of the year, and his crew lead small guided horseback and backpacking camping trips into the Wind River Mountains as well as day trips along smaller streams.

HORSEBACK RIDING **Allen's Diamond Four Ranch,** the highest-altitude dude ranch in Wyoming, arranges mountain horse-pack trips, big-game hunts, and guided fishing and other horseback excursions. Some trips originate at the ranch, where you stay in cabins and take day rides; others are overnight backcountry adventures. Children must be seven or eight years old to go on extended pack trips. Also available are drop-camp services. No pets are allowed. Call or check the Web site for directions. ⊠ *Off U.S. 287, 35 mi northwest of Lander* ☎ *307/332–2995 or 307/349–6784* ⊕ *www. diamond4ranch.com.*

WHERE TO EAT

$$$
ECLECTIC
✕ **Cowfish.** At this funky restaurant you can dine on a cozy, outdoor patio and select from sandwiches and haute cuisine from both land and water. For starters try pot stickers and seared ahi tuna. Entrées range from 16-ounce rib-eye steaks, fillets, prime rib (served Friday and Saturday only), slow-cooked baby back ribs, and hamburgers made from local beef, to wild Alaskan salmon and beer-battered shrimp. Rounding out the menu are fun twists on standby dishes like fish tacos with chipotle aioli or fillet tips on penne pasta smothered in tequila cream sauce. An on-site microbrewery and an organic garden of fresh vegetables and herbs add a distinctive touch to each meal. ⊠ *128 Main St.* ☎ *307/332–7009* ⊕ *www.landerbar.com* ⊟ *AE, D, MC, V.*

$
AMERICAN
✕ **Gannett Grill.** This crowded, noisy place serves large sandwiches, never-frozen half-pound hamburgers, and hand-tossed New York–style pizzas. In spring and summer you can sit on the garden deck while the kids play in the yard. ⊠ *126 Main St.* ☎ *307/332–7009* ⊕ *www.landerbar.com* ⊟ *AE, D, MC, V.*

$$$
STEAK
Fodor'sChoice
★
✕ **Svilars' Bar & Dining Room.** This small, dark, family-owned restaurant with vinyl booths has what many locals say are the best steaks in all of Wyoming. A meal here usually begins with *sarma* (cabbage rolls) and other appetizers. Your server will then place before you one of the biggest, if not *the* biggest, and best steaks you've likely ever seen. There's even baked lobster. ⊠ *173 S. Main St., 10 mi east of Lander, Hudson* ☎ *307/332–4516* ⊟ *AE, D, MC, V* ⊙ *Closed Sun., Labor Day–Memorial Day closed alternate Mon. No lunch.*

WHERE TO STAY

$–$$
▦ **The Inn at Lander.** This two-story Best Western motel sits on a hill overlooking Lander and is within walking distance of restaurants and discount-store shopping. The small outdoor area has picnic tables. Children 12 and under stay free with one paying adult. **Pros:** good-size, clean rooms; close to downtown; bar/café. **Cons:** close to highway; can get crowded during conferences; no indoor pool. ⊠ *260 Grandview Dr., at U.S. 287/789* ☎ *307/332–2847* ⊕ *www.bestwesternwyoming.com* ⇌ *109 rooms* ⏍ *In-room: safe, refrigerator (some), Wi-Fi. In-hotel: pool, spa, no-smoking rooms* ⊟ *AE, D, MC, V* ▯◉*EP.*

¢–$$
▦ **Two Sisters Bed & Breakfast.** Highlights of this 1918 Arts and Crafts–style home include an enormous yard with a creek running through, a sunny deck for breakfasts, and extremely gracious owners and staff.

Rooms are handsome, with lots of old oak and handmade quilts, but not so "B&B precious" that you feel like you're sleeping in a museum exhibit. Students from the local Catholic college sometimes use the common space downstairs as a study and conversation space, which can give the place a salon-type vibe or infringe a tiny bit on privacy, depending on your take. **Pros:** gorgeous old home; hospitable innkeepers; close to downtown; loaner bikes available. **Cons:** parlor area is a sometime-hangout for students; Catholic-theme decorating motif may be slightly off-putting to some. ✉ *768 S. 3rd St.* ☎ *307/349–7191* 🌐 *www.twosistersbnb.com* ⇨ *5 rooms, 3 with bath* ♨ *In-room: refrigerator, Wi-Fi. In-hotel: Internet terminal, no-smoking rooms* ▭ *AE, D, MC, V* 🍽 *BP.*

CAMPING ⛺ **Dallas Dome Ranch.** There's a re-created Old West ghost town of Dallas, Wyoming, at this RV park and campground that sits beside the Little Popo Agie River. There are lots of amenities here, including a restaurant, shops, and horseshoes, and you can take a hayride or swim in the river. Horses and pets are welcome. ♨ *Flush toilets, full hookups, drinking water, guest laundry, showers, picnic tables, general store, play area, swimming (river), Wi-Fi* ⇨ *58 full hookups, 8 partial hookups, 7 cabins, tents welcome* ✉ *U.S. 287, 9 mi southeast of Lander, 1 mi east of Rawlins turnoff* ☎ *307/332–3836* ▭ *D, MC, V.*

⛺ **Sleeping Bear RV Park.** Next to a golf course, this campground and RV park has lots of grass and shade trees. You can enjoy various activities here, including basketball, horseshoes, volleyball, and a couple of old-school arcade games. There's often evening entertainment in the form of campfires and storytelling. ♨ *Flush toilets, full hookups, partial hookups (electric and water), drinking water, guest laundry, showers, picnic tables, public telephone, general store, play area, Wi-Fi* ⇨ *32 full hookups, 12 partial hookups, 10 tent sites, 3 cabins* ✉ *715 E. Main St.* ☎ *307/332–5159 or 888/757–2327* 🌐 *www.sleepingbearrvpark.com* ▭ *AE, D, MC, V.*

NIGHTLIFE

On weekends the **Lander Bar & Grill** (✉ *126 Main St.* ☎ *307/332–7009*) gets crowded with people who come to dance and listen to live country bands.Local bands often jam at **Folklore Coffeehouse** (✉ *311 Main St.* ☎ *No phone*).

THE ARTS

June through August the **Native American Cultural Program** (☎ *307/856–4801 or 800/433–0662*) has dance exhibitions in nearby Riverton City Park most Thursday evenings. Native American traditional dancing is part of the **Yellow Calf Memorial Powwow** (☎ *307/332–6120 or 800/433–0662*), usually held in early June in Ethete to honor Chief Yellow Calf, the last chief of the Arapaho tribe, 16 mi north of Lander on the Wind River Indian Reservation. For information on area cultural events, such as the Shoshone tribe's Chokecherry Festival in Lander's City Park (3rd and Fremont streets) in late August, call 307/332–5542. You can also find a calendar of Wind River cultural activities at (🌐 *www.wind-river.org*) under "What to Do."

SHOPPING

The shelves at **Main Street Books** (✉ *300 W. Main St.* ☎ *307/332–7661*) are lined with classic, regional, and best-selling books that you can peruse at the coffee bar. Antiques and one-of-a-kind treasures are sold at **Charlotte's Web** (✉ *228 Main St.* ☎ *307/332–5884*).

Distinctive, flamboyant clothing, unique jewelry, and local art are available at **Whippy Bird** (✉ *232 Main St.* ☎ *307/332–3444* ⊕ *www. whippybird.com*).

DUBOIS

86 mi east of Jackson via U.S. 26, U.S. 287, and U.S. 89/191.

The mountains around Dubois attracted explorers as early as 1811, when members of the Wilson Price Hunt party crossed through the region en route to Fort Astoria in Oregon. These high peaks still attract folks who like to hike, climb, ride horses, camp, and experience wilderness. The largest concentration of free-ranging bighorn sheep in the country—more than 1,400—lives here, roaming the high country in summer and wintering just above town on Whiskey Mountain.

South and east of Grand Teton and Yellowstone, Dubois is the least well known of the gateway communities to the parks, but this town of 1,000 provides all the services a visitor in Jackson or Cody might need. You can still get a room during the peak summer season without making a reservation months in advance, although it's a good idea to call a week or so before you arrive.

GETTING HERE AND AROUND

Leave Grand Teton National Park headed east on Highway 26/287 to reach Dubois, heading over the 9,658-foot Togwotee Pass. The drive can be a real bear in the winter, when Togwotee sees as much as an astounding 25 feet of snow. The highway becomes Ramshorn Avenue in Dubois, the town's main drag, and then continues 75 mi southeast to Lander. A lot of Dubois's best lodging is on dude ranches way outside of town, but you can walk anywhere with ease inside the city limits.

VISITOR INFORMATION

Dubois Chamber of Commerce (✆ *Box 632, Dubois 82513* ☎ *307/455–2556* 🖷 *307/455–3168* ⊕ *www.duboiswyoming.org*).

EXPLORING

Displays at the **Wind River Historical Center** focus on Wind River tie hacks (workers who cut ties for railroads), local geology, and the archaeology of the Mountain Shoshone. Outbuildings include the town's first schoolhouse, a saddle shop, a homestead house, and a bunkhouse. The center also offers periodic tours in the summer to nearby petroglyphs. With advance notice you can examine the historical-photograph collection, oral-history tapes, and library. ✉ *909 W. Ramshorn Ave.* ☎ *307/455–2284* 🖾 *$2* ☉ *June–mid-Sept., daily 9–6; mid-Sept.–May, Tues.–Sat. 10–4.*

☾ Friday nights at 8 in the summer, cowboys at the **Dubois Rodeo** kick up a ruckus in the downtown Clarence Allison Memorial Arena, one of the West's best rodeos. Tickets are $7; children under six get in free.

☾ You can learn about bighorn sheep, including Rocky Mountain big-
★ horn, at the **National Bighorn Sheep Interpretive Center** on the north side
of Dubois. Among the mounted specimens here are the "super slam,"
with one of each type of wild sheep in the world, and two bighorn
rams fighting during the rut. Hands-on exhibits illustrate a bighorn's
body language, characteristics, and habitat. Winter tours (reserve
ahead) to Whiskey Mountain provide an opportunity to see the wild
sheep in its natural habitat; reservations are required and cost $25
per person. ✉ *907 Ramshorn Ave.* ☎ *307/455–3429 or 888/209–2795*
🖃 *$2.50 adults; $6 family* ☉ *Memorial Day–Labor Day, daily 9–7;
Labor Day–Memorial Day, Mon.–Sat. 9–5; wildlife-viewing tours
mid-Nov.–Mar.*

**OFF THE
BEATEN
PATH**

Brooks Lake Recreation Area. About 20 mi west of Dubois, easy-to-mod-
erate hiking trails lead around Brooks Lake, across alpine meadows,
and through pine forest to high mountain points with expansive views
of Brooks Lake Mountain and the Pinnacles. You can picnic here, and
boat, fish, or swim on the lake. Brooks Lake Lodge, a private dude
ranch, stands on the lakeshore. ✉ *20 mi west of Dubois on U.S. 26/287,
then 7 mi northeast on gravel road to Brooks Lake Recreation Area*
☎ *307/455–2466* ⊕ *www.fs.fed.us/r2/shoshone.*

SPORTS AND THE OUTDOORS

CROSS-
COUNTRY
SKIING

Among the best places for cross-country skiing is **Togwotee Pass,** east of
Jackson and north of Dubois on U.S. 26/287, in the Bridger-Teton and
Shoshone national forests.

MOUNTAIN
CLIMBING

Much of the appeal of the Wind River Range, which you can access
from the west near Pinedale, or the east near Lander and Dubois, is the
(relatively difficult) access to major peaks, the most significant of which
is Gannett Peak, at 13,804 feet the highest mountain in Wyoming. The
trip to the base of Gannett Peak can take two days, with considerable
ups and downs and stream crossings that can be dangerous in late
spring and early summer. The reward for such effort, however, is seclusion: climbing Gannett Peak might not be as dramatic as climbing the
Grand Teton to the west, but you won't have to face the national-park
crowds at the beginning or end of the climb. Wind River is a world
of granite and glaciers, the latter (though small) being among the last
active glaciers in the U.S. Rockies. Other worthy climbs in the Wind
River Range are Gannett's neighbors Mount Sacajawea and Fremont
Peak. **Jackson Hole Mountain Guides** (✉ *165 N. Glenwood St., Jackson*
☎ *307/733–4979* ⊕ *www.jhmg.com*) leads trips in the area.

WHERE TO EAT

$
AMERICAN

✗**Cowboy Café.** Among the homemade, blue-ribbon dishes served at
this small restaurant in downtown Dubois are sandwiches, steaks,
buffalo burgers, chicken, pork, baby back ribs, and fish. For dessert
the peach caramel crisp and chocolate bourbon pecan pie are not soon
forgotten. You can also grab a hearty breakfast and sip coffee alongside the cowboy clientele. ✉ *115 E. Ramshorn Ave.* ☎ *307/455–2595*
🖃 *AE, D, MC, V.*

$$ ✕ **Paya Deli Pizza & Catering.** Don't be fooled by the Podunk picnic tables
AMERICAN where you can hang out and eat on the sheltered porch while people-
☉ watching on the main drag in this one-horse cow town. Inside, amid
★ the pastel walls, whimsical photos, and pub-style table seating, chef
Barb from Seattle tosses perhaps the tastiest gourmet pizzas baked in
a wood oven in Wyoming. She's also stocking the soup and salad bar
with hot broths and chowders. In the deli you'll find fresh antipasto
and big-city sandwiches like a Reuben on real rye bread. ✉ *112 Ram-*
shorn Ave. ☎ *307/455–3331* ⊕ *www.payadeli.com* ▭ *AE, D, MC, V*
☉ *Closed Mon. and Tues.*

$$$ ✕ **Rustic Pine Steakhouse.** The 1930s-era, 40-foot, hand-carved pinewood
STEAK bar reveals a menagerie of trophy game. This is one of Wyoming's more
Fodor's Choice memorable package stores and watering holes, where locals and visitors
★ congregate to shoot pool and share news about hunting or hiking. The
adjoining restaurant serves mouthwatering steaks, seafood, and pastas
in a quaint, remodeled barn with a stone fireplace, white tablecloths,
and candles. Get your greens at the salad bar. ✉ *119 E. Ramshorn*
Ave. ☎ *307/455–2772 restaurant, 307/455–2430 bar* ⊕ *www.rustic-*
pinetavern.com ▭ *D, MC, V* ☉ *Closed Thurs.*

WHERE TO STAY

$$$$ ▦ **Brooks Lake Lodge.** This mountain lodge on Brooks Lake combines
Fodor's Choice great scenery with service and amenities. Built in 1922, the lodge has
★ massive open-beam ceilings, spacious rooms, subtle lighting, and log,
leather, and wicker furnishings. Each of the lodge bedrooms and cabins
has handcrafted lodgepole-pine furniture. Some cabins have wood-
burning stoves; the lodge suite has a full kitchen, living room, two-per-
son Jacuzzi tub, and king-size beds. All cabins have panoramic views
of the Wind River Range; some overlook Brooks Lake. Take a guided
hike, go horseback riding, or fly-fish or canoe on the lake in summer.
In winter you can take dogsled or snowmobile rides with outfitters.
Dinner is served in the lodge dining room, or you can enjoy a drink in
the small bar or tea in the adjoining den. Many evenings include music
and other entertainment before or during dinner. **Pros:** warm, hospitable staff; diverse menu; year-round activities; rustic location. **Cons:**
no TV/phone; not accessible by car in winter. ✉ *458 Brooks Lake Rd.,*
23 mi west of Dubois, ☎ *307/455–2121* ⊕ *www.brookslake.com* ⟿ *7*
rooms, 8 cabins ☉ *In-room: no a/c, no TV, Wi-Fi. In-hotel: restaurant,*
bar, gym, spa, no-smoking rooms ▭ *AE, MC, V* ❏ *FAP.*

¢–$$ ▦ **Longhorn RV & Motel.** Remodeled in 2007, this family-owned lodging
has cabins and a small camping area/RV park in a cottonwood grove.
It's 2 mi east of Dubois, with a view of the painted badlands. **Pros:**
good shade and trees; long pull-throughs. **Cons:** a drive from town;
Wi-Fi signal varies. ✉ *5810 U.S. 26* ☎ *307/455–2337 or 877/489–2337*
⊕ *www.duboislonghornrvresort.com* ⟿ *24 rooms, 51 RV sites, 3 tent*
sites ☉ *In-room: Wi-Fi. In-hotel: laundry facilities, some pets allowed,*
no-smoking rooms ▭ *D, MC, V* ❏ *EP.*

¢–$$ ▦ **Stagecoach Motor Inn.** This locally owned downtown motel has a large
backyard with a picnic area and playground equipment, and there's even
a reproduction stagecoach for kids to climb on. The play area is bordered by Pretty Horse Creek, so young children need some supervision.

4

Some rooms have full kitchens; others have refrigerators only. **Pros:** walking distance to town; pool; friendly staff; pets allowed. **Cons:** interiors are a little dated. ⊠ *103 E. Ramshorn Ave.* ☎ *307/455–2303 or 800/455–5090* 🖷 *307/455–3903* ⊕ *www.stagecoachmotel-dubois.com* ⏎ *50 rooms, 4 suites* ⚸ *In-room: kitchen (some), refrigerator (some), Wi-Fi. In-hotel: pool, laundry facilities, some pets allowed, no-smoking rooms* ⊟ *AE, D, MC, V.*

$$$$ ⚇ **T Cross Ranch.** At this traditional guest ranch in an isolated valley 15 mi north of Dubois, the eight cozy cabins have porches with rocking chairs, fireplaces or woodstoves, and handmade log furniture. You can snuggle under a down quilt by night and spend your days riding horses. Hosts Gretchen and Mark Cardall were raised in the ranching tradition, and they know how to match people to horses. Weeklong and three-night stays are available. **Pros:** a genuine dude ranch, surrounded by the beautiful Shoshone National Forest, with a focus on horses, hiking, backpacking, and fishing; eco-emphasis includes power supplied by wind turbines. **Cons:** tennis players and golfers should book elsewhere. Those wishing to vacation closer to Yellowstone and Grand Teton national parks might find themselves too far and on the wrong side of the mountains here. ⊠ *15 mi north of Dubois off Horse Creek Rd.* ☎ *307/455–2206 or 877/827–6770* ⊕ *www.tcross.com* ⏎ *9 cabins* ⚸ *In-room: no a/c, no phone, no TV. In-hotel: children's programs (ages 6 and up), laundry facilities, no-smoking rooms* ⊟ *No credit cards* ☾ *Closed mid-Sept.–mid-June* ⏐⊙⏐ *FAP.*

SHOPPING

Fodor's Choice
★ From leather couches to handmade lamps, painted hides, and lodgepole-pine and aspen furniture, you can furnish your home with the Western-style items sold at **Absaroka Western Designs & Tannery** (⊠ *1414 Warm Springs Dr.* ☎ *307/455–2440* ⊕ *www.absarokawesterndesign.com*). The sounds of Native American music set the tone at **Stewart's Trapline Gallery & Indian Trading Post** (⊠ *120 E. Ramshorn Ave.* ☎ *307/455–2800*). You'll find original oil paintings, old-pawn silver Native American jewelry, Navajo rugs, katsina dolls, Zuni fetishes, and high-quality Plains Indian artwork.

Southwest Montana

BOZEMAN, HELENA, NORTH OF YELLOWSTONE

5

WORD OF MOUTH

"Bozeman—can't say enough about this delightful town. We LOVED it. The Museum of the Rockies is a MUST for kids—the dinosaur egg clutches are worth the ticket alone. Be sure to catch the film as it shows how they find and extract the dino bones."

—explorefamily

Updated by
Joyce Dalton
and Ray
Sikorski

Glistening, glaciated, and grand, the Absarokas, Cra-
zies, Gallatins, and other mountains send cooling summer
winds to roil among the grasslands and forests of southwest Montana. This is a wild place inhabited by hundreds
of animal species.

Abundant wildlife is a daily sight, from the pronghorn sprinting across
grasslands to the 17,000-strong northern elk herd in and north of Yellowstone National Park. Bald eagles and ospreys perch in tall snags
along the rivers, watching for fish. Mules and white-tailed deer spring
over fences (and across roads, so watch out when driving). Golden
eagles hunt above hay fields. Riparian areas come alive in spring with
ducks, geese, pelicans, and great blue herons. The south-central area
known as Yellowstone Country shares the topography, wildlife, rivers,
and recreational opportunities of its namesake national park.

Critters outnumber people in southwest Montana, which should come
as no surprise when you consider that some counties have fewer than
one person per square mile. The region's ranches are measured in the
thousands of acres, though they are bordered by ranchettes of fewer
than 20 acres around the towns of Bozeman, Big Timber, Red Lodge,
and Dillon. But even the most densely populated area, Yellowstone
County, has only about 34 people per square mile. That leaves thousands of square miles in the region wide open for exploration. Hiking,
fishing, mountain biking, and rock climbing are popular outdoor activities in summer, and in winter the thick pillows of snow make skiing and
snowmobiling conditions near perfect.

Southwest Montana's human history reaches back only about 12,000
years, and the non–Native American presence dates back only 200
years. Yet this place is full of exciting tales and trails, from the path
followed by the Lewis and Clark Expedition to the Bozeman and Nez
Perce trails. To the west, in Montana's southwesternmost corner, is Gold
West Country, which includes the gold-rush towns of Helena, Virginia
City, and Bannack. Roadside signs along various routes in the region
indicate the sites of battles, travels, and travails.

ORIENTATION AND PLANNING

GETTING ORIENTED

Southwest Montana encompasses a multitude of landscapes, from
rolling plains and creek-carved coulees to massive mountain ranges
and raging rivers fed by snowfields atop towering peaks. The region's
beauty is best experienced at a leisurely pace—one that allows you to
do some wildlife viewing, spend an afternoon on the banks of a stunning stream, and watch the slow descent of the sun as it drops behind
ragged mountains.

A private vehicle is far and away the best means of exploring southwest Montana, as it allows you to appreciate the grandeur of the area. Wide-open terrain affords startling vistas of mountains and prairies, where you're likely to see abundant wildlife. I–90 is the major east–west artery through the region; I–15 is the major north–south route. Most of the other routes here are paved and in good shape, but be prepared for gravel and dirt roads the farther off the beaten path you go. Driving through the mountains in winter can be challenging; a four-wheel-drive vehicle, available from most car-rental agencies, is best.

PLANNING

WHEN TO GO

December through March is the best time to visit for skiers, snowboarders, snowshoers, and people who love winter. Summer draws even more visitors. That's not to say that southwest Montana gets crowded, but you may find more peace and quiet in spring and fall, when warm days and cool nights offer pleasant vacationing under the Big Sky.

Temperatures will drop below freezing in winter (and in fall and spring in the mountains) and jump into the 80s and 90s in summer. The weather can change quickly, particularly in the mountains and in the front range area north of Helena, and temperatures have been known to vary by as much as 70°F within a few hours, bringing winds, thunderstorms, and the like.

PLANNING YOUR TIME

For the best tour of southwest Montana, drive the unforgettable roadways that seem to reach the top of the world, make frequent stops in historic towns and parks. Drive up the Beartooth Pass from Red Lodge and, between late May and early October, hike along myriad trails right from the highway. Stop in Big Timber to sample small-town Western life, ride a white-water raft on the Stillwater River, or fly-fish the Yellowstone River with a knowledgeable outfitter. From Livingston, home to several museums, drive south into ever more beautiful countryside, through the Paradise Valley toward Yellowstone National Park. A float trip on this section of the Yellowstone, combined with a stay at Chico Hot Springs, is the stuff of which great memories are made.

In summer in Virginia City, Ennis, or Three Forks, return to gold-rush days along the historic streets or live for today with a fly rod in hand and a creel waiting to be filled beside you. Trail rides, float trips, steam trains—not to mention long walks in the long-gone footsteps of Lewis and Clark, Sacajawea, and a few thousand forgotten trappers, traders, cavalry soldiers, and Native Americans—all await you around these towns.

Bozeman, Big Sky, and the Gallatin Canyon are premier destinations in any season, with more than enough museums, galleries, historic sites, and scenic stops to fill your itinerary. Southwest Montana offers ample opportunities for outdoor recreation even when the snow flies. In places like Big Sky, Bridger Bowl, the Gallatin National Forest, and Moonlight Basin you can experience some of the best skiing and snowmobiling in America, and after a day on the slopes or the trails plunge into the

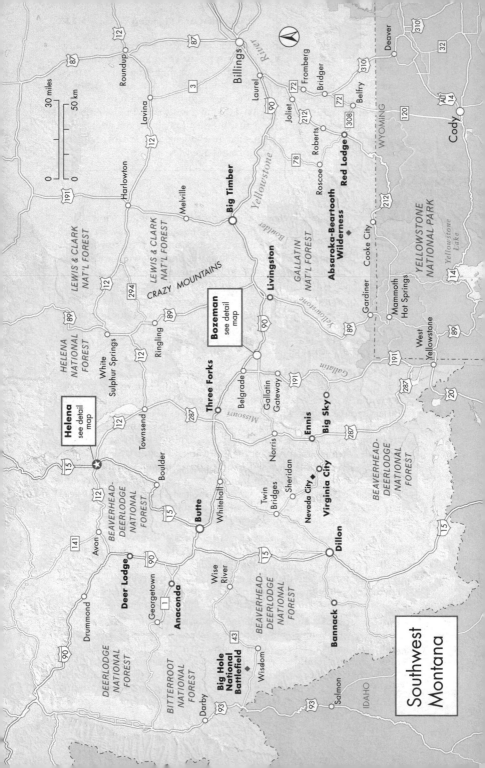

hot springs in Bozeman, Butte, or Boulder.

In making the most of your time, pause to breathe in the air filtered through a few million pines, to listen to the sounds of nature all around, to feel the chill of a mountain stream or the welcome warmth of a thermal spring. Small moments like these stick with you and become the kind of memories that will beckon you back to this high, wide, and handsome land.

GETTING HERE AND AROUND

AIR TRAVEL

Several daily flights link Bozeman's Gallatin Field Airport to Great Falls, Denver, Minneapolis, Salt Lake City, and Seattle. Butte Airport has service from Salt Lake City. Helena Airport has service from Billings, Great Falls, Minneapolis, Denver, Seattle, and Salt Lake City. Note that major air carriers tend to use smaller planes to serve the area.

TOP REASONS TO GO
■ Fly-fishing the gorgeous Gallatin River.
■ For a scenic and exhilarating drive, the Beartooth Highway can't be topped.
■ State Capitol, Helena: from Charlie Russell's Lewis and Clark painting to the Goddess of Liberty crowning the copper dome, the capitol is a masterpiece inside and out.
■ The Museum of the Rockies houses the world's largest collection of dinosaur fossils.
■ Wilderness skiing at the remote Big Sky Ski Resort.

Airlines Alaska Airlines/Horizon Air (☎ 800/547-9308 ⊕ www.alaskaair. com).**Delta/Skywest** (☎ 800/221-1212 ⊕ www.delta.com). **Northwest** (☎ 800/225-2525 ⊕ www.nwa.com). **United/United Express** (☎ 800/241-6522 ⊕ www.united.com).

Airports Butte Airport (⊠ 101 Airport Rd., Butte ☎ 406/494-3771 ⊕ www.butteairport.com). **Gallatin Field Airport** (⊠ 850 Gallatin Field Rd., Belgrade ☎ 406/388-8321 ⊕ www.bozemanairport.com). **Helena Airport** (⊠ 2850 Skyway Dr., Helena ☎ 406/442-2821 ⊕ www.helenaairport.com).

BUS TRAVEL

Greyhound Lines serves several communities along I–90, including Billings, Livingston, Bozeman, and Butte. Karst Stage/4x4 Stage has regional service in the Bozeman area, plus service from Bozeman to Big Sky. Rimrock Trailways, which is based in Billings, serves major communities in the state. Skyline is a Big Sky area bus service that also provides service between Bozeman and Big Sky.

Information Greyhound Lines (☎ 800/231-2222 ⊕ www.greyhound.com). **Karst Stage/4x4 Stage** (☎ 800/845-2778 ⊕ www.karststage.com). **Rimrock Trailways** (☎ 800/255-7655 ⊕ www.rimrocktrailways.com). **Skyline** (☎ 406/995-6287 ⊕ www.skylinebus.com).

CAR TRAVEL

Major routes are paved and well maintained, but there are many gravel and dirt roads off the beaten track. When heading into remote regions, be sure to fill up the gas tank, and check road reports for construction delays or passes that may close in severe winter weather. Always carry a flashlight, drinking water and some food, a first-aid kit, and emergency overnight gear (a sleeping bag and extra, warm clothing). Most important, make sure someone is aware of your travel plans. While driving, be prepared for animals crossing roads, livestock on open ranges along the highway, and other hazards such as high winds and dust- or snowstorms.

When driving in the mountains in winter, make sure you have tire chains, studs, or snow tires.

Contacts Montana Highway Patrol (☎ *406/388–3190 or 800/525–5555* ⊕ *www.doj.mt.gov/enforcement/highwaypatrol/*). **Statewide Road Report** (☎ *800/226–7623* ⊕ *www.mdt.mt.gov/travinfo/*).

RESTAURANTS
This is ranch country, so expect numerous Angus-steer steak houses. Many restaurants also serve bison meat and various vegetarian meals, but you'll find few ethnic dishes. Restaurants here are decidedly casual: blue jeans, crisp shirts, and cowboy boots are dressy for the region.

HOTELS
Lodging varies from national chain hotels to mom-and-pop motor inns. More and more guest ranches are inviting lodgers, historic hotels are being restored, and new bed-and-breakfasts are opening their doors. If you plan to visit in summer or during the ski season (December–mid-March), it's best to reserve rooms far in advance.

WHAT IT COSTS					
	¢	$	$$	$$$	$$$$
Restaurants	under $8	$8–$12	$13–$20	$21–$30	over $30
Hotels	under $70	$70–$100	$101–$150	$151–$200	over $200

Restaurant prices are for a main course at dinner. Hotel prices are for two people in a standard double room in high season, excluding service charges and a 7% bed tax.

CAMPING
There are numerous campsites throughout the region, and they vary from rustic (with pit toilets) to relatively plush (with cabins and heated swimming pools). When camping, ask about bears in the area and whether or not food must be stored inside a hard-sided vehicle (not a tent). Avoid bringing pets to campgrounds—it can lead to confrontations with the wildlife, and it's against the rules at most campgrounds.

Contact Montana Fish, Wildlife & Parks for information on camping in state parks and the U.S. Forest Service for information on camping at national parks in the area.

Contacts Montana Fish, Wildlife & Parks (☎ *406/444–2535* ⊕ *www.fwp.state. mt.us/parks*). **U.S. Forest Service** (☎ *406/329–3511* ⊕ *www.fs.fed.us/*).

NORTH OF YELLOWSTONE

This mountainous stretch of land from the town of Red Lodge west to the resort region at Big Sky is mostly roadless, glaciated, and filled with craggy heights. Winter often refuses to give up its grasp on this high alpine region until late spring. Snowpack assures that streams feeding the mighty Yellowstone River will flow throughout the hot summer, satiating the wildlife, native plants, and numerous farms downstream.

RED LODGE

60 mi southwest of Billings via I–90 and U.S. 212. 60 mi northwest of Cody via Rte.120/Rte. 72 and Rte. 308.

Nestled against the foot of the pine-draped Absaroka-Beartooth Wilderness, this little burg is listed on the National Register of Historic Places and has become a full-blown resort town, complete with a ski area, trout fishing, access to backcountry hiking, horseback riding, and a golf course. Red Lodge was named for the Crow Indians' custom of marking their tepee lodges with paintings of red earth. It became a town in the late 1880s, when the Northern Pacific Railroad laid tracks here to take coal back to Billings. One of Red Lodge's most colorful characters from this time was former sheriff "Liver Eatin'" Jeremiah Johnston, the subject of much Western lore and an eponymous movie starring Robert Redford. This area is a favored stopover for motorcyclists and others heading over the Beartooth Highway to Yellowstone National Park. Free brochures for self-guided historical walking tours of the town and driving tours of the county are available at the chamber of commerce and the museum.

GETTING HERE AND AROUND

You need a car to get to Red Lodge. Once here, shops, galleries, and restaurants are walkable from most lodging facilities. There is no public transportation and only one taxi (as in vehicle, not company); no traffic lights or parking meters, but plenty of stop signs. When passing through Joliet on U.S. 212, obey the frequently changing speed-limit signs to the letter. The nearest airport is in Billings.**VISITOR INFORMATIONRed Lodge Chamber of Commerce** (⊠ *601 N. Broadway, Red Lodge* ☎ *406/446–1718 or 888/281–0625* ⊕ *www.redlodge.com*).

EXPLORING

Joliet, a neonless ranching community midway between I–90 and Red Lodge along Highway 212, claims a bit of glamour at **The Homestead Café** (⊠ *606 W. Front Ave.* ☎ *406/962–3911*). The owners spent years in Las Vegas as Marilyn Monroe and Elvis Presley impersonators, and the resemblance to these icons is still astounding.Along Highway 212 in Joliet you'll find the **Charles Ringer Studio & Gallery** (⊠ *418 E. Front Ave.* ☎ *406/962–3705* ⊕ *www.charlesringer.com*). Ringer's metal kinetic sculptures, from the huge and strange to the small and lovely, are in collections around the world, including that of former president Bill Clinton.

EN ROUTE

5

The folks in Red Lodge, all 2,450 of them, relish festivals. For a complete list and exact dates, contact the **Red Lodge Area Chamber of Commerce.**

Each August the **Festival of Nations** (⊕ *www.festivalofnations.us*) celebrates the varied heritages of early settlers, many of whom migrated to work in now-defunct coal mines. The weekend festival includes ethnic music, food, and dance.

From kindergartners to seniors, fiddlers of all ages head for Red Lodge each July to compete in the two-day **Montana State Old-Time Fiddlers Contest** ⊕ *www.montanafiddlers.org.*

For 10 days in July the fur-trade/mountain-man era lives again during **Rendezvous at Red Lodge** (⊕ *www.redlodge.com/rendezvous*). Participants from around the country set up tents, don period dress, and trade tools, beads, and other items at this historical reenactment.

Fourth of July weekend means the **Home of Champions Rodeo** (⊕ *www. redlodgerodeo.com)*has come to town. Now in its eighth decade, this three-day event sees many of the country's rodeo greats taking part in all the usual events. Some also join in the Saturday parade along the town's main street.

The **Beartooth Nature Center** provides a home for more than 70 injured or orphaned mammals and raptors, including bears, mountain lions, bobcats, wolves, and golden eagles. ⊠ *615 2nd Ave. E* ☎ *406/446–1133* ⊕ *www.beartoothnaturecenter.org* ⊠ *$6* ⊙ *June–Oct., daily 10–5; Nov.–May, daily 10–2.*

In addition to memorabilia that once belonged to rodeo greats, the Ridin' Greenoughs and Bill Linderman, the **Carbon County Historical Society Museum** houses a historic gun collection, simulated coal and hardrock mines, and Crow Indian and Liver Eatin' Johnston exhibits. ⊠ *224 N. Broadway* ☎ *406/446–3667* ⊕ *www.carboncountyhistory.com* ⊠ *$5* ⊙ *Late May–early Sept., Mon.–Sat. 10–5, Sun. 11–3; early Sept.–late May, Thurs. and Fri. 10–5, Sat. 10–3.*

OFF THE BEATEN PATH

A bar and a museum may seem an unlikely pairing, but Shirley Smith, owner of the **Little Cowboy Bar & Museum** (⊠ *105 W. River St., Fromberg, 20 mi east on Hwy. 308, then 19 mi north on Hwy. 72* ☎ *406/668–9502* ⊠ *Free*), makes it work. A rodeo enthusiast and lover of local lore, Smith has packed the one-room museum with rodeo memorabilia and objects ranging from projectile points to bottled beetles.

SPORTS AND THE OUTDOORS

DOWNHILL SKIING ❅

There are 84 ski trails on 1,600 acres at **Red Lodge Mountain Resort** (⊠ *305 Ski Run Rd.* ☎ *406/446–2610 or 800/444–8977* ⊕ *www.red-lodgemountain.com*). The family-friendly resort has a 2,400-foot vertical drop, a large beginner area, plenty of groomed intermediate terrain, and 30 acres of extreme chute skiing. Slopes are accessed by two high-speed quads, one triple, and four double chairs. Lift tickets are $47. The season runs late November–mid-April, conditions permitting.

NORDIC SKIING
At the **Red Lodge Nordic Ski Center,** escape to the solitude of forests along 14½ km (9 mi) of groomed trails at the base of the Beartooth Mountains. You also can experience on- and off-trail backcountry skiing and snowboarding. Trails are maintained by volunteers, and there is no lodge. ✛ *1 mi from town on Hwy. 78, then 2 mi west on Fox Trail* ☎ *406/425–0698* ⊕ *www.beartoothtrails.org* ⊠ *$5* ☉ *Dec.–Mar.*

FISHING
Montana Trout Scout (⊠ *213 W. 9th St.* ⬡ *Box 412 59068* ☎ *406/855–3058* ⊕ *www.montanatroutscout.com*) conducts fly-fishing float trips and wade fishing on local streams and rivers such as the Yellowstone, Clark's Fork, Stillwater, and Rock Creek.

GOLF
The surrounding mountains form a backdrop for the 18-hole, par-72 **Red Lodge Mountain Golf Course** (⊠ *828 Upper Continental Dr.* ☎ *406/446–3344 or 800/444–8977*). The season generally runs from mid-May to mid-September.

HORSEBACK RIDING ☉
With **Whispering Winds Horse Adventures** (⊠ *55 Ladvala Rd., Roberts* ✛ *10 mi north of Red Lodge* ☎ *406/671–6836*) enjoy riding lessons in the ranch's arena or daytime or sunset trail rides among rolling hills. Lunch or dinner is optional; reservations for rides are required. A half-day Family Fun program customizes the riding experience.

WHITE-WATER RAFTING
The Stillwater River's foaming white water flows from the Absaroka-Beartooth Wilderness, providing exhilarating rafting from mild to wild with **Adventure Whitewater** (⊠ *310 W. 15th St.* ⬡ *Box 639 59068* ☎ *406/446–3061 or 800/897–3061* ⊕ *www.adventurewhitewater.com*).

WHERE TO EAT

$
MEXICAN
✕ **Bogart's.** Not surprisingly, Bogie's photos and memorabilia cover the walls. But this casual eatery's most notable features are great Mexican food, margaritas, burgers, and specialty pizzas. The biggest seller is chicken enchiladas with homemade sour-cream sauce. ⊠ *11 S. Broadway* ☎ *406/446–1784* ▭ *AE, D, MC, V.*

$$$
NEW AMERICAN
✕ **Bridge Creek Backcountry Kitchen & Wine Bar.** Locally raised all-natural beef and fresh seafood are popular dinner entrée choices here. For lunch, the various half-sandwich and soup combos are winners. Bridge Creek has an extensive wine list, occasional wine tastings, theme buffets in the off-season, and patio dining in summer. ⊠ *116 S. Broadway* ☎ *406/446–9900* ⊕ *www.eatfooddrinkwine.com* ▭ *MC, V.*

$
AMERICAN
✕ **Foster and Logan's Pub & Grill.** Multiple TVs, each tuned to a different sport, line the brick walls of this friendly place. The bar claims 20 beers on tap, the better to enjoy what locals call the town's best hamburgers. In winter opt for buffalo chili. ⊠ *17 S. Broadway* ☎ *406/446–9080* ▭ *AE, D, MC, V.*

WHERE TO STAY

$$–$$$
🛏 **Gallagher's Irish Rose B&B.** A large stone fireplace serves as the focal point of the living room, and gas or electric stoves or fireplaces lend a cozy feel to each guest room, as do quilts and artwork, both by the owners. Baked apple-pecan French toast with homemade syrup is a popular breakfast choice. A separate private house, which can sleep

5

eight, also is available. **Pros:** food products organically grown; easy walk to shops, galleries, and restaurants. **Cons:** stairs pose a problem for some; no parking lot but street parking plentiful. ✉ *302 S. Broadway* ☎ *Box 1237* 🖹 *406/446–0303 or 877/446–0303* ⊕ *www.irishrosehost. com* ⟿ *3 rooms* 🔊 *In-room: no phone, DVD, Wi-Fi.* ▤ *AE, D, MC, V* ☉ *Closed Nov., Apr., and May* ⦿*BP.*

$$–$$$ 🖼 **Pollard Hotel.** This 1893 landmark in the heart of Red Lodge's his-
★   toric district has been restored to the charms of an earlier era, when the likes of Calamity Jane and Liver Eatin' Johnston frequented the hotel. Reproduction Victorian furniture gives a fin de siècle feel, and handsome oak paneling adds a rich touch to some public rooms. Favorites on the dinner menu ($$$–$$$$) include pan-seared duck breast with toasted almond couscous, fresh herbs, and a pomegranate reduction, and the 14-ounce rib eye with horseradish crème fraiche. **Pros:** near most shops and attractions; sauna and hot tub welcome after a day on the ski slopes. **Cons:** standard rooms, though attractive, are on the small size; restaurant not open for lunch. ✉ *2 N. Broadway* ☎ *Box 650 59068* 🖹 *406/446–0001 or 800/765–5273* 🖷 *406/446–0002* ⊕ *www. pollardhotel.com* ⟿ *38 rooms* 🔊 *In-room: DVD (some), Wi-Fi. In-hotel: restaurant, gym, Internet, Wi-Fi* ▤ *AE, D, MC, V* ⦿*BP.*

$$–$$$ 🖼 **Rock Creek Resort.** A wooden bear's raised paw welcomes you to this 35-acre getaway, where a Southwestern motif decorates the wood, log, and stone lodge, cabin, condos, and town homes perched beside a babbling, boulder-strewn creek. Some of the rooms have hot tubs and/or fireplaces. A historic old cabin holds the wonderful Old Piney Dell restaurant ($$$–$$$$), where the steaks, Wiener schnitzel, and Sunday brunch are especially popular. In summer the Kiva restaurant serves breakfast and lunch. **Pros:** creek and woods make for pleasant surroundings; restaurant offers superb food and views. **Cons:** lack of public transport necessitates a car; restaurant phone unmanned, even by machine, until near dinnertime. ✉ *6380 U.S. 212 S, 5 mi south of Red Lodge* ☎ *406/446–1111 or 800/667–1119* 🖷 *406/237–9851* ⊕ *www.rockcreekresort.com* ⟿ *38 rooms, 48 condos, 1 cabin, 2 town homes* 🔊 *In-room: kitchen (some), Wi-Fi. In-hotel: 2 restaurants, bar, tennis courts, pool, gym, bicycles, laundry facilities, Wi-Fi* ▤ *AE, D, DC, MC, V* ⦿*CP.*

CAMPING   🔺 **Greenough Campground and Lake.** Pine trees, a small trout-stocked lake, and gentle hiking trails provide summer respite at Greenough, named after a local family of rodeo greats and one of a dozen U.S. Forest Service campgrounds in the Red Lodge vicinity. There's fishing in Greenough Lake ¼ mi from the campground. 🔊 *Pit toilets, drinking water, fire grates, picnic tables* ⟿ *18 sites* ✉ *10½ mi south of Red Lodge on U.S. 212, then 1 mi west on Hwy. 421* ☎ *406/446–2103* ⊕ *www. fs.fed.us/r1/custer* 🔊 *Reservations essential* ▤ *AE, D, MC, V only if reservations made through National Reservation Service* ☎ *877/444–6777* ⊕ *www.recreation.gov* ☉ *Closed Oct.–Apr.*

⟳   🔺 **Red Lodge KOA.** With its heated pool, playground, trout-filled brook, and access to Rock Creek for fishing, this tidy campground is ideal for families. Sites are along the banks of small creeks and among shady willows and pine trees. 🔊 *Flush toilets, full hookups, partial hookups* *(water), drinking water, guest laundry, showers, fire grates, picnic tables, food service, electricity, public telephone, play area, swimming (pool), Wi-Fi ⚡ 13 full hookups, 35 partial hookups, 20 tent sites; 6 cabins ✉ 7464 U.S. 212, 4 mi north of Red Lodge ☎ 406/446–2364 (disconnected in winter) or 800/562–7540 ⊕ www.koa.com ⚭ Reservations essential during July ▤ AE, D, MC, V ◔ Closed mid-Sept.–mid-May.*

NIGHTLIFE AND THE ARTS

NIGHTLIFE Sit back with a beer and a steak while you watch the Bearcreek Downs' Pig Races at the **Bearcreek Saloon & Steakhouse** (✉ 108 W. Main St., 7 mi east of Red Lodge on Hwy. 308, Bearcreek ☎ 406/446–3481). Oinkers in numbered jerseys streak around an outdoor oval while patrons bet on their favorites; proceeds fund local scholarships. The races take place summer evenings at 7, Thursday through Sunday.

THE ARTS Located in a 1889 train depot, the **Carbon County Arts Guild & Depot Gallery**
★ (✉ 11 W. 8th St. ☎ 406/446–1370 ⊕ www.carboncountydepotgallery. org) showcases paintings and sculptures by Western artists. The **Coleman Gallery and Studio** (✉ 223 S. Broadway ☎ 406/446–1228 or 800/726–2228 ⊕ www.colemangallery.biz) features works by photographer Merv Coleman. Natural scenery and wildlife are his specialties. Internationally recognized painter Kevin Red Star, whose works draw on his Crow Indian heritage, displays his oils, acrylics, lithographs, and etchings at **Kevin Red Star Gallery** (✉ 19 S. 1st St. Roberts ☎ 406/445–2549 ⊕ www. kevinredstar.com). Red Star's works are in the permanent collections of the Smithsonian Institution, the Institute of American Indian Art, and the Pierre Cardin Collection in Paris. The **Red Lodge Clay Center** (✉ 123 S. Broadway ☎ 406/446–3993 ⊕ www.redlodgeclaycenter.com) promotes local, regional, and national ceramic artists. Exhibits change monthly.

EN
ROUTE
Fodor's Choice
★

Driving south from Red Lodge along the 68-mi **Beartooth Highway** (U.S. 212) will take you over the precipitous 11,000-foot **Beartooth Pass** as the road winds its way through lush alpine country to the "back door" of Yellowstone National Park. With multiple steep climbs and switchbacks, this officially designated Scenic Byway and All American Road was a feat of 1930s engineering. The highway is usually open from mid-May to mid-October, but snow can close it at any time of the year. Several hiking trails lead off the highway; for hiking maps and more information, contact the **Beartooth Ranger District** (☎ 406/446–2103) in Red Lodge.

ABSAROKA-BEARTOOTH WILDERNESS

Although millions of summer visitors swarm into Yellowstone National Park to the south, the Absaroka-Beartooth Wilderness is blissfully unpeopled year-round, except for dedicated backcountry travelers who come precisely for its emptiness. Unlike in Yellowstone, no paved roads lead into the wilderness area, although a four-wheel-drive vehicle is not essential for access. The wilderness encompasses Montana's highest mountains, including 12,799-foot Granite Peak; because of that, the prime hiking season (August) is relatively short. Many of the 640 high-mountain lakes may remain partially frozen even into August, especially in the high plateau region. Hikes are moderate to strenuous. Perhaps the most popular trails are those in the East Fork–Rosebud Creek area (35 mi one-way), where numerous lakes rest in alpine basins above 9,000 feet. Keep in mind that this is grizzly-bear country. You can get information and permits from Custer National Forest in Billings, or Gallatin National Forest in Bozeman.

GETTING HERE AND AROUND

The two main access routes are 12 mi south of Red Lodge via Beartooth Highway and 10 mi west of Red Lodge via Rock Creek Road. You'll need a car to get around.

> **WORD OF MOUTH**
>
> "I go to Yellowstone frequently, but had never driven the Beartooth. Last summer I finally made it. I went out the Silvergate entrance and drove to Red Lodge and stayed overnight. Really enjoyed Red Lodge! From there I cut over northwest to meet Interstate 90, past Billings and down through the gorgeous Paradise Valley to Gardiner."   —Dayle

For information on the western half of the wilderness, contact **Gallatin National Forest** (⊠ *Federal Bldg., 3017 Fallon St., Suite C, Bozeman* ☏ *406/522–2520* ⊕ *www.fs.fed.us/r1/gallatin*).

For information on the eastern half of the wilderness, contact **Custer National Forest** (⊠ *1310 Main St., Billings* ☏ *406/657–6200* ⊕ *www. fs.fed.us/r1/custer*).

SPORTS AND THE OUTDOORS

Because the Beartooths are rugged and remote, it's best to get outfitted in Billings, Red Lodge, or another city before heading here. Climbing guides and horse-pack trail guides—recommended unless you are familiar with the backcountry—can lead trips to remarkable and scenic places, safely. Most important, know backcountry rules regarding travel in grizzly-bear country.

HORSEBACK RIDING
Wranglers, guides, a cook, tents, and cots accompany you on four- and five-day fly-fishing pack trips with **Beartooth Plateau Outfitters** (⊠ *819 Clear Creek Rd., 13 mi north of Red Lodge on U.S. 212, Roberts* ☏ *406/445–2293 or 800/253–8545* ⊕ *www.beartoothoutfitters.com*).

MOUNTAIN CLIMBING
Experienced climbers from **Beartooth Mountain Guides** (⌂ *Box 1985, Red Lodge 59068* ☏ *406/446–9874* ⊕ *www.beartoothmountainguides.com*) lead climbs to the top of Montana's tallest mountain, the challenging 12,799-foot Granite Peak. They also offer one-day and multiday backpacking trips devoted to rock climbing, alpine and ski mountaineering, and ice climbing for beginners and experts.

BIG TIMBER AND THE BOULDER RIVER

88 mi northwest of Red Lodge via Hwy. 78 north and I–90 west; 81 mi west of Billings via I–90.

People come to Big Timber for its small-town (population 1,600) Western ambience, to fly-fish the blue-ribbon trout streams, float the Yellowstone River, or unwind in front of the Crazy Mountains (so called because a homesteader supposedly went crazy from living in such a remote setting). South of town you can follow the Boulder River in its mad dash out of the Absaroka-Beartooth Wilderness. This journey along Highway 298 will take you into wild country, with craggy peaks rising on either side of a lush, ranch-filled valley.

GETTING HERE AND AROUND

To get around, you'll need a vehicle, as there is no public transportation. There are also no parking meters. The nearest airport is Billings.

VISITOR INFORMATION

The **Sweet Grass Chamber of Commerce** (✉ *I–90, Exit 367* ✆ *Box 1012, Big Timber, 59011* ☎ *406/932–5131* ⊕ *www.bigtimber.com*) can provide information about sightseeing in the region. You'll find a stand with maps and brochures outside the chamber. ☉ *June–early Sept.*

EXPLORING

Drop by the **Yellowstone River Trout Hatchery,** a five-minute drive from the town center, to view and learn about cutthroat trout. The best time to visit the hatchery is in spring, when you can see the fingerlings. ✉ *Fairgrounds Rd.* ☎ *406/932–4434* 🏷 *Free* ☉ *Daily 9–4.*

The small but well-organized **Crazy Mountain Museum** houses exhibits on Big Timber's history and people, as well as the Crazy Mountains. Highlights include the famous Cremer Rodeo, sheep and wool exhibits, a collection of chaps and cattle brands, and a room dedicated to pioneers that includes artifacts dating from the late 1890s. An early-20th-century schoolhouse and a Norwegian stabbur, or storehouse, also stand on the grounds. ✉ *2 Cemetery Rd., Exit 367 off I–90* ☎ *406/932–5126* 🏷 *Donations accepted* ☉ *June–Sept., Mon.–Sat. 10–4:30, Sun. 1–4:30.*

The comical critters at **Greycliff Prairie Dog Town State Park** pop out of their underground homes, stand upright, sound their chirping alarms, and dash to another hole. Explorers Meriwether Lewis and William Clark referred to these "barking squirrels" in their journals. At this 98-acre protected habitat you can catch the action from your car. ✉ *I–90, Exit 377, Greycliff* ☎ *406/247–2940* ⊕ *www.fwp.state.mt.us* 🏷 *Free* ☉ *Daily dawn–dusk.*

At **Natural Bridge State Monument** the Boulder River disappears underground, creating a natural bridge, then reappears as roaring falls in the Boulder River canyon. Hiking trails and interpretive signs explain how this geologic wonder occurred. The Main Boulder Ranger Station, a few miles past the bridge, is one of the oldest in the United States and is now an interpretive center. ✉ *Hwy. 298, 27 mi south of Big Timber* ☎ *406/247–2940* ⊕ *www.fs.fed.us/r1/gallatin/* 🏷 *Free* ☉ *Daily.*

OFF THE BEATEN PATH

Indian Caves Pictographs. Native Americans lived in the area for more than 10,000 years, leaving evidence of their presence on cave walls here, including a depiction of a bison hunt. To get to the cave you'll have to hike 1½ mi along the Grouse Creek Trail, near the main Boulder Ranger Station on U.S. 298. The cave is always open, but in poor weather the trail can be difficult to hike. From the trail, it's a hands-and-knees scramble, not recommended for small children, to the cave entrance. A flashlight is useful for visiting the cave. ✉ *U.S. 298, 26 mi south of Big Timber on the Main Boulder River* ☎ *406/932–5155.*

SPORTS AND THE OUTDOORS

FISHING You're likely to see white pelicans, bald eagles, white-tailed deer, and cutthroat trout on single- or multiday float and fishing trips on the Yellowstone River with **Big Timber Guides and Rollin' Boulder Outfitters** (✉ *529 E. Boulder Rd., last 6 mi on gravel ⌂ Box 328, McLeod 59052* ☎ *406/932–4080* ⊕ *www.finditlocal.com/bigtimber/flyfish.html*).

You can fish in a private lake or streams at the vast working cattle ranch, **Burns Ranch** (✉ *333 Swamp Creek Rd.* ☎ *406/932–4518* ☉ *Apr.–Oct.*). The 40-acre Burns Lake, with rainbow, cutthroat, brown, and brook trout, is limited to a few anglers a day. This is a registered lake, so no license is necessary. The cost is $100 per rod, and reservations are required. The ranch is 4 mi north of Big Timber on U.S. 191 and then another 4 mi west on Swamp Creek Road.

HORSEBACK RIDING **Montana Bunkhouses Working Ranch Vacations LLC** is an organization of more than 20 ranches working cooperatively on the European agrotourism model to give visitors a non-gussied-up ranching experience. At least eight are in the Big Timber area. Join the rancher in his daily tasks, take part in cattle drives, take a trail ride, head for the nearest trout stream, or just relax. Accommodations range from ranch houses to remote cabins to bunkhouses. ⌂ *Box 693, Livingston 59047* ☎ *406/222–6101* ⊕ *www.montanaworkingranches.com.*

WHERE TO EAT

$ ✕ **Country Skillet.** From 6 in the morning until 10 at night you'll find the
CAFE welcome mat out here. For those who love their eggs and pancakes, breakfast is served all day. A variety of burgers, salads, and entrées, including pork chops and ham steak, are also on the menu. ✉ *Big Timber Loop Rd., just off I–90, Exit 367* ☎ *406/932–4580* ⊟ *AE, D, DC, MC, V.*

$ ✕ **Peking Garden.** Chinese lanterns hang here from the pressed tin ceiling—a nice blending of cultures. Select from the expected array of shrimp, chicken, pork, beef, and vegetable dishes, both spicy and mild, offered at lunch and dinner. ✉ *121 McLeod St.* ☎ *406/932–4848* ⊟ *MC, V.*

WHERE TO STAY

¢–$ 🏨 **Grand Hotel.** Fine dining and an 1890s saloon are two of the attractions of this classic Western hotel, listed on the National Register of Historic Places, in downtown Big Timber. The attractive 1890 Room ($$$$) serves steaks, seafood, and lamb for dinner, plus decadent desserts. For lunch, the 1890 Saloon claims to have served "cattlemen, cowboys, sheepherders, miners, railroad men and travelers" for more than 100 years. Guest rooms are small, clean, and comfortable, with

---

THE RUNNING OF THE SHEEP

The annual one-day **Running of the Sheep** (✉ *I–90, Exit 392, 25 mi west of Big Timber, Reed Point* ☎ *406/326–2325*), held the Sunday of Labor Day weekend, celebrates the sturdy Montana-bred sheep and the state's agriculture history with humor. In addition to the sheep run (the sheep are let loose down the main street, sort of like the bulls in Pamplona, Spain, only a lot tamer), you can see a parade of antique cars, covered wagons, and a stagecoach (robbed, of course, by bandits on horseback).

period furnishings—the kind of accommodations you might find over the Longbranch Saloon in *Gunsmoke*. **Pros:** virtually shrieks once-grand Old West; restaurant decor and food still qualify as grand. **Cons:** claw-foot tubs in hallway baths notwithstanding, the dearth of en suite facilities won't please all; on a given day the "chef's choice" breakfast might not coincide with "guest's choice." ✉ *139 McLeod St.* 📫 *Box 1242* ☎ *406/932–4459* 📠 *406/932–4248* 🌐 *www.thegrand-hotel.com* 🛏 *11 rooms, 4 with bath* 👍 *In-room: no TV (some). In-hotel: 2 restaurants, bar* 💳 *MC, V* 🍴 *BP.*

$$–$$$ **The Homestead Bed & Breakfast.** There's nothing rustic about this homestead. Situated in a tree-lined historic residential district, this 1903 house claims period furnishings throughout, a 52-inch TV for guests, and fireplaces in the parlor, library, music room, and one guest room. The original oak staircase leads to three of the guest rooms, each with private bath and individually controlled thermostat. Popular breakfast dishes include puffed pancakes filled with fresh fruit. During the winter the Homestead hosts concerts sponsored by the local Jazz Society. **Pros:** quiet neighborhood; most bathrooms are quite large. **Cons:** town offers few dining options; no parking lot, but street parking no problem. ✉ *614 McLeod St.* 📫 *Box 466* ☎ *406/932–3033* 🛏 *4 rooms* 💳 *MC, V* 🍴 *BP.*

5

CAMPING **Halfmoon Campground.** At the end of a dusty road leading into the lovely Crazy Mountains, this respite with tent and trailer sites (up to 32 feet) is ideal for scenic picnicking, hiking, and fishing. Be aware that the altitude is 6,400 feet. 👍 *Pit toilets, drinking water (summer only), fire grates, picnic tables* 🛏 *12 sites* ✉ *11 mi north of Big Timber on U.S. 191, then 12 mi west on Big Timber Canyon Rd.* ☎ *406/932–5155* 🌐 *www.fs.fed.us/r1/gallatin* ✍ *Reservations not accepted* 💳 *No credit cards.*

West Boulder Campground and Cabin. Shady and cool, this remote setting is known for good fishing, access to the Absaroka-Beartooth Wilderness, and quiet camping. The cabin has electricity, a woodstove, a refrigerator, and water in summer. Reservations, available through National Reservation Service (☎ *877/444–6777* 🌐 *www.recreation.gov*), are essential for the cabin. 👍 *Pit toilets, drinking water (summer only), fire pits, picnic tables* ✉ *West Boulder Rd.; head 16 mi south of Big Timber on U.S. 298 to McLeod, 6½ mi southwest on Rd. 30, and 8 mi southwest on West Boulder Rd.* ☎ *406/932–5155* 🌐 *www.fs.fed.us/r1/gallatin* 🛏 *10 tent sites; 1 cabin* ✍ *Reservations not accepted for campsites* 💳 *No credit cards for campsites; AE, D, MC, V for cabin.*

NIGHTLIFE

The name may evoke unsavory images, but that doesn't stop fly-fishing anglers, ranchers, and curious tourists from filling the **Road Kill Cafe and Bar** (✉ *1557 Boulder Rd., U.S. 298, 15 mi south of Big Timber, McLeod* ☎ *406/932–6174*). Beer, burgers, and Road Kill T-shirts are big sellers. Weekly movie nights are complete with popcorn.

LIVINGSTON AND THE YELLOWSTONE RIVER

35 mi west of Big Timber via I–90, 116 mi west of Billings via I–90.

The stunning mountain backdrop to the town of Livingston was once Crow territory, and a chief called Arapooish said about it, "The Crow country is good country. The Great Spirit has put it in exactly the right place. When you are in it, you fare well; when you go out of it, you fare worse."

Livingston, along the banks of the beautiful Yellowstone River, was built to serve the railroad and the settlers it brought. The railroad still runs through this town of around 7,500, but now tourism and outdoor sports dominate the scene. Many writers and artists call Livingston home, and there are some 15 art galleries here. Robert Redford chose the town, with its turn-of-the-20th-century flavor, to film parts of the movie *A River Runs Through It*.

GETTING HERE AND AROUND

Livingston is reachable by I–90 from the east and west, and U.S. 89 from the north and south. The historic section, with its restaurants and attractions, is compact and walkable. There is one taxi company, but not one parking meter. The nearest airport is in Bozeman.

EXPLORING

The 1902 **Livingston Depot Center** is situated in the former Northern Pacific depot, which served as the gateway to Yellowstone for the park's first 25 years. It is now a museum with displays on Western and railroad history. ⊠ *200 W. Park St.* ☎ *406/222–2300* ⊕ *www.livingstonmuseums.org* ⊠ *Free* ☉ *Late May–early Sept., Mon.–Sat. 9–5, Sun. 1–5.*

The **Yellowstone Gateway Museum,** on the north side of town in a turn-of-the-20th-century schoolhouse, holds an eclectic collection, including finds from a 10,000-year-old Native American dig site, a flag fragment associated with the Battle of the Little Bighorn, and a Native cultures interpretive exhibit. Outdoor displays include an old caboose, a sheep wagon, a stagecoach, and other pioneer memorabilia. ⊠ *118 W. Chinook St.* ☎ *406/222–4184* ⊠ *$6, good for 2 consecutive days* ☉ *Late May–early Sept., daily 10–5; rest of Sept., Tues.–Sat. noon–4.*

Just south of Livingston and north of Yellowstone National Park, the **Yellowstone River** comes roaring down the Yellowstone Plateau and flows through Paradise Valley. Fifteen fishing access sites are found in this area, some with primitive public campsites (available on a first-come, first-served basis; for information contact Montana Fish, Wildlife & Parks Department at ☎ 406/247–2940). In addition to trout fishing, rafting and canoeing are popular here. With snowcapped peaks, soaring eagles, and an abundance of wildlife, a float on this section of the Yellowstone is a lifetime experience. U.S. 89 follows the west bank of the river, and East River Road runs along the east side.

Since the 1920s cowboys and cowgirls have ridden and roped at the annual **Livingston Roundup Rodeo,** held at the Park County Fairgrounds. All members of the Professional Rodeo Cowboy Association, participants descend on Livingston from around the United States and

Canada. ⊠ *46 View Vista Dr.* ☏ *406/222–0850 Livingston Chamber* ⊕ *www.livingston-chamber.com* ✉ *$12* ☉ *July 2–4, nightly at 8* PM.

Since the 1950s the **Wilsall Rodeo** (⊠ *U.S. 89 N, east on Clark St. past grain elevator to rodeo grounds, Wilsall* ☏ *406/578–2371*) has been showcasing cowboy and cowgirl events in mid-June at this ranching community at the base of the Crazy Mountains 35 mi east of Livingston.

OFF THE
BEATEN
PATH

Paradise Valley Loop. A drive on this loop takes you along the spectacular Yellowstone River for a short way and then past historic churches, schoolhouses, hot springs, and expansive ranches, all behind the peaks of the Absaroka-Beartooth Wilderness. From Livingston head 3 mi south on U.S. 89, turn east onto East River Road, and follow it over the Yellowstone River and for 32 mi through the tiny towns of Pine Creek, Pray, Chico, and Emigrant. You'll eventually hit U.S. 89 again, where roadside historic markers detail early residents' lives; follow it north to Livingston. ☏ *406/222–0850* ⊕ *www.livingston-chamber.com.*

SPORTS AND THE OUTDOORS

The Yellowstone River and its tributary streams draw fly-fishers from around the globe for Yellowstone cutthroat, brown, and rainbow trout. Hiking trails lead into remote accesses of surrounding peaks, often snowcapped through June.

BOATING With **River Source Outfitters** (⊠ *5237 Hwy. 89 S* ☏ *406/223–5134* ⊕ *www.riversourcerafting.com*) you can take multiday canoe trips on the Yellowstone or Marias rivers, half- or full-day white-water (class II and III rapids) rafting trips, or kayak lessons and tours. From November through April the company organizes dogsledding adventures. Boaters eager to explore the Yellowstone River will find a one-stop shop at **Rubber Ducky River Rentals** (⊠ *15 Mt. Baldy Dr.* ☏ *406/222–3746* ⊕ *www.riverservices. com*). Aside from guide and drop-off services, the store rents and sells boats and equipment, including its own line of rafts and kayaks.

FISHING **George Anderson's Yellowstone Angler** (⊠ *5256 U.S. 89 S* ☏ *406/222–7130* ⊕ *www.yellowstoneangler.com*) specializes in catch-and-release fly-fishing float trips on the Yellowstone River, wade trips on spring creeks, access to private lakes, and fly-casting instruction.

The fishing experts at **Dan Bailey's Fly Shop** (⊠ *209 W. Park St.* ☏ *406/222–1673 or 800/356–4052* ⊕ *www.dan-bailey.com*) can help you find the right fly, tackle, and outdoor clothing. Rental equipment, fly-fishing clinics, and float and wade trips are also available at this world-renowned shop.

HORSEBACK **Bear Paw Outfitters** (⊠ *136 Deep Creek Rd.* ☏ *406/222–6642 or 406/222–*
RIDING *5800*) ⊕ *www.bearpawoutfittersmt.com*) runs one-hour to full-day rides, pack trips of up to three days, and fly fishing/riding combos in Paradise Valley and Yellowstone National Park. **Rockin' HK Outfitters** (✉ *Box 123, Pray, 17 mi south of Livingston 59065* ☏ *406/333–4505* ⊕ *www.rockinhk.com*) will customize your multiday pack trip into the backcountry of Yellowstone National Park. The focus can be on fly-fishing or photography, as well as the riding experience itself.

5

CLOSE UP

Welcome to Fly-Fishing Heaven

Montana has the best rainbow, brown, and brook trout fishing in the country. This is the land of *A River Runs Through It,* the acclaimed Norman Maclean novel that most people know as a movie. Although the book was set in Missoula, the movie was filmed in the trout-fishing mecca of southwest Montana, and the Gallatin River played the role of Maclean's beloved Big Blackfoot. Several rivers run through the region, notably the Madison, Gallatin, and Yellowstone (more or less parallel to one another flowing north of Yellowstone National Park), as well as the Big Hole River to the west. All are easily accessible from major roads, which means that in summer you might have to drive a ways to find a fishing hole to call your own.

If you're only a casual angler, all you'll really need is a basic rod and reel, some simple tackle (hooks, sinkers, floaters, and extra line) and a few worms, which can all be bought at most outfitting and sporting-goods stores for less than $40. Many non-fly-fishers use open-face reels with lightweight line and spinners, which makes for a nice fight when they connect with trout. If you would like to try your hand at the more elegant stylings of fly-fishing, hire a local guide. Not only will he show you the good fishing holes, but a knowledge-able outfitter can teach you how not to work waters into a froth. Many guide services will provide you with fly-fishing equipment for the day.

WHERE TO EAT

$$ ✕ **Adagio Trattoria.** Baskets of corks here and there lend a proper Mediter-ranean ambience to this popular Italian eatery. Chef Jim Liska serves up a variety of homemade pastas, including penne with a choice of Tuscan or Sicilian meat sauce, plus veal, beef, and seafood dishes. ⊠ *101 N. Main St.* ☎ *406/222–7400* ▤ *AE, MC, V* ⊘ *Closed Sun. No lunch Fri. and Sat.*

$$ ✕ **Montana's Rib & Chop House.** Here, in the middle of cattle country,
STEAK you can expect the juiciest, tenderest steaks—such as the hand-cut rib eye—all made from certified Angus beef. Jambalaya, salmon, and baby back ribs marinated for 24 hours are also on the menu. ⊠ *305 E. Park St.* ☎ *406/222–9200* ▤ *AE, D, MC, V.*

¢ ✕ **Paradise Valley Pop Stand & Grill.** You can dine in or order takeout from
FAST FOOD this 1950s-style burger and ice-cream joint. The ice cream is made locally. ⊠ *5060 U.S. 89, 2 mi south of Livingston* ☎ *406/222–2006* ▤ *MC, V.*

$ ✕ **Park Place Tavern.** Chances are good that the next table or bar stool
AMERICAN here will be occupied by one of Livingston's many writers or artists. The long patio and equally long bar are popular in summer, and the interior, with yet another bar, displays art by Russell Chatham along with his world-record striped bass. Open from 11 to 10, the restaurant serves salads, burgers, and pasta along with seafood and steak entrées. ⊠ *106 E. Park St.* ☎ *406/222–5277* ▤ *AE, D, MC, V.*

WHERE TO STAY

$$$$ ▦ **63 Ranch.** Owned by the same family since 1929, this 2,000-acre working cattle ranch is one of Montana's oldest dude ranches. Only weeklong packages are available, and they include a full range of

activities, from horseback riding to fishing to helping check or move cattle. The rustic cabins are commodious yet comfortable, with log furniture and private baths. **Pros:** guests describe the number of riding trails as inexhaustible; even cautious riders report feeling secure accompanied by wranglers. **Cons:** 5,600-foot altitude might take some getting used to; no-credit-card policy equals loss of air miles. ⊠ *Off Bruffey La., 12 mi southeast of Livingston ✆ Box 979 59047 ☎ 406/222–0570 🖷 406/222–6363 ⊕ www.sixtythree.com ⇆ 12 cabins ⚹ In-room: no a/c, no phone, no TV. In-hotel: laundry facilities, Wi-Fi* ⊟ *No credit cards* ⊗ *Closed mid-Sept.–mid-June* ⍓❙ *FAP.*

$$$$ 🖃 **B Bar Ranch.** In winter this 9,000-acre working cattle ranch invites
★ guests for spectacular winter adventures in cross-country skiing and wildlife tracking. The ranch shares a 6-mi boundary with Yellowstone National Park, in Tom Miner Basin, 36 mi south of Livingston. Sleigh rides and naturalist-led trips into Yellowstone are some of the activities. Rates include meals and activities, and there's a two-night minimum stay. Four-wheel drive is recommended for reaching the ranch. **Pros:** a rare chance to enjoy winter ranch activities; owners' strong commitment to ecology is evident. **Cons:** ranch access involves travel on gravel roads. Pros: or con: absence of phone and TV is a blessing or a curse. ⊠ *818 Tom Miner Creek Rd., Emigrant (24 mi south of Livingston)* ☎ *406/848–7729* 🖷 *406/848–7793* ⊕ *www.bbar.com* ⇆ *6 cabins, 3 lodge rooms* ⚹ *In-room: no a/c, no phone, no TV, Wi-Fi. In-hotel: Wi-Fi* ⊟ *D, MC, V* ⊗ *Closed Mar.–mid-Dec.* ⍓❙ *FAP.*

¢–$$ 🖃 **Chico Hot Springs Resort & Day Spa.** The Chico Warm Springs Hotel
★ opened in 1900, drawing famous folks such as painter Charlie Russell (1864–1926) to the 96°F–103°F hot-spring pools. The hotel is surrounded by two large outdoor soaking pools, a convention center, and upscale cottages that open to views of 10,920-foot Emigrant Peak and the Absaroka-Beartooth Wilderness beyond. The least expensive rooms share a bath. The dining room ($$$–$$$$) is considered among the region's best for quality of food, presentation, and service. Pine nut–encrusted halibut with fruit salsa and Gorgonzola filet mignon are among the biggest draws. **Pros:** chef can't be beat; setting encourages closeness to nature. **Cons:** all guest rooms are not equal; not situated well for dining around. ⊠ *1 Old Chico Rd., Pray* ☎ *406/333–4933 or 800/468–9232 (outside MT only)* 🖷 *406/333–4694* ⊕ *www.chicohotsprings.com* ⇆ *82 rooms, 4 suites, 16 cottages* ⚹ *In-room: no a/c (some), kitchen (some), refrigerator (some), no TV, Wi-Fi. In-hotel: restaurant, bar, pool, spa, Wi-Fi, some pets allowed* ⊟ *AE, D, MC, V.*

$$$$ 🖃 **Mountain Sky Guest Ranch.** This full-service guest-ranch resort in the middle of scenic Paradise Valley and 30 mi north of Yellowstone National Park is a family favorite. The cabins feel luxurious after a day in the saddle. The children's programs offer age-appropriate activities such as hiking, swimming, crafts, hayrides, campfires, and a talent show. Dinners range from Western barbecue to gourmet treats such as grilled lamb loin topped with fig-and-port-wine glaze. There's a seven-night minimum stay in summer only. **Pros:** variety, preparation, and abundance of food win raves; fresh fruit delivered to cabins daily. **Cons:** big: 100% occupancy means 90 guests. ⊠ *Big Creek Rd.; U.S. 89 S, then west 4½ mi*

5

on Big Creek Rd., Emigrant (24 mi south of Livingston) ✆ *Box 1219, Emigrant 59027* ☎ *406/333–4911 or 800/548–3392* 📠 *406/333–4537* ⊕ *www.mtnsky.com* ➾ *32 cabins* ♿ *In-room: no a/c, no phone, refrigerator, no TV. In-hotel: bar, tennis court, pool, children's programs (ages 1–18), laundry facilities, Internet* ☰ *MC, V* 🍽 *FAP.*

$ 🏨 **The Murray Hotel.** Even cowboys love soft pillows, which is why they come to this 1904 town centerpiece, whose floors have seen silver-tipped cowboy boots, fly-fishing waders, and the polished heels of Hollywood celebrities. Antiques reflect a different theme in each guest room. Ask to see the third-floor suite that film director Sam Peckinpah once called home. Historic photos, a player piano, and stuffed game animals decorate the lobby and surround the antique elevator, which is still in use. **Pros:** easy stroll to shops and galleries; metal beds, claw-foot tubs, and pedestal sinks maintain period ambience. **Cons:** elevator requires an operator; some areas show their age. ⊠ *201 W. Park St.* ☎ *406/222–1350* 📠 *406/222–2752* ⊕ *www.murrayhotel.com* ➾ *30 rooms* ♿ *In-room: kitchen (some), Wi-Fi. In-hotel: restaurant, bar, Wi-Fi, some pets allowed* ☰ *AE, D, MC, V.*

CAMPING ⛺ **Paradise Valley/Livingston KOA.** Set among willows, cottonwoods, and small evergreens, this full-service campground is well situated along the banks of the Yellowstone River, 40 mi north of Yellowstone National Park. Pull-throughs accommodate RVs up to 95 feet. It's popular with families, who enjoy the heated pool, so it's a good idea to reserve ahead. ♿ *Flush toilets, full hookups, dump station, drinking water, guest laundry, showers, fire grates, picnic tables, public telephone, general store, swimming (indoor pool)* ➾ *82 RV sites, 27 tent sites; 22 cabins, 2 cottages* ⊠ *163 Pine Creek Rd.; 10 mi south of Livingston on U.S. 89, then ½ mi east on Pine Creek Rd.* ☎ *406/222–0992 or 800/562–2805* ⊕ *www.livingstonkoa.com* ☰ *D, MC, V* ⊙ *Closed mid-Oct.–Apr.*

⛺ **Pine Creek Campground.** A thick growth of pine trees surrounds this Paradise Valley campground at the base of the mountains. It's near the trailhead for challenging hikes to Pine Creek Waterfalls and the Absaroka-Beartooth Wilderness. ♿ *Pit toilets, drinking water, fire pits, picnic tables* ➾ *25 sites* ⊠ *9 mi south of Livingston on U.S. 89, then 6 mi east on Pine Creek Rd.* ☎ *406/222–1892 or 877/444–6777 (latter is National Reservation Service)* ⊕ *www.fs.fed.us/r1/gallatin* ☰ *AE, MC, V (cards through National Reservation Service only)* ⊙ *Closed early Sept.–late May.*

NIGHTLIFE

With dancing and country music, microbrews, video poker, and keno, the **Buffalo Jump Steakhouse & Saloon** (⊠ *5237 U.S. 89 S* ☎ *406/222–2987*) has livened up many a Saturday night in Livingston. Locals voted the jukebox at the **Murray Bar** (⊠ *201 W. Park St.* ☎ *406/222–6433* ⊕ *www.themurraybar.com*) the best in town, and its staff the friendliest. There's live music most weekends. Friday and Saturday evenings June through August, the **Pine Creek Cafe** (⊠ *2496 E. River Rd. [about 12 mi from town]* ☎ *406/222–3628*) serves live bluegrass music, barbecue burgers, and beer under the stars. The fun starts at 7.

SHOPPING

★ Livingston's beauty has inspired artists, as evidenced by the many fine-art galleries in town. The **Danforth Gallery** (✉ *106 N. Main St.* ☎ *406/222–6510*) is a community art center that displays and sells paintings, sculptures, and jewelry. **Visions West Gallery** (✉ *108 S. Main St.* ☎ *406/222–0337* ⊕ *www.visionswestgallery.com*) specializes in contemporary Western and wildlife art, including numerous works on the fly-fishing theme, from paintings and bronzes to hand-carved flies.

At the **Cowboy Connection** (✉ *110 S. Main St.* ☎ *406/222–0272*) you'll find two rooms filled with pre-1940 Western boots, art, photos, spurs, holsters, even the occasional bullet-riddled hat. For contemporary Western and Native American items, such as fringed jackets and skirts, and rattlesnake earrings, visit **Gil's Indian Trading Post** (✉ *207 W. Park St.* ☎ *406/222–0112*). The floorboards creak as you walk through **Sax and Fryer** (✉ *109 W. Callender St.* ☎ *406/222–1421*), an old-time bookstore specializing in Western literature, especially books by Montana authors. It's the oldest store in Livingston.

In addition to selling outdoor clothing, boots, and bicycles, **Timber Trails** (✉ *309 W. Park St.* ☎ *406/222–9550*) helps mountain bikers, hikers, and cross-country skiers with trail maps, directions, bike rentals and repairs, and friendly advice.

THREE FORKS

51 mi west of Livingston via I–90, 29 mi west of Bozeman via I–90.

Although the scenery in Three Forks is striking, it's the historic sites that make this place worth a visit. Sacajawea (circa 1786–1812) traveled in the area with her Shoshone family before she was kidnapped as a child by a rival tribe, the Hidatsas. Five years later she returned here as part of the Lewis and Clark expedition. In 1805 they arrived at the forks (of the Madison, Jefferson, and Gallatin rivers), now in Missouri Headwaters State Park, looking for the river that would lead them to the Continental Divide. A plaque in the city park commemorates her contribution to the expedition's success.

GETTING HERE AND AROUND

The town of Three Forks is easily walkable, but you'll want a car to reach the Headwaters and Buffalo Jump areas. There's ample free parking downtown. The nearest airport is Bozeman's Gallatin Field.

EXPLORING

★ The Madison, Jefferson, and Gallatin rivers come together to form the mighty Missouri River within **Missouri Headwaters State Park,** a National Historic Landmark. At 2,540 mi, the Missouri is the country's longest river. Lewis and Clark named the three forks after Secretary of the Treasury Albert Gallatin, Secretary of State James Madison, and President Thomas Jefferson. The park has historical exhibits, interpretive signs, picnic sites, hiking trails, and camping. ✉ *Trident Rd., 3 mi northeast of Three Forks on I–90, exit at Three Forks off-ramp, then go east on 205 and 3 mi north on 286* ☎ *406/994–4042* ⊕ *www.fwp.mt.gov* ✄ *$5* *per vehicle, includes admission to Madison Buffalo Jump; free with Montana license plate* ⊙ *Daily dawn–dusk.*

Within the **Madison Buffalo Jump** historic site is a cliff where Plains Indians stampeded bison to their deaths for more than 2,000 years, until European guns and horses arrived in the West. An interpretive center explains how the technique enabled Native Americans to gather food and hides. Picnic areas provide a restful break from touring. Be on the lookout for rattlesnakes here, and avoid wandering off the paths. ✉ *Buffalo Jump Rd., 5 mi east of Three Forks on I–90, exiting at Logan, then 7 mi south on Buffalo Jump Rd.* ☎ *406/994–4042* ⊕ *www.fwp. mt.gov* ✑ *$5 per vehicle, includes admission to Missouri Headwaters State Park; free with Montana license plate* ⊙ *Daily dawn–dusk.*

ⓒ The **Lewis and Clark Caverns,** Montana's oldest state park, hold some of the most beautiful underground landscapes in the nation. Two-hour tours lead through narrow passages and vaulted chambers past colorful, intriguingly varied limestone formations. The temperature stays in the 50s year-round; jackets and rubber-sole shoes are recommended. Note that the hike to the cavern entrance is mild. A campground sits at the lower end of the park. ✉ *Hwy. 2, 19 mi west of Three Forks* ☎ *406/287–3541* ✑ *$10* ⊙ *Mid-June–mid-Aug., daily 9–6:30; May–mid-June and mid-Aug.–Sept., daily 9–4:30.*

Thousands of local historical artifacts are on display in the **Headwaters Heritage Museum,** including a small anvil and all that is left of a trading post, Fort Three Forks, established in 1810. ✉ *Main and Cedar Sts. 59752* ☎ *406/285–4778* ✑ *Donations accepted* ⊙ *June–Sept., Mon.– Sat. 9–5, Sun. 1–5; Oct.–May by appointment.*

SPORTS AND THE OUTDOORS

BOATING In addition to arranging guided fly-fishing float trips, **Canoeing House and Guide Service** (✉ *11227 U.S. 287* ☎ *406/285–3488*) rents canoes and kayaks.

WHERE TO STAY AND EAT

¢ ✕ **Wheat Montana.** At Wheat Montana's Three Forks headquarters and
CAFE flagship restaurant/store, you can enjoy tasty sandwiches, freshly baked bread, and pastries such as gigantic cinnamon rolls. You can even purchase grind-your-own flour from their Prairie Gold Whole Wheat. ✉ *10778 Hwy. 287, I–90 at Exit 274* ☎ *406/285–3614 or 800/535–2798* ✉ *AE, MC, V* ⊙ *Daily 6 AM–7 PM; summer, 6 AM–8 PM.*

CAMPING ⚠ **Missouri Headwaters State Park.** Tent and trailer sites are strewn among the cottonwood trees of the campground at this park. Three pavilions detail the Lewis and Clark adventure through the area, and 4 mi of trails lead visitors through meadows and to vista points along the rivers. Reservations are taken only for groups. ⚺ *Flush toilets, pit toilets, drinking water, fire grates, picnic tables* ⟐ *17 sites* ✉ *Hwy. 286; 4 mi northeast of Three Forks on Hwy. 205, then north on Hwy. 286* ☎ *406/994–4042* ⊕ *www.fwp.mt.gov* ✉ *No credit cards* ⊙ *May–Sept.*

BIG SKY AND GALLATIN CANYON

75 mi southeast of Three Forks via I–90 and then U.S. 191; 43 mi southwest of Bozeman via I–90, then U.S. 191.

GETTING HERE AND AROUND

Bozeman has the nearest airport. **Karst Stage** (⊕ *www.karststage.com*) offers year-round airport shuttle service to Big Sky. The region known as "Big Sky" is actually three areas: the Mountain Village at the top of the 9-mi-long Lone Mountain Trail (Highway 64); the Meadow Village, 3 mi west of Highway 191 on Lone Mountain Trail; and the area around the intersection of Highway 191 and Lone Mountain Trail. **Skyline Bus** (⊕ *www.skylinebus.com*) offers year-round rides between these areas, as well as routes to Bozeman and back.

EXPLORING

The name of Lone Peak, the mountain that looms over the isolated community beneath Big Sky, is a good way to describe **Big Sky Resort,** one of the most remote major ski resorts in the country. Here you can ski a true wilderness. Yellowstone National Park is visible from the upper mountain ski runs, as are 11 mountain ranges in three states. The park's western entrance at West Yellowstone is about 50 mi away, along a route frequented by elk, moose, and bison (use caution when driving U.S. 191).

Conceived in the 1970s by national TV newscaster Chet Huntley, the resort area is the solitary node of civilization in otherwise undeveloped country, between Bozeman and West Yellowstone. Getting here invariably means at least one plane change en route to Bozeman and about an hour's drive to the resort through Gallatin Canyon, a narrow gorge of rock walls, forest, and the frothing Gallatin River.

This is not to suggest that Big Sky is primitive. Indeed, being just a few decades old and growing rapidly, the resort is quite modern in its design and amenities. You won't find crowds among all this rugged nature, but you will discover that all the perks of a major summer and ski vacation spot are readily available in Big Sky's three villages. One is in the Gallatin Canyon area along the Gallatin River and U.S. 191. Another, Meadow Village, radiates from the 18-hole Big Sky Golf Course. The third enclave, 9 mi west of U.S. 191, is the full-service ski resort itself, overlooking rugged wilderness areas and Yellowstone National Park.

Major real-estate developments around Big Sky have started to impinge upon the resort-in-the-wild atmosphere with exclusive developments such as Spanish Peaks and the gated Yellowstone Club. Still, outdoor pleasures abound. In addition to skiing, golfing, hiking, horseback riding, and other activities, Big Sky hosts many festivals, musical events, races, and tournaments. ⊠ *1 Lone Mountain Trail, Big Sky* ⅅ *Box 160001* ☎ *406/995–5000 or 800/548–4486* ⊕ *www.bigskyresort.com.*

In 1902 Frank Crail picked this spot for the headquarters of his 960-acre homestead and cattle ranch. Now the **Historic Crail Ranch** makes a pleasant picnic spot in the midst of Big Sky's Meadow Village area. To get here, drive west on Big Sky Spur Road, make a right on Little Coyote, go past the chapel, and make a left onto Spotted Elk Road in Meadow

Village. ⊠ *Spotted Elk Rd.* ☎ *406/995–2160* ⊕ *www.bigskychamber.com* ⊠ *Free* ☉ *Memorial Day–Labor Day, daily dawn–dusk.*

SPORTS AND THE OUTDOORS

FISHING
Fodor'sChoice
★

Rivers such as the **Gallatin,** which runs along U.S. 191, the Madison (one valley west), and the Yellowstone (one valley east) have made southwest Montana famous among fly-fishers, most of whom visit during the non-winter months.

East Slope Outdoors (⊠ *47855 Gallatin Rd., U.S. 191* ☎ *406/995–4369 or 888/359–3974* ⊕ *www.eastslopeoutdoors.com*) arranges guides for winter and summer fly-fishing. You can also rent or buy flies, rods and reels, clothing, and gifts here. Flies, rods and reels, clothing, equipment rentals, and guides are available at **Gallatin Riverguides** (⊠ *47430 Gallatin Rd., U.S. 191* ☎ *406/995–2290 or 888/707–1505* ⊕ *www.montana-flyfishing.com*). **Wild Trout Outfitters** (⊠ *47520 Gallatin Rd., U.S. 191* ☎ *406/995–2975 or 800/423–4742* ⊕ *www.wildtroutoutfitters.com*) offers fly-fishing instruction, full-day horse-pack fishing trips, float-tube fishing, and drift boat trips with stops for wade fishing at prime runs.

GOLF
The 18-hole Arnold Palmer–designed **Big Sky Golf Course** (⊠ *Black Otter Rd., Meadow Village* ☎ *406/995–5780 or 800/548–4486*) has challenging holes along the north fork of the Gallatin River, breezes from snowy Lone Peak, and the occasional moose, elk, or deer on the green.

HORSEBACK
RIDING
☙

Jake's Horses & Outfitting (⊠ *U.S. 191 and Beaver Creek Rd.* ☎ *406/995–4630 or 800/352–5956* ⊕ *www.jakeshorses.com*) will take you on one- to six-hour rides along mountainous trails on Forest Service lands year-round. Summer dinner rides and multiday pack trips inside Yellowstone National Park are also available. **Canyon Adventures** (⊠ *47200 Gallatin Rd., U.S. 191* ☎ *406/995–4450 or 800/520–7533* ⊕ *www.montanacanyonadventures.com*) leads one- and two-hour trail rides May through September in the Gallatin Canyon. There's also a ride-and-raft combo.

KIDS'
ACTIVITIES
☙

The kids-only Outdoor Youth Adventures program at **Lone Mountain Ranch** (⊠ *4 mi west of U.S. 191 on Lone Mountain Trail, Hwy. 64 and ½ mi down gravel Lone Mountain Ranch Rd.* ☎ *406/995–4644 or 800/514–4644*) includes building snow caves, tubing, snowshoeing, playing snow kickball, and cross-country skiing over snowy trails and through obstacle courses. From June through August, **Camp Big Sky** (⊠ *Box 161433 59716* ☎ *406/995–3194*) runs a day camp for visiting and local kids ages pre-kindergarten through middle school. Activities such as tennis, dance, golf, nature study, and soccer are held at Big Sky Community Park in Meadow Village and at other sites.

RAFTING
Geyser Whitewater Expeditions (⊠ *46651 Gallatin Rd., U.S. 191* ☎ *406/995–4989 or 800/914–9031* ⊕ *www.raftmontana.com*) has guided raft trips on the Gallatin River. **Montana Whitewater** (⊠ *63960 Gallatin Rd., U.S. 191* ☎ *406/763–4465 or 800/799–4465* ⊕ *www.montanawhitewater.com*) arranges half- or full-day rafting trips on the Gallatin, Madison, and Yellowstone rivers. The company also offers paddle-and-saddle combos and a five-day teen kayaking school.

Hitting the Slopes

It's called "cold smoke"—the exceedingly light, dry snow that falls on the mountains of southwest Montana—and it doesn't go to waste. All told, the region has six downhill ski areas and more than 390 km (245 mi) of cross-country trails. The season generally begins in late November or early December and runs through early to mid-April.

Downhill ski areas such as Bridger Bowl, Discovery, Moonlight Basin, Maverick, and Red Lodge Mountain are family-friendly, inexpensive, and relatively uncrowded. For steep skiers, one of the country's largest resorts, Big Sky, has more than 500 turns on a single slope; it's also a fine mountain for beginner and intermediate skiers.

The cross-country tracks of Lone Mountain Ranch stand out among the 40 or 50 trails in southwest Montana. They're groomed daily or weekly and are track-set for both classic and skate skiing. Backcountry skiing has no limits, with hundreds of thousands of skiable acres on public land.

5

SNOWMO-
BILING
Far and away the most popular nonskiing activity in the region is snowmobiling into and around Yellowstone National Park. West Yellowstone, about 50 mi south of Big Sky on U.S. 191, prides itself on being the "Snowmobile Capital of the World." The most popular excursion is the 60-mi round-trip between West Yellowstone and Old Faithful; the park allows in a few hundred commercially guided snowmobiles each day. **Canyon Adventures** (⊠ *47200 Gallatin Rd., U.S. 191* ☎ *406/994–4450 or 800/520–7533*) arranges snowmobiling excursions.

SNOWSHOEING
You can rent snowshoes through **Big Sky Rentals** (⊠ *Snowcrest Lodge, Plaza Area* ☎ *406/995–5841*) for use on the resort's 2-mi Moose Tracks trail, which wends through aspen groves. Quiet and picturesque snowshoe trails lead through the woods and meadows of **Lone Mountain Ranch** (⊠ *4 mi on Lone Mountain Trail, Hwy. 64, and ½ mi down gravel ranch road* ☎ *406/995–4644 or 800/514–4644*), where you can get a trail map and rent snowshoes and poles.

DOWNHILL SKIING AND SNOWBOARDING

For many years the attitude of more advanced skiers toward Big Sky was "big deal." There wasn't nearly enough challenging skiing to keep expert skiers interested for long, and certainly not for an entire ski week. As a remedy, the Big Sky people strung up the Challenger chairlift, one of the steepest in the country, and then installed a tram to the summit of Lone Peak, providing access to an array of steep chutes, open bowls, and at least one scary-steep couloir. The tram also gave Big Sky the right to claim the second-greatest vertical drop—4,350 feet—of any resort in the country.

None of that, however, has diminished Big Sky's otherwise easy-skiing reputation. There is still a good deal of intermediate and lower-intermediate terrain, a combination of wide-open bowl skiing higher up and trail skiing lower down. Additionally, there are 85 km (51 mi) of groomed cross-country skiing trails nearby at Lone Mountain Ranch.

MOONLIGHT BASIN

The Big Sky resort dominates downhill skiing in the area, but don't overlook the resort at **Moonlight Basin** (✉ *34 Madison Rd.* ✆ *Box 160040* ☎ *406/993–6000 or 877/822–0432* ⊕ *www.moonlightbasin.com*), with north-facing slopes overlooking the Lee Metcalf Wilderness Area.

The runs aren't as lengthy as they are next door at Big Sky, but Moonlight's

1,900 acres offer some unique knolls, chutes, and glades. Vertical drop is 4,150 feet, and runs are rated 21% beginner, 26% intermediate, 14% advanced, and 39% expert. Lift tickets cost $55. Purchase of "The Biggest Skiing in America" ticket ($94) gives access to 5,500 connected skiable acres at both Moonlight and Big Sky. The resorts share two lifts, making it easy to access both areas.

The other plus about skiing Big Sky is its wide variety of exposures. Many of the ski areas here are built on north-facing slopes, where snow usually stays fresher longer, protected from the sun. In addition to these, Big Sky also has plenty of runs facing south and east, and the differing snow textures that result make for more interesting skiing.

FACILITIES 4,350-foot vertical drop; 3,812 skiable acres; 150 runs on 3 mountains; 14% beginner, 26% intermediate, 40% advanced, 20% expert; 1 aerial tram, 4 high-speed quads, 1 quad chair, 5 triple chairs, 5 double chairs, 5 surface lifts.

LESSONS & PROGRAMS Half-day group-lesson rates at the **ski school** (☎ *406/995–5000 or 800/548–4486*) are $67. Powder, mogul, and snowboarding clinics are also available. There's also a ski school just for kids—whether they're first-timers or speedsters—with enthusiastic instructors.

LIFT TICKETS Lift tickets cost $79. Multiday tickets (up to 10 days) offer savings of up to $9 per day. Kids 10 and under ski free. "The Biggest Skiing in America" lift ticket ($94) allows access to both Big Sky Resort and Moonlight Basin, which make up the largest connected skiable terrain in the United States (5,500 acres).

RENTALS The resort's **Big Sky Ski Rentals** (☎ *406/995–5841*) at the base of the mountain offers rental packages for $35, and high-performance ski packages for $50. At **Gallatin Alpine Sports** (✉ *3091 Pine Dr., Meadow Village* ☎ *406/995–2313*) rentals run $25 with discounts for multidays; performance skis are $35 and demos, $45.

NORDIC SKIING

★ **Lone Mountain Ranch** (☎ *406/995–4644 or 800/514–4644* ⊕ *www.lmranch. com*) is a rare bird in cross-country and snowshoeing circles. Not only are there 85 km (51 mi) of groomed trails, but the network is superb, with everything from a flat, open, golf-course layout to tree-lined trails with as much as 1,600 feet of elevation gain (and loss). Much of the trail network provides a genuine sense of woodsy mountain seclusion. If there is a drawback, it's that moose sometimes wander onto the trails.

WHERE TO EAT

$$$$
STEAK
✕ **Buck's T-4 Lodge and Restaurant.** Within a historic log lodge and bar, this restaurant is known for its dinners of seafood, wild game, and hand-cut Montana steaks. ✉ *U.S. 191* ☎ *406/995–4111* ▤ *AE, D, MC, V*

$$
CAFÉ
✕ **Bugaboo Cafe.** This spacious café, possibly the best value in the area, serves contemporary fare, from breakfasts that feature a blue-crab omelet to dinners centered on rib eye, fish, and pork. On weekends, brunch is set out from 7 AM to 2 PM. ✉ *47995 Gallatin Rd., U.S. 191 59716* ☎ *406/995–3350* ▤ *AE, D, MC, V* ☉ *Closed Mon. No dinner Sun.*

$$$
AMERICAN
✕ **By Word of Mouth.** At night this restaurant fills with the boisterous merrymaking of the après-ski crowd—particularly Friday night, when a throng gathers for an all-you-can-eat fish fry. The menu includes coriander-dusted Alaskan sockeye salmon with apricot, pine nut, and sun-dried tomato, and sugar-and-spice-rubbed baby back ribs. The wine list is lengthy, and there are several local beers on tap. ✉ *2815 Aspen Dr., in Westfork Meadows* ☎ *406/995–2992* ⊕ *www.bigskycatering.com* ▤ *AE, D, MC, V* ☉ *No lunch.*

$$$$
CONTINENTAL
✕ **Moonlight Dinners.** For a unique dining experience, rendezvous at the Summit Hotel in Mountain Village to ride a Sno-Cat into the pristine land of Big Sky for a meal under the stars. While the chef prepares French onion soup, filet mignon, garlic mashed potatoes, and chocolate fondue with fresh fruit on a woodstove, you can sled on hills under the light of the moon and tiki lamps or relax around a bonfire. Yurt dining is accompanied by live music and candlelight. ⊡ *Box 160815, 59716* ☎ *406/995–3880* ⊕ *www.skimba.com* ⚲ *Reservations essential* ▤ *MC, V* ☉ *Late Nov.–mid-Apr.*

Westfork Meadows has several tasty eat-in or take-out spots. At **Wrap Shack** (☎ *406/995–3099*) wraps start out the size of a pizza, and stuffed, aren't a whole lot smaller. Choose as many fillings as you can handle. **Hungry Moose** (☎ *406/995–3045*) serves deli sandwiches as well as basic grocery items. **Blue Moon Bakery** (☎ *406/995–2305*) sets out a tempting array of scones, muffins, cakes, and cookies.

WHERE TO STAY

$$$$
Fodor'sChoice
★
🏨 **The Big EZ.** Atop a mountain at a 7,500-foot elevation, the Big EZ lodge overlooks other mountains and the Gallatin River drainage. All guest rooms are appointed with Western-style furnishings, an eclectic collection of fine art, and flat-screen TVs. Guests are housed in the main lodge and the Inn (a separate structure); the suite is in its own little stone building. The property includes a wine cellar, a 9-hole, par-72 championship putting course, and one of the state's largest outdoor hot tubs. Dinners are unusual, elegant, and savory: try pan-roasted caribou loin or African pheasant, and save room for Tasmanian-honey crème brûlée. **Pros:** river-rock fireplaces in guest rooms; massage room. **Cons:** not the easiest property to reach; not best choice for singles or those with disabilities. ✉ *7000 Beaver Creek Rd.* ⊡ *Box 160070 59716* ☎ *406/995–7000 or 877/244–3299* ▤ *406/995–7007* ⊕ *www. bigezlodge.com* ⇌ *12 rooms, 1 suite* ⚇ *In-room: no a/c (some), Wi-Fi. In-hotel: restaurant, bar, laundry service* ▤ *MC, V* ▥ *FAP.*

$$$$
🏨 **Lone Mountain Ranch.** Four-night to one-week packages include seasonal activities such as naturalist-guided trips to Yellowstone, cross-country

ski passes, and kids' camps. The ranch, known for its Nordic Ski Center, maintains 85 km (51 mi) of groomed trails for classic and skate cross-country skiing. An additional four trails totaling 10 km (6 mi) are for snowshoers only. Some activities cost extra, such as horse-packing trips to alpine lakes, fly-fishing, and downhill skiing. Lodging ranges from historic cabins to an elegant log lodge. Partake of a night of backcountry sleigh rides, dinner, and entertainment. **Pros:** guests praise the cozy lodgings; wide variety of adventure and nature-oriented activities. **Cons:** not a working ranch; accommodations range from old cabins to modern lodge. ⊠ *4 mi on Lone Mountain Tr., and ½ mi down gravel ranch road* ✆ *Box 160069, 59716* ☎ *406/995–4644 or 800/514–4644* 🖷 *406/995–4670* ⊕ *www.lmranch.com* ➩ *23 cabins, 7 rooms* ⚭ *In-room: no a/c, no phone, no TV. In-hotel: restaurant, bar, children's programs (ages 4–18)* ⊟ *D, MC, V* ⊘ *Closed Oct., Nov., Apr., and May* ⑩ *FAP.*

$$$$
Fodor's Choice
★
Rainbow Ranch Lodge. An April 2008 fire burned down the Rainbow Ranch Lodge's original 1919 main building, but a painstaking rebuilding effort has returned the lodge to its former glory. Log-accented cabins perch alongside the Gallatin River, where guests can fish from the riverbank or in the rainbow trout–stocked pond (catch and release). An outdoor fireplace stands beside the infinity hot tub. Animal and fishing motifs decorate the spacious guest rooms, which have wood-burning fireplaces (most), TVs discreetly hidden behind pictures, filtered water, lodgepole-pine beds, and down comforters. The exceptional restaurant ($$$$), decorated with Western paintings, has one of the state's largest collections of wines, 8,500 bottles, displayed in the Bacchus Room, where groups of up to 10 can dine. Fresh fish is flown in daily. Among the game dishes are mesquite-grilled elk tenderloin and Gorgonzola-crusted bone-in buffalo rib eye. **Pros:** guest room decks overlook the river; great use of wood, even in baths. **Cons:** situated along highway rather than in resort area; only coffee, tea, and some pastries put out in morning. ⊠ *42950 Gallatin Rd., U.S. 191* ✆ *Box 160336* ☎ *406/995–4132 or 800/937–4132* 🖷 *406/995–2861* ⊕ *www.rainbowranchbigsky.com* ➩ *21 rooms, 2 cabins, 2 private homes* ⚭ *In-room: Wi-Fi. In-hotel: restaurant, bar, spa* ⊟ *AE, D, MC, V* ⑩ *CP.*

$$$–$$$$
★
Summit at Big Sky. Along with having an absolute prime location at the foot of Big Sky's chairlifts, the Summit Hotel now has bragging rights for having hosted the First Family during President Obama's August 2009 visit to Montana. A Euro-Western flavor decorates the spacious rooms and suites, which are ideal for discriminating business travelers and families looking to be at the center of the mountain action. The best things about the Summit just may be the underground, heated parking garage, unusual in Montana, and the outdoor, year-round soaking pool. **Pros:** all the facilities one could wish; near slopes, shops, and restaurants. **Cons:** some miss the intimacy of smaller properties; attracts conventions. ⊠ *1 Lone Mountain Trail, Mountain Village* ✆ *Box 160001* ☎ *406/995–5000 or 800/548–4486* ⊕ *www.bigskyresort.com* ➩ *213 rooms, 8 suites* ⚭ *In-room: kitchen, Wi-Fi. In-hotel: 2 restaurants, room service, bar, pool, gym, spa, bicycles, children's programs (ages 2–12)* ⊟ *AE, D, DC MC, V* ⊘ *Closed mid-Apr.–late May and early Oct.–late Nov.* ⑩ *FAP.*

CAMPING   ⚠ **Greek Creek.** This Forest Service campground with RV and tent sites snuggles up to the Gallatin River under a canopy of tall evergreens. ⚒ *Pit toilets, drinking water, fire grates, picnic tables, swimming (river)* ⌁ *15 sites* ✉ *U.S. 191, 30 mi south of Bozeman* ☎ *406/587–9054 or 877/444–6777 (latter is National Reservation Service)* ⊕ *www.recreation.gov (National Reservation Service)* ⊟ *AE, D, MC, V (cards through National Reservation Service only)* ⊘ *Early May–late Sept.*

NIGHTLIFE AND THE ARTS

NIGHTLIFE   Some weekends the **Corral** (✉ *42895 Gallatin Rd., U.S. 191* ☎ *406/995–4249*) rocks to regional live bands. Other entertainment comes from quirky bartenders, pool-table bets, and legions of skiers, snowmobilers, and locals in for the Montana brews. With live music year-round on weekends the dance floor at **Half Moon Saloon** (✉ *45130 Gallatin Rd., U.S. 191* ☎ *406/995–2928*) rivals the saloon's long bar, mountain views, and pool tables as a draw. There's live rock music at **Whiskey Jack's** (✉ *Mountain Mall, 1 Lone Mountain Trail* ☎ *406/995–5786*), where the dancing often spills out onto the deck for a boogie in ski boots.

THE ARTS   Every July and August the **Music in the Mountains** (✉ *Meadow Village* ★ *Pavilion* ☎ *406/995–2742 or 877/995–2742*) summer concert series showcases such headliners as Taj Mahal, Willie Nelson, and the Bozeman Symphony Orchestra in outdoor venues.

SHOPPING

Top-of-the-line ski and snowboard equipment and outerwear are sold at **Big Sky Sports** (✉ *Mountain Mall, 1 Lone Mountain Trail* ☎ *406/995–5840*). Jewelry and women's and children's clothing, including ski wear, are among the offerings at **Willow Boutique** (✉ *Meadow Village* ☎ *406/995–4557*). Be sure to check out the fancy belts.

BOZEMAN

This recreation capital offers everything from trout fishing to whitewater river rafting to backcountry mountain biking to skiing. The arts have also flowered in Bozeman, the home of Montana State University. The mix of cowboys, professors, students, skiers, and celebrities make it one of the more diverse communities in the northern Rockies as well as one of the fastest-growing towns in Montana.

Bozeman has a strong Western heritage, readily evident at local museums, downtown galleries, and even the airport. In 1864 a trader named John Bozeman led his wagon train through this valley en route to the booming goldfields of Virginia City and southwest Montana. For several years this was the site of Fort Ellis, established to protect settlers making their way west along the Bozeman Trail, which extended into Montana Territory.

GETTING HERE AND AROUND

Several daily flights link Bozeman's Gallatin Field Airport to Great Falls, Denver, Minneapolis, Salt Lake City, and Seattle. The bright yellow **Streamline buses** (☎ *406/587–2434* ⊕ *www.streamlinebus.com*) offer free weekday and Saturday service between downtown, Montana State University, Bozeman Deaconess Hospital, and outlying shopping areas, as well as weekend late-night service and a route to and from Livingston. Free two-hour parking is available on and near Main Street; there's also a parking garage between Tracy and Black avenues on East Mendenhall Street.

You can easily maneuver downtown Bozeman's mix of Old West bars, saddle shops, upscale stores and restaurants, and espresso cafés on foot or by bicycle. To appreciate the town's diversity, stroll the residential area near the university, where mansions, bungalows, and every style in between coexist side by side. A vehicle is necessary—in winter, a four-wheel-drive vehicle is best—to explore the parks, trails, and recreation areas in the mountain ranges surrounding Bozeman.

VISITOR INFORMATION

Free maps for self-guided historical walking tours are available at the **Bozeman Area Chamber of Commerce** (⊠ *2000 Commerce Way* ☎ *406/586–5421*) and at the Gallatin Pioneer Museum.

EXPLORING BOZEMAN

TOP ATTRACTIONS

❷ Emerson Cultural Center. A school until 1992, this 1920 Gothic Revival brick building now houses 37 galleries, studios, and classrooms, plus a performing-arts hall. You can watch craftspeople at work, purchase artwork, take a class, or catch a performance here, plus enjoy a tasty lunch or dinner at the on-site Emerson Grill. ⊠ *111 S. Grand Ave.* ☎ *406/587–9797, 406/586–5247 for Grill* ⊕ *www.theemerson.org* ⌫ *Free* ☉ *Daily 10–5 and for scheduled evening performances.*

❸ Museum of the Rockies. Here you'll find a celebration of the history of the
⟳ Rockies region, with exhibits ranging from prehistory to pioneers, plus
Fodor'sChoice a planetarium with laser shows. Most renowned is the museum's Siebel
★ Dinosaur Complex housing one of the world's largest dinosaur fossil collections along with the largest-known T-rex skull, a Mesozoic Media Center, and a Hall of Giants complete with sound effects. Children love the hands-on science activities in the Explore Yellowstone Children's Discovery Center and the outdoors Tensley Homestead, with home-crafts demonstrations, including butter churning, weaving, and blacksmithing. May through mid-September, sheep, donkeys, and horses graze among the tall pasture grasses of the homestead. ⊠ *600 W. Kagy Blvd., south end of university campus* ☎ *406/994–2251* ⊕ *www.museumoftherockies.org* ⌫ *$10 museum and planetarium combo, $5 planetarium laser shows* ☉ *Mon.–Sat. 9–5, Sun. 12:30–5; daily 8–8 in summer.*

❶ Pioneer Museum. West of downtown, this redbrick former jail, built in 1911, serves as a reminder of the rough-and-tumble days of the past. Inside, the Gallatin Historical Society displays Native American artifacts, a model of Fort Ellis, a reconstruction of an 1870s log cabin, a research library, photo archives, and a bookstore. ⊠ *317 W. Main St.* ☎ *406/522–8122* ⊕ *www.pioneermuseum.org* ⌫ *$5* ☉ *June–Sept., Mon.–Sat. 10–5; Oct.–May, Tues.–Sat. 11–4.*

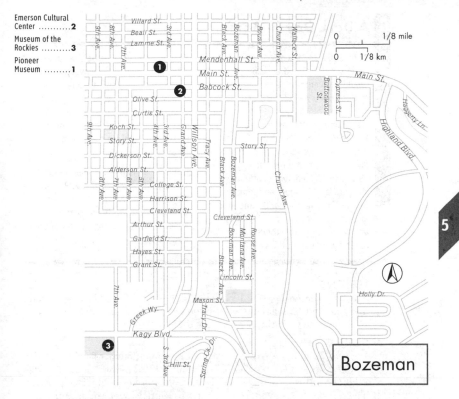

WORTH NOTING

Bozeman Hot Springs. You can soak for an hour or a day at Bozeman Hot Springs, with nine indoor pools, one outdoor pool, a sauna, spa, gym, and juice bar. ✉ *81123 Gallatin Rd., Hwy. 191, 5 mi west of Bozeman at Four Corners Junction of Huffine La. and U.S. 191* ☎ *406/586–6492* 🎫 *$8.50* ☉ *Mon.–Thurs. 7 AM–10 PM, Fri. 6 AM–dusk, Sat. dusk–11 PM, Sun. 8 AM–10 PM.*

SPORTS AND THE OUTDOORS

BICYCLING

Bozeman bike shops can supply all the equipment, repairs, and info that bike addicts might wish. **Bangtail Bicycle Shop** (✉ *137 E. Main St.* ☎ *406/587–4905*) is a full-service shop selling bikes, gear, and maps. **Chalet Sports** ✉ *108 W. Main* ☎ *406/587–4595*) rents mountain and road bikes in the summer, and cross-country and downhill skis in the winter. The staff at **Summit Bike & Ski** (✉ *26 S. Grand* ☎ *406/587–1064*) sells bikes, supplies, maps, and biking guidebooks. They don't do rentals.

A Dark Day in Bozeman

At 8:12 am on March 5, 2009, a natural gas leak sparked an explosion that would forever change the landscape of Bozeman's Main Street. The blast was heard blocks away, and windows were shattered as far down as the Baxter Hotel on West Main Street. When the fire and ash settled, one life was lost, half a historic city block had been leveled, two buildings were structurally damaged, and nine businesses were displaced. It happened at a time of economic uncertainty, and the community wondered what, if anything, would fill the void.

Things may not ever be the same, but there were signs of recovery in short order. Montana Trails Gallery moved to East Main Street, as did Boodles Restaurant. The iconic Rockin' R Bar and the American Legion launched plans to rebuild on their former locations.

Bozeman's Pioneer Museum (⊠ 317 *W. Main St.* ☎ *406/522–8122* ⊕ *www. pioneermuseum.org*) features an exhibit called The Block That Was Rocked, explaining the events of the tragic day.

FISHING

The **Bozeman Angler** (⊠ *23 E. Main St.* ☎ *406/587–9111*) sells fly rods and gear and arranges guided trips on several lakes, streams, and rivers, including the Gallatin, Madison, and Yellowstone rivers.

SKIING

☞ Located 20 minutes from downtown Bozeman, **Bridger Bowl** (⊠ *15795 Bridger Canyon Rd.* ☎ *406/587–2111 or 800/223–9609* ⊕ *www.bridgerbowl.com*) is known for skiing in "cold smoke," light, dry powder. The terrain, from steep, rocky chutes to gentle slopes and meadows, is the headline act at this community-owned mountain, where lift tickets ($45) are almost half the price of those at upscale resorts. One quad, five double, and two triple chair lifts access 71 named runs, which are ranked 20% beginner, 30% intermediate, 20% advanced, and 30% expert only. There are 311 acres of expert-only terrain, reached by the Schlasman's lift; skiers are required to carry avalanche transceivers. The mountain is open early December–early April. Fresh powder on the mountain? Look for a flashing blue beacon atop the former Baxter Hotel on Main Street.

Bohart Ranch & Cross-Country Ski Center (⊠ *16621 Bridger Canyon Rd.* ☎ *406/586–9070* ⊕ *www.bohartranchxcski.com*) maintains 29 km (18 mi) of groomed trails on ranch and Forest Service permit land for classic and skate technique skiing. Lessons and rentals are available. The season runs early December to late March. In summer the trails are open for hiking, mountain biking, and horseback riding. There's also an 18-hole Frisbee golf course.

WHERE TO EAT

$$ ✕**Cafe Internationale.** African batiks and masks decorate the walls of
CONTEMPORARY this popular eatery, where a large selection of hot and cold salads and
sandwiches greet the lunch crowd. For dinner the portobello-mushroom
lobster soup and fillet Madagascar are big favorites. ✉ *622 W. Mend-
enhall* ☎ *406/586–4242* ⊟ *AE, D, MC, V.*

$ ✕**Cateye Café.** Some call it funky; all call it good food at a fair price.
AMERICAN Named for the shape of Grandma Annable's glasses, this small restau-
★ rant serves breakfast and lunch, including a "Cat'serole" (the café's
term) of the Day at lunch. ✉ *23 N. Tracy Ave.* ☎ *406/587–8844* ⊕ *www.
cateyecafe.com* ⊟ *MC, V* ⊘ *No dinner.*

$$$$ ✕**John Bozeman's Bistro.** Located in Bozeman's historic downtown dis-
ECLECTIC trict, this contemporary café changes its menu regularly. Expect dishes
such as Jamaican jerk chicken, coconut fried shrimp, Sonoran pork
roulade, and fettuccine carbonara, and check out the "Superfoods"
gluten-free menu. ✉ *125 W. Main St.* ☎ *406/587–4100* ⊕ *www.john-
bozemansbistro.com* ⊟ *AE, D, MC, V* ⊘ *Closed Sun. and Mon.*

$$$ ✕**Looie's Downunder.** Situated in the historic downtown area, this res-
ECLECTIC taurant is popular for both the atmosphere (casual and intimate) and
the food. In addition to the sushi bar, Looie's is known for its certified
Angus beef, rack of lamb, extensive seafood selection, and a lengthy
wine list. ✉ *101 E. Main St.* ☎ *406/522–8814* ⊟ *AE, D, MC, V.*

$$ ✕**Montana Ale Works.** A cavernous brick building, the former North-
ern Pacific Railroad depot houses a full bar with a huge selection
of Montana microbrews, and a restaurant with a choice of quiet or
boisterous seating areas. In addition to the 40 beers on tap, the Ale
Works serves bison burgers, baked pasta dishes, Caribbean and Span-
ish dishes, and nightly specials such as fresh grilled halibut, scallops,
Kobe burgers, and steaks. ✉ *611 E. Main St.* ☎ *406/587–7700* ⊟ *AE,
D, MC, V* ⊘ *No lunch.*

$ ✕**Western Café.** A deer head sporting sunglasses surveys the cowboys
and families that pack the counter stools and tables at this down-home
breakfast and lunch spot. Peruse the local paper as you work your way
through biscuits and gravy, eggs with corned-beef hash, or pork chops.
There's nothing fancy outside or in, but for local color, this is it. ✉ *443
E. Main St.* ☎ *406/587–0436* ⊟ *D, MC, V* ⊘ *No dinner.*

WHERE TO STAY

$$–$$$ ⊞ **Gallatin Gateway Inn.** Back in 1927 the Milwaukee Railroad built this
inn as a stopping-off point for visitors to Yellowstone National Park.
Carved beams crisscross the 23-foot ceiling of the long, rectangular
lobby, and a modern, Western style decorates the guest rooms painted
in soothing earth tones. The bathrooms are fitted with original tile
work and brass fixtures. Crisp white linens and candlelight set the for-
mal tone in the restaurant ($$$–$$$$), which serves regional cuisine.
Pros: tile and brass uphold early-20th-century ambience; handicapped-
accessible rooms. **Cons:** staff could be a bit friendlier; long, somewhat
sparse lobby doesn't invite relaxation. ✉ *76405 Gallatin Rd., U.S.
191, Gallatin Gateway* ☎ *406/763–4672 or 800/676–3522* ⊕ *www.*

gallatingatewayinn.com ⚃ *33 rooms* ♿ *In-room: Wi-Fi In-hotel: restaurant, bar, tennis court, pool* ▭ *AE, D, MC, V* ⦿| *CP.*

$$$–$$$$ ⌂ **Gallatin River Lodge.** On the property of a 350-acre ranch, this full-service, year-round fly-fishing lodge has 2 mi of waterfront on the river for which it is named. Fly-fishing packages include a guide, three meals per day, airport transfers, and accommodations; a three-day minimum applies for packages. The elegant country inn has six suites, with Mission-style furniture, Western art, Jacuzzi tubs, fireplaces, and views of the river. **Pros:** lodge earns praise for matching guests with activities. **Cons:** most opt for three- to seven-night packages, so single-night reservations scheduled only two weeks in advance.; if fly-fishing isn't your thing, not the best choice. ✉ *9105 Thorpe Rd.* ☎ *406/388–0148 or 888/387–0148* 🖷 *406/388–6766* ⊕ *www.grlodge.com* ⚃ *6 suites* ♿ *In-room: no a/c, Wi-Fi. In-hotel: restaurant, bar* ▭ *AE, MC, V* ⦿| *BP.*

$$–$$$ ⌂ **Hilton Garden Inn.** This comfortable property with a friendly staff is a 10-minute drive from downtown. Since the hotel attracts business travelers, guest rooms are equipped with additional phone lines, microwaves, and other extras. There is a sumptuous breakfast buffet (extra charge) with omelets made to order. **Pros:** decor a step up from usual chain hotel look; staff helpful and pleasant. **Cons:** located in busy mall area. ✉ *2023 Commerce Way* ☎ *406/582–9900 or 877/782–9444* 🖷 *406/582–9903* ⊕ *www.bozeman.stayhgi.com* ⚃ *122 rooms* ♿ *In-room: refrigerator, Wi-Fi. In-hotel: room service, pool, gym, laundry facilities* ▭ *AE, D, DC, MC, V.*

$$–$$$
Fodor'sChoice
★
⌂ **Lehrkind Mansion Bed and Breakfast.** Built in 1897 for a wealthy master brewer, this B&B's gables, bays, and corner tower exemplify Queen Anne architecture. The current owners scoured antiques stores in five states to find the perfect furniture, art, and decorative items, including a 7-foot-tall Regina music box that plays 27-inch tin disks. Guest rooms have en-suite bath. **Pros:** grand oak staircase and carefully selected antique furnishings; proprietors are former Yellowstone National Park rangers who are happy to relate sightseeing itineraries as well as the history of the home. **Cons:** opt for Garden House if stairs are a problem; breakfast at set time. ✉ *719 N. Wallace Ave.* ☎ *406/585–6932 or 800/992–6932* ⊕ *www.bozemanbedandbreakfast.com* ⚃ *9 rooms* ♿ *In-room: no a/c, no TV.* ▭ *AE, D, MC, V* ⦿| *BP.*

$$–$$$
★
⌂ **Voss Inn.** This B&B occupies an elegant 1883 Victorian house and is lavishly furnished with antiques and knickknacks. Three guest rooms have fireplaces. Upon request, you can have afternoon tea in the parlor. Huge breakfasts are served in rooms or in the dining room. **Pros:** fringed lamps and metal beds true to Victorian era; bun warmer for morning muffins built into hallway radiator upstairs. **Cons:** decor, such as dark flowered wallpaper, lends formal touch; only one guest room on first floor, so not ideal if stairs are a problem. ✉ *319 S. Willson Ave.* ☎ *406/587–0982* 🖷 *406/585–2964* ⊕ *www.bozeman-vossinn.com* ⚃ *6 rooms* ♿ *In-room: no a/c (some), no TV.* ▭ *AE, D, MC, V* ⦿| *BP.*

NIGHTLIFE AND THE ARTS

NIGHTLIFE

The Filling Station, affectionately dubbed the Filler by locals (⊠ *2005 N. Rouse* ☎ *406/587–5009*) features live music on weekends and often during the week, ranging from bluegrass to hip-hop. Ranchers and students share the dance floor.

THE ARTS

The **Bozeman Symphony Society** (⊠ *1822 W. Lincoln, Suite B* ☎ *406/585– 9774* ⊕ *bozemansymphony.org*) runs a year-round concert series, often featuring talented university students and traveling artists. Performances take place at the Willson Auditorium, and there's one outdoor summer concert each year in Big Sky. During the summer months **Shakespeare in the Parks** performs several plays in repertoire. Most performances take place on the Montana State University campus. ⊠ *354 Strand Union Bldg., MSU* ☎ *406/994–1220* ⊕ *www2.montana.edu/shakespeare/* 🖭 *Free.*

SHOPPING

The two levels of **Country Bookshelf** (⊠ *28 W. Main St.* ☎ *406/587–0166* ⊕ *www.countrybookshelf.com*) house a large Montana and Western section, including many autographed works, as well as more general offerings. They'll ship all over the world. Outdoor wear, cross-country-skiing equipment, and boating gear are sold at **Northern Lights Trading Co.** (⊠ *1716 W. Babcock St.* ☎ *406/586–2225* ⊕ *www.northernlightstrading.com*). Don't be surprised to see any of the helpful staff members out on the trails, tracks, or rivers beside you. **Schnee's Powderhorn Outfitters** (⊠ *35 E. Main St.* ☎ *406/587–7373* ⊕ *www.schnees.com*), in business since 1946, sports two rooms filled with fishing gear and Western clothing.

HELENA

Montana's state capital is a city of 28,000, with 25 city parks, several museums, a thriving arts community, and its own minor-league baseball team. The southern part of the city, near the state Capitol and neighboring museums, mansions, and parks, is hilly and thick with lush greenery in summer. This quiet town started as a rowdy mining camp in 1864 and became a banking and commerce center in the Montana Territory. At the turn of the 20th century Helena had more millionaires per capita than any other town in the country. Some of that wealth came from ground now occupied by Main Street: called Last Chance Gulch, it was the first of several gulches that yielded more than $15 million in gold during the late 1800s. With statehood came a fight between the towns of Anaconda and Helena over which would be the capital. In a notoriously corrupt campaign in which both sides bought votes, Helena won. The iron ball of urban renewal has since robbed the town of much of its history, but Helena still has ornate brick-and-granite historic buildings along Last Chance Gulch.

GETTING HERE AND AROUND

Helena Airport has service from Billings, Great Falls, Minneapolis, Denver, Seattle, and Salt Lake City. The downtown historic area has a pedestrian-only mall on Last Chance Gulch with shops, coffeehouses, and restaurants. There are several historic sights here that you can see on foot, but other sights are spread out in the city and best accessed by automobile. A trolley (☎ *406/447–1580* ⊕ *www.downtownhelena. com* ☒ *50 cents*) travels between the Great Northern Town Center, Last Chance Gulch, and the Capitol area Monday through Friday, 10–6, stopping every half hour at designated points.

VISITOR INFORMATION

The **Helena Area Chamber of Commerce** (✉ *225 Cruse Ave.* ☎ *406/442–4120* ⊕ *www.helenachamber.com*) near Helena's historic downtown, can provide a brochure for a self-guided walking tour.

EXPLORING HELENA

TOP ATTRACTIONS

⑩ Cathedral of St. Helena. Modeled after the cathedral in Vienna, Austria, this Gothic Revival building has stained-glass windows from Bavaria and 230-foot-tall twin spires that are visible from most places in the city. Construction began in 1908 and was completed six years later. Note the white-marble altars, statues of Carrara marble, and gold leaf decorating the sanctuary. Free guided tours are given between 1 and 3 pm in the summer (Memorial Day–Labor Day) or with one day's advance notice. ✉ *530 N. Ewing St.* ☎ *406/442–5825* ☒ *Donations accepted* ☉ *Daily 7–6.*

⑫ Exploration Works. Rotating exhibits and interactive displays—which
☾ can include a transparent anatomical woman or the dissection of sheep
★ brains—are the main attractions at Helena's science museum. ✉ *995 Carousel Way* ☎ *406/457–1800* ⊕ *www.explorationworks.org* ☒ *$8 adults, $5.50 kids* ☰ *MC, V* ☉ *Tues.–Sat. 10–5, Sun. noon–5; closed Sun. mid-May–mid-Sept.*

⑪ Great Northern Carousel. Hand-carved grizzly bears, mountain goats, big-
☾ horn sheep, and river otters gallop through the center of town on this carousel, open 363 days a year (closed Thanksgiving and Christmas). You can buy locally made premium ice cream and fudge here. ✉ *989 Carousel Way* ☎ *406/457–5353* ⊕ *www.gncarousel.com* ☒ *$1.50* ☉ *Mon.–Thurs. 10:30–9, Fri. 10:30–10, Sat. 10–10, Sun. 11–8.*

❸ Last Chance Gulch. Four down-and-out prospectors designated this spot their "last chance" after they'd followed played-out gold strikes across the West. Their perseverance paid off when they discovered the first of several gold deposits here, which propelled Helena to the ranks of Montana's leading gold producers. Many of the mansions and businesses that resulted from the discovery of gold still stand on this historic route, also known as Main Street.

❼ Montana Governor's Mansion. Governors lived in this Victorian mansion between 1913 and 1959. You can take a scheduled guided tour, but call ahead, because some tours are unexpectedly canceled. ✉ *304*

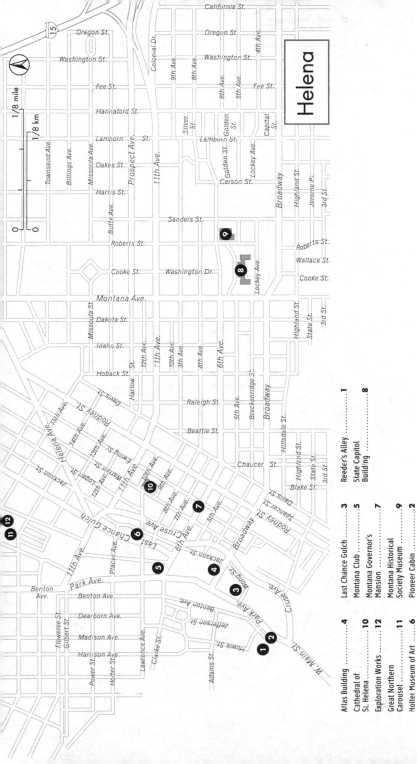

Helena

N. Ewing St. ☎ *406/444–4789* ⊕ *www.montanahistoricalsociety.org* 🖅 *$4* ⊙ *Tours May–Sept., Tues.–Sat. noon, 1, 2, and 3; Oct.–Apr., Sat. noon, 1, 2, and 3.*

❾ Montana Historical Society Museum. Highlights here include the MacKay
⟳ Gallery, which displays one of the most important collections of Western artist Charlie Russell's work, and the Haynes Gallery, where early black-and-white photos of Yellowstone National Park taken by F. Jay Haynes are on display. The expansive Montana Homeland exhibit, which contains nearly 2,000 historical artifacts, documents, and photographs, takes a thorough look at Montana from the time of the first settlers to the present. The venue also hosts special events and family days in summer, including programs on folk music, Native American culture, and cowboys. Call ahead for information on upcoming events. Out in front of the Historical Society Museum, catch the **Last Chance Train Tour** (☎ *406/442–1023 or 888/423–1023*) for an hour-long tour through historic neighborhoods of miners' mansions on the west side to the site where four miners made their first gold discovery on the gulch. Train tours cost $7.50 and take place Monday–Saturday at 11, 1, 3, and 5:30 in July and August, at 11, 1, and 3 Memorial Day weekend–June 30, and at 11 and 3 September 1–15. ⊠ *225 N. Roberts St., across from state capitol* ☎ *406/444–2694 or 800/243–9900* ⊕ *www.montanahistoricalsociety.org* 🖅 *$5* ⊙ *Memorial Day–Labor Day, Mon.–Sat. 9–5; Labor Day–Memorial Day, Mon.–Sat. 9–5.*

❷ Pioneer Cabin. This 1864 hand-hewn log structure now houses a museum of the gold-rush days of the 1860s. This is Helena's oldest surviving home. ⊠ *212 S. Park Ave.* ☎ *406/449–6688* ⊕ *www.reedersalley.com* 🖅 *Donation* ⊙ *Mid-May–mid-Sept., call for tour schedule; group tours available year-round by appointment.*

❶ Reeder's Alley. Miners' houses and distinctive shops built in the 1870s line this carefully restored area of Old Helena along with restaurants and a visitor center. Note the stone pillars and wooden stringers of the Morelli Bridge, spanning a walking trail that leads to the Mount Helena Trail System. ⊠ *Near south end of Last Chance Gulch* ⊕ *www.reedersalley.com.*

❽ State Capitol Building. The Greek Renaissance Capitol is topped by a dome of Montana copper and holds Charlie Russell's largest painting, a 12-by-25-foot depiction of Lewis and Clark. Self-guided-tour booklets are available. This building was thought so beautiful that South Dakota modeled its capitol in Pierre on the same design. ⊠ *6th Ave. and Montana Ave.* ☎ *406/444–4789* 🖅 *Free* ⊙ *May–Sept., Mon.–Sat. 9–3; Oct.–Apr., Sat. 10–2.*

WORTH NOTING
❹ Atlas Building. Stylized flames lap at dancing salamanders on the rooftop of this restored 1887 neo-Romanesque building, which a statue of Atlas appears to be hoisting on his shoulders. Once an insurance building, it's now home to the Upper Missouri Artists Gallery. ⊠ *7 Last Chance Gulch* ☎ *406/457–8240 or 800/457–8240* 🖅 *Free* ⊙ *Mid-May–mid-Sept., Tues.–Fri. 10–5:30, Sat. 10–5, Sun. 11–3; mid-Sept.–mid-May, Wed.–Sat. 11–5.*

6 **Holter Museum of Art.** Displays at this museum include folk art, crafts, photography, painting, and sculpture, with an emphasis on homegrown Montana artists. ⊠ *12 E. Lawrence Ave.* ☎ *406/442–6400* ⊕ *www.holtermuseum.org* ✉ *Donations accepted* ⊙ *Tues.–Sat. 10–5:30, Sun. noon–4. Closed Mon.*

5 **The Montana Club.** Built in 1905 by architect Cass Gilbert, who also designed the United States Supreme Court Building, the Montana Club was once the tallest building in the state. It's notable for its stone archways and contemporary I-beam construction underneath its classical facade. ⊠ *24 W. 6th Ave., corner of Fuller* ☎ *406/442–5980* ✉ *Free.*

SPORTS AND THE OUTDOORS

To stretch your legs, consider taking an hour-long hike to the top of Mt. Helena, which towers over the Last Chance Gulch pedestrian mall on the west edge of town. From the summit, you'll have panoramic views of the city, the Helena Valley, and the Rocky Mountains to the west.

BICYCLING
Helena is quickly gaining a reputation as a go-to place for mountain biking, in no small part because of the free **Saturday shuttle service** (⊕ *www. downtownhelena.com* ⊙ *Mid-June–mid-Sept.*) from Last Chance Gulch to Mount Helena's Ridge Trail, providing easy access to 8 mi of downhill single-track back to town. Other trails such as the Birdseye Loop and the Helena Valley Loop lead to mining towns and thick forests.

To find out more about bike routes, check the Web site of the **Helena Bicycle Club** (⊕ *www.helenabicycleclub.org*). The **Helena National Forest** (☎ *406/449–5201*) can provide bike route information by phone.**Great Divide Cyclery** (⊠ *336 N. Jackson* ☎ *406/443–5188*) rents full-suspension mountain bikes as well as road bikes.

BOATING
The more than 75 mi of shoreline of the **Canyon Ferry Recreation Area** (⊠ *Hwy. 284, near Helena, Townsend* ☎ *406/475–3310*) make a great place to fish, boat, sail, camp, and watch wildlife. The Missouri River once flowed freely here, though now a dam has created a lake. You can rent pontoon, fishing, and pedal boats from **Kim's Marina, RV Park and Store** (⊠ *8015 Canyon Ferry Rd., 2 mi east of dam on Hwy. 284* ☎ *406/475–3723* ⊕ *www.kimsmarina.com*).

★ In their travels on the Missouri River, Lewis and Clark made note of towering limestone cliffs. **Gates of the Mountains** (⊠ *Off I–15, 20 mi north of Helena* ☎ *406/458–5241* ⊕ *www.gatesofthemountains.com* ⊙ *Memorial Day–mid-Sept.*) boat tours take you past these same great stone walls, which rise 1,200 feet above the river.

FISHING
Western Rivers Outfitters (⊞ *Box 772, East Helena 59635* ☎ *406/227–5153*) offers day trips, overnight camping, and base-camp fishing excursions, and float trips on the Bitterroot, Blackfoot, Clark Fork, Missouri, Madison, Gallatin, and Jefferson rivers.

5

On the Trail of Lewis and Clark

America's greatest adventure began with the stroke of a pen, when in 1803 President Thomas Jefferson purchased the vast Louisiana Territory from cash-strapped France, effectively doubling the size of the United States. The land, stretching from the Gulf of Mexico to Canada and from the Mississippi River to the Rockies, was unmapped and virtually unknown to outsiders.

To understand what his $16 million had bought, Jefferson appointed a secret "Corps of Discovery" to venture west, make contact with native peoples, chart the landscape, and observe the growing British presence in the Pacific Northwest. The group would be headed by Jefferson's personal secretary, Meriwether Lewis, and another intrepid explorer, William Clark.

TIME IN MONTANA

On May 14, 1804, Lewis and Clark set out from St. Louis on their expedition with a party of 45 seasoned soldiers, scouts, interpreters, and others, poling up the Missouri River in well-stocked flatboats and keelboats. After wintering with the Mandans in North Dakota, the corps continued upriver in canoes and keelboats as soon as ice jams had cleared the waterway.

They entered what is now Montana on April 27, 1805, and followed the Missouri to its Montana headwaters—the confluence of the Jefferson, Madison, and Gallatin rivers. After they reached the Continental Divide, Shoshone Indians helped them cross the Rockies. The party then followed the Snake, Clearwater, and Columbia rivers, reaching the Pacific Ocean that fall.

On the return trip, the expedition split into two groups in Montana and explored several rivers, including the

Yellowstone. The explorers arrived back in St. Louis on September 23, 1806, having traveled more than 8,000 mi. They had spent more than a quarter of their time in Montana, where much of the land they observed remains unchanged today.

FOLLOWING IN THEIR FOOT-STEPS

If you want to trace Lewis and Clark's path, the best place to start is the Lewis and Clark National Historic Trail Interpretive Center in Great Falls, where the 200-year-old adventure unfolds before you. Nearby Giant Springs State Park marks the place where Clark discovered a large "fountain or spring" during an 18-mi portage around a series of waterfalls.

Missouri Headwaters State Park near Three Forks preserves the spot where the explorers traced the river to its origin. The Lolo Pass Visitor Center, on U.S. 12 at the Montana-Idaho border, also interprets the expedition.

Another way to connect with Lewis and Clark history is a boat tour on the "Mighty Mo." Several operators offer tours at Gates of the Mountains, north of Helena off I–15, and also at the White Cliffs area of the Upper Missouri National Wild and Scenic River below Fort Benton. A canoe rental and shuttle service on the Missouri near Loma gives you a self-guided option. And look for Lewis and Clark Trail signs along state, U.S., and interstate highways that follow the expedition's route.

WHERE TO EAT

$$ ✕ **Benny's Bistro.** An art deco–inspired interior fills out this small but CONTEMPORARY spacious restaurant, which started out serving comfort food but has ★ branched into more exotic fare. It's known for its creamy tomato soup with fresh rosemary and its smoked-trout martini appetizer: local smoked trout with capers, cucumbers, baguette, and seasoned cream cheese, served in a martini glass. The bistro features live music, usually jazz, on Friday and Saturday at 7 PM. ⊠ *108 E. 6th Ave.* ☎ *406/443–0105* ⊟ *AE, D, MC, V* ⊗ *Closed Sun. No dinner Mon. and Tues.*

$$$ ✕ **The Caretaker's Cabin.** Located next to the Pioneer Cabin, the 1865- CONTEMPORARY built Caretaker's Cabin is one of the oldest houses in Helena. The cabin has been transformed into a cozy fine-dining restaurant that offers a constantly changing menu emphasizing locally raised, organic food, as well as a five-course, prix-fixe menu on Saturday evening. Dishes could include herbed rack of lamb, king crab legs, Greek shrimp, pork enchiladas, or New York strip teriyaki stir-fry. Price of the prix-fixe meal includes two appetizers, soup and salad du jour, dessert, and coffee or tea. Wine and beer are BYOB. ⊠ *212 S. Park Ave.* ☎ *406/449–6848* ⚑ *Reservations essential* ⊟ *No credit cards* ⊗ *Closed Sun.–Tues.*

$$$$ ✕ **Last Chance Ranch.** An all-you-can-eat prime-rib dinner follows a AMERICAN wagon ride (included in the price). Dinner, served family-style at 7 PM ★ in Montana's largest tepee, includes salads, potatoes, and huckleberry cheesecake, all accompanied by a singing cowboy. ⊠ *Transportation from Helena to ranch, 8 mi southwest of town, is included in price* ☎ *406/442–2884 or 800/505–2884* ⊕ *www.lastchanceranch.biz* ⚑ *Reservations essential* ⊟ *MC, V* ⊗ *Closed Oct.–May.*

$$$ ✕ **Lucca's.** This cozy restaurant was quietly impressing locals before it ITALIAN made its move to Last Chance Gulch, where out-of-towners now regularly enjoy the Italian fare, steaks, lamb chops, and impressive wine list. Try Pollo alla Lucca's, the house specialty: chicken breast stuffed with Genoa salami and provolone cheese in a light, crispy crust. Limited hours and a small dining area make reservations a must. ⊠ *56 N. Last Chance Gulch59601* ☎ *406/457-8311* ⚑ *Reservations essential* ⊟ *AE, D, MC, V* ⊗ *Closed Mon. and Tues. No lunch.*

¢ ✕ **No Sweat Cafe.** Wooden booths give this restaurant an old-time, casual AMERICAN feel. Potatoes figure heavily into the breakfast menu, in items such as the Bakery Ladies' Special: potatoes and sausage, with garlic, green onions, and cheese. There are vegetarian specials on weekdays, and the lunch menu includes burgers and enchiladas. ⊠ *427 N. Last Chance Gulch* ☎ *406/442–6954* ⊟ *No credit cards* ⊗ *Closed Mon.*

$$ ✕ **On Broadway.** Wooden booths, discreet lighting, and brick walls con- ITALIAN tribute to the comfortable ambience at this Italian-fusion restaurant. Popular dishes include rib-eye steak and pasta puttanesca (sautéed Greek olives, artichoke hearts, red bell peppers, red onions, capers, and pine nuts tossed in linguine). When the state legislature is in session, representatives make this a boisterous place. ⊠ *106 Broadway* ☎ *406/443–1929* ⚑ *Reservations not accepted* ⊟ *AE, D, MC, V* ⊗ *Closed Sun. No lunch.*

5

¢ ✗ **The Staggering Ox.** The unique deli sandwiches here have even more
AMERICAN unique, often political, names. Try the Capitol Complex (loaded with
different deli meats and cheese), or the Nuke (ham, turkey, roast beef,
and three cheeses). The "clubfoot" sandwiches are served on specialty
breads shaped like a can of beans. Zany decor ranges from old records
dangling from the ceiling to various artists' paintings. ⊠ *Lundy Center,
400 Euclid Ave.* ☎ *406/443–1729* ▤ *MC, V.*

$ ✗ **Toi's Thai.** Possibly the best Thai restaurant in Montana, the tiny Toi's
THAI is always crowded. Every dish is hand-cooked by Thai native Toi Areya
★ Tyler. Specialties include pad thai, panang—a beef curry dish—and
green curries. ⊠ *423 N. Last Chance Gulch* ☎ *406/443–6656* ⌖ *Reservations essential* ▤ *MC, V* ☉ *Closed Mon.and Tues.*

$$$ ✗ **Windbag Saloon & Grill.** This historic restaurant in the heart of down-
AMERICAN town was called Big Dorothy's until 1973, when a crusading county attor-
★ ney forced Dorothy to shut down. Now it's a family restaurant, named for
the political debates you're likely to hear while dining on burgers, quiche,
salads, and sandwiches, or steaks and seafood at dinnertime. It also has a
large selection of imported beer, on tap and in bottles. A bounty of cher-
rywood gives the place a warm, comfortable feel. ⊠ *19 S. Last Chance
Gulch* ☎ *406/443–9669* ▤ *AE, D, MC, V* ☉ *Closed Sun.*

WHERE TO STAY

¢–$$$ ▦ **Canyon Ferry Mansion.** Saved from inundation in 1954 when the Can-
★ yon Ferry Reservoir was created, this former cattle baron's home was
relocated to a premier perch above the lake. Antiques accent the frilly
modern furnishings and lovingly restored woodwork throughout the
B&B. In addition to several private rooms, there's a dorm-style bunkhouse that sleeps seven, as well as a "honeymoon cabin" with Jacuzzi.
Outdoorsy types come here for summer water sports, winter ice boating, and year-round fishing; impatient lovers come for no-wait elop-
ing at the on-site chapel. **Pros:** meticulously restored home; friendly
host. **Cons:** remote location; price-tagged furnishings give the feel of
staying in an antiques store. ⊠ *7408 U.S. 287, 30 mi southeast of Helena at mile marker 74, Townsend* ☎ *406/266–3599 or 877/933–7721*
▦ *406/266–4003* ⊕ *www.canyonferrymansion.com* ⇖ *7 rooms, 3 with
bath; 1 bunkhouse; 1 wheelchair-accessible cabin* ⌂ *In-room: Wi-Fi. In-
hotel: spa, beachfront, bicycles* ▤ *AE, D, MC, V* ⦿❘ *BP.*

$–$$ ▦ **Holiday Inn Express.** This hotel is staffed with pleasant locals who
know the region and just may share a favorite fishing spot with you.
At the junction of U.S. 12 and I–15, the motel provides easy access to
those just needing a place to sleep for the night. **Pros:** convenient; reasonably priced. **Cons:** doesn't offer much beyond a typical chain-hotel
experience. ⊠ *701 Washington St.* ☎ *406/449–4000 or 800/465–4329*
⊕ *www.hiexpress.com* ⇖ *75 rooms, 7 suites* ⌂ *In-room: Wi-Fi. In-
hotel: gym, laundry facilities* ▤ *AE, D, DC, MC, V* ⦿❘ *CP.*

$$ ▦ **The Sanders Bed and Breakfast.** Colonel Wilbur Sanders, one of the first
Fodor'sChoice senators of Montana, built this three-story Victorian mansion in 1875.
★ The colonel's rock collection is still in the front hall, and the B&B has
retained his furnishings. Most of the rooms overlook mountain-ringed
downtown Helena. Breakfasts are a work of art: Grand Marnier French

toast, orange soufflé, or gingerbread waffles. **Pros:** incredibly accommodating hosts; first-class breakfasts; warm, relaxing atmosphere. **Cons:** dim reading light in room. ⊠ *328 N. Ewing St.* ☎ *406/442–3309* 🖷 *406/443–2361* ⊕ *www.sandersbb.com* ⇘ *7 rooms* ⚛ *In-room: Internet.* ▤ *AE, MC, V* ⏀ *BP.*

CAMPING ⚠ **Cromwell-Dixon Campground.** High above Helena on MacDonald Pass at 6,320 feet, this forested spot is frequented by migrating birds in spring and fall. ⚛ *Pit toilets, drinking water, fire grates, picnic tables* ⇘ *15 sites* ⊠ *MacDonald Pass, U.S. 12* ☎ *406/449–5490* ⊕ *www.fs.fed.us/r1/helena* ☉ *Early June–mid-Sept.*

NIGHTLIFE AND THE ARTS

Late May through mid-September, live music plays in downtown parks and plazas Wednesday evening from 5 to 9 as part of the **Alive at Five** (☎ *406/447–1535* ⊕ *www.downtownhelena.com*) series. The type of music and the venues vary, but it's always free and good family fun.

In a remodeled historic stone jail, the **Myrna Loy Center for the Performing Arts** (⊠ *15 N. Ewing St.* ☎ *406/443–0287* ⊕ *www.myrnaloycenter.com*)—named after the Montana-born actress—hosts live performances by nationally and internationally recognized musicians and dance troupes. Two theaters show foreign and independent films.

SHOPPING

★ Since 1951 many of the nation's best ceramic artists have come to work in residency at the **Archie Bray Foundation** (⊠ *2915 Country Club Ave.* ☎ *406/443–3502* ⊕ *www.archiebray.org*). Wander near the five antiquated, 8-foot-high, dome-shape brick kilns on a self-guided walking tour, and visit the gift shop, which sells work produced by foundation artists. It's open Monday–Saturday 10–5 and Sunday 1–5.

A refreshing stop in the historic center of town, the independent **Montana Book and Toy Company** (⊠ *331 N. Last Chance Gulch* ☎ *406/443–0260* ⊕ *www.mtbookco.com*) lines its shelves with regional and hard-to-find books, unique toys, games, and gifts.

Most every need of the outdoor recreationist can be met at **The Base Camp** (⊠ *5 W. Broadway* ☎ *406/443–5360* ⊕ *www.thebasecamp.com*) which rents camping, kayaking, and cross-country ski equipment, as well as offering clothing, books, maps, gear galore, and friendly information.

☽ For an old-fashioned sweet treat, pull up a stool at the **Parrot Confectionery** (⊠ *42 N. Last Chance Gulch* ☎ *406/442–1470*), a soda fountain and candy store built in the 1920s that sells everything from chocolate malts with homemade ice cream to hand-dipped chocolates and a regional favorite, cherry phosphates.

THE SOUTHWEST CORNER

In Montana Territory days, the mineral wealth of this remote area drew hard-drinking miners, women of easy virtue, thieves, and the people who became rich on it all. Abundant winter snowfall coats the mountains and feeds the lush valleys, where ranching and forestry are the main industries and where remnants of the mining era abound.

DEER LODGE

60 mi southwest of Helena via U.S. 12 and I–90, 80 mi southeast of Missoula via I–90, and 60 mi northwest of Butte via I–90.

Deer Lodge, a quiet community of 3,400 residents, maintains a complex of history museums in and near its old state penitentiary. Many locals make their living by ranching, which came to the 55-mi-long Deer Lodge Valley in 1862, when John Grant built the area's first cabin and began a cattle operation, selling beef to miners. Ranching remained the primary industry as the town of Deer Lodge developed. Its name derives from a 40-foot-high geothermal mound that used to emit steam from its top; Native Americans thought it resembled a large medicine lodge. The minerals and water attracted deer, and so the Native Americans named the place Deer Lodge. The mound is hidden behind trees and buildings at the Warm Springs State Hospital.

GETTING HERE AND AROUND

Deer Lodge is small and easily walkable, with most of the attractions on or near Main Street. There's plenty of free on-street parking. The nearest airports are in Helena and Butte.

EXPLORING

A single admission charge ($9) grants you access to the Old Montana Prison Museum, the Montana Auto Museum, the Frontier Montana Museum, and Yesterday's Playthings.

Built in 1871, the old Montana Territorial Prison did not shut down until 1979. It's now the **Old Montana Prison Museum,** where you can enter cells and learn about early Montana law. Also on display is the gallows tree taken from town to town in territorial days to hang convicted prisoners. ⊠ *1106 Main St.* ☏ *406/846–3111* ⊕ *www.pcmaf.org* ☞ *$9, includes admission to other 3 complex museums* ☉ *June–Aug., daily, call for hrs; Sept.–Oct. and April–May, Wed.–Sun., call for hrs.*

The **Montana Auto Museum** is a car buff's delight. Displays include more than 150 vintage Mopars, Chevys, Fords, and Studebakers dating from 1903 to the 1970s, including such rarities as a 1928 REO Speedwagon. ⊠ *1106 Main St.* ☏ *406/846–3111* ⊕ *www.pcmaf.org* ☞ *$9, includes admission to other 3 complex museums* ☉ *June–Aug., daily, call for hrs; Sept.–Oct. and Apr.–May, Wed.–Sun., call for hrs.*

The **Frontier Montana Museum** displays hats, saddles, spurs, chaps, and all things cowboy. Also here are Civil War items, Native American artifacts, and Desert John's Saloon, complete with whiskey memorabilia. ⊠ *1106 Main St.* ☏ *406/846–0026* ⊕ *www.pcmaf.org* ☞ *$9, includes admission to other 3 complex museums* ☉ *Mid-May–mid-Sept., daily, call for hrs.*

Whimsical old toys inhabit **Yesterday's Playthings.** Admission here grants you access to the Montana Auto Museum, Frontier Montana Museum, and Old Montana Prison Museum. ✉ *1106 Main St.* ☎ *406/846–1480* ⊕ *www.pcmaf.org* ✆ *$9, includes admission to 3 other museums* ⊙ *Mid-May–mid-Sept., daily, call for hrs.*

The **Powell County Museum** focuses on local history; it includes a hand-carved wood folk-art collection, photographs, mining memorabilia, and vintage furniture and household items. ✉ *1193 Main St.* ☎ *406/846–1694* ⊕ *www.pcmaf.org* ✆ *Free* ⊙ *June–Sept., daily noon–5.*

⟳ Daily tours of the 1,600-acre **Grant-Kohrs Ranch National Historic Site,** a working cattle ranch run by the National Park Service, provide insight into ranching life in the 1860s. You can learn about roping steers, watch blacksmithing demonstrations, and bounce along in a covered wagon. The annual Grant-Kohrs Ranch Days, with demonstrations and kids' programs, takes place in mid-July. ✉ *Grant Circle, ½ mi off I–90* ☎ *406/846–2070* ⊕ *www.nps.gov/grko* ✆ *Free* ⊙ *June–Aug., daily 8–5:30; Sept.–May, daily 9–4:30.*

WHERE TO EAT AND STAY

¢ ✗ **Yak Yak's.** Save room for one of the 40 different milk shakes and malts
AMERICAN at this Western-front eatery, which serves a bit of everything: breakfast fare, burritos, cold and grilled sandwiches, salads, and soups. ✉ *200 Main St.* ☎ *406/846–1750* ⚓ *Reservations not accepted.*

¢–$ 🏨 **Scharf's Motor Inn.** Directly across from the Old Montana Prison complex of museums, this nondescript, conveniently located motel offers a family-style restaurant (¢–$$) with no-nonsense fare such as ham and eggs, burgers, and chicken-fried steak. **Pros:** near museums and town; playground for the kids; the price is right. **Cons:** generic rooms. ✉ *819 N. Main St.,* ☎ *406/846–2810* 🖷 *406/846–3412* ⊕ *www.scharfsmontana.com* ↻ *42 rooms, 1 9-person house* ⚭ *In-room: Wi-Fi. In-hotel: some pets allowed* ▭ *AE, D, DC, MC, V.*

CAMPING ⛺ **Indian Creek Campground.** Set among brush and flats, this campground along tiny Indian Creek has large campsites, plus cable TV hookups and Wi-Fi. It's a good idea to make reservations. ⚭ *Flush toilets, full hookups, drinking water, guest laundry, showers, picnic tables, electricity* ↻ *51 full hookups, 10 partial hookups, 10 tent sites* ✉ *745 Maverick La.* ☎ *406/846–3848 or 800/294–0726* ▭ *MC, V* ⊙ *Mid-Apr.–Oct. 15.*

ANACONDA

22 mi south of Deer Lodge via I–90, 24 mi west of Butte via I–90 and Rte. 1.

Nicknamed the Smelter City, Anaconda is a window on the age of the copper barons, who ran this town from the 1880s through the 1950s. A number of sites preserve traces of Anaconda's rough-and-tumble history, including the dormant 585-foot smokestack, visible for miles, of the copper-smelting works around which the town was built. Copper is no longer the chief industry here, but even the Jack Nicklaus–designed golf course uses smelter-tailings slag for sand traps. Anaconda is also an ideal spot for fishing and hiking, and it sits at the base of the rugged

5

Pintler Mountains, popular for cross-country skiing, downhill skiing, and backcountry adventures.

GETTING HERE AND AROUND

Anaconda is motorist- and pedestrian-friendly; streets are uncrowded, and parking is free.

EXPLORING

The **Anaconda Visitor Center,** in a replica railroad depot, displays memorabilia of the town's copper history. Here you can board a 1936 **Vintage Bus** for a tour of historic Anaconda. ✉ *306 E. Park Ave.* ☎ *406/563–2400* ⊕ *www.anacondamt.org* ✆ *Visitor center free, bus $8* ☉ *Visitor center weekdays 9–5, mid-May–mid-Sept., Sat. 9:30–4. Bus mid-May–mid-Sept., Mon.–Sat. at 10 and 2.*

The **Copper Village Museum and Arts Center** houses displays on the area's history along with local artwork. The center also hosts musical performances and special events. ✉ *401 E. Commercial St.* ☎ *406/563–2422* ⊕ *www.coppervillageartcenter.com* ✆ *Free* ☉ *Tues.–Sat. 10–4.*

The classic art deco **Washoe Theatre** (✉ *305 Main St.* ☎ *406/563–6161*), built in 1931, was ranked by the Smithsonian as the fifth-most-beautiful theater in the nation. Murals and ornamentation in silver, copper, and gold leaf are some of the highlights of this theater, which is open nightly for movies and other events.

At 585 feet tall, "the Stack" at **Anaconda Smoke Stack State Park** is a solid reminder of the important role the Anaconda Copper Company played in the area's development. Built in 1919, the stack, one of the tallest freestanding brick structures in the world, is listed on the National Register of Historic Places. Smelting operations ceased in 1980. There's a viewing and interpretive area with displays and historical information, but you cannot access the smokestack itself. ✉ *Hwy. 1* ☎ *406/542–5500* ⊕ *fwp.mt.gov* ✆ *Free* ☉ *Daily dawn–dusk.*

OFF THE BEATEN PATH

Anaconda-Pintler Wilderness. Overlapping three ranger districts of the Beaverhead-Deerlodge National Forest, the 159,000-acre Anaconda-Pintler wilderness area extends more than 30 mi along the Continental Divide to the southwest of Anaconda. Elevations range from 5,400 feet near the Bitterroot River to 10,793 feet at the summit of West Goat Peak. Glaciation formed many spectacular cirques, U-shape valleys, and glacial moraines in the foothills. The habitat supports mountain lions, deer, elk, moose, bears, and many smaller animals and birds. About 280 mi of Forest Service trails cross the area. If you hike or ride horseback along the Continental Divide, at times you can view the Mission Mountains to the northwest and the mountains marking the Idaho-Montana border to the southwest. If you want to explore the wilderness, you must obtain a detailed map and register your plans with a Forest Service office. Stock forage is scarce, so if you're riding a horse, bring concentrated feed pellets. Note that no motorized travel is permitted in the wilderness area. There are more than 20 access points to the area, including popular ones at Moose Lake, Georgetown Lake, and the East Fork of the Bitterroot River. ✉ *Access to East Fork of Bitterroot River via U.S. 93* ☎ *406/821–3201* ✆ *Free* ☉ *Daily 24 hrs.*

Pintler Scenic Highway. The 63 mi of mountain road on this highway pass a ghost town, historic burgs, and Georgetown Lake. The road begins in Anaconda and ends on I–90 at Drummond, backdropped by the 159,000-acre Anaconda-Pintler Wilderness. ☎ 406/563–2400 *for information on highway.*

SPORTS AND THE OUTDOORS

BICYCLING Check with **Sven's Bicycles of Anaconda** (⊠ 220 Hickory St. ☎ 406/563–7988) for local advice, including the best mountain-biking routes, from back roads to challenging mile-high trails. In winter Sven's rents ice skates, and offers ski and snowboard tunes and repairs.

CROSS-COUNTRY SKIING Beautifully groomed skate and classic-ski trails climb nearly to the Continental Divide at the **Mt. Haggin Cross-Country Ski Trails** area, the state's largest wildlife management area, with more than 54,000 acres. Twenty-five kilometers of trails are maintained by volunteers from the Mile High Nordic Ski Club (⊕ *www.milehighnordic.org*). There's a warming hut but there are no services. Information is available at Sven's Bicyclesat Hickory St. and Commercial Ave. (☎ 406/563–7988). To get to the area from Anaconda, head southwest on Highway 1, cross the railroad tracks, and look for the sign to Wisdom; from here make a left onto Highway 274 and follow it for 11 mi to the parking area.

DOWNHILL SKIING Powder skiing at **Discovery Ski Area** (⊠ *Hwy. 1, 23 mi northwest of Anaconda at Georgetown Lake* ☎ 406/563–2184 ⊕ *www.skidiscovery. com*), an inexpensive family resort, offers thrills on the extreme steeps and extensive beginner and intermediate runs.

GOLF At the public 18-hole, Jack Nicklaus-designed **Old Works Golf Course** (⊠ *1205 Pizzini Way* ☎ 406/563–5989 ⊕ *www.oldworks.org*), on the site of Anaconda's historic Old Works copper smelter, hazards are filled with smelter-tailings slag instead of sand.

WHERE TO EAT AND STAY

$$–$$$$ 🏨 **Fairmont Hot Springs Resort.** This resort between Anaconda and Butte is a great option for families. Although not much to look at, the Fairmont has naturally heated indoor and outdoor swimming pools, a 350-foot waterslide, a playground, and a wildlife zoo in a beautiful setting. There's also an 18-hole golf course on the grounds. **Pros:** huge, hot pools are great for kids of any age. **Cons:** waterslide not included with room charge; detractors point to outdated facilities and lackluster food. ⊠ *1500 Fairmont Rd., Anaconda* ☎ 406/797–3241 or 800/332–3272 🖶 406/797–3337 ⊕ *www.fairmontmontana.com* ⇆ *153 rooms, 23 suites* ⚑ *In-room: Wi-Fi. In-hotel: restaurant, bar, golf course, tennis courts, pools* ▤ *AE, D, MC, V.*

¢–$ 🏨 **Seven Gables Resort.** At Georgetown Lake, this simple, clean lodge has views of the Pintler Mountains and is 4 mi from skiing and across the road from fishing. The restaurant ($–$$$) serves simple fare such as pressure-fried chicken and burgers; there's also a salad bar. **Pros:** convenient to fishing. **Cons:** miles from most services. ⊠ *20 Southern Cross Rd.* ☎ 406/563–5052 ⊕ *www.sevengablesmontana.com* ⇆ *9 rooms* ⚑ *In-room: no a/c, refrigerator, Wi-Fi. In-hotel: restaurant, bar, beachfront* ▤ *AE, D, MC, V.*

5

CAMPING   ⚠ **Lost Creek State Park.** A short trail at this scenic recreation area leads to the Lost Creek Falls. Views of limestone cliffs rising 1,200 feet above the canyon floor, and frequent sightings of bighorn sheep and mountain goats are some of the attractions of this park. The campground has hiking trails and creek fishing. ♿ *Pit toilets, drinking water, fire grates, picnic tables, swimming (creek)* ⛺ *25 sites, 1 wheelchair-accessible with toilet* ✉ *1½ mi east of Anaconda on Hwy. 1, then 2 mi north on Hwy. 273, then 6 mi west* ☎ *406/542–5500* ⊕ *fwp.mt.gov/lands/site_280851.aspx* ⚓ *Reservations not accepted* ☺ *May 1–Nov. 30.*

> ## WORD OF MOUTH
>
> "Butte is rich in mining history, the city itself is built half on a hill dotted with gallows frames and the 'no longer operational' Berkely Pit. Butte was once known as the richest hill on earth. So if you have an interest in mining, etc., Butte's your place." —Lynn 5

BUTTE

30 mi east of Anaconda via Hwy. 1 and I–90, 79 mi northwest of Virginia City via Hwy. 287 and Hwy. 55, 68 mi south of Helena via I–15.

Dubbed the "Richest Hill on Earth," Butte was once a wealthy and rollicking copper-, gold-, and silver-mining town. During its heyday, 100,000 people from around the world lived here; by 1880 Butte had generated about $22 billion in mineral wealth. The revived historic district, Uptown Butte, is now a National Historic Landmark area. Numerous ornate buildings recall the Old West, and several museums preserve the town's past. Today about 34,000 people live in the Butte–Silver Bow County area. The city maintains a strong Irish flavor, and its St. Patrick's Day parade is one of the nation's most notorious.

GETTING HERE AND AROUND
Uptown Butte's attractions are easily accessible on foot, but you'll want some kind of motorized vehicle if you'll be staying in "The Flats" south of I-90. A **municipal bus** (⊕ *www.co.silverbow.mt.us/transit/* ⛟ *60 cents*) plies four routes within the city. Other than during St. Patrick's Day and other festivals, free parking is plentiful. Delta/Skywest is currently the only major carrier operating out of Butte's Bert Mooney Airport, offering two flights a day to and from Salt Lake City.

VISITOR INFORMATION
You can catch hour-and-a-half narrated tours on a red trolley ($10 for adults) at the **Butte–Silver Bow Chamber of Commerce Visitor and Transportation Center** (✉ *1000 George St.* ☎ *800/735–6814 or 406/723–3177* ⊕ *www.buttechamber.org*), just off I–90 at Exit 126. You also can pick up free information about the area and take a stroll down the scenic Blacktail Creek Walking Path.

EXPLORING
Keeping watch over Butte is **Our Lady of the Rockies,** on the Continental Divide. The 90-foot-tall, 80-ton statue of the Virgin Mary is lighted at night. For a 2½-hour bus tour, stop by the visitor center, run by a nonprofit, nondenominational organization. ✉ *3100 Harrison Ave., at Butte Plaza Mall* ☎ *406/782–1221 or 800/800–5239* ⊕ *www.ourladyoftherockies.*

com 🖥 *$15* ⊙ *June–Sept., Mon.–Sat. at 10 and 2, Sun. at 11 and 2, weather permitting.*

Thanks to old mining waste, Butte has the dubious distinction as the location of the largest toxic-waste site in the country. Some underground copper mines were dug up in the 1950s, creating the **Berkeley Open Pit Mine,** which stretches 1½ by 1 mi, reaches 1,800 feet deep, and is filled with toxic water some 800 feet deep. A viewing platform allows you to look into the now-abandoned mammoth pit where more than 20 billion pounds of copper, 704 million ounces of silver, and 3 million ounces of gold were extracted from the Butte mining district. ✉ *Continental Dr. at Park St.* ☎ *406/723–3177 or 800/735–6814* 🖥 *$2* ⊙ *May–Sept., Mon.–Sat. 8–8, Sun. 9–6, weather permitting.*

★ The **Clark Chateau Museum,** an elegant 1898 four-story Victorian mansion that was built by William Clark as a wedding gift for his son Charles, is open for guided tours. The house, a replica of one wing of the Chateau de Chenonceau in France's Loire Valley, displays 18th- and 19th-century furniture, textiles, and collectibles as well as artwork. ✉ *321 W. Broadway* ☎ *406/723–7600* 🖥 *$4* ⊙ *May–Sept., Tues.–Sat. 10–4.*

William Clark, one of Butte's richest copper barons, built the **Copper King Mansion** between 1884 and 1888. Tours of the house take in the hand-carved oak paneling, nine original fireplaces, antiques, a lavish ballroom, and frescoes. The house doubles as a bed-and-breakfast. ✉ *219 W. Granite St.* ☎ *406/782–7580* ⊕ *www.thecopperkingmansion. com* 🖥 *$7.50* ⊙ *May–Sept., daily 9–4; Oct.–Apr. by appointment.*

More than 1,300 mineral specimens are displayed at Montana Tech University's **Mineral Museum,** including a 27½-troy-ounce gold nugget and a 400-pound smoky quartz crystal. ✉ *1300 W. Park St.* ☎ *406/496–4414* ⊕ *www.mbmg.mtech.edu* 🖥 *Free* ⊙ *June 15–Sept. 15, daily 9–5; Sept. 16–June 14, weekdays 9–4.*

The **Mai Wah Museum** contains exhibits on the history of the Chinese and other Asian settlers of Butte. The two historic buildings it occupies were constructed to house Chinese-owned businesses: the Wah Chong Tai Company and the Mai Wah Noodle Parlor. ✉ *17 W. Mercury St.* ☎ *406/723–3231* ⊕ *www.maiwah.org* 🖥 *Donations accepted* ⊙ *June–Sept., Tues.–Sat. 11–5; open in winter by appointment.*

For a behind-the-scenes look at the shadier side of Butte's heyday, **Old Butte Historical Adventures** leads guided walking tours to underground speakeasies, brothels of the Red Light District, and the former city jail, known as the "Butte Bastille." ✉ *117 N. Main St.* ☎ *406/498–3424* ⊕ *www.buttetours.info.*

OFF THE BEATEN PATH

Sheepshead Recreation Area. At this designated Wildlife Viewing Area you might glimpse elk, deer, moose, waterfowl, and birds of prey. The area is wheelchair accessible, and offers paved walking trails, a fishing dock, picnic tables, a rentable pavilion, horseshoe pits, and drinking water. ✉ *13 mi north of Butte on I-15 to Exit 138, Elk Park, west on Forest Service Rd. 442, follow signs for 6 mi* ☎ *406/494–2147* 🖥 *Free* ⊙ *June 15–Labor Day, daily.*

5

SPORTS AND THE OUTDOORS

FISHING   **Tom's Fishing and Bird Hunting Guide Service** (⊠ *3460 St. Ann St.* ☎ *406/723–4753 or 800/487–0296*) arranges float and wade trips for blue-ribbon trout fishing.

HORSEBACK   **Cargill Outfitters** (⊠ *40 Cedar Hills Rd., Whitehall* ☎ *406/494–2960*
RIDING   ⊕ *www.ironwheel.com*), which is just over the Continental Divide, 20 minutes east of Butte, offers two-hour to full-day horseback trips into the Highland Mountain range.

WHERE TO EAT

$$ ✗ **Broadway Café.** This turn-of-the-20th-century building is the place
PIZZA   for gourmet pizzas and salads. Salad dressings, sauces, and dough are
★   all made on the premises, and the enclosed deck's panoramic view of the city can be enjoyed year-round. Pizza by the slice is available at lunchtime. On Friday night there's live music. ⊠ *302 E. Broadway* ☎ *406/723–8711* ⊟ *AE, D, MC, V* ☉ *Closed Sun.*

$$ ✗ **Freds Mesquite Grill.** This spacious newcomer to the Butte scene has
AMERICAN   made its mark by offering contemporary spins on old favorites, all of which are cooked in the restaurant's mesquite grill. Choices range from hamburgers and barbecue chicken sandwiches to halibut, filet mignon, and kebabs. The Caesar dressing is made fresh every day, and the bar offers a wide variety of cocktails and specialty drinks as well as Northwestern microbrews. ⊠ *205 S. Arizona* ☎ *406/723–4440* ⊟ *D, MC, V.*

¢   ✗ **Town Talk Bakery.** No visit to Butte is complete without trying a pasty,
AMERICAN   the traditional miner's dinner of meat, potatoes, and onion baked inside a pastry shell. This bakery is one of the best of several eateries that serve these pocket-size meals; they also sell doughnuts, cookies, cakes, and breads. There are no tables; all items are takeout. ⊠ *611 E. Front St.* ☎ *406/782–4985* ⊟ *No credit cards* ☉ *Closed Sun. and Mon.*

$$$ ✗ **Uptown Café.** Fresh seafood, steaks, poultry, and pasta are served in
CONTEMPORARY   this elegant, low-key restaurant that's one of southwest Montana's finest
Fodor's Choice   eateries. Try the scallops Provençal, sautéed with tomatoes, feta cheese,
★   and garlic. A rotating exhibit of paintings by local artists lines the walls. ⊠ *47 E. Broadway* ☎ *406/723–4735* ⊟ *AE, D, MC, V.*

WHERE TO STAY

$–$$$ ▦ **Best Western Butte Plaza Inn.** Butte's largest lodging is convenient to shopping, sports events, and the interstates. The rooms are clean and comfortable, if somewhat bland. **Pros:** no surprises; decent breakfast bar; full-service restaurant attached. **Cons:** generic; can be loud; not walking distance to the Uptown Butte sights. ⊠ *2900 Harrison Ave.* ☎ *406/494–3500 or 800/543–5814* ᛫ *406/494–7611* ⊕ *www.bestwestern.com* ⟳ *134 rooms* ⚬ *In-room: Wi-Fi. In-hotel: restaurant, bar, pool, laundry facilities, parking (free), some pets allowed* ⊟ *AE, D, MC, V* ⊚⊙ *BP.*

¢–$$ ▦ **Copper King Mansion Bed and Breakfast.** Completed in 1888 as the home of notorious Copper King William Andrews Clark, the mansion remains much in its original state, and is the only privately owned mansion in Montana accessible to the public through seasonal tours. Six of the mansion's 35 rooms are used as a bed-and-breakfast, and the owners have attempted to re-create the experience of living like a turn-of-the-century millionaire, with such furnishings as a hand-carved fireplace, burled walnut bed, and a circular shower that hits you from all sides. Pros: where else can you live like a Copper King? The furniture, the stories, and the history are all genuine and first-rate. Cons: even kings get hot without air-conditioning. ☒ *219 W. Granite St.* ☎ *406/782–7580* ⊕ *www.thecopperkingmansion.com* ⬚*4 rooms, 2 suites* ⚹ *In-room: no a/c.* ⎜Oⵏ *BP* ⊟ *MC, V.*

¢–$ 🏨 **Hotel Finlen.** In continuous operation since it opened in 1924, Finlen, with its lobby of ornate chandeliers and pillars, stands in testament to Butte's heyday, when the hotel played host to the likes of Charles Lindbergh and Mrs. Herbert Hoover. Once boasting more than 200 rooms under the mansard roof of this nine-story, French Second Empire structure, most of those are now apartments, with only 20 hotel rooms remaining—plus another 32 in the adjacent Finlen Motor Inn. The rooms are unremarkable, but some provide excellent views of Uptown Butte. Pros: elegant, historic lobby; excellent value; best location in Uptown Butte. Cons: not all rooms have views; small parking lot; tiny bathrooms. ☒ *100 E. Broadway* ☎ *406/723–5461* ⬚*20 hotel rooms, 3 suites, 32 motel rooms* ⚹ *In-hotel: Wi-Fi, laundry services* ⊟ *AE, D, DC, MC, V.*

$$–$$$ 🏨 **Toad Hall Manor Bed and Breakfast.** Built as a private home in the early
Fodor'sChoice 1990s, this mansion has a historic feel thanks to hardwood accents, mar-
★ ble tile, and a classic redbrick exterior. Each of the four guest rooms is named after a character from Kenneth Grahame's *The Wind in the Willows.* The ground-floor Papa Otter's Place, with its Victorian-style furnishings, marble-accented Jacuzzi, and French doors opening to a private garden, probably offers the best value. Sir Badger's Suite, which takes up the entire fifth floor with two bedrooms, a two-person Jacuzzi, walk-in closet, and loft-style windows, ranks as the most luxurious option. Pros: a classic B&B experience. Cons: only four rooms, so you need to book well in advance. ☒ *1 Green La.* ☎ *406/494–2625 or 866/443–8623* ⬚ *406/494–8025* ⊕ *www.toadhallmanor.com* ⬚*4 rooms* ⚹ *In-hotel: Wi-Fi* ⊟ *AE, D, MC, V* ⎜Oⵏ*BP.*

CAMPING ⛺ **Butte KOA.** This large and grassy campsite with cottonwood trees has a playground and allows fishing in the on-site Silver Bow Creek. It's next to the Butte visitor center and is easily accessed from the interstate. It's a good idea to reserve ahead. ⚹ *Flush toilets, full hookups, partial hookups (water), dump station, drinking water, guest laundry, showers, picnic tables, food service, electricity, public telephone, general store, swimming (pool)* ⬚ *100 RV sites (full or partial hookups), 20 tent sites; 4 cabins* ☒*1601 Kaw Ave., off I–90 at Exit 126* ☎ *406/782–8080 or 800/562–8089* ⊕ *www.koa.com* ⊟ *D, MC, V* ⊙ *Mid-Apr.–Oct.*

VIRGINIA CITY

72 mi southeast of Butte via Hwys. 2, 41, and 287; 68 mi southwest of Bozeman via Rte. 84, U.S. 287, and Rte. 287.

Remnants of Montana's frontier days, Virginia City and its smaller neighbor, Nevada City, are two of the state's standout attractions. Boardwalks pass in front of partially restored historic buildings, and 19th-century goods stock the stores. Virginia City prospered when miners stampeded into Montana Territory after the 1863 discovery of gold. The diggings were rich in Alder Gulch, and Virginia City eventually became Montana's second territorial capital. Enticed by the city's wealth, criminals came to prey on the miners. In turn, vigilance committees held lightning-fast trials and strung up the bad guys. The outlaws were buried atop Boot Hill, overlooking town.

GETTING HERE AND AROUND

Virginia City is easily walkable; the smaller Nevada City is 1 mi west on Hwy. 287. Except during busiest times, free parking is readily available on Wallace Street or nearby side streets.

VISITOR INFORMATION

At the **Virginia City Depot Visitor Center** you can get information on theater, historic accommodations, and gold panning, and buy train tickets to Nevada City. ⊠ *430 W. Wallace St.* ☎ *406/843–5247* ⊕ *www.virginiacitymt.com* ✉ *Free* ☉ *Memorial Day–Labor Day, daily 9–5.*

EXPLORING

The eclectic assortment of items dating from 1860 to 1900 at the **Thompson-Hickman Memorial Museum** includes a petrified wedding cake, the eponymous limb of "Club Foot" George Lane, rifles, and numerous photographs. The collection is made up of the heirlooms of three local families. The local library is upstairs. ⊠ *Wallace St.* ☎ *406/843–5238* ✉ *Donations accepted* ☉ *Memorial Day–Labor Day, daily 10–5.*

A 1910 narrow-gauge steam train, the **Baldwin Locomotive No. 12,** Montana's only operating steam locomotive run by volunteer crews, travels between Virginia City and Nevada City on weekends from July 4 through Labor Day, as well as Memorial Day weekend. On weekdays a smaller gas-powered locomotive, the C.A. Bovey No. 8, makes the same journey. ☎ *406/843–5247* ⊕ *www.virginiacitymt.com* ✉ *$15 round-trip for the Baldwin, $8 round-trip for the C.A. Bovey.*

Full-moon evenings of June, July, and August feature **Moonlight and Steam Trains,** in which a moonlight steam locomotive ride is topped off with drinks and munchies at Virginia City's Bale of Hay Saloon. ✉ *$20, includes drink* ☉ *Memorial Day–Labor Day, one trip per month during full moon, 10 pm–11:30 pm.*

★ The living-history **Nevada City Open Air Museum,** down the road from Virginia City, preserves the town as it was at the turn of the 20th century, with restored buildings, thousands of artifacts from the gold-rush era, and weekend demonstrations. Included in the collection is the **Depuis House,** from the PBS television series *Frontier House.* ⊠ *U.S. 287, 1½ mi west of Virginia City* ☎ *406/843–5247* ⊕ *www.virginiacitymt.com* ✉ *$8* ☉ *Mid-May–mid-Sept., daily 9–6.*

After they were hanged by vigilantes, the outlaws who preyed on miners ended up in graves at **Boot Hill** cemetery. Have a look at the old markers and take in the hill's view. ⊠ *From Wallace St. turn north on Spencer St. and follow signs for* ROAD AGENTS' GRAVES ☎ *406/843–5555* or *800/829–2969* ⊕ *www.virginiacitychamber.com.*

WHERE TO EAT AND STAY

$$ × **Star Bakery Restaurant.** Opened in 1863, Star Bakery made beer and
AMERICAN bread for area miners. Open almost continually ever since, it's now a
breakfast, lunch, and dinner restaurant specializing in ribs and chicken
smoked on the premises, as well as "The John Henry," purported to be
the largest cheeseburger in Madison County. ⊠ *1576 Hwy. 287, Nevada
City* ☏ *406/843–5525* ⌂ *Reservations not accepted* ▤ *AE, D, MC, V*
⊘ *Closed Labor Day–Memorial Day.*

¢–$$ ⬚ **Fairweather Inn and the Nevada City Hotel and Cabins.** Virginia City's
Fairweather Inn is a classic Western-Victorian hotel with balconies in
the heart of the area's gold-mining country. The two-story 1863 Nevada
City Hotel is 1½ mi away in Nevada City; there are Victorian-style
hotel rooms, plus rustic miners' cabins. **Pros:** historic hotel; convenient
location; comfortable rooms. **Cons:** no air-conditioning; most rooms
have shared bath; no frills. ⊠ *305 W. Wallace St.* ☏ *406/843–5377 or
800/829–2969* ⊟ *406/843–5235* ⇝ *Fairweather Inn: 14 rooms, 6 with
bath. Nevada City Hotel: 11 rooms, 2 suites, 17 cabins* ⅋ *In-room: no
phone, no TV.* ▤ *MC, V* ⊘ *Closed Sept. 15–mid-May.*

$–$$ ⬚ **Stonehouse Inn Bed & Breakfast.** Period charm pervades this 1884
Gothic Revival home with antiques, brass beds, 12-foot ceilings, and
a teddy-bear collection. The full breakfast might include strawberry
French toast with cream cheese and fresh fruit. ⊠ *306 E. Idaho St.*
☏ *406/843–5504* ⊕ *www.stonehouseinnbb.com* ⇝ *5 rooms* ⅋ *In-room:
no a/c, no phone. In-hotel: laundry facilities, Wi-Fi* ▤ *MC, V* ⍍ *BP.*

$$–$$$ ⬚ **Upper Canyon Outfitters.** Along with cattle herding, hunting, and fly-
fishing adventures, this secluded guest ranch offers rooms in its spacious Western-style lodge or kitchen-equipped log cabins. Hearty ranch
meals are available in the lodge. **Pros:** an all-inclusive Western experience. **Cons:** a far cry from Disneyland. ⊠ *2149 Upper Ruby Rd., 35 mi
southwest of Virginia City* ☏ *800/735-3973* ⊕ *www.ucomontana.com*
⇝ *Lodge: 5 rooms, 1 suite. Cabins: 3 2-bedroom cabins, 1 1-bedroom
cabin.* ⅋ *In-room: Lodge: Refrigerator. Cabins: Kitchen.*

CAMPING ⚠ **Virginia City RV Park.** It's a good idea to reserve ahead at this RV park,
which also has four grassy campsites and two cabins. ⅋ *Flush toilets, full
hookups, partial hookups, dump station, drinking water, showers, picnic
tables, electricity* ⇝ *10 full hookups, 15 partial hookups, 4 tent sites*
⊠ *Hwy. 287, ¼ mi east of Virginia City* ☏ *406/843–5493 or 888/833–
5493* ⊕ *www.virginiacityrvpark.com* ▤ *MC, V* ⊘ *Mid-May–mid-Sept.*

NIGHTLIFE AND THE ARTS

NIGHTLIFE For a no-holds-barred, singing comedy cabaret, leave the kids at home
and hit the bawdy **Brewery Follies** (⊠ *H. S. Gilbert Brewery building,
201 E. Wallace* ☏ *406/843–5218 or 800/829–2969*) (ages 13 and up);
shows take place daily Memorial Day through Labor Day.

THE ARTS The historic **Opera House** (⊠ *338 W. Wallace St.* ☏ *406/843–5314 or
★ 800/829–2969* ⊕ *www.virginiacityplayers.com*) is the oldest continuously
operating summer theater in the West, in operation since 1949. Early
June through early September, the theater hosts an amusing vaudeville
show by the Virginia City Players Tuesday through Sunday at 7 PM, with
Wednesday, Saturday, and Sunday matinees at 2 PM. The cost is $18.

5

SHOPPING

Opened in 1864, **Rank's Mercantile** (⊠ *211 W. Wallace St.* ☎ *406/843–5454 or 800/494–5442*) is Montana's oldest continuously operating store. Period clothing, books, toys, gifts, and groceries are for sale here.

ENNIS

14 mi east of Virginia City via Hwy. 287, 53 mi southwest of Bozeman via Rte. 84 and U.S. 287.

In addition to being a hub of ranching in the area, this tiny town sits among some of the best trout streams in the West. People come from around the world for the area's blue-ribbon fishing, particularly in the area of Beartrap Canyon. Welcoming you to town is a sign that reads 600 PEOPLE, 11,000,000 TROUT.

GETTING HERE AND AROUND

Ennis is easily walkable, and has free parking on Main Street and in side-street lots.

EXPLORING

Consistently rated among the most exciting and challenging rodeos in Montana, the July 3 and 4 **Ennis Rodeo** (☎ *406/682–4700*) attracts top cowpokes.

Each year at the **Ennis National Fish Hatchery** six strains of rainbow trout produce 23 million eggs used to stock streams throughout the United States. ⊠ *180 Fish Hatchery Rd.* ☎ *406/682–4847* ⊕ *www.fws.gov/ ennis/* ☒ *Free* ☉ *Daily 7:30–5.*

For a bit of relaxation, nothing beats soaking in the natural hot water of the **Norris Hot Springs** pool. Live musical acts perform on the poolside stage Friday through Sunday nights, starting at 7 PM. ⊠ *Hwy. 84, 16 mi north of Ennis on U.S. 287, then ¼ mi east through town, or 33 mi west of Bozeman on Hwy. 84, Norris* ☎ *406/685–3303* ⊕ *www.norris- hotsprings.com* ☒ *$5, $7 with music* ☉ *Memorial Day–Labor Day, Wed.–Sat. 4–10, Sun. noon–10; Labor Day–Memorial Day, Wed.–Fri. 4–10, weekends noon–10.*

OFF THE BEATEN PATH | **Beartrap Canyon.** In this part of the Lee Metcalf Wilderness you can hike, fish, and go white-water rafting on the Madison River. A picnic area and access to Trail Creek are at the head of the canyon below Ennis Lake. To get here, drive north out of Ennis on U.S. 287 to the town of McAllister and turn right down a bumpy dirt road (no number), which takes you around to the north side of the lake across the dam. Turn left after the dam onto an unmarked road and drive across the river to the Trail Creek access point. ☎ *406/683–8000* ☒ *Free* ☉ *Daily.*

SPORTS AND THE OUTDOORS

FISHING | The fly-fishing specialists of **Eaton Outfitters** (⊠ *307 Jeffers Rd.* ☎ *406/682– 4514 or 800/755–3474*) lead trips on the Madison, Beaverhead, Big Hole, and Ruby rivers. The **Tackle Shop** (⊠ *127 E. Main St.* ☎ *406/682– 4263 or 800/808–2832*) offers guided float and wade fishing on the Madison, Big Hole, and other rivers. The full-service Orvis fly shop also sells luggage, clothing, and fishing accessories.

WHERE TO EAT AND STAY

$$$
CONTEMPORARY

✕ **Continental Divide.** This bistro-style restaurant is a pleasant surprise in an area with numerous steak houses. Among the specials are Hawaiian swordfish with citrus aioli, and slow-roasted Long Island duck with apricot mango glaze. ✉ *47 Geyser St., 1½ mi north of Ennis on Hwy. 287* ☎ *406/682–7600* ▤ *AE, D, MC, V* ☺ *Closed Dec.–Apr.*

¢–$

▥ **Fan Mountain Inn.** This simple but clean family motel has wonderful views of the Madison Range and is within walking distance of downtown shops and galleries. There's a cozy fireplace in the lobby. **Pros:** good location; reasonably priced. **Cons:** very basic—just a place to rest your head. ✉ *204 N. Main St.* ☎ *406/682–5200 or 877/682–5200* ⊕ *www. fanmountaininn.com* ⊠ *27 rooms* ♿ *In-room: refrigerator (some), Wi-Fi. In-hotel: some pets allowed* ▤ *AE, D, MC, V.*

CAMPING

⚠ **Ennis RV Village.** An 8-acre wetlands park with hiking trails is adjacent to this RV park, with views of the Madison, Gravelly, and Tobacco Root ranges. Reservations are recommended. ♿ *Flush toilets, full hookups, partial hookups, dump station, drinking water, guest laundry, showers, picnic tables, electricity, public telephone, general store* ⊠ *76 full hookups, 10 partial hookups, 4 tent sites* ✉ *15 Geyser St., just off Hwy. 287 1 mi north of Ennis* ☎ *406/682–5272 or 866/682–5272* ⊕ *www. ennisrv.com* ▤ *AE, D, MC, V* ☺ *Apr.–Oct.*

NIGHTLIFE

Live music on Friday night during the summer at the **Claim Jumper Saloon** (✉ *305 E. Main St.* ☎ *406/682–5558*) ranges from blues to classic rock. The saloon's **Roadmaster Grille** features booths crafted from 1950s-era American automobiles, as well as outside dining.

DILLON

65 mi south of Butte via I–90 west and I–15 south.

Blue-ribbon trout fishing on the Beaverhead River attracts thousands of anglers here year-round. A capital of southwest Montana's ranch country, Dillon began as a cattle- and wool-shipping point between Utah and the goldfields of Montana. From the mid-1860s until the early 1900s cattle and sheep remained the primary cargo shipped out of here on the Union Pacific Railroad.

GETTING HERE AND AROUND

Dillon's downtown area is easily accessed on foot, and there's plenty of free parking in town. From Dillon you can hike and mountain-bike into the nearby Ruby and Tendoy mountains.

EXPLORING

The **Beaverhead County Museum** exhibits Native American artifacts, ranching and mining memorabilia, a homesteader's cabin, agricultural artifacts, a one-room schoolhouse, a Lewis and Clark diorama, a model train, a research center, and a boardwalk imprinted with the area's ranch brands. ✉ *15 S. Montana St.* ☎ *406/683–5027* ⊠ *$3* ☺ *Memorial Day–Labor Day, weekdays 9–5, Sat. 11–3; Labor Day–Memorial Day, weekdays 9–5.*

Everyone is a cowboy for the annual **Dillon Jaycee Labor Day Rodeo and Parade** (⊠ *Fairgrounds, Railroad St.* ☎ *406/683–5511*), which has been staged here since 1914. Among the activities that take place at this week-long celebration leading up to Labor Day are a fair, rodeo, and concert.

William Clark of the Lewis and Clark Expedition climbed to the top of this limestone bluff at what's now **Clark's Lookout State Park** and took three compass readings; the maps he made from these readings became an important resource for future travelers. A ¼-mi gravel loop trail takes visitors to the top of the bluff, where interpretive signs include a replica of Clark's sketched map of the area. ⊠ *1 mi north of Dillon on Hwy. 91* ⊕ *www.fwp.state.mt.us* 🖾 *Free* ⊘ *Daily 8–dusk.*

OFF THE BEATEN PATH

Red Rock Lakes National Wildlife Refuge. In the undeveloped and remote Centennial Valley, this almost-50,000-acre refuge shelters moose, deer, and antelope, but is primarily a sanctuary for 230 species of birds, including trumpeter swans. Once threatened with extinction, these elegant birds have survived thanks to refuge protection; today they build their nests and winter here among the 16,500 acres of lakes and marshes. ⊠ *27650B South Valley Rd., 60 mi south of Dillon on I–15 to Monida; follow signs east 28 mi on gravel road, Lima* ☎ *406/276–3536* ⊕ *www.fws.gov/redrocks* 🖾 *Free* ⊘ *Daily 7–4:30.*

SPORTS AND THE OUTDOORS

FISHING

Whether they're discussing nymphs, caddis flies, or crane flies, the guides of **Backcountry Angler** (⊠ *426 S. Atlantic St.* ☎ *406/683–3462* ⊕ *www.backcountryangler.com*) know the art of fly-fishing. They lead overnight fishing-lodging trips, plus wade- and float-fishing day adventures. **Uncle Bob's Outdoors, Inc.** (⊠ *11 Pierce Dr.* ☎ *406/683–2692 or 888/683–7637*) arranges float- and wade-fishing trips on private creeks and ponds and the Beaverhead, Big Hole, Jefferson, and Ruby rivers.

HORSEBACK RIDING

Horse and mule day rides and pack trips traverse the Continental Divide and the Lima Peaks with **Centennial Outfitters** (⊠ *Box 92, 45 mi south of Dillon via I–15, Lima* ☎ *406/276–3463*). **Diamond Hitch Outfitters** (⊠ *3405 10 Mile Rd., 4 mi west of Dillon* ☎ *406/683–5494 or 800/368–5494* ⊕ *www.diamondhitchoutfitters.com*) takes you by horse or mule to high rocky summits, past endless flowery meadows, and along trout fisheries on hourly rides, cookout rides, and overnight pack trips.

SKIING
Ⓒ

A fun family attraction, **Maverick Mountain Ski Area** (⊠ *Hwy. 278 [Maverick Mountain Rd.], 40 mi west of Dillon in Polaris* ☎ *406/834–3454* ⊕ *www.skimaverick.com*) has a top elevation of 8,820 feet, a vertical drop of 2,020 feet, and 24 runs. Lessons and ski and snowboard rentals and sales are available for kids and adults.

WHERE TO EAT

$$
CONTEMPORARY
★

✕ **Cross Ranch Cookhouse.** Three meals a day are served at set hours at this cookhouse with working ranch hands: breakfast at 6:30, lunch at noon, and dinner at 6 pm. In addition to salads, bread, and dessert, "pitchfork fondue" is available on special request—Angus beef sirloin, skewered and served on a pitchfork. ⊠ *12775 Bannack Rd.; south on I–15, Exit 44, on Hwy. 324 12 mi to Bannack turnoff, right 2 mi ahead on right* ☎ *406/681–3133* ⚭ *Reservations essential* ▤ *No credit cards* ⊘ *Closed Sun. and Jan.*

$
CONTEMPORARY ✗ **Sweetwater Coffee.** This warm and friendly coffee shop offers salads, sandwiches, and pasta along with its espresso drinks. Try the Blue Dorris Salad. ⊠ *26 E. Bannack* ☎ *406/683–4141* ▭ *No credit cards* ⊘ *Closed Sat. and Sun.*

WHERE TO STAY

$$ ⛺ **Goose Down Ranch.** Darling cabins, one log and one clapboard, have mountain views all around and are near the famed Poindexter Slough blue-ribbon fly-fishing spot on the Beaverhead River. The cabins both have two bedrooms, fireplaces, and cozy couches. **Pros:** great fishing; full-service cabins. **Cons:** only two cabins means advance reservations are essential. ⊠ *2409 Carrigan La.* ☎ *406/683–6704 or 406/925–1619* ⊕ *www.goosedownranch.com* ⇝ *2 cabins* ♿ *In-room: no phone, kitchen, laundry facilities.* ▭ *MC, V.*

¢–$ ⛺ **The Grasshopper Inn.** In the spectacular Pioneer Mountains, this mountain lodge is ideally situated for snowmobiling, hiking, and fishing. The tidy, colorful rooms have log beds and views of the mountains. The restaurant's back bar dates from the 1800s. The simple yet filling meals ($$) include burgers, steak, and fish. You can rent snowmobiles nearby in winter. **Pros:** cozy, secluded getaway; reasonably priced. **Cons:** miles from services. ⊠ *9601 Pioneer Scenic Byway, 45 mi west of Dillon, Polaris* ☎ *406/834–3456* 🖷 *406/834–3507* ⇝ *10 rooms, 2 apartments* ♿ *In-room: no phone, no a/c. In-hotel: restaurant, bar* ▭ *D, MC, V.*

$ ⛺ **Guest House Inn & Suites.** This hotel is affordable, clean, and quiet, and has an outdoor sundeck off the indoor pool. The staff can direct you to interesting local sights, scenic viewpoints, and perhaps even a good local fishing hole. **Pros:** full breakfast; indoor pool; not overpriced—it's one of the nicer places to stay in Dillon. **Cons:** detractors speak of inattentive management and a buffet that didn't last until the advertised time. ⊠ *580 Sinclair St.* ☎ *406/683–3636 or 800/214–8378* ⊕ *www.guesthouseintl. com* ⇝ *58 rooms* ♿ *In-room: kitchen (some), refrigerator, DVD, Wi-Fi. In-hotel: pool, gym, some pets allowed* ▭ *AE, D, MC, V* ⦿ *BP.*

$$ ⛺ **The River's Edge Lodge Bed and Breakfast.** Located 10 mi south of Dillon on a stretch of the Upper Beaverhead River, this year-round bed-and-breakfast caters to fishermen. Although the amenities of town may be a good way down the road, this secluded barnlike lodge—constructed from wood of a wide variety of species—was designed to put its guests as close to this first-class fly-fishing river as possible. **Pros:** great location and atmosphere if you're here to fish. **Cons:** if you're not fishing, you may feel out of your element. ⊠ *765 Henneberry Rd.* ☎ *406/683–6214 or 406/925–1494* ⊕ *www.riversedgelodgebb.com* ⇝ *5 rooms* ♿ *In-room: no a/c. In-hotel: some pets allowed* ▭ *No credit cards* ⦿ *BP.*

CAMPING △ **Dillon KOA.** Pine, aspen, and birch trees shade this campground on the banks of the Beaverhead River. The campground, which is on the edge of Dillon, has views of the Pioneer Mountains and other peaks. ♿ *Flush toilets, full hookups, dump station, drinking water, guest laundry, showers, picnic tables, electricity, public telephone, general store, play area, swimming (pool)* ⇝ *18 full hookups, 43 partial hookups, 34 tent sites; 4 cabins* ⊠ *735 W. Park St.* ☎ *406/683–2749 or 800/562–2751* ⊕ *www. koa.com* ▭ *D, MC, V.*

5

BANNACK

24 mi west of Dillon via I–15 and U.S. 278.

GETTING HERE AND AROUND

Bannack State Historic Park has a large parking lot for visitors. Once inside the gates, everything is accessed on foot. To get to Bannack from Dillon, follow Highway 278 west for 17 mi and watch for a sign just after Badger Pass; take the paved road for 4 mi.

EXPLORING

Bannack was Montana's first territorial capital and the site of the state's first major gold strike, on July 28, 1862, at Grasshopper Creek. Now **Bannack State Historic Park,** this frontier boomtown has historic structures lining the main street, and picnic and camping spots. It was here that the notorious renegade Sheriff Henry Plummer and two of his deputies were caught and executed by vigilantes for murder and robbery. A re-creation of the gallows on which Plummer was hanged still stands. Rumors persist that Plummer's stash of stolen gold was hidden somewhere in the mountains near here and never found. ☎ *406/834–3413* ⊕ *www.bannack.org* ✉ *$5 per out-of-state vehicle; free for vehicles with Montana license plates* ☉ *Park Memorial Day–Labor Day, daily 8–9; Labor Day–Memorial Day, daily 8–5. Visitor center late May–early Sept., daily 10–6; Sept., daily 11–5; Oct., weekends 11–5; limited hrs in May.*

Bannack Days (☎ *406/834–3413* ⊕ *www.bannack.org* ✉ *$5 per vehicle*), always the third weekend in July, celebrates life in Montana's first territorial capital with wagon rides, a main-street gunfight, black-powder weapons shoots, gold panning, a stagecoach robbery, old-time music and dancing, and pioneer-crafts demonstrations.

OFF THE BEATEN PATH

Pioneer Mountain Scenic Byway. Mountains, meadows, lodgepole-pine forests, and willow-edged streams line this road, which runs north–south between U.S. 278 (west of Bannack) and Highway 43. Headed north, the byway skirts the Maverick Mountain Ski Area and Elkhorn Hot Springs and ends at the town of Wise River on the Big Hole River. ☎ *406/683–5511.*

CAMPING

⚠ **Bannack Campgrounds.** Grasshopper Creek, where gold was discovered in 1862, flows right by these two rustic campgrounds, which have few amenities but are close to Bannack. Grocery stores and restaurants are in nearby Dillon. It's a good idea to reserve ahead for the single tepee. ♿ *Pit toilets, drinking water, fire pits, picnic tables* ⊃ *35 tent sites; 1 tepee* ✉ *4200 Bannack Rd.* ☎ *406/834–3413* ⊕ *www.bannack.org* ▤ *MC, V.*

BIG HOLE NATIONAL BATTLEFIELD

60 mi northwest of Bannock via Hwy. 278 northwest and Hwy. 43 west; 87 mi southwest of Butte via I–90 west, I–15 south, and Hwy. 43 west.

GETTING HERE AND AROUND

Big Hole is 6,300 feet above sea level, so you may need to slow your pace while walking its trails; visitors are encouraged to drink plenty of fluids. Nearest facilities are in Wisdom, 10 mi east of the battlefield, which has a gas station, store, and restaurants.

EXPLORING

At **Big Hole National Battlefield,** a visitor center overlooks meadows where one of the West's greatest and most tragic stories played out. In 1877 Nez Perce warriors in central Idaho killed some white settlers as retribution for earlier killings by whites. Knowing the U.S. Army would make no distinction between the guilty and the innocent, several hundred Nez Perce fled, beginning a 1,500-mi, five-month odyssey that has come to be known as the Nez Perce Trail. The fugitives engaged 10 separate U.S. commands in 13 battles and skirmishes. One of the fiercest of these was at Big Hole, where both sides suffered losses. From here the Nez Perce headed toward Yellowstone. The Big Hole battlefield remains as it was when the battle unfolded; tepee poles erected by the park service mark the site of a Nez Perce village and serve as haunting reminders of what transpired here. Ranger-led programs take place daily in summer; group tours can be arranged with advance request. The park stays open for winter snowshoeing and cross-country skiing on a groomed trail through the battlefield's sites. Big Hole National Battlefield is one of 38 sites in four states that make up the **Nez Perce National Historic Park** (☎ *208/843–7001 ⊕ www.nps.gov/nepe*), which follows the historic Nez Perce Trail. ⊠ *16425 Hwy. 43 West, 10 mi west of Wisdom* ☎ *406/689–3155 ⊕ www.nps.gov/biho* ⊠ *Free* ☉ *May–Labor Day, daily 9–6; Labor Day–Apr., daily 9–5.*

The annual **Commemoration of the Battle of Big Hole** (☎ *406/689–3155 ⊕ www.nps.gov/nepe*), in early August, includes traditional Nez Perce music, ceremonies, and demonstrations, along with cavalry exhibitions.

WHERE TO STAY

¢–$ ⌂ **Jackson Hot Springs Lodge.** William Clark (of Lewis and Clark) cooked his dinner in the hot springs near the site of this spacious log lodge decorated with elk antlers, a stuffed mountain lion, and other critters. Accommodations are in cabins, many with fireplaces, and there's also tent and RV camping. The Olympic-size outdoor pool is filled with artesian hot water that averages 103°F year-round. The dining room ($$$) specializes in wild game dishes such as pheasant, bison, and elk steaks. **Pros:** first-class dining; relaxing pool; classic Western lodge. **Cons:** detractors complain of stubborn room temperatures; facilities in need of upkeep; overpriced. ⊠ *Main St., Box 808; 30 mi northwest of Big Hole, Jackson* ☎ *406/834–3151 or 888/438–6938 ⊕ www.jacksonhotsprings.com/jack-acc.htm* ➾ *16 cabins, 4 hotel rooms* ⅋ *In-room: no a/c, no phone, no TV. In-hotel: restaurant, bar, pool, some pets allowed* ⊟ *AE, D, MC, V.*

CAMPING ⚠️**Miner Lake Campground.** Campsites have a view of the Beaverhead Mountains at this quiet, out-of-the-way lakeside spot. You can fish in 30-acre Miner Lake, which is also popular for nonmotorized boats. *♿ Pit toilets, drinking water, fire grates, picnic tables, swimming (lake) ⇱ 18 tent sites ✉ Forest Rd. 182, 9 mi west of Hwy. 278, 12 mi southwest of Jackson Jackson ☎ 406/689–3243 🖶 406/689–3245 ⊕ www. fs.fed.us/r1/ ⊟ No credit cards ⊙ June–Sept.*

Glacier
National Park

WITH WATERTON NATIONAL PARK

WORD OF MOUTH

"And then it was time for the sunrise . . . The sun hit that pyramidal mountain that stands alone, directly across the lake from the lodge, and set it afire. First pink, then gold, hovering above the still-dark lake—the stuff of famous photographs."

—Enzian

WELCOME TO GLACIER NATIONAL PARK

TOP REASONS TO GO

★ **Witness the Divide:** The rugged mountains that weave their way through Glacier and Waterton along the Continental Divide seem to have glaciers in every hollow melting into tiny streams, raging rivers, and icy-cold mountain lakes.

★ **Just hike it:** There are hundreds of miles of trails that cater to hikers of all levels—from all-day hikes to short strolls. It's little wonder the readers of *Backpacker Magazine* rated Glacier the number-one backcountry hiking park in America.

★ **Go to the sun:** Crossing the Continental Divide at the 6,646-foot-high Logan Pass, Glacier's Going-to-the-Sun Road is a spectacular drive.

★ **View the wildlife:** This is one of the few places in North America where all native carnivores, including grizzlies and wolves, still survive. Bighorn sheep, mule deer, coyotes, grizzly bears, and black bears can often be seen from roadways.

1 West Glacier. Known to the Kootenai people as "sacred dancing lake," Lake McDonald is the largest glacial water-basin lake in Glacier National Park.

2 Logan Pass. At 6,646 feet, this is the highest point on the Going-to-the-Sun Road. From mid-June to mid-October a 1½-mi board-walk leads to an overlook that crosses an area filled with lush meadows and wildflowers.

3 East Glacier. St. Mary Lake and Many Glacier are the major highlights of the eastern side of Glacier. Services and amenities are located at both sites.

4 Backcountry. This is some of the most incredible terrain in North America, and provides the right combination of beautiful scenery and isolation. Although Waterton is a much smaller park, its backcountry trails connect with hiking trails in both Glacier and British Columbia's Akamina-Kishinena Provincial Park.

5 Waterton Lakes. The Canadian national park is the meeting of two worlds: the flatlands of the prairie and the abrupt upthrust of the mountains.

MONTANA

Polebridge

GETTING ORIENTED

In the rocky northwest corner of Montana, Glacier National Park encompasses 1.2 million acres (1,563 square mi) of untrammeled wilds. Within the park there are 37 named glaciers (which are ever-so-slowly diminishing), 200 lakes, and 1,000 mi of streams. Neighboring Waterton Lakes National Park, across the border in Alberta, Canada, covers another 130,000 acres. In 1932 the parks were unified to form the Waterton-Glacier International Peace Park—the first international peace park in the world—in recognition of the two nations' friendship and dedication to peace.

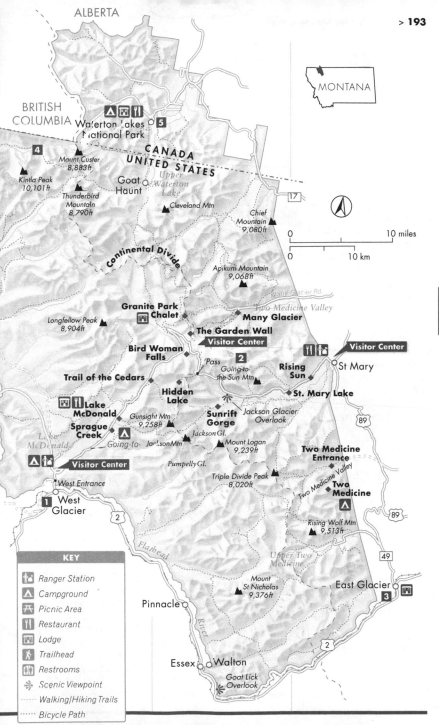

ALBERTA

MONTANA

BRITISH COLUMBIA

Waterton Lakes National Park

△🖼🍴 5

CANADA
UNITED STATES

4

Mount Custer
8,883ft

Kintla Peak
10,101ft

Thunderbird
Mountain
8,790ft

Goat
Haunt

Upper
Waterton
Lake

Cleveland Mtn

Chief
Mountain
9,080ft

17

Continental Divide

Apikuni Mountain
9,068ft

Many Glacier Rd.

Two Medicine Valley

6

Longfellow Peak
8,904ft

Granite Park
Chalet 🖼

Many Glacier

The Garden Wall
Visitor Center

Visitor Center 🍴👥

St Mary

Bird Woman
Falls

Trail of the Cedars

2

Pass

Going-to-
the-Sun Mtn

Rising
Sun

Hidden
Lake

St. Mary Lake

🖼🍴 Lake
McDonald

Gunsight Mtn
9,258ft

Sunrift
Gorge

Jackson Glacier
Overlook

Sprague
Creek

△

JacksonMtn

Jackson Gl.

Mount Logan
9,239ft

89

Lake
McDonald

Going-to-

Pumpelly Gl.

Two Medicine
Entrance

△ 🚺 Visitor Center

West Entrance

Triple Divide Peak
8,020ft

Two Medicine Valley

Two
Medicine

1 West
Glacier

2

Rising Wolf Mtn
9,513ft

89

49

Flathead

Upper Two
Medicine

Mount
St Nicholas
9,376ft

East Glacier 🖼

Pinnacle

3 △

River

Essex

Walton

Goat Lick
Overlook

2

KEY

🏠 Ranger Station
△ Campground
🌲 Picnic Area
🍴 Restaurant
🖼 Lodge
🚶 Trailhead
🚻 Restrooms
⛷ Scenic Viewpoint
···· Walking/Hiking Trails
···· Bicycle Path

0 ————— 10 miles
0 ————— 10 km

GLACIER NATIONAL PARK PLANNER

When to Go

Of the 2 million annual visitors to Glacier and 400,000 to Waterton, most come between July 1 and September 15, when the streams are flowing and wildlife is roaming. Snow removal on the alpine portion of Going-to-the-Sun Road is usually completed by mid-June; the opening of Logan Pass at the road's summit marks the summer opening of Glacier. Canada's Victoria Day in late May marks the beginning of the season in Waterton. Spring and fall are quieter. By October, snow forces the closing of most park roads.

AVG. HIGH/LOW TEMPS

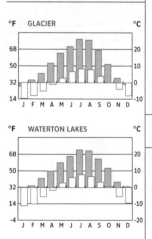

Flora and Fauna

In summer, a profusion of new flowers, grasses, and budding trees covers the landscape high and low. Spring attracts countless birds, from golden eagles riding thermals north to Canada and Alaska to rare harlequin ducks dipping in creeks. Snow-white mountain goats, with their wispy white beards and curious stares, are seen in alpine areas, and sure-footed bighorn sheep graze the high meadows in the short summers. The largest population of grizzly bears in the lower 48 states lives in the wild in and around the park. Feeding the animals is illegal.

Visiting Glacier in winter makes for easy tracking of many large animals like moose, elk, deer, mountain lions, wolf, lynx, and their smaller neighbors—the snowshoe hare, pine marten, beaver, and muskrat.

In park lakes, sportfishing species include burbot (ling), northern pike, whitefish, grayling, cutthroat, rainbow, lake (Mackinaw), kokanee salmon, and brook trout.

Tours

Glacier Park Inc. schedules driver-narrated van tours that cover most of the park accessible by road. The tour of Going-to-the-Sun Road is a favorite, with plenty of photo opportunities at roadside pull-outs. Some of the tours are conducted in "jammers," vintage 1936 red buses with roll-back tops. Short trips and full-day trips are available. Reservations are essential. ⌂ *P.O. Box 2025, Columbia Falls, MT 59912* ☎ *406/892–2525 or 403/236–3400* ⊕ *www.glacierparkinc.com* ✉ *$45–$90* ☯ *June–Sept.*

Getting Here and Around

On the east, U.S. 89 accesses Many Glacier and St. Mary, Route 49 reaches Two Medicine. On the west, U.S. 2 goes to West Glacier. Take the Chief Mountain Highway to access Waterton Lakes during the summer or Highway 89 to Alberta Highway 2 through Cardston and then west to the park via Highway 5 any time of the year. The nearest airports to Glacier are in Great Falls and Kalispell, Montana. The nearest airport to Waterton Lakes is in Calgary.

The roads in both parks are either paved or gravel, and become deteriorated from freezing and thawing. Drive slowly and anticipate that rocks and wildlife may be around the corner. Road reconstruction is part of the park experience, as there are only a few warm months in which road crews can complete projects. Scenic pull-outs are frequent; watch for other vehicles pulling in or out, and watch for children in parking areas. Most development and services center around St. Mary Lake on the east and Lake McDonald on the west.

Glacier Park Inc. (☎ 406/226–5666 ⊕ www.glacierpark-inc.com) operates a shuttle along the Going-to-the-Sun Road July 1 to Labor Day. Buses make stops at major trailheads, campgrounds, and other developed areas between Lake McDonald Lodge and Rising Sun Motor Inn.

Border Crossings

A passport is required of everyone crossing the Canadian/ U.S. border. Kids traveling with only one parent need a notarized letter from the other parent giving permission to enter Canada or the United States. If you are traveling with pets, you need proof of up-to-date immunizations to cross the border in either direction. Citizens from most countries (Canada, Mexico, and Bermuda are exceptions) entering the United States from Canada must pay $6 (cash only) at the border for a required I–94 or I–94W Arrival-Departure Record form, to be returned to border officials when leaving the U.S. Contact United States Customs (☎ 406/335–2611 ⊕ www.cbp.gov) or the Canada Border Services Agency (☎ 403/344–3767 ⊕ www.cbsa-asfc.gc.ca) for more information.

Safety Tips

Never approach a bear or any other park animal, no matter how cute, cuddly, and harmless it appears. If you encounter a bear, don't run. Back away slowly and assume a nonthreatening posture. If a brown or grizzly bear charges, drop into the fetal position, protect your head and neck, and do not move. It's the opposite if you encounter a black bear or mountain lion: act aggressively, throw rocks or sticks, and try to look large by holding up a pack or branches. If attacked, fight back, aiming for the nose.

To minimize the risk of contact with bears and mountain lions, hike only during the day, hike in groups, and make lots of noise by singing, talking loudly, and clapping hands, especially near blind corners and streams.

Check for ticks after walking through shrubs and high grasses. They are a problem especially in the spring.

Prepare for winter storms with survival kits that include snow tires or chains, a shovel and window scraper, flares or a reflector, a blanket or sleeping bag, a first-aid kit, sand, gravel or traction mats, a flashlight with extra batteries, matches, a lighter and candles, paper, nonperishable foods, drinking water, and a tow chain or rope.

6

By Debbie Olsen

The massive peaks of the Continental Divide in Northwest Montana are the backbone of Glacier National Park and its sister park in Canada, Waterton Lakes, which together make up the International Peace Park. From their slopes, melting snow and alpine glaciers yield the headwaters of rivers that flow west to the Pacific Ocean, north to the Arctic Ocean, and southeast to the Atlantic Ocean via the Gulf of Mexico. Coniferous forests, thickly vegetated stream bottoms, and green-carpeted meadows provide homes and sustenance for all kinds of wildlife.

PARK ESSENTIALS

ACCESSIBILITY

All visitor centers are wheelchair accessible, and most of the campgrounds and picnic areas are paved, with extended-length picnic tables and accessible restrooms. Three of Glacier's nature trails are wheelchair accessible: the Trail of the Cedars, Running Eagle Falls, and the Oberlin Bend Trail, just west of Logan Pass. In Waterton, the Linnet Lake Trail, Waterton Townsite Trail, Cameron Lake day-use area, and the International Peace Park Pavilion are wheelchair accessible.

ADMISSION FEES AND PERMITS

Entrance fees for Glacier are $25 per vehicle, or $12 for one person on foot or bike, good for seven days; it's $35 for a one-year pass. A day pass to Waterton Lakes costs C$7.80, and an annual pass costs C$39. *Passes to Glacier and Waterton must be paid separately.*

At Glacier the required backcountry permit is $5 per person per day from the Apgar Backcountry Permit Center after mid-April for the upcoming summer. Advance reservations cost $20. Mail a request and a check after mid-April to Backcountry Reservations, Glacier National Park Headquarters, P.O. Box 395, West Glacier, MT 59936.

Waterton requires backcountry camping permits for use of its 13 backcountry camp spots, with reservations available up to 90 days in advance. Buy the permit for C$9.80 per adult per night—reserve for an additional C$11—at the visitor reception center (☎ 403/858–5133).

ADMISSION HOURS

The parks are open year-round, but most roads and facilities close October through May. The parks are in the mountain time zone.

ATMS/BANKS

You'll find cash machines at Lake McDonald, Many Glacier, St. Mary Lodge, and Glacier Park lodges and in Waterton's Tamarack Village Square. Waterton has a full-service bank in the Waterton Townsite. The closest full-service bank in the Glacier area can be found in Columbia Falls, where there are several.

CELL-PHONE RECEPTION

Cell phones do not generally work in the mountains. Find pay phones at Avalanche Campground, Glacier Highland Motel and Store, Apgar, St. Mary Visitor Center, Two Medicine Campstore, and all lodges except Granite Park Chalet and Sperry Chalet.

RELIGIOUS SERVICES

In the summer you can attend either Christian Ministry or Catholic services at Glacier, and Anglican, United, Catholic, or Mormon services in Waterton.

PARK CONTACT INFORMATION

Glacier National Park ⓘ *P.O. Box 128, West Glacier, MT 59936* ☎ *406/888–7800* ⊕ *www.nps.gov/glac.* **Waterton Lakes National Park** ⓘ *P.O. Box 200, Waterton Park, AlbertaCanada T0K 2M0* ☎ *403/859–2224 or 800/748–7275* ⊕ *www.pc.gc.ca/waterton.*

GLACIER NATIONAL PARK

6

SCENIC DRIVES

Fodor'sChoice
★ **Going-to-the-Sun Road.** This magnificent 50-mi highway—the only American roadway designated both a National Historic Landmark and a National Civil Engineering Landmark—crosses the crest of the Continental Divide at Logan Pass and traverses the towering Garden Wall. Open from mid-June to mid-September, this is one of the most stunning drives in Glacier National Park. A multiyear Sun Road rehabilitation project will result in some driving delays due to reconstruction.

Many Glacier Road. This 12-mi drive enters Glacier on the northeast side of the park, west of Babb, and travels along Sherburne Lake for almost 5 mi, penetrating a glacially carved valley surrounded by mountains. It passes through meadows and a scrubby forest of lodgepole pines, aspen, and cottonwood. The farther you travel up the valley, the more clearly you'll be able to see Grinnell and Salamander glaciers. The road passes Many Glacier Hotel and ends at the Swift Current Campground. It's usually closed from October to May.

WHAT TO SEE

HISTORIC SITES

Ⓒ **Apgar.** On the southwest end of Lake McDonald, this tiny hamlet has a few stores, an ice-cream shop, motels, ranger buildings, a campground, and an historic schoolhouse. From November to mid-May no services remain open, except the weekend-only visitor center. Across the street from the Apgar visitor center, **Apgar Discovery Cabin** is filled with animal posters, kids' activities, and maps. ⊠ *2 mi north of west entrance* ☎ *406/888–7939* ☉ *Cabin: mid-June–Labor Day, daily 1:30–3.*

GLACIER IN ONE DAY

It's hard to beat the **Going-to-the-Sun Road** for a one-day trip in Glacier National Park. This itinerary takes you from west to east—if you're starting from St. Mary, take the tour backward. First, however, call the Glacier Park Boat Company (☎ 406/257–2426) to make a reservation for the **St. Mary Lake or Lake McDonald boat tour,** depending on where you end up. Then, drive up Going-to-the-Sun Road to **Avalanche Creek Campground,** and take a 30-minute stroll along the fragrant **Trail of the Cedars.** Afterward, continue driving up—you can see views of waterfalls and wildlife to the left and an awe-inspiring, precipitous drop to the right. At the summit, **Logan Pass,** your arduous climb is rewarded with a gorgeous view of immense peaks, sometimes complemented by a herd of mountain goats. Stop in at the **Logan Pass Visitor Center,** then take the 1½-mi **Hidden Lake Nature Trail** up to prime wildlife-viewing spots. Picnic at the overlook above Hidden Lake. In the afternoon, continue driving east over the mountains. Stop at the **Jackson Glacier Overlook** to view one of the park's largest glaciers. Continue down; eventually the forest thins, the vistas grow broader, and a gradual transition to the high plains begins. When you reach **Rising Sun Campground,** take the one-hour St. Mary Lake boat tour to St. Mary Falls. If you'd rather hike, the 1.2-mi **Sun Point Nature Trail** also leads to the falls. (Take the boat tour if you're driving from east to west.) The Going-to-the-Sun Road is generally closed from mid-September to mid-June.

SCENIC STOPS

⇨ *Going-to-the-Sun Road close-up for stops along that famous route.*

Goat Lick Overlook. Mountain goats frequent this natural salt lick on a cliff above the Middle Fork of the Flathead River. ⊠ *2½ mi east of Walton Ranger Station on U.S. 2.*

Grinnell and Salamander Glaciers. These glaciers formed as one ice mass, but in 1926 they broke apart and have been shrinking ever since. The best viewpoint is reached by the 5½-mi Grinnell Glacier Trail from Many Glacier. ⊠ *Trailhead for Grinnell Glacier Trail at the far northwestern end of Lake Josephine. Catch a boat to this trailhead or hike there via the trail behind the Many Glacier Hotel.*

Lake McDonald. This beautiful 10-mi-long lake is accessible year-round on Going-to-the-Sun Road. Take a boat ride to the middle for a view of the surrounding glacier-clad mountains. You can go fishing and horseback riding at either end, and in winter, snowshoe or cross-country ski. ⊠ *2 mi north of west entrance.*

Running Eagle Falls (Trick Falls). Cascading near Two Medicine, these are actually two different waterfalls from two different sources. In spring, when the water level is high, the upper falls join the lower falls for a 40-foot drop into Two Medicine River; in summer the upper falls dry up, revealing the lower 20-foot falls that start midway down the precipice. ⊠ *2 mi east of Two Medicine entrance.*

Two Medicine Valley. Rugged, often windy, and always beautiful, the valley is a remote 9-mi drive from Route 49 and is surrounded by some of the park's most stark, rocky peaks. On and around the valley's lake you can rent a canoe, take a narrated boat tour, camp, and hike. Be aware that bears frequent the area. The road is closed from late October through late May. ⊠ *Two Medicine entrance, 9 mi east of Hwy. 49* ☎ *406/888–7800, 406/257–2426 boat tours.*

VISITOR CENTERS

↻ **Apgar Visitor Center.** This is a great first stop if you're entering the park from the west. Here you can get all kinds of information, including maps, permits, books, and the *Junior Ranger* newspaper. You can plan your route on a large relief map to get a glimpse of where you're going. In winter the rangers offer free snowshoe walks. Snowshoes can be rented for $2 at the visitor center. ⊠ *2 mi north of West Glacier in Apgar Village* ☎ *406/888–7800* ☉ *Mid-May–Oct., daily 8–8; Nov.–mid-May, weekends 9–4.*

Logan Pass Visitor Center. Built of stone, this center stands sturdy against the severe weather that forces it to close in winter. Books, maps, and more are stocked inside. Rangers staff the center and give 10-minute talks on the alpine environment. ⊠ *34 mi east of West Glacier, 18 mi west of St. Mary* ☎ *406/888–7800* ☉ *Mid-June–mid-Sept., daily 9–7.*

St. Mary Visitor Center. The park's largest visitor complex, it has a huge relief map of the park's peaks and valleys and provides a 15-minute video that orients visitors. Rangers host evening presentations during the peak summer months. Traditional Blackfeet dancing and drumming performances are offered throughout the summer. Check with the center for exact dates and times. The center has books and maps for sale, backcountry camping permits, and large viewing windows facing the 10-mi-long St. Mary Lake. ⊠ *Going-to-the-Sun Rd., off U.S. 89* ☎ *406/732–7750* ☉ *Mid-May–mid-Oct., daily 8–4:30 with extended hours during the peak summer months.*

SPORTS AND THE OUTDOORS

BICYCLING

Cyclists in Glacier must stay on roads or bike routes and are not permitted on hiking trails or in the backcountry. The one-lane, unpaved Inside North Fork Road from Apgar to Polebridge is well suited to mountain bikers. Two Medicine Road is an intermediate paved route, with a mild grade at the beginning, becoming steeper as you approach Two Medicine Campground. Much of the western half of Going-to-the-Sun Road is closed to bikes from 11 to 4. Other restrictions apply during peak traffic periods and road construction. You can find thrilling off-road trails just outside the park near Whitefish. There are no bike-rental shops inside the park, but there is one in the nearby town of Whitefish.

OUTFIT-
TER AND
EXPEDITIONS
Guided cycling tours inside the park with plenty of stops to identify plants, animals, and habitats can be arranged with **Glacier Adventure Guides** (⌂ *P.O. Box 4833, Whitefish 59937* ☎ *406/891–2173 or*

6

Going-to-the-Sun Road

Going-to-the-Sun Road, arguably the most beautiful drive in the country, connects Lake McDonald on the west side of Glacier with St. Mary Lake on the east. Turnoffs provide views of the high country and glacier-carved valleys. The sights below are listed in order from west to east.

The Garden Wall. An abrupt and jagged wall of rock juts above the road and is visible for about 10 mi as it follows Logan Creek from just past Avalanche Creek Campground to Logan Pass. ⊠ *24–34 mi northeast of West Glacier.*

★ **Logan Pass.** At 6,660 feet, this is the highest point in the park accessible by motor vehicle. It presents unparalleled views of both sides of the Continental Divide and is frequented by mountain goats, bighorn sheep, and grizzly bears. It is extremely crowded in July and August. ⊠ *34 mi east of West Glacier, 18 mi west of St. Mary.*

Hidden Lake Overlook. Take a walk from Logan Pass up to see the crystalline Hidden Lake, which often still has ice clinging to it in early July. It's a 1½-mi hike on an uphill grade, partially on a boardwalk that protects the abundant wildflowers. ⊠ *Trailhead behind Logan Pass Visitor's Centre.*

Jackson Glacier Overlook. On the east side of the Continental Divide you come into view of Jackson Glacier

looming in a rocky pass across the upper St. Mary River valley. If it isn't covered with snow, you'll see sharp peaks of ice. The glacier is shrinking and may disappear in another 100 years. ⊠ *5 mi east of Logan Pass.*

St. Mary Lake. When the breezes calm, the lake mirrors the snow-capped granite peaks that line the St. Mary Valley. The Sun Point Nature Trail follows the lake's shore 1 mi each way. ⊠ *1 mi west of St. Mary.*

■ TIP→ **The drive is susceptible to frequent delays in summer.** To avoid traffic jams and parking problems, take the road early in the morning or late in the evening (when the lighting is ideal for photography and wildlife is most likely to appear).

Vehicles must be under 21 feet long, 10 feet high, and 8 feet wide, including mirrors, between Avalanche Creek Campground and Sun Point. This roadway is open only from mid-June to mid-September, due to heavy snowfalls.

If you don't want to drive the Going-to-the-Sun Road, consider making the ride in a "jammer," an antique red bus operated by **Glacier Park Inc.** (☎ *406/892–2525* ⊕ *www.glacierpark-inc.com*). The drivers double as guides and can roll back the tops of the vehicles to give you improved views. Reservations are required.

877/735–9514 ⊕ *www.glacierparkskitours.com*). Rental bikes are included with the tours (but the company doesn't rent bikes otherwise). **Glacier Cyclery** (⊠ *326 E. 2nd St., Whitefish* ☎ *403/862–6446* ⊕ *www. glaciercyclery.com*) has daily and weekly bike rentals on touring, road, and mountain bikes for all ages and skill levels. It also sells bikes and does repairs.

BOATING AND RAFTING

Glacier has many stunning lakes and rivers, and boating is a popular park activity. Glacier Park Boat Company offers guided tours of Lake McDonald, St. Mary Lake, and Two Medicine Lake, as well as Swiftcurrent Lake and Lake Josephine at Many Glacier from June to mid-September. You can rent small boats at Lake McDonald, Apgar, Two Medicine, and Many Glacier through the Glacier Park Boat Company. Watercraft such as Sea-Doos or Jet Skis are not allowed in the park.

Many rafting companies provide adventures along the border of the park on the Middle and North Forks of the Flathead River. The Middle Fork has some excellent white water, while the North Fork has both slow-moving and fast-moving sections. If you bring your own raft or kayak, stop at the Hungry Horse Ranger Station in the Flathead National Forest near West Glacier to obtain a permit.

OUTFIT-
TERS AND
EXPEDITIONS
★

Glacier Park Boat Company (☎ 406/257–2426 ⊕ *www.glacierparkboats. com* 🖅 *Tours $11.25–$22, rentals $18–$24 per hour ☉ May–Sept.*) gives tours on five lakes. A **Lake McDonald cruise** takes you from the dock at Lake McDonald Lodge to the middle of the lake for an unparalleled view of the Continental Divide's Garden Wall. **Many Glacier tours** on Swiftcurrent Lake and Lake Josephine depart from Many Glacier Lodge and provide views of the Continental Divide. **Two Medicine Lake cruises** leave from the dock near the ranger station and lead to several trails. **St. Mary Lake cruises** leave from the launch near Rising Sun Campground and head to Red Eagle Mountain and other spots. The tours last 45–90 minutes. You can rent kayaks, canoes, rowboats ($18 per hour), and small motorboats ($24 per hour) at Lake McDonald, Apgar, Two Medicine, and Many Glacier.

For rafting outfitters and expeditions, ⇨ *Multisport Outfitters.*

FISHING

Within Glacier there's an almost unlimited range of fishing possibilities, with a catch-and-release policy encouraged. You can fish in most waters of the park, but the best fishing is generally in the least accessible spots. A fishing license is not required inside the park boundary, but you must stop by a park office to pick up a copy of the regulations. The fishing season runs from the third Saturday in May to November 30. There are several companies that offer guided fishing trips in the area. ■ **TIP→ Fishing on both the North Fork and the Middle Fork of the Flathead River requires a Montana conservation license ($10) plus a Montana fishing license ($15 for two consecutive days or $60 for a season). They are available at most convenience stores, sports shops, and from the Montana Department of Fish, Wildlife, and Parks (☎ 406/752–5501 ⊕ www. fwp.mt.gov).**

⇨ *Multisport Outfitters for additional fishing outfitters and expeditions.*

HIKING

With 730 mi of marked trails, Glacier is a hiker's paradise. Trail maps are available at all visitor centers and entrance stations. Before hiking, ask about trail closures due to bear or mountain lion activity. Never hike alone. For backcountry hiking, pick up a permit from park

6

MULTISPORT OUTFITTERS

Glacier Guides and Montana Raft Company. Take a raft trip through the stomach-churning white water of the Middle Fork of the Flathead and combine it with a hike, horseback ride, or a barbecue. The company also offers guided hikes and fly-fishing trips. ⊠ *11970 U.S. 2 E, 1 mi west of West Glacier* ☎ *406/387–5555 or 800/521–7238* ⊕ *www.glacierguides.com* 🖃 *$48–$87* ⊗ *May–Oct.*

Glacier Raft Company and Outdoor Center. In addition to running fishing trips, family float rides, and high-adrenaline white-water adventure rafting (including multiday excursions), this outfitter will set you up with camping, backpacking, and fishing gear. There's a full-service fly-fishing shop and outdoor store. You can stay in one of nine log cabins that sleep six to 14 people. ⊠ *11957 U.S. 2 E, West Glacier* ☎ *406/888–5454 or 800/235–6781* ⊕ *www.*

glacierraftco.com 🖃 *$48–$87* ⊗ *Year-round; rafting mid-May–Sept.*

Great Northern Whitewater. Sign up for daily white-water, kayaking, and fishing trips. This outfitter also rents Swiss-style chalets with views of Glacier's peaks. ⊠ *12127 Hwy. 2 E, 1 mi south of West Glacier* ☎ *406/387–5340 or 800/735–7897* ⊕ *www.gnwhitewater.com* 🖃 *$48–$82* ⊗ *May–Oct.*

Wild River Adventures. Brave the white water in an inflatable kayak or a traditional raft, or enjoy a scenic float with these guys, who will paddle you over the Middle Fork of the Flathead and peddle you tall tales all the while. They also provide trail rides and scenic fishing trips on rivers around Glacier Park. ⊠ *11900 U.S. 2 E, 1 mi west of West Glacier* ☎ *406/387–9453 or 800/700–7056* ⊕ *www.riverwild.com* 🖃 *$48–$115* ⊗ *Mid-May–Sept.*

headquarters or the Apgar Backcountry Permit Center near Glacier's west entrance (☎ *406/888–7939*).

EASY

Avalanche Lake Trail. From Avalanche Creek Campground, take this 3-mi trail leading to mountain-ringed Avalanche Lake. The walk is relatively easy (it ascends 500 feet), making this one of the most accessible backcountry lakes in the park. Crowds fill the parking area and trail during July and August, and on sunny weekends in May and June. ⊠ *Trailhead across from Avalanche Creek Campground, 15 mi north of Apgar on Going-to-the-Sun Rd.*

☾ **Baring Falls.** For a nice family hike, try the 1.3-mi path from the Sun Point parking area. It leads to a spruce and Douglas fir wood; cross a log bridge over Baring Creek, and you arrive at the base of gushing Baring Falls. ⊠ *Trailhead 11 mi east of Logan Pass on Going-to-the-Sun Rd. at the Sun Point parking area.*

★ **Hidden Lake Nature Trail.** This uphill, 1½-mi trail runs from Logan Pass southwest to Hidden Lake Overlook, from which you get a beautiful view of the lake and McDonald Valley. In spring ribbons of water pour off the rocks surrounding the lake. ⊠ *Trailhead directly behind Logan Pass Visitor Center.*

☺ **Trail of the Cedars.** This wheelchair-
★ accessible, ½-mi boardwalk loop
through an ancient cedar and hem-
lock forest is a favorite of families
with small children and people
with disabilities. Interpretive signs
describe the habitat and natural
history of the rain forest. ⊠ *Trailhead across from Avalanche Creek
Campground, 15 mi north of Apgar
on Going-to-the-Sun Rd.*

MODERATE

Fodor'sChoice **Highline Trail.** From the Logan Pass
★ parking lot, hike north along the Garden Wall and just below the craggy
Continental Divide. Wildflowers dominate the 7.6 mi to Granite Park
Chalet, a National Historic Landmark, where hikers with reservations
can overnight. Return to Logan Pass along the same trail or hike down
4½ mi (a 2,500-foot descent) on the Loop Trail. ⊠ *Trailhead at the
Logan Pass Visitor Center.*

Iceberg Lake Trail. This moderately strenuous 9-mi round-trip hike passes
the gushing Ptarmigan Falls, then climbs to its namesake, where icebergs
bob in the chilly mountain loch. Mountain goats hang out on sheer cliffs
above, bighorn sheep graze in the high mountain meadows, and grizzly
bears dig for glacier lily bulbs, grubs, and other delicacies. Rangers lead
hikes here almost daily in summer, leaving at 8:30 AM. ⊠ *Trailhead at
the Swiftcurrent Inn parking lot off Many Glacier Rd.*

DIFFICULT

★ **Grinnell Glacier Trail.** The strenuous 5½-mi hike to Grinnell Glacier, the
park's largest and most accessible glacier, is marked by several spectacular viewpoints. You start at Swiftcurrent Lake's picnic area, climb a
moraine to Lake Josephine, then climb to the Grinnell Glacier overlook.
Halfway up, turn around to see the prairie land to the northeast. You
can shortcut the trail by 2 mi each way by taking two scenic boat rides
across Swiftcurrent Lake and Lake Josephine. From July to mid-September, a ranger-led hike departs from the Many Glacier Hotel boat dock
most mornings at 8:30. ⊠ *Trail begins at Lake Josephine boat dock.*

Sun Point Nature Trail. This short, 1.3-mi well-groomed trail allows you to
walk along the cliffs and shores of picturesque St. Mary Lake. There is a
stunning waterfall at the end of the hike. You may choose to hike one-
way and take a boat transfer back. ⊠ *Trailhead is 11 mi east of Logan
Pass on Going-to-the-Sun Rd. at the Sun Point parking area.*

Two Medicine Valley Trails. One of the least-developed parts of Glacier,
the lovely southeast corner of the park is a good place for a quiet day
hike, although you should look out for signs of bears. The trailhead to
Upper Two Medicine Lake and Cobalt Lake begins west of the boat
dock and camp supply store where you can make arrangements for a
boat pick-up or drop-off across the lake. ⊠ *Trailhead is west of the
boat dock and camp supply store at Two Medicine Campground, 9 mi
west of Rte. 49.*

GLACIERS AWAY?

Call it global warming or call it
a natural progression, but the
glaciers at Glacier National Park
are feeling the heat. By 2050, or
earlier, it is estimated that all of
the glaciers in the park will have
melted. Currently there are 50
glaciers in the park (at one time
there were 200).

6

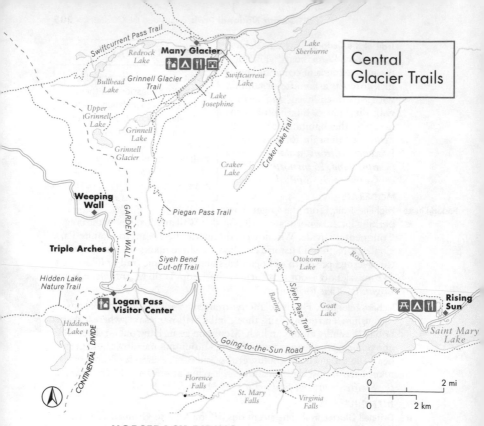

HORSEBACK RIDING

Horses are permitted on many trails within the parks; check for seasonal exceptions. Horseback riding is prohibited on paved roads. You can pick up a brochure about suggested routes and outfitters from any visitor center or entrance station. The Sperry Chalet Trail to the view of Sperry Glacier above Lake McDonald is a tough 7-mi climb.

OUTFIT-
TERS AND
EXPEDITIONS
At **Glacier Gateway Outfitters** (☎ *406/226–4408, 406/338–5560* ✉ *$25–$175* ☉ *May–Sept.*), in East Glacier, a Blackfoot cowboy guides riders through the park's Two Medicine area. Rides, which are one hour or one day, begin at Glacier Park Lodge and climb through aspen groves to high-country views of Dancing Lady and Bison mountains. Riders must be 8 and older, and reservations are essential. **Swan Mountain Outfitters** (☎ *877/888–5557 central reservations, 406/888–5010 Apgar Corral, 406/888–5121 Lake McDonald Corral, 406/732–4203 Many Glacier Corral* ⊕ *www.swanmountainoutfitters.com/glacier* ✉ *$40 for 1 hr, $58 for 2 hrs, $105 for ½ day, $150 for full day* ☉ *Late May–mid-Sept.*) begins its rides at Apgar, Lake McDonald, and Many Glacier, and is the only outfitter that offers horseback riding inside the park. Trips for beginning to advanced riders cover both flat and mountainous territory. Riders must be 7 or older and weigh less than 250 pounds. Reservations are essential.

SKIING AND SNOWSHOEING

Cross-country skiing and snowshoeing are increasingly popular in the park. Glacier distributes a free pamphlet titled *Ski Trails of Glacier National Park*, with 16 noted trails. You can start at Lake McDonald Lodge and ski cross-country up Going-to-the-Sun Road. The 2½-mi Apgar Natural Trail is popular with snowshoers. No restaurants or stores are open in winter in Glacier.

> **NOTABLE QUOTATION**
>
> "Get off the tracks at Belton Station (now West Glacier), and in a few minutes you will find yourself in the midst of what you are sure to say is the best care-killing scenery on the continent."
>
> —John Muir

OUTFITTERS AND EXPEDITIONS **Glacier Park Ski Tours** (🖰 *P.O. Box 4833, Whitefish 59937* 🕿 *406/891–2173 or 877/735–9514* ⊕ *www.glacierparkskitours.com* ✉ *$30–$150* ☽ *Mid-Nov.–May*) leads one-day or multiday guided ski or snowshoe trips on the park's scenic winter trails. On overnight trips you stay in snow huts or tents. Just outside the southern edge of the park, the **Izaak Walton Inn** (✉ *290 Izaak Walton Inn Rd. [off U.S. 2], Essex 59916* 🕿 *406/888–5700* ⊕ *www.izaakwaltoninn.com* ▤ *MC, V* ✉ *$85–$200 full day [includes lunch]* ☽ *Mid-Nov.–May*) has more than 20 mi of groomed cross-country ski trails on the property and offers guided ski and snowshoe tours inside the park. The hotel is one of the few places in the area that is both open during the winter months and accessible by Amtrak train—a nice perk, because then you don't have to worry about driving on icy mountain roads.

6

EDUCATIONAL OFFERINGS

CLASSES AND SEMINARS

☾ **Glacier Institute.** Based near West Glacier at the Field Camp and on the remote western boundary at the Big Creek Outdoor Education Center, this learning institute offers more than 75 field courses for kids and adults. Year-round, experts in wildlife biology, native plants, and river ecology lead treks into Glacier's backcountry on daylong and multiday programs. 🖰 *P.O. Box 7457, Kalispell 59901* 🕿 *406/755–1211* ⊕ *www.glacierinstitute.org*.

KIDS' CAMPS

☾ **Adventure Camps.** Youngsters ages six to eight can partake of one-day naturalist courses, while kids 11–13 can take weeklong hiking and rafting trips. Some camps involve backcountry camping, while others are based out of the Big Creek or Glacier Park field camps. Subjects range from ecology and birding to wildflowers, predators and prey, and backcountry medicine. ✉ *137 Main St., Kalispell* 🕿 *406/755–1211* ⊕ *www. glacierinstitute.org* ✉ *$20–$300* ☽ *June–Aug.*

RANGER PROGRAMS

These programs are free to visitors. Most run daily, July through Labor Day. For information on ranger programs, call 🕿 *406/888–7800*.

The Crown of the Continent

The history of Glacier National Park started long before Congress named the spectacular wilderness a national park. American Indians, including the Blackfeet, Kootenai, and Salish, regularly traversed the area's valleys for centuries before white immigrants arrived. For the most part, these migratory people crossed the Rocky Mountains in search of sustenance in the form of roots, grasses, berries, and game. Many tribes felt that the mountains, with their unusual glacier-carved horns, cirques, and arêtes, were spiritually charged. Later, white people would be similarly inspired by Glacier's beauty and would nickname the area atop the Continental Divide the "Crown of the Continent."

White trappers arrived in the area as early as the 1780s. Then in 1805 Lewis and Clark passed south of what is now Glacier National Park. Attracted by the expedition's reports of abundant beaver, many more trappers, primarily British, French, and Spanish, migrated to the region. For most of the early to mid-1800s, human activity in the area was limited to lone trappers and migrating Indians.

On their journey west, Lewis and Clark sought but did not find the elusive pass over the Rockies, now known as Marias Pass on the southern edge of the park. Whether their scouts were unaware of the relatively low elevation—5,200 feet—of the pass, or whether they feared the Blackfeet that controlled the region, is unknown. The pass went undiscovered until 1889, when surveyors for the Great Northern Railway found it in the dead of winter. By 1891 the Great Northern Railway's tracks had crossed Marias Pass, and by 1895 the railroad had completed its westward expansion.

As homesteaders, miners, and trappers poured into the Glacier area in the late 1800s, the American Indian population seriously declined. The Blackfeet were devastated by smallpox epidemics—a disease previously unknown in North America—from the mid-1800s until the early 1900s. The disease, and a reduced food supply due the overhunting of buffalo, stripped the Blackfeet of their power and, eventually, their land. In 1895 the tribe sold the area now within the park to the U.S. government, which opened it to miners. Returns on the mines were never very substantial, and most were abandoned by 1905.

Between the late 1880s and 1900, *Forest and Stream* magazine editor George Grinnel made several trips to the mountains of northwestern Montana. He was awed by the beauty of the area and urged the U.S. government to give it park status, thus protecting it from mining interests and homesteaders. At the same time, the Great Northern Railway company was spreading the word about the area's recreational opportunities. The company built seven backcountry chalets to house guests, and promised tourists from the East a back-to-nature experience with daylong hikes and horseback rides between the chalets. Visitors arrived by train at West Glacier, took a stagecoach to Lake McDonald, a boat to the lakeside Snyder Hotel, and began their nature adventures from there. Between Grinnel's political influence and the Great Northern's financial interests, Congress found reason enough to establish Glacier National Park; the bill was signed by president William Howard Taft in 1910.

⚙ **Children's Programs.** Kids learn about bears, wolves, geology, and more via hands-on activities, such as role-playing skits and short hikes. Check the Apgar Education Cabin located near the Apgar Visitor Center for schedules and locations.

Evening Campfire Programs. Rangers lead discussions on the park's wildlife, geology, and history. The programs occur at park campgrounds, beginning at 8 or 9 PM. Topics and dates are posted at campgrounds, lodges, and the St. Mary Visitor Center.

⚙ **Junior Ranger Program.** Year-round, children ages 6–12 can become a Junior Ranger by completing activities in the *Junior Ranger* newspaper available at the park Visitor Centers.

Naturalist Activities. Evening slide programs, guided hikes, and boat tours are among the ranger-led activities held at various sites in the park. A complete schedule of programs is listed in *Glacier Explorer,* a National Park Service publication distributed at the visitor centers.

TOURS

★ **Sun Tours.** Tour the park and learn the Blackfeet perspective with these native guides who concentrate on how Glacier's features are relevant to the Blackfeet Nation, past and present. In summer, tours depart daily from East Glacier at 29 Glacier Avenue at 8 AM and the St. Mary Visitor Center at 9:15 AM in air-conditioned coaches. ⊠ *29 Glacier Ave., East Glacier* ☎ *406/226–9220 or 800/786–9220* ⊕ *www.glacierinfo. com* ⌨ *$35–$55* ☉ *June–Sept., daily at 8 AM (East Glacier) and 9:15 AM (St. Mary).*

6

WATERTON LAKES NATIONAL PARK

SCENIC DRIVES

Akamina Parkway. Take this winding 16-km (10-mi) road up to Cameron Lake. A relatively flat, paved, 1.6-km (1-mi) trail hugs the western shore and makes a nice walk. Bring your binoculars, because it's common to see grizzly bears on the lower slopes of the mountains at the far end of the lake.

Red Rock Parkway. The 15-km (9-mi) route takes you from the prairie up the Blakiston Valley to Red Rock Canyon, where water has cut through the earth, exposing red sedimentary rock.

WHAT TO SEE

HISTORIC SITES

First Oil Well in Western Canada. Alberta is known worldwide for its oil and gas production, and the first oil well in western Canada was established in 1902 in what is now the park. Stop at this National Historic Site to explore the wellheads, drilling equipment, and remains of the Oil City boomtown. ⊠ *Watch for sign 7.7 km (4.8 mi) up the Akamina Pkwy.* ☎ *No phone.*

★ **Prince of Wales Hotel.** Named for the prince who later became King Edward VIII, this lovely hotel was constructed between 1926 and 1927 and was designated a National Historic Site in 1995. The lobby window affords a pretty view, and afternoon tea is a treat here. ⊠ *Off Hwy. 5* ☎ *406/756–2444 or 403/859–2231 mid-May–late Sept.* ⊕ *www.glacierparkinc.com* ⊙ *Mid-May–late Sept.*

SCENIC STOPS

★ **Cameron Lake.** The jewel of Waterton, Cameron Lake sits in a land of glacially carved cirques (steep-walled basins). In summer hundreds of varieties of alpine wildflowers fill the area, including 22 kinds of wild orchids. Canoes and pedal boats can be rented here. ⊠ *Akamina Pkwy., 13 km (8 mi) southwest of Waterton Park Townsite.*

Goat Haunt Ranger Station. Reached only by foot trail or tour boat from Waterton Townsite, this spot on the U.S. end of Waterton Lake is the stomping ground for mountain goats, moose, grizzlies, and black bears. The ranger posted at this remote station gives thrice-daily 10-minute overviews of Waterton Valley history. ⊠ *South end of Waterton Lake* ☎ *406/888–7800 or 403/859–2362* ⊕ *www.watertoncruise.com* ⊠ *Tour boat $22 one-way* ⊙ *Mid-May–Oct.*

★ **Waterton Townsite.** This is a decidedly low-key community in roughly the geographical center of the park. In summer it swells with tourists, and local restaurants and shops open to serve them. In winter only a few motels are open, and services are limited.

VISITOR CENTER

Waterton Information Centre. Stop here on the eastern edge of Waterton Townsite to pick up brochures, maps, and books. Park interpreters are on hand to answer questions and give directions. ⊠ *On Waterton Rd. before you reach the townsite* ☎ *403/859–5133 or 403/859–2224* ⊙ *Mid-May–mid-June, daily 8–6; mid-June–early Sept., daily 8–8; early Sept.–Oct. 8, daily 9–6.*

SPORTS AND THE OUTDOORS

The park contains numerous short hikes for day-trippers and some longer treks for backpackers. Upper and Middle Waterton and Cameron lakes provide peaceful havens for boaters. A tour boat cruises across Upper Waterton Lake, crossing the U.S.–Canada border, and the winds that rake across that lake create an exciting ride for windsurfers—bring a wet suit, though; the water remains numbingly cold throughout summer.

BICYCLING

Bikes are allowed on some trails, such as the 3-km (2-mi) Townsite Loop Trail. A ride on mildly sloping Red Rock Canyon Road isn't too difficult. Cameron Lake Road is an intermediate route.

OUTFITTER **Pat's Waterton.** Choose from surrey bikes, mountain bikes, or motorized scooters. Pat's also rents tennis rackets, strollers, and binoculars. ⊠ *Corner of Mt. View Rd., Waterton Townsite* ☎ *403/859–2266.*

WATERTON IN ONE DAY

Begin your day with a stop at the **Waterton Information Centre** to pick up free maps and information about interpretive programs and schedules.

Behind the reception center is the **Bear's Hump Trailhead,** where you can enjoy a relatively easy 1.4-km (0.9-mi) hike to a beautiful scenic overlook. After the hike, drive up the hill to the historic **Prince of Wales Hotel** to enjoy the view.

Next, visit **Waterton Townsite** for an early lunch. Afterward, walk the easy 3-km (2-mi) **Townsite Loop Trail,** stopping to view **Cameron Falls** and explore the trail behind the falls.

End the day with a scenic, two-hour **Waterton Inter-Nation Shoreline Cruise** across the border to **Goat Haunt Ranger Station** and back.

BOATING

Nonmotorized boats can be rented at Cameron Lake in summer; private craft can be used on Upper and Middle Waterton lakes.

OUTFITTERS AND EXPEDITIONS
☾
★

Waterton Inter-Nation Shoreline Cruise Co. This company's two-hour round-trip boat tour along Upper Waterton Lake from Waterton Townsite to Goat Haunt Ranger Station is one of the most popular activities in Waterton. (*Note that because Goat Haunt is in the United States, you must clear customs if you want to stay at Goat Haunt and hike into Glacier from there.*) The narrated tour passes scenic bays, sheer cliffs, and snow-clad peaks. ✉ *Waterton Townsite Marina, on the northwest corner of Waterton Lake near the Bayshore Inn* ☎ *403/859–2362* ⊕ *www.watertoncruise.com* ✉ *C$34* ☉ *May–early Oct., cruises several times daily.*

HIKING

There are 225 km (191 mi) of trails in Waterton Lakes that range in difficulty from short strolls to strenuous treks. Some trails connect with the trail systems of Glacier and British Columbia's Akamina-Kishenina Provincial Park. The wildflowers in June are particularly stunning along most trails.

EASY

☾
★

Bear's Hump Trail. This 2.7-km (1.7-mi) trail climbs up the mountainside to an overlook with a great view of Upper Waterton Lake and the town site. ✉ *Trailhead directly behind the Waterton Information Centre bldg.*

☾

Cameron Lake Shore Trail. This relatively flat paved 1½-km (1-mi) trail is a peaceful place for a walk. Look for grizzlies on the lower slopes of the mountains at the far end of the lake. ✉ *Trailhead at the lakeshore in front of the parking lot, 13 km (8 mi) southwest of Waterton Townsite.*

Crandell Lake Trail. This easy 2½-km (1½ mi) trail follows an old wagon road to lead to Oil City. ✉ *Trail begins about halfway up the Akamina Pkwy.*

MODERATE

Bertha Lake Trail. This 13-km (8-mi) trail leads from the Waterton Townsite through a Douglas fir forest to a beautiful overlook of Upper Waterton Lake, then on to Lower Bertha Falls. If you continue on, a steeper climb will take you past Upper Bertha Falls to Bertha Lake. The wildflowers are particularly stunning along this trail in June. ⊠ *Trailhead on south end of Waterton Townsite; head toward the lake and you will find a parking lot on the west side of the road.*

> ### HIKER'S SHUTTLE
>
> **Tamarack Outdoor Outfitters.** This is the headquarters for hiker shuttle services that run throughout Waterton to most of the major trailheads; they can also arrange certified hiking guides for groups. You can reserve shuttles two months in advance. ⊠ *Tamarack Village Sq., Waterton Lakes National Park* ☎ *403/859–2378* ⊕ *www.watertonvisitorservices. com* ⊙ *May–Sept.*

DIFFICULT

Fodor's Choice ★ **Crypt Lake Trail.** This awe-inspiring, strenuous, 9-km (5½-mi) trail is proclaimed by some to be one of the most stunning hikes in the Canadian Rockies. Conquering the trail involves a boat taxi across Waterton Lake, a climb of 2,300 feet, a crawl through a tunnel that measures almost 100 feet, and a climb along a sheer rock face. The reward is a 600-foot-tall cascading waterfall and the turquoise waters of Crypt Lake. ⊠ *Trailhead at Crypt Landing accessed by ferry from Waterton Townsite.*

HORSEBACK RIDING

Rolling hills, grasslands, and rugged mountains make riding in Waterton Lakes a real pleasure. Scenery, wildlife, and wildflowers are easily viewed from the saddle, and many of the park trails allow horses.

OUTFITTERS AND EXPEDITIONS With **Alpine Stables** (⊠ *P.O. Box 53, Waterton Lakes National Park* ☎ *403/859–2462 May–Sept., 403/653–2449 Oct.–Apr.* ⊕ *www.alpinestables.com* ⊙ *May–Sept.*) you can arrange hour-long trail rides and all-day guided excursions within the park as well as multiday pack trips through the foothills of the Rockies.

SWIMMING

ʘ **Waterton Lakes.** These lakes are chilly year-round, but they are still a great place to cool off after a long hot day of hiking. Most visitors wade, but a few join the "polar bear club" and get completely submersed. ⊠ *Along the shoreline in Waterton Townsite.*

Waterton Health Club. This club, at the Waterton Lakes Lodge Resort, has an 18-meter (56-foot) saltwater pool, a hot tub, a sauna, and a gym. A one-week membership to the facility costs C$18 (or C$52 for a family). ⊠ *101 Clematis Ave. Waterton Townsite.*

EDUCATIONAL OFFERINGS

Evening interpretive programs are offered from late June until Labor Day at the Falls Theatre, near Cameron Falls and the townsite campground. These one-hour sessions begin at 8 PM. A guided International Peace Park hike is held every Wednesday and Saturday in July and

FAMILY PICKS

Hidden Lake Nature Trail. This uphill, 1½-mi, self-guided trail runs from Logan Pass southwest to Hidden Lake Overlook, from which you get a beautiful view of the lake and McDonald Valley. In spring, ribbons of water pour off the rocks surrounding the lake. A boardwalk protects the abundant wildflowers and spongy tundra on the way.

Lake McDonald. Rent a canoe and enjoy paddling around the lake. If you work up a sweat, you can go for a swim in the lake afterwards.

Climb Bear's Hump. This 2.7-km (1.7-mi) trail takes you from the Waterton Information Centre up the mountainside to an overlook with a great view of Upper Waterton Lake and the townsite.

A surrey and a swim. Rent a surrey bike at Pat's Waterton store and enjoy peddling around the townsite. A surrey bike has a flat seat and a canopy and can hold up to three people, so it is great for families. Cool off afterwards with a swim in icy-cold Waterton Lake.

6

August. The 14-km (9-mi) hike begins at the Bertha trailhead, and is led by Canadian and American park interpreters. You take lunch at the International Border, before continuing on to Goat Haunt in Glacier National Park, Montana, and returning to Waterton via boat. A fee is charged for the return boat trip. You must pre-register for this hike at the Waterton Information Centre.

WHAT'S NEARBY

Early tourists to Glacier National Park first stopped in **East Glacier,** where the Great Northern Railway had established a station. Although most people coming from the east now enter by car through St. Mary, East Glacier, population about 400, attracts visitors with its quiet, secluded surroundings and lovely Glacier Park Lodge. **Browning,** 35 mi to the east of Glacier, is the center of the Blackfeet Nation, whose name is thought to have been derived from the color of their painted or dyed black moccasins; there are about 13,000 enrolled tribal members. The green waters of the Flathead River's Middle Fork and several top-notch outfitters make **West Glacier** an ideal base for river sports. The small town of **Columbia Falls,** only 15 mi west of Glacier National Park, has restaurants, services and accommodations.

The best base for the park is **Whitefish,** 25 mi west of Glacier and with a population of 6,000. The town has a well-developed nightlife scene, good restaurants, galleries, and shops. The village of **Essex** borders the southern tip of the park and is the site of the main rail and bus terminals for visitors coming to the park. About 45 minutes from Glacier's west entrance on Flathead Lake's pristine northeast shore, **Bigfork** twinkles with decorative lights that adorn its shops, galleries, and restaurants. Just 28 mi east of Waterton, **Cardston** is home to the Alberta Temple, built by the Mormon pioneers who established the town. The

Remington Carriage Museum contains North America's largest collection of horse-drawn vehicles.

⇨ *For further information about nearby attractions and towns, see Chapter 7.*

WHERE TO EAT AND STAY

ABOUT THE RESTAURANTS

Steak houses featuring certified Angus beef are typical of the region; in recent years resort communities have diversified their menus to include bison meat, fresh fish, and savory vegetarian options. Small cafés offer hearty, inexpensive meals, and you can pick up on local history through conversation with the local denizens. Trout, venison, elk, moose, and bison appear on the menus inside the park. Attire everywhere is decidedly casual.

ABOUT THE HOTELS

Lodgings in the parks tend to be fairly rustic and simple, though there are a few grand lodges and some modern accommodations. There are a few modern hotels that offer facilities such as swimming pools, hot tubs, boat rentals, guided excursions, or fine dining. Although there is a limited supply of rooms within both parks, the prices are relatively reasonable. It's best to reserve well in advance, especially for July and August.

ABOUT THE CAMPGROUNDS

There are 10 major campgrounds in Glacier National Park and excellent backcountry sites for backpackers. Reservations for Fish Creek and St. Mary campgrounds are available through the National Park Reservation Service (☎ *877/444–6777 or 518/885–3639* ⊕ *www.recreation.gov*). Reservations may be made up to five months in advance. Parks Canada operates four campgrounds in Waterton Lakes that range from fully serviced to unserviced sites. There are also some backcountry campsites. Visitors can prebook campsites for a fee of C$11. To do so, visit ⊕ *www.pc.gc.ca* or call ☎ *905/426–4648 or 877/737–3783*.

Outside the park, campgrounds vary from no-services, remote state or federal campsites to upscale commercial operations. During July and August it's best to reserve a site. Ask locally about bears, and always store food inside a bear box or a closed hard-side vehicle (not a tent).

WHAT IT COSTS				
	¢	$	$$	$$$	$$$$
Restaurants	under $8	$8–$12	$13–$20	$21–$30	over $30
Hotels	under $70	$70–$100	$101–$150	$151–$200	over $200
Campgrounds	under $10	$10–$17	$18–$35	$36–$49	over $50

Restaurant prices are per person for a main course at dinner. Hotel prices are per night for two people in a standard double room in high season, excluding taxes and service charges. Camping prices are for a standard (no hookups, pit toilets, fire grates, picnic tables) campsite per night.

WHERE TO EAT

GLACIER

$$
AMERICAN
☾
✕ **Eddie's Café, Gifts & Grocery.** Whether you stop in for burgers and fries or enjoy a salad with a trout dinner, the food is simple and good at Eddie's. Try the huckleberry cobbler or pop next door to the ice-cream shop and enjoy some huckleberry ice cream for dessert. Eddie's serves breakfast, lunch, and dinner, and they can even pack up a picnic lunch to go. ⌂ *P.O. Box 69, Apgar Village 59936* ☎ *406/888–5361* ⚲ *Reservations not accepted* ▭ *D, DC, MC, V* ⊕ *www.eddiescafegifts.com* ⊗ *Closed mid Sept.–late May.*

$$–$$$
AMERICAN
★
✕ **Lake McDonald Lodge Restaurants.** In Russell's Fireside Dining Room, take in a great view while choosing between standards such as pasta, steak, wild game, and salmon. There are also some delicious salads and other local favorites on the menu. Don't miss the apple bread pudding with caramel-cinnamon sauce for dessert. The restaurant has an excellent breakfast buffet and a children's menu, and box lunches are available on request. Across the parking lot is a cheaper alternative, Jammer Joe's Grill & Pizzeria (¢–$),which serves burgers and pasta for lunch and dinner. ⊠ *10 mi north of Apgar on Going-to-the-Sun Rd.* ☎ *406/888–5431 or 406/892–2525* ▭ *AE, D, MC, V* ⊗ *Closed early Oct.–early June.*

$$
AMERICAN
✕ **Ptarmigan Dining Room.** Sophisticated cuisine is served in the dining room of early-20th-century, chaletlike Many Glacier Hotel. As the sun sets over Swiftcurrent Lake just outside the massive windows, French-American cuisine is served amid Swiss-style decor. Signature dishes include the wild game sausage sampler, buffalo Stroganoff, and Rocky Mountain trout. Each night there's a chef's special such as fresh fish or pork prime rib with a huckleberry demi-glace. For a true Montana creation, have a huckleberry daiquiri. ⊠ *Many Glacier Rd.* ☎ *406/732–4411* ▭ *AE, D, MC, V* ⊗ *Closed late Sept.–early June.*

PICNIC AREAS
There are picnic spots at most campgrounds and visitor centers. Each has tables, grills, and drinking water in summer.

★
Sun Point. On the north side of St. Mary Lake, this is one of the most beautiful places in the park for a picnic. ⊠ *Sun Point Trailhead.*

WATERTON LAKES

$$$
CANADIAN
✕ **Prince of Wales Dining Room.** Enjoy upmarket cuisine before a dazzling view of Waterton Lake in the dining room of this century-old chalet high on a hill. Choose from a fine selection of wines to accompany your meal. Every afternoon the lodge's main culinary event unfolds: a British high tea served in the lobby includes finger sandwiches, scones and other pastries, and chocolate-dipped fruits, and is enjoyed with live piano music. ⊠ *Off Hwy. 5 in the Prince of Wales Hotel outside Waterton Townsite* ☎ *403/859–2231* ▭ *AE, D, MC, V* ⊗ *Closed Oct.–May.*

OUTSIDE THE PARKS

$$$
AMERICAN
★
✕ **Belton Chalet Grill Dining Room.** This is a lovely dining room with original wainscoting and leaded-glass windows, but if the weather is nice you should ask for a table on the deck where you can see the sunset behind the mountains or watch the trains roll by. Menu specialties include buffalo meatloaf, chili-rubbed wild Alaska salmon, and the bacon-wrapped

6

bourbon-and-brown-sugar-cured beef fillet. The restaurant remains open most of the year (weekends only in the winter months). ⊠ *Rte. 49, next to railroad station, East Glacier* ☎ *406/226–5600* ⏦ *Reservations recommended* ⊟ *AE, D, MC, V* ⊘ *Closed early Oct.–early Dec. and late Mar.–late May. Closed Mon.–Thurs. early Dec.–late Mar. (brunch only on Sun. Dec.–Mar.) No lunch.*

$ ✕ **Serrano's.** After a day on the dusty trail, fresh Mexican food is quite
MEXICAN   a treat, whether dining inside or on the back patio. Try a taco salad, a
★   beef burrito, or a chicken enchilada with one of the restaurant's famous margaritas. Don't be surprised if there's a lineup during July, August, and early September—the restaurant is a favorite with locals and visitors alike, and doesn't take reservations. ⊠ *29 Dawson Ave., East Glacier* ☎ *406/226–9392* ⊕ *www.serranosmexican.com* ⏦ *Reservations not accepted* ⊟ *AE, D, DC, MC, V* ⊘ *Closed Oct.–Apr.*

WHERE TO STAY

GLACIER

$$$ ⛺ **Granite Park Chalet.** Early tourists used to ride horses through the park 7 to 9 mi each day and stay at a different chalet each night. The Granite Park is one of two chalets still standing (the other one is the Sperry Chalet). You can reach it only via hiking trails. You must bring sleeping bags and your own food and water, and you need a reservation. A rustic kitchen, limited refrigeration, and pit toilets are near the chalet. You can park at Logan Pass Visitor Center and hike 7.6 mi or at the Loop Trailhead and hike uphill 4 mi. **Pros:** beautiful scenery; secluded. **Cons:** difficult to access; rustic; far from services. ⊠ *7.6 mi south of Logan Pass on Going-to-the-Sun Rd.* ☎ *888/345–2649* ⊕ *www.graniteparkchalet. com* ⏦ *12 rooms* ☖ *In-room: no a/c, no TV. In-hotel: kitchen, refrigerator* ⊟ *AE, D, MC, V* ⊘ *Closed mid-Sept.–late June.*

$$$ ⛺ **Lake McDonald Lodge.** One of the great historic lodges of the West
Fodor's Choice   anchors this complex on the shore of lovely Lake McDonald. On the
★   Going-to-the-Sun Road not far from Apgar and West Glacier, this lodge is an ideal base for exploring the western side of the park. Scenic cruises of the park's largest lake depart from the boat docks right behind the lodge, or you can rent private boats by the hour or by the day. Take a room in the lodge itself, where public spaces are filled with massive timbers, stone fireplaces, and animal trophies. Rooms are located on the second and third floors of the lodge and there is no elevator. Cabins sleep up to four and don't have kitchens; there are also motel-style rooms separate from the lodge. All rooms are no-smoking, and four are wheelchair accessible. **Pros:** lovely lakeside setting; historic property; close to Apgar, West Glacier, and Going-to-the-Sun Road. **Cons:** rustic; no TV; small bathrooms. ⊠ *Going-to-the-Sun Rd.* ⏦ *P.O. Box 2025, Columbia Falls 59912* ☎ *406/892–2525 or 406/888–5431* ⊕ *www.glacierparkinc.com* ⏦ *32 lodge rooms, 38 cabins, 30 motor-inn rooms* ☖ *In-room: no a/c, no TV. In-hotel: restaurant, bar* ⊟ *AE, D, MC, V.*

$$$ ⛺ **Many Glacier Hotel.** The most isolated of the grand hotels—it's on
★   Swiftcurrent Lake on the northeast side of the park—this is also one of the most scenic, especially if you nab one of the lake-view balcony rooms. There's a large fireplace in the lobby where guests gather on

chilly mornings. Rooms are small and sparsely decorated, but the location and the view can't be beat. There are several wonderful hikes to enjoy in this area, including ranger-guided hikes to Grinnell Glacier and Iceberg Lake. You can combine the hikes with a scenic boat tour to substantially decrease the hiking distance. Wildlife is often seen in this part of the park, and bear sightings are common in August when the huckleberries ripen. All rooms at the hotel are no-smoking. **Pros:** stunning views from lodge; secluded; good hiking trails nearby. **Cons:** rustic rooms; no TV; no Internet. ⊠ *Many Glacier Rd., 12 mi west of Babb* ✆ *P.O. Box 2025, Columbia Falls 59912* ☏ *406/892–2525 or 406/732–4411* ⊕ *www.glacierparkinc.com* ⇝ *206 rooms, 6 family rooms, 2 suites* ⚹ *In-room: no a/c, no TV. In-hotel: restaurant, bar-* ▭ *AE, D, MC, V.*

$$$$ ⛱ **Sperry Chalet.** This elegant backcountry lodge, built in 1913 by the Great Northern Railway, is accessible only by a steep, 6.7-mi trail with a 3,300-foot vertical rise. Either hike in or arrive on horseback. Guest rooms have no electricity, heat, or running water, but who cares, when the view includes Glacier's Gunsite Mountain, Mt. Edwards, Lake McDonald, and mountain goats in wildflowers. Informal meals, such as turkey with the trimmings, are simple yet filling. Note that the reservations office is closed in September and October. **Pros:** spectacular views; lovely secluded mountain setting; meals included. **Cons:** difficult to access; far from services; no electricity or running water. ⊠ *On the west side of Gunsite Mountain. Trail to chalet begins at Lake Macdonald Lodge on the Going-to-the-Sun Rd.* ✆ *P.O. Box 188, West Glacier 59936* ☏ *406/387–5654 or 888/345–2649* ⊕ *www.sperrychalet.com* ⇝ *17 rooms* ⚹ *In-room: no a/c, no phone, no TV. In-hotel: restaurant* ▭ *AE, MC, V* ⊗ *Closed mid-Sept.–early July* ⋈ *FAP.*

$$ ⛱ **Village Inn.** On Lake McDonald, this motel could use some updating, but it is very popular and offers a great view. All of the plain but serviceable rooms, some with kitchenettes, face the lake. A restaurant, bar, and coffee shop are nearby. **Pros:** great views; nice location in Apgar Village. **Cons:** rustic motel; smaller property; few amenities. ⊠ *Apgar Village* ✆ *P.O. Box 2025, Columbia Falls 59912* ☏ *406/756–2444* ⊕ *www.villageinnatapgar.com* ⇝ *36 rooms* ⚹ *In-room: no a/c, kitchen (some)* ▭ *AE, D, MC, V.*

CAMPING **$$** ⛺ **Apgar Campground.** This popular and large campground on the southern shore of Lake McDonald has many activities and services. From here you can hike, boat, fish, or swim and sign up for trail rides. About 25 sites are suitable for RVs. **Pros:** close to many activities and services; scenic spot; many campground amenities. **Cons:** large campground; less secluded. ⊠ *Apgar Rd.* ☏ *406/888–7800* ⛺ *169 tent sites, 25 RV sites* ⚹ *Flush toilets, pit toilets, dump station, drinking water, bear boxes, fire grates, picnic tables, food service, public telephone, general store, ranger station, swimming (lake)* ▭ *AE, D, MC, V* ⊗ *Closed mid-Oct.– early May.*

$$ ⛺ **Avalanche Creek Campground.** This peaceful campground is shaded by huge red cedars and bordered by Avalanche Creek. Trail of the Cedars begins here, and it's along Going-to-the-Sun Road. Some campsites and the washroom facilities are wheelchair accessible. There are 50 sites

6

for RVs up to 26 feet. **Pros:** nice setting near a creek; wheelchair accessible. **Cons:** 10-minute drive to most services. ✉ *15.7 mi. from the West entrance on the Going-to-the-Sun Rd.* ☎ *406/888–7800* ⚠ *37 tent sites, 50 RV sites,* ⚥ *Flush toilets, drinking water, fire grates, picnic tables, public telephone* ▤ *AE, D, MC, V* ⊘ *Closed early Sept.–early June.*

$$ ⚠ **Kintla Lake Campground.** Beautiful and remote, this is a trout fisherman's favorite. Trails lead into the backcountry. The dirt access road is rough, so RVs are not recommended. **Pros:** beautiful setting; remote; good fishing nearby. **Cons:** difficult to access; not good for trailers or RVs. ✉ *14 mi north of Polebridge Ranger Station on Inside North Fork Rd.* ⚠ *13 tent sites* ⚥ *Pit toilets, dump station, bear boxes, fire grates, picnic tables* ⚱ *Reservations not accepted* ▤ *No credit cards* ⊘ *Closed mid-Sept.–mid-May.*

$$ ⚠ **Many Glacier Campground.** One of the most beautiful spots in the
★   park is also a favorite for bears. Several hiking trails take off from here, and often ranger-led hikes climb to Grinnell Glacier. Always check posted notices for areas closed because of bears. **Pros:** beautiful scenery; nice hiking trails in the area; ranger-led hikes nearby. **Cons:** beware of bears. ✉ *Next to the Swiftcurrent Motor Inn on Many Glacier Rd.* ☎ *406/888–7800* ⚠ *97 tent sites, 13 RV sites* ⚥ *Flush toilets, pit toilets, drinking water, showers, bear boxes, fire grates, picnic tables, food service, public telephone, ranger station, swimming (lake)* ▤ *AE, D, MC, V* ⊘ *Closed Oct.–Apr.*

$$$ ⚠ **St. Mary Campground.** This large, grassy spot alongside the lake and stream has mountain views and cool breezes. It always seems to be the campground that fills first. **Pros:** beautiful scenery; flush toilets and showers. **Cons:** large, busy campground. ✉ *0.9 mi from the St. Mary entrance to the Going-to-the-Sun Rd.* ☎ *406/888–7800* ⚠ *123 tent sites, 25 RV sites* ⚥ *Flush toilets, pit toilets, drinking water, showers, bear boxes, fire grates, picnic tables, food service, public telephone, swimming (lake)* ▤ *AE, D, MC, V* ⊘ *Closed Oct.–Apr.*

$$ ⚠ **Sprague Creek Campground.** This sometimes noisy roadside campground for tents, RVs, and truck campers (no towed units) offers spectacular views of the lake and sunsets, fishing from shore, and great rock skipping on the beach. Restaurants, gift shops, and a grocery store are 1 mi north on Going-to-the-Sun Road. Sites are first-come, first-served. **Pros:** small campground; spectacular views; 1 mi from stores and services. **Cons:** can be noisy; no trailers allowed. ✉ *Going-to-the-Sun Rd., 1 mi south of Lake McDonald Lodge* ☎ *406/888–7800* ⚠ *25 tent/ RV sites* ⚥ *Flush toilets, drinking water, bear boxes, fire grates, picnic tables* ⚱ *Reservations not accepted* ▤ *No credit cards* ⊘ *Closed mid-Sept.–mid-May.*

$$ ⚠ **Two Medicine Campground.** Because of its distance from the Going-to-the-Sun Road, this is often the last campground to fill during the height of summer. A general store, snack bar, and boat rentals are available. **Pros:** lots of onsite amenities; flush toilets and showers; pretty setting. **Cons:** farther away from popular areas along the Going-to-the-Sun Rd. ✉ *14 mi from East Glacier at the end of Two Medicine Rd.* ☎ *406/888–7800* ⚠ *86 tent sites, 13 RV sites* ⚥ *Flush toilets, pit toilets, drinking water, showers, bear boxes, fire grates, picnic tables,*

food service, public telephone, general store, swimming (lake) ▭ AE, D, MC, V ◎ Closed Oct.–Apr.

WATERTON

$$$$ ⊞ **Prince of Wales Hotel.** Perched between two lakes, with a high mountain backdrop, this hotel has the best view in town. A high steeple crowns the building, which is fantastically ornamented with eaves, balconies, and turrets. The two-story windows in the lobby have stunning views of the valley and the townsite. Even if you don't choose to stay in the hotel, you should stop by and visit the well-stocked gift shop or enjoy afternoon tea, which is served in the lobby daily. Expect creaks and rattles at night—the old hotel, built in the 1920s, is exposed to rough winds. Rates decrease by about 25% off-season. **Pros:** spectacular view; historic property; bellmen wear kilts. **Cons:** rustic rooms; no TV; no a/c. ⊠ *Off Hwy. 5; access road is opposite the Waterton Information Center ⊕ P.O. Box 33, Waterton Park T0K 2M0 ☎ 406/756–2444, 403/859–2231 mid-May–late Sept. ⊕ www.glacierparkinc.com ↪ 86 rooms ♿ In-room: no a/c, no TV. In-hotel: restaurant ▭ AE, MC, V ◎ Closed late Sept.–mid-May.*

$$$$ ⊞ **Waterton Glacier Suites.** Located in the heart of the townsite, this property is within walking distance of restaurants, shopping, and the boat dock on beautiful Waterton Lake. It is one of the newer accommodations in the park and is particularly nice for couples. Rooms come in several different configurations and have microwaves, mini-refrigerators, and fireplaces. All rooms here are no-smoking. **Pros:** modern convenient suites; good for couples; open year-round. **Cons:** no view; pull-out sofas uncomfortable. ⊠ *107 Wildflower Ave. ⊕ P.O. Box 51, Waterton Park T0K 2M0 ☎ 403/859–2211 or 866/621–3330 ⊕ www.watertonsuites. com ↪ 26 rooms ♿ In-room: safe, refrigerator, DVD, Wi-Fi. In-hotel: laundry facilities, laundry service, Wi-Fi ▭ AE, MC, V.*

CAMPING △ **Waterton Townsite Campground.** Though the campground is busy,
$$ noisy, and windy, sites here are grassy and flat, with access to kitchen shelters and have views down the lake into the U.S. part of the peace park. The town's restaurants and shops are within walking distance. **Pros:** right in town; walking distance to restaurants and other amenities; flush toilets and showers. **Cons:** busy campground; windy. ⊠ *Waterton and Vimy Aves. ☎ 905/426–4648 or 877/737–3783 ⊕ www.pc.gc.ca/ waterton △ 143 tent sites, 95 RV sites ♿ Flush toilets, full hookups, dump station, drinking water, guest laundry, showers, fire grates, picnic tables, public telephone ▭ AE, MC, V ◎ Closed early Oct.–late Apr.*

OUTSIDE THE PARKS

$$$ ⊞ **Belton Chalet.** This carefully restored 1910 railroad hotel, the original winter headquarters for the park, has a great location just outside the West Glacier entrance. Rooms are cozy and bright, with original woodwork around the windows and period furnishings. Some rooms open up to a private deck area with lovely views. The Lewis and Clark Cottages, which remain open in winter, are snug up against the evergreen forest behind the lodge. If train noise bothers you, ask for a room at the back of the hotel. **Pros:** excellent restaurant on site; wraparound decks with lovely views; historic property. **Cons:** train noise; rustic; no a/c or

TV. ⊠ *12575 U.S. 2 E, West Glacier, MT 59936* ☎ *406/888–5000 or 888/235–8665* ⊕ *www.beltonchalet.com* ⟿ *25 rooms, 2 cottages* ⚭ *In-room: no a/c, no phone, no TV. In-hotel: restaurant, bar, spa, bicycles* ▭ *MC, V* ⊺◯⫮ *BP.*

$$ **⊡ Glacier Park Lodge.** Just outside the east side of the park, across from
★ the Amtrak station, you'll find this beautiful hotel built in 1913. The full-service lodge is supported by 500- to 800-year-old fir and 3-foot-thick cedar logs. Rooms are sparsely decorated, but there are historic framed posters on the walls in the halls. Cottages and a house are also available on the grounds next to the golf course. If you golf on the spectacular course, watch out for moose. Entertainers delight guests with storytelling and singing in the great hall. **Pros:** on-site golf course; scenic location; lots of activities. **Cons:** small bathrooms; no elevator; no a/c. ⊠ *Off U.S. 2, East Glacier* ✆ *P.O. Box 2025, Columbia Falls, MT 59912* ☎ *406/892–2525 or 406/226–9311* ⊕ *www.glacierparkinc. com* ⟿ *161 rooms* ⚭ *In-room: no a/c, no TV. In-hotel: restaurant, bar, golf course, pool, spa* ▭ *AE, D, MC, V.*

CAMPING   **⚹ Sundance RV Park and Campground.** This older campground, 6 mi
$$ south of West Glacier, was built with families in mind. It's close to a water park, and offers free Wi-Fi. Bicyclists and hikers drop in for $4 showers. You can also rent a tepee or a cabin here. **Pros:** close to water park; flush toilets and showers; free Internet. **Cons:** outside the park. ⊠ *10545 U.S. 2 E, Coram, MT* ☎ *406/387–5016* ⚹ *31 RV sites, 2 cabins, 1 tepee* ⚭ *Flush toilets, partial hookups (electric and water), dump station, drinking water, guest laundry, showers, fire grates, picnic tables, play area* ▭ *MC, V* ⊝ *Closed Oct. 15–May 15.*

Northwest Montana

7

WORD OF MOUTH

"The trip from Missoula up through Big Fork, Flathead Lake and Glacier Park is full of so much beauty, charm and scenery. And some rolling hills, too."

—slangevar

"Downtown Missoula has a lot of really interesting architecture . . . There are also wonderful "ghost" signs painted on old brick buildings, a visual treat."

—Ackislander

Updated by
Jessica Gray

With more than 6 million acres of public land, northwest Montana might be America's largest outdoor destination. More than 1,000 secluded mountain lakes with crystal-clear waters provide peaceful isolation for anglers. On Flathead Lake you can sail and water-ski. Thousands of miles of hiking and biking trails lace the Missoula and Bitterroot valleys and climb Big Mountain and the Mission Mountains region. In winter the land settles under a blanket of snow, and the water under sheets of ice, creating a winter-sports paradise, particularly for skiers.

The region's rivers, streams, lakes, and mountains attract outdoor adventurers, but once here, they discover playhouses, art galleries, and summer festivals and rodeos. In winter visitors seek out northwest Montana's six ski areas and scores of cross-country ski trails. But some of the best times to visit are the shoulder seasons, particularly in September, when there are fewer crowds and gorgeous days.

ORIENTATION AND PLANNING

GETTING ORIENTED

Much of the area's population is concentrated in the Bitterroot, Missoula, Mission, and Flathead valleys. Missoula, with a population of approximately 82,000, is the largest. Home of the University of Montana, it's a business and shopping center and offers many arts and cultural attractions. In friendly towns such as Hamilton, Stevensville, Kalispell, Polson, and Whitefish you'll find well-preserved historic sites and small yet resourceful museums. However, civilization here perches on the edge of seemingly endless wilderness: visit this part of the world for its wildlife, its water, and its pristine lands.

PLANNING

WHEN TO GO

Most visitors to northwest Montana come in July and August, enticed by lakes, rivers, golf courses, trails, and fresh mountain air. Arts festivals, rodeos, powwows, and farmers' markets fill the summer calendar. Even during this busiest season, though, you're unlikely to feel cramped among Montana's wide-open spaces. Winter is the second peak season; deep snows attract snowboarders and skiers to the region's six alpine ski areas. It's also an excellent time to explore cross-country-ski and snowshoe trails through the light, fluffy snow.

Spring and fall are the quiet seasons, but they're becoming increasingly popular. In spring wildlife sightings include newborn elk calves, fawns, and an occasional bear cub. Mountain air cools the nights, and the occasional late-spring storm can cloak the region in snow, if only for a day. Fall's dry, warm days and blessedly cool nights offer the best of weather; there are few other tourists, and most attractions are still open. Lodgings offer off-season rates and there are no crowds, unless it's at a local high-school event, where nearly the entire town shows up. No matter the time of year, keep in mind that weather in this part of the world can change rapidly. Be prepared with extra clothing.

> **TOP REASONS TO GO**
>
> ■ The Daly Mansion gives a glimpse into Montana's affluent past.
>
> ■ The Carousel for Missoula is an old-fashioned thrill ride.
>
> ■ Big Mountain's slopes are awash in wildflowers in summer.
>
> ■ The Bison Range comes alive in the spring with all the new babies.

PLANNING YOUR TIME

Among the best in the state, northwest Montana's six alpine ski areas are led by the Whitefish Mountain Resort at Big Mountain in the Flathead Valley. If you come in summer, be sure to take a chairlift ride to the top: from there you can see the Canadian Rockies, the peaks of Glacier, and the valley. Nearby, railroad fans and history buffs will appreciate Whitefish's Stumptown Historical Museum and Kalispell's Central School Museum, both crammed full of local history, plus a few humorous exhibits. Water lovers find ample room for all kinds of sports on Flathead Lake, the West's largest natural freshwater lake. Artsy types should stop in Bigfork, on the lake's northeast shore, where galleries dominate the main street and eateries are often galleries, too.

If your travels include Missoula, you can figure out the lay of the land via a short hike to the м on the mountainside above the University of Montana's Washington-Grizzly Football Stadium. From here you'll see the Clark Fork River, downtown's Missoula Art Museum, and, way off to the west, the Rocky Mountain Elk Foundation Wildlife Visitor Center.

In the forested Bitterroot Valley, where many travelers follow Lewis and Clark's trail, stop at Traveler's Rest State Park for perspective on the expedition. Plan on floating and fishing the Bitterroot and other local rivers, and in early July watch the Senior Pro Rodeo if you're in Hamilton. At one of the valley's guest ranches, be sure to sign up for a trail ride into the Bitterroot or Selway wilderness areas and along surrounding U.S. Forest Service trails. Wherever you go, don't forget your cowboy hat and your "howdy."

GETTING HERE AND AROUND

AIR TRAVEL

Northwest Montana has two principal airports: Missoula International, on U.S. 93 just west of Missoula, and Glacier Park International, 8 mi northeast of Kalispell and 11 mi southeast of Whitefish on U.S. 2. Both are serviced by major airlines; if you're coming from outside the Rockies

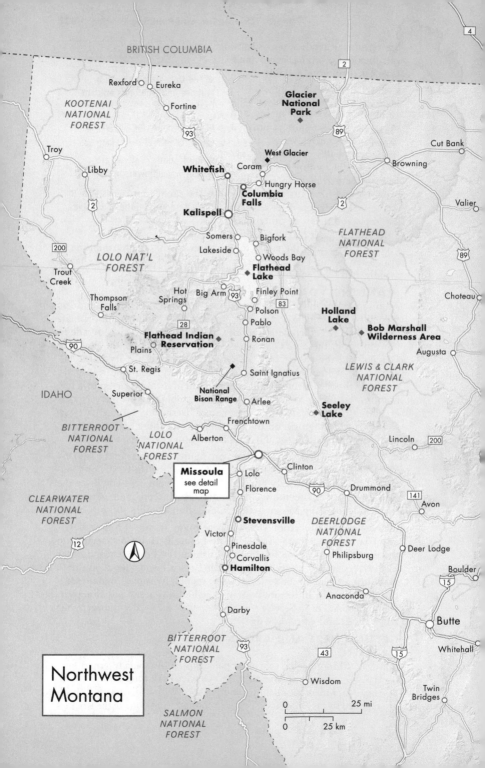

area, the odds are that you'll have a connecting flight through a larger hub such as Denver, Salt Lake City, Minneapolis/St. Paul, Phoenix, or Calgary, Alberta.

Airlines Alaska/Horizon (☎ 800/547-9308 ⊕ www.horizonair.com). **Allegiant Airlines** (☎ 720/505-8888 ⊕ www.allegiantair.com). **America West** (☎ 800/428-4322 ⊕ www.usairways.com/awa). **Delta** (☎ 800/221-1212 ⊕ www.delta-air.com). **Northwest** (☎ 800/225-2525 ⊕ www.nwa.com). **Skywest** (☎ 800/453-9417 ⊕ www.skywest.com). **United/United Express** (☎ 800/864-8331 ⊕ www.united.com).

Airport Information Glacier Park International Airport (⊠ 4170 U.S. 2 E, Kalispell ☎ 406/257-5994 ⊕ www.iflyglacier.com). **Missoula International Airport** (⊠ 5225 U.S. 10 W, Missoula ☎ 406/728-4381 ⊕ www.flymissoula.com).

BUS TRAVEL

Commercial buses that travel along U.S. 93 between Missoula and Whitefish depart daily and stop at several small towns en route.

Bus Information Greyhound (☎ 800/231-2222 ⊕ www.greyhound.com).

CAR TRAVEL

Of Montana's 69,000 mi of public roads, there are certainly more gravel and dirt roads than paved. Many of the unpaved routes are in good shape, yet you'll need to slow down and, as on any Montana road, be on the lookout for wildlife, open-range livestock, farm equipment, unexpected hazards such as cattle crossing guards, and changing weather and road conditions. Snow can fall any month of the year. In more remote areas, carry an emergency kit with water, snacks, extra clothing, and flashlights. Gasoline is available along most paved roads. However, if you are traveling in more remote areas, be sure to gas up before leaving town. Note that in mountainous terrain it's unlikely that you will have cell-phone reception.

Information Statewide Road Report (☎ 511 or 800/226-7623 ⊕ www.mdt.mt.gov/travinfo). **Montana Highway Patrol** (☎ 911, 406/329-1500, 406/755-6688, or 800/525-5555 ⊕ www.doj.mt.gov/enforcement/highwaypatrol).

TRAIN TRAVEL

Amtrak chugs across the Highline and the northwest part of the state, stopping in East Glacier, West Glacier, and Whitefish daily. Flathead Travel partners with Amtrak to offer package excursions to Glacier National Park and other northwest Montana destinations.

Train Information Amtrak (☎ 800/872-7245 ⊕ www.amtrak.com). **Flathead Travel** (⊠ 500 S. Main St., Kalispell ☎ 800/223-9380 or 406/752-8700 ⊕ www.flatheadtravel.com).

RESTAURANTS

Although Montana generally isn't known for elegant dining, several sophisticated restaurants are tucked away among the tamaracks and cedars, where professionally trained chefs bring herbed nuances and wide-ranging cultural influences to their menus. More typical of the region are steak houses featuring certified Angus beef; in recent years, particularly in resort communities, these institutions have diversified their menus to include bison meat, fresh fish, and savory vegetarian options. Small cafés offer hearty, inexpensive meals, and you can pick up on local history through photographs and artwork on walls and conversation with the local denizens. Attire everywhere is decidedly casual: blue jeans, a clean shirt, and cowboy boots or flip-flops are dress-up for most Montana restaurants.

HOTELS

From massive log lodges to historic bed-and-breakfasts to chain hotels, you'll find the range of lodging options here that you'd expect from a region that makes a business of catering to tourists. Many historic lodges and cabins do not offer air-conditioning, but in general you won't miss it, since summers here are never humid and temperatures rarely reach 90 degrees and can get downright cold at night. During ski season and the summer vacation months, reservations are necessary. Some hotels are open only in summer and early fall.

WHAT IT COSTS					
	¢	$	$$	$$$	$$$$
Restaurants	under $8	$8–$12	$13–$20	$21–$30	over $30
Hotels	under $70	$70–$100	$101–$150	$151–$200	over $200

Restaurant prices are for a main course at dinner, excluding sales tax of 2%–4% in some resort communities. Hotel prices are for two people in a standard double room in high season, excluding service charges and 7% bed tax.

CAMPING

Campgrounds across the region vary from no-services, remote state or federal campsites, to upscale commercial operations. During July and August it's best to reserve a camp spot. Ask locally about bears, and whether or not food must be stored inside a hard-side vehicle (not a tent). Avoid leaving pets alone at campgrounds because of wildlife confrontations, and because it's against the rules at most campgrounds.

Information **KOA, Kampgrounds of America** (☎ 406/248-7444 ⊕ www.koa.com). **Montana Fish, Wildlife & Parks** (☎ 406/444-2535 ⊕ www.fwp.mt.gov). **U.S. Forest Service** (☎ 406/329-3511 ⊕ www.fs.fed.us/r1).

FLATHEAD AND MISSION VALLEYS

Between the Canadian border and Missoula, tree-lined lakes and snowy peaks punctuate glaciated valleys scoured out by ice sheets some 12,000 years ago. A growing destination for golf, boating, skiing, and other outdoor recreation, the fertile Flathead and Mission valleys support ranching and farming, and are becoming known for some of the state's best restaurants.

FLATHEAD INDIAN RESERVATION

20 mi north of Missoula via U.S. 93.

Home to the Salish and Kootenai tribes, this 1.2-million-acre reservation is a fascinating historical site. Archaeological evidence indicates that Native Americans were here some 14,000 years ago, but it wasn't until the 1700s that the Kootenai, Salish, and Pend d'Oreille shared common hunting grounds in this area. The people hunted bison, descendants of which you can see at the National Bison Range. When Catholic "Black Robes" arrived to convert the Indians, they built the St. Ignatius Mission.

GETTING HERE AND AROUND

The southern border to the reservation is a quick 20-minute drive on U.S. Highway 93 from Missoula International Airport. Glacier International Airport is 35 mi to the north.

EXPLORING

For nature lovers, the main attractions of the **Flathead Indian Reservation** are fishing and water recreation on numerous lakes and streams and bird-watching in Ninepipe National Wildlife Refuge. A tribal fishing license is required, and is available at most licensing agents. Of the approximately 6,950 enrolled tribal members of the **Confederated Salish and Kootenai Tribes** (✉ *Box 278, Pablo 59855* ☎ *406/675–2700, 406/657–0160, or 888/835–8766* ⊕ *www.cskt.org*), about 4,500 live on the reservation, which is interspersed with non–Native American ranches and other property. Both tribes celebrate their heritage during the annual July Powwow. ☎ *406/675–0160* ⊕ *www.indiannations.visitmt.com/flathead.shtm* ☐ *Free* ⊙ *Weekdays 9–5.*

★ The **Sqelix'u/Aqfsmakni-k Cultural Center (The People's Center)** exhibits artifacts, photographs, and recordings concerning the Salish, Kootenai, and Pend d'Oreille people. The People's Center oversees educational programs, guided interpretive tours, outdoor traditional lodges, and annual festivals. A gift shop sells both traditional and nontraditional work by local artists and craftspeople. ✉ *53253 U.S. 93 W, 6 mi south of Polson, Pablo* ☎ *406/883–5344* ⊕ *www.peoplescenter.net* ☐ *$5* ⊙ *Memorial Day–Labor Day, Mon.–Sat. 9–5; Labor Day–Memorial Day, weekdays 9–5.*

Fodor's Choice
★ The Red Sleep Mountain Drive, a 19-mi loop road at the **National Bison Range,** allows close-up views of bison, elk, pronghorn, deer, and mountain sheep. The gravel road rises 2,000 feet and takes about two hours to complete; you're required to begin the drive no later than 6 PM and to finish before the gate closes at dark. The 19,000-acre refuge at the foot of the Mission Mountains was established in 1908 by Theodore Roosevelt. Today the U.S. Fish and Wildlife Service ranches a herd of 400 bison. A visitor center explains the history, habits, and habitat of the bison. To reach the bison range, follow the signs west, then north from the junction of U.S. 93 and Route 200 in Ravalli. ✉ *58355 Bison Range Rd., Moiese* ☎ *406/644–2211* ⊕ *www.fws.gov/bisonrange/* ☐ *$5 per vehicle* ⊙ *Range 7 AM–dark throughout year; visitor center mid-May–Sept., daily 8 AM–6 PM; Oct.–mid-May, weekdays 8–4.*

Established in 1846 as a Hudson's Bay Company trading post, **Fort Connah** was used by fur traders until 1871. Of the original three buildings, one remains today; it's believed to be the oldest building still standing in Montana. You can't go inside, but a historical marker details events and inhabitants. ✉ *U.S. 93 at Post Creek, between St. Ignatius and Charlo*

☎ *406/676–0256 or 406/549–4431* ⊕ *www.visitmt.com* ✉ *Donations accepted* ☉ *By appointment.*

The **St. Ignatius Mission**—a church, cabin, and collection of other buildings—was built in the 1890s with bricks made of local clay by missionaries and Native Americans. The 61 murals on the walls and ceilings of the church were used to teach Bible stories to the Indians. In the St. Ignatius Mission Museum (an old log cabin) there's an exhibit of early artifacts and arts and crafts. The mission is still a functioning church; Mass is offered every Sunday morning in the rectory. To reach the mission from St. Ignatius, take Main Street south to Mission Drive. ⊠ *300 Bear Track Ave.* ☎ *406/745–2768* ✉ *Donations accepted* ☉ *Memorial Day–Labor Day, daily 9–7; Labor Day–Memorial Day, daily 9–5.*

Sprawling **Ninepipe National Wildlife Refuge** is *the* place for bird-watchers. This 2,000-acre wetland complex in the shadow of the Mission Mountains is home to everything from marsh hawks to kestrels to red-winged blackbirds. Flanking both sides of U.S. 93 are rookeries for double-crested cormorants and great blue herons; bald eagles fish here in the winter. Roads (including U.S. 93, where stopping is prohibited within the boundaries) through the center of the refuge are closed March through mid-July during nesting season, but you can drive along the periphery throughout the year. Maps are available from the nearby National Bison Range, which manages Ninepipe. ⊠ *58355 Bison Range Rd.* ☎ *406/644–2211* ⊕ *www.fws.gov/bisonrange/ninepipe/.*

OFF THE BEATEN PATH

Symes Hot Springs Hotel and Mineral Baths. Truly a unique find on the western edge of the Flathead Indian Reservation, this rustic 1928 hotel has hot mineral pools from continuously flowing springs, spa treatments, massage, and live music on weekends. In the restaurant ($–$$$), steak, seafood, and pasta satisfy hungry soakers. The hotel itself isn't a standout, though the rates (¢–$$) are reasonable. Several historic hot springs in the area attracted Native Americans for centuries. **Pros:** a great place to get away from crowds. **Cons:** quite a way from larger towns. ⊠ *209 Wall St., Hot Springs* ☎ *406/741–2361 or 888/305–3106* ⊕ *www.symeshotsprings.com* ✉ *Pools and baths $7* ☉ *Sun.–Thurs. 7 AM–10:15 PM. Fri. and Sat. 7 AM–MIDNIGHT.* ▭ *AE, D, DC, MC, V*

WHERE TO EAT AND STAY

$$

CONTEMPORARY

✕ **Ninepipes Lodge.** On the edge of the Ninepipe National Wildlife Refuge, the lodge has views of the snow-tipped Mission Mountains and the native-grass-edged wetlands full of birds. The restaurant is open seven days a week, and dinners include tasty all-natural Angus beef steaks, seafood, and specials like beer-battered catfish. You can find reasonable lodging here, too ($), as well as an art gallery, a museum, and a trading post next door. ⊠ *69286 U.S. Hwy. 93, Charlo* ☎ *406/644–2588* ▭ *AE, D, DC, MC, V.*

$–$$$$

▦ **Cheff Guest Ranch and Outfitters.** This 20,000-acre working cattle ranch at the base of the Mission Mountains lets you take part in ranching life in summer and conducts pack trips from September through November. Hearty breakfasts start off days of trail rides; fishing for trout, bass, bullhead, and perch; and exploration on the nearby Ninepipe National Wildlife Refuge and Kicking Horse Reservoir in the valley below. You can join in on fencing projects, moving stock, and bucking bales of hay. A full range of options is available, from rooms with no services to cabins with all-inclusive packages. **Pros:** the Cheffs have been taking care of folks for a long time, and are excellent hosts; their horses and mules are some of the best in the outfitting world, and they do a good job matching a rider's skill with the right horse. **Cons:** a significant drive coming from either Kalispell or Missoula. ⊠ *30888 Eagle Pass Trail, Charlo* ☎ *406/644-2557* ⊕ *www.cheffguestranch.com* ☞ *7 rooms, 3 with bath; 2 cabins* ⚐ *In-room: no a/c, no phone, kitchen in cabins. In-hotel: laundry facilities* ▤ *AE, MC, V* ☯ *Closed Dec.–May* ⎆ *FAP.*

¢–$$ ⚏ **Twin Creeks B&B.** The setting is first-rate at this contemporary B&B:
☾   two creeks meander through the property, under the spectacular Mission Mountains, with views of Mission Valley farmland. Three tepees—you may stay in them for the ultimate Western night—and the resident St. Bernard dogs, Hansel and Gretel, are popular with kids. Breakfast consists of homemade biscuits and huckleberry jam, ham, eggs any way you like them, or steel-cut oats. **Pros:** fresh cookies always at hand; a beautiful property with stunning views. **Cons:** owners are sometimes difficult to reach for questions. ⊠ *33292 Twin Creek Way, Ronan* ☎ *406/676-8800 or 877/524-8946* ⊕ *www.twincreeksbb.com* ☞ *7 rooms, 3 tepees* ⚐ *In-room: no a/c, DVD, Internet. In-hotel: room service, laundry facilities, parking (free), some pets allowed, no-smoking rooms* ▤ *MC, V* ⎆ *BP.*

CAMPING   ⚠ **Mission Meadows RV.** Tucked away beneath shady pines, this conveniently located RV park is near the bison range and fishing. ⚐ *Flush toilets, full hookups, dump station, drinking water, guest laundry, showers, fire pits, picnic tables, electricity, public telephone, general store* ☞ *20 full hookups, 70 partial hookups, 30 tent sites* ⊠ *44457 Mission Meadow Dr., 2 mi north of Ronan* ☎ *406/676-5182* 🖷 *406/676-0854* ▤ *D, MC, V.*

THE ARTS

☾   For more than a century, the four-day powwow during the **Arlee 4th of July Celebration** (⊠ *Pow-Wow Rd., ½ mi east of U.S. 93, Arlee* ☎ *406/675-2700 Ext. 1222* ⊕ *www.arleepowwow.com*) has drawn Native Americans from all over the West. Highlights are drumming, dancing, and singing contests; the parade; the traditional encampment; and arts, crafts, and food vendors. Gambling includes traditional stick games and live cards.

SHOPPING

The **Flathead Indian Museum and Trading Post** (⊠ *1 Museum La., on U.S. 93, St. Ignatius* ☎ *406/745-2951*) has an extensive collection of authentic artifacts from local Native American tribes. On sale are arts, crafts, books, maps, and gifts.

FLATHEAD LAKE

12 mi north of Ronan via U.S. 93.

The 370-foot-deep Flathead Lake, with 180 mi of shoreline, is the largest natural freshwater lake in the western United States. It's a wonderful—and popular—place for sailing, fishing, and swimming. Wildhorse

Island State Park, in the lake, is home to bighorn sheep and other wildlife; the 2,165-acre island can be reached only by private boat. Cherry groves line the lake's shores, and toward the end of July farmers harvest them and sell cherries at roadside stands along the two highways that encircle the lake.

GETTING HERE AND AROUND

Seven miles south of Kalispell the road splits, and you can choose which route along the lake you would like to take. U.S. Highway 93 is the more traveled, winding around the west side of the lake through the towns of Lakeside, Polson, and Ronan. Montana Highway 35 goes along the east side of the lake and through the town of Bigfork.

VISITOR INFORMATION

Glacier Country (✉ Box 1035, Bigfork 59911 ☎ 800/338-5072 ⊕ www. glaciermt.com).**Bigfork Chamber of Commerce** (✉ Box 237, Bigfork 59911 ☎ 406/837-5888 ⊕ www.bigfork.org).

EXPLORING

Polson, a quiet community of 4,000 on the southern edge of Flathead Lake, sits under the morning shadow of the jagged Mission Mountains. It's the largest town on the Flathead Indian Reservation. Picnic spots, lake access, and playgrounds are found at Boettcher, Sacajawea, and Riverside parks. Some other parks are for tribal members only; signs identify picnic areas that are closed to the public.

The Swan River empties into Flathead Lake at the small, idyllic resort community of **Bigfork.** The small town is filled with shops, galleries, restaurants, and a cultural center. Many summer events are so popular that you should make dinner and playhouse reservations a month in advance. This is a great spot to browse after you're finished with your outdoor activities.

The rotating exhibits at **Bigfork Museum of Art and History** (✉ *525 Electric Ave.* ☎ *406/837-6927* ⊕ *www.bigforkmuseum.org*) display bronzes, paintings, and works in other mediums by Montana artists.

SPORTS AND THE OUTDOORS

BOATING **Absolute Water Sport Rentals** (✉ *49708 U.S. 93, Polson* ☎ *406/883-3900 or 800/358-8046*) inside the Best Western Kwa TaqNuk Resort, has everything from canoes and sea kayaks to Jet Skis. At **Dayton Yacht Harbor** (✉ *399 C St., Dayton* ☎ *406/849-5423 or 800/775-2990*) you can rent a sailboat, take sailing lessons, or moor your own sailboat near Wild Horse and Cromwell islands.

★ One of the most pleasant ways to see the lake is to take a **two-hour sail** (✉ *150 Flathead Lodge Rd., Bigfork* ☎ *406/837-4391*) on the historic *Questa* or the *Nor'Easter,* both 51-foot Q-class racing sloops built in the 1920s. They depart from Flathead Lake Lodge.

FISHING Take a charter trip on Flathead Lake with **A-Able Fishing Charters & Tours** (✉ *688 Lakeside Blvd., Lakeside* ☎ *406/844-0888*) to fish for enormous lake trout, as well as pike, perch, and whitefish, or just enjoy the spectacular scenery. They take individuals and groups of up to 18 people. Fly-fish with **Two River Gear and Outfitter** (✉ *603 Electric Ave., Bigfork* ☎ *406/837-3474*) on local streams, rivers, and lakes.

GOLF   Wonderful views of mountains and Flathead Lake from **Eagle Bend Golf Club** (⊠ *279 Eagle Bend Dr., Bigfork* ☎ *406/837–7310 or 800/255–5641*) are matched by the golfing on the 27-hole course. Each of the 27 holes of the **Polson Bay Golf Club** (⊠ *111 Bayview Dr.* ☎ *406/883–8230*) has a view of the Mission and Swan mountain ranges and Flathead Lake.

HIKING   **Jewel Basin Hiking Area** (⊠ *10 mi east of Bigfork via Hwy. 83 and Echo Lake Rd. to Jewel Basin Rd., No. 5392*) provides 35 mi of well-main-
Fodor's Choice   tained trails among 27 trout-filled alpine lakes. You'll find the near-
★   est phone and hearty to-go trail lunches at the Echo Lake Café at the junction of Highway 83 and Echo Lake Road. The **Swan Lake Ranger District Office** (⊠ *200 Ranger Station Rd.* ☎ *406/837–7500*) in Bigfork sells hiking maps.

KAYAKING   World-class kayaking on the Swan River's Wild Mile draws boaters and spectators to the white water during spring and summer runoff. The annual **Bigfork Whitewater Festival** (⊠ *8155 Hwy. 35, Old Town Center, Bigfork* ☎ *406/837–5888* ⊕ *www.bigfork.org*) celebrates the torrent every Memorial Day weekend with a water rodeo, races, and entertain-ment at local pubs and eateries.

RAFTING   Eight white-water miles of the lower Flathead River are covered by **Flat-
☾   head Raft Co.** (⊠ *1503 U.S. 93 S, across from Super 1 Foods in Polson* ☎ *406/883–5838 or 800/654–4359* ⊕ *www.flatheadraftco.com*). From June through September it provides wild rafting adventures, kayaking, and Native American interpretive trips between Kerr Dam and Buffalo Bridge, overnight trips, charter fishing, and tours of Wild Horse Island. The outfitter will design family floats suitable for any age.

SKIING   As you schuss runs of **Blacktail Mountain Ski Area** (⊠ *Blacktail Mountain*
☾   *Rd., Lakeside* ☎ *406/844–0999* ⊕ *www.blacktailmountain.com*), you'll glimpse Flathead Lake and surrounding peaks. This family-friendly mountain is known for inexpensive lift tickets; uncrowded, mostly inter-mediate slopes; a lovely log-accented lodge; and friendly staff.

WHERE TO EAT

$$$ ✕ **Bigfork Inn.** The Swiss-chalet style of the Bigfork Inn is reminiscent of
AMERICAN   the lodges in Glacier National Park. Inside, you'll find a lively atmo-sphere, with seating for more than 200 patrons between the main dining room, library, deck (summer), balcony, and two private rooms. They have live music Friday and Saturday evenings, and all are welcome on the dance floor. Splurge with Crispy Farmhouse Duck (served with a pecan, cherry, and red currant sauce) or the Australian lobster tail. Only slightly less decadent but delicious nonetheless is the Bigfork Inn Fet-tuccini made with chicken, red peppers, onions, and basil and topped with an asiago sauce. ⊠ *604 Electric Ave., Bigfork* ☎ *406/837–6680* ▤ *AE, D, MC, V* ☾ *No lunch.*

$$$ ✕ **La Provence.** The garden dining here offers a flower-studded view
AMERICAN   down Bigfork's main street. Local artists' work decorates the white-
★   washed walls. The owner-chef specializes in French onion soup with Gruyère cheese served inside a large onion, and specials like venison tenderloin with figs and Bordeaux sauce. An international wine list and a traditional chocolate soufflé round out the Mediterranean meals. They also have a deli, La Petit Provence, located inside, which serves

Big Country, Brief History

Scraped by receding glaciers and chiseled by weather, the landscape of northwest Montana has a long history, but the region's human history is relatively recent. The earliest Native Americans probably settled here between 10,000 and 12,000 years ago, or traveled through in search of bison herds east of the Rockies. Today the Confederated Salish and Kootenai Tribes live on the Flathead Indian Reservation, spread out across the Mission and Flathead valleys; their People's Center is one of the state's best displays of native culture and history.

Explorers such as Lewis and Clark looked at but mostly didn't touch the riches—timber, wild game, and emerald lakes—of northwest Montana, and more permanent white settlers didn't arrive until they had depleted goldfields in other areas of the West. Many of the frontier communities are only now celebrating centennial

anniversaries. Even so, the area claims some of Montana's oldest structures, such as St. Mary's Mission, the first Catholic mission in the Northwest, and Fort Connah, a Hudson's Bay Company fur-trading post. During the race across the continent, three railroads laid track through Glacier Country, leaving in their wake elegant train stations and a heritage of rail travel.

Historic sites throughout northwest Montana offer a glimpse back at the rough-and-tumble old days, but the wild lands and wildlife are what you'll write home about. On the National Bison Range you'll see descendants of the last few free-roaming American bison. Watch for birds of prey wherever you go. From the Lee Metcalf National Wildlife Refuge to the Bob Marshall Wilderness to Glacier National Park, elk, bighorn sheep, mountain goats, and bears thrive. All of these critters are living reminders of centuries of Montana history.

---

gourmet sandwiches, soups, and quiches for lunch. ⊠ *408 Bridge St., Bigfork* ☎ *406/837–2923* ▭ *AE, MC, V* ☻ *Labor Day–Memorial Day, closed Sun. and Mon.*

$$$　✕ **Showthyme!** In Bigfork's former bank building, built in 1908, diners
AMERICAN　opt for street- or bay-side seating, or a table in the snug bank vault. The
★　menu changes seasonally, but signature dishes include fresh ahi tuna with sweet soy ginger and wasabi over jasmine rice, and roasted elk tenderloin with porcini mushrooms. Save room for Benedictine chocolate truffle pie. ⊠ *548 Electric Ave., Bigfork* ☎ *406/837–0707* ▭ *AE, D, MC, V* ☻ *Closed Sun. and Mon. No lunch.*

WHERE TO STAY

$$$$　🏨 **Averill's Flathead Lake Lodge.** Since 1945 Averill's has been providing
☺　families a wholesome and active Western getaway. The beautiful green grounds are on the shore of the lake, where beach fires, canoeing, and sailing take place. The lodge, accommodations, and other buildings are all log-and-stone structures. Horseback rides set out both in the morning and evening, and you can learn to rope in the rodeo arena. Many activities such as rafting and guided fishing trips are available for an extra cost. It's BYOB at the bar. October through May the lodge is open for corporate retreats only. **Pros:** watching large herd of horses being

turned out to pasture at end of day is breathtaking; well-kept facility with many family activities. **Cons:** sign on the east side of Highway 35 can easily be missed; price takes this facility out of reach of most travelers. ⊠ *150 Flathead Lodge Rd., Bigfork* ☎ *406/837–4391* ⊕ *www. flatheadlakelodge.com* 🔊 *20 rooms, 20 cottages* ⚭ *In-room: no a/c, no phone, no TV. In-hotel: tennis courts, pool, beachfront, children's programs (ages 3 and up), Wi-Fi in lodge, no-smoking rooms* ☰ *AE, MC, V* ⦿ *FAP.*

$$$$ ★ ⚏ **Mountain Lake Lodge.** This resort perched above crystalline Flathead Lake offers 30 well-appointed suites surrounding an outdoor pool on meticulously groomed grounds. From your room, enjoy sweeping views of the lake (best from the lakeside lodges) and surrounding mountains. The hotel is well situated for hiking, golfing, rafting, and lake cruising. The log-accented dining room is designed to let you watch the sunset while enjoying smoked pheasant and other delicacies. The dining room is open seasonally; the bar serves light dinners year-round. **Pros:** beautiful facility with stunning views; great central location. **Cons:** it's a short drive to Bigfork, but Highway 35 is narrow and winding; be very aware of logging trucks during certain times of the year. ⊠ *14735 Sylvan Dr., at Hwy. 35 mile marker 26.5, Bigfork* ☎ *406/837–3800 or 877/823–4923* ⊕ *www.mountainlakelodge.com* 🔊 *30 suites* ⚭ *In-hotel: 2 restaurants, bar, pool, Wi-Fi, no-smoking rooms* ☰ *AE, D, MC, V* ⦿ *EP.*

$$–$$$$ ⚏ **Swan River Inn.** Situated in downtown Bigfork with views overlooking Bigfork Bay, the Swan River Inn has eight opulent suites decked out with themes such as Victorian, country French, safari (decorated with antiques gathered from world travels), or Montana-made furnishings. They also have three houses in Bigfork, such as the Carriage House or Trapper Cabin, with the same luxurious amenities. The restaurant ($$–$$$) at the Swan River Inn exudes European elegance, serving filet mignon wrapped in bacon, rack of lamb with a huckleberry demi-glace, and Margrit's Famous Spaghetti. There is a brunch on Sunday, and look for celebrations, such as Oktoberfest, at different times of the year. **Pros:** all except one room have great views of the bay; terrific location for all the restaurants, shops, and entertainment in Bigfork. **Cons:** downtown Bigfork is a busy place in summer, particularly during festivities such as Whitewater Days. ⊠ *360 Grand Ave., Bigfork* ☎ *406/837–2328* ⊕ *www.swanriverinn.com* 🔊 *8 suites, 3 cottages* ⚭ *In-room: refrigerator, Wi-Fi* ☰ *D, MC, V* ⦿ *EP.*

CAMPING ⚲ **Flathead Lake state parks.** Five lakeside parks are scattered around Flathead, offering quiet camping, boat launches, and good views. Bigfork's Wayfarers, Lakeside's West Shore, and Polson's Big Arm, Finley Point, and Yellow Bay parks are all owned by the state of Montana and run by Montana Fish, Wildlife & Parks. ⚭ *Flush toilets, drinking water, showers (some), fire grates, picnic tables, swimming (lake)* 🔊 *273 tent sites* ⊠ *490 N. Meridian Rd., Kalispell* ☎ *406/752–5501* ⊕ *www.fwp. mt.gov* ☰ *No credit cards* ⊙ *May–Sept.*

☾ ⚲ **Polson Motorcoach and RV Resort/ KOA.** Perched above Flathead Lake with incredible views of the Mission and Swan mountains, this grassy spot is convenient to the lake and town, and hosts can direct you to

7

fossil and arrowhead hunting. Not just for campers, this resort has a cottage complete with its own kitchenette and private hot tub. ♿ *Flush toilets, full hookups, dump station, drinking water, guest laundry, showers, fire pits, picnic tables, electricity, public telephone, general store, play area, swimming (pool), Wi-Fi* ⤳ *31 full hookups; 23 partial hookups; 1 cottage with kitchenette, fireplace, and private hot tub* ✉ *200 Irving Flats Rd., Polson* ☎ *406/883–2130 or 800/562–2130* ⊕ *www. polsonrvresort.com* ⊟ *AE, D, MC, V* ⊗ *Mid-Apr.–mid-Oct.*

SHOPPING

Bigfork's Electric Avenue is lined with galleries and eclectic gift shops, and is recognized for unparalleled dining and sweets. Try the soft cookies and hot-out-of-the-oven cinnamon rolls baked daily and shipped nationwide from **Brookies Cookies** (✉ *191 Mill St.* ☎ *406/837–2447*). **Electric Avenue Gifts** (✉ *490 Electric Ave.* ☎ *406/837–4994*) carries unique Flathead cherry designs in everything from dishes to napkins, custom wood signs, and a multitude of unique gifts. See award-winning sculptor Eric Thorsen at work daily on clay sculptures and wood carvings in his studio. **Eric Thorsen Fine Art Gallery** (✉ *547 Electric Ave.* ☎ *406/837–4366*). You can pick up a tiny jar of huckleberry jam or flavored honey at **Eva Gates Homemade Preserves** (✉ *456 Electric Ave.* ☎ *406/837–4356 800/682–4283*), or have one of the family-size jars of various treats shipped back home.

▌**EN ROUTE**

Between the Bitterroot Valley and the Flathead Valley, Highway 93 winds its way around the west side of Flathead Lake. Known for the two-lane, often slow-going traffic, this route has many places to stop and drink in the mountain backdrop that frames the lake. Along the way, wine lovers should check out **Mission Mountain Winery** (✉ *82420 Hwy. 93, 23 mi north of Polson, Dayton* ☎ *406/849–5524*) where you can sample wines from Montana's first bonded winery. The Pinot Noir and Pinot Gris, from pinot grapes grown on the property's vineyard, are award-winners.

KALISPELL

20 mi northwest of Bigfork via Hwy. 35.

Main Street (U.S. 93) in busy downtown Kalispell is lined with galleries, jewelry stores, boutiques, and restaurants. This century-old city, the Flathead County seat, is a regional business and retail center for people from northwest Montana. An Andrew Carnegie library is now home to the Hockaday Museum of Art, and just a few blocks away Kalispell's first school building has been turned into the Central School Museum. Pick up visitor information at the historic Great Northern Depot.

GETTING HERE AND AROUND

Daily flights fly into Glacier International Airport in Kalispell. Amtrak arrives daily in Whitefish, which is 15 mi to the north on Highway 93. From Glacier National Park, U.S. Highway 2 West will lead right into the heart of Kalispell.

EXPLORING

You can ring the old school bell at the **Central School Museum,** an 1894 Romanesque building. In the museum are galleries, activities, and displays about regional heritage and history, including local Native American culture. You'll also find a café, a museum store, conference rooms, and a reference library. ⊠ *124 2nd Ave. E* ☎ *406/756–8381* ⊕ *www.yourmuseum.org* ⌗ *$5* ⊘ *June–Sept., Mon.–Sat. 10–5; Oct.–May, weekdays 10–5.*

☾ A town highlight is the **Conrad Mansion National Historic Site Museum,** a 26-room Norman-style mansion that was the home of C. E. Conrad, the manager of a freighter on the Missouri River and the founder of Kalispell. Docents offer specialized tours for kids that focus on the clothing, activities, and food of the turn-of-the-20th-century era. The "Christmas at the Mansion" kicks off the holiday season in October, and the mansion is decorated for the season. There is a special "Tea and Tour" offered every Saturday from late November to the end of December. ⊠ *4th St. between 6th and Woodland* ☎ *406/755–2166* ⊕ *www.conradmansion.com* ⌗ *$8* ⊘ *Guided tours mid-May–mid-Oct., Tues.–Sun. 10–4 on the hr; Christmas tours Thanksgiving–late Dec., Fri.–Sun. 11, 1, and 3.*

The **Hockaday Museum of Art,** housed in the renovated Carnegie library, presents contemporary art exhibits focusing on Montana artists. ⊠ *302 2nd Ave. E, at 3rd St.* ☎ *406/755–5268* ⊕ *www.hockadayartmuseum.org* ⌗ *$5* ⊘ *June–Aug., Tues.–Fri. 10–6, Sat. 10–5, Sun. noon–4; Sept.–May, Tues.–Sat. 10–5.*

☾ One of 20 city green spaces, **Woodland Park** has a playground, ball fields, rose gardens, and a picnic area. Geese, ducks, peacocks, and black swans flutter to the pond, which in winter opens for ice skating; there's a warming hut nearby. Open June–August, Woodland Water Park is a popular attraction with a pool, waterslides, and the "Lazy River" float. ⊠ *Conrad Dr. and Woodland Dr.* ☎ *406/758–7812 or 406/758–7778* ⊕ *www.kalispell.com/parks* ⌗ *Woodland Park free, water park $6* ⊘ *Daily dawn–dusk.*

☾ Inside the historic **Great Northern Depot** is visitor information from the Kalispell Chamber of Commerce and the Flathead Convention and Visitors Bureau. Outside is the lovely Depot Park, where live music, arts shows, a gazebo, picnicking, and a playground attract both locals and travelers. ⊠ *15 Depot Park* ☎ *406/758–2800 or 888/888–2308* ⊕ *www.kalispellchamber.com* ⌗ *Free* ⊘ *Weekdays 8–5.*

OFF THE BEATEN PATH

Lone Pine State Park. At an elevation of 2,959 feet, you can view Kalispell, Flathead Lake, and the Whitefish Mountain Range from this 186-acre park. Features include a self-guided nature trail, a visitor center, nature interpretive programs, picnic areas and shelters, horse trails, and a horseshoe pit. Be sure to bring your camera. ⊠ *4 mi southwest of Kalispell on Foyes Lake Rd., then 1 mi east on Lone Pine Rd.* ☎ *406/755–2706* ⊕ *www.fwp.mt.gov* ⌗ *$5 per out-of-state vehicle* ⊘ *Mid-Apr.–Oct., daily dawn–dusk.*

7

SPORTS AND THE OUTDOORS

GOLF   At **Big Mountain Golf Club** (✉ *3230 U.S. 93 N* ☎ *406/751–1950 or 800/255–5641*) the challenging 18-hole links-style course has rolling fairways lined with native grasses and giant pine trees along the Stillwater River. At one time a private herd of bison grazed on what's now **Buffalo Hill Golf Club** (✉ *1176 N. Main* ☎ *406/756–4530 or 888/342–1619* ⊕ *www.golfbuffalohill.com*) in the heart of Kalispell. This municipal 27-hole course, built in 1936, has tree-lined fairways along the Stillwater River.

HIKING   Every year from May through October the **Montana Wilderness Association** (✉ *307 1st Ave. E, Suite 1* ☎ *406/755–6304* ⊕ *www.wildmontana. org*) offers free Wilderness Walks booklets describing dozens of trails in state. Join one of their free guided backcountry hikes, which vary from short wildflower walks to strenuous climbs.

TRAIL RIDING   Ride for a couple of hours or an entire day on the beautiful rolling hills and open meadows of this 800-acre ranch with **High Country Trails.** Kids seven years and older are welcome. (✉ *2800 Foy's Lake Rd.* ☎ *406/755– 1283 or 406/755–4711*).

WHERE TO EAT

$$ ✗ **Capers.** For more than a decade Capers was known as Café Max, and
CONTEMPORARY   it was the place for upscale dining in Kalispell. The owners decided it
★   was time to provide more moderately priced meals with the same delicious flair. The revamped menu still offers upscale fare, such as the grilled Montana buffalo tenderloin or melt-in-your-mouth seared ahi, but also includes less pricey but equally impressive brick oven pizzas and vegetarian lasagna. Capers serves outstanding wine and a surprisingly varied selection of local and imported beer. For dessert, try their tiramisu. ✉ *121 Main St.* ☎ *406/755–7687* ☐ *AE, MC, V* ⊘ *Closed Mon. No lunch.*

$$ ✗ **The Knead Cafe.** Come here for the best bread and soup in the val-
CONTEMPORARY   ley. The café's baked goods, including croissants, fresh baguettes, and chocolate cakes, will entice you in, but it's worth your while to stay for breakfast or lunch—their Reuben sandwiches are sublime, and any one of their salads makes a great lunch. The funky, mismatched dining tables and chairs are surrounded by local artwork. ✉ *25 2nd Ave. W* ☎ *406/755–7510* ☐ *AE, MC, V* ⊘ *Closed Sun.*

WHERE TO STAY

$$$–$$$$ ▦ **Hampton Inn Kalispell.** This hotel 1 mi west of downtown features an indoor 24-hour guest pool, fitness center, gift shop, and shuttle service. Guests will enjoy their free "on the house" hot buffet breakfast. The spacious rooms, Western decor, and river-rock fireplace in the lobby give the place a homey feel. They also have suites with private hot tubs and fireplaces. **Pros:** very spacious; great room rates often available from end of September through April. **Cons:** pool is directly off lobby; hotel is on west side of town, which can be bogged down during high traffic times coming from either Whitefish or through Kalispell; no restaurant on-site. ✉ *1140 U.S. 2 W* ☎ *406/755–7900 or 800/426–7866* ⊕ *www. hamptoninnkalispell.com* ⇌ *120 rooms* ⚿ *In-room: refrigerator, Inter-*

net, Wi-Fi. In-hotel: pool, gym, no-smoking rooms ☰ AE, D, DC, MC, V ⓘ◯ CP.

$$ ▦ **The Kalispell Grand Hotel.** The
★ smell of freshly baked cookies greets travelers in the afternoon as soon as they walk into the Kalispell Grand. The hotel has been a local landmark for nearly a century, welcoming guests since 1912, shortly after Glacier became a national park. The Grand's lobby has wildlife mounts, rich wood, and comfortable furniture, and local artists

showcase their works in the art gallery. The rooms are clean and comfortable, with nice-size work desks for business travelers. But for those who would rather relax, they have a certified massage therapist available to work out any sore muscles. **Pros:** feels like a step back in time; very friendly staff; delicious cookies every afternoon; they also make their own pound cake for the continental breakfast. **Cons:** no Wi-Fi in rooms; an older property—although clean and updated, may not appeal to those who like newer hotels. ✉ *100 Main St.* ☎ *406/755–8100 or 800/858–7422* ⊕ *www.kalispellgrand.com* ⮫ *38 rooms, 2 suites* ⚷ *In-room: Internet. In-hotel: spa, Wi-Fi* ☰ *AE, D, DC, MC, V* ⓘ◯ *CP.*

$$$$ ▦ **The Master Suite.** If you've ever dreamed of living in a castle overlooking spectacular countryside, this is the place to stay. As the name implies, there is one grand, private suite—actually the entire ground floor of the home—for people seeking privacy as well as plenty of room to stretch out. The 1,500-square-foot accommodation includes two bathrooms, living area, partial kitchen, bedroom, and patio. Guests are welcome on the main level of the house, as well as on the outdoor decks and gorgeous grounds. Hors d'oeuvres and cocktails are served in the afternoon. Gourmet breakfasts are often made with organic ingredients and can be modified to meet dietary needs. **Pros:** you're the guest of honor here; ideal for a romantic getaway; you can board your horses at a nearby facility. **Cons:** having only one room takes away the camaraderie of a typical bed-and-breakfast. ⌂ *1031 S. Main St., 59901* ☎ *406/752–8512* ⊕ *www.mastersuitebedandbreakfast.com* ⮫ *1 room* ⚷ *In-room: DVD, Internet* ☰ *MC, V* ⓘ◯ *BP.*

CAMPING ⚠ **Glacier Pines RV Park.** A bit of forest in the city, this spacious campground set among pines has paved roads and no maximum size limit or time limit. There are no tent sites, and it's open year-round. ⚷ *Flush toilets, full hookups, dump station, drinking water, guest laundry, showers, fire pits, picnic tables, electricity, general store, play area, swimming (pool), Wi-Fi* ⮫ *75 full hookups* ✉ *1850 Hwy. 35 E, 1 mi east of Kalispell* ☎ *406/752–2760 or 800/533–4029* ⊕ *www.glacierpines. com* ☰ *MC, V.*

7

NIGHTLIFE

Cowboy boots and sneakers kick up the sawdust and peanut shells on the floor at **Moose's Saloon** (✉ *173 N. Main St.* ☎ *406/755–2337*), where tunes from the jukebox get the raucous crowd moving. You can order pizza or a hearty sandwich to go with your beer.

SHOPPING

Sportsman Ski Haus (✉ *145 Hutton Ranch Rd.* ☎ *406/755–6484 or 406/862–3111*) has a brand-new facility in Kalispell to satisfy any outdoor-equipment need. There's also a store in the Whitefish Mountain Mall off Highway 93.

WHITEFISH

15 mi north of Kalispell via U.S. 93.

A hub for golfing, lake recreation, hiking, mountain biking, and skiing, Whitefish sits at the base of Big Mountain Ski and Summer Resort. Nine lifts serve 3,000 acres of powder skiing and provide outstanding winter and summer views (the mountain is closed mid-April–early June and late September–mid-November) into Glacier National Park and the Canadian Rockies. At Whitefish Lake, Native Americans once caught and dried whitefish. Euro-American settlers came a century ago to farm or join the timber or railroad industries; the sporty resort town now has 5,000 residents. Skiers descend Big Mountain late fall through early spring, and summer attracts hikers to the Danny On Trail. The trail leads to the mountain summit, which can also be accessed via the Glacier Chaser chairlift. Numerous other activities, such as a kids' bike academy, art treks, art and music festivals, and nighttime stargazing events, keep the mountain busy throughout the warmer months. You can tackle mountain-bike trails, rent mountain scooters, try a 9-hole folf (Frisbee golf) course, and walk in the trees along an 800-foot path in the treetops, 60 feet above the forest floor. A nature center and a few gift shops and restaurants remain open mid-June–mid-September, daily 9–4:30.

GETTING HERE AND AROUND

Amtrak's Empire Builder arrives daily right in downtown Whitefish, making this an economical choice for some travelers. When eastbound, it arrives in the early morning, making it difficult to check into hotels. Glacier International Airport has daily flights and is 15 mi away. Many hotels have shuttles back and forth. From Glacier National Park it's an easy 30-minute trip via U.S. Highway 2 and then U.S. Highway 40.

VISITOR INFORMATION

Whitefish Chamber of Commerce (✉ *520 E. 2nd St., Whitefish* ☎ *406/862–3501 or 877/862–3548* ⊕ *www.whitefishchamber.org*).

EXPLORING

If you want to check out a cross section of American life, drop by the Whitefish train station at 6 AM as a sleepy collection of farmers, cowboys, and skiers awaits the arrival of Amtrak's *Empire Builder,* en route from Seattle to Chicago. Inside the half-timber depot is the **Stumptown Historical Society's Museum.** The focus here is the Great Northern

Railway, the nation's first unsubsidized transcontinental railway that passed through Whitefish. On display are lanterns, old posters, and crockery, as well as reminders of local history, such as the books of author Dorothy M. Johnson and photos of the Whitefish football team from 1922 through 1954, plus some real fun (look for the fur-covered trout). You can pick up a walking-tour map of Whitefish's historic district here. ⊠ *500 Depot St.* ☎ *406/862–0067* ⊠ *Donations accepted* ⊙ *June–Sept., weekdays 10–4, Sat. noon–3; Oct.–May, weekdays 11–3, Sat. noon–3.*

SPORTS AND THE OUTDOORS

BICYCLING   Of the 2,000 mi of county roads in the area, only 400 mi are paved, leaving dirt and gravel roads and innumerable trails open for discovery. You can rent bikes suitable to the terrain at **Glacier Cyclery** (⊠ *326 E. 2nd St.59937* ☎ *406/862–6446* ⊕ *www.glaciercyclery.com*). Monday-night group rides begin at the shop courtyard and lead to a variety of trails of varying degrees of difficulty. Bike maps, gear, and free air are available at this full-service shop.

DOGSLEDDING   The dogs are raring to run at **Dog Sled Adventures** (⊠ *U.S. 93, 20 mi north of Whitefish, 2 mi north of Olney* ☎ *406/881–2275* ⊕ *www.dogsledadventuresmt.com*). Your friendly musher will take care to gear the ride to the passengers, from kids to senior citizens; bundled up in a sled, you'll be whisked through Stillwater State Forest on a 1½-hour ride over a 12-mi trail. The dogs mush trails such as the Eskimo Rollercoaster late November–mid-April. Reservations are necessary.

FISHING   Toss a fly on one of the region's trout streams or lakes and you might snag a west slope cutthroat, rainbow trout, or grayling. In winter you can dangle a line through a sawed hole in the ice of Whitefish Lake. The best place for fishing gear in Whitefish is **Lakestream Fly Fishing Shop** (⊠ *334 Central Ave.* ☎ *406/862–1298* ⊕ *www.lakestream.com*). Guided trips to secluded private lakes, equipment, and fly-fishing gear are sold at the shop. Advice is free. The **Tally Lake Ranger District** (⊠ *1335 Hwy. 93 W* ☎ *406/863–5400*) can recommend good fishing spots and provide maps to the Flathead National Forest.

SKIING AND SNOWBOARDING

The **Whitefish Mountain Resort on Big Mountain** has been one of Montana's top ski areas since the 1930s. Eight miles from Whitefish, it's popular among train travelers from the Pacific Northwest and the upper Midwest. Whitefish Mountain Resort is undergoing major changes, including the greatly improved Big Mountain Road and a brand new Base Lodge, which houses the Kid's Center, a cafeteria, MacKenzie River Pizza, the Snowsports Center, and the office for lift tickets, rentals, and lockers. Chair 6 is directly out the upper-level exit. The snow season runs from early December through early April.

The mountain's most distinctive features are its widely spaced trees, which—when encased in snow—are known as snow ghosts. With

3,000 skiable acres, plus out-of-bounds areas for Sno-Cat skiing, the Big Mountain offers a lot of terrain to explore and many different lines to discover among those widely spaced trees. The pleasure of exploration and discovery—such as finding a fresh cache of powder many days after a snowstorm—is perhaps the main reason to ski the Big Mountain. Easy discovery comes with the help of free mountain tours by mountain ambassadors. They meet intermediate skiers near the bottom of the main quad chair, Glacier Chaser, at 10:30 AM and 1:30 PM daily.

In general the pitch is in the intermediate to advanced-intermediate range; there's not a whole lot of super-steep or super-easy skiing. A sameness in pitch, however, doesn't mean a sameness in skiing. With trails falling away on all sides of the mountain, there is a tremendous variation in exposure and hence in snow texture; also take into consideration the number of trees to deal with and the views (the best being northeast toward Glacier National Park). Kids love the Super Pipe on the front side's Chair 3; they can spend the whole day on the north side, especially in the natural half pipe of George's Gorge, under Chair 7 (the Big Creek Express).

One of the Big Mountain's best features is its long high-speed quad, the Glacier Chaser, meaning that runs using most of the mountain's 2,300-foot vertical are interrupted by less than 10 minutes of lift-riding time. A negative is weather. Foggy days are not uncommon; at those times you're thankful that those snow ghosts are around as points of reference.

During the summer months the mountain comes alive with wildflowers and an abundance of activities provided by the resort. Ride the lift up the mountain and rent one of their mountain bikes down. Go for a "walk in the treetops" from a boardwalk suspended in the treetops and guided by expert naturalists. The new zip-line tour will carry you at 50 miles per hour to a height of over 100 feet in the air. Children and adults alike will enjoy the thrill of the Alpine Slide as you race down the mountain on your own sled. ⌂ *Box 1400 59937* ☏ *406/862–2900 or 877/754–3474* ⊕ *www.skiwhitefish.com* ⊙ *Early Dec.–early Apr. and mid-June–mid-Sept., daily 10–6; Fri. and Sat. night skiing late Dec.– early Mar. until 8:30.*

Backcountry Skiing & Snowboarding Because of an unusually liberal policy regarding skiing out-of-bounds, backcountry powder skiing and boarding are possible from the top of the Big Mountain. For the most part, the Big Mountain ski patrol does not prevent riders from crossing ski-area boundary ropes, although if you do so and get into trouble, you're responsible for paying rescue costs. Those who choose to travel out-of-bounds run a high risk of getting lost: it's easy to ski too far down the wrong drainage, creating the prospect of a tiring and excruciating bushwhack back to the base. For an introduction to the nearby backcountry, you might want to sign up with Big Mountain Ski and Snowboard School's **Sno-Cat-skiing** (☏ *406/862–2909*) operation, which takes skiers on a four-hour off-piste adventure for the price of a lift ticket plus $120. Although the backcountry avalanche danger varies with the winter snowpack, it's best to check the local avalanche forecast with **Glacier Country Avalanche Center** (☎ *406/257–8402*) and to carry transceivers, probe poles, shovels, and, most important, a knowledge of backcountry safety and first aid.

Facilities 2,300-foot vertical drop; 3,000 skiable acres; 20% beginner, 50% intermediate, 30% advanced; 3 high-speed quad chairs, 1 quad chair, 5 triple chairs, 3 surface lifts. Snow report ☎ *406/862–7669 or 877/754–3474.*

Lessons and Programs Group instruction in downhill is offered for $56 for a half day (plus a lift ticket); cross-country, telemark skiing, and snowboarding lessons are also available. Specialty clinics such as racing, mogul, and telemark techniques are provided, as well as children's programs. For information, call the **Ski and Snowboard School** (☎ *406/862–2909*).

Lift Tickets A full-day ticket is $61; for night skiing the charge is $16.

Nordic Skiing There are two machine-groomed track systems in the Whitefish area: both systems serve their purpose well enough, but don't expect inspiring views or a sense of wilderness seclusion. The **Big Mountain Nordic Center** (☎ *406/862–1900*) has its own 10 mi of groomed trails; the daily fee is $12. One advantage that the **Glacier Nordic Touring Center** (✉ *1200 U.S. 93 W* ☎ *406/862–4000 for snow report*) on Whitefish Lake Golf Course has is that 1.6 mi of its 7 mi of groomed trail is for night skiing. An $8 per person donation is suggested. Rentals and trail maps are available at **the Outpost Lodge on Big Mountain** (☎ *406/862–2946*). Arrangements for cross-country lessons can be made through the **Ski and Snowboard School** (☎ *406/862–2909*).

Rentals Full snowboard- or ski-rental packages including skis/snowboard, boots, and poles start at $30 per day (☎ *406/862–1995*).

Snowmobiling There are more than 200 groomed snowmobile trails in the Flathead region. Unless you are an experienced snowmobiler and expert at avalanche forecasting, you should take a guided trip. **Extreme Motorsports** (✉ *6191 Hwy. 93* ☎ *406/862–8594*) rents machines and clothing and leads guided tours.

WHERE TO EAT

$ ✗ **Buffalo Cafe.** For the classic small-town café experience, this is the
AMERICAN place. Locals and visitors happily blend in a casual, friendly atmosphere
Fodor's Choice as they dig into well-prepared breakfasts and lunches. You can start
★ your day with huckleberry pancakes, biscuits and gravy, or any of a dozen egg dishes. At lunchtime it's burgers, salads, grilled sandwiches, and Tex-Mex-style burritos and tacos; homemade milk shakes are worth the calories. Dinner provides a home-cooked-meal-away-from-home experience such as stroganoff made with sirloin steak and ground beef, steak sandwiches, and wild Alaskan salmon tacos. ✉ *514 3rd St.* ☎ *406/862–2833* ⊕ *www.buffalocafewhitefish.com* ▤ *AE, MC, V.*

¢ ✗ **Montana Coffee Traders.** Coffees, fresh roasted locally, pastries, and
CAFE homemade gelato are favorites with downtown shoppers. Unique hand-painted furniture, gifts, and bulk coffees and teas line the hangout's brick walls. Browse through the Saddest Pleasure Bookstore in the back of the café for local works, used books, and cards. Or visit the shop

where their roasting is done at 5810 Highway 93 South. ⊠ *110 Central Ave.* ☎ *406/862–7667* ⌂ *Reservations not accepted* ⊟ *AE, MC, V.*

$$
MEXICAN

✗ **Pescado Blanco.** Mountain-Mexican fusion—fine Mexican cuisine with a Rocky Mountain flair—includes handmade tacos, burritos, enchiladas, fresh seafood, wild game, and a fresh-salsa bar. Enjoy a cold beer or glass of wine in the summer on the patio with mountain views. ⊠ *235 1st St.* ☎ *406/862–3290* ⊟ *MC, V.*

¢–$
MEXICAN

✗ **Quickees Cantina.** You can count on great sandwiches and authentic Mexican dishes here. Try the fish tacos—a Quickees' specialty. ⊠ *28 Lupfer* ☎ *406/862–9866* ⊟ *MC, V* ۞ *Closed Sun.*

$$

✗ **Rising Sun Bistro.** On the way to Big Mountain sits this charming bistro brightly decorated a sunny French blue. Dishes are prepared with fresh local ingredients; look for daily quiche specials, salmon Cobb salad, and cider-and-mustard-braised short ribs. For dessert, try their specialty lemon cake. This is also a good choice for breakfast. ⊠ *549 Wisconsin Ave.* ☎ *406/862–1236* ⊟ *AE, D, MC, V* ۞ *Closed Mon. Brunch only Sun.*

$$$
SOUTHERN

✗ **Tupelo Grille.** In homage to the South, Louisiana native chef-owner Pat Carloss cooks up excellent dishes such as Low Country shrimp and grits, herb-crusted rack of lamb, Cajun creole gumbo, and Thai beef tenderloin tips served in a red sauce that is worth cleaning your plate for. Carloss rotates his well-chosen art collection in the dining room and further enlivens the atmosphere with piped-in New Orleans jazz, Dixieland, or zydeco music. ⊠ *17 Central Ave.* ☎ *406/862–6136* ⊟ *AE, MC, V* ۞ *No lunch.*

$$$
JAPANESE

✗ **Wasabi Sushi Bar and Ginger Grill.** Not your typical Western ski-town eatery, Wasabi is the place for your sushi fix and Japanese cuisine. The restaurant has an urban sophistication with lavender-and-red walls accented in black, with a huge fish mural along one wall. For cooked dishes, the Ginger Grill serves a variety of meals to please the whole family. As eclectic and innovative as the sushi bar, the grill has small and large plates, including lamb, duck, chicken, seafood, vegetarian dishes, and gluten-free entrées. ⊠ *419 E. 2nd St.* ☎ *406/863–9283* ⊟ *MC, V* ۞ *Closed Mon. No lunch.*

$$$
CONTEMPORARY

✗ **Whitefish Lake Restaurant.** In the historic clubhouse on the municipal golf course, dine on locals' favorites such as hand-cut steaks and prime rib, or fresh fish dishes such as halibut steak wrapped in herbs and phyllo dough, baked and served with your choice of rice, garlic mashed potatoes, or the unique horseradish potato pancakes. The Napoléon, made with eggplant, caramelized onions, roasted red peppers, and provolone, and topped with a spicy tomato sauce, makes a delicious vegetarian entrée. You can also get a burger at the bar, but always save room for dessert: coffee–ice cream mud pie with Oreo cookie–crumb crust and fudge or the owner's homemade peppermint ice cream. ⊠ *1200 U.S. 93 N* ☎ *406/862–5285* ⊕ *www.whitefishlake-restaurant.com* ⌂ *Reservations essential* ⊟ *AE, D, MC, V* ۞ *No lunch mid-Oct.–mid-Apr.*

WHERE TO STAY

For lodging at the base of the Big Mountain Ski and Summer Resort, contact **central reservations** (☎ 800/858–4152), which handles everything from upscale Kandahar Lodge to dormitory-like Hibernation House, and various new-and-chic to older-yet-updated condominiums.

$$$$ ⊡ **Bar W Guest Ranch.** Just a short drive north of Whitefish, the Bar W is a playground for horse people and outdoor-recreation enthusiasts. You can ride the nearby trails or in the indoor arena, watch trainers work with horses, or take lessons yourself. There are also unlimited hiking opportunities, and there's fishing in nearby Spencer Lake, skeet shooting, archery, and more. The rooms are clean and comfortable with a distinct Western flair. The cabin overlooks pasture and the nearby woods, and it's not uncommon to sit on the deck and watch deer and other wildlife. **Pros:** horse boarding provided, so you can bring your own to ride the 3,000-plus acres on state land; this is a great facility for business or family gatherings, with lots of activities and plenty of room. **Cons:** children under seven not allowed on trail rides, though the ranch provides a miniature pony for them. ⊠ *2875 Hwy. 93 W* ☎ *406/863–9099 or 888/828–2900* ⊕ *www.barwguestranch.com* ⇆ *6 rooms, 2 cabins* ☾ *In-room: refrigerator. In-hotel: Wi-Fi* ⊟ *AE, D, MC, V* ⊺⊙⊺ *BP.*

$$–$$$ ⊡ **Garden Wall Inn B&B.** Most of what you see in this 1923 home is
★ antique, from first-edition books about Glacier National Park and local history to bed linens with lace borders. All rooms are individually decorated and have down duvets. Special extras include a wake-up coffee and tea tray delivered to your room and afternoon beverages and hors d'oeuvres in front of the fireplace. The three-course breakfast in the dining room is served on china from a Glacier National Park lodge. The innkeeper lives on the premises and shares cooking duties with the vivacious owner. The snow bus to the ski resort stops one block away. **Pros:** industrious chef uses fresh, local produce in many of the dishes; fresh flowers from the garden complement each room's decor; deep claw-foot tubs can't be beat for a soak after a hard day of hiking or skiing. **Cons:** Spokane Avenue is a very busy street in Whitefish, and it might be tricky making a turn during the morning and afternoon traffic. ⊠ *504 Spokane Ave.* ☎ *406/862–3440 or 888/530–1700* ⊕ *www. gardenwallinn.com* ⇆ *3 rooms, 1 suite* ☾ *In-room: no a/c, no phone, no TV, Wi-Fi. In-hotel: restaurant, parking (free), no-smoking rooms* ⊟ *AE, MC, V* ⊺⊙⊺ *BP.*

$$$$ ⊡ **Grouse Mountain Lodge.** Always a Whitefish favorite, Grouse Mountain is consistently booked solid in July and August. Public tennis courts and cross-country trails border the lodge, and there's a 36-hole golf course next door. Off-season you can book some bargain activity packages. Thoroughly modern, it has a sunny lounge area with a lacquered slate floor, elk-horn chandeliers, soft-cushioned furniture, and a tall fireplace. The Grill at Grouse ($$–$$$$) focuses on steaks, ribs, and Pacific Northwest salmon baked on a cedar plank. Food is also served outside from mid-April to mid-October on the Deck and Patio ($–$$$), where there's shade and a large stone fire pit. The Wine Room can be reserved for a five-course dinner expertly paired with wines from their

7

impressive collection. Recently renovated guest rooms are less refined but have standard modern furnishings and features, including 24-inch flat-screen TVs and high-speed Wi-Fi. Also updated, with a refrigerator, wet bar, and microwave, the loft units are a good choice for families. During the holidays the lodge is decorated with twinkly flair. **Pros:** Grouse Mountain provides shuttle service from the airport or Amtrak station, daily trips into town, and four trips each day up Big Mountain; they can also provide a rental car at the lodge for those who wish to travel to Glacier or the surrounding area. **Cons:** must walk outside across parking lot to reach fitness room; hotel is too far from town to walk in for shopping or restaurants. ⊠ *2 Fairway Dr.* ☎ *406/862–3000, 877/862–1505* ⊕ *www.grousemountainlodge.com* ⤳ *133 rooms, 12 loft suites* ⟠ *In-hotel: 3 restaurants, bar, pool, gym, bicycles* ☰ *AE, D, DC, MC, V.*

$$$ 🏨 **Hidden Moose Lodge B&B.** At the foot of the road that climbs to Big Mountain, this two-story log lodge has a lively ski motif—a child's sled for a coffee table, an antique ski for a handrail. Some of the rooms have their own Jacuzzis, and there's one outdoors as well. Rooms are individually decorated with rough-hewn pine furniture and ironwork, and each has its own entrance off a small deck. The living room's vaulted ceiling creates space for plenty of light and a 20-foot-high fireplace; the scene can be quite social, especially in summer. Breakfasts are a standout, and come evening a glass of wine or bottle of locally brewed beer is on the house. The skier-owners may even share their favorite powder run on Big Mountain. **Pros:** lodge is easy to find and away from hectic downtown traffic; atmosphere is very welcoming, and you may not want to leave. **Cons:** stairs could be difficult for some people with physical challenges, or who are stoved up after hitting the slopes for the first time; not close enough to town to walk for shopping or restaurants. ⊠ *1735 E. Lakeshore Dr., 1.9 mi from downtown* ☎ *406/862–6516 or 888/733–6667* ⊕ *www.hiddenmooselodge.com* ⤳ *13 rooms* ⟠ *In-room: refrigerator, DVD, Wi-Fi. In-hotel: no-smoking rooms* ☰ *AE, D, MC, V* ⑩ *BP.*

$$$–$$$$ 🏨 **Kandahar–The Lodge at Big Mountain.** Cafe Kandahar (no lunch, reservations recommended), the small, rustic dining room in this lovely mountain lodge, serves the finest dinners ($$$–$$$$) on the mountain. In addition to dressed-up standards such as tournedos of beef and New York strip steak, you can choose from game dishes such as roast quail, elk roulade, and duck with a spice-and-orange-vanilla-bean jus, all prepared with a French provincial touch. In the rest of the lodge, the massive lobby fireplace and the Snug Bar are attractive public spaces, and the wood-accented guest rooms feature tile-and-granite finishes, leather furniture, and down comforters on the beds. Remedies Day Spa provides massage services daily and is on-site. You can catch a free two-minute shuttle to the slopes, then ski back to the lodge. **Pros:** very accommodating staff knows some of the best ski areas; spa is a plus, especially after that first day on the slope. **Cons:** even though it isn't ski season, they're closed to the public during some of the nicest times to be on the mountain; restaurant isn't open for breakfast or lunch, but they do provide a small continental breakfast. ⊠ *3824*

Big Mountain Rd. ⊕ *Box 278 59937* ☎ *406/862–6247 café, 800/862–6094, 406/862–6098* ⊕ *www.kandaharlodge.com* ↻ *50 rooms* & *In-room: kitchen (some), refrigerator, Wi-Fi. In-hotel: restaurant, bar, gym, laundry facilities, Wi-Fi, parking (free), no-smoking rooms* ⊟ *AE, D, MC, V* ⊗ *Closed early Apr.–May and Oct.–late Nov.* ⓄⓁ BP.

$$$$ ⊡ **Kristianna Mountain Resort.** With a selection of condos, town houses, and luxury private homes, Kristianna can accommodate everyone from couples seeking an intimate getaway to large gatherings of family or friends. You can ski to the door in many places, or walk a short distance to the lifts. The places are adorned in Montana-style decor, with comfort, including down comforters and fireplaces, a priority. The owners/managers take superb care of their guests, including stocking your kitchen ahead of time, if requested, and picking you up at the airport or train station. **Pros:** all properties are very well kept, and most guests want for nothing. **Cons:** not a typical hotel or rental complex, since the room or homes are in different locations on the mountain, but some of the private homes are large enough to house a large group. ⊠ *3842 Winter Lake* ☎ *406/862–2860 or 800/754–0040* ⊕ *www.kristianna.com* ↻ *15 condos, 10 town houses, 5 private homes* & *In-room: kitchen.* ⊟ *AE, D, MC, V* ⓄⓁ EP.

$$$$ ⊡ **The Lodge at Whitefish Lake.** Set on the edge of the lake, this luxury resort has beautifully appointed rooms with rich wood tones, granite countertops, and slate bathrooms with large walk-in showers and deep soaking tubs. You can spend an afternoon on the private beach or use their marina for sailing, jet-skiing, or kayaking. In winter daily shuttle service is available to the ski slopes. The only lakefront restaurant in the area, the Boat Club ($$$$) offers high-end dining with a large selection of beer and wine. Relax in front of the fire after a long day of skiing and snack on their famous Boat Club sweet-potato chips, served with bleu cheese cream. **Pros:** free valet parking; lakefront location with stunning views; courteous staff. **Cons:** no Wi-Fi in rooms; not within walking distance of downtown. ⊠ *1380 Wisconsin Ave.* ☎ *406/863–1000 or 866/872–6310* ⊕ *www.lodgeatwhitefishlake.com* ↻ *63 rooms, 21 condos* & *In-room: safe, kitchen, refrigerator, Internet. In-hotel: restaurant, room service, bar, pool, gym, spa, beachfront, water sports, laundry service, Wi-Fi, parking (free)* ⊟ *AE, D, DC, MC, V*

CAMPING ⚠ **Whitefish Lake State Park.** On Whitefish Lake in a shady grove of tall pines, this clean campground is very popular and fills early. It has a shallow bay for swimming, a boat launch, and views of the Whitefish Range. One downside is that trains rumble through at all hours. & *Flush toilets, pit toilets, drinking water, showers, fire grates, picnic tables, swimming (lake), boat launch* ↻ *25 sites* ⊠ *State Park Rd., ½ mi from downtown on U.S. 93 N, then 1 mi north on State Park Rd.* ☎ *406/862–3991* ⊕ *www.fwp.mt.gov* ⊟ *No credit cards* ⊗ *May–early Oct.; limited services Oct.–Apr.; no reservations.*

NIGHTLIFE AND THE ARTS

THE ARTS The **O'Shaughnessy Cultural Arts Center** (⊠ *1 Central Ave.* ☎ *406/862–5371*) hosts a variety of year-round live performances and concerts, as well as classic and independent films, in an intimate theater setting.

The wild and the woolly show up in February for the annual **Whitefish Winter Carnival** (✆ *Box 1120 59937* ☎ *406/862–3501* ⊕ *www.whitefishwintercarnival.com*), where you may be chased by a yeti or kissed by a mountain man at the parade. There are activities on the Big Mountain, including a torchlight parade and the Spirit of Winter show by the Ski School. In town, events include snow-sculpting contests and skijoring races (skiers pulled by horse and riders).

NIGHTLIFE   A locals' hangout, particularly for the singles crowd, **the Great Northern Bar and Grill** (☎ *27 Central Ave.* ☎ *406/862–2816*) rocks with local bands, open-mike nights, and the occasional sort-of-big-name gig. The stage is surrounded by signs from Whitefish enterprises that are now defunct. Hang out inside or head out to the patio to enjoy a brew and a pile of nachos on cool summer evenings. The microbrewery **Great Northern Brewing** (✉ *2 Central Ave.* ☎ *406/863–1000*) is open for free tastings of eight different beers, including the Wild Huckleberry Wheat and Wheatfish. They're open daily noon–8.

SHOPPING

ᗢ   The largest toy shop in northwest Montana, **Imagination Station** (✉ *221 Central Ave.* ☎ *406/862–5668*) has fun, educational, and creative toys and gifts in all price ranges. It also has a downtown Kalispell location.

COLUMBIA FALLS

8 mi east of Whitefish via U.S. 93 and Hwy. 40.

GETTING HERE AND AROUND

Glacier International Airport is 7 mi south via Highway 2. Amtrak in Whitefish is 7 mi to the west. Glacier National Park via U.S. Highway 2 is only 15 mi away.

EXPLORING

ᗢ   Many roadside attractions open during summer between the hardworking lumber town of Columbia Falls and Glacier National Park. Hands down, the most popular place on hot summer days is the **Big Sky Waterpark,** the largest water park in Montana. Besides the 10 waterslides the park has a huge whirlpool, a kids' pool, a beach volleyball court, a golf course, arcade games, bumper cars, a carousel, barbecue grills, a picnic area, a souvenir shop, and food service. ✉ *7211 U.S. 2 E, junction of U.S. 2 and Hwy. 206* ☎ *406/892–5025 or 406/892–2139* ⊕ *www.bigskywp.com* ☒ *$24* ⊙ *Memorial Day–Labor Day, daily 11–7.*

ᗢ   Get lost in the maze at the **Amazing Ventures Fun Center,** a circuitous outdoor route made of plywood walls and ladders, with viewing areas where parents can watch their kids (and give directions when necessary). Other attractions include Bankshot Basketball, go-karts, 18 holes of miniature golf, thriller bumper boats in a pond, and a picnic area. ✉ *10265 U.S. 2 E, Coram* ☎ *406/387–5902* ☒ *$6 per activity or $17.25 fun pass* ⊙ *Memorial Day–mid-Sept., daily 9:30–an hr before dark.*

ᗢ   You've found the power center of Montana at the **House of Mystery–Montana Vortex,** a wacky roadside attraction where the laws of physics don't apply and other mystifying phenomena prevail. ✉ *7800 U.S. 2 E* ☎ *406/892–1210* ☒ *$8* ⊙ *Apr.–Oct., daily 10–5.*

WHERE TO EAT AND STAY

$ ✕**The Back Room of the Nite Owl.** Locals wait in line for the fall-off-the-
AMERICAN bone barbecue ribs, broasted chicken, and fry bread served with honey
butter. The atmosphere is very casual, with a large main room, several
smaller eating areas (great for families), and a spacious patio. A typical
combination platter includes your choice of ribs (country-style or spare)
and either broasted or rotisserie chicken served with sides of fry bread,
baked beans, coleslaw, and red potatoes—or opt for a side salad. They
also serve pasta and have excellent pizza with homemade sauce. ⊠ *Hwy.*
2 E ☎ *406/892–3131* ⊟ *AE, D, MC, V* ⊘ *No lunch.*

$$$–$$$$ ⊞ **Meadow Lake Golf Resort.** As the name indicates, the links are front
⟳ and center here. The inn is just a few steps from the pro shop, and the
veranda has views of the course as well as the surrounding mountains
and a pond. Condos and vacation homes, with private decks, barbecue
grills, fireplaces, and simple, comfortable furnishings, line the fairways.
The spa has some of the best treatments in the area, including Mon-
tana's only Vichy shower. Truby's restaurant ($$–$$$$) specializes in
pastas, burgers, and brick-oven pizzas. You can dine outside in summer.
Troop Meadow Lake has many activities for the kids, including swim-
ming-pool games, arts and crafts, outdoor adventures, and movie night.
Pros: free shuttle service to Whitefish Mountain Resort; very accommodating for families. **Cons:** fine dining is limited in the Columbia Falls
area; although centrally located between the Big Mountain, Flathead
Lake, or Glacier National Park, it's a fair distance to any of the places.
⊠ *100 St. Andrew's Dr.* ☎ *406/892–8700 or 800/321–4653* ⊕ *www.*
meadowlake.com ⤺ *24 rooms, 100 condos, 20 vacation homes* ⚒ *In-*
room: kitchen (some), refrigerator (some), Wi-Fi. In-hotel: restaurant,
bar, golf course, pools, gym, Internet, laundry facilities, no-smoking
rooms ⊟ *AE, D, DC, MC, V* ⎟⚉⎟ *EP.*

CAMPING ⛺ **Columbia Falls RV Park.** The in-town location, with tall trees to shelter
against the breeze, is convenient to the Big Sky Waterpark, shopping,
the city pool, and the Flathead River. Pull-through spaces are adequate
for large RVs, and the tent area is grassy, with electricity for some sites.
⚒ *Flush toilets, full hookups, showers, picnic tables, electricity, public*
telephone, general store, Wi-Fi ⤺ *50 full hookups, 6 tent sites* ⊠ *1000*
3rd Ave. E, on U.S. 2 ☎ *406/892–1122 or 888/401–7268* ⊕ *www.*
columbiafallsrvpark.com ⊟ *D, MC, V* ⊘ *May–Oct.*

NIGHTLIFE AND THE ARTS

THE ARTS Enjoy plenty of holiday cheer and local color at the early December
nighttime parade, **Night of Lights** (⊠ *Nucleus Ave.* ☎ *406/892–2072*
⊕ *www.columbiafallschamber.com*).

The outdoors echoes with the **Lion's Club Summer Concert Series** (⊠ *Ma-*
rantette Park on U.S. 2 E ☎ *406/892–2072*) in the Don Lawrence
Amphitheater Thursday at 8 PM from mid-June through late August.
Types of music vary but are aimed toward a broad audience; the Don
Lawrence Big Band has a performance every year.

NIGHTLIFE Whether the owner's band is playing on the stage or cowboys are ser-
enading a sparse crowd of locals during karaoke, the **Blue Moon Nite Club,**
Casino and Grill (⊠ *Hwy. 40 and U.S. 2* ☎ *406/892–9925*) is a hoot. The
wooden dance floor gets a good scuffing on Western dance and country-

swing nights. Two stuffed grizzly bears rear up near the entrance, and other species decorate the large saloon as well.

SHOPPING

Huckleberry Patch Restaurant & Gift Shop (✉ *8868 U.S. 2 E, Hungry Horse* ☏ *406/387–5670 or 800/527–7340* ⊕ *www.huckleberrypatch.com*) has been the huckleberry headquarters of the state for more than 50 years, selling the purple wild berry native to the region. It has an excellent selection of jams, candies, coffee, fudge, barbecue sauce, and huckleberry-scented lotions (best not worn while hiking in bear country!). Don't miss their outstanding huckleberry pie or milk shakes.

SEELEY–SWAN VALLEY

Squeezed between two magnificent mountain ranges—the Missions on the west and the Swan Range on the east—the glacially formed Swan Valley is littered with lakes, sprinkled with homesteads, and frosted with snow for five months of the year. One road, Highway 83, winds along an 80-mi course that follows the Clearwater and Swan rivers, popular for boating and fishing—both winter ice fishing and summer trout fishing. Several trailheads lead into the Bob Marshall Wilderness from the Swan Valley. Modern amenities are as sparse as the population. Only about a thousand people reside here year-round, so you are much more likely to encounter a dozen deer than a dozen humans. With that in mind, it's imperative that you look out for deer and elk on the road, day and night. Summer visitors fill campgrounds and the few guest lodges. Besides snowmobiling and cross-country skiing, winters bring snow, drippy weather, and low clouds. Do as the locals do: put up your hood, grab the gloves and boots, and head outdoors.

SEELEY LAKE

120 mi south of Glacier National Park via U.S. 2, Hwy. 206, and Hwy. 83.

Bordered by campgrounds, hiking trails, and wildlife-viewing opportunities, this community of 2,400 centers on lovely Seeley Lake. Nearby is the Big Blackfoot River, a setting in *A River Runs Through It*, Norman McLean's reflection on family and fishing. Host to races and leisure outings, the Seeley Creek Nordic Ski Trails roll across hills and meadows. In winter 350 mi of snowmobile trails rip through the woods. The major industry, logging, which began in 1892, is evident on some hillsides.

GETTING HERE AND AROUND

Missoula International is the nearest airport, 60 mi and just over an hour away via Montana Highway 200 and U.S. Highway 83. It is best to have a car, since few places provide a shuttle.

EXPLORING

Paddling on the 3½-mi **Clearwater Canoe Trail,** along an isolated portion of the Clearwater River, you may see moose and will likely see songbirds, great blue herons, and belted kingfishers. The Seeley Lake Ranger Station has free maps and directions to the put-in for the two-hour paddle. ✉ *3 mi north of Seeley on Hwy. 83* ☎ *406/677–2233* ⊕ *www. fs.fed.us/r1* ✆ *Free* ☉ *May–Oct.*

Ten days of events celebrate winter during the January **Seeley Lake Area Winterfest,** including a snow-sculpture contest, Christmas tree bonfire, parade, biathlon, kids' games, cross-country ski events, and snowmobile poker runs. ✉ *Hwy. 83 S* ☎ *406/677–2880* ⊕ *www.seeleylakechamber. com* ☉ *Mid–late Jan., daily.*

Logging's colorful past is displayed in the big log barn at **Seeley Lake Museum and Visitors Center,** along with tools of the trade and visitor information. ✉ *2920 Hwy. 83 S at mile marker 13.5* ☎ *406/677–2880* ⊕ *www.seeleylakechamber.com* ✆ *Free* ☉ *Memorial Day–Labor Day, daily 9–5; Labor Day–Memorial Day, Mon., Thurs., and Fri. 11–4.*

OFF THE BEATEN PATH

Morrell Falls National Recreation Trail #30. A 2½-mi hike (one way) leads to the lovely cascades of Morrell Falls. It is actually a series of falls, with the longest about a 100-foot drop. This is a moderately difficult family hike, perfect for a picnic (although it's wise to remember this is bear country), and often used by bicyclists and horsemen. Maps and travel information are available at the Seeley Lake Ranger District office. ✉ *From Hwy. 83, turn east on Morrell Creek Rd. and follow signs* ☎ *406/677–2233* ⊕ *www.fs.fed.us/r1* ✆ *Free* ☉ *Daily.*

SPORTS AND THE OUTDOORS

★ You can romp in deep snows on the **Seeley Creek Nordic Ski Trails** at the edge of town. Trails are groomed for skate and classic skiing. Nearby are dogsled trails. The trail systems share a parking lot and covered picnic area, where you can join a campfire to warm your toes. ✉ *Forest Rd. 477; from Hwy. 83, turn east on Morrell Creek Rd., aka Cottonwood Lakes Rd., and drive 1 mi to trailhead* ☎ *406/677–2233* ⊕ *www.seeley-lakechamber.com* ✆ *$4 donation requested* ☉ *Dec.–Mar., daily.*

CROSS-COUN-TRY SKIING

You can ski a few kilometers on the **Double Arrow Resort** (✉ *Hwy. 83 at milepost 12, 2 mi south of Seeley Lake* ☎ *406/677–2777 or 800/468–0777*), where you may see moose in the willows.

Ski-touring equipment and maps from **Seeley Lake Recreational Rentals** (✉ *Hwy. 83 N* ☎ *406/677–7368* ⊕ *www.seeleylakerecrentals.com*) will take you to the winter trails. You can also rent snowmobiles, snowshoes, and summer toys like boats and bikes—reserve online.

SNOWMO-BILING

Rent snowmobiles, snowshoes, cross-country skis, and all of the accessories from **Seeley Sport Rentals** (✉ *3112 Hwy. 83 S* ☎ *406/677–3680* ⊕ *www.seeleysportrentals.com*), which also offers a guide service. When the weather warms up, they have pontoon boats, ski boats, wave runners, canoes, and mountain bikes for summer adventures.

WHERE TO EAT AND STAY

$$$
STEAK

✗**Lindey's Steak House.** Locals will send you here to watch the sun set over the lake while dining on the only thing on the menu: steak. Select cuts, all 16-ounce portions, are served with potatoes, garlic bread, and pickled watermelon rind served family-style. During the summer, grab a burger or chicken breast sandwich at Bay Burgers ($–$$) and enjoy the outside dining. October through March, Bay Burgers moves inside the steak house from 11 to 3. ⊠ *Hwy. 83, downtown Seeley Lake* ☎ *406/677–9229* ▬ *MC, V.*

$$–$$$$ 🖫 **Double Arrow Resort.** The handsome log main lodge built in 1929 combines European grace and Western trimmings on a 200-acre spread. The great room's stone fireplace is a guest gathering spot; nearby in Seasons restaurant ($$$) the sophisticated and changing menu features blackened buffalo sirloin, cedar-planked salmon, and their very own double-arrow-branded rib eye. Guest rooms and log cabins are simply furnished with a few antiques and fluffy comforters. Early-20th-century log homes with antiques, knotty-pine interiors, and modern kitchens are popular with families. The resort sits adjacent to one of the finest golf courses in northwestern Montana. **Pros:** excellent location for a family reunion, with all the amenities to keep people of all ages entertained. **Cons:** closest airport is in Missoula, which is 55 mi from Double Arrow; it's 100 mi to Whitefish for those traveling by Amtrak. ⊠ *Hwy. 83, milepost 12, 2 mi south of Seeley Lake* ⬧ *Box 747, 301 Lodge Way, Seeley Lake 59868* ☎ *406/677–2777 or 800/468–0777* ⊕ *www. doublearrowresort.com* ⇥ *3 rooms, 12 cabins, 6 homes* ⅙ *In-room: no a/c, kitchen (some), Internet. In-hotel: restaurant, bar, golf course, tennis courts, pool, laundry facilities, Wi-Fi, no-smoking rooms* ▬ *D, MC, V* ⑩ *CP.*

CAMPING △ **Big Larch.** Giant larch trees shade the large site, where fishing and boating are popular. There's a good beach for swimming, a horseshoes pit, wheelchair-accessible picnicking, and marked nature trails. Shopping, laundry, and services are nearby. ⅙ *Flush toilets, dump station, drinking water, fire grates, picnic tables, ranger station, swimming (lake)* ⇥ *50 sites* ⊠ *Forest Rd. 2199; 1 mi north of Seeley Lake on Hwy. 83, and ½ mi west on Forest Rd. 2199* ☎ *406/677–2233* ⊕ *www.fs.fed.us/ r1* ▬ *No credit cards* ☉ *Mid-May–Sept.; primitive camping (no services or fees) mid-Sept.–May.*

△ **Seeley Lake Forest Service Campground.** This busy campground among tall pines is on the lake, so mosquitoes can be pesky. Groceries, sports rentals, and restaurants are about 4 mi away. Reservations are recommended. ⅙ *Flush toilets, dump station, drinking water, fire grates, picnic tables, ranger station, swimming (lake)* ⇥ *29 sites* ⊠ *Boy Scout Rd.* ☎ *406/677–2233* ⊕ *www.fs.fed.us/r1* ▬ *No credit cards* ☉ *Late May–Labor Day.*

HOLLAND LAKE

19 mi north of Seeley Lake via Hwy. 83.

Outdoorsy types come to this 400-acre lake for fishing, boating, swimming, hiking, trail riding, and camping in summer and ice fishing, cross-country skiing, snowshoeing, and snowmobiling in winter. To pursue any of the activities available in this remote setting, you must come equipped with your own canoe, motor launch, or snowmobile: your company will be kokanee salmon, rainbow trout, and bull trout, plus the handful of people who run Holland Lake Lodge. Maps for the numerous trails that depart from the lake area are available at the lodge or through the Forest Service office. Some routes climb the Swan Range into the Bob Marshall Wilderness.

GETTING HERE AND AROUND

Both Missoula International Airport and Glacier International Airport in Kalispell are approximately 85 mi away via U.S. Highway 83, otherwise known as the Seeley Swan Highway. A car is a must.

EXPLORING

The hike to **Holland Falls** is about 1½ mi from the lodge. The last bit is a steep climb, but it's well worth it for the view. ⊠ *Holland Lake Rd.; from Hwy. 83, turn east on Forest Rd. 44 for 3 mi to Holland Lake Rd.* ☎ *406/837–7500* ⊕ *www.fs.fed.us/r1* ⊠ *Free* ☉ *Daily.*

WHERE TO STAY

$–$$ ☶ **Holland Lake Lodge.** When the snow flies, this lodge is nearly buried, which makes for cozy fireside dining and relaxing. The log lodge sits on the lakeshore, where you can cross-country ski or snowshoe from the door. In summer, step off the cabin porch for a hike or a swim. Cabins are updated yet rustic. You can dine on trout in the restaurant ($$–$$$) while watching the trout rise. **Pros:** incredible place nestled at the foot of the mountains; you can't ask for a better place to relax, particularly during the shoulder seasons. **Cons:** the 4 mi of unpaved road can be a bit rough and very congested during the summer; this is a heavily used area in July and August for packers and hikers heading into the backcountry. ⊠ *1947 Holland Lake Rd., Swan Valley* ☎ *406/754–2282 or 877/925–6343* ⊕ *www.hollandlakelodge.com* ⇌ *9 rooms, 6 cabins* ♨ *In-room: no a/c, no phone, no TV. In-hotel: restaurant, room service, bar, no-smoking rooms* ☰ *AE, D, MC, V* ☉❘ *FAP.*

CAMPING ⚠ **Holland Lake Campground.** Large trees provide lots of shade for campers near the lake. The spot is popular with outfitters who pack horses into the nearby Bob Marshall Wilderness. Food service is available nearby at Holland Lake Lodge. ♨ *Pit toilets, dump station, drinking water, bear boxes, fire grates, picnic tables, swimming (lake)* ⇌ *40 sites* ⊠ *Holland Lake Rd.* ☎ *406/837–7500* ⊕ *www.fs.fed.us/r1* ☰ *No credit cards* ☉ *Mid-May–Sept.*

BOB MARSHALL WILDERNESS AREA

5 mi east of Hwy. 83 via Pyramid Pass Trail, Lion Creek Pass Trail, or Smith Creek Pass Trail.

The Bob Marshall, Scapegoat, and Great Bear wilderness areas take up 1.5 million rugged, roadless, remote acres within the Flathead National Forest. Preservation pioneer, forester, and cofounder of the Wilderness Society, Bob Marshall pushed Congress in 1964 to create the wilderness area that bears his name. Since then, little has altered the landscape, which runs 60 mi along the Continental Divide. More than 1,000 mi of trails enter the wilderness from near Seeley Lake at Pyramid Pass Trail and Holland Lake at Pyramid Pass, Condon's Lion Creek Pass, and Smith Creek Pass, where hikers are sure to meet outfitters and packhorses. An old airstrip at Shafer Meadows is used for float parties on the wild white-water Middle Fork of the Flathead.

GETTING HERE AND AROUND

The Bob Marshall Wilderness can be accessed from the west near Seeley Lake and Holland Lake via Highway 83, from the east near Choteau and Bynum via Highway 89, and from the northwest near Hungry Horse via Highway 2 and the East Reservoir Road. The latter is a long, winding gravel road that's impassable during the winter; a four-wheel-drive vehicle is a good idea.

EXPLORING

Information on the Bob Marshall Wilderness is available through the **Flathead National Forest,** which has maps, listings of outfitters and access points, and safety information about travel in bear country. ⊠ *650 Wolfpack Way, Kalispell* ☎ *406/758–5200* ⊕ *www.fs.fed.us/r1* 🖭 *Free* ☻ *Weekdays 8–4.*

A complete list of trails, elevations, and backcountry campsites can be found in the book *Hiking Montana's Bob Marshall Wilderness* by Erik Molvar, available at **Books West** (⊠ *101 Main, Kalispell* ☎ *406/752–6900 or 800/471–2270*).

OFF THE BEATEN PATH

Spotted Bear. At the end of a long and often washboarded gravel road, Spotted Bear is a remote entrance into the Bob Marshall Wilderness. You'll find there a ranger station, outfitter's ranch, campground, swimming, and rafting a short distance down the South Fork of the Flathead River to the Hungry Horse Reservoir. ⊠ *Forest Service Rd. 38; 55 mi from Hungry Horse on either E. or W. Hungry Horse Reservoir Rd.* ☎ *406/387–3800* ⊕ *www.fs.fed.us/r1* 🖭 *Free* ☻ *Apr.–Oct.*

SPORTS AND THE OUTDOORS

FISHING

Five-day pack and float trips with **Bob Marshall Wilderness Horse Pack and Float Expeditions** (⊠ *55 mi from Hungry Horse on either E. or W. Hungry Horse Reservoir Rd. toward Spotted Bear Ranger Station* ☎ *800/223–4333* ⊕ *www.spottedbear.com*) go deep into the backcountry for fly-fishing in the wilderness. This Orvis-endorsed expedition is limited to 12 people per trip. **Wilderness Lodge** (⊠ *West Side Hungry Horse Reservoir Rd., 55 mi east of Hungry Horse* ☎ *406/387–4051*) conducts five-day or longer float and fishing trips in the wilderness area from the end of June to mid-September.

TRAIL RIDES

Take a day ride or an overnight pack trip into the wilderness with **Diamond R Guest Ranch** (⊠ *East Side Hungry Horse Reservoir Rd., 55 mi from Hungry Horse* ☎ *406/756–1573 or 800/597–9465*). **A-Rawhide Trading Post** (⊠ *12000 Hwy. 2 E, West Glacier* ☎ *406/387–5999 or 800/388–5727* ⊕ *www.glacierrawhide.com*) takes riders on excursions from one hour to 11 days in the Flathead National Forest, or try a "Saddle and Paddle" adventure, where you ride a horse upstream alongside the Middle Fork of the Flathead River and raft down.

WHERE TO STAY

$$$$ 🖭 **Rich Ranch.** At this small, personal, and beautiful guest ranch bordering the Bob Marshall Wilderness, all-inclusive packages are the rule. You get traditional Western meals and a horse to ride for the duration of your stay; some packages emphasize riding, others fishing or hunting, and they have snowmobile tours in the winter. **Pros:** there is plenty to do even if you never leave the ranch; owners are very accommodating

and helpful. **Cons:** it's several hours to get to Glacier National Park and at least an hour to reach the shopping in Missoula. ⊠ *939 Cottonwood Lakes Rd., Seeley Lake* ☎ *406/677–2317 or 800/532–4350* ⊕ *www. richranch.com* ➟ *4 rooms, 8 cabins, 2 tepees* ⅁ *In-room: no a/c, no phone, DVD (some). In-hotel: bicycles, Wi-Fi in the lodge, no-smoking rooms* ⊟ *MC, V* ⑂ *FAP.*

$$$
Fodor's Choice
★
🏨 **Seven Lazy P Guest Ranch.** A snug haven in a rugged landscape, this 1,200-acre ranch is surrounded by pines and aspens deep in Teton Canyon, an eastern gateway to the Bob Marshall Wilderness. The duplex cabins feel like a second home, with comfortable furniture, wood-paneled ceilings, rough-hewn wainscoting, and picture windows; enveloping sofas and chairs, a large stone fireplace, and more golden wood fill the main lodge. Their 3,600-square-foot log home has three suites, each with room for four or more people, making it ideal for larger groups. Three meals daily (included in the room rate) are served family-style, and the food is memorable: a sausage-egg-and-cheese bake with homemade muffins for breakfast, grilled lemon-glazed salmon for dinner, and pies just out of the oven. They'll fortify you for a day of hiking, wildlife viewing, or guided horseback riding (also included in the room rate). In summer multiday pack trips into the Bob Marshall give riders a glimpse of the Rockies as Lewis and Clark saw them. **Pros:** true Montana experience; clean, rustic wood cabins; longtime Montana natives as hosts; set in the heart of the wilderness. **Cons:** nearest airport is an hour and a half away; no cell-phone service. ⌂ *Box 178 Choteau 59422* ☎ *406/466–2044* ⊕ *www.sevenlazyp.com* ➟ *3 duplex cabins, 4 family-type cabins, 1 3-bedroom house* ⅁ *In-room: no a/c, no phone, refrigerator, no TV. In-hotel: Wi-Fi* ⊟ *MC, V* ⊗ *Closed end of Nov.–Apr.* ⑂ *FAP.*

$$$$
★
🏨 **Spotted Bear Ranch.** Book well in advance if you wish to stay at this remote yet upscale lodge. The two-bedroom log cabins here among the evergreens are cozy, yet have generator power, flush toilets, showers, fireplaces, and views. The ranch, reachable by a rough road, specializes in fly-fishing expeditions. Dinners are for guests only, and are served family-style in the historic main lodge. **Pros:** Bob Marshall Wilderness is at your fingertips; fly-fishing opportunities are phenomenal. **Cons:** plan on a two- or three-hour drive on a winding and teeth-rattling road to reach the lodge; very remote and out of range for those dependent on cell phones. ⊠ *55 mi from Hungry Horse on either E. or W. Hungry Horse Reservoir Rd. toward Spotted Bear Ranger Station, Whitefish* ⌂ *Winter address, Box 4940* ☎ *800/223–4333* ⊕ *www.spottedbear.com* ➟ *6 cabins* ⅁ *In-room: no a/c, no phone, no TV. In-hotel: no-smoking rooms* ⊟ *AE, D, MC, V* ⊗ *Closed mid-Sept.–mid-June* ⑂ *FAP.*

CAMPING
🏕 **Spotted Bear Campground.** Alongside the South Fork of the Flathead River, this remote campground offers flat sites shaded by tall pines. Grizzly bears frequent the area, so a clean camp is imperative. Trailheads lead into wilderness areas. ⅁ *Vault toilets, dump station, drinking water, bear boxes, fire grates, picnic tables, ranger station, swimming (river)* ➟ *13 sites* ⊠ *Forest Service Rd. 38, 55 mi southeast of U.S. 2 at Hungry Horse* ☎ *406/758–5376* ⊕ *www.fs.fed.us/r1* ⊟ *No credit cards* ⊗ *Memorial Day–Labor Day.*

7

Of Dudes and Ranches

By the late 1800s stories of the jagged peaks and roaring rivers in the Rocky Mountains had caught the nation's imagination. Travelers headed west on the recently completed transcontinental railroads to see these wonders firsthand. They stayed where they could, which often meant rustic ranches. It worked out well—ranchers, starved for fresh faces and news from back home, were pleased to have the company. Soon ranches began hosting paying guests. These "dudes" stayed for weeks or months, and participated in day-to-day operations. By 1940 there were more than 300 dude ranches in the United States and Canada. Today you'd be hard pressed to find one of these places calling itself a dude ranch—"guest ranch" sounds better—and the typical stay is about a week. Activities include trail rides, barbecues, hoedowns, and sometimes opportunities to work the livestock. The week often culminates in an O-Mok-See, a series of competitive horseback events.

MISSOULA

A fertile valley hemmed in by mountains cradles Missoula, the cultural center of northwest Montana. The largest metropolis around (population 57,000) is the home of the University of Montana. In the aptly nicknamed Garden City, maple trees line the residential streets and the Clark Fork River slices through the center of town; a 6-mi riverside trail passes the university en route to Hellgate Canyon. Missoula makes a good base for regional exploration by way of Interstate 90 east–west, U.S. 93 north–south, and numerous back roads.

In 1860 French trappers dubbed this trading settlement the Hell Gate when they discovered bones and bodies in the canyon after a bloody battle between Blackfeet and other Indians. Settlers did not arrive until more than 50 years after the Lewis and Clark expedition traveled through the area. Gold speculators, homesteaders, and the coming of the Northern Pacific Railroad in 1883 all helped establish the town.

GETTING HERE AND AROUND

Missoula International Airport operates flights daily with several major airlines. Most hotels have shuttles to and from the airport. Greyhound bus lines provide service to Missoula also. By car, it is 120 mi south of Kalispell via U.S. Highway 93, and 200 mi north of Bozeman via Interstate Highway 90.

Missoula is home to the Adventure Cycling Association (formerly Bike Centennial), so it's no surprise that the city has more bicycles than people. Exploring by bicycle is popular and easy: downtown and the university district are relatively flat and have bike paths and bike traffic lanes; many storefronts are adorned with bike racks. Within the center of the city walking is a good option, too, particularly given that parking is at a premium and that the university itself is a car-free zone. Dozens of walking and biking paths wend through town. The Missoula Valley and sights on the outskirts of town are best explored by car.

VISITOR INFORMATION
Missoula Chamber of Commerce (✆ *Box 7577, Missoula 59807* ☎ *406/543–6623 or 800/526–3465* ⊕ *www.missoulachamber.com*).

EXPLORING MISSOULA

Numbers in the margin correspond to numbers on the Missoula map.

TOP ATTRACTIONS

❹ **A Carousel for Missoula.** In downtown Caras Park, kids hop in the saddles
☺ of hand-carved steeds. The carousel's horses and chariots gallop on a lovingly restored 1918 frame, accompanied by tunes from the largest band organ in continuous use in the United States. The Dragon Hollow play area next to the carousel features a dragon, a castle, and many play structures. ⊠ *101 Carousel Dr.* ☎ *406/549–8382* ⊕ *www.carrousel. com* 🖃 *Adults $1.50, under 16 and over 55 50¢ per ride; play area free* ⊙ *Memorial Day–Labor Day, daily 11–7; Labor Day–Memorial Day, daily 11–5:30.*

❼ **Clark Fork River.** The heart of Missoula is defined by the Clark Fork River, which cuts through Hellgate Canyon between Mount Sentinel and Mount Jumbo, passes by the university, and slices through downtown. A 6-mi-long riverside trail and the connecting 2½-mi Kim Williams trail make for easy, pleasant walks, with picnic spots and benches along the way where you can watch the river. Take note: the powerful currents of the Clark Fork are dangerous—they've taken many lives over the years.

⓫ **Historical Museum at Fort Missoula.** Fort Missoula, at the western edge of town, was established in 1877 at the height of the U.S. Army's conflict with the Nez Perce, led by Chief Joseph. The museum's indoor and outdoor exhibits, including 13 historic structures relocated from nearby sites, depict and explain the early development of Missoula County. The black 25th Infantry of bicycle soldiers arrived in 1888 to test bicycles for military use; near-life-size photos depict the soldiers during an expedition to Yellowstone National Park's Mammoth Terraces. Uniforms and artifacts are also on display. They ultimately rode one-speed bicycles from Missoula to St. Louis. Guided tours are available by appointment. ⊠ *Fort Missoula, Bldg. 322, accessed via South Ave.* ☎ *406/728–3476* ⊕ *www.fortmissoulamuseum.org* 🖃 *$3* ⊙ *Memorial Day–Labor Day, Mon.–Sat. 10–5, Sun. noon–5; Labor Day–Memorial Day, Tues.–Sun. noon–5.*

❷ **Missoula Art Museum.** Each year two-dozen changing contemporary art
★ exhibits join a permanent collection featuring works by E.S. Paxson, Walter Hook, Rudy and Lela Autio, and modern-day Native American artists. The 1903 Carnegie Library building, reopened in summer 2006 after extensive remodeling adding handicapped accessibility, has much more gallery space and classrooms. ⊠ *335 N. Pattee St., 1 block from intersection with W. Broadway* ☎ *406/728–0447* ⊕ *www.missoulaart-museum.org* 🖃 *Donations accepted* ⊙ *Wed.–Fri. 10–5, Sat. 10–3; call for occasional extended hrs.*

7

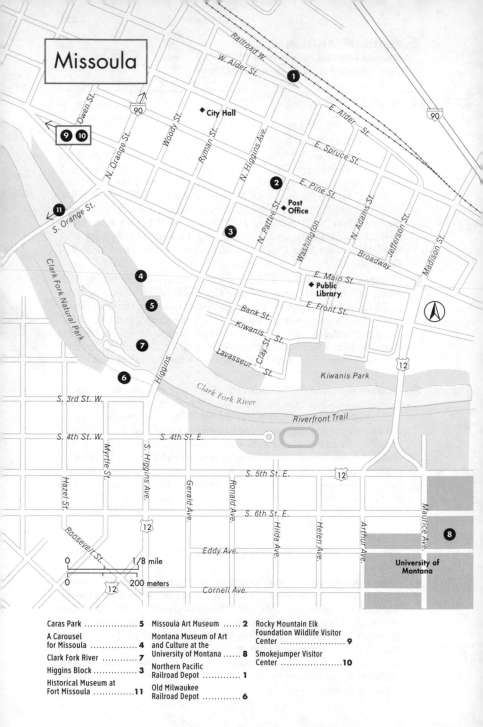

Missoula

City Hall

Post Office

Public Library

Railroad W.

W. Alder St.

E. Alder St.

E. Spruce St.

E. Pine St.

E. Main St.

E. Front St.

Bank St.

Kiwanis St.

Lavasseur St.

Clay St.

Broadway

Jefferson St.

Madison St.

N. Adams St.

Washington

N. Pattee St.

N. Higgins Ave.

Ryman St.

Woody St.

N. Orange St.

Owen St.

S. Orange St.

Clark Fork Natural Park

Clark Fork River

Kiwanis Park

Riverfront Trail

Higgins

S. 3rd St. W.

S. 4th St. W.

S. 4th St. E.

S. 5th St. E.

S. 6th St. E.

Myrtle St.

Hazel St.

Roosevelt St.

S. Higgins Ave.

Gerald Ave.

Ronald Ave.

Hilda Ave.

Helen Ave.

Arthur Ave.

Maurice Ave.

Eddy Ave.

Cornell Ave.

University of Montana

0   1/8 mile

0   200 meters

Rocky Mountain Elk Foundation Wildlife Visitor Center. The new visitor center features natural-history displays (including hands-on displays for kids), films, art, taxidermied animals, a world-record-size pair of elk antlers, and an outdoor nature trail. The foundation works to preserve wild lands for elk and other wildlife; since 1984 the nonprofit organization has saved almost 5 million acres from development. ✉ *5705 Grant Creek Rd.; look for big bronze elk* ☎ *406/523–4500 or 800/225–5355* ✇ *Donations accepted* ⊙ *Jan. 1–Memorial Day, weekdays 8–5, Sat. 10–5; Memorial Day–Dec. 30, weekdays 8–6, weekends 9–6.*

> ### WORD OF MOUTH
>
> "Missoula has great downtown, good restaurants, and a fun atmosphere. You should check out the carousel and the kayaking park downtown."   —kureiff

⑩ ★ **Smokejumper Visitor Center.** A replica 1930s lookout tower, fire photos, videos, and murals explain wildland fire ecology and behavior, fire-fighting technique, and the nation's history of smoke jumping, which began here in 1942. Today it's the largest smoke-jumper base in the nation. From Memorial Day through Labor Day the center offers five tours daily, given by guides who provide firsthand accounts of jumping into blazing forests. ✉ *5765 W. Broadway, 6 mi west of town, next to airport* ☎ *406/329–4934* ⊕ *www.smokejumpers.com* ✇ *Donations accepted* ⊙ *Memorial Day–Labor Day, weekdays 8:30–5; Labor Day–Memorial Day by appointment; summer tours on the hr 10–11 and 2–4.*

WORTH NOTING

⑤ **Caras Park.** Downtown's favorite green space, the park has a walking path along the Clark Fork River. A summer pavilion hosts live musical performances such as those at Downtown ToNight, a Thursday evening event that also features food and what the chamber of commerce likes to call a "beverage garden." ✉ *Front and Ryman Sts.* ☎ *406/543–4238* ⊕ *www.missouladowntown.com* ✇ *Free* ⊙ *Daily 6 AM–11 PM.*

❸ **Higgins Block.** This Queen Anne–style commercial structure, a granite, copper-domed corner building with red polychromed brick, occupies a block in the heart of downtown. On the National Register of Historic Places, it's now home to a deli, a bank, and several shops. ✉ *202 N. Higgins Ave.* ⊕ *www.missouladowntown.com* ✇ *Free* ⊙ *Tues. noon–8, Wed.–Sat. noon–6.*

❽ **Montana Museum of Art and Culture at the University of Montana.** The university's art museum, divided into the Meloy and Paxson galleries, hosts traveling exhibitions and has a permanent collection of more than 10,000 works, with an emphasis on historic and contemporary art from the West. ✉ *Performing Arts and Radio/Television Center, University of Montana* ☎ *406/243–2019* ⊕ *www.umt.edu/montanamuseum* ✇ *Donations accepted* ⊙ *June–Aug., Wed.–Sat. 11–3; Sept.–May, Tues.–Thurs. 11–3, Fri. and Sat. 11–2.*

❶ **Northern Pacific Railroad Depot.** The construction of the Northern Pacific Railroad was instrumental in opening up the West to settlers, and the arrival of the line in Missoula is a key point in the city's history. The depot, opened in 1901, is an example of the Renaissance Revival architecture that dominates the north end of downtown. Today the depot houses private offices, but you can still look around inside, enjoy a picnic outside, and examine the Crossings, a sculpture of giant red enamel Xs representing railroad trestles over mountain ravines. ⊠ *N. Higgins Ave.* ☎ *406/543–4238* ⊕ *www.missouladowntown.com* 🖃 *Free* ⊙ *Weekdays 9–5.*

6 **Old Milwaukee Railroad Depot.** A Missoula landmark along the river's south shore, this 1910 passenger depot, with Romanesque windows, a Spanish-style roof, two towers, and Mission-style parapet walls, is on the National Register of Historic Places. It's now the site of the Boone and Crockett Club national headquarters, an organization founded in 1887 by Theodore Roosevelt to establish conservation of wild habitats. Open to the public is a display of a world-record-size taxidermied elk, bighorn sheep, and other wildlife. ⊠ *250 Station Dr., near Higgins Ave. Bridge* ☎ *406/542–1888, 888/840–4868 for orders* ⊕ *www.boonecrockett.org* 🖃 *Free* ⊙ *Weekdays 8–5.*

SPORTS AND THE OUTDOORS

BICYCLING

Nearly 30 trails thread through Missoula and can be found on the *Missoulian's* Hike, Bike, Run map, free online or by calling the **Bicycle and Pedestrian Office** (☎ *406/721–7275* ⊕ *www.missoulian.com/app/hikebike/*).

★ The folks at **Adventure Cycling** (⊠ *150 E. Pine St.* ☎ *406/721–1776 or 800/755–2453* ⊕ *www.adv-cycling.org*) in downtown Missoula have good suggestions for nearby bike routes and an extensive selection of regional and national bike maps for sale. You can find bikes to rent or buy, cycling accessories, and cross-country ski gear at **Open Road Bicycles & Nordic Equipment** (⊠ *517 S. Orange St.* ☎ *406/549–2453*).

FISHING

Grizzly Hackle (⊠ *215 W. Front St.* ☎ *406/721–8996*) offers guided flyfishing and outfitting for half-day float trips on the Bitterroot, Blackfoot, and Clark Fork rivers. Pick up supplies in the retail shop or sign up for a lesson.

RAFTING

Raft and kayak adventures with **Montana River Guides** (⊠ *80 Sawmill Gulch Rd., 35 mins west of Missoula on I-90, Exit 70 at Cyr, cross Cyr Bridge, turn left on Sawmill Gulch, and look for yellow rafts* ☎ *406/273–4718 or 800/381–7238*) splash down the Blackfoot and Bitterroot rivers and the rowdy Alberton Gorge of the Clark Fork River.

SKIING

Montana Snowbowl (⊠ *Grant Creek Rd.* ☎ *800/728–2695 or 406/549–9777* ⊕ *www.montanasnowbowl.com*) has slopes for advanced skiers who are hooked on steep, challenging runs, and powdery views of nearby Rattlesnake Wilderness. Telemarkers and geländesprung alpine ski jumpers add a colorful element to the scene. New skiers aren't neglected: groomed beginner and intermediate runs make up more than half the trails on the 950 acres here, 12 mi northwest of Missoula.

Services include a restaurant, bar, and Geländesprung Lodge in the base area.

WHERE TO EAT

¢ ✕ **Bernice's Bakery.** Missoula's best bakery sells buttery croissants, muffins, scones, quiches, and other treats plus a tempting array of desserts, breads, and coffee from 6 AM to 8 PM. For a quick lunch, there's a small selection of sandwiches, such as hummus with roasted red pepper and basil vinaigrette. There's seating inside and out, or you can eat alongside the nearby river. ✉ *190 S. 3rd W* ☎ *406/728–1358* ⊕ *www.bernicesbakerymt.com* ⚖ *Reservations not accepted* ▭ *D, MC, V.*

AMERICAN

$$$$ ✕ **Blue Canyon Kitchen and Tavern.** Blue Canyon brings a new game to Missoula by pairing the casual Montana atmosphere with excellent food and a unique dining experience. The open kitchen creates hearty dishes for their seasonally inspired, innovative menu. Try the pretzel-crusted trout served in a whole-grain-mustard–caper-butter sauce, or go all out with the beef rib-eye steak with a smoked blue cheese–maple butter. Better yet, plan ahead and reserve the private table to create your own five-course culinary meal with their inventive head chef. ✉ *3720 N. Reserve St.* ☎ *406/451–2583* ⊕ *www.bluecanyonrestaurant.com* ▭ *AE, D, DC, MC, V.*

CONTEMPORARY
★

¢ ✕ **Hoagieville.** For a quick bite to eat, this local drive-in is a good alternative to the chains. As the name suggests, they serve mouthwatering hoagies, complete with special sauce, along with nationally renowned Hoagie cheese fries. Kids will love the authentic drive-in with friendly carhops who deliver the food right to your window. ✉ *2413 S. Higgins Ave.* ☎ *406/543–5265* ▭ *AE, D, MC, V.*

AMERICAN

$$$$ ✕ **Lolo Creek Steakhouse.** For a real taste of Montana, head for this steak house in a rustic log structure 8 mi south of Missoula, in Lolo. The dining room has a hunting-lodge atmosphere, replete with taxidermied wildlife on the walls. Although most diners opt for one of their signature sirloins—cooked over a crackling open-pit barbecue and available in three sizes—there are other well-prepared meat, chicken, and seafood dishes from which to choose. ✉ *6600 U.S. 12 W, Lolo* ☎ *406/273–2622* ▭ *AE, D, MC, V* ☉ *Closed Mon. No lunch.*

STEAK
★

$$$$ ✕ **The Red Bird.** Intimate tables and innovative cuisine make this restaurant the best fine-dining experience in Missoula. The owners use locally grown ingredients from area farmers and ranchers. The private candlelit tables and extensive wine list make the Red Bird an ideal spot for a romantic dinner. The menu changes seasonally, with dishes such as grilled bison tenderloin with smoked-tomato-mashed Yukon gold potatoes and Tuscan pork loin with house-made ricotta. A wine bar serves less expensive yet equally delicious meals in a more casual setting. ✉ *111 N. Higgins, Suite 100, through lobby of historic Florence building* ☎ *406/549–2906* ⊕ *www.redbirdrestaurant.com* ☉ *Restaurant Tues.–Sat. 5:30–9:30; wine bar weekdays 11:30–10:30, Sat. 4:40–10:30* ▭ *AE, D, MC, V.*

AMERICAN
★

$$ ✕ **The Shack Cafe.** A longtime Missoula favorite for any meal, this elegant restaurant isn't in a shack but rather in a tastefully remodeled auto dealership. Swinging doors take you into the saloon, where there's an

CONTEMPORARY
★

7

oak bar that arrived in Montana via steamship up the Missouri River a century ago. For dinner try the pork-loin cutlets or one of the specials. Breakfasts of hearty omelets and huge pancakes are popular with the locals. ⊠ *222 W. Main* ☎ *406/549–9903* ⊕ *www.theshackcafe.com* ▤ *AE, MC, V.*

¢ ✗**Worden's Market & Deli.** Floorboards creak beneath you as you explore
DELI this old-fashioned market, which spills over with deli delicacies. There's an impressive selection of groceries, along with imported beer, microbrews, and wine, plus a knowledgeable staff to help you make the best selections. With 150 cheeses to choose from, the sandwich possibilities are endless; have them pile on Black Forest ham and horseradish for a creation that will get you down the trail. There's limited seating both inside and outside, where Worden's espresso bar has a walk-up window. ⊠ *451 N. Higgins Ave.* ☎ *406/549–1293* ⊕ *www.wordens.com* ⚱ *Reservations not accepted* ▤ *AE, MC, V.*

WHERE TO STAY

$$ 🖵 **C'mon Inn.** This hotel at the bottom of Grant Creek, near the Snow-
☾ bowl ski area, has easy access to recreation and business in Missoula. The best family lodging in town, it features a spacious, tree-filled indoor courtyard with a pool, baby pool, five hot tubs, and a waterfall. The large guest rooms equipped with flat-screen TVs open onto the pool on the first floor and have balconies on the second. Some rooms have kitchens. **Pros:** easily accessible off the interstate; ideal location for those skiing at Snowbowl; pool and hot tubs make this a good choice for families. **Cons:** away from the downtown's restaurants and entertainment. ⊠ *2775 Expo Pkwy., off I–90* ☎ *406/543–4600 or 888/989–5569* ⊕ *www.cmoninn.com* ⇒ *119 rooms* ☾ *In-hotel: pool, gym, no-smoking rooms* ▤ *AE, DC, MC, V* ⊙l *CP.*

$$ 🖵 **Goldsmith's Bed and Breakfast.** Built in 1911 for the first president of
★ the University of Montana, this lodging is on the bank of the Clark Fork River, at the end of a footbridge that leads to the campus. Within the prairie-style building, with big white eaves and a huge porch, are period furnishings, wool carpets, and fresh flowers. Each private room is unique; the honeymoon suite has a Japanese soaking tub, and two suites have gas fireplaces. Public rooms include a library and sitting area. Breakfast offerings include frittatas with a basil/cream sauce and apple-walnut pancakes, served in the dining room or on the deck overlooking the Clark Fork River. **Pros:** very convenient to walk to many of the outstanding shops and restaurants from here; chef obviously loves what he does, judging by the quality of the breakfasts. **Cons:** downtown location also puts you near the railroad, where the train whistle frequently blows; main entrance is next to the honeymoon suite's private deck. ⊠ *809 E. Front St.* ☎ *406/728–1585 or 866/666–9945* ⊕ *www. goldsmithsinn.com* ⇒ *3 rooms, 4 suites* ☾ *In-hotel: Wi-Fi, no-smoking rooms* ▤ *D, MC, V* ⊙l *BP.*

$$–$$$ 🖵 **Hilton Garden Inn Missoula.** This upscale facility is a business traveler's dream. There's a fully equipped business center near the lobby, and the spacious rooms donned in Montana-lifestyle decor are set up with large desks, as well as flat-screen TVs, adjustable beds, DVD players,

and video games. The Blue Canyon Kitchen and Silver Creek Tavern next door serve lunch and dinner, and the Great American Grill next to the lobby serves breakfast. The Pavilion Pantry convenience mart has the sundries that you forgot, and the helpful staff is able to direct you to the sights and recreational opportunities in the area. **Pros:** business amenities make working on the road fun; smoke-free tavern with live games is an enjoyable place to unwind. **Cons:** view from the Grill overlooks the parking area; because restaurants are not directly affiliated with the Hilton chain, you have to walk outside to enter the restaurant and tavern. ⊠ *3720 N. Reserve St.* ☏ *406/532–5300 or 877/782–9444* ⊕ *www.missoula.stayhgi.com* ⤳ *146 rooms* � *In-room: refrigerator, Internet, Wi-Fi. In-hotel: 2 restaurants, bar, pool, gym, laundry facilities, no-smoking rooms* ▭ *AE, DC, MC, V* ⧀ *EP.*

$$–$$$ ▦ **Holiday Inn Missoula–Downtown at the Park.** The Missoula member of the Holiday Inn chain is a large, comfortable hotel with a lush atrium in the center and recently remodeled rooms, some with a lovely river view. The property's greatest asset is its location in Missoula's riverfront Bess Reed Park, a stone's throw from the Clark Fork River and across the river from the university, a ¾-mi walk. Pets are welcome. Pros: great area for walks along the river trail and an easy walk into town for eating and shopping; restaurant and bar serve both terrific food and tasty mixed drinks. Cons: rooms overlooking the atrium can be noisy when the hotel is hosting big functions. ⊠ *200 S. Pattee St.* ☏ *406/721–8550 or 800/399–0408* ⊕ *www.himissoula.com* ⤳ *200 rooms* � *In-room: Internet, Wi-Fi. In-hotel: restaurant, bar, pool, gym, no-smoking rooms* ▭ *AE, D, DC, MC, V* ⧀ *EP.*

$$$$ ▦ **The Resort at Paws Up.** At this resort you go "glamping"—glamorous
◑ camping. With linens and a "camping butler," even staying in one of
★ the tents at Paws Up is a long way from roughing it. For more refinement, try one of the luxury homes, each with its own outdoor hot tub. Included in your stay is use of an electric car to navigate around the ranch. For the wilderness traveler, ride 12 mi back to the Encampment at Bull Creek, where gourmet food and featherbeds await. During your stay, fly-fish in the Blackfoot River, go horseback riding on Paws Up's nearly 40,000-acre "backyard," or pamper yourself at "spa city." Never worry about the kids becoming bored with the Kids Corps of Discovery offering daily activities lasting a full or half day. **Pros:** property is one of a kind in Montana; true luxury accommodations and first-class service. **Cons:** this is a very exclusive resort, and the price tag is steep. ⊠ *40060 Paws Up Rd., Greenough* ☏ *406/244–5200 or 866/894–7969* ⊕ *www. pawsup.com* ⤳ *28 homes, 10 tents (including the Encampment at Bull Run)* � *In-room: kitchen (some), Wi-Fi. In-hotel: spa, laundry facilities (some)* ▭ *AE, D, MC, V* ⧀ *FAP.*

$$ ▦ **Wingate by Wyndham.** Oversize guest rooms and a 24-hour self-service
◑ business center here are designed with the business traveler in mind, but two waterslides and a splash pool please kids as well. Rooms have cordless phones, lounge chairs, and large TVs; a few have Jacuzzis. The inn serves a hot breakfast complete with omelets and waffles. It is right off the interstate and near the airport. **Pros:** great waterslides for the kids; friendly staff; good free breakfast. Cons: no restaurants

within walking distance. ⊠ *5252 Airway Blvd.* ☎ *406/541–8000 or
866/832–8000* ⊕ *www.wingateinnmissoula.com* 🖙*100 rooms* ☆ *In-
room: refrigerator, Wi-Fi. In-hotel: pool, gym, laundry facilities, no-
smoking rooms* ☰ *AE, D, DC, MC, V* �🍽️*CP.*

CAMPING   🏕️ **Jellystone RV Park.** On the outskirts of town, this lively park is popu-
☙   lar with families for the playground, miniature golf, swimming pools,
and, a kid favorite, pictures with Yogi Bear. The friendly owners serve
huckleberry ice cream nightly. Camping cabins, which sleep four com-
fortably, have air-conditioning, refrigerators, and microwaves. ☆ *Flush
toilets, full hookups, partial hookups, dump station, drinking water,
guest laundry, showers, picnic tables, food service, electricity, general store, swimming (pool)* 🖙*110 full hookups, 7 tent sites; 6 cabins* ⊠ *I–90, Exit 96, ½ mi north* ☎ *406/543–9400 or 800/318–9644*
⊕ *www.campjellystonemt.com* ☰ *MC, V* ☯ *May–Oct. 1.*

☙   🏕️ **Missoula KOA.** This lovely campsite in the Montana-born KOA chain
is easy to reach from the interstate. It has a pool and two hot tubs, a
game center, miniature golf, bike rentals, a playground, and a bonfire
pit area. Nightly ice-cream socials and weekend activities during the
summer make this more of a community than a campground. ☆ *Flush
toilets, full hookups, dump station, drinking water, guest laundry, showers, picnic tables, food service, electricity, public telephone, general
store, swimming (pool)* 🖙*146 full hookups, 31 tent sites; 19 cabins*
⊠ *3450 Tina Ave., I–90, Exit 101, 1½ mi south, right on England Blvd.*
☎ *406/549–0881 or 800/562–5366* ⊕ *www.missoulakoa.com* ☰ *AE,
D, MC, V.*

NIGHTLIFE AND THE ARTS

☙   The wildest film stars in the world are up on the big screen at the
weeklong **International Wildlife Film Festival** (⊠ *718 S. Higgins Ave.*
☎ *406/728–9380* ⊕ *www.wildlifefilms.org*), which shows natural-history documentaries in early May at the Wilma and Roxy theaters in
downtown Missoula. The festival includes seminars, panel discussions,
a parade, and art displays. The organization also offers a fall festival,
MontanaCINE: Cultures and Issues on Nature and Environment, at
the Roxy.

☙   At the **Missoula Children's Theatre** (⊠ *200 N. Adams* ☎ *406/728–1911
or 406/728–7529* ⊕ *www.mctinc.org*), year-round productions vary
from Broadway musicals to community theater for and by children
from 5 to 18 years old. From October to June you can see local talent
and guest artists (usually professionals) perform family favorites like
Seussical. In summer there's a theater camp where kids are the stars of
the productions.

The University of Montana's Department of Drama and Dance manages
the **Montana Repertory Theatre** (☎ *406/243–6809* ⊕ *www.montanarep.
org*). This professional company provides the region with a steady diet
of popular Broadway shows on campus as well as in national tours.

SHOPPING

Take a break while touring downtown Missoula and have a cappuccino or chai shake at **Butterfly Herbs** (⊠ *232 N. Higgins Ave.* ☎ *406/728–8780*), or try the Butterfly Ice Cream Coffee Soda—a cold drink with multiple layers of sweetness. The shop sells herbs and spices in bulk, candies, soaps, candles, china, and other odds and ends.

Works by Montana authors, a fine selection of regional books, and gifts are found at **Fact and Fiction** (⊠ *220 N. Higgins Ave.* ☎ *406/721–2881*). Readings, signings, and other literary events are scheduled year-round at this comfortable shop, where you're likely to rub elbows with an author browsing the shelves.

At the outdoor **Missoula Farmers' Market** (⊠ *N. Higgins Ave. on Circle Sq. between Railroad and Alder Sts.* ☎ *406/543–4238* ⊕ *www.missouladowntown.com*) you can buy flowers, fresh fruits and vegetables, and unique handmade goods. It's held on Market Plaza, a two-block area downtown, every Saturday morning from mid-May to mid-October and Tuesday evenings from July through mid-September.

Whimsical artistry by Missoula natives is available at the **Monte Dolack Gallery** (⊠ *139 W. Front* ☎ *406/549–3248* ⊕ *www.montedolack.com*), open Monday–Saturday for your laughing pleasure.

For locally made crafts, come to the **Saturday Arts and Craft Market** (⊠ *Pine St. between Higgins Ave. and Pattee St.* ☎ *406/543–4238* ⊕ *www.missouladowntown.com*), open Saturday mornings from mid-May to mid-October.

BITTERROOT VALLEY

This history-filled valley south of Missoula was once home to Nez Perce who helped Lewis and Clark find their way through the mountains. The expedition's campsites, plus historic mansions and missions, are scattered in and around Stevensville, Hamilton, and Darby, towns founded by early settlers attracted by temperate weather and fertile soil. Flanked by the Bitterroot and Sapphire mountains, the valley is named for the state flower, the delicate pink rosette-shape bitterroot, which blooms in late spring; its roots were a staple of the Salish Indian diet. U.S. 93 threads through the heart of the verdant valley and along the Bitterroot River, an excellent fly-fishing spot. Back roads lead to wildlife refuges and numerous remote trailheads for biking and hiking.

STEVENSVILLE

30 mi south of Missoula via U.S. 93.

Stevensville, population 1,550, sits on the site of the state's first non–Native American settlement, St. Mary's Mission, a restored treasure that dates back to 1841. Nearby Fort Owen is a partially restored 1850s trading post. The town itself is named for General Isaac Stevens, who was in charge of the Northwest Territory's military posts and Native American affairs. Today it's a mix of beautiful old homes and haphazard modern construction in a lush valley.

GETTING HERE AND AROUND
Stevensville is 30 mi south of Missoula via U.S. Highway 93. The road was widened in 2009 and is a relaxing, scenic drive.

EXPLORING

♻ The **Lee Metcalf National Wildlife Refuge,** on the edge of town, is nearly as pristine as it was before development encroached upon the wilds in this part of the state. Within its 2,800 acres reside 235 species of birds, 41 species of mammals, and 17 species of reptiles and amphibians. Bald eagles, osprey, deer, and muskrats are frequently seen along the preserve's 2 mi of nature trails and in the wildlife-viewing area. There are children's fishing and waterfowl clinics in the summer and fall. Fishing is permitted on the river, but not on the refuge ponds. Archery season for deer and waterfowl hunting occur during their specific seasons in autumn. ⊠ *4567 Wildfowl La., 2 mi north of Stevensville* ☎ *406/777–5552* ⊕ *www.fws.gov/leemetcalf/* ☜ *Free* ☉ *Daily dawn–dusk.*

★ **St. Mary's Mission,** established by Father Pierre DeSmet in 1841, was the first Catholic mission in the Northwest and the site of the first permanent non–Native American settlement in Montana. The site is run by a nonsectarian, nonprofit organization that encourages tour groups, school groups, and individuals to explore the home of Father Anthony Ravalli, an Italian priest recruited to the mission by Father DeSmet in 1845. Ravalli was also Montana's first physician and pharmacist. On the site are a photogenic chapel, a priest's quarters, a pharmacy, Father Ravalli's log house, and the cabin of Chief Victor, a Salish Indian who refused to sign the Hell Gate Treaty and move his people onto the Flathead Reservation. A burial plot has headstones bearing the names of both Native Americans and white settlers. ⊠ *4th St.; from Main St., turn west at 4th and drive 3 blocks* ☎ *406/777–5734* ⊕ *www.saintmarysmission.org* ☜ *$7* ☉ *Mid-Apr.–mid-Oct., daily 10–4.*

Major John Owen established **Fort Owen** as a trading post in 1850. The property also served as the headquarters of the Flathead Agency until 1860. It's worth a half hour to visit the museum to see the restored barracks, artifacts, and some of the fort's original furnishings. ⊠ *Hwy. 269, ½ mi east of U.S. 93 at Stevensville* ☎ *406/542–5500* ⊕ *www.fwp. mt.gov* ☜ *$4* ☉ *Daily dawn–dusk.*

Historical artifacts in the **Stevensville Museum** include the belongings of early settlers, particularly the missionaries who came to convert the Native Americans of the West. Other exhibits provide an overview of the area's original cultures (Salish, Nez Perce, and Lemhi Shoshone), background on Lewis and Clark's two visits, and a look at later residents, from orchard farmers to today's cybercommuters. ⊠ *517 Main St.* ☎ *406/777–1007* ☜ *Donations accepted* ☉ *Memorial Day–Labor Day, Thurs.–Sat. 11–4, Sun. 1–4.*

SPORTS AND THE OUTDOORS

FISHING **Anglers Afloat, Inc.** (⊠ *2742 Alpenglow Rd.* ☎ *406/777–3421*) leads serious fly-fishermen after the really big trout on floats on the Bitterroot and Blackfoot rivers. During the mayfly, caddis, and salmon fly hatches, fish with **Backdoor Outfitters** (⊠ *227 Bell Crossing E* ☎ *406/777–3861*), along spring creeks, in private ponds, or on river float trips on the Bitterroot, Clark Fork, Blackfoot, and Big Hole rivers.

WHERE TO EAT AND STAY

$ ✕ **Frontier Cafe.** For a bit of town gossip and great burgers, stop in this
CAFÉ classic small-town café, a dressed-down spot where the locals love to hang out. ⊠ *3954 U.S. 93 N* 🕾 *406/777–4228* ▤ *AE, D, MC, V.*

$$ ✕ **Marie's Italian Restaurant.** This family-run sit-down restaurant is known
CONTEMPORARY for its gourmet Italian cuisine and fresh seafood. A good way to decide what you like best is to try the sampler, which includes handmade pasta stuffed with different fillings, spinach gnocchi, fettuccine Alfredo, shrimp, vegetables, and another side. All meals include soup or salad. ⊠ *4040 Hwy. 93 N* 🕾 *406/777–3681* ▤ *No credit cards* ⊙ *Closed Dec.–Feb. and Mon.–Thurs. No lunch.*

¢ ✕ **Olde Coffee Mill Bakery and Eatery.** For those looking for delicious baked
CONTEMPORARY goods, an espresso/cappuccino fix, or hearty sandwiches, including the popular veggie sandwich, as well as homemade soups and quiches, this place fits the bill at lunch. Or join the hungry crowd for dinner on the first Friday of every month. ⊠ *225 Main St.* 🕾 *406/777–2939* 🍴 *Reservations not accepted* ▤ *No credit cards* ⊙ *Closed Sun. Dinner 1st Fri. of month only.*

$$ 🏠 **Bitterroot River Bed and Breakfast.** Views of the Bitterroot River give this inn a peaceful, country feel even though it's within walking distance of many of the shops and restaurants in downtown Stevensville. The rooms are made with comfort in mind, including down comforters and featherbeds in some rooms, and a cozy fireplace in another. Breakfasts are casual, but with egg casseroles, banana-bread French toast, and locally roasted coffee, they'll be sure to fuel you for the day. Children over six are welcome. **Pros:** owners are longtime Montana residents who know the area and are happy to offer advice on activities. **Cons:** no phones in the rooms for private conversation, but cell phones should work. ⊠ *501 South Ave.* 🕾 *406/777–5205* ⊕ *www.bitterrootriverbb. com* 🛏 *4 rooms* ⚷ *In-room: no TV (some), Wi-Fi. In-hotel: bicycles* ▤ *MC, V* 🍴❘*BP.*

CAMPING ⛺ **Charles Waters Campground.** Located in the historic area of Stevensville, this is an access point to the Selway-Bitterroot Wilderness. Trails, fishing, picnic spots, and a bicycle campsite are sheltered among trees, affording glimpses of the surrounding mountains. A fire-ecology interpretive trail explores regrowth after recent forest fires. ⚷ *Pit toilets, drinking water, fire grates, picnic tables* 🛒 *22 sites* ⊠ *2 mi west of U.S. 93 on County Rd. 22 (Bass Creek Rd.), then 1 mi northwest on Forest Rd. 1316* 🕾 *406/777–5461* ⊕ *www.fs.fed.us/r1/bitterroot/* ▤ *No credit cards* ⊙ *Late May–early Sept.*

EN
ROUTE A refreshing stop for wildlife viewing is the **The Teller** (⊠ *1288 Eastside Hwy., Corvallis* 🕾 *406/961–3507* ⊕ *www.theteller.org*), a 1,200-acre private wildlife conservation property intended to inspire, educate, and demonstate conservation in action. Situated along 3 mi of the Bitterroot River, about 8 mi north of Hamilton, the refuge is home to otters, beavers, spotted frogs, and salamanders, as well as pileated woodpeckers, birds of prey, waterfowl, whitetail deer, and many native plants. Visitors can take a stroll on the half-loop walking trail along the Bitterroot

7

River. An education center conducts numerous conservation programs for the public. Conference groups and wedding parties may arrange to stay in the three homes on the refuge. To get here, take Route 269 (Eastside Highway) to Quast Lane and follow the signs.

HAMILTON

21 mi south of Stevensville via U.S. 93.

Home to retirees, gentleman ranchers, and the Ravalli County Museum, Hamilton (pop. 5,000) is a gateway to the Selway-Bitterroot Wilderness. It was established by 19th-century industrialist Marcus Daly to house employees at his 22,000-acre Bitterroot Stock Farm. There he raised thoroughbred racehorses, funding the venture with part of the fortune he made mining copper in Montana. His own home, the Daly Mansion, is open for tours.

GETTING HERE AND AROUND

Hamilton is 50 mi south of Missoula via U.S. Highway 93. A car is essential, since few hotels have an airport shuttle and many of the places to see are far apart and off the beaten path.

VISITOR INFORMATION

Bitterroot Valley Chamber of Commerce (✉ *105 E. Main St., Hamilton* ☎ *406/363–2400* ⊕ *www.bitterrootvalleychamber.com*).

EXPLORING

☾ Copper king Marcus Daly's 24,000-square-foot, 56-room **Daly Man-**
★ **sion,** with 25 bedrooms, 15 baths, and five Italian marble fireplaces, is the showplace of Hamilton, and is undergoing a $1.7 million ongoing renovation to preserve its history and elegance. The Georgian Revival-style house is open to the public, and tours run on the hour. There's also a printed walking guide available to the extensive grounds. The Kids in the Garden event is held in August. Frequent festivities at the mansion include crafts shows and a Kentucky Derby Gala that celebrates Daly's dedication to racehorses. Call the chamber of commerce or the mansion to learn about events. ✉ *251 Eastside Hwy.* ☎ *406/363–6004* ⊕ *www.dalymansion.org* ☒ *$8* ☉ *Mid-Apr.–mid-Oct., daily 10–3; and for special events.*

The **Ravalli County Museum,** in the former courthouse, contains exhibits on natural history, fly-fishing, Native Americans, Lewis and Clark, and other subjects related to the region. During the Saturday Series (most Saturdays 2 PM, $5), speakers share local history and lore. ✉ *205 Bedford* ☎ *406/363–3338* ⊕ *www.brvhsmuseum.org* ☒ *Couple $5, single $3, families $6* ☉ *Tues.–Fri. 10–4, Sat. 9–1.*

Hamilton is in the midst of the 1.6-million-acre **Selway-Bitterroot National Forest.** It includes the Bitterroot and Sapphire mountains and parts of the Selway-Bitterroot, Anaconda-Pintler, and Frank Church–River of No Return wildernesses, and is traversed by the Salmon and Selway rivers. More than 1,600 mi of trails wend through the forest, where visitors may encounter bears, elk, moose, deer, and bighorn sheep. There are also songbirds and birds of prey such as eagles and owls. The forest has three historically significant trails: the Continental Divide Scenic

Trail, the Lewis and Clark Trail, and the Nez Perce Trail; some parts of the trails are open to hikers, other parts to bikes and vehicles. Wildfires of 2000 scorched parts of the forest; hikers should be alert to the danger of falling trees in the burned-out areas. ⊠ *1801 North Ave.* ☎ *406/777–5461* ⊕ *www.fs.fed.us/r1* ⊠ *Free* ⊙ *Daily.*

OFF THE BEATEN PATH

Skalkaho Highway. Three miles south of Hamilton, turn east onto Route 38, also known as the Skalkaho Highway, and you'll find yourself on a beautiful, seldom-traveled route leading into the Sapphire Mountains and on to the Georgetown Lake area near Anaconda. This fair-weather road is best traveled in summer, since 20 mi of it are gravel. Mountain bikers tour here, and there are plenty of hiking trails through the 23,000-acre Skalkaho Wildlife Preserve. Note that trailers are not recommended. Forest Road 1352 into the preserve is closed October 15 to December 1, making that a fine time for nonmotorized travel. Only 10 mi of the Skalkaho Highway are plowed in winter, which means the area is excellent for cross-country skiing and snowshoeing.

SPORTS AND THE OUTDOORS

FISHING
There are two good options for fishing excursions in the area. You can float and fish with **Fly Fishing Adventures** (⊠ *10739 Limber Pine Street, Lolo* ☎ *406/363–2398*) on the Bitterroot River and Clark Fork River. Fishing trips with **Fly Fishing Always** (⊠ *714 S. 4th St.* ☎ *406/360–4346*) amble down the Bitterroot River looking for brown trout and west slope cutthroat. Scenic float trips on the Missouri and Clark Fork rivers are also available.

TRAIL RIDES
Spend a few hours or a full day in the saddle with **Wildlife Adventures** (⊠ *1765 Pleasant View Dr Victor* ☎ *888/642–1010*).

WHERE TO EAT

$
CONTEMPORARY
✕ **Bitter Root Brewing.** Meet the brewmaster, sample a Sawtooth Ale or "the Brewer's Whim," and enjoy the live music (Thursday and Saturday). This smoke-free brewpub offers free tastings daily and an eclectic menu from the grill, and their specialty, hand-dipped fresh fish-and-chips. ⊠ *101 Marcus St., 1 block east of town center* ☎ *406/363–7468* ⊕ *www.bitterrootbrewing.com* ▭ *AE, D, DC, MC, V.*

$
CONTEMPORARY
✕ **Naps Grill.** This local favorite is known throughout the Bitteroot Valley as the place with the best burger in the region. The locally owned family restaurant serves burgers, steaks, and sandwiches, all made with fresh ingredients and Montana beef. For those who want to eat lighter, they serve a fresh Mandarin salad. ⊠ *220 N. 2nd St.* ☎ *406/363–0136* ⊕ *www.napsgrill.homestead.com* ▭ *MC, V* ⊙ *Closed Sun.*

¢–$$
CONTEMPORARY
✕ **Spice of Life.** Wednesday night, when live music fills the air, is the time to visit this romantic spot in a historic building. Eclectic fare includes pasta, seafood, steak, Mexican, Thai, and Japanese specials. ⊠ *163 2nd St. S* ☎ *406/363–4433* ⊕ *www.thespiceinhamilton.com* ▭ *AE, MC, V* ⊙ *Closed Sun. No dinner Mon. and Tues.*

WHERE TO STAY

$
☷ **Best Western Hamilton Inn.** This clean and convenient hotel is typical of the chain's smaller properties. It's within walking distance of many of the town's sites and restaurants. A continental breakfast and a newspaper are available in the lobby each morning. Pros: easy to

find and centrally located; pets welcome. **Cons:** rooms are pretty basic; one of the older facilities in the area. ⊠ *409 S. 1st St.* ☎ *406/363–2142 or 800/426–4586* ⊕ *www.bestwestern.com* ⇆ *39 rooms, including 3 larger family-size rooms* ⚷ *In-room: refrigerator, Wi-Fi. In-hotel: some pets allowed, no-smoking rooms* ☰ *AE, D, DC, MC, V* ⑂ *CP.*

$–$$ ⊞ **Deer Crossing B&B.** On this homestead two deluxe rooms, two luxury suites, and two cabins are set on 25 acres surrounded by pastureland, pines, the Sapphire Mountains, and Como Peak. Accommodations are outfitted with fireplaces, hot tubs, and Western furnishings. The friendly owners serve a hearty breakfast on the deck in summers. Horses and pets are welcome. **Pros:** facilities for horses; family-friendly accommodation can host large groups. **Cons:** carpet in the main lodge is a little dated; no Wi-Fi. ⊠ *396 Hayes Creek Rd.* ☎ *406/363–2232 or 800/763–2232* ⊕ *www.deercrossingmontana.com* ⇆ *2 rooms, 2 suites, 2 cabins* ⚷ *In-room: no a/c, no phone. In-hotel: parking (free), some pets allowed, no-smoking rooms* ☰ *AE, D, MC, V* ⑂ *BP.*

CAMPING   ⚠ **Blodgett Canyon Campground.** From this undeveloped campsite along a canyon creek you have easy access to hiking and biking trails, fishing, and rock climbing. There's no garbage haul, so cleanliness depends on good camping etiquette. ⚷ *Pit toilets, drinking water, fire grates, picnic tables* ⇆ *6 sites* ⊠ *Blodgett Canyon, 5 mi northwest of Hamilton* ☎ *406/777–5461* ⊕ *www.fs.fed.us/r1* ⚼ *Reservations not accepted* ☰ *No credit cards.*

The Montana Plains

8

Updated
by Andrew
Mckean

Space, lots of space, is the hallmark of eastern Montana's gently rolling plains. If you're looking to escape stifling crowds and urban sprawl, you'll take well to the wide-open plains of Big Sky Country.

The state as a whole averages six people per square mi, but some of its prairies measure in reverse: one person per 6 square mi. Although largely devoid of the epic snow-covered peaks of the towering Rockies, the eastern two-thirds of Montana have an expansive beauty that seems to stretch endlessly beyond the horizon, beckoning you to bask in the isolated serenity of one of the least-populated places in the country—in a land of almost too much sky.

That's not to say that eastern Montana is flat and boring. In fact, the grassy plains are often broken up by geographical oddities such as badlands, glacial lakes, and ice caves. Occasional pine-covered foothills or snowcapped mountains even pop up, looking strangely out of place rising from the surrounding prairie. This topographical diversity makes the region a playground for lovers of the outdoors. Hiking, horseback riding, wrangling, boating, skiing, snowmobiling, caving, and some of the best fishing and hunting in the world are among the greatest attractions here. Beyond the blessings nature has bestowed upon the state are an ample number of historic sites, state parks, museums, and even paleontological digs.

ORIENTATION AND PLANNING

GETTING ORIENTED

Paradoxically, the first- and third-largest cities in Montana are in the state's highly rural eastern region. The largest city in a 500-mi radius, Billings is a center for culture, shopping, entertainment, and medical care. Great Falls, straddling the Missouri River near a handful of thundering waterfalls, is one of Montana's greatest historical centers, with dozens of museums and interpretive centers that trace the state's varied cultural influences. Scattered in between these two cities are more than 100 small communities, some with no more than two dozen inhabitants living in the shadow of towering clapboard grain elevators. Although diminutive, sleepy, and dependent on the larger cities, each of these towns has its own distinct Western character, adding to the larger flavor of the region.

Major roads are few and far between. I–94 sweeps westward from North Dakota to Billings, where it joins I–90, which comes up from Wyoming's Bighorn Mountains and snakes west through the Rockies into Idaho. The only other interstate is I–15, which threads north out of Idaho and onto the plains outside Helena before looping around Great Falls and heading to Canada. In the vast stretches of prairie out of reach of the interstates, the key thoroughfares are U.S. 2, also known as the Hi-Line, running east–west across the top of the state; U.S. 212, running southeast out of Billings into South Dakota; and U.S. 87, running north out of Billings.

PLANNING

WHEN TO GO

Each season offers something different in Montana: summer brings warm, dry weather perfect for hiking, biking, and horseback riding; autumn yields throngs of wildlife for animal watchers, and anglers; winter means plenty of snow for skiing, snowmobiling, and ice fishing. Although summer is the busiest season here—with good reason, since freezing temperatures can arrive as early as September and depart as late as May—many travelers are only passing through on their way farther west. The roads may be crowded, but the attractions, hotels, and restaurants are likely not. Winter can sometimes be just as busy as summer, as thousands of avid skiers rush through on their way to the slopes.

PLANNING YOUR TIME

Space, one of Montana's most abundant natural resources, can make traveling between major communities and attractions tedious. The drive from Great Falls to Billings, for instance, takes four hours. It's tempting to rush the drive to get from point A to point B, but that tactic can make you—and your traveling companions—batty with the vehicular version of cabin fever.

Break up long drives with side trips and random stops. Even if the trip could take only four or five hours, give yourself the entire day. Survey your route on a map before you set out and choose two or three possible stops along the way. Between Great Falls and Billings you might pause in the Big Snowy Mountains for a brisk hike. Break up the drive from Great Falls to Havre with lunch in Fort Benton, at the Union Grille in the Grand Union Hotel. Don't hesitate to stop in the random small town. You may not find much more than a gas station and a diner, but the locals will almost always offer friendly conversation and a few tall tales.

There is plenty to do in the two largest cities on the Montana plains. Lake Elmo State Park, ZooMontana, and Pictograph Cave State Monument are good stops in Billings, and the C. M. Russell Museum, Giant Springs State Park, and the Lewis and Clark National Historic Trail Interpretive Center are must-sees in Great Falls. Both cities make good base camps for further exploration: most of the region's attractions are day trips from these communities.

If you have the time, explore some of the state's smaller towns. These mini-municipalities have few obvious visitor attractions. You just have to do a little creative thinking in these remote villages. It may look a little primitive next to its big-city counterparts, but don't hesitate to pay a visit to the local museum. Remember outdoor recreation opportunities, too: for example, Miles City may look a little dull at first glance, but it's the perfect base from which to float down the Yellowstone River

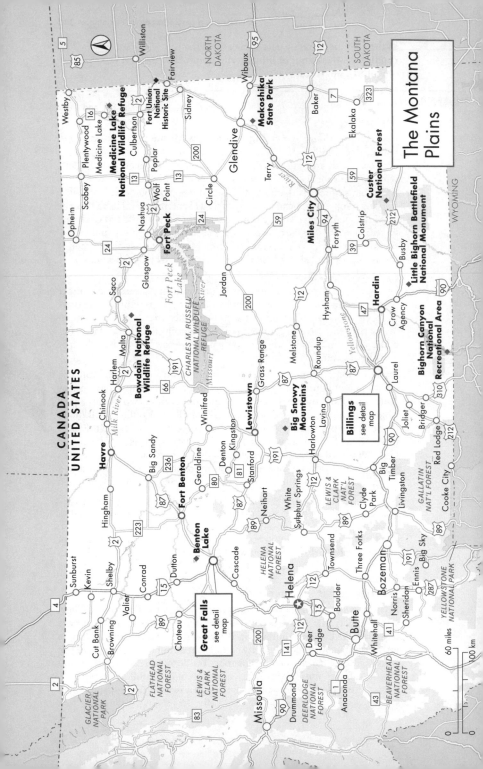

The Montana Plains

to Pirogue Island State Park or kick around on the rocky shorelines for agates and arrowheads.

Indeed, the great outdoors are probably why you're in Montana to begin with. If you are unaccustomed to so much space, the state's endless plains and wide-open skies may become wearisome after a while, but they can be every bit as beautiful as the mountain peaks that tower in the distance. Appreciate the empty countryside while you can, and stop on the side of the road in this strangely deserted landscape and marvel at the scale of the sky and the horizon. Once you're back home, you'll miss it.

GETTING HERE AND AROUND

AIR TRAVEL

Within eastern Montana, frequent commercial flights—generally via Salt Lake City, Seattle, Denver, or Phoenix—are available only to Billings and Great Falls. Thanks to subsidies, regularly scheduled flights on small twin-engine turboprops are available in many small towns, and charter flights can be arranged. Because the region is so isolated, flights here from anywhere in the country can be pricey—often more expensive than coast-to-coast flights. Some residents of the region drive as far as Bismarck, North Dakota; Rapid City, South Dakota; or Gillette, Wyoming, to catch departing flights.

Airlines Allegiant Air(☎ 702/505-8888⊕ www.allegiantair.com). **Delta** (☎ 800/221-1212 ⊕ www.delta.com). **Great Lakes Airlines** (☎ 800/554-5111 ⊕ www.greatlakesav.com). **Horizon** (☎ 800/547-9308 ⊕ www.horizonair.com). **Northwest** (☎ 800/225-2525 ⊕ www.nwa.com). **United** (☎ 800/864-8331 ⊕ www.united.com).

Airports Billings Logan International Airport (☎ 406/238-3420 ⊕ www.flybillings.com). **Great Falls International Airport** (☎ 406/727-3404 ⊕ www.gtfairport.com).

BUS TRAVEL

A dwindling number of bus companies connect most communities of 1,000 residents or more; smaller towns may not have service. Expect high ticket prices; depending on where you're going, taking the bus can be almost as expensive as flying, and because of the great expanse of Montana, it can take infinitely longer.

Information Greyhound Bus Lines (☎ 406/245-5116 or 800/231-2222 ⊕ www.greyhound.com). **Karst Stage** (☎ 406/556-3500 ⊕ www.karststage. com). **Powder River Transportation** (☎ 307/674-6188). **Rimrock Stages**

TOP REASONS TO GO

■ Charles M. Russell Wildlife Refuge: Marvel at the eroded breaks, see elk bugling in the fall, and soak in the quiet beauty.

■ Downtown Great Falls: The solid Edwardian architecture and the quirky shops satisfy contemporary visitors.

■ Billings Rimrocks: Possibly the best spot in the West for Kodachrome sunsets.

■ Fort Peck Reservoir: Rent a boat and ride down this sprawling lake in June or July.

■ Big Springs Trout Hatchery: Tote a picnic to this oasis outside Lewistown.

8

(☎ *406/245–7696 or 800/255–7655* ⊕ *www.rimrocktrailways.com*). **Silver Eagle Shuttle Inc.** (☎ *406/256–9793* ⊕ *www.montanacustomtours.com*).

CAR TRAVEL

It is virtually impossible to travel around the Montana plains without a car. One of the best things about driving here is the lack of traffic. Aside from a little bustle in Great Falls or Billings on weekdays in the late afternoon, gridlock and traffic jams are unheard of. The largest driving hazards will be slow-moving farming or ranching equipment, wranglers on horseback, herds of grazing livestock that refuse to move off the highway, and deer bounding over ditches in the evening. Driving gets a little hairy in winter, but not because of the amount of snow that falls, which is generally very little. Whiteouts, when winds tearing across the plains whip up the tiniest bit of snow into ground blizzards, are the most common hazard. Large drifts and slick roads become more problematic at higher elevations.

For information on road conditions, contact the Montana Department of Transportation.

Information **Montana Department of Transportation** (☎ *800/226–7623 or 511* ⊕ *www.mdt.mt.gov/travinfo*). **Montana Highway Patrol** (☎ *406/444–3780* ⊕ *www.doj.mt.gov/enforcement/highwaypatrol*).

TRAIN TRAVEL

Amtrak serves the isolated communities of the Hi-Line with its Empire Builder line, running one train each way daily from Chicago to Seattle. The tracks run nearly parallel to U.S. 2 the entire length of the state. Trains stop in the towns of Glasgow, Malta, Havre, Wolf Point, and Cut Bank, among others.

Information **Amtrak** (☎ *800/872–7245* ⊕ *www.amtrak.com*).

RESTAURANTS

Showy dress and jewelry matter little to most Montanans. A cowboy in dusty blue jeans, flannel shirt, and worn boots leaning against his rust-eaten Chevy could be a millionaire rancher and stockbroker, and the ponytailed woman behind the counter of the general store might be the town mayor. Because of this, no matter where you go to eat—whether the food is extravagant or simple, the prices expensive or dirt-cheap—dress is casual. But despite the universal informality in dining, eastern Montana has a surprising number of upscale restaurants turning out sophisticated dishes. Good ethnic food, with the possible exception of Mexican and Native American cuisine, is scarce, however. Classic steak houses and local ma-and-pa eateries are ubiquitous.

HOTELS

The strength of eastern Montana's hospitality doesn't lie in luxury resorts, bustling lodges, or crowded dude ranches, which are confined almost entirely to the western third of the state. The crown jewels of lodging on the plains are historic hotels and bed-and-breakfasts. Nearly every town with more than a few hundred residents has at least one of these properties, but no two are alike. From turreted Victorian mansions and rustic log ranch houses to Gothic manors and hulking sandstone inns with intricately carved facades, these lodgings have their own appeal and local flavor that set them apart from chain accommodations and commercial strip motels.

WHAT IT COSTS					
	¢	$	$$	$$$	$$$$
Restaurants	under $8	$8–$12	$13–$20	$21–$30	over $30
Hotels	under $70	$70–$100	$101–$150	$150–$200	over $200

Restaurant prices are for a main course at dinner. Hotel prices are for two people in a standard double room in high season, excluding service charges and 4% tax.

CAMPING

Many federal and state-owned lands allow camping for little or no charge, and you can often set up camp wherever you like, so long as you don't light a fire. In the more developed towns and cities there is almost always a campground or two with more modern conveniences, such as hot showers and flush toilets. It's a testament to this treeless terrain that most commercial campgrounds advertise their shade before their other amenities.

Contact Montana Fish, Wildlife & Parks for information on camping in state parks and the U.S. Forest Service and Bureau of Land Management for information on camping on federal land in the area.

Information **Montana Fish, Wildlife & Parks** (☎ 406/444–2535 ⊕ www.fwp. mt.gov). **U.S. Bureau of Land Management** (☎ 406/896–5000 ⊕ www.blm.gov/ mt/). **U.S. Forest Service** (☎ 406/329–3511 ⊕ www.fs.fed.us/r1).

GREAT FALLS

One of Great Falls' greatest assets is its sense of history. Here, along the banks of the Missouri where the plains meet the Rockies, explorers Meriwether Lewis and William Clark encountered one of the more daunting obstacles of their expedition: the thundering waterfalls that gave the city its name. The waterfalls have since been tamed by hydropower dams, but an interpretive center, guided boat trips, and paved trails that recall the passage of the two explorers in 1805 are impressive, and a slew of other museums and attractions celebrate other chapters in the city's history. From prehistoric buffalo jumps and famous Western artists to pioneering cowboys and the Missouri River fur trade, Great Falls has a storied past rich enough to make its people proud. And they are.

With 56,690 residents, Great Falls is no longer Montana's second-largest city, demoted in the 2000 census to third place, below the burgeoning mountain town of Missoula and its 363 extra residents. But Great Falls is still the commercial and social hub for northern Montana and southern Alberta, with a bi-level mall, thriving downtown district, bustling civic center, and near-boundless opportunities for outdoor recreation.

EXPLORING GREAT FALLS

This is a beautiful city for a sightseeing drive. Maple and linden trees line the residential streets, the Missouri River slices through the center of town, and the Rockies sink their teeth into the western horizon. The Highwoods and Little Belts mountains frame the views to the north and east of town. Despite the curves of the river, most streets are straight and relatively easy to navigate, thanks largely to the flat terrain. However, with an Air Force base on the east side of town, a commercial airport on the west side, and only four bridges spanning the river in between, traffic can get heavy, especially in late afternoons and on weekends. Pedestrian paths are far less congested. A gorgeous 33-mi-long riverside trail, ideal for walking and cycling, passes the city's largest green space, Gibson Park, and one of the largest cold-water springs in the world at Giant Springs State Park.

GETTING HERE AND AROUND

Many roads lead to Great Falls, and drivers have several options for getting here, depending on whether scenery or speed is the goal. From points west, one of the prettiest routes is dropping down from Highway 2 just east of Browning to Highway 89. The winding road has great views of the Rockies, and the little town of Choteau is a perfect place to stop to stretch your legs. If efficiency is the aim, take Highway 2 east to I–15 at Shelby.

The street layout in Great Falls is a standard grid, with avenues running east–west and streets north–south. Several one-ways make it easier to get from one end of town to the other while avoiding the busy traffic on Central and 10th Avenue South. Great Falls Transit, the city bus system, runs six days a week. And Great Falls is a bicycle-friendly town.

VISITOR INFORMATION

Great Falls Convention and Visitors Bureau (☎ *406/735–8535* ⊕ *great-fallscvb.visitmt.com*).

TOP ATTRACTIONS

 Black Eagle Falls. On the north side of the historic part of town is 40-foot-high, 500-foot-wide Black Eagle Falls, one of the places where the Missouri River takes a sharp dive on its 500-foot descent through town. A pedestrian bridge from the parking area leading to an island alongside the falls makes a nice place to watch birds or the water. The adjacent golf courses and baseball diamond give the area plenty of green space and a seminatural feel, although it's hard not to notice the concrete dam looming above. ⊠ *Intersection of U.S. 87 and 25th St. N.*

❻ C.M. Russell Museum Complex. This 76,000-square-foot complex houses
Fodor's Choice the largest collection of original art and personal objects of legendary
★ cowboy artist Charlie Russell (1864–1926). Russell's more than 4,000 works of art—sculptures, watercolors, oil paintings—primarily portray the vanishing era of the Old West. His log studio and home, built at the turn of the 20th century, are adjacent to the main galleries. A highlight is the bison exhibit: more than 1,000 objects are used to tell the epic story of this Western icon, and you feel the floor tremble as you experience the sensation of being in the middle of a stampede. Also here are

collections of paintings by other 19th-century and modern Western artists, interactive exhibits, and a research library. ✉ *400 13th St. N* ☎ *406/727-8787* ⊕ *www.cmrussell.org* 🎫 *$9* ⊙ *May–Sept., daily 9–6; Oct.–Apr., Tues.–Sat. 10–5.*

2 **Giant Springs State Park.** The freshwater springs here feed a state fish hatchery that covers 400 acres of parkland. According to residents, the waters that flow from the springs form the shortest river in the world, the 200-foot-long Roe River (Oregonians hold that their D River is shorter, but most independent record keepers side with Montana on the issue). In addition to the hatchery, a visitor center, picnic grounds, a river drive, hiking and biking trails, and a playground are all on-site, and you can walk up the hill to Fish, Wildlife & Parks' regional headquarters, filled with educational displays featuring life-size mounts of area wildlife. You can also fish, attend educational programs, and take tours. Kids will enjoy feeding the hatchery's fish. ✉ *4600 Giant Springs Rd.* ☎ *406/454-5840* ⊕ *www.fwp.mt.gov* 🎫 *$5 for nonresidents, free for Montana residents* ⊙ *Daily dawn–dusk.*

8 **Gibson Park.** This park, named for the insightful founder of Great Falls, is the crown jewel of the city's 400-acre park system. The most popular features are the duck pond and extensive flower gardens. There are also jogging paths, outdoor exercise equipment, basketball courts, horseshoe pits, restrooms, a playground, a band shell, and prime picnicking spots. Riverside Railyard Skate Park, reputed to be one of the best in the Northwest, connects to Gibson Park via the walking path leading underneath the railroad overpass. The restored log cabin of Vinegar Jones, reportedly Great Falls' first permanent resident, is also on display in the park near the gardens. ⊠ *Park Dr. N and 1st Ave. N* ☎ *406/771–1265* ⊕ *www.greatfallsmt.net/people_offices/park_rec/* ▨ *Free* ☉ *Daily dawn–dusk.*

WORTH NOTING

❼ Historic district. Great Falls has many stories to tell in its historic homes and businesses, including the beautiful brick buildings of the railroad era. There are more than 200 historic houses and small businesses along the east bank of the Missouri River. The structures reflect various architectural styles, including bungalow, prairie, colonial, Queen Anne, Victorian, and Second Empire. You can obtain brochures for one- to two-hour self-guided walking tours at the **Great Falls Information Center** (⊠ *15 Upper River Rd.* ☎ *406/771–0885 or 800/735–8535*). Or catch the Great Falls Historic Trolley (☎ *406/771–1100 or 888/707–1100* ⊕ *www.greatfallshistorictrolley.com*) for a comprehensive tour given by people passionate about the area.

❸ Lewis and Clark National Historic Trail Interpretive Center. At this hands-on interpretive center overlooking the Missouri River you can trace the trail that the Corps of Discovery traveled from 1804 to 1806 while in search of an overland route to the Pacific Ocean. The center exhibits materials used by the travelers and the Native Americans they met on their journey. Films, a self-guided tour, and costumed interpreters who conduct daily demonstrations further illuminate the history. Don't miss the pirogue pull, a muscle-straining simulation of the arduous task of pulling the expedition's dugout boats up cactus-studded canyons. The corps spent a month dragging their boats through the rugged prairie to avoid Great Falls' namesake waterfalls. ⊠ *4201 Giant Springs Rd.* ☎ *406/727–8733* ⊕ *www.fs.fed.us/r1/lewisclark/lcic.htm* ▨ *$5* ☉ *Memorial Day–Sept., daily 9–6; Oct.–Memorial Day, Tues.–Sat. 9–5, Sun. noon–5.*

❺ Paris Gibson Square Museum of Art. Contemporary artwork of the northwest United States makes up the bulk of the collection here. There is an educational resource room where kids and adults can try hands-on puzzles and projects, along with several exhibition halls and a photography collection. A perennial and butterfly garden on the south side of the building is a perfect spot for a summer picnic. ⊠ *1400 1st Ave. N* ☎ *406/727–8255* ⊕ *www.the-square.org* ▨ *$5* ☉ *Weekdays 10–5, Tues. also 7 PM–9 PM, Sat. noon–5.*

❶ Rainbow Falls. One of the waterfalls that gives the city its name, 50-foot-high Rainbow Falls is below Rainbow Dam, about 1½ mi east of Giant Springs State Park. An overlook has informational signs about the history of the area, as well as excellent views of the river. The surrounding land is mostly owned by ranchers, although there are some trails cut into the hills near the falls. ⊠ *Giant Springs Rd.*

OFF THE
BEATEN
PATH

Smith River. Flowing out of the Helena National Forest in the heart of Montana is the 60-mi Smith River. Like most other waterways in the state, it fluctuates with the seasons, ranging from a trickle in September to a raging torrent in June (thanks to the melting mountain snowpack). Although the river is popular for numerous activities, including camping on its banks, fishing, and swimming, the most prevalent activity on the Smith is floating. Floating is so popular, in fact, that Montana Fish, Wildlife & Parks limits the number of groups boating down the river to 700 per year. (It also prohibits dogs.) Despite the river's popularity, this is still Montana, and the sense of serene isolation that comes from the sight of towering mountains and open prairie will far outweigh any annoyance at seeing a few other boats during your journey. ⊠ *Between I–15 and U.S. 85* ☎ *406/454–5840* ⊕ *www.fwp.mt.gov* ⊠ *Charges for use permits vary; call for details. Float applications due mid-Feb.*

First Peoples Buffalo Jump State Park. For centuries Native Americans hunted bison by stampeding them off a cliff at this 2,000-acre park, which is sacred to the state's original residents. This is one of the largest and best-interpreted buffalo jumps in the United States. The mile-long cliff affords a spectacular view of the Rocky Mountains, the Missouri River, and the plains. An interpretive center focuses on the culture of the Plains Indians before white settlement. You can hike the 1.5-mile-long trail to the top of the hill where buffalo runners led herds over the cliff to their demise. ⊠ *342 Ulm-Vaugh Rd., 10 mi south of Great Falls on I–15 to Ulm exit, then 3½ mi northwest* ☎ *406/866–2217* ⊕ *www. fwp.mt.gov* ⊠ *$5 for nonresidents, free for Montana residents* ☉ *Memorial Day–Sept., daily 8–6; Oct.–Memorial Day, Wed.–Sat. 10–4, Sun. noon–4.*

SPORTS AND THE OUTDOORS

Unlike some of Montana's more westerly cities, Great Falls does not lie at the base of world-class ski runs or sheer cliffs for rock climbing. It is nevertheless popular with outdoor enthusiasts, largely because of its central location. Ski lodges and climbing trails are a short drive west, and stretching out north and south are Montana's famed blue-ribbon fishing streams. Not to be forgotten is the "Mighty Mo"—the Missouri River, a recreational playground that runs straight through the middle of the city.

The 33-mi **River's Edge Trail** (☎ *406/788–3313* ⊕ *www.thetrail.org*) follows the Missouri River through the city on both banks; four bridges connect the trail's two branches. The trail, which attracts bikers, joggers, and strollers, passes Gibson Park, the West Gate Mall, Giant Springs State Park, and several waterfalls and dams. More primitive and challenging trails extend downstream of Rainbow Dam. More than 15 mi of the path, which is still under development, are paved; the remaining 18 mi are gravel. You can get a brochure on the mining-related landmarks seen along the trail from the Great Falls Information Center (⊠ *15 Upper River Rd.* ☎ *406/771–0885 or 800/735–8535*) or**Knicker Biker** (⊠ *117 2nd Ave. N* ☎ *406/454–2912*), three blocks from the River's

8

Edge Trail near Gibson Park. They have the best selection of bikes and bicycle accessories in town.

In downtown Great Falls, **Bighorn Outdoor Specialists** (✉ *206 5th St. S* ☎ *406/453–2841*) is an outdoors specialty store with everything from camping-stove fuel and freeze-dried food to ice-climbing equipment and kayaks. The store also rents canoes and kayaks. **Craig Madsen's Montana River Outfitters** (✉ *923 10th Ave. N* ☎ *406/761–1677 or 800/800–8218*), facing the river on the north side of town, is known for its guided trips along the river by canoe, raft, or kayak. You can also get outfitted for a float trip with a wide selection of rental equipment.

WHERE TO EAT

$$
CONTEMPORARY
✗ **Bert & Ernie's.** A casual atmosphere and consistent food have made this downtown eatery a locals' favorite, and live entertainment in its Irish-flavored bar is drawing a younger crowd on weekday evenings. Burgers, hearty beef, chicken, and seafood selections, and full-meal salads are featured. The bar has more than a dozen Montana microbrews on tap and a respectable wine list. There's live entertainment, including bluegrass pickers, classical guitarists, and Irish pub bands, on Thursday throughout the summer, and on many weekends as well. ✉ *300 1st Ave. S* ☎ *406/453–0601* ⊕ *www.bertandernies.com* ▤ *AE, D, MC, V* ⊙ *Closed Sun.*

$$$
AMERICAN
✗ **Borrie's.** The dining is family-style at this restaurant in Black Eagle, a small community that borders the northeast edge of Great Falls. Regulars favor the steaks, fried chicken, lobster, and burgers, and the huge portions of spaghetti, ravioli, and rigatoni are legendary. Historic photos of Great Falls line the walls, but they're hard to appreciate in the dim lighting. ✉ *1800 Smelter Ave. NE, Black Eagle* ☎ *406/761–0300* ▤ *AE, D, MC, V* ⊙ *No lunch.*

$$$
AMERICAN
✗ **The Breaks Ale House & Grill.** Upstairs in this historic warehouse just south of downtown is a wine bar and restaurant offering something for every appetite. On the lighter side are an impressive number of salads, as well as an herb-broiled walleye. For heartier fare, consider the veal piccata, roasted duck, or a Montana buffalo T-bone steak. Sushi is available on weekends. Downstairs is Machinery Row, a pub where you can shoot pool, throw darts, and enjoy live music on weekends. An outdoor lounge has the only outdoor fire pit in the city. The wine bar offers more than two dozen appetizers in an intimate, casual setting. ✉ *202 2nd Ave. S* ☎ *406/453–5980* ⊕ *www.thebreaksgrill.com* ▤ *AE, D, MC, V* ⊙ *Closed Sun.*

$$$$
AMERICAN
✗ **Eddie's Supper Club.** Campfire steak, lobster, prime rib, and shrimp are the entrées of choice at this casual Great Falls mainstay. The large booths and tables may hark back to the 1950s, but Eddie's serves some of the best burgers and steaks in town. There's live piano music on Friday and Saturday. ✉ *3725 2nd Ave. N* ☎ *406/453–1616* ▤ *AE, D, MC, V.*

WHERE TO STAY

¢–$ Great Falls Inn. The furniture in the common areas of this small but well-appointed downtown hotel is so comfortable you'll want to meet friends in the lobby. Many of the guests of the inn stay here while using the services of the Great Falls Clinic and Benefis Healthcare Center next door. **Pros:** off the busy main drag of 10th Avenue South; comfortable, no-nonsense rooms. **Cons:** not easy to find; views of the back of the hospital. ⊠ *1400 28th St. S* ☎ *406/453–6000 or 800/454–6010* 📠 *406/453–6078* ⊕ *www.greatfallsinn.com* 🛏 *60 rooms* ⚐ *In-room: refrigerator (some). In-hotel: gym, Wi-Fi, some pets allowed* ☰ *D, MC, V* ⍾⎮ *CP.*

$$–$$$$ La Quinta Inn & Suites Great Falls. Overlooking the Missouri River just southwest of downtown and within easy walking distance of casual restaurants and watering holes, this clean, trendy property is a nice balance between bland franchise hotels and pricey upper-end lodging. Decor is decidedly Western, with a stone fireplace and exposed log beams. **Pros:** River's Edge Trail is outside the door; well-kept grounds give the property a luxury resort feel; off the main thoroughfares but close to downtown and the 10th Avenue South retail district. **Cons:** can be difficult to find; few restaurants within walking distance. ⊠ *600 River Dr. S* ☎ *406/761–2600* ⊕ *www.lq.com* 🛏 *91 rooms, 21 suites* ⚐ *In-room: Wi-Fi. In-hotel: laundry facilities, some pets allowed* ☰ *AE, D, MC, V* ⍾⎮ *CP.*

$–$$ Townhouse Inn. Frequent travelers to Great Falls return again and again to this modern hotel for its low prices and well-furnished, spacious rooms. Shades of beige, green, red, and blue decorate the motel-style rooms. An indoor courtyard has plants, a swimming pool, and a large hot tub. There's a game room with air hockey and foosball. **Pros:** hearty breakfast; easy to find; convenient single level. **Cons:** casino in the hotel; heavy traffic on 10th Avenue. ⊠ *1411 10th Ave. S* ☎ *406/761–4600* 📠 *406/761–7603* ⊕ *www.townhouseinngreatfalls. com* 🛏 *109 rooms* ⚐ *In-hotel: pool, Wi-Fi, some pets allowed* ☰ *AE, D, DC, MC, V.*

CAMPING Fort Ponderosa Campground. Horseshoes, proximity to outdoor recreation along Belt Creek and in the Little Belt Mountains, and helpful hosts are some of the attractions of this friendly campground tucked in the Belt Creek Canyon, 20 mi south of Great Falls just off U.S. Highway 89. A small store here stocks propane and some basic provisions, and larger stores are in the nearby town of Belt, a short drive—or tube ride down the creek—away. An A-frame chalet is available as a monthly rental for those who want an extended stay in this beautiful area. There's an extra $5 charge per night if you plan to use your RV's electric heater or air conditioner. ⚐ *Flush toilets, full hookups, partial hookups (electric and water), drinking water, guest laundry, showers, fire pits, picnic tables, food service, electricity, public telephone, general store, play area, swimming (creek)* 🛏 *9 full hookups, 25 partial hookups, 10 tent sites; 1 house* ⊠ *568 Armington Rd.* ☎ *406/277–3232* ☰ *D, MC, V.*

Great Falls KOA. Regular evening entertainment at this campsite on the south edge of town includes bluegrass music, country humor, and

8

a little cowboy poetry. Facilities are kid-friendly, with a small petting zoo, playground, horseshoe pits, basketball hoops, and a sand volleyball court. The site is near three golf courses, and has a large outdoor pool with a hot tub and sauna, spacious tent sites, and even rental cottages. ☼ *Flush toilets, full hookups, partial hookups (electric and water), drinking water, showers, picnic tables, food service, electricity, public telephone, general store, swimming (pool), Wi-Fi* ↩ *80 full hookups, 60 partial hookups, 30 tent sites; 25 cabins* ⊠ *1500 51st St. S* ☎ *406/727–3191 or 800/562–6584* ⊕ *www.koa.com/where/mt/26153/* ▭ *AE, D, MC, V.*

SHOPPING

★ Thanks to insightful city planners, Great Falls is blessed with a beautiful and extensive **downtown shopping district** full of the kind of old-fashioned stores—including galleries, toy stores, and clothiers—that in other parts of the country are rapidly giving way to chain stores and shopping malls. During the summer the downtown area comes alive with events such as the Great Falls Farmer's Market, held outside the Civic Center from June through September, and Alive at Five, which brings live music downtown one evening a week. Most of these businesses are in an area bounded by the Missouri River, 8th Street, 4th Avenue North, and 4th Avenue South.

★ A co-op run by a dozen local artists, **Gallery 16** (⊠ *608 Central Ave.* ☎ *406/453–6103*) has creations from more than 100 craftspeople, whose works include paintings, jewelry, furniture, pottery, and sculptures.

CENTRAL MONTANA

Although central Montana consists mostly of rolling plains carpeted with golden grasses, the general uniformity of the landscape is broken up by the occasional mountain range or swath of forest. There are other contrasts here as well, in this land where the pinnacles of the Rockies abut the ranches and farms of the prairie, and where old mining camps lie only a few miles from historic cow towns. Among the highlights of the region are its rivers: the Missouri, the Judith, and the Smith. They might not provide the kind of fishing found in Montana's famed Madison and Gallatin rivers, but they also aren't as crowded, and their rich history and stunning landscape make them the most popular Montana destinations you've probably never heard of. If you require regular doses of culture, you'll easily get bored in this land of seeming sameness, where you're considered a newcomer unless your grandparents are buried in the local cemetery.

FORT BENTON

40 mi northeast of Great Falls via U.S. 87.

The gateway to the Upper Missouri River, this town of 1,594 people has a rich and rugged past that's captured in a trio of excellent museums. Lewis and Clark first camped at this site less than an hour downriver from Great Falls in 1805. As a quick and easy way to move people, the Missouri River was the lifeblood of 19th-century Fort Benton. The first steamboat arrived here from St. Louis in 1859, and the city once claimed distinction as the farthest inland port in the world. Throughout the 1860s gold taken from mines across Montana was shipped down-river via Fort Benton; in 1866 alone, the town shipped 2½ tons of gold dust. The river still moves people today, not to seek their fortune in the goldfields but to paddle its placid waters amid the peaceful, serene, and beautiful countryside.

GETTING HERE AND AROUND

Highway 87, also known as the Havre Highway, travels from Great Falls to Havre, and is the most logical route to Fort Benton from either direction. The fact that there are no major hills or sharp turns along the way encourages speed; be on the lookout for reckless motorists.

Fort Benton is set up in a grid, with most of the travel-related sights situated near the river between Main Street and River Street. It's an easy town to walk or bicycle.

EXPLORING

★ The **Missouri Breaks Interpretive Center** puts the fabled Missouri Breaks in perspective, and offers a virtual glimpse of the river to those not float-ing down the Mighty Mo and maps for those who do. The front of the building, on Fort Benton's historic levee, looks like the stunning White Cliffs of the Missouri; the rear resembles the deck of a paddlewheel steamer. Inside, photos and films of the river and its wildlife, interactive exhibits, and history lessons await. A complete set of lithographs by Karl Bodmer, a Swiss artist who documented the area in 1933, graces one wall of the center. ⊠ *701 7th St.* ☎ *406/622–4000 or 877/256–3252* ⌨ *$2 or $10 for area museum pass* ☯ *Memorial Day–Sept. 30, daily 8–5; Oct. 1–Memorial Day, weekdays 8–5.*

Montana's official agriculture museum, the **Museum of the Northern Great Plains** tells the story of three generations of farmers from 1908 until 1980. The 30,000 square feet of exhibition space hold a village of busi-nesses from the homestead era and a library. On display are the Hor-naday-Smithsonian Bison, specimens taken from the Montana plains when it seemed likely that the species faced extinction. In 1886 the six buffalo were stuffed, then exhibited in the Smithsonian for more than 70 years before being returned to their native state. ⊠ *1205 20th St.* ☎ *406/622–5316* ⊕ *www.fortbenton.com/museums/ag.html* ⌨ *$10 for area museum pass* ☯ *May–Sept., Mon.–Sat. 10–4, Sun. noon–4; other months by appointment only.*

Fodor's Choice

★ Covering the era from 1800 to 1900, the **Museum of the Upper Missouri** highlights the importance of Fort Benton and the role it played as a trad-ing post, military fort, and the head of steamboat navigation. There are daily guided tours at the adjacent Old Fort Benton, considered the birth-place of Montana; its 1846 blockhouse is the oldest standing structure in the state. Highlights of the museum include tours of the restored fron-tier-era fort. The $10 fee also gives you access to the nearby Museum of the Northern Great Plains and the Missouri Breaks National Monument Interpretive Center. ⊠ *Old Fort Park* ☎ *406/622–5316* ⌨ *$10 for area* *museum pass* ◯ *May–Sept., Mon.–Sat. 10–4, Sun. noon–4, tours of fort at 10:30 and 1:30; other months by appointment only.*

In 1805–06 Lewis and Clark explored the upper Missouri River and camped on its banks. Today the stretch designated the **Upper Missouri National Wild and Scenic River** runs 149 mi downriver from Fort Benton. Highlights include the scenic White Cliffs area, Citadel Rock, Hole in the Wall, Lewis and Clark Camp at Slaughter River, abandoned homesteads, and abundant wildlife. Commercial boat tours, shuttle service, and boat rentals—including rowboats, powerboats, and canoes—are available in Fort Benton and Virgelle. Be aware of seasonal restrictions that prohibit motorized boats and limit campsites on the river. ✉ *Missouri Breaks Interpretive Center, 701 7th St.* ☎ *406/622–4000* 🖅 *Free.*

SPORTS AND THE OUTDOORS

Although sparsely inhabited, this calm stretch of the Mighty Mo is becoming more and more popular with visitors. There's no shortage of outfitters and guides offering their services at competitive prices.

★ The **Lewis and Clark Canoe Expeditions** (✉ *812 14th St.* ☎ *406/622–3698 or 888/595–9151* ⊕ *www.lewisandclarkguide.com*) guided trips last from one to seven days and can include horseback riding. You can also arrange for canoe rentals and a guide-only service, in which you provide transportation and food for your escort. The **Missouri River Canoe Company** (✉ *7485 Virgelle Ferry Rd. N, Loma* ☎ *406/378–3110 or 800/426–2926* ⊕ *www.canoemontana.com*), in the tiny town of Virgelle, provides canoe and kayak rentals by the day, outfitted excursions, and one- to four-day guided trips. Trips with lodging at Virgelle Merc, a restored homestead-era settlement with accommodations in cabins and B&B rooms, are also available.

WHERE TO EAT AND STAY

$$–$$$ 🏨 **Grand Union Hotel.** Perhaps the oldest hotel in Montana, the Grand
Fodor's Choice   Union was built on the bank of the Missouri in 1882 to serve steamboat
★   and stage travelers. Filled with period pieces, the two-story building is as elegant as ever. With its dark-wood accents and Victorian-style lighting, the Union Grille Restaurant ($$$–$$$$) brings to mind the refinement cultivated by the Western frontier's elite. The seasonal menu features Montana regional cuisine and fare from afar, including local roasted chicken, cocoa-dusted elk loin with espresso-whipped mashed potatoes, and grilled buffalo rib eye. The varied wine list is populated predominantly by choices from California and Washington vineyards, and offers a number of exceptional beer choices from Montana microbreweries. **Pros:** the hotel has a colorful history; easy walking around town; friendly atmosphere. **Cons:** hard to get a room at the last minute; no lunch at the Union Grille. ✉ *1 Grand Union Sq.* 🕭 *P.O. Box 1119* ☎ *406/622–1882 or 888/838–1882* ⊕ *www.grandunionhotel.com* 🛏 *26 rooms* ☖ *In-hotel: restaurant, bar* ⊟ *AE, D, MC, V* ◯ *Restaurant closed Mon. and Tues. in winter. No lunch* ⑂ *CP.*

LEWISTOWN

90 mi southeast of Fort Benton via Hwys. 80 and 81.

Started as a small trading post in the shadow of the low-lying Moccasin and Judith mountains, Lewistown has evolved into a pleasant town of nearly 7,000 residents. Several locations are listed on the National Register of Historic Places, including the Silk Stocking and Central Business districts, Courthouse Square, Judith Place, and Stone Quarry.

GETTING HERE AND AROUND

Lewistown is in the geographic center of the state, but there's no easy way to arrive here. Two-lane state roads are the only option, and the most popular route is Highway 87/200 running from Great Falls to Billings. Like most small towns in these parts, Lewistown is easy to navigate. Highway 87/200 becomes Main Street.

VISITOR INFORMATION

Self-guided-tour brochures are available at the **Lewistown Area Chamber of Commerce** (⊠ *408 N.E. Main St.* ☎ *406/535–5436 or 866/912–3980* ⊕ *www.lewistownchamber.com*).

EXPLORING

Nearly half the town—and several hundred visitors from across the country—turn out each year for the **Lewistown Chokecherry Festival.** Held the first Saturday after Labor Day, the annual harvest celebration includes arts and crafts booths, a farmers' market, a cook-off starring the wild-growing sour fruit, and a variety of contests for visitors of all ages, including a chokecherry pit–spitting contest that awards distance and accuracy. ⊠ *Along Main St.* ☎ *406/535–5436 or 866/912–3980* ⊕ *www.lewistownchamber.com.*

Pioneer relics, blacksmith and cowboy tools, guns, and Native American artifacts are displayed at the **Central Montana Museum.** Guided tours are available in the summer; from Labor Day through Memorial Day visitors are on their own to view the array of exhibits, most of which illuminate the human history of the Judith Basin and central Montana. ⊠ *408 N.E. Main St.* ☎ *406/535–3642* ▣ *Free* ☉ *Memorial Day–Labor Day, daily 10–4.*

☼
★ Discover the vistas that inspired Western artist Charlie Russell on the **Charlie Russell Chew-Choo,** a vintage 1950s-era train that travels on the old Milwaukee Road tracks through some of the most beautiful and remote landscapes in the state. The tour, which departs from Kingston, about 10 mi northwest of Lewiston, lasts 3½ hours and includes a prime-rib dinner and a cash bar. On weekends before Christmas the Chew-Choo transforms into a prairie Polar Express, and there are special Oktoberfest and New Year's Eve runs. ⊠ *U.S. 191 north 2 mi, then Hanover Rd. west for 7½ mi* ☎ *406/535–5436 or 866/912–3980* ⊕ *www.montanacharlierussellchewchoo.com* ▣ *$90–$125, including dinner* ☉ *June–Oct. and Dec., Sat. Call for departure times.*

☼ At the head of one of the purest cold-water springs in the world is the **Big Springs Trout Hatchery.** The state's largest cold-water production station nurtures several species of trout and kokanee salmon. The show pond, where you can view albino rainbow trout and fish weighing a monstrous

8

15 pounds, is a popular attraction, but the hatchery grounds are a sight in and of themselves and a wonderful spot to enjoy a picnic under giant willow and cottonwood trees. You can see the place where Big Spring Creek spurts from the earth, and the native wildlife—including white-tailed deer, beavers, wood ducks, and belted kingfishers—makes frequent appearances. ⊠ *Hwy. 466, 7 mi southeast of Lewistown; 2035 Fish Hatchery Rd.* ☎ *406/538–5588* ☒ *Free* ☉ *Daily dawn–dusk.*

OFF THE BEATEN PATH

Judith River. The tame, deserted Judith flows more than 60 mi from the Lewis and Clark National Forest through arid plains and sandy mesas before emptying into the Missouri. The scenery is stunning, but the variably low water levels and stifling hot summer sun are not conducive to float trips. This is, however, excellent fossil-hunting ground, and the **Judith River Dinosaur Institute**, based in Malta, sponsors frequent digs here. Most of the land surrounding the river is private, though, so check before you start wandering the banks looking for bones. As always, remember to leave fossils where you find them, and report anything significant to the Dinosaur Institute. ⊠ *North of Hwy. 200* ☎ *406/696– 5842 Dinosaur Institute* ⊕ *www.montanadinosaurdigs.com.*

War Horse National Wildlife Refuge. In 1958 this 3,192-acre area was established as a refuge and breeding ground for migratory birds and other wildlife. The refuge comprises three units: War Horse Lake, Wild Horse Lake, and Yellow Water Reservoir. The three units are geographically separate, but all are part of the larger Charles M. Russell National Wildlife Refuge, which encompasses more than 1 million acres along the Missouri River. Note that it's necessary to take gravel roads, which can be particularly tough going after a heavy rain or snow, to reach the fishing and wildlife areas. ⊠ *48 mi east of Lewistown on U.S. 87* ☎ *406/538–8706* ⊕ *www.fws.gov/cmr/* ☒ *Free* ☉ *Daily; headquarters weekdays 8–4.*

SPORTS AND THE OUTDOORS

Lewistown has access to water—and plenty of it. From natural springs to alpine lakes to crystal-clear creeks fed by melting snow, there are all kinds of ways to get wet in town, or within a few short miles. Big Springs Creek flows right through downtown, and even underneath several establishments on Main Street.

☾ **Ackley Lake State Park** (⊠ *U.S. 87 to Hwy. 400, then 7 mi southwest* ☎ *406/454–5840* ⊕ *www.fwp.mt.gov*) has two boat ramps, great fishing for rainbow trout, and a 23-site campground. It's to the north of the Little Belt Mountains, about 26 mi southwest of Lewistown. In a clearing roughly 9 mi outside Lewistown you can swim in the **Gigantic Warm Springs** (⊠ *North on U.S. 191, then west on Hwy. 81 for 9 mi*), a small spring-fed lake that keeps a constant temperature of 68°F. One of the most popular places in Frank Day City Park is the **Lewistown Municipal Swimming Pool** (⊠ *S. 5th Ave.* ☎ *406/535–4503*), a 13,000-square-foot water park with two large slides. For a more relaxing experience at the city park, stroll the seven-circuit labyrinth garden planted in annuals and perennials.

WHERE TO EAT AND STAY

$$ ✕**The Mint Bar & Grill.** This quaint bar and grill serves an exceptional
CONTINENTAL   array of dishes, but you won't find most of them on the menu. You have
★   a choice of 7 to 10 specials each night, ranging from the duck breast
with a cognac cream sauce to walleye, salmon, and halibut selections.
The separate full bar serving a fine selection of microbrews is housed in
the same restored 1914 brick building. ✉ *113 4th Ave. S* ☎ *406/535–
9925* ▭ *D, MC, V* ☺ *Closed Sun.*

$$ ▣ **Yogo Inn of Montana.** This sprawling modern hotel on the east side
of Lewistown takes its name from the Yogo sapphires mined nearby.
Rooms are contemporary, spacious, and well furnished; some have four-
poster beds. Many rooms face an indoor courtyard with a swimming
pool and hot tub. The hotel and convention center is built around the
Centermark Courtyard, which takes its name from surveyor documents
buried here in 1912: they proclaimed the spot the geographical center
of Montana. You can arrange for Western buggy and sleigh rides and
guided tours of nearby ghost towns and Native American petroglyphs.
Pros: accommodating staff; single story means easy access; good restaurant. **Cons:** noise is an issue when it's busy; has an "old hotel" smell.
✉ *211 E. Main St.* ☎ *406/535–8721 or 800/860–9646* ⊕ *www.yogoinn.
com* ⤸ *123 rooms* ⚹ *In-hotel: restaurant, bar, pool, Wi-Fi, some pets
allowed* ▭ *AE, D, MC, V.*

BIG SNOWY MOUNTAINS

40 mi south of Lewistown via Red Hill Rd.

South of Montana's geographical center an island of rocky peaks rises
more than 3,000 feet from the sea of windswept prairie, beckoning
scenery lovers and hard-core adventurers alike. A combination of pine
and fir forests and barren tundra, much of the Big Snowy Mountains
area is undeveloped. More than 80% of its 106,776 acres are designated federal wilderness study area—there are no homes, no commercial services, no industry, and very few roads. The result is almost total
solitude for anyone who treks into the Big Snowies to explore their
rocky pinnacles, icy caves, and tranquil forests. The best road accesses
are Red Hill Road about 40 mi south of Lewistown or Trail and Niel
creeks east of the small town of Judith Gap.

GETTING HERE AND AROUND

The Big Snowies are close to Lewistown and easy to access via county
roads. Once up there, most of them turn into fairly decent gravel roads.
On the west side, head west on Highway 87/200 to Eddie's Corner and
drop down to Judith Gap. To reach points east, take Highway 238 all
the way past Big Spring Creek where it turns into Red Hill Road.

VISITOR INFORMATION

Few of the features of the Big Snowies are marked, but you can pick
up a map of the area from any of the Lewis and Clark National Forest
ranger stations scattered around central Montana, including the **Musselshell Ranger Station** (✉ *809 2nd St. NW, Harlowton* ☎ *406/632–4391*
⊕ *www.fs.fed.us/r1/lewisclark*), 25 mi southwest of the mountains.

8

EXPLORING

At 8,681 feet, **Greathouse Peak** is the tallest mountain in the Big Snowies. Vehicles are permitted on Forest Service roads that reach partially to the peak, but the simplest way up is to hike the 6 mi of unmarked trails that zigzag up the slope from Halfmoon Canyon. The main trail, which is only mildly strenuous, doesn't quite make it to the top; to reach the summit, you'll need to hike a few yards off the main path. You'll know you've reached the highest point when you see the two stone cairns. The Judith Ranger Station in Stanford is your best source for Snowies information. ⊠ *Pack Trail* ☎ *406/566–2292* ☉ *Daily; automobile access seasonally restricted by deep snow.*

The second-highest point in the Big Snowies is **Big Snowy**, also called Old Baldy. Just 41 feet shorter than Greathouse Peak, the 8,640-foot-high mountain makes an enjoyable climb. A designated path, Maynard Ridge Trail, follows an old jeep road almost to the summit. The peak is a barren plateau with a small rocky outcropping marking the highest point. ⊠ *Red Hill Rd.* ☎ *406/566–2292* ☉ *Daily; automobile access seasonally restricted by deep snow.*

★   In the higher reaches of the mountains is pristine **Crystal Lake.** There's excellent hiking along interpretive and wildflower trails as well as camping, fossil hunting, and ice-cave exploration. The ice cave is a 6-mi hike from the 28-site campground; June is the best time to see the 30-foot ice pillars formed over the winter. There's a cabin 6 mi from the gate for snowmobilers, cross-country skiers, and snowshoers, but it's closed when the snow is too deep to navigate (which is most of the winter). No motorized boats are allowed on the lake. ⊠ *Crystal Lake Rd.* ☎ *406/566–2292* ☜ *Free* ☉ *Daily; automobile access generally June–Nov., but can be seasonally restricted by deep snow.*

A pair of 1909 sandstone buildings in the town of Harlowton, 25 mi southwest of the mountains, house the **Upper Musselshell Museum.** The collection primarily contains artifacts of the people who lived in, worked, and developed the land around the Upper Musselshell River. There are also fossils of bison and dinosaurs (including a full-size reproduction of "Ava," from the recently discovered species Avaceratops) in the two buildings in Harlow's small but picturesque commercial district. ⊠ *11 and 36 S. Central St., Harlowton* ☎ *406/632–5519* ☜ *$5* ☉ *Memorial Day–Labor Day, Tues.–Sat. 10–5, Sun. 1–5.*

SPORTS AND THE OUTDOORS

In the evergreen forests and rocky slopes of the Big Snowies and the Judith and Little Belt mountains you can pursue numerous outdoor activities, including fishing, hiking, rock climbing, snowmobiling, and cross-country skiing. The utter isolation of the region enhances the experience, but be sure to get supplied in the larger communities of Lewistown, Great Falls, or Billings before making the trek out to the mountains.

A well-appointed local outfitter, **Don's Store** (⊠ *120 2nd Ave. S, Lewistown* ☎ *406/538–9408 or 800/879–8194*) carries a wide selection of fishing and hunting gear and outdoor wear, plus optics equipment such as binoculars and spotting scopes. **High Plains Bike & Ski** (⊠ *924 W. Water*

St., Lewistown ☎ 406/538–2902) sells many brands of alpine and bicycling equipment and can rush-order cross-country-skiing equipment. Call before you go, because hours vary.

WHERE TO STAY

¢–$ 🏨 **Corral Motel.** Family units, some with two bedrooms, and three full kitchenette units are the specialty of this hotel filled with modern furniture. Most rooms afford unobstructed views of the Musselshell River and the Castle, Crazy, and Big Snowy mountains. **Pros:** perfect base camp for three different mountain ranges; bring your well-behaved bird dog. **Cons:** traffic noise from U.S. 191; nothing fancy. ⊠ *U.S. 12 and U.S. 191 E, Harlowton* ☎ 406/632–4331 or 800/392–4723 ⬛ 406/632–4748 ⏋ *18 rooms, 6 2-bedroom units* ⅙ *In-room: refrigerator (some). In-hotel: restaurant, bar, some pets allowed* ⊟ *AE, D, MC, V.*

CAMPING ⛺ **Crystal Lake Campground.** Tucked inside the lip of the crater that contains the waters of Crystal Lake, this primitive Forest Service campground may be one of the most dramatic (and cold) places to pitch a tent in the state. There are year-round ice caves nearby, and snow can fly just about any month of the year. There's plenty of space separating the campsites. ⅙ *Pit toilets, drinking water, picnic tables, swimming (lake)* ⏋ *28 sites* ⊠ *Crystal Lake Rd., 22 mi west of U.S. 87* ☎ 406/566–2292 ⬛ 406/566–2408 ⊟ No credit cards ⊙ *Mid-May–late Sept.; call to verify.*

EN ROUTE Any combination of U.S. 12, U.S. 191, U.S. 87, and I–90 will make a quick route to Billings. However, if you have the time, try getting off the main roads. The square of beautiful country between these four highways is the location of **Halfbreed Lake National Wildlife Refuge** (⊠ *Molt-Rapelje Rd.* ☎ 406/538–8706), part of the Charles M. Russell National Wildlife Refuge. The several thousand acres of Halfbreed encompass a seasonally wet lake and wetlands, creeks, and grassy plains. Wildlife includes grouse, waterfowl, grasslands birds, deer, and antelope. This is a favorite spot for birders.

BILLINGS

A bastion of civilization on an otherwise empty prairie, Billings is a classic Western city, full of the kind of history that shaped the frontier. The Minnesota and Montana Land and Improvement Company founded the town simply to serve as a shipping point along the Northwestern Railroad. In the spring of 1882 the settlement consisted of three buildings—a home, a hotel, and a general store—but before six months passed 5,000 city lots had been sold and more than 200 homes and businesses had been erected. The city's immediate and consistent growth earned Billings the nickname "the Magic City."

Billings's population has doubled every 30 years since its founding. In 2007 the population for the city proper hit the 100,000 mark, making it not only the largest city in Montana, but the largest for 500 mi in any direction. Since the 1951 discovery of an oil field that stretches across Montana and the Dakotas into Canada, refining and energy production have played a key role in keeping Billings vibrant and productive.

GETTING HERE AND AROUND

Several exits access Billings from I–90. Livingston lies 116 mi to the west and Miles City 145 mi to the east along the same highway. Great Falls, 219 mi northwest, is reached by following I–90 to U.S. 287, then I–15, or by taking U.S. 87 via Lewistown. A number of airlines serve Logan International Airport.

Although city planners in its first century did a fine job of laying out the constantly growing community of Billings, most growth in recent years, both residential and commercial, has been in what is commonly called the West End. The primary residential districts are on the northern and western sides, the industrial parks are on the city's southern and eastern perimeters, and a historic downtown district is a bit east of center. Major avenues ease the flow of traffic between the sectors, and downtown streets, which are primarily one-way, are logically numbered. Although most of the newer hotels and motels are in the western part of the city, the majority of tourist sights and better restaurants are downtown. Therefore, expect to do far more driving than walking to reach your destination. Locals complain mightily about rush-hour traffic, but gridlock is unheard of, and those from bigger metropolitan areas will wonder what the gripe is.

VISITOR INFORMATION

Billings Area Visitor Center and Cattle Drive Monument. In front of the center, a hero-size bronze sculpture of a cattle drover with two longhorns commemorates the Great Montana Centennial Cattle Drive of 1989 (which commemorated the drive of 1889). Images of mountains, a stream, and pine trees are etched in the glass entry doors. Helpful personnel and numerous brochures will orient you to area attractions. ⊠ *815 S. 27th St.* ☎ *406/252–4016 or 800/735–2635* ⊕ *www.visitbillings.com* ☉ *Daily 9–6.*

EXPLORING BILLINGS

TOP ATTRACTIONS

6 Alberta Bair Theater. In the 1930s, 20th Century Fox built this art deco movie theater on land homesteaded by a successful sheep-ranching family. Saved from the wrecking ball by community groups in the 1980s, it is now a cultural center for the region. Aside from being home to the Billings Symphony Orchestra, the Alberta Bair hosts a variety of national and international companies each year. It is open only during performances. ⊠ *2801 3rd Ave. N* ☎ *406/256–6052 or 877/321–2074* ⊕ *www.albertabairtheater.org.*

4 Lake Elmo State Park. Surrounding a 64-acre reservoir in the Billings Heights area, this park is a popular spot for hiking, swimming, fishing, and nonmotorized boating. Although it's not far from downtown, the park is still wild enough to seem miles away from civilization. The regional on-site headquarters for Montana Fish, Wildlife & Parks is a source of recreational information and museum-quality wildlife displays. ⊠ *2400 Lake Elmo Dr.* ☎ *406/247–2940* ⊕ *www.fwp.mt.gov* *Free for vehicles with Montana license plates, $5 per vehicle for others* ☉ *Daily 5 am–10 pm.*

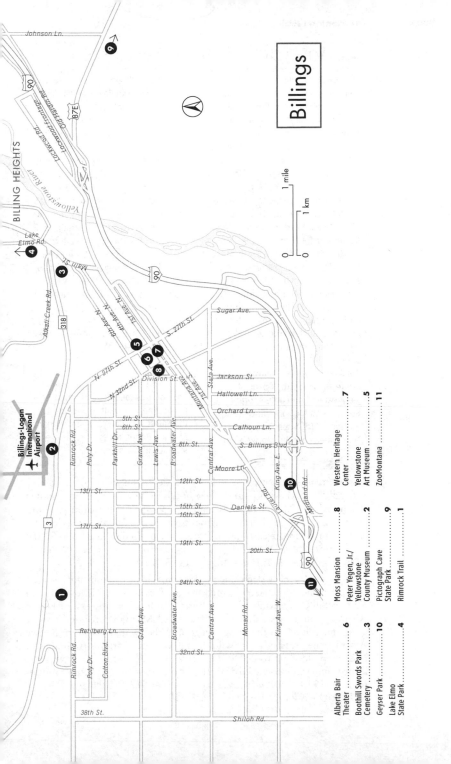

Billings

Alberta Bair
Theater **6**
Boothill Swords Park
Cemetery **3**
Geyser Park **10**
Lake Elmo
State Park **4**

Moss Mansion **8**
Peter Yegen, Jr./
Yellowstone
County Museum **2**
Pictograph Cave
State Park **9**
Rimrock Trail **1**

Western Heritage
Center **7**
Yellowstone
Art Museum **5**
ZooMontana **11**

A GOOD TOUR OF BILLINGS

The center of Billings is tucked beneath a distinct rock wall, aptly named the Rimrocks. Running along part of the wall is the **Rimrock Trail** ❶, made up of several smaller trails, which has outstanding views. After your hike, drive east on Highway 3 to **Peter Yegen, Jr./Yellowstone County Museum** ❷ at the entrance to Logan International Airport. Continue east on Route 318, passing **Boothill Swords Park Cemetery** ❸ before heading north on Main Street to **Lake Elmo State Park** ❹, a popular recreational spot on the edge of town near Billings Heights. Head back down Main Street and then drive southwest on 6th Avenue North into the commercial district, where several sights are grouped together. Make a left onto North 27th Street and drive to 4th Avenue North for the **Yellowstone Art Museum** ❺, displaying Western and contemporary art. Continue on foot one block south on North 27th Street to 3rd Avenue North; make a right and walk one

block to North 28th Street to reach the **Alberta Bair Theater** ❻. Walk south down North 28th Street to Montana Avenue, where you'll find the **Western Heritage Center** ❼. To reach the turn-of-the-20th-century **Moss Mansion** ❽, head north on North 28th Street for two blocks; make a left onto 2nd Avenue North and follow it west for several blocks to Division Street. Return to your car and drive south on 27th Street until you reach I–90; follow the interstate east for 2 mi to Exit 452. Turn right and follow Highway 87 south a few miles to the border of the Crow Indian Reservation, where you'll find the fascinating **Pictograph Cave State Park** ❾. For a bit of fun, head back into Billings and take I–90 west to **ZooMontana** ⓫.

TIMING

You could easily spend two or more days on this tour, depending on how much time you want to allocate to the sights and parks. In winter, many of the outdoor sights close or are significantly less enjoyable.

❽ **Moss Mansion.** Dutch architect Henry Hardenbergh, who worked on the original Waldorf-Astoria and Plaza hotels in New York City, designed this house in 1903 for businessman P. B. Moss. The mansion still contains many of the elaborate original furnishings, ranging in style from Moorish to art nouveau. Guided tours are offered on the hour. ⌧ *914 Division St.* ☎ *406/256–5100* ⊕ *www.mossmansion.com* ⌦ *$7* ۞ *Sept.–May, Tues.–Sun. 1–3; June–Aug., Tues.–Sat. 10–3, Sun. 1–3.*

❷ **Peter Yegen, Jr./Yellowstone County Museum.** This log cabin once served as a gentlemen's club, frequented by the likes of Teddy Roosevelt and Buffalo Bill Cody. Today the structure, standing near the exit of Logan Airport, houses a small but artifact-filled Montana frontier history museum. Check out the chuck wagon, barbed-wire collection, Native American items, taxidermic wildlife, a Lewis and Clark fur-trading post, and creepy-looking tools from the city's first dentist office. A veranda affords unparalleled views of the Bighorn, Pryor, and Beartooth mountains. ⌧ *1950 Terminal Circle* ☎ *406/256–6811* ⊕ *www.pyjrycm.org* ⌦ *Free* ۞ *Weekdays 10:30–5, Sat. 10:30–3.*

⑨ **Pictograph Cave State Park.** Once home to prehistoric hunters, this spot
Fodor's Choice has yielded more than 30,000 artifacts related to early human history.
★ A paved trail affords views of the 2,200-year-old cave paintings depicting animal and human figures; if you bring binoculars, you'll be able to
appreciate better the subtle detail of the artwork. A visitor center houses
an interpretive area and a gift shop. ⊠ *3401 Coburn Rd., off U.S. 87*
☎ *406/254–7342* ⊕ *www.pictographcave.org* ⊠ *Free for vehicles with
Montana license plates, $5 per vehicle for others* ⊙ *May–Aug., daily
8–8; Sept.–Apr., daily 11–7.*

❶ **Rimrock Trail.** This trail system on the northern edge of Billings is a pleasant mix of paved urban paths and rugged dirt tracks, where elderly
locals out for a Sunday stroll are just as content as extreme mountain
bikers. Several individual trails make up the Rimrock system, which
starts at Boothill Cemetery and winds past the airport up into the rocky
formations that surround the city and give the trail its name. Expect
fantastic views of the open plains and five distinct mountain ranges in
some places, and the roar of jet engines and the sight of oil-refinery
smokestacks in others. ⊠ *Airport Rd.* ☎ *406/245–4111.*

❼ **Western Heritage Center.** The permanent exhibits here include oral histories,
⟁ artifacts, and kid-friendly interactive displays tracing the lives of Native
Americans, ranchers, homesteaders, immigrants, and railroad workers
who lived in the area from 1880 onward. Native American interpretive
programs also are offered. The impressive castlelike building that houses
the center is almost as interesting as the exhibits. ⊠ *2822 Montana Ave.*
☎ *406/256–6809* ⊕ *www.ywhc.org* ⊠ *$5* ⊙ *Tues.–Sat. 10–5*

❺ **Yellowstone Art Museum.** One of the premier art museums in a four-
state region, the Yellowstone displays Western and contemporary art
by nationally and internationally known artists. The permanent collection numbers more than 4,000 works, including pieces by Charles
M. Russell and cowboy author and illustrator Will James. (It has the
largest collection of art by James in the country.) Beyond the Palette,
the attractive museum café ($), serves lunch Tuesday through Saturday
and has a tapas night on Thursday. ⊠ *401 N. 27th St.* ☎ *406/256–6804*
⊕ *yellowstone.artmuseum.org* ⊠ *$5* ⊙ *Mon.–Wed., Fri., and Sat. 10–5,
Thurs. 10–8, Sun. noon–5.*

⓫ **ZooMontana.** Ranging over 70 acres of zoological park and botanical
⟁ gardens, ZooMontana has inhabitants evenly divided between those
native to the region, such as grizzlies, grey wolves, and bighorn sheep,
and the exotic, including Siberian tigers, red pandas, and pygmy mar-
mosets. There's a farm and ranch area, complete with a petting zoo.
Because there are few zoos in the region, it can be extremely busy here in
summer. ⊠ *2100 S. Shiloh Rd.* ☎ *406/652–8100* ⊕ *www.zoomontana.
org* ⊠ *$6* ⊙ *May–late Sept., daily 10–5; late Sept.–Apr., daily 10–4.*

WORTH NOTING

❸ **Boothill Swords Park Cemetery.** Atop the Rimrocks, north of downtown,
lie the graves of H. M. Muggins Taylor, the army scout who carried
word of Custer's defeat through 180 mi of hostile territory; Western
explorer Yellowstone Kelly; and several outlaws executed in territorial
days. A sign tells the story of Crow warriors who blindfolded their

Guest Ranches on the Plains

CLOSE UP

Most eastern Montana ranchers are busy enough with making a living that their concession to visitors is a two-fingered wave through the windshield. But a few ranches, most in the mountains south of Billings, cater to guests, who take part in calving and branding, trailing cows to summer pasture, fixing fence, and other staples of ranch life.

Dryhead Ranch (☎ 307/548–6688) is headquartered in Lovell but sprawls up the arid east slopes of the Pryor Mountains in Montana. A dozen horse-loving guests a week visit from April through November, helping Iris Basset and her family run their thousand head of cattle and 300 horses. "They come for as much horseback riding as we can give them, and we can wear them out in four or five days," says Basset.

Nestled in the Clarks Fork Valley to the west, **Lonesome Spur Ranch** (☎ 406/662–3460) also caters to

horsey guests, more than half of whom hail from overseas. This is where Nicholas Evans, author of *The Horse Whisperer*, lived as he researched the best-selling novel, and a week at the ranch revolves around saddle horns and bridle bits and includes a trip to see the Pryor Mountains' wild-horse herd.

Just to the west, in the shadow of the Beartooth Mountains, the **Lazy E-L Ranch** (☎ 406/328–6858) is similarly devoted to horses and includes ranch work.

Don't expect wine tastings or hot-towel spas at these working ranches, but if you want to spend a week in the saddle experiencing authentic Western landscapes from the back of a horse, these ranches are worth a look. Rates range from $1,500 to $1,800 per week per adult, and some ranches allow groups to book the entire facility.

horses before riding them off what's now known as Sacrifice Cliff in hopes that the gods would end a smallpox epidemic. ⊠ *East end of Black Otter Trail, parallel to Airport Rd.* ☎ *406/657–8371.*

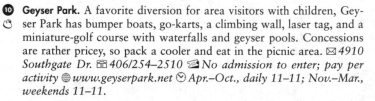 **Geyser Park.** A favorite diversion for area visitors with children, Geyser Park has bumper boats, go-karts, a climbing wall, laser tag, and a miniature-golf course with waterfalls and geyser pools. Concessions are rather pricey, so pack a cooler and eat in the picnic area. ⊠ *4910 Southgate Dr.* ☎ *406/254–2510* ☞ *No admission to enter; pay per activity* ⊕ *www.geyserpark.net* ⊘ *Apr.–Oct., daily 11–11; Nov.–Mar., weekends 11–11.*

SPORTS AND THE OUTDOORS

The Rimrocks are easily the dominant feature of Billings. These 400-foot sandstone rock walls provide a scenic backdrop for numerous recreational pursuits. One of the most popular is mountain biking; suitable terrain for beginners, experienced thrill seekers, and everyone in between can be found within a short driving distance. The Yellowstone River flows through town; best access points are East Bridge on the east side of Billings and South Hills southeast of town off Blue Creek Road.

GOLF

Billings has more than half a dozen public golf courses. Ranging from quick 9-hole executives in the middle of town to grand 18-hole country-club courses set against the Rimrocks, the golfing venues around the city are diverse in design and often have exceptional views of the surrounding country. Greens fees are generally very reasonable. A public 18-hole, par-72 course near Lake Elmo State Park in the Billings Heights section, the **Lake Hills Golf Club** (⊠ *1930 Clubhouse Way* ☎ *406/252–9244* ⊕ *www.lakehillsgolf.com*) is in a wooded area frequented by grouse, antelopes, and pheasants. Its two lakes and 444-yard 18th hole are its most famous features. The **Yegen Golf Club** (⊠ *1390 Zimmerman Trail* ☎ *406/656–8099* ⊕ *www.yegengolfclub.com*), an 18-hole, par-71 public course, is set against the walls of the Rimrocks. Although not very wooded, the course has plenty of water hazards and bunkers. **Eagle Rock Golf Course** (⊠ *5624 Larimer La.* ☎ *406/655–4445* ⊕ *www. eaglerockgolfcourse.com*) provides both the expected facilities, including a Western-style wood-and-stone clubhouse, and the challenging hazards of an 18-hole, par-72 course. Take U.S. 87 north, then U.S. 312 to Larimer Lane.

MOUNTAIN BIKING

The **Bike Shop** (⊠ *1934 Grand Ave.* ☎ *406/652–1202*), owned by a local family since the 1970s, sells, rents, and services mountain and road bikes. **Scheels All Sports** (⊠ *Rimrock Mall, 1233 W. 24th St.* ☎ *406/656–9220*) sells mountain and road bikes. Head to the **Spoke Shop** (⊠ *1910 Broadwater Ave.* ☎ *406/656–8342*) for road bikes, mountain bikes, and equipment.

WHERE TO EAT

$$
ITALIAN
✕ **Bruno's.** "A Touch of Italy" serves as this West End eatery's motto, and it's an apt one. Traditional music, antique pasta machines, and old olive-oil cans set the stage for 10 or so homemade pasta dishes, plus shrimp, chicken, veal, and specialty pizzas. The full bar includes a modest selection of Italian wines and beers. ⊠ *1911 King Ave. W* ☎ *406/652–4416* ▭ *AE, D, MC, V* ⊘ *No lunch Sun.*

$$$
NEW AMERICAN
✕ **Enzo Bistro.** People come to this attractive chalet-style building for European, pan-Asian, and American specialties such as pasta, the catch of the day, Moroccan couscous, and grilled pork rack with Glacier Ale barbecue sauce. ⊠ *1502 Rehberg La., at Grand Ave.* ☎ *406/651–0999* ▭ *AE, DC, MC, V* ⊘ *No lunch. Closed Mon.*

$$$
NEW AMERICAN
★
✕ **George Henry's.** With its stained glass and tearoom-style table settings, this restaurant in an 1882 Victorian house is elegant but cozy. Favorites include steak Oscar (with béarnaise sauce, crab, and asparagus), veal piccata, and walleye pike with almonds. Flower boxes hang from the iron fence enclosing the patio tables. ⊠ *404 N. 30th St.* ☎ *406/245–4570* ▭ *AE, D, DC, MC, V* ⊘ *Closed Sun. No lunch Sat.*

$$$
NEW AMERICAN
✕ **The Granary.** A restored flour mill houses this restaurant, which ages its own beef and changes its eclectic menu every few months. Seafood,

veal, lamb, and organic chicken are mainstays. Like outdoor seating options at most Billings restaurants, the veranda here is very popular in summer. ⊠ *1500 Poly Dr.* ☎ *406/259–3488* ▭ *AE, D, MC, V* ⊘ *No lunch weekends.*

$$$
NEW AMERICAN
Fodor's Choice
★

✕ **Juliano's.** Award-winning Hawaiian-born chef Carl Kurokawa's menu changes monthly, but you can count on fresh fish each Wednesday, flown in the day before from Hawaii. Other offerings might include grilled twin quails with cranberry wine sauce and pine nuts, and baked apricot-glazed baby spring chicken stuffed with cashew fried rice. Inspired by Pacific and European flavors, yet distinctly American, Carl's cooking is some of the best in the state. The intimate dining areas' decor is impressive, with a pressed tin ceiling in one room and painted scenes of a grape-carrying Bacchus in another. Situated behind a hedge on a residential street, and thus not easily spotted, the building was formerly a stable for the turn-of-the-20th-century sandstone mansion next door. In warm weather patio dining is a popular option. Lunch runs $8–$10. ⊠ *2912 7th Ave. N* ☎ *406/248–6400* ▭ *AE, D, MC, V* ⊘ *Closed Sun. No dinner Mon. and Tues. No lunch Sat.*

$$
IRISH

✕ **Pug Mahon's.** Good Irish stews, pasties, pork-chop sandwiches, fish-and-chips, and corned beef and cabbage are highlights of this authentic Irish pub, which serves dozens of imported beers and whiskies. ⊠ *3011 1st Ave. N* ☎ *406/259–4190* ▭ *D, MC, V*

$$$$
AMERICAN

✕ **The Rex.** Built in 1910 by Buffalo Bill Cody's chef, this restaurant was saved from the wrecking ball and restored in 1975. Today it's one of the best steak houses in the city. The bar area features wooden ceiling beams, and the main dining room's oak paneling exudes a clubby ambience. In warm weather the outdoor patio is perhaps the most popular place to dine on such dishes as buffalo fillet, prime rib, shrimp po'boy, or jerk steak with mango chutney. The kitchen stays open until 11 PM, later than at most Billings eateries, and there's a piano bar on weekends. ⊠ *2401 Montana Ave.* ☎ *406/245–7477* ▭ *AE, D, DC, MC, V.*

$$
ASIAN

✕ **Sweet Ginger.** Large sepia photos of the proprietors as children and as newlyweds line one wall, a hint of the personal pride and attention evident here. In addition to what the owners term "modern Chinese" dishes, the menu offers tempting satays, soba, tempura, sashimi, and sushi. It's open for lunch and dinner Tuesday–Friday and from 3 pm on Saturday. ⊠ *2515 Montana Ave.* ☎ *406/245–9888* ▭ *AE, MC, V* ⊘ *Closed Sun. and Mon; no lunch Sat.; closed Sept.*

$
MEXICAN

✕ **Santa Fe Red's.** Wooden beams, greenery, strings of chilies, and colorful weavings bring a touch of the Southwest to this northern eatery. Tasty Mexican white prawns and stuffed poblano peppers, as well as the expected array of enchiladas, tacos, fajitas, and other favorites, make ordering no easy matter. ⊠ *1223 Grand Ave.* ☎ *406/252–2221* ▭ *AE, D, MC, V.*

$$$
AMERICAN

✕ **Walkers.** Situated downtown near the Alberta Bair Theater, this restaurant has a loyal dinner following, understandable considering its casual yet elegant decor, pleasant, attentive service, and such entrées as duck breast, jumbo prawns, oven-roasted pork roulade, and made-from-scratch pastas. Walkers also has an upscale bar scene, attracted, in part, by a tempting selection of hot and cold tapas. ⊠ *2700 1st Ave. N* ☎ *406/245-9291* ▤ *AE, D, MC, V.*

WHERE TO STAY

$$-$$$$ ⊡ **Crowne Plaza.** With 23 stories, this property is one of the few highrises in Billings, making it a handy orientation point. Guest rooms are spacious and well appointed, with some providing mountain views. The hotel is noted for its superb Western art collection, which hangs in both public areas and guest rooms. The appropriately named Montana Sky Restaurant ($$$), open for breakfast and dinner, features regional game dishes such as elk loin medallions, along with more usual fare. **Pros:** a $16.5 million renovation completed in 2008; lobby Starbucks; concierge floors; complimentary gym and airport shuttle. **Cons:** some complain of noise from trains passing a couple of blocks away; front desk staff gets mixed reviews. ⊠ *27 N. 27th St.* ☎ *406/252-7400 or 800/588-7666* ⊕ *www.crowneplaza.com* ⇨ *289 rooms* ⚷ *In-room: refrigerator (some), Wi-Fi. In-hotel: restaurant, room service, bar, gym, laundry service, Wi-Fi* ▤ *AE, D, DC, MC, V.*

$ ⊡ **Dude Rancher Lodge.** As you might expect, a Western theme pervades this downtown institution, right down to the lantern-style light fixtures, wood paneling, and custom-made carpet "branded" with the symbols of area ranches. The hotel has one suite with a full kitchen, and Room 226 is known for its resident ghost. An on-site restaurant serves breakfast and lunch. **Pros:** within easy walking distance of attractions and restaurants; some baths have jetted tubs. **Cons:** rooms and baths are on the small side; you'll love or hate the brightly colored bathroom vanities. ⊠ *415 N. 29th St.* ☎ *406/259-5561 or 800/221-3302* ⊕ *www. duderancherlodge.com* ⇨ *57 rooms* ⚷ *In-room: refrigerator (some), Wi-Fi. In-hotel: restaurant, room service (breakfast, lunch), Wi-Fi, some pets allowed* ▤ *AE, D, DC, MC, V.*

$$ ⊡ **Hilton Garden Inn.** A double-sided fireplace serves as the lobby focal point for this West End property. Guest rooms are well appointed, with good work space, nice art, and comfortable mattresses topped by white duvets. The heated indoor pool, whirlpool, 24-hour business center, and airport shuttle are complimentary. There's a buffet, as well as à la carte, breakfast for an extra charge. **Pros:** pleasant front desk staff; comfortable conversation areas in lobby. **Cons:** duvets are not the bedding of choice for some; situated in a busy (rather than attractive) part of town. ⊠ *939 S. 25th St. W* ☎ *406/655-8800 or 877/782-9444* ⇨ *128 rooms* ⚷ *In-room: refrigerator, Wi-Fi. In-hotel: restaurant (breakfast only), room service, pool, gym, laundry facilities, laundry service, Wi-Fi* ▤ *AE, DC, MC, V.*

$-$$$ ⊡ **The Josephine Bed and Breakfast.** Within walking distance of downtown, this lovely home, built in 1912, offers five theme guest rooms, including the Garden Room, with its floral fabrics, and the Captain's Room, complete with a mahogany four-poster bed and a claw-foot tub. You're welcome to relax in the guest parlor, with a piano, coffeetable books, and newspapers, or in the library. Breakfast is served at your convenience; sourdough pancakes topped with homemade chokecherry syrup are a favorite among return guests. **Pros:** like staying in

8

a favorite aunt's house; guest passes to the local YMCA. **Cons:** finely furnished B&Bs are seldom the ideal environment for kids. ☒ *514 N. 29th St.* ☎ *406/248–5898 or 800/552–5898* ⊕ *www.thejosephine.com* ⇨ *5 rooms* ♿ *In-room: Wi-Fi. In-hotel: Internet terminal, Wi-Fi* ▭ *AE, D, MC, V* ⦿ *BP.*

$$ 🛏 **Springhill Suites by Marriott.** Among the newish properties in the West End, this all-suite hotel has a lot going for it. A partial wall divides the two-queen or one-king bedroom from the sitting area, where a sofa, armchair, and desk provide good work and relaxation space. A nook houses a compact sink, refrigerator, microwave, and cabinets. No fewer than seven pictures, including one in the bathroom, add warmth. The lobby breakfast room has ample space and is separate from the serving counter. **Pros:** excellent value; friendly front desk staff; several restaurants nearby. **Cons:** situated just off a busy street; limited lobby seating. ☒ *1818 King Ave.* W ☎ *406/652–9313* ⇨ *79 rooms* ♿ *In-room: refrigerator, Internet. In-hotel: restaurant (breakfast only), pool, gym, laundry facilities, Internet terminal, Wi-Fi* ▭ *AE, DC, MC, V* ⦿ *CP.*

$–$$ 🛏 **Wingate by Wyndham.** If you've brought the kids along, this is the
☻   choice, hands down, for one clear reason: a 35,000-square-foot indoor water park ($10 per person per day) with two three-story slides, four mini-slides, a wave pool, and a hot tub for the older set. If that's not enough, there's a games arcade. On the other hand, those who find swimsuited, barefoot kids racing around annoying rather than cute should choose another property. Because the hotel opened in 2007, guest rooms are still spiffy, though not overly imaginative. **Pros:** free bottled water is a small, but appreciated, touch; Montana's Rib & Chop House is right next door. **Cons:** sort of out by itself, so call for directions; between handling reservations and selling water-park tickets, front desk staff are too busy for speedy service. ☒ *1801 Majestic La. 59102* ☎ *406/839–9300 or 877/995–8999* ⇨ *109 rooms* ♿ *In-room: safe, refrigerator, Wi-Fi. In-hotel: restaurant (breakfast only), pool, gym, Wi-Fi* ▭ *AE, DC, MC, V* ⦿♡ *P.*

NIGHTLIFE AND THE ARTS

NIGHTLIFE

★   The **Carlin Martini Bar and Nightclub** (☒ *Carlin Hotel, 2501 Montana Ave.* ☎ *406/245–2503*) offers live jazz on Friday evening, comedy acts one Wednesday per month, and outdoor rock music during the summer. Live country and classic rock music make the dance floor the place to be Tuesday through Saturday evenings at **Montana Chads** (☒ *3953 Montana Ave.* ☎ *406/259–0111*). The kitchen serves a real cowboy breakfast sandwich (cheese, egg, sausage, onion, and tomato on sourdough), along with equally filling fare throughout the day. A friendly bar, plus pool and poker tables, is part of the experience. Call for directions.

Tiny's Tavern (☒ *323 N. 24th St. [corner of 3rd Ave.]* ☎ *406/259–0828*) a corner bar dubbed a "local treasure" by some, has live jazz on Saturday night, Cajun chicken wings and homemade french fries plus 11 types of burgers all day every day, and multiple TVs turned to multiple sports. Sunday from 10 am to 1 pm, Tiny's sets out an all-you-can-eat chicken buffet for $6.50. The passenger trains are gone, but Billings's

19th-century depot has a new life as **McCleary's Tavern** (✉ *2314 Montana Ave.* ☎ *406/839–9041*). Solid food and beverages make this a consistent lunch spot for downtowners, but at night the bar is a favorite hangout for the younger set.

THE ARTS

Upward of 20 downtown galleries host free receptions during the bimonthly Friday evening **Billings Art Walks** (☎ *406/259–6563* ⊕ *www.artwalkbillings.com*). A free bus ferries nonwalkers around. Maps are available at participating galleries.

The **Alberta Bair Theater** (✉ *2801 3rd Ave. N* ☎ *406/256–6052 or 877/321–2074* ⊕ *www.albertabairtheater.org*) presents music, theater, dance, and other cultural events. It's the home theater for the Billings Symphony Orchestra.

Venture Theatre (✉ *2317 Montana Ave.* ☎ *406/591–9535* ⊕ *www.venture-theatre.org*) brings productions, ranging from works for young people to cutting-edge dramas, to its small stage most weekends. Though the actors are nonprofessional, you wouldn't know it.

SHOPPING

Al's Bootery (✉ *1820 1st Ave. N* ☎ *406/245–4827 or 800/745–4827* ⊕ *www.alsbootery.com*) corrals your toes into no-nonsense work boots, moccasins, and fancy cowboy boots with prices to suit the ranch hand's wallet as well as the millionaire ranch owner's. For a sweet souvenir for the folks back home (and for yourself), don't miss **Paula's Edibles** (✉ *2712 2nd Ave. N* ☎ *406/655–0865*) where you'll find dark, milk, and white chocolate in the shape of cowboy boots and hats, bears, moose, and trout, all made on the premises and individually wrapped. **Lou Taubert Ranch Outfitters** (✉ *123 N. Broadway* ☎ *406/245–2248* ⊕ *www.LouTaubert.com*) carries an impressive collection of ladies' and men's upscale Western wear and accessories, including belts, scarves, and jewelry. Decorative items for the home, all Western-themed, are displayed as well.

Rand's Custom Hats (✉ *2205 1st Ave. N* ☎ *406/248–7688 or 800/346–9815* ⊕ *www.randhats.com*) creates cowboy hats for working cowboys and movie stars, and will custom-fit a felt fur hat. Prices range from $300 to $2,000.

EN ROUTE ★

Although the route will take you slightly out of the way, take I–94 on your way to Hardin and stop at **Pompey's Pillar National Monument** (✉ *I–94, 25 mi east of Billings* ☎ *406/875–2400* ⊕ *www.pompeyspillar.org* 🎟 *$7 per vehicle or free when interpretive center is closed* ⊙ *Apr. 30–Labor Day, daily 8–8; Labor Day–Oct. 28, 9–4*), the only on-site physical evidence of the Lewis and Clark expedition. When William Clark saw this small sandstone mesa rising out of the prairie along the Yellowstone River on July 25, 1806, he climbed to the top to survey the area and then marked it with his signature and the date. His graffiti, along with other engravings by early-19th-century fur traders and homesteaders, is still visible. You can climb to the top of the mesa and view the signature year-round during daylight hours. Festive "Clark

Days" are held the last weekend in July, the anniversary of the explorer's visit to the knob. To get to Hardin, continue east on I–94 for a few miles and then head south on Highway 47.

SOUTHEAST MONTANA

Characterized by badlands, shallow canyons, grassy hills, and, above all, treeless plains, the land here survives on annual rainfall that just barely exceeds that of a desert. Aside from the livestock, this land belongs to ranchers and Native Americans—specifically the Crow and Northern Cheyenne, who both have reservations here. Few settlements in the region have more than 1,000 people, but most are friendly and almost always willing to show you around town—which sometimes consists of their home and the general store they run next door.

HARDIN

50 mi east of Billings via I–90.

Although its roots are firmly planted in cattle ranching, Hardin makes a significant portion of its living as a visitor gateway to the Little Bighorn Battlefield National Monument just a few miles to the south. It's also a popular base for exploring the several state parks and national recreation areas nearby. With 3,334 residents, Hardin is among the largest communities in southeast Montana.

GETTING HERE AND AROUND

It's difficult to get lost in the small town of Hardin. Arriving from the south on Interstate 90, exiting at Old U.S. 87 will get you to the Bighorn County Historical Museum and its visitor information center. Restaurants, hotels and campgrounds are easily accessed via Route 47 and North Central Avenue, and the downtown center is found on 3rd Street.

EXPLORING

The **Arapooish Fishing Access Site,** 2½ mi northeast of Hardin, is a favorite spot among locals, who pack the family up, set up in a shaded picnic area, cast a line into the Bighorn River, and have a cookout. It's also a prime bird-watching venue. ⊠ *½ mi north of Hardin on Hwy. 47, then 2 mi east on undesignated county road (signage will direct you to the site)* ☎ *406/247–2940* ⊕ *www.fwp.mt.gov* ✉ *Free* ☾ *Daily dawn–dusk.*

Focusing on Native American and early homestead settlement, the 35-acre **Bighorn County Historical Museum and Visitor Information Center** complex comprises 24 historic buildings that have been relocated to the site. The buildings are open May 1–October 1, and interpretive exhibits in the museum explore the region's Native American and pioneer history. Friendly staff and volunteers help bring life to the museum. ⊠ *I–90, Exit 497* ☎ *406/665–1671* ⊕ *www.museumonthebighorn.org* ✉ *Free* ☾ *May–Sept., daily 8–6; Oct.–Apr., daily 9–5.*

★   During the third week in August, a stretch of land along the Bighorn River becomes the "tepee capital of the world" when the **Crow Fair and Rodeo,** official fair of the Crow tribe, begins north of the town of Crow

Agency. The festival focuses on traditional dances, activities, and sports tournaments. ⊠ *Bighorn River north of Crow Agency, 14 mi south of Hardin on I–90* ☎ *406/638–3793* ☙ *Free.*

OFF THE
BEATEN
PATH

The Montana Dinosaur Trail. Eastern Montana 200 million years ago was a swampy, wet place populated by seashore jungles, swamps, and dinosaurs. Today the badlands and breaks of the region are the nation's paleontological hot spots. Many of the best dinosaur fossils have been taken to New York's Museum of Natural History and the Smithsonian, but you can see original inhabitants of the region at dust-country museums and state-of-the-art interpretive centers across eastern Montana. The Dinosaur Trail includes 15 stops, from Jack Horner's collection at the Museum of the Rockies in Bozeman to a field station at Fort Peck. A free brochure is available by calling the toll-free number for the Montana Office of Tourism or by visiting the Dinosaur Trail Web site. ☎ *Montana Tourism: 800/847–4868* ⊕ *www.mtdinotrail.org.*

WHERE TO EAT AND STAY

$ AMERICAN   Fodor's Choice   ★

✕ **Purple Cow.** This family eatery with a friendly staff is a favorite among travelers, largely because heading eastward it's one of the last restaurants for more than 200 mi. The shakes and malts are fantastic, as are the burgers and steaks. Portions are generous, so you might want to consider splitting some items, such as the delectable BLT. If you're starved, or have the family in tow, check out the Montana Breakfast, complete with ¾ pound of bacon, sausage, or ham, four eggs, 12 pancakes, ¾ pound of hash browns, and a pint of O.J. ⊠ *I–90, Exit 495, 1485 N. Hwy. 47* ☎ *406/665–3601* ⊟ *AE, D, MC, V.*

¢–$$

🖹 **American Inn.** The massive waterslide that towers above the outdoor pool is the most noticeable feature of this lodging off I–90. Tans, browns, and blues decorate the guest rooms, a bracing change from the sterile beiges and pastels of most chain hotels. As a bonus, you can make free telephone calls anywhere in the United States. **Pros:** easy access off I–90; great for families; half a dozen restaurants nearby. **Cons:** bathrooms are small. ⊠ *1324 N. Crawford Ave.* ☎ *406/665–1870* 🖨 *406/665–1492* ➥ *43 rooms* ♿ *In-room: refrigerator. In-hotel: pool, laundry facilities, Wi-Fi, some pets allowed* ⊟ *AE, D, MC, V* ⏇ *CP.*

CAMPING

⚠ **Grandview Campground.** Cable TV, nightly ice-cream socials, and movie rentals are some of the extras at this full-service campground. On the edge of town, in the narrow corridor between downtown Hardin and I–90, it is near the Hardin Community Activity Center, giving you access to an Olympic-size indoor pool and fitness facilities (fee). The owner is a font of knowledge and takes great pride in the community. The Grandview is open year-round, but only a few full hookup sites are available in winter. ♿ *Flush toilets, full hookups, dump station, drinking water, guest laundry, showers, picnic tables, electricity, public telephone, play area, Wi-Fi* ➥ *50 full hookups, 30 tent sites.* **Pros:** easy access off I–90; all city services; extra-long campsites for RVs. **Cons:** not exceptionally kid friendly; no pool on-site. ⊠ *1002 N. Mitchell* ☎ *406/665–2489 or 800/622–9890* ⊕ *www.grandviewcamp. com* ⊟ *MC, V.*

8

LITTLE BIGHORN BATTLEFIELD NATIONAL MONUMENT

15 mi south of Hardin via I–90.

When the smoke cleared on June 25, 1876, neither Lieutenant Colonel George Armstrong Custer (1839–76) nor the 200 soldiers, scouts, and civilians were alive to tell the story of their part of the battle against several thousand Lakota-Sioux and Northern Cheyenne warriors inspired by Sitting Bull (circa 1831–90) and Crazy Horse (1842–77). It was a Pyrrhic victory for the tribes; the loss pushed the U.S. government to redouble its efforts to remove them to the Great Sioux Reservation in Dakota Territory. Now the Little Bighorn Battlefield, on the Crow Indian Reservation, memorializes the warriors and the men of the Seventh Cavalry who took part in the conflict, with monuments and an interpretive center. The site, made up of broken river bluffs and river bottoms along the Little Bighorn River, remains largely undeveloped. Note that there are rattlesnakes around the area. During the summer visiting season, daytime temperatures hover in the 80–90°F range. Bring clothing that is comfortable in hot weather, as well as sunscreen and water, both of which will make your outdoor experience here safer and more enjoyable.

GETTING HERE AND AROUND

The national monument is 15 mi south of Hardin, off Interstate 90, Exit 510, and Highway 212. The site is 3 mi south of Crow Agency, Montana.

EXPLORING

The interpretive exhibits at the **Little Bighorn Battlefield Visitor Center** explain the events that led to and resulted from the battle, as well as the deeper issues regarding the historical conflict between white and Native American culture. Talks by park rangers contain surprises for even the most avid history buff. ⊠ *Battlefield Rd.* ☎ *406/638–3204* ⊘ *Memorial Day–July, daily 8–9; Aug.–Labor Day, daily 8–8; Sept. and Oct., daily 8–6; Nov.–Mar., daily 8–4:30; Apr.–late May, daily 8–6.*

The old stone superintendent's house is now the **White Swan Memorial Library,** which has one of the most extensive collections of research material on the Battle of the Little Bighorn. You can view the material by appointment only; contact the visitor center for more information.

Among those interred at **Custer National Cemetery,** near the visitor center, are Custer's second-in-command, Marcus Reno; some of Custer's Native American scouts; and many soldiers from more modern wars, from World Wars I and II to Korea and Vietnam. Note that you can visit the cemetery without paying the park entrance fee.

For more than 120 years the only memorial to those killed in the battle was the towering obelisk of the **7th Cavalry Monument** at the top of Last Stand Hill. Although the hill isn't particularly high, it affords a good overall view of the battlefield site.

★ Until the **Indian Memorial** was unveiled in 2003, the battlefield's only monument paid tribute to the immediate losers. Although they are meant to honor Native Americans who died on both sides (Custer had a few Crow and Arikara scouts), the three bronze riders of this memorial represent the united forces of the Lakota Sioux, Northern Cheyenne, and Arapahoe, who defeated the government troops. The stone opening off to the side forms a "spirit gate" welcoming the dead riders.

Scattered around the battlefield are short white **markers** indicating the places where soldiers died. Although the markers may look like graves, the actual bodies are interred elsewhere, including that of Custer, whose remains rest at the military academy at West Point. One marker belongs to Custer's younger brother, Thomas, one of the most decorated soldiers of the Civil War. Nineteen red markers represent Native American warriors, in part because no one knows exactly where they fell: the Native American survivors buried their dead immediately after the battle in traditional fashion.

After Custer's defeat, two of his officers held their ground against the Native American forces at **Reno-Benteen Battlefield.** The seven companies lost only 53 men during the two-day siege; more soldiers might have shared Custer's fate had not the advance of several thousand fresh troops caused the Native Americans to break camp and flee the region. ⊠ *Battlefield Rd.* ☎ *406/638–3204* ⊕ *www.nps.gov/libi* ⊠ *$10 per vehicle* ⊘ *Memorial Day–July, daily 8–9; Aug.–Labor Day, daily 8–8; Sept. and Oct., daily 8–6; Nov.–Mar., daily 8–4:30; Apr.–late May, daily 8–6.*

WHERE TO EAT

$ ✕ **Custer Battlefield Trading Post and Cafe.** With its stock of T-shirts, inexpensive jewelry, Indian fry bread mix, and dream catchers, the trading post is touristy, but the small attached restaurant is quite good—as evidenced by the locals who regularly congregate here. Steak is the dish of choice, and there are no fewer than three ways to get it on a sandwich. The several variations of Indian taco made by the Crow cooks are especially popular. ⊠ *I–90 at U.S. 212, Exit 510* ☎ *406/638–2270* ⊕ *www.laststand.com* ▤ *D, MC, V.*

SOUTHWESTERN

8

BIGHORN CANYON NATIONAL RECREATION AREA

40 mi southwest of Little Bighorn Battlefield National Monument via I–90 and Hwy. 313.

Centered on a 60-mi-long lake, this park stretches between the Pryor and Bighorn mountains, well into Wyoming. Really just a wide spot on the Bighorn River, the lake fills much of Bighorn Canyon, whose steep walls, carved by geological upheaval and the force of wind and water, are too rugged for casual access. ☎ *307/548–2251 or 406/666–2412* ⊕ *www.nps.gov/bica/* ⊠ *$5 per vehicle* ⊘ *Daily 24 hrs.*

GETTING HERE AND AROUND

Most people visit the park by boat, which is the only way within the park to get directly from the northern unit, in Montana, to the southern unit, much of which is in Wyoming. Most of the major sights are accessible by boat, but you can also reach them by driving north from Wyoming on Highway 37. If you're visiting from Wyoming, Lovell makes a good base for exploring the area. Check locally about useable boat ramps; fluctuating lake levels can leave the upper 15 mi mostly dry.

EXPLORING

The **Yellowtail Dam Visitor Center** in the northern unit features exhibits focusing on the life of Crow Chief Robert Yellowtail, the Crow people, the history of the Bighorn River, the dam's construction, and the wildlife in the area, including the wild mustangs that roam the high grasslands of the Pryor Mountains above the canyon. ⊠ *Hwy. 313, Fort Smith* ☎ *406/666–2412 or 406/666–3218* ⊕ *www.nps.gov/bica/* ⊠ *Included in $5 admission to recreation area* ⊙ *Memorial Day–Labor Day, daily 9–5.*

The old **Hillsboro Dude Ranch** complex is probably the best known and easiest to reach of the four ranch ruins within the recreation area. There are old log cabins, cellars, chicken coops, and other buildings that belonged to Grosvener W. Barry, one of the area's more colorful characters in the early 20th century. He attempted three gold-mining ventures, all of which failed, before opening a dude ranch here. ⊠ *Hwy. 37* ⊕ *www.nps.gov/bica* ⊠ *Included in $5 admission to recreation area.*

Fodor'sChoice ★ When Spanish explorers introduced horses to the Americas, some of the animals inevitably escaped and roamed wild across the land. You can see some of the last members of these breeds in the **Pryor Mountain Wild Horse Range**, the first such nationally designated refuge. Some 200 horses, generally broken into small family groupings, roam these arid slopes with bighorn sheep, elk, deer, and mountain lions. Coat variations such as grulla, blue roan, dun, and sabino indicate Spanish lineage, as do markings such as dorsal stripes, zebra stripes on the legs, and a stripe on the withers. The best way to view the herds is simply to drive along Highway 37 and look out your window. ⊠ *Hwy. 37* ☎ *406/896–5013* ⊕ *www.kbrhorse.net/wclo/blmdak01.html* ⊠ *Included in $5 admission to recreation area.*

★ **Devil's Canyon Overlook**, a few miles north of the Wyoming border, affords breathtaking views of the point where narrow Devil's Canyon joins sheer-walled Bighorn Canyon. The overlook itself is on a cliff 1,000 feet above the lake. Look for fossils in the colorful rock layers of the canyon walls. ⊠ *Hwy. 37* ⊕ *www.nps.gov/bica/* ⊠ *Included in $5 admission to recreation area.*

The **Crooked Creek Ranger Station**, past the south entrance of the park in Wyoming, houses exhibits about the four historic ranches within the recreation area. A small shop sells books related to the local history and geology. ⊠ *Hwy. 37, WY* ☎ *307/548–7326* ⊕ *www.nps.gov/ bica/* ⊠ *Included in $5 admission to recreation area* ⊙ *Daily; hrs vary by season.*

The main visitor center for the park, the **Bighorn Canyon Visitor Center** has geological and historical exhibits on the area, as well as a film about the canyon. Two shorter movies, one on the Pryor Mountain wild horses and the other about Medicine Wheel National Historic Landmark (east of Lovell), are shown on request. A small store sells books and other regional items. ⊠ *U.S. 310 at U.S. 14A, Lovell, WY* ☎ *307/548–5406* ⊕ *www.nps.gov/bica/* ⊠ *Free* ⊙ *Memorial Day–Labor Day, daily 8–6; Labor Day–Memorial Day, daily 8–5.*

Chief Plenty Coups State Park. Although many Plains Indian tribes opposed the intrusion of whites into their lands, the Crow did not. Hoping that U.S. troops would keep the rival Cheyenne and Lakota off their lands, the Crow allied themselves with the U.S. government. Ultimately, the army protected Crow territory from the other tribes—but only so it could be settled by whites. Despite the betrayal, the last traditional chief of the Crow, Plenty Coups, strongly encouraged his people to adopt modern ways and cooperate with the U.S. government. At his request, his home and general store in the town of Pryor were preserved as a state park after his death. Note the blending of modern and traditional ways, such as the room of honor in the rear of his log home, meant to parallel the place of honor along the back wall of a tepee. Parks Passports are not valid here. ⊠ *1 mi west of Pryor on county road, Pryor* ☎ *406/252–1289* ⊕ *www.mt.gov/parks/* ⊠ *Free to Montana residents, $5 per vehicle for others* ☉ *May–Sept., daily 8–8.*

SPORTS AND THE OUTDOORS
The Lewis and Clark expedition, and later, fur traders avoided the Bighorn River at all costs, for the narrow channel, high canyon walls, and sharp rocks were treacherous. With the construction of the Yellowtail Dam in the 1960s, however, the water levels in the canyon rose above most rocky obstacles and created new access points along the shore of the now-tamed river. The fishing here—for smallmouth bass, rainbow and brown trout, walleye, yellow perch, and more—is excellent above the dam. Below the dam, the cold, clear water exiting the hydropower facility has created a world-class trout fishery. Many visitors never wet a line, opting instead to simply rest on the water and enjoy the calm winds and pleasant views.

Fluctuating reservoir levels, caused by extended drought and light mountain snowpack, can periodically shut down the lake's marinas and boat launches. Because canyon walls create sharp turns and bottlenecks in the lake, there are some boating speed limits. All the marinas on Bighorn Lake operate during the peak summer season and are closed in the fall, winter, and early spring. Boats can be docked or rented in the northern unit of the park at **Ok-A-Beh Marina** (⊠ *Off Hwy. 313, on north end of lake* ☎ *406/666–2349*). The facilities here aren't luxurious, but you'll find a basic eatery, a few groceries, tackle, a swimming area, and reasonable rates. One of the most popular boat launches in the southern unit is **Barry's Landing** (⊠ *Hwy. 37* ☎ *406/666–2412*). There isn't much here—not even electricity—but the scenic campground, shaded picnic area, and central location are big draws. Many boats in the southern unit are based at **Horseshoe Bend Marina** (⊠ *Hwy. 37, WY*), which has boat rentals, a beach, a small general store, a modest restaurant, and the largest campground in the park. A nearby buildup of silt from the Shoshone and Bighorn rivers has made boat launching here a tricky business.

CAMPING
Black Canyon Campground. This campground, about 5 mi south of the Ok-A-Beh Marina up the tight Black Canyon Creek, is accessible only by boat, and only during high water. It's very primitive, but the

isolation is unmatched. ⚐ *Pit toilets, bear boxes, fire pits, picnic tables, swimming (lake)* ⭾ *17 sites* ⊠ *Black Canyon Creek* ☎ *406/666–3218* ⊕ *www.nps.gov/bica/* ⚐ *Reservations not accepted.*

🛆 **Horseshoe Bend Campground.** The proximity to the marina in the southern unit makes this, the largest campground in the park, especially popular, although never very busy. It's open all year, but most services are unavailable in winter. ⚐ *Flush toilets, dump station, drinking water, fire pits, picnic tables, food service, electricity, public telephone, general store, swimming (lake)* ⭾ *54 sites* ⊠ *Hwy. 37, WY* ☎ *307/548–7230* ⊕ *www.nps.gov/bica/* ⚐ *Reservations not accepted.*

🛆 **Medicine Creek Campground.** Just north of Barry's Landing, the isolated site offers a good central location without the summer bustle of some other camping spots. You can boat or hike in. ⚐ *Pit toilets, picnic tables, swimming (lake)* ⭾ *6 sites* ⊠ *Medicine Creek* ☎ *307/548–2251* ⊕ *www.nps.gov/bica/* ⚐ *Reservations not accepted.*

MILES CITY

160 mi northeast of Bighorn Canyon National Recreation Area via Hwy. 313 and I–94.

History buffs enjoy the ranch town of Miles City (population 8,120), at the confluence of the cottonwood-lined Tongue and Yellowstone rivers. The federal Fort Laramie Treaty of 1868 stated that this land would be "Indian country as long as the grass is green and the sky is blue." The government reneged on its promise only six years later, when gold was found in the Black Hills of South Dakota to the southeast. White settlers streamed into the area, setting in motion events that led to the Battle of the Little Bighorn. After the battle the army built a new post less than 2 mi from where Miles City would be founded. In time the ranchers took over, and in 1884 the last of the great herds of bison was slaughtered near here to make room for cattle. Ranching has been a way of life ever since.

GETTING HERE AND AROUND

Hugging the north side of Interstate 94, Miles City is easily traversed via the I–94 Business Loop, which takes motorists through the heart of the town. Alternatively, travelers may take Route 59 from I–94 past Miles Community College, then left on Main Street to the downtown area. To reach Pirogue Island State Park, follow Valley Drive East northeast from downtown.

EXPLORING

★ The third weekend in May, Miles City holds its famed **Bucking Horse Sale,** a three-day event with a rodeo, a concert, and a giant block party. Rodeo-stock contractors come from all over the country to buy the spirited horses sold here. Faded Wranglers and cowboy boots are proudly displayed downtown, along with open containers and a sort of rowdy civic pride. ⊠ *Fairgrounds Rd. at Main St.* ☎ *406/234–2890* ⊕ *www. buckinghorsesale.com* ⭍ Ticket prices vary for concerts.

★ Although the holding tanks of an old water-treatment plant don't seem like the best location for fine art, the **Custer County Art & Heritage Center,** in the town's 1910 wastewater facility overlooking the Yellowstone

River, is actually very attractive. The permanent exhibit reflects the town's Western heritage; the traveling shows are a bit more varied. The museum store features a variety of original artworks, reproductions, ceramics, and a good selection of Western history books. ⊠ *85 Water Plant Rd.* 🖾 *406/234–0635* ⊕ *www.ccac.milescity.org* 🖾 *Free* ☉ *Oct.– Apr., daily 1–5; May–Sept., daily 9–5.*

★ Wind and water carved holes in the sandstone pillars north of Ekalaka, creating an eerie and barren landscape. Embracing the terrain's mystery, Native Americans used the site for rituals to conjure spirits centuries ago. Teddy Roosevelt was struck by the area's unique beauty when he visited in the late 19th century. In 1957 the area was designated **Medicine Rocks State Park.** The 320-acre park is largely undeveloped; aside from a few picnic tables, a short hiking trail, and a handful of unmarked campsites, the land is exactly how it was when Native Americans first performed their ceremonies here. ⊠ *Hwy. 7 north of Miles City between Baker and Ekalaka* 🖾 *406/234–0900* ⊕ *www.fwp.mt.gov/parks/* 🖾 *Free* ☉ *Daily 24 hrs.*

The **Range Riders Museum,** built on the site of the 1877 Fort Keogh cantonment, is jammed to the rafters with saddles, chaps, spurs, guns, and other frontier artifacts. Some of the 12 museum buildings of this complex were once part of the fort, which was abandoned in 1924 after being used as a remount station during World War I. The volunteers and staff love to talk about local history and are great sources for information about modern amenities, too. ⊠ *435 L.P. Anderson Rd., across Tongue River Bridge on west end of Main St., Exit 135 off I-94* 🖾 *406/232–6146* 🖾 *$5* ☉ *Apr.–Oct., daily 8–5:30.*

Pirogue Island State Park, a 269-acre chunk of land in the middle of the Yellowstone River, is completely undeveloped; the only way to access the park is by floating down the river or fording in times of low water. The cottonwood trees are an excellent habitat for waterfowl, raptors, and deer, and the geology of the island makes it prime agate-hunting ground. ⊠ *1 mi north of Miles City on Hwy. 59, 2 mi east on Kinsey Rd., then 2 mi south on county road* 🖾 *406/234–0900* ⊕ *www.fwp. mt.gov/lands/site_283962.aspx* 🖾 *Free*

WHERE TO EAT AND STAY

$ ✕ **Mama Stella's Pizza.** You can always opt for traditional pies, but you
PIZZA may want to try one of Mama Stella's imaginative creations, such as pizza topped with white Alfredo sauce. Unusual toppings include sauerkraut and asparagus, and there are several sandwiches with Italian and domestic flairs. Mama also offers breakfast starting at 8 AM, delivers, and stays open until 10 PM on weeknights and until midnight on weekends—no small accomplishment in a town with fewer than 9,000 residents. ⊠ *Trail's Inn Bar and Comedy Club, 607 Main St.* 🖾 *406/234–2922* ▭ *AE, D, MC, V.*

$–$$ 🖾 **Best Western War Bonnet Inn.** The two-room family suites and complimentary hot breakfast make this chain hotel stand out. It's on the edge of town near I-94. **Pros:** easy access off Interstate 90, and fairly easy walk or short drive to the vehicle-friendly cafés and gas stations off the highway; serviceable rooms and decent breakfast. **Cons:** restaurant

8

across the street is dated and even a little dingy; stay here for a quick overnight, not for the amenities; truck traffic can be distracting. ⊠ *1015 S. Haynes Ave.* ☎ *406/234–4560* ⊕ *www.bestwestern.com* ⤴ *54 rooms, 4 suites* ⚓ *In-hotel: pool, gym, Wi-Fi* ⊟ *AE, D, DC, MC, V* ⍾ *CP.*

CAMPING   ⚠ **Medicine Rocks Campground.** Although these campsites are primitive—they aren't even marked—the weathered rocks here make an incredible backdrop for a night sleeping under the stars. ⚓ *Pit toilets, drinking water, picnic tables* ⤴ *12 tent sites, 12 RV sites* ⊠ *Off Hwy. 7 north of Miles City between Baker and Ekalaka* ☎ *406/234–0900* ⊕ *www.fwp. mt.gov/parks/* ⚓ *Reservations not accepted.*

NIGHTLIFE

The downtown **Trail's Inn Bar and Comedy Club** (⊠ *607 Main St.* ☎ *406/234–2922*) draws regional and national comedy acts. Satisfy your munchies at the on-site Mama Stella's Pizza restaurant.

SHOPPING

★   The craftspeople at **Miles City Saddlery** (⊠ *808 Main St.* ☎ *406/232–2512* ⊕ *www.milescitysaddlery.com*), in business since 1909, custom-design saddles of legendary quality. They also craft saddlebags, holsters, and other leather goods. Even if you're not buying, this is worth a stop.

OFF THE BEATEN PATH   **Custer National Forest, Sioux Ranger District.** The name of these expansive federal lands is misleading: it should really be "Custer National Forests." Composed of dozens of discrete tracts dotting the land from Red Lodge (60 mi southwest of Billings, near Yellowstone National Park) all the way into South Dakota, Custer National Forest is one of the most ecologically diverse federally managed lands. The units in southeast Montana are called the Ekalaka Hills, and like their nearby neighbors in South Dakota, these pine-covered bluffs and mesas are often referred to as "an island of green in a sea of prairie," for good reason. Visible from miles away, the tiny forested ridges appear like mountains in the middle of the grassy plains. Drive any of the four-wheeler roads off Highway 212 between Ashland and Broadus and climb to a timbered ridge. Get out and hike to a vista, where you can breathe in the prairie from what appears to be a great height but is only a couple of hundred feet above the prevailing landscape. Deer, turkey, and even elk fill the woods, and many species of raptors are known to nest here. The area is completely undeveloped and offers no services. ⊠ *11 mi southeast of Ekalaka on Hwy. 323, 6 mi east of Ashland on U.S. Hwy. 212* ☎ *605/797–4432* ⊕ *www.fs.fed.us/r1/custer/.*

THE BIG OPEN

Revel in wild grasslands, stark badlands, unhindered skylines, and spectacular sunsets, far from the rumble of jetliners, the roar of traffic, and the ringing of cell phones. A great triangle bounded by the Yellowstone River to the south, the Missouri River to the north, and U.S. 87 to the west, the region comprises nearly 10% of the state of Montana. Its residents, however, represent less than 1% of the state's total population, and the number is shrinking. This is a region with barely 1,000 people between the two largest towns (Jordan, with 364 residents, and Circle, with 644), where the livestock outnumbers the people 100 to 1. One winter the tumbleweeds clogged a highway so badly that the state had to send out snowplows to clear the way.

MAKOSHIKA STATE PARK

84 mi northeast of Miles City via I–94 and N. Merrill Ave.

GETTING HERE AND AROUND

Interstate 94, which vectors across eastern Montana, provides quick access to Miles City, Billings, and Bismarck, North Dakota, and even farther east, Minneapolis. Glendive is one of several communities in the area with regularly scheduled air service, from Great Lakes Airlines, with connections to Billings and Denver. It's hard to get around here without a car.

★ Named after the Lakota word for "bad land," Makoshika State Park encompasses more than 11,000 acres of Montana's badlands, distinct rock formations also found in Wyoming and the Dakotas. The bare rock walls and mesas of the park create an eerie moonscape that is only occasionally broken by a crooked pine or juniper tree warped by the hard rock and lack of water. Practically a desert, the badlands are excellent fossil grounds, and the remains of tyrannosaurs and triceratops have been found here.

At the entrance to the park, the largest in Fish, Wildlife & Parks' state-parks system, is the small **Visitor Information Center,** with information on the park's history and geology. A few fossils are on display, including a triceratops skull. ☎ *406/377–6256* ⊕ *www.fwp.mt.gov/lands/site_283890.aspx* ☼ *Daily 9–5.*

Interpretive signs explain the geology of the rock layers visible on the ½-mi loop of the **Cap Rock Nature Trail,** which begins on Cains Coulee Road, a few miles from the park entrance. The trail affords excellent views of a natural rock bridge. Beginning at the campground, the 1.5-mi **Diane Gabriel Trail** loops through both badlands and prairie terrain. At the halfway point a duck-billed-dinosaur fossil is embedded in a cliff. The .5-mi **Kinney Coulee Trail** starts about 4 mi south of the park entrance and leads 300 feet down a canyon. The terrain here is a bit more forested than elsewhere in the park, but the rock formations are the real stars. ✉ *Makoshika State Park Rd.* ☎ *406/377–6256* ⊕ *www.fwp.mt.gov/parks/* 🔖 *$5 per vehicle for nonresidents, free for Montana residents* ☼ *Daily 24 hrs.*

WHERE TO STAY

$–$$ 🛏 **Charley Montana Bed & Breakfast.** Built by ranching mogul Charles Krug in 1907, this solid brick home looks like a fortress compared with its stick-built Victorian contemporaries. Indeed, with more than 25 rooms and 8,000 square feet, the place sometimes seems more like a castle than a B&B. The interior is decidedly soft, however, and much of the Krug family's period furniture is still in use. **Pros:** owners are friendly and helpful; this is a comfortable, plush base from which to explore the Yellowstone River and nearby badlands. **Cons:** building and some fixtures feel old; downtown location is handy, but there are few remarkable places to eat or drink. ⊠ *103 N. Douglas, Glendive* ☎ *888/395–3207* ⊕ *charley-montana.com* ☞ *5 rooms* ⚭ *In-room: refrigerator (some)* ☰ *AE, D, MC, V* ⊚ *BP.*

CAMPING ⚠ **Makoshika State Park Campground.** This small campground doesn't offer much in the way of amenities, but the views of the surrounding sheer cliffs and stone bluffs are incredible. There's a Frisbee-golf course nearby. Some facilities are at the nearby visitor center. ⚭ *Flush toilets, drinking water, fire pits, picnic tables, electricity, public telephone, ranger station* ☞ *22 sites* ⊠ *Makoshika State Park Rd.* ☎ *406/377–6256* ⊕ *www.fwp.mt.gov/parks/* ☰ *No credit cards.*

EN ROUTE The drive from Makoshika State Park to Fort Peck will take you along the Hi-Line, otherwise known as U.S. 2. Drive Highway 200 to Circle, then north on Highway 13, one of Montana's designated Scenic Backcountry Byways, or drive north through the wide, fertile Yellowstone River valley on Highway 16 to Sidney, then Culbertson, where you'll catch U.S. Highway 2. Either way, you'll travel through the **Fort Peck Indian Reservation** (⊠ *U.S. 2* ☎ *406/768–5155*). Like most of eastern Montana, much of the land here is beautifully austere; at nearly 2 million acres, the reservation is home to only 6,800 tribal members. However, the reservation does have a bustling industrial center, a community college, and an interesting tribal cultural center and museum in Poplar.

FORT PECK

147 mi northwest of Makoshika State Park via Hwy. 200 S, Hwy. 13, U.S. 2, and Hwy. 117.

Fort Peck itself is mostly a quiet retirement town today, with 240 residents; at night the lights of ranch houses here are few and far between. It owes its existence to massive Fort Peck Dam, built on the Missouri River during the Great Depression. One of President Franklin Roosevelt's earliest and largest New Deal projects, the Fort Peck Dam provided a source of water and jobs. Now the 6-mi-long dam holds back sprawling Fort Peck Reservoir and wows visitors with the sheer scale of the earthen works. Fort Peck is a great base from which to fish for walleye, northern pike, and smallmouth bass on the reservoir, or camp and hike the remote Missouri River Breaks on either side of the lake.

GETTING HERE AND AROUND

Get to Fort Peck town site from Nashua—turn south off U.S. 2 onto Route 117 and drive 10 mi south. From Glasgow, drive 17 mi on Highway 24. And from Circle, drive Highway 24 north for about 65 mi. For its size, Fort Peck Reservoir has the fewest public access points of any big reservoir and recreation area in America. That means you have to carefully plan your route if you want to get anywhere near the water up-lake from the dam, and you have to watch the weather when you go, for the region's infamous gumbo can bog you down. Managed access points on the northern shore include Duck Creek Bay, just west of the marina; The Pines, a remote cluster of private cabins about 20 mi up-lake from the dam; Bone Trail, a remote fishing access site and campground about halfway up the lake; and Fourchette Bay, another boat ramp and campground south of Malta. On the south shore of the lake the best access is at Hell Creek State Park north of Jordan, reachable by a well-maintained gravel road. Fort Peck Reservoir's Big Dry Arm, which juts due south from the dam, hosts Rock Creek Marina.

EXPLORING

★ The 18,000-square-foot **Fort Peck Interpretive Center** features interpretive displays recounting the history and significance of the dam's construction, wildlife of the lower river and Missouri River Breaks, and one of the most striking life-size dinosaur displays in the West. It's a reproduction of Peck's Rex, a tyrannosaurus rex unearthed near Fort Peck, and other local dinosaur discoveries are also detailed here. The center also features the largest aquariums in Montana, filled with the native and introduced fish species of Fort Peck Reservoir and the Missouri River. Guided tours of the dam and its power plants are available April through October. ⊠ *Lower Yellowstone Rd.* ☎ *406/526–3493* ⊕ *www. corpslakes.us/fortpeck* ⌨ *Free* ☉ *Oct. 1–Apr. 30, weekdays 10–4; May 1–Sept. 30, daily 9–5.*

At the peak of dam construction, nearly 11,000 workers lived in Fort Peck; together with their families, they made up a thriving population center of 50,000. To help keep the populace entertained, the Army Corps of Engineers built a movie house in 1934. It was supposed to be a temporary structure, but instead it eventually became the **Fort Peck Summer Theatre.** The chalet-style building is a venue for live entertainment weekend nights in summer. ⊠ *110 5th St.* ☎ *406/228–9219* ⊕ *www. fortpecktheatre.org/* ⌨ *$15* ☉ *June–Aug., Fri.–Sun. 7–midnight.*

SPORTS AND THE OUTDOORS

Stretching 134 mi across the border between the Big Open and the Hi-Line (U.S. 2), Fort Peck Reservoir is a prime outdoor-adventure destination. Fishing is especially popular here, with walleye being the lake's most well-known and hotly pursued fish. Other species include northern pike, lake trout, smallmouth bass, and Chinook salmon. Outfitters are hard to come by, so be sure to get most of your supplies before you arrive. The lake is the venue for the annual **Governor's Cup Walleye Tournament** (☎ *406/228–2222* ⊕ *www.mtgovcup.com/*) held the second weekend in July.

The **Fort Peck Dredge Cuts** (⊠ *Hwy. 117* ☎ *406/228–3700*), also known as the Fort Peck Trout Pond, is a state fishing access site just below Fort Peck Dam off the Missouri River. It has a boat launch and family-friendly swimming beaches. The **Rock Creek Marina** (⊠ *652 S. Rock Creek Rd.* ☎ *406/485–2560*) has marina facilities, a boat launch, and a modern campground on the remote Big Dry Arm of the lake. **Fort Peck Marina** on the west side of Fort Peck Dam is probably the most accessible concession on the big lake. The store has basic and walleye-specific fishing tackle, basic groceries, bait, boat gas, and a boat-repair facility. The associated bar has beverages to go or for on-site consumption, and a simple restaurant. (⊠ *West End Dr.* ☎ *406/526–3442*)

8

WHERE TO STAY

¢–$ ⊡ **Fort Peck Hotel.** Just about every piece of furniture in this lodgelike wooden building dates from the hotel's construction during the Great Depression. Inside, the thick beams, sturdy rafters, and Western style transport you back to the 1930s. Accommodations are small and modest, and most bathrooms have showers, but some have massive clawfoot bathtubs. During the summer season the adjoining rustic dining room serves three square meals a day for an additional charge. The hotel, listed on the National Historic Registry, is popular with hunters in the fall and with arts patrons in the summer. Packages that include lodging, meals, and theater tickets are available. **Pros:** authentic 1930s feel; the restaurant is spacious, and the front porch is a wonderful place to wind down. **Cons:** creaking floors, dripping faucets, and creaking beds make this seem more like a summer camp than a hotel; in the summertime the mosquitoes can drive you inside; off-season hours are erratic. ⊠ *175 S. Missouri St.* ☎ *406/526–3266 or 800/560–4931* 📠 *406/526–3472* ⬎ *38 rooms* & *In-room: no phone, no TV. In-hotel: Wi-Fi* ⊟ *D, MC, V.*

CAMPING   ⚠ **Downstream Campground.** Known locally as Kiwanis Park, this large wooded campground sits just below Fort Peck Dam on the shores of the Missouri River. If Kiwanis is full—and it's popular with Hi-Liners on holiday weekends—then drive past Fort Peck Marina to West End Campground. & *Flush toilets, pit toilets, partial hookups (electric), dump station, drinking water, showers, picnic tables, electricity, public telephone, play area, swimming (lake)* ⬎ *71 partial hookups, 3 tent sites* ⊠ *Hwy. 24 N* ☎ *406/526–3224* 📠 *406/526–3593* ⊟ *AE, D, MC, V.*

CHARLES M. RUSSELL NATIONAL WILDLIFE REFUGE

1 mi south of Fort Peck via Missouri Ave.

Bordering the shores of Fort Peck Lake—and extending west more than 100 mi to U.S. 191—is the massive Charles M. Russell National Wildlife Refuge, a 1.1-million-acre preserve teeming with more than 200 species of birds, including bald eagles and game birds; 45 different mammals, including elk, bighorn sheep, antelope, prairie dogs, and deer; and a variety of fish and reptiles. But this is also a refuge for history: each year scientists from around the country march into the preserve, and each year they find something new, whether it's dinosaur bones, buffalo jumps, tepee rings, or an old homesteader's shack. The refuge, one of the largest under the U.S. Fish & Wildlife Service's management, is open for hiking, horseback riding, fishing, boating, and other activities. Several access roads run through the area; most of these are unpaved, aside from U.S. 191, which runs north–south through the western edge of the refuge. ☎ *406/538–8706* ⊕ *cmr.fws. gov* ⊠ *Free* ☉ *Daily 24 hrs.*

GETTING HERE AND AROUND

Visitors shouldn't treat this landscape casually. It's remote, desolate, and given to wild swings in weather. This is four-wheel-drive country, and if you travel off paved roads, pack enough food to stay for at least three days longer than you planned. That's because once the dirt and gravel roads get wet with rain or snow, they become as greasy as Crisco and often become impassable. Bring extra fuel, because gas stations are as distant as Malta and Glasgow to the north and Grassrange to the south. But the remote nature of the Breaks makes these endless prairies, deep canyons, and remote timbered ridges wonderful places for hiking and backcountry exploration. Bring good boots, sunscreen, and insect repellent. You are unlikely to see other people besides local ranchers out checking fences and cattle.

EXPLORING

There are three staffed **field stations** (✉ *U.S. 91, Hwy. 200, and Hwy. 24* ☎ *406/538–8706* ⊕ *cmr.fws.gov*) in the refuge: the **Sand Creek Wildlife Station**, the **Jordan Wildlife Station**, and the **Fort Peck Wildlife Station**. Although they have no public facilities, they are conveniently scattered around the park, and are sources for maps, road conditions, and points of interest. If they're in, the rangers will help you with directions or problems.

★ Hundreds of elk congregate in evening in the fall at the **Slippery Ann Wildlife Viewing Area** (✉ *U.S. 191*). During the autumn mating season the bulls violently lock horns while herds of cows come to watch and be courted. Be sure to bring binoculars and zoom lenses for your camera, because you must keep your distance from these massive animals.

A refuge within a refuge, the **UL Bend National Wildlife Refuge** consists of more than 20,000 acres of wilderness entirely within the boundaries of the Charles M. Russell National Wildlife Refuge. Its primary mission at the moment is to rescue one of the nation's most endangered animals: the black-footed ferret. The ferrets depend on the high concentration of prairie dog towns for food. There are also plenty of grouse and burrowing owls, who use abandoned prairie-dog tunnels for homes. ✉ *UL Bend National Wildlife Refuge Rd.* ☎ *406/538–8706* ⊕ *cmr.fws.gov* ✉ *Free* ☉ *Daily 24 hrs.*

THE HI-LINE

The Hi-Line is named for U.S. 2, which connects Houlton, Maine, with Everett, Washington. The most northerly road traveling east–west across the United States, the highway plows a path almost straight through northern Montana until it reaches the Rockies. Remote prairies, northern wetlands, and scattered forests make this area a haven both for wildlife and for the few people who live here. There may not be a Starbucks on every corner, or even a movie theater within 100 mi, but Hi-Line residents wouldn't have it any other way. The Hi-Line is a favorite for travelers who want to get away from the sterile interstate culture of the West, and in the summer you'll see droves of cross-country bicyclers laden with camping gear making a season-long trek, usually headed east to get a push from the prevailing wind.

MEDICINE LAKE NATIONAL WILDLIFE REFUGE COMPLEX

230 mi northeast of Charles M. Russell National Wildlife Refuge via Larb Creek Rd. and U.S. 2.

GETTING HERE AND AROUND

State Highway 16, which heads north to one of the few 24-hour ports on the Canadian border, cuts right through the refuge. Medicine Lake's main roads are well maintained, but the secondary roads are rutted and slippery in wet weather.

EXPLORING

Established in 1935, this refuge sandwiched between U.S. 2 and the Canadian border encompasses more than 30,000 acres of wetlands that provide habitat for dozens of mammal species, including beavers, muskrats, and bobcats, and a variety of shorebirds and upland birds. Medicine Lake hosts one of the largest concentrations of American pelicans in the nation. There are few facilities available, but that's the point.

The refuge has a relatively high visitation from hard-core birders who view migrating waterbirds in the spring and hunters who pursue upland game birds and waterfowl in the fall. Other than those seasons, you'll have the refuge to yourself. Bring good boots and long pants and hike into remote ponds and prairie potholes that hold an unbelievable amount of wildlife.

Winding through the central unit of the refuge is the **Auto Tour Route,** an excellent way to get a peek at the animals that call this pristine park home. Most of the route is open only during daylight hours.

The **Observation Tower,** adjacent to the refuge headquarters, provides a good overview of the lakes in the refuge and the surrounding terrain. From above the trees and tall reeds you can see the distinct lakes and ponds, as well as the sand hills around the borders. Birders often congregate in the **Grouse Observation Blind,** 2¼ mi east of the refuge headquarters, to take a good look at the resident bird species. The covered area is also good for watching other wildlife. ⊠ *223 North Shore Rd.* ☎ *406/789–2305* ⊕ *www.fws.gov/medicinelake* 🎫 *Free* 🕙 *Daily dawn–dusk.*

BOWDOIN NATIONAL WILDLIFE REFUGE

200 mi west of Medicine Lake National Wildlife Refuge via U.S. 2.

GETTING HERE AND AROUND

Bowdoin is just off U.S. 2 between Glasgow and Malta. The best all-weather road to the refuge turns off the highway just 3 mi east of Malta. Turn onto Old Highway 2 at the brown-and-white refuge sign and drive the well-maintained gravel road to the two stone pillars marking the entrance to the refuge and its headquarters complex. Two-wheel-drive sedans can navigate most roads, but a higher-clearance four-wheel-drive is a better option.

EXPLORING

An oxbow of the Missouri River before the last ice age, Bowdoin National Wildlife Refuge is a massive series of lakes and wetlands a few miles east of Malta. Before the government started to administer the refuge, water levels would drastically vary by season, making it a poor breeding ground for birds—but an excellent breeding ground for disease. Since the construction of several dikes and water channels in the 1930s, however, the water levels of the lakes have remained fairly constant, and the 15,000-acre preserve now shelters numerous birds and mammals. Aside from typical prairie animals and field songbirds, there are sizeable populations of pelicans, gulls, and herons. Several protected species also live here, including the piping plover, black-footed ferret, bald eagle, and peregrine falcon.

As the main road through the refuge, the **Bowdoin Refuge Auto Tour Route** affords excellent views of the terrain and wildlife. Old U.S. 2 is another main route, but it doesn't compare to the slower and far more scenic experience of the Auto Tour.

The **Bowdoin Wildlife Refuge Headquarters,** at the main entrance to Bowdoin, provides information on refuge conditions, species lists, a variety of mounted birds and mammals, and instructions for a drivable tour route. ⊠ *Bowdoin Refuge Auto Tour Rte.* ☎ *406/654–2863* ⊕ *bowdoin.fws.gov* ✉ *Free* ☾ *Weekdays 8–5.*

Birders and wildlife photographers come to the **Pearce Waterfowl Production Area Bird Blind,** on the northeast edge of the refuge, for great views. ☎ *406/654–2863* ⊕ *bowdoin.fws.gov* ✉ *Free* ☾ *Daily during daylight hrs.*

OFF THE BEATEN PATH

Phillips County Historical Museum. This museum, and the Dinosaur Field Station next door, is an official repository for fossils found in the Judith River basin. The highlight of the dinosaur display is a reconstructed albertosaur skeleton, which towers above the rest of the collection. There are also exhibits on outlaws who spent time here: Butch Cassidy, the Sundance Kid, Kid Curry, the Tall Texan, and other members of the Wild Bunch gang. Ask about tours of the Robinson House and gardens next door. The house, ordered from a Sears & Roebuck catalog and erected in 1900, is an example of frontier simplicity. ⊠ *431 U.S. 2, Malta* ☎ *406/654–1037* ⊕ *www.phillipscountymuseum.org* ✉ *$4* ☾ *Mon.–Sat. 10–5, Sun. 12:30–5.*

Great Plains Dinosaur Museum and Field Station. Surprisingly sophisticated given the location, this great little museum is right next door to the Phillips County Historical Museum. The station houses some of Montana's finest fossils and includes a fossil preparation laboratory that visitors can view. Specimens on display include Roberta, a well-preserved Brachylophosaur, and Leonardo, which has been celebrated as the best-preserved dinosaur fossil ever discovered. Both specimens were unearthed near Malta. Other gems include rotating exhibits of fossil collections and a great kids' education program. The station includes a gift shop. Amateur dino hounds can sign up here for a guided dig. ⊠ *U.S. Highway 2 East, Malta* ☎ *406/654–5300* ⊕ *www.greatplainsdinosaurs.org* ✉ *$5* ☾ *Mon.–Sat. 10–5, Sun. 12:30–5.*

8

WHERE TO STAY

¢–$ ⚐ **Maltana Hotel.** Easy to find, this downtown hotel is within walking distance of Malta's Amtrak station and a few blocks from the junction of U.S. 2 and 191. The rooms are modest but modern, with Wi-Fi and coffeemakers—unusual finds in a small, isolated town. **Pros:** well-tended small hotel with great service and comfortable rooms. **Cons:** hot in the summer and a little breezy in the winter; beds are lumpy. ✉ *138 1st Ave. E, Malta* ☎ *406/654–2610* 🖷 *406/654–2905* 🛏 *19 rooms* ⚐ *In-room: refrigerator* ⊟ *AE, D, MC, V.*

$ ⚐ **Edgewater Inn and RV Park.** One of the nicer of a cluster of so-so motels in Malta, the Edgewater is also the easiest to find. It's on U.S. 2 on the west end of town, across from the busy Westside Conoco gas station, convenience store, and restaurant. Nice, clean rooms, abundant parking, and even an indoor pool make this a favorite of regular Hi-Line travelers. Tent and RV sites are behind the motel. **Pros:** accessible, clean, and fairly quiet. **Cons:** location along the Milk River can be buggy in the summer. ✉ *47176 U.S. Highway 2, Malta* ☎ *406/654–1302* or *800/821–7475* 🛏 *40 rooms* ⚐ *In-room: refrigerator, Wi-Fi. In-hotel: pool, gym, laundry facilities* ⊟ *AE, DC, MC, V* ⊙ *EP*

> **RESTORING THE PRAIRIE**
>
> The **American Prairie Foundation** wants to heal the prairie by returning bison and associated wildlife species to the landscape, and they're starting south of Malta, where ranch managers are building a small herd of bison, restoring streams and rangeland, and even rehabilitating a country school. You can visit their properties and learn more about their vision of temperate grasslands conservation around the world by arranging tours. ✉ *Dry Fork Rd., Malta* ☎ *406/585–4600* ⊕ *www. americanprairie.org.*

HAVRE

103 mi west of Bowdoin National Wildlife Refuge via U.S. 2.

Mainly a place to stay when visiting Fort Assinniboine, the town of Havre (population 9,621) is the trading center for a wide area of extreme north-central Montana and southern Alberta and Saskatchewan. It lies in the Milk River valley in the shadow of the Bears Paw Mountains, and in a preserve south of town you can fish, picnic, or just enjoy the view.

GETTING HERE AND AROUND

Havre is in many ways the buckle of the Hi-Line belt that runs across northern Montana. It has by far the most amenities of any community and lies at a crossroads between the Canadian cities of Swiftcurrent and Lethbridge and Great Falls to the south. The highway is the main travel route, but Amtrak also stops here, and because this is the crew-changing point, train travelers are afforded a few minutes to stretch their legs. If you have a day, there are some appealing destinations here, from the bustling downtown to its wonderful museums and historical centers.

EXPLORING

Displays at the **H. Earl Clack Memorial Museum** include murals, artifacts, dioramas, and military exhibits that explore the lives of Plains Indians and Havre's early settlers and ranchers. The museum arranges tours of Fort Assinniboine and the Wahkpa Chu'gn Archaeological Site, a major buffalo jump. ⊠ *1753 U.S. Hwy. 2 West, #30* ☎ *406/265–4000* 🖅 *Free* ⊙ *Labor Day–Memorial Day, Tues.–Sat. 1–5; Memorial Day– Labor Day, daily 11–6.*

★ Once the largest military reservation west of the Mississippi, **Fort Assinniboine** was established in 1879 in the aftermath of the Battle of the Little Bighorn. At its peak, the fort had more than 100 brick and stone buildings and nearly 500 men. The soldiers stationed here brought along their families, who lived on the post. As a result, the Victorian-era fort became a cultural center as well as a military one, hosting plays and dances along with parades and training exercises. The fort is now a museum, and many of the imposing buildings still stand, although they appear eerily deserted. In fact, a few are storage or administrative facilities for the Northern Research Agricultural Center. Others are open to public tours, which begin at the H. Earl Clack Memorial Museum. ⊠ *1753 U.S. Hwy. 2 W in Holiday Village Mall* ☎ *406/265–4000* 🖅 *$6* ⊙ *May–Sept., tours at 11:30 and 5 daily or by appointment.*

★ The **Havre Beneath the Streets** tour takes you to a bordello, an opium den, a bakery, and other stops in an underground business center dating from the early days of the frontier—the equivalent of a modern underground mall. The subterranean businesses were mainly built and operated by the town's Asian population, drawn to the area by the Great Northern Railroad and its attendant business opportunities. Reservations for tours are recommended. ⊠ *120 3rd Ave.* ☎ *406/265–8888* 🖅 *$10* ⊙ *Sept.–May, Mon.–Sat. 10–4; June–Aug., daily 9–5.*

Set in the ancient Bears Paw Mountains, about 10 mi south of town, is the 10,000-acre **Beaver Creek Park,** the largest county park in the country. It's a favorite spot for locals, who come here to fish in the two lakes and winding Beaver Creek, camp, picnic, and enjoy the grassy foothills and timbered ridges of this island mountain range surrounded by dryland wheat fields. ⊠ *1786 Beaver Creek Rd.* ☎ *406/395–4565* 🖅 *$7 per vehicle* ⊙ *Daily 24 hrs.*

WHERE TO EAT AND STAY

¢–$$ ✕ **Lunch Box.** There are daily soup and sandwich specials at this fam-
AMERICAN ily-style deli; two soups are made fresh daily. The menu lists a lot of healthful choices, with 70 sandwiches, as well as salads, nachos, baked potatoes, lattes, and espresso. ⊠ *213 3rd Ave.* ☎ *406/265–6588* 🖃 *AE, D, MC, V* ⊙ *Closed Sun.*

$$ 🏨 **AmericInn.** A handsome hotel and convention center, this roomy complex anchors the west end of Havre just south of U.S. 2. Amenities include a few suites with whirlpools, conference rooms for small group meetings, and a well-appointed fitness center. **Pros:** the most modern motel along the Hi-Line, with fixtures that are elegant and in working order; location is convenient to Havre's modest mall, Kmart, and Walmart on the city's west side. **Cons:** twice the price of most lodging

in town. ⊠ *2520 Highway 2 West* ☎ *406/395–5000 or 800/396–5007*
⊕ *www.americinn.com/hotels/MT/Havre* ➾ *52 rooms* ☐ *In-room:*
DVD, Wi-Fi. In-hotel: pool, gym, laundry facilities, laundry service,
parking (free), some pets allowed ⊟ *AE, DC, MC, V* ⦿| *BP*

$ ⊞ **Best Western Great Northern Inn.** A clock tower, colorful flags, and
off-white stones and bricks decorate the proud exterior of this spacious hotel that offers one of the best breakfasts on the Hi-Line. Contemporary furnishings fill the rooms. **Pros:** great hot breakfast in the
morning and comfortable rooms; good beds and spacious bathrooms.
Cons: parking can be tight; the rail yard behind the hotel can get noisy.
⊠ *1345 1st St.* ☎ *406/265–4200 or 888/530–4100* ⊕ *www.bestwestern.*
com ➾ *63 rooms, 12 suites* ☐ *In-hotel: bar, pool, laundry facilities,*
Wi-Fi ⊟ *AE, D, DC, MC, V* ⦿| *CP.*

THE ARTS

Focusing on the pencil drawings of local artist Don Graytak, the **Old
Library Gallery** (⊠ *439 4th Ave.* ☎ *406/265–8165*) also displays paintings
and pottery; most have a connection with local history and culture.

Northern Wyoming

WITH CODY AND SHERIDAN

WORD OF MOUTH

"The Bighorn Mountains in north-central Wyoming are spectacular. Frankly, I found this better than Yellowstone. . . . Nearby is Bighorn Canyon, well worth stopping at the Devils Canyon Overlook—1000 foot sheer drop to the river below. Up the mountains thru Shell Canyon and up near the top is one of the most increible waterfall scenes: Bucking Mule Falls, which is about 500 feet and has a great view down the canyon."

—weimarer

Updated by
Joyce Dalton,
T. D. Griffith,
and Shauna
Stephenson

Pine-carpeted hillsides and snowy mountain summits give way to windswept prairies and clean-flowing rivers where the Great Plains meet the mighty Rocky Mountains. Northern Wyoming's epic landscape is replete with symbols of the American frontier: the ranch, the rodeo, and the cowboy.

It may be that no state in the union exalts cowboy life as Wyoming does. The concept of the dude-ranch vacation—where urban folk learn to rope, ride, and rodeo with weathered ranchers and professional cattle drivers—started in northern Wyoming, at Eatons' Guest Ranch 18 mi outside Sheridan in the town of Wolf. Numerous other guest ranches are strewn across the grassy plains here, from the dusty prairies east of Cody to the alpine meadows of the Big Horn Mountains. Most Big Horn–area dude ranches run pack trips into these high, rugged peaks, sometimes for days at a time. Even if you prefer a warm bed to sleeping under the stars, don't be deterred, and certainly don't leave the state without getting on a horse at least once: try a shorter trail ride or a pack trip that ends at a furnished cabin.

The outdoors is northern Wyoming's primary draw. Take the time to appreciate the wide-open spaces before you: take a hike, go fishing, ride a bike, or get out into the snow. Much of this territory is just as empty as it was when the first white people arrived here two centuries ago. Even though Europeans settled in Wyoming as early as 1812, the state's population is the smallest in the nation, at only 515,004 permanent residents. But the few who have dwelt in this place have been history makers. This part of Wyoming has a rich and storied past that encompasses icons such as gunslingers, gamblers, miners, mule skinners, and warriors. Some of the most famous (and infamous) figures of the Old West passed through here, including Buffalo Bill Cody, Wild Bill Hickok, Calamity Jane, Chief Washakie, Butch Cassidy, and the Sundance Kid, the latter of whom took his name from one of the region's towns.

ORIENTATION AND PLANNING

GETTING ORIENTED

Northern Wyoming is a point of convergence. Here mountains meet prairies, forests meet ranches, and country towns meet Western cities. Most settlements have no more than a few hundred people; only three surpass 10,000 residents. Casper, on the banks of the North Platte River in the center of Wyoming, is on or near five of the major pioneer trails of the mid-19th century, including the Oregon and Mormon trails. Gillette, in the Powder River Basin near Devils Tower National Monument, and Sheridan, on the edge of the Big Horn Mountains 104 mi to the northwest, are both in Wyoming's energy country, although ranching (both dude and cattle) are mainstays of the communities. Cody, with about 9,100 residents, is the largest community between the Big Horn Mountains and Yellowstone National Park, a convenient stop for visitors on their way to the natural treasures farther west.

PLANNING

WHEN TO GO

People come to experience northern Wyoming in all four seasons—sometimes all in the same week. The weather here is notoriously difficult to predict, as warm Chinook winds can shoot January temperatures into the 70s and freak storms can drop snow in July. On the whole, however, Mother Nature behaves herself and gives the area pleasantly warm summers and refreshingly snowy winters. Most travelers flock to the region between June and August, availing themselves of the higher temperatures optimal for outdoor activities. Many more come to ski or snowmobile the pristine powder of the Big Horn Mountains in winter.

Temperatures in both seasons can be extreme, however. Thermometers often register a week of triple digits in August in the lower elevations. Snow begins to blanket the mountain slopes in late September and begins to recede only in late May. Spring, especially in the mountains, is sometimes nothing more than a week or two of rain between the last winter snowfall and the warm sunshine of summer. Autumn, on the other hand, is full of pleasantly warm days, cooler nights, and vivid colors. Additionally, the only crowds to fight are small pockets of hunters, anglers, and local leaf peepers.

PLANNING YOUR TIME

Many people travel through northern Wyoming on their way to visit the wonders of Yellowstone National Park to the west. This is one of the most logical ways to see the area, but beware: the empty spaces between towns and the wide-open road might tempt you to speed through the region too quickly. Give yourself enough time to allow for occasional stops, and don't hesitate to overnight in one of the area's small towns. You won't just be breaking up the car ride; you'll get to visit some of the American West's hidden gems. Planning ahead is imperative—hotels, gas stations, and restaurants can be few and far between, and with the recent energy-production boom it can be difficult to get reservations.

If you're headed into Wyoming from the east along I–90, be sure to stop at Sundance and Devils Tower National Monument. The towns of Gillette, Buffalo, and Sheridan are also worth your time, and are ideal places to spend the night. You have your choice of guest ranches and mountain lodges here, and you can take the opportunity to explore both the Wyoming plains and the foothills of the Big Horns. Take either U.S. 14 or U.S. 16 through the mountains and stretch your legs in the Cloud Peak Wilderness Area, a prime spot for outdoor recreation, whether it's a 15-minute hike or a daylong ski trip. West of the Big Horns, the two highways meet up near Basin; from here, U.S. 14 is a straight shot to Cody and U.S. 310 is a scenic route through the arid plains near Lovell and Deaver.

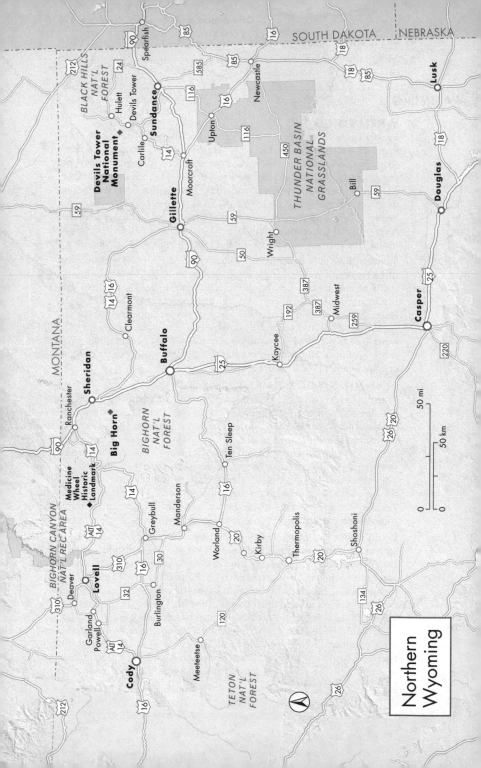

Northern Wyoming

An alternative for those interested in pioneer trails and stagecoach routes is to head south from Buffalo via I–25 to the eastern Wyoming towns of Casper, Douglas, and Lusk. They lie in flatter landscape and offer less in the way of visitor services, but this is where you'll find the National Historic Trails Interpretive Center, Fort Fetterman State Historic Site, and similar attractions. From here, head back north on U.S. 20 to Thermopolis and travel either northeast into the Big Horns on U.S. 16 or northwest toward Cody and Yellowstone National Park on Highway 120.

TOP REASONS TO GO

■ For a good meal, visit the Chophouse in Gillette.

■ Jaunt around Devils Tower to marvel at one of nature's most impressive edifices.

■ Hogadon Ski Area has something for the whole family.

■ A visit to Eagle Butte Coal Mine will give you a taste of what powers Wyoming's economy.

GETTING HERE AND AROUND
AIR TRAVEL
For the most part, airlines connect the region only to Denver, Minneapolis, or Salt Lake City, although some carriers occasionally have seasonal routes to smaller cities such as Billings. Delta Air Lines serves Casper and Cody from Salt Lake City. Northwest Airlines connects Casper and Minneapolis. United Airlines flies from Denver into Casper, Gillette, Sheridan, and Cody.

The region's major airports are Casper's Natrona County International Airport, Gillette's Campbell County Airport, and Cody's Yellowstone Regional Airport. Sheridan County Airport has one or two flights daily to and from Denver, plus charter service.

The Campbell County Airport is 6 mi north of Gillette and 106 mi east of Sheridan. Natrona County International Airport is 12 mi west of Casper. Yellowstone Regional Airport is on the edge of Cody, about a mile from downtown.

Airlines Delta Air Lines (☎ 800/221–1212 ⊕ www.delta.com). **Northwest Airlines** (☎ 800/225–2525 ⊕ www.nwa.com). **United Airlines** (☎ 800/241–6522 ⊕ www.ual.com).

Airports Campbell County Airport (✉ 2000 Airport Rd., Gillette ☎ 307/686–1042 ⊕ www.ccgov.net/departments/airport/index.html). **Natrona County International Airport** (✉ 8500 Airport Pkwy., Casper ☎ 307/472–6688 ⊕ www.iflycasper.com). **Sheridan County Airport** (✉ 908 W. Brundage La. ☎ 307/674–4222 ⊕ www.sheridancountyairport.com). **Yellowstone Regional Airport** (✉ 3001 Duggleby Dr., Cody ☎ 307/587–5096 ⊕ www.flyyra.com).

BUS TRAVEL
National bus service from Greyhound Lines is available only through Powder River Transportation, a regional carrier that connects the area to the larger hub cities of Cheyenne and Rapid City, South Dakota. Casper, Gillette, Sheridan, Cody, and nearly every smaller town in northern and central Wyoming are well served by Powder River Transportation.

Information **Greyhound Lines** (☎ *307/587–6993 or 800/231–2222* ⊕ *www. greyhound.com*). **Powder River Transportation** (☎ *307/682–0960*).

CAR TRAVEL

Unless you're traveling with a package tour, a car is essential here. I–90 cuts directly through northeastern Wyoming, hitting the towns of Sheridan, Buffalo, Gillette, and Sundance. I–25 runs south from Buffalo through the Big Horns to Casper, Douglas, Cheyenne, and eventually Denver. There are no interstate highways west of the Big Horns, so U.S. 14—one of two routes that cross the mountain range—is the main road in this part of the state, connecting Cody with I–90.

Because the territory in this part of the world is so sparsely populated, it's almost impossible to find gas and repair shops at your convenience. There are few towns along the major routes here, including the interstates, so it's wise to plan your trip in advance. Although most of the country has gone to 24-hour credit-card gas pumps, these pieces of technology haven't hit the smaller towns in Wyoming, and it's rare to find a gas station open past the early evening unless you're in Gillette, Sheridan, Casper, or Cody. If you're driving in a particularly remote region, it's wise to take along extra water. Although the communities here employ great fleets of snowplows in the winter, it can sometimes take them time to clear the upper elevations. Some passes in the Big Horns close entirely. Keep in mind, too, that residents are used to driving in a little snow and ice, so the plows will come out only if accumulations are substantial.

Contact the Wyoming State Highway Patrol for information on road conditions.

Information **Wyoming State Highway Patrol** (☎ *888/996–7623 or 800/442–9090* ⊕ *dot.state.wy.us*).

RESTAURANTS

Although not every community here has the eclectic mix of dining options common in more urban areas, there are plenty of small restaurants and local cafés with inimitable appeal. The larger communities often have several ethnic eateries from which to choose, serving everything from traditional Mexican and Native American specialties to Old World Italian and modern Korean dishes. The real strength of the region's dining, however, lies with the basics. In almost any small-town watering hole you can order up some of the freshest and best-tasting beef and buffalo in the world. Whether it's prime rib and mashed potatoes with sunflower bread or charred rib eye with corn on the cob, the area's best meals are simple yet filled with a flavor found only in the West.

ABOUT THE HOTELS

Just as diverse as the area's landscape, which fades from small Western cities into vast lengths of open prairie and forested mountains, are its accommodations. In the population centers lodgings range from new chain hotels with wireless Internet access to elegant and historic stone inns decorated with buffalo skins and Victorian furniture. Move beyond these cities, however, and everything changes. Campgrounds abound in the open countryside. On the prairie, expect sprawling guest ranches alongside cold mountain-fed creeks. In the higher elevations, look for charming bed-and-breakfasts on mountain slopes with broad alpine vistas. But whatever the type of accommodation, all kinds of amenities are available, from the ordinary to the unconventional, including saunas, hot tubs, horseback riding, fly-fishing lessons, and square dancing. Perhaps the greatest benefit of all, however, is the isolation. In what some might call a welcome change in this era of information overload, many rural lodgings don't have in-room televisions or telephones, and vast stretches don't have cell-phone service.

WHAT IT COSTS					
	¢	$	$$	$$$	$$$$
Restaurants	under $8	$8–$12	$13–$20	$21–$30	over $30
Hotels	under $70	$70–$100	$101–$150	$151–$200	over $200

Restaurant prices are for a main course at dinner, excluding sales tax of 4%–7%. Hotel prices are for two people in a standard double room in high season, excluding service charges and 5%–10% tax.

CAMPING

The opportunities to camp in this region are almost limitless. There are countless campgrounds in the Big Horns, and a few on the prairies below. Most of the public land within the national forests and parks is open for camping, provided that you don't light any fires. Keep in mind when selecting your campsite that the majestic peaks of the Big Horns are home to black bears and mountain lions.

THE BIG HORN BASIN

9

Rich in Native American history, Old West flavor, and natural wonders, this broad basin is flanked by the Absaroka and Owl mountains to the west and the Big Horns to the east. The Bighorn River flows north along the eastern edge of the basin and up into Montana. Here, straddling the two states, is Bighorn Canyon National Recreation Area; most of the recreation area lies in Montana, but the southern portion is easily accessible in Wyoming via Highway 37.

LOVELL

49 mi northeast of Cody via Alternate U.S. 14.

This small community makes a convenient, if bare-bones, base for exploring the Bighorn Canyon National Recreation Area, which overlaps the Wyoming–Montana border. On the Wyoming side, Bighorn Lake is popular with boaters and anglers; most of the main attractions, including the majority of the Pryor Mountain Wild Horse Range, lie on the Montana side. (⇨ *Chapter 8.*)

GETTING HERE AND AROUND

You'll need your own vehicle here.

The main visitor center for the Bighorn Canyon National Recreation Area, the **Bighorn Canyon Visitor Center,** has geological and historical exhibits, as well as two free films about the canyon and area geology. The National Park Service personnel are welcoming and helpful. ⊠ *20 Hwy. 14A, just east of town* ☎ *307/548–2251* ⊕ *www.nps.gov/bica/* ⊠ *$5, 1-yr pass $30* ⊙ *Memorial Day–Labor Day, daily 8–6; Labor Day–Memorial Day, daily 8:30–4:30.*

Practically next door to the Bighorn Canyon Visitor Center, the **Pryor Mountain Wild Mustang Center** uses photos, printed information, and helpful volunteers to introduce people to the 25 to 30 stallions and their bands that roam over 38,000 acres of range. Although many of the mustangs will likely be up in the mountains, you're almost sure to see some right from the paved road, Highway 37. This could include White Cloud, a stallion featured in two books by Ginger Kathrens. ⊠ *1106 Road 12* ☎ *307/548–9453* ⊕ *www.pryormustangs.org* ⊙ *May–Sept., daily 9–5, though days and hours may vary.*

More than 155 species of birds, including white pelicans, pheasants, bald eagles, and great blue herons, inhabit the 19,424-acre **Yellowtail Wildlife Habitat Management Area,** as do numerous other animal species, including red fox, mule deer, and cottontail rabbits. ⊠ *Hwy. 37, 33 mi northeast of Lovell* ☎ *307/527–7125* ⊠ *Free* ⊙ *Daily.*

OFF THE BEATEN PATH

Fodor'sChoice

★

Medicine Wheel National Historic Landmark. A ring of rocks 75 feet in diameter, this ancient site is the best preserved of nearly 150 Native American stone wheels found in Wyoming, South Dakota, Montana, Alberta, and Saskatchewan. Evidence such as the 28 spokes (one for each day of the lunar cycle) leading from the edge of the wheel to a central cairn has persuaded some that the wheel was an ancient spiritual observatory much like England's Stonehenge may have been. To protect the area, access to the wheel is restricted to foot travel; it's a 1.5-mi hike to the site from the parking lot (people with disabilities may drive to the site). Up in the Big Horn Mountains, at an elevation of 9,642 feet, the site affords views of the entire Big Horn Basin. At this elevation you'll want to bring a coat or sweatshirt. ⊠ *30 mi east of Lovell on Alternate U.S. 14* ☎ *307/548–6541* ⊠ *Free* ⊙ *Daily 24 hrs.*

Hyart Theatre, an arty-looking, 975-seat movie palace built in 1950 by film lover Hyrum Bischoff, is the heart and soul of this 2,300-person outpost, known as the Rose City, at the foot of the Big Horn Mountains. Because of the popularity of home video rentals, the Hyart shut down in 1992, but it was revived by a citizens' committee of volunteers who raised funds to restore the theater, its spacious lobby, sunken lounge, sloping balcony, "cry room" for babies, and neon painter's palette high above the marquee to its former Truman-era glory. It reopened in 2004. ⊠ *251 E. Main St.* ☎ *307/548–7021* ⊕ *www.hyarttheater.com* ⊠ *Tickets $4* ⊙ *Fri. at 7 and 9:30, Sat. at 3 and 7.*

WHERE TO EAT AND STAY

There's a somewhat wider choice of basic, low- to mid-range motels and eateries in Powell, about 20 mi west.

$

AMERICAN

✕ **Lange's Kitchen.** This homey diner-style grill is a local institution, where folks come for the kind of down-home cooking that sticks to your ribs:

biscuits and gravy, oatmeal, hamburgers, shrimp baskets, tacos, halibut strips, and liver and onions. For lighter meals, they also serve soups, salads, and hot and cold sandwiches. Lange's is open from 6 AM to 2 PM. ⊠ *483 Shoshone Ave.* 🕾 *307/548–9370* ⊟ *MC, V* ⊘ *No dinner.*

¢ ✕ **The Switchback Grill.** Catering to lunch and early-bird dinner crowds,
AMERICAN this place serves Philly cheesesteak sandwiches, fried chicken, hoagies, hamburgers, and steaks with grilled onions and fries. ⊠ *384 W. Main St.* 🕾 *307/548–9595* ⊟ *MC, V.*

¢ 🆃 **Horseshoe Band Motel.** This low-slung, one-story throwback from 1969 is straight out of a Sam Shepard play. You'll find a gas grill for guests, and picnic tables. The property is popular with hunters, allowing their dogs to stay, too. **Pros:** clean rooms, some with kitchenettes; on main road through town. **Cons:** fills up quickly; front desk staff may or may not be friendly, depending who's on duty. ⊠ *375 E. Main St.,* 🕾 *307/548–2221* 🛏 *22 rooms* ⚷ *In-room: Refrigerator (some). In-hotel: Wi-Fi, some pets allowed* ⊟ *AE, MC, V.*

CODY

60 mi southeast of Red Lodge, Montana, via Rte. 308, then 72/120; 52 mi east of Yellowstone via U.S. 14/16/20.

Cody, founded in 1896 and named for Pony Express rider, army scout, Freemason, and entertainer William F. "Buffalo Bill" Cody, is the eastern gateway community for Yellowstone National Park. But this town of 9,100 is much more than a base for exploring the surrounding area. Five excellent museums under one roof make up the outstanding Buffalo Bill Historical Center, and the Western lifestyle is alive and well on dude ranches and in both trendy and classic shops. Part of the fun in Cody is sauntering down Sheridan Avenue, stopping by the Irma Hotel (built by Buffalo Bill and named for his daughter) for some refreshment, and attending the nightly rodeo.

GETTING HERE AND AROUND

The North Fork Highway—as the route leading west to Yellowstone is locally known—follows the North Fork of the Shoshone River past barren rock formations strewn with tumbleweeds, then enters lush forests and green meadows as the elevation increases roughly 3,000 feet in 70 mi. Cody is within easy reach of the Shoshone National Forest, the Absaroka Range, the Washakie Wilderness, and the Buffalo Bill Reservoir. If you're staying downtown, shops, restaurants, and even the Buffalo Bill Historical Center are within easy walking distance. Otherwise, you'll need a car, as there is no public transportation and only one taxi company.

VISITOR INFORMATION

Cody Country Chamber of Commerce (⊠ *836 Sheridan Ave., Cody* 🕾 *307/ 587–2777 or 800/393–2639* ⊕ *www.codychamber.org*) has a helpful visitors' desk and a wealth of free maps and brochures, including a self-guided walking tour of the town's historic sites.

9

EXPLORING CODY

The **Wyoming Vietnam Veterans Memorial** is a small-scale version of the Vietnam Veterans Memorial wall in Washington, D.C. The Cody memorial recognizes the Wyoming residents who died during the conflict. ⊠ *U.S. 14/16/20, east of Cody* .

The **Cody Mural,** at the Church of Jesus Christ of Latter-day Saints, is an artistic interpretation of Mormon settlement in the West. Edward Grigware painted the 36-foot-diameter scene on the domed ceiling in the 1950s. ⊠ *1719 Wyoming Ave.* ☎ *307/587–3290* ☒ *Free* ⊙ *June–mid-Sept., Mon.–Sat. 9–7, Sun. 3–7.*

Fodor'sChoice On the west side of Cody are some of the finest museums anywhere and
★ true jewels of the West: the **Buffalo Bill Historical Center,** which houses five world-class museums in one. On summer weekdays special programs are held for kids and adults. The **Buffalo Bill Cody Museum** is dedicated to this larger-than-life figure. Shortly after Cody's death, friends took mementos of the famous scout and Wild West showman and opened the Buffalo Bill Museum in a small log building. The museum has since been moved to the historical center and includes films, posters from the original Wild West shows, and illustrated books as well as personal effects such as clothing, guns, saddles, and furniture. The **Cody Firearms Museum** traces the history of firearms through thousands of models on display, from European blunderbusses to Gatling guns and modern firearms. Included are examples of Winchester and Browning arms, as well as a model of an arms-manufacturing plant. There are also the 1881 Navy revolvers belonging to Cody friend James "Wild Bill" Hickok. Through exhibits, outdoor activities, and tours, the **Draper Museum of Natural History** explores the Yellowstone ecosystem. There are children's discovery areas in addition to life-size animal mounts. Recordings play the sounds of wolves, grizzly bears, birds, and other animals that make their home in the Yellowstone area. At the **Plains Indian Museum,** interactive exhibits and life-size dioramas explore the history and culture of the Lakota, Blackfeet, Cheyenne, Shoshone, and Nez Perce tribes. Among the exhibits are rare medicine pipes, clothing, a travois, and an earth-house interpretive area. The **Whitney Gallery of Western Art,** devoted to the West's greatest artists, is organized by subject, such as wildlife, scenery, and Native American life. On display are works by famed masters, including Frederic Remington, Charles M. Russell, Albert Bierstadt, George Catlin, and Thomas Moran, plus contemporary artists such as Harry Jackson, James Bama, and Peter Fillerup. ⊠ *720 Sheridan Ave.* ☎ *307/587–4771* ⊕ *www.bbhc.org* ☒ *$15 (2 consecutive days)* ⊙ *Apr., daily 10–5; May–mid-Sept., daily 8–6; mid-Sept.–Oct., daily 8–5; Nov.–Mar., Thurs.–Sun. 10–5.*

🖰 **Cody Nite Rodeo,** more dusty and intimate than big rodeos such as Cheyenne Frontier Days, offers children's events, such as goat roping, in addition to the regular adult events. Tickets are sold online and at the hotels, and restaurants, as well as the rodeo grounds. ⊠ *Stampede Park on Hwy. 14/16/20W* ☎ *307/587–5155 or 800/207–0744* ⊕ *www.cody-stampederodeo.com* ☒ *$18* ⊙ *June–Aug., daily at 8* PM.

⟲ On summer evenings the **Cody Gunslingers Shootout** takes place in front of the Irma Hotel. ✉ *1192 Sheridan Ave.* ☎ *307/587–4221* ⊕ *www. codygunfighters.com* 🎟 *Free* ☉ *June–Sept., Mon.–Sat. at 6 PM.*

If you give the folks at **Cody Trolley Tours** an hour of your time, they'll take you on a journey through 100 years of Cody history. The tour takes in historic sites, scenery, geology, and wildlife attractions. A combination ticket also grants you admission to the Buffalo Bill Historical Center. Reservations are a good idea. ✉ *Ticket booth in front of Irma Hotel, 1192 Sheridan Ave.* ☎ *307/527–7043* 🎟 *Tour ticket $22, combination ticket with Buffalo Bill Historical Center $32* ☉ *June–Sept., daily at 11, 1, and 3.*

⟲ On Cody's western outskirts, off the West Yellowstone Highway, is **Old Trail Town,** a collection of historic buildings from Wyoming's frontier days, housing photos and pioneer and Native American artifacts. A small cemetery serves as resting place for some famous mountain men, including Liver Eatin' Johnston. With the authentic buildings and rustic displays, you really get a feel for an Old West town. ✉ *1831 Demaris Dr.* ☎ *307/587–5302* 🎟 *$8* ☉ *Mid-May–Sept., daily 8–7.*

Fishing and boating on the Buffalo Bill Reservoir are popular activities at **Buffalo Bill State Park,** west of Cody. A visitor center here focuses on the history of the reservoir, which was completed in 1910. ✉ *47 Lakeside Rd., west of Cody on U.S. 14/16/20; then Rte. 291* ☎ *307/587–9227* ⊕ *wyoparks.state.wy.us/Site/SiteInfo.asp?siteID=3* 🎟 *Park $4 with Wyoming license plate, $6 otherwise; camping $10 with Wyoming license plate, $17 otherwise* ☉ *Park daily 24 hrs, visitor center May–Sept., daily 8–8.*

The **Shoshone National Forest** was the country's first national forest, established in 1891. You can hike on 1,500 mi of trails, fish, mountain bike, and ride horses in warmer weather, and snowmobile and cross-country ski in winter. There are picnic areas and campgrounds. ✉ *U.S. 14/16/20, west of Cody* ☎ *307/527–6921* ⊕ *www.fs.fed.us/r2/shoshone/* 🎟 *Free* ☉ *Daily 24 hrs.*

9

OFF THE BEATEN PATH

Chief Joseph Scenic Highway. In 1877 a few members of the Nez Perce tribe killed some white settlers in Idaho as retribution for earlier killings by whites. Fearing that the U.S. Army would punish the guilty and innocent alike, hundreds of Nez Perce fled on a five-month journey toward Canada along what came to be known as the Nez Perce Trail. On the way they passed through what is now Yellowstone National Park, across the Sunlight Basin area north of Cody, and along the Clarks Fork of the Shoshone River before turning north into Montana. To see the rugged mountain area they traveled through, follow Highway 120 north 17 mi to Highway 296, the Chief Joseph Scenic Highway. The highway eventually leads to Cooke City, Montana, and Yellowstone National Park. Along the way you'll see open meadows, pine forests, and a sweeping vista of the region from the top of Dead Indian Pass.

SPORTS AND THE OUTDOORS

CANOEING, KAYAKING, AND RAFTING

Gradient Mountain Sports (⊠ *1725 Sheridan Ave.82414* ☎ *307/587–4659* ⊕ *www.gradientmountainsports.net*) provides kayaking excursions, instruction, sales, and rentals of recreational and sit-on-top kayaks plus white-water demos. Family river trips on the Shoshone River are offered by **River Runners** (⊠ *1491 Sheridan Ave.* ☎ *307/527–7238 or 800/535–7238* ⊕ *www.riverrunnersofwyoming.com*).**Wyoming River Trips** (⊠ *233 Yellowstone Ave. or 1701 Sheridan Ave.* ☎ *307/587–6661 or 800/586–6661* ⊕ *www.wyomingrivertrips.com*) arranges Shoshone River trips.

FISHING

The fish are big at the private **Monster Lake** (☎ *307/797–4109*), filled with rainbow, brook, and brown trout weighing up to 10 pounds. For a fee you can fish all or part of the day at this lake on the east side of town.

You can buy fishing tackle, rent equipment, get information on fishing in the area, or take a guided half- or full-day trip with **Tim Wade's North Fork Anglers** (⊠ *1107 Sheridan Ave.* ☎ *307/527–7274* ⊕ *northforkanglers.com*). **Wyoming Trout Masters** (⊠ *63 Bartlett La.* ☎ *307/250–0043* ⊕ *www.troutmasters.us*) will arrange trips on the Shoshone, Clark's Fork, and Bighorn rivers, plus several lakes around Cody. Choose from pontoon boat, lake trolling, river wading, or float-tube adventures, as well as fishing/photo combos.

GOLF

Olive Glenn Golf and Country Club (⊠ *802 Meadow La.* ☎ *307/587–5551, restaurant 307/587–5688*) is a highly rated 18-hole course open to the public; a Jacuzzi, pool, and two tennis courts are also here. The club's restaurant is open to the public for lunch Monday–Friday; reservations are essential.

HORSEBACK RIDING

Ride from one hour to all day or take a pack trip for fishing and photography with **Cedar Mountain Trail Rides** (⊠ *U.S. 14/16/20, 1 mi west of rodeo grounds* ☎ *307/527–4966*). For a list of Cody-area outfitters, contact **Cody Country Outfitters and Guides Association** (☎ *307/587–6178* ⊕ *ccoga.org*).

SKIING

In the Wood River valley near Meeteetse, 22 mi southeast of Cody, **Wood River Ski Touring Park** (⊠ *1010 Park Ave.* ☎ *307/868–2603*) has 40 km (25 mi) of groomed cross-country trails in the Shoshone National Forest.

WHERE TO EAT

$$ ✕ **Granny's.** This family-style diner has a kids' and senior menu and is
ⓒ popular with locals as well as visitors. Offerings include good coffee, omelets, biscuits with gravy (breakfast menu available all day), patty melts, hot sandwiches, fried chicken, soups, and salads. ⊠ *1550 Sheridan Ave.* ☎ *307/587–4829* ⊟ *MC, V.*

$ | **✕ La Comida.** Making no claim to authentic Mexican cooking, this res-
MEXICAN | taurant nevertheless receives praise for its "Cody-Mex" cuisine. You may order enchiladas, burritos, tacos, and chiles rellenos, but they won't be as spicy as similar foods would be in the Southwest. Mexican wall hangings contribute to the festive atmosphere. Tables on the large front porch are great for people-watching. ✉ *1385 Sheridan Ave.* ☎ *307/587–9556* ☰ *AE, D, DC, MC, V.*

$$$ | **✕ Proud Cut Saloon.** At this popular downtown eatery and watering hole
STEAK | owner Del Nose serves what locals call "kick-ass cowboy cuisine": nine cuts of beef headlined by a 22-ounce porterhouse. The non-carnivorous will find a couple of shrimp and fish offerings. Western paintings, vintage photographs of Cody country, and large-game mounts decorate the place. ✉ *1227 Sheridan Ave.* ☎ *307/527–6905* ☰ *AE, D, MC, V.*

$$ | **✕ Wyoming Rib & Chop House.** Limited to a few locales in Wyoming
AMERICAN | and Montana, this not-quite-a-chain facility attracts quite a following. Expect as many locals as visitors among your fellow diners at lunch or dinner. Baby back ribs, Angus beef, and fresh seafood are favorites. ✉ *1367 Sheridan Ave.* ☎ *307/527–7731* ⊕ *www.ribandchophouse.com* ☰ *AE, D, MC, V.*

WHERE TO STAY

$$$ | **⊡ Chamberlin Inn.** Situated less than a block off bustling Sheridan Ave-
Fodor's Choice | nue, the inn and its three separate guest structures (one the old county
★ | courthouse, another a two-story former barn) seem a peaceful oasis. Dating to 1904, this beautifully restored property once hosted Ernest Hemingway; his room, number 18, features a leather bed and a Winslow Homer fly-fisherman painting copied on tile. **Pros:** pressed tin ceilings and a sunroom recall an earlier era; art throughout, including many Alphonse Mucha works copied on tile. **Cons:** no elevator (request first-floor rooms if stairs are a problem); no pool. ✉ *1032 12th St.,* ☎ *307/587–0202 or 888/587–0202* ⊕ *www.chamberlininn.com* ⇱ *18 rooms in main building, 2 apartments, 1 cottage, 1 2-story house* ♿ *In-room: kitchen (some), refrigerator (some), DVD (some), Wi-Fi. In-hotel: room service (breakfast only), Wi-Fi* ☰ *AE, MC, V* ⦿| *BP.*

$$–$$$ | **⊡ Cody Cowboy Village.** The individual and duplex log cabins here are pure Western, right down to the open-beam ceilings, iron bedsteads with horseshoe designs, and bathroom wallpaper printed with boots and cowboy hats. High-thread-count sheets and soft duvets ensure a restful sleep, as does the 35-person hot tub. **Pros:** great room décor; cabin porches to take in mountain views. **Cons:** sometimes a wait at check-in; 2 mi from historic center and downtown. ✉ *203 W. Yellowstone Ave.* ☎ *307/587–7555* ⊕ *www.codycowboyvillage.com* ⇱ *50 rooms* ♿ *In-room: Wi-Fi. In-hotel: Wi-Fi* ☰ *AE, DC, MC, V* ☯ *Closed mid-Oct.–Apr.* ⦿| *CP.*

$$ | **⊡ Irma Hotel.** Built in 1902 by Buffalo Bill and named for his daughter, the original section of this hotel is listed on the National Register of Historic Places. The property retains both frontier charm and rough edges, with period furniture and pull-chain commodes in many rooms, a large restaurant open all day ($$–$$$), and an elaborate cherrywood bar said to have been a gift from Queen Victoria to Buffalo Bill. For

9

those looking for modern amenities and trappings, this probably isn't it. But if you want true history, choose one of the 15 rooms, named after local legends, in the original hotel rather than in the annex, which has standard contemporary rooms. Scared of ghosts? Don't book Room 35. **Pros:** tons of character, history and charm; in the heart of town. **Cons:** location not for those seeking peace and quiet; front desk staff could be more helpful. ⊠ *1192 Sheridan Ave.* ☎ *307/587–4221 or 800/745–4762* ⊕ *www.irmahotel.com* ⟿ *40 rooms* ᐸ *In-room: Wi-Fi. In-hotel: restaurant, bar, some pets allowed* ⊟ *AE, D, DC, MC, V.*

$$$
Fodor's Choice
★

⊡ **K3 Guest Ranch B&B.** Here you have the chance to stay at a Western ranch, this one only a 15-minute drive from town, without spending a mint. There's no minimum stay required, and decor is decidedly upscale-Western. In one guest room a wooden fence stands before a wall-to-wall picture of the Tetons, and in another you can bed down in quilted comfort in an old chuck wagon. More options? Sleep in a genuine sheepherder's wagon, circa 1897. Guests don cowboy hats for breakfast, which is cooked over an open campfire, while an Australian sheepdog and two horses show off their repertoire of tricks. Ask Jerry about his autographed guest soap collection. **Pros:** no detail spared in creating this unique ambience; trips to wild-mustang range on request. **Cons:** several miles' travel on well-posted gravel road; driving into town for dinner may not please some. ⊠ *30 Nielsen Tr.* ☎ ⊕ *www.k3guestranch.com* ⟿ *4 rooms* ᐸ *In-room: no phone, DVD (some), Wi-Fi. In-hotel: Wi-Fi* ⊟ *MC, V* ᐅᐊ *BP.*

$$

⊡ **Lambright Place B&B.** Illuminated deer figures and a wood-burning fireplace welcome you to this comfortable gray-frame B&B a couple of blocks off Cody's main street. Four light, airy guest rooms are in the main house, and a partition separates the queen bed from three singles in the backyard bunkhouse. The breakfast crème-brûlée French toast and artichoke soufflé win special praise. **Pros:** bunkhouse is ideal for families; guests laud warmth of hosts. **Cons:** some don't like the set breakfast hour; no coffeemakers in rooms. ⊠ *1501 Beck Ave.* ☎ *307/527–5310 or 800/241–5310* ⊕ *www.lambrightplace.com* ⟿ *4 rooms, 1 bunkhouse* ᐸ *In-room: refrigerator (some), no TV (some), Wi-Fi. In-hotel: Wi-Fi* ⊟ *MC, V* ᐅᐊ *BP.*

$$–$$$$

⊡ **The Mayor's Inn.** Built in 1909 for Cody's first elected mayor, this B&B's decor is Victorian with a Western flair. A claw-foot tub, a jetted tub, or a private hot tub highlight guest-room baths. A separate cottage equipped with full kitchen stands behind the main building. For breakfast, appealing options include the frittata (an Italian omelet) and sourdough flapjacks with buffalo sausage. Thursday through Saturday, the inn is open for dinner ($$), offering such choices as wild salmon, tenderloin medallions, and lamb chops. Nonguests are welcome. **Pros:** breakfast tables indoors, on veranda, and on patio; one guest room downstairs. **Cons:** a little walk from the main drag; no guest computer for non–laptop carriers. ⊠ *1413 Rumsey Ave.* ☎ *307/587–0887* ⊕ *www.mayorsinn.com* ⟿ *4 rooms, 1 cottage* ᐸ *In-room: no phone, Wi-Fi. In-hotel: restaurant, Wi-Fi* ⊟ *AE, DC, MC, V* ᐅᐊ *BP.*

$$$$

⊡ **Rimrock Dude Ranch.** Dating to 1926, this is one of the oldest guest ranches on the North Fork of the Shoshone River. Your week (minimum stay) at Rimrock includes activities ranging from horseback riding in the surrounding mountain country to rafting, an all-day excursion in Yellowstone National Park, and an evening at the rodeo. There are no overnights in winter, but visitors to the area can join a snowmobile day trip into the park. Lodging is in one- and two-bedroom cabins. **Pros:** excellent long-standing reputation, near Yellowstone. **Cons:** minimum stay; might be too expensive for those on tight budgets. ⊠ *2728 North Fork Hwy.* ☎ *307/587–3970* ⊕ *www.rimrockranch.com* ⊸ *9 cabins* �findroom: no a/c, refrigerator, no TV. In-hotel: pool ☰ MC, V for deposit only ☺ Closed Oct.–Apr. ⸙ FAP.*

$$$–$$$$ ⛺ **UXU Ranch.** One of the cabins at the UXU guest ranch is a historic
☼ late-19th-century stage stop moved to the site and decorated with Molesworth-style furnishings; other cabins here date to the 1960s or 1920s. The ranch, along the North Fork of the Shoshone River, offers outstanding horseback riding, pack trips into the nearby mountains, superb fly-fishing, white-water rafting arrangements, and a location near the Sleeping Giant ski area. There's a minimum one-week stay. It's open year-round; inquire about winter rates. **Pros:** gorgeous setting; 17 mi from Yellowstone; expert management. **Cons:** altitude could bother some; hot tub but no pool. ⊠ *1710 Yellowstone Hwy., Wapiti* ☎ *307/587–2143 or 800/373–9027* ⊕ *www.uxuranch.com* ⊸ *11 cabins* ⚐ *In-room: no a/c, no phone, Wi-Fi. In-hotel: restaurant, bar, children's programs (ages 3 and up), Wi-Fi* ☰ *MC, V* ⸙ *FAP.*

$ ⛺ **Yellowstone Valley Inn & RV.** Located 16 mi west of Cody and 30 mi east of Yellowstone National Park's east entrance, this sprawling property offers basic accommodations in a mountain setting on the Shoshone River. Rooms are in the motel or duplex cabins, plus two suites in the main lodge; campsites are available. **Pros:** rustic but clean rooms; beautiful location; pleasant front desk staff. **Cons:** bar crowd can be noisy, but is unlikely to disturb guests in motel or cabins; same for live music in dance hall five nights a week. ⊠ *3324 North Fork Hwy.,* ☎ *307/587–3961 or 877/587–3961* ⊕ *www.yellowstonevalleyinn.com* ⊸ *15 motel rooms, 20 cabin rooms* ⚐ *In-room: no phone, Wi-Fi. In-hotel: restaurant, bar, pool, laundry facilities, some pets allowed* ☰ *AE, D, MC, V.*

CAMPING

There are 31 campgrounds within **Shoshone National Forest** (☎ *307/527–6921* ⊕ *www.fs.fed.us/r2/shoshone*); some have only limited services, and others have hookups and campground hosts.

$ ⛺ **Absaroka Bay RV Park.** This campground stands across the street from Beck Park, where lake fishing is free (but you must have a Wyoming fishing license). All RV spots are pull-through, and there's a big tenting area, though tent sites are not individually marked off. The camp has picnic tables but no cabins or store, and Sheridan Avenue's shops and restaurants are a major trek. ⊠ *2002 Mountain View* ☎ *307/527–7440 or 800/557–7440* ⊸ *99 full hookups* ☰ *MC, V* ☺ *Closed Nov.–Apr.*
⛺ **Cody KOA.** At breakfast, this campground on the southeast side of town serves all the pancakes you can eat for $2. There's also a free shuttle to the Cody Nite Rodeo, and you can arrange to take a horseback ride. ⚐ *Flush toilets, full hookups, partial hookups (electric and*

water), drinking water, guest laundry, showers, picnic tables, general store, swimming (pool) ⟋*78 tent sites, 68 full hookups, 54 partial hookups; 21 camping cabins, 1 cottage with bath and kitchen* ⊠*5561 U.S. 20 (Greybull Hwy.)* ☎*307/587–2369 or 800/562–85077* ⊕*www. codykoa.com* ⊟*D, MC, V* ☉ *Closed Nov.–Apr.*

⚠ **Dead Indian Campground.** You can fish in the stream at this tent campground adjacent to the Chief Joseph Scenic Byway (Highway 296). There are hiking and horseback-riding trails, plus nearby corrals for horses. ⚲ *Pit toilets, drinking water, bear boxes, fire grates, picnic tables, swimming (creek)* ⟋*12 sites* ⊠*17 mi north of Cody on Hwy. 120, then 25 mi northwest on Hwy. 296* ☎*307/527–6921* ⊕*www. fs.fed.us/r2/shoshone* ⊟*No credit cards* ☉ *Closed Nov.–Apr.*

⚠ **Ponderosa Campground.** Within walking distance (three blocks) of the Buffalo Bill Historical Center plus restaurants and shops, this is a large family-run facility with separate areas for tents and RVs. Each RV spot has its own picnic table. You can even stay in a tepee or pitch your own tent in a primitive camping area (without any nearby facilities) known as the OK Corral in the canyon above the Shoshone River. ⚲ *Flush toilets, full hookups, dump station, drinking water, guest laundry, showers, picnic tables, public telephone, play area, Wi-Fi* ⟋*137 full hookups, 50 tent sites; 6 tepees, 7 camping cabins* ⊠*1815 8th St.* ☎*307/587–9203* ⊟*No credit cards* ☉ *Closed mid-Oct.–mid-Apr.*

NIGHTLIFE AND THE ARTS

NIGHTLIFE

A trip to Cody isn't complete without a chance to scoot your boots to live music, usually provided by the local group West the Band, at **Cassie's** (⊠*214 Yellowstone Ave.* ☎*307/527–5500* ⊕ *www.cassies.com*). The tunes are a mix of classic country, the band's Western originals, and today's hits. Opened in 1922 by a local "sportin' lady," Cassie's today has three levels with a restaurant, a dance floor, and three bars.

THE ARTS

During summer months free live concerts are held each Friday evening at the **park on Sheridan Avenue.** Jazz, country, or soft rock could be on the program. **The Yellowstone Jazz Festival** (☎*307/587–2777 or 800/393–2639*) takes place during a mid-July weekend. Venues are spread around town. Contact the Chamber of Commerce for exact dates and time.

After dinner, Monday through Saturday from May through September, head to the art deco Cody Theater for **Dan Miller's Cowboy Music Revue** (⊠*1171 Sheridan Ave.* ☎*307/272–7855* ⊕ *www.cowboymusicrevue. com* ⊠ *$14)*. Miller, a radio and TV host, singer, and actor, performs all three roles, along with his Empty Saddles band.

⟳
Fodor's Choice
★

The two-day **Plains Indian Powwow** (⊠*720 Sheridan Ave.* ☎*307/587–4771* ⊕ *www.bbhc.org*), in late June, brings together hoop dancers, traditional dancers, and jingle dancers from various tribes. The performances take place outdoors at the Buffalo Bill Historical Center.

Open Range Images (⊠*1201 Sheridan Ave.* ☎*307/587–8870* ⊕ *www. openrangeimages.com*) displays and sells the work of regional photographers. Wyoming's wildlife, flora, and landscapes provide the primary scenes, but less traditional themes also are presented.Sculptures and paintings by such artists as James Bama, Chris Navarro, and Kevin Red Star are displayed at **Big Horn Galleries** (✉ *1167 Sheridan Ave.* ☎ *307/527–7587* ⊕ *www.bighorngalleries.com*). **Simpson Gallagher Gallery** (✉ *1161 Sheridan Ave.* ☎ *307/587–4022* ⊕ *www.simpsongallaghergallery.com*) showcases and sells contemporary representational art by Harry Jackson, Margery Torrey, Greg Scheibel, and others.

SHOPPING

★ Sheridan Avenue, Cody's main drag, is a great place to browse and shop among its many Native American and Western-theme shops. Most carry high-quality goods, but for those desiring the real McCoy, one way to judge an item's authenticity is to determine whether it's made from natural or artificial materials. Head to the **Custom Cowboy Shop** (✉ *1286 Sheridan Ave.* ☎ *800/487–2692*) to stock up on top-quality cowboy gear and clothing, ranging from hats and vests for men to women's shirts and jackets; there's even gear for your horse here. Also available are CDs by top Western recording artists such as Ian Tyson, Don Edwards, and Michael Martin Murphey.

Women shop at the **Plush Pony** (✉ *1350 Sheridan Ave.* ☎ *307/587–4677*) for "uptown Western clothes" ranging from leather belts to stylish skirts, jeans, jackets, and dresses. The **Wyoming Buffalo Company** (✉ *1270 Sheridan Ave.* ☎ *307/587–8708 or 800/453–0636*) sells buffalo-meat products, such as sausage and jerky, in addition to specialty foods such as huckleberry honey.

POWDER RIVER BASIN AND THE BLACK HILLS

9

The rolling grassland of the Powder River Basin, in the far northeastern corner of Wyoming, is the ancestral homeland of the Lakota Sioux. On its western edge the Big Horn Mountains are both a popular winter recreational area and a beautiful backdrop for the communities of Sheridan, Big Horn, and Buffalo. As you drive east the mountains give way to coal mines (particularly around Gillette), oil fields, and family ranches, many of which were established in the 19th century by Basque sheepherders. Now one of the least-populated parts of America, the basin encompasses the vast Thunder Basin National Grasslands.

The Black Hills border the Powder River Basin to the east, where a couple of hundred thousand acres of Black Hills National Forest spill out of South Dakota into Wyoming. Thickly wooded with pine, spruce, and fir trees, the rocky slopes stand in stark contrast to the prairie below. Some of the most famous characters of the American West roamed across this soil, including Wild Bill Hickok, Calamity Jane, and the Sundance Kid, who took his name from a local town.

Dropping a Line

Casting into a clear stream or placid blue lake is a popular pastime all over Wyoming, with good reason: the waters of the entire state teem with trout, pike, whitefish, catfish, and bass of all kinds. Most fishing enthusiasts stick to the land near Yellowstone, leaving the blue-ribbon streams of northern Wyoming relatively underutilized. The Bighorn River, Powder River, Crazy Woman Creek, Keyhole Reservoir, and Buffalo Bill Reservoir are all excellent angling venues.

Fly-fishing is especially big here, and there's no shortage of outfitters to equip you, both in the towns and in the wilderness. Anyone with a pole—be it an experienced fly-fisher or novice worm dangler—is respected out here. All the same, if you're a beginner, you'd do well to hire a guide. Tackle-shop staff can direct you to some good fishing spots, but you're more likely to find the choicest locations if you have an experienced local at your side.

SHERIDAN

147 mi north of Casper via I–25 and I–90.

Proximity to the Big Horn Mountains and Bighorn National Forest makes Sheridan (population 15,804) a good base for hiking, mountain biking, skiing, snowmobiling, and fly-fishing, and the small city's European-flavored cowboy heritage makes it an interesting stop for history buffs. Soon after trappers built a simple cabin along Little Goose Creek in 1873, the spot became a regional railroad center. Cattle barons, many of them English and Scottish noblemen, established ranches that remain the mainstay of the economy. Sheridan still has ties to Britain's aristocracy; in fact, Queen Elizabeth II herself has paid the town a visit. Recently, coal mines and oil wells to the east have brought much-needed jobs and tax income to this community of 16,429 residents.

GETTING HERE AND AROUND

Whether you're arriving from the northwest or east via Interstate 90 or the south via Interstate 25, the Big Horn Mountains provide an impressive backdrop to this decidedly Western town. Take the East 5th Street or East Brundage Lane exits to Big Horn Avenue and the downtown core, and then park and walk to a host of art galleries, Western stores, restaurants, and outfitters. You'll also discover 30 bronzes on permanent display and another 27 sculptures on extended display throughout downtown.

VISITOR INFORMATION

Sheridan Chamber of Commerce (⌂ Box 707, Sheridan 82801 ☎ 307/672-2485 or 800/453-3650 ⊕ www.sheridanwyomingchamber.org).

EXPLORING

Built in 1923 as a vaudeville theater called the Lotus, the **Wyo Theater** was closed and nearly demolished in the early 1980s. A strong show of support from the community saved the building, and now the refurbished art deco structure hosts everything from orchestras and ballets to lectures and Broadway revivals, especially in the summer. ⊠ *42 N. Main St.* ☎ *307/672–9084* ⊕ *www.wyotheater.com.*

Although local cowboy legend Don King died in 2007, his sons still operate **King's Saddlery and Ropes,** where they've been hand-tooling saddles since the 1940s. They also make high-quality equipment for area ranchers and professional rodeo performers. King's has crafted gear for many celebrities, including Queen Elizabeth II. The real treat is found across a small alley directly behind the store, where a small museum is chock-full of Western memorabilia, ranging from more than 400 vintage firearms and hand-crafted spurs to historical photographs, wildlife mounts, and arguably the largest collection of Western saddles anywhere. ⊠ *184 N. Main St.* ☎ *307/672–2702.*

★ A Flemish Revival mansion built in 1913 for John B. Kendrick, cattleman and one of Wyoming's first governors and senators, is now the **Trail End State Historic Site.** The furnishings and exhibits in the home are designed to depict early-20th-century ranching on the Plains. Highlights include elegant hand-carved woodwork and a third-floor ballroom. ⊠ *400 Clarendon Ave.* ☎ *307/674–4589* ⊕ *www.trailend.org* ☞ *$2 for Wyoming residents, $4 for others* ⊙ *Apr. and Sept.–mid-Dec., daily 1–4; June–Aug., daily 9–6.*

Fodor'sChoice
★ Evidence of the area's Old World ties can be found at the **Sheridan Inn,** just a few blocks from downtown near the old railroad depot. Modeled after a hunting lodge in Scotland, the 1893 building sports 69 gables in a show of architectural splendor not often seen around these parts. On the National Register of Historic Places, the inn once lured the likes of Herbert Hoover, Will Rogers, and Ernest Hemingway, and Buffalo Bill auditioned performers here for his Wild West Show. The Inn underwent a $4.8 million restoration from 2006 to 2009, employing "green" technologies, and an additional $2.8 million is expected to be spent on 22 refurbished guest rooms slated to open in mid-2010. The original Buffalo Bill Bar, an oak-and-mahogany monstrosity on the main floor, is purported to be a gift sent from England by Queen Victoria. Lunch and dinner are served all year in the restored 1893 Grille & Spirits restaurant, although patrons are no longer permitted to bring their horses inside. ⊠ *856 Broadway* ☎ *307/674–2777* ⊕ *www.sheridaninn. com* ☞ *Free; self-guided tour $2* ⊙ *Mon.–Sat. 11–9.*

SPORTS AND THE OUTDOORS

FLY-FISHING More of a custom adventure company than an outfitter, **Angling Destinations** (⊠ *151 Powder Horn Rd.* ☎ *800/211–8530*) arranges multi-day fishing trips to some of the most remote locations of Wyoming, Montana, and Idaho, as well as international destinations. For the less experienced angler, **Big Horn Mountain Sports** (⊠ *334 N. Main St.* ☎ *307/672–6866*) provides fly-fishing lessons and guided trips and rents and sells complete fly-fishing gear (including flies, rods, reels, waders, and hats), as well as travel gear and other outdoor apparel. The full-service **Fly Shop of the Big Horns** (⊠ *227 N. Main St.* ☎ *307/672–5866*) offers rentals, fishing apparel and gear, guided trips on private and public waters, and a fly-fishing school, as well as the largest fly selection in the region.

9

WHERE TO EAT

$$$$
CONTEMPORARY
Fodor's Choice
★

✕ **Oliver's Bar and Grill.** Yellows, greens, and soft light accent this industrial-feeling restaurant with big-city ambience. Oliver's has an open kitchen, paintings from local artists on the walls, and perennially high marks from its loyal clientele. The ever-changing and eclectic menu carries Western favorites like burgers, salads, and chicken dishes as well as osso buco, pan-roasted Alaskan halibut, gnocchi, shrimp, and pasta. Seasonal items include Copper River salmon from Alaska, available here in early summer for only three weeks. From the kitchen bar you can watch chefs prepare your meal, and there's a diverse and inviting wine list, too. Afterward, such fine desserts as crème brûlée and cheesecake with port or cognac offer decadent possibilities. ⌂ *55 N. Main St.* ☎ *307/672–2838* ▭ *AE, D, MC, V.*

$$
AMERICAN
☾

✕ **Sanford's Grub and Pub.** This replica of a hole-in-the-wall founded by a bunch of college buddies inhabits a massive old building but evokes the TV Land junk alley that inspired its name. With its mishmash of vintage signs, crusty car tags, sports team ephemera, and scrap heaps of memorabilia, it's no surprise that Sanford's menu of miscellany would be unlike most found in Wyoming. Here Cajun and Southwestern-style dishes, seafood pasta, and big juicy steaks compete with whimsically named half-pound burgers, salads, sandwiches, and Dixieland favorites, including a huge selection of beers and a couple of in-house brews that might offend some finer folks. Oh yeah, try the Rocky Mountain Oysters if you dare! ⌂ *1 E. Alger St.* ☎ *307/674–1722* ▭ *D, DC, MC, V.*

WHERE TO STAY

$$$–$$$$
▦ **Eatons' Guest Ranch.** This spread is credited with inventing the dude ranch, back in the late 19th century, and it's still going strong as a working cattle ranch. Its location, west of Sheridan on the edge of the Bighorn National Forest, makes it ideal for horseback riding, fishing, cookouts, and pack trips. The ranch can accommodate 125 guests, and reservations for the summer should be made by March. The facilities are a collection of one-, two-, and three-bedroom cabins and the main lodge. There's a one-week minimum stay mid-June through August and a three-day minimum stay the rest of the season. **Pros:** a pleasantly rustic experience, with plenty of chances to spend time in the saddle. **Cons:** with the minimum stay, if you find you don't like ranch life you're stuck for a few days. ⌂ *270 Eatons' Ranch Rd., Wolf* ☎ *307/655–9285 or 800/210–1049* ⎙ *307/655–9269* ⊕ *www.eatonsranch.com* ↩ *51 cabins* ⚅ *In-room: no a/c, no TV. In-hotel: pool, laundry facilities* ▭ *MC, V* ☻ *Closed Oct.–May* ▯ *FAP.*

$–$$
▦ **The Mill Inn.** A former flour mill near a bridge has been converted into this motel, listed on the National Register of Historic Places, with a lobby featuring wood accents and Native American art. Some rooms face a busy street. The building has six stories, but the top four floors are business offices. Furniture from a dude ranch fills much of the motel, giving it a definite Western style. **Pros:** near downtown; complimentary breakfast; historic accents with great photography by L. A. Huffman. **Cons:** some think the inn is overpriced, with some rooms too close to outside traffic and the bathrooms unaccommodating to those with disabilities. ⌂ *2161 Coffeen Ave.* ☎ *307/672–6401 or 888/357–6455*

307/672–6401 ⊕ *www.sheridanmillinn.com* ⇱ *45 rooms* ♺ *In-room: (refrigerator some), Wi-Fi. In-hotel: gym, some pets allowed* ☰ *AE, D, MC, V* ⧫ *CP.*

$$$$ ⊡ **The Ranch at Ucross.** If you're looking to get in touch with yourself— or your traveling companion—the banks of Piney Creek may well be the place. In the foothills of the Big Horns, this tranquil Old West–style ranch is as relaxed as it gets. The four bedrooms in the restored 1912 house, as well as modern rooms and cabins around the property, are given a warm Western feel by gnarled wood lamps, quilt-covered beds, and comfy throws for cool nights. Most accommodations open onto spacious decks where you can read, watch the sun set, or just gaze at the Canada geese, grazing horses, and towering cottonwoods. Do some mountain-stream fishing or take a pack trip to mountain lakes. Good for family reunions and retreats. **Pros:** stay one night, and you'll wish you owned the place; quiet and relaxing. **Cons:** a long way from any- where. ⊠ *2673 U.S. Hwy. 14, Clearmont* ☎ *307/737–2281 or 800/447– 0194* ⊕ *www.blairhotels.com* ⇱ *31 rooms, 6 cabins* ♺ *In-room: no TV, Wi-Fi. In-hotel: bar, tennis courts, pool, some pets allowed* ☰ *AE, D, MC, V* ⧫ *FAP.*

$$–$$$$ ⊡ **Sheridan Holiday Inn.** The soaring atrium of this five-story lodging, which is five minutes from downtown by car, has a waterfall and is filled with overstuffed chairs and couches, as well as Scooter's Sports Bar. With white-and-blue accents and tan walls, the rooms are typical of chain hotels, but most have some Western-style touches, and some look out on the Big Horn Mountains. Three restaurants ($–$$$$), the Brew Garden, The Greenery, and Sugarland Mining Company, serve burgers, steak, chicken, and pasta. The Sunday brunch buffet starts at $12.95. **Pros:** large and modern; good dining options; a putting green in the lobby; a fun and friendly staff. **Cons:** this is a big hotel with a busi- ness feel, even though it's not right downtown. ⊠ *1809 Sugarland Dr.* ☎ *307/672–8931 or 888/752–5338* 🖳 *307/672–6388* ⊕ *www.meetin- sheridan.com* ⇱ *212 rooms, 7 suites* ♺ *In-hotel: 3 restaurants, bar, pool, gym, Wi-Fi, some pets allowed* ☰ *AE, D, DC, MC, V.*

CAMPING ⌂ **Big Horn Mountain KOA Campground.** On the banks of Big Goose Creek minutes away from downtown Sheridan is this KOA, a well-developed campground with a basketball court, horseshoe pits, and a miniature- golf course. ♺ *Flush toilets, full hookups, drinking water, guest laundry, showers, picnic tables, electricity, public telephone, play area, swim- ming (pool), Wi-Fi* ⇱ *45 full hookups; 33 tent sites, 14 with electricity; 6 cabins* ⊠ *63 Decker Rd.* ☎ *307/674–8766* ⊕ *www.koakampgrounds. com* ☰ *AE, D, MC, V.*

SHOPPING

The suburban malls that have drained so many downtowns are absent in Sheridan; instead, Main Street is lined with mostly homegrown—and sometimes quirky—shops.

In a break from typical gift stores stocked with rubber tomahawks, the **Best Out West Mall** (⊠ *109 N. Main St.* ☎ *307/674–5003*) is a two-story bazaar of Western paraphernalia, with booths hawking everything from spurs to rare books. Some items are new, but most are antiques. You can find a great selection of cowboy boots, hats, and other Western apparel at **Dan's Western Wear**(✉ *226 N. Main St.* ☎ *307/672–9378* ⊕ *www. danswesternwear.com*), which boasts of the largest sign on Main Street. The **Crazy Woman Trading Company** (✉ *120 N. Main St.* ☎ *307/672–3939* ⊕ *crazywomantradingco.com*) sells unique gifts and antiques, including deluxe coffees and T-shirts picturing a black bear doing yoga. Murphy McDougal, the store's CEO (and the owners' golden retriever), is usually sleeping near the front door.

BIG HORN

9 mi south of Sheridan via Hwy. 335.

Now a gateway to Bighorn National Forest, this tree-lined town with mountain views was originally a rest stop for emigrants heading west. An outpost on the Bozeman Trail, which crossed Bozeman Pass, Big Horn City in the mid-19th century was a lawless frontier town of saloons and roadhouses. After pioneers brought their families to the area in the late 1870s, the rowdy community quieted down. It never officially incorporated, so although it has a post office, fire department, and school, there is no bona-fide city government.

GETTING HERE AND AROUND

Located between the vast Bighorn National Forest and Interstate 90 south of Sheridan, the town of Big Horn can be reached via State Highway 335 south to County Road 28 East. It's a town of just 198 residents; you won't have trouble finding your way around.

EXPLORING

⟳ A hand-hewn-log blacksmith shop, built in 1879 to serve pioneers on their way to the goldfields of Montana, houses the **Bozeman Trail Museum**, the town's historical repository and interpretive center. The jewel of its collection is the Cloud Peak Boulder, a stone with names and dates apparently carved by military scouts just two days before the Battle of the Little Bighorn, which was fought less than 100 mi to the north in 1876. The staff is very friendly to children, and there are some old pipe organs that kids are encouraged to play. ✉ *335 Johnson St.* ☎ *307/674– 1600* ▭ *Free* ☉ *Memorial Day–Labor Day, weekends 11–6.*

If you're not staying at a ranch and you want to get a look at one of the West's finest, visit the **Bradford Brinton Memorial**, south of Big Horn on the old Quarter Circle A Ranch. The Brinton family didn't exactly rough it in this 20-room clapboard home, complete with libraries, fine furniture, and silver and china services. A reception gallery displays changing exhibits from the Brinton art collection, which includes such Western artists as Charles M. Russell and Frederic Remington. ✉ *239 Brinton Rd.* ☎ *307/672–3173* ⊕ *www.BBMandM.org* ▭ *$4* ☉ *Memorial Day–Labor Day, daily 10–4.*

Big Horn is an access point to the 1.1-million-acre **Bighorn National Forest**, which has lush grasslands, alpine meadows, rugged mountaintops, canyons, and deserts. There are numerous hiking trails and camping spots for use in the summer, and it's a popular snowmobiling area in the winter. ✉ *Ranger station, 2013 Eastside 2nd St., Sheridan* ☎ *307/674– 2600* ⊕ *www.fs.fed.us/r2/bighorn.*

WHERE TO EAT AND STAY

$$$$
AMERICAN

✗**Bozeman Trail Inn.** A wood-slat building with a false front and tin roof, this is the oldest operating bar in Wyoming, established in 1882. The inn's only sign is painted on a mock covered wagon that's perched above the door. The kitchen serves standard burgers and sandwiches for lunch, steak and seafood for dinner, and prime rib on weekends. Try the 14-ounce hand-cut buffalo rib-eye steak. ✉ *158 Johnson St.* ☎ *307/672–9288* ☐ *MC, V.*

$$–$$$

▦ **Spahn's Big Horn Mountain Bed and Breakfast.** Ron and Bobbie Spahn have guest rooms at their soaring log home in the Big Horn Mountains. The rooms have tongue-and-groove woodwork, peeled-log beams, ruffled curtains, and peeled-log beds, and overlook Native American lands, mountain peaks, and Montana in the distance. It's more than a traditional B&B: you can participate in cookouts and guided tours that include a wildlife-viewing trip. Family-style dinners, including fresh grilled steaks, are served by arrangement. **Pros:** 40-acre property adjoining a million acres of public forests; you can literally see 100 mi; secluded; short drive to Big Horn (7.5 mi). **Cons:** solar-powered electricity and limited-hot-water showers might exasperate some; doesn't take credit cards. ✉ *Hwy. 335, 7 mi south of Big Horn, Box 579* ☎ *307/674–8150* ☐ *307/674–8150* ⊕ *www.bighorn-wyoming. com* ⊃ *3 rooms* ☐ *In-room: no a/c, no phone, no TV* ☐ *No credit cards* ❖⊙ *BP.*

THE PLACE TO BE IN BUFFALO

Buffalo's Occidental Hotel may be the best place to begin your visit to the Big Horn region, particularly on a Thursday night. That's when you'll find bluegrass music flowing through the doors of its Western-style saloon, and virtually the entire town assembled there. It's a good chance to meet the locals, enjoy some great music and refreshments, and contribute to local charities, for which the gathering has raised thousands of dollars. This is as friendly as the West gets.

BUFFALO

34 mi south of Big Horn via I–90, U.S. 87, and Hwy. 335.

Buffalo is a trove of history and a hospitable little town in the foothills below Big Horn Pass. Here cattle barons who wanted free grazing and homesteaders who wanted to build fences fought it out in the Johnson County War of 1892. Nearby are the sites of several skirmishes between the U.S. military and Native Americans along the Bozeman Trail. Buffalo is 182 mi due west on I–90 of Sturgis, South Dakota. The first week of every August, Sturgis hosts a very popular and legendary bikers' conclave. So, if you're passing through at this time of year, don't be surprised to hear the occasional roar of hogs.

GETTING HERE AND AROUND

Arriving in the region via Interstate 25, take the U.S. 87 or East Hart Street exit west to South Main Street and the downtown business district. Then park and explore area parks, shops, museums, and the famed

Occidental Hotel. For a quiet, shaded picnic, check out City Park and Prosinski Park a block southwest of the Occidental.

VISITOR INFORMATION

Buffalo Chamber of Commerce (✉ 55 N. Main St. ☎ 307/684–5544 or 800/227–5122 ⊕ www.buffalowyo.com).

EXPLORING

Fodor'sChoice The **Jim Gatchell Memorial Museum** is the kind of small-town museum
★ that's worth stopping for if you're interested in the frontier history of the region, including the Johnson County Cattle War. It contains Native American, military, outlaw, and ranching artifacts collected by a local pharmacist who was a close friend of area Native Americans. Starting in 2007 the museum began a $300,000 renovation expected to be completed in 2011. Visitors will discover new exhibits and interpretive opportunities. ✉ 100 Fort St. ☎ 307/684–9331 ⊕ www.jimgatchell. com ⊠ $5 ☉ Memorial Day–Labor Day, Mon.–Sat. 9–6, Sun. noon–6; Sept., weekdays 9–5.

★ Signs bearing a buffalo symbol mark the **Clear Creek Trail** (☎ 307/684–5544 or 800/227–5122), which consists of about 13 mi of trails following Clear Creek through Buffalo and past historic areas. The trail has both paved and unpaved sections that you can traverse on foot or by bicycle. Along it you see the Occidental Hotel (made famous by Owen Wister's novel *The Virginian*), a brewery and mill site, and the site of Fort McKinney, now the Veterans' Home of Wyoming. You can also use the trail for wildlife viewing, photography, and access to fishing.

★ **Fort Phil Kearny State Historic Site** was the focal point of Red Cloud's War, and Phil Kearny was probably the most fought-over fort in the West. This is the largest 8-foot stockaded, Hollywood-style fort ever built by the U.S. military, covering 17 acres; it experienced almost daily skirmishing against Cheyenne or Lakota warriors. Its location eventually led to major battles, including the December 21, 1866, Fetterman Fight, in which 81 soldiers were killed (the only time in American military history that a whole command was defeated to the last man) and the August 2, 1867, Wagon Box Fight, in which 32 men held their position in a daylong fight against more than 800 Lakota. This battle was considered a victory by both sides.

The fort's mission was to protect travelers on the Bozeman Trail going to the goldfields in southern Montana. However, there are theories that it may have been placed in what were the last and best hunting grounds of the Northern Plains tribes in order to draw them away from the railroad construction across southern Wyoming that was occurring at the same time. In the fall of 1868 the U.S. government signed the Fort Laramie Treaty, ending Red Cloud's War—the only war Native Americans won against the United States. The treaty closed the Bozeman Trail, making all the land between the Black Hill and Big Horn Mountains, and the land between the Yellowstone and North Platte rivers, unceded Indian land where whites could not go. However, it also for the first time established Indian Agencies along the Missouri River for the different Lakota tribes. So, although the Indians won the war, they lost the peace. As part of the treaty, Fort Phil Kearny was abandoned in

August 1868. Within two weeks, it is believed, Cheyenne, under Two Moon, occupied and then burned the fort to the ground. No original buildings remain at the site, but fort building locations are marked, and the visitor center has good details. The stockade around the fort was re-created after archaeological digs in 1999. ⊠ *528 Wagon Box Rd., Banner* ✛ *15 mi north of Buffalo on I–90* ☏ *307/684–7629* ⊕ *www. philkearny.vcn.com* ⊠ *$2 for Wyoming residents, $4 others* ☉ *Interpretive center mid-May–Sept., daily 8–6.*

SPORTS AND THE OUTDOORS

The forested canyons and pristine alpine meadows of the Big Horn Mountains teem with animal and plant life, making this an excellent area for hiking and pack trips by horseback. The quality and concentration of locals willing to outfit adventurers are high in Buffalo, making it a suitable base camp from which to launch an expedition.

The folks at **South Fork Mountain Lodge & Outfitters** (⊠ *7558 Hwy. 16 W, 16 mi west of Buffalo on U.S. 16* ☏ *307/267–2609* ⊕ *southfork-lodge. com*) can customize about any sort of adventure you'd like to undertake in the Big Horns, whether it's hiking, hunting, fishing, horseback riding, snowmobiling, or cross-country skiing. The company can arrange for all of your food and supplies and provide a guide, or render drop-camp services for more experienced thrill seekers.

HORSEBACK
RIDING AND
PACK TRIPS

Located on a 24,000-acre working ranch, the **Powder River Experience** (⊠ *297 Upper Powder River Rd., 6 mi. south of U.S. 14, Arvada* ☏ *307/758–4381 or 888/736–2402*) gives you the chance to ride on the open range or to pack into the backcountry for an overnight stay at a log cabin. You're also encouraged to watch or personally experience as many ranch activities as you wish, whether it's branding, cattle driving, or calving.

Trails West Outfitters (⊠ *140 Flagstaff Way, Buffalo* ☏ *307/684–5233 or 888/283–9793* ⊕ *www.trailswestoutfitters.com*) arranges multiday pack trips in the Shoshone National Forest. The company also operates shorter wilderness excursions and drop camps for more independent adventurers.

WHERE TO EAT

$$
AMERICAN

✕ **Colonel Bozeman's Restaurant and Tavern.** This eatery, which is literally on the Bozeman Trail, serves decent food, from chicken, taco, and Cobb salads to local favorites such as prime-rib melts and club sandwiches or bison steak, burgers, and king-cut prime-rib plates amid Western memorabilia. You can also dine outdoors on the deck and sip from the large selection of microbrews. ⊠ *675 E. Hart St.* ☏ *307/684–5555* ⊟ *D, MC, V.*

$$$
CONTEMPORARY
Fodor'sChoice
★

✕ **The Virginian Restaurant.** Named for the 1902 Owen Wister novel that made Buffalo famous, this is the dining salon of the beautifully restored Occidental Hotel. Dishes made from organic beef range from buffalo rib eye to chateaubriand and filet mignon with béarnaise sauce. Further delights include shrimp scampi, swordfish, and chicken marsala, all served amid the splendor of antique mirrors, Western art, and Victorian lamps; many fixtures are from the original building. Period lamps light the 19th-century brass-color tin ceiling, and wainscoting accents the maroon-colored walls. There's also a kids' menu, and starry-eyed couples can dine in candlelit seclusion within the old Stockmen's bank vault. ⊠ *10 N. Main St.* ☎ *307/684–0451* ═ *AE, D, MC, V.*

$$$
STEAKHOUSE
★

✕ **Winchester Steak House.** You can tie up your car in front of the hitching racks before this Western-style eatery in a false-front building. The Winchester has prime rib, steak, and more steak, plus appetizers, a good wine list, and a large rock fireplace and small bar. Locals rave about the place. ⊠ *117 Hwy. 16 E* ☎ *307/684–8636* ═ *MC, V* ☺ *Closed Sun. and Mon. No lunch.*

WHERE TO STAY

$–$$$
Fodor'sChoice
★

🏨 **Occidental Hotel.** This enchanting, fully restored grand hotel, founded in 1880, served emigrants on the Bozeman Trail, two U.S. presidents, and some of Wyoming's most colorful characters. Owen Wister immortalized the Occidental in his 1902 novel *The Virginian,* about the Johnson County Cattle War. After winning a high-stakes poker game in 1918, one family held on to the hotel for 58 years, keeping intact all of its original furnishings and architectural accents. A lavish $1 million–plus restoration under current owners John and Dawn Wexo spruced up the Victorian-style rooms and tin-ceiling lobby, saloon, and restaurant, sparing this living treasure from the wrecking ball. Most spectacular among the many nostalgic suites are the Clear Creek, with its six-post cherrywood bed, adjoining sitting room, and spacious bathroom, and the elegant Teddy Roosevelt Suite, furnished with a high-back walnut bed, an antique hardwood desk, and a claw-foot tub. Down in the saloon, the 25-foot bar, stained-glass shade, and tin ceiling look brand new—except for 23 bullet holes, revealing origins in the cutthroat, quick-draw era. On Thursday nights nowadays there's a bluegrass hootenanny jam-packed with friendlies. **Pros:** well-stocked library; gracious service; owners on premises; well-appointed rooms; gourmet restaurant. **Cons:** no pool; old plumbing (but it doesn't leak). ⊠ *10 N. Main St.* ☎ *307/684–0451* ⊕ *occidentalwyoming.com* ➷ *6 rooms, 8 suites* ⚐ *In-hotel: 2 restaurants, Wi-Fi, some pets allowed* ═ *AE, D, MC, V.*

$$$$
☺
Fodor'sChoice
★

🏨 **Paradise Guest Ranch.** Not only does this dude ranch 13 mi west of Buffalo have a stunning location at the base of some of the tallest mountains in the range, but it's also one of the oldest (circa 1907) and most progressive, as evidenced by its adults-only month (September) and two ladies' weeks. The rest of the summer has extensive children's programs, with everything from overnight pack trips to a kids' rodeo. Adult programs involve sing-alongs and fancy barbecues. The wranglers are very careful about matching riders to appropriate horses; multiday trips venture into the Bighorn National Forest and Cloud Peak Wilderness Area. Three full-time guides on staff take guests on fly-fishing excursions. Cabins are simple. Some have fireplaces; all have full baths and kitchenettes. There's a one-week minimum stay. **Pros:** clean cabins with rustic, beautiful views; hospitable staff; good children's programs; ask about 30% June discounts. **Cons:** minimum stays; 11.5 mi to Buffalo; cold mornings until late spring. ⊠ *282 Hunter Creek Rd., off U.S. 16, Box 790* ☎ *307/684–7876* 🖷 *307/684–7380* ⊕ *www.paradise-ranch.com* ➷ *18 cabins* ⚐ *In-room: no a/c, no phone, kitchen, no TV.*

In-hotel: bar, pool, children's programs (ages 6–18), laundry facilities ⊟ *No credit cards* ☉ *Closed Oct.–Apr.* ❍⌶ *FAP.*

CAMPING ⚠ **Deer Park Campground.** Although one section of this campground is quiet and relaxed, reserved for campers over 55, the main campsites are busy. In addition to a heated pool and a hot tub, Deer Park offers ice-cream socials at night for $1. ♿ *Flush toilets, full hookups, partial hookups (electric and water), drinking water, showers, guest laundry, general store, picnic tables, electricity, swimming (pool), Wi-Fi* ✇ *33 full hookups, 33 partial hookups, 34 tent sites; 3 cabins* ✉ *146 U.S. 16* ☎ *307/684–5722 or 800/222–9960* ⊕ *www.deerparkrv.com* ⊟ *D, MC, V* ☉ *May–Sept.*

NIGHTLIFE

Regulation pool tables and live country music and dancing every Friday and Saturday night (no cover charge) make the **Buffalo Sports Bar** (✉ *106 U.S. 16* ☎ *307/684–9999)* a local favorite. You'll find flat screens and pub fare.

GILLETTE

70 mi east of Buffalo on I–90.

With a population that's boomed from 17,000 in 1981 to 32,000 in 2009, Gillette, the metropolis of the Powder River Basin, has many relatively new properties, restaurants, and shopping opportunities. Thanks to the region's huge coal mines, it's one of Wyoming's wealthiest cities, and as a result it has an excellent community infrastructure that includes the Cam-Plex, a multiuse events center that hosts everything from crafts bazaars and indoor rodeos to concerts and fine-arts exhibits. Gillette is also a gateway town for Devils Tower National Monument, the volcanic plug that is one of the nation's most distinctive geological features and a hot spot for rock climbers.

Gillette has worked hard to make itself presentable, but you don't have to look very hard to find a shovel bigger than a house at one of its giant strip mines. Once a major livestock center, from which ranchers shipped cattle and sheep to eastern markets, the city now mines millions of tons of coal each year and ships it out to coal-fired power plants. In fact, if Gillette (and surrounding Campbell County) were its own nation, it would be the world's sixth-greatest producer of coal. Currently the county turns out nearly a third of all American-mined coal. Gillette, however, is a big fish in a small pond, one of only two incorporated towns in the county (the other is Wright, population 1,347).

GETTING HERE AND AROUND

Gillette may well serve as the heartbeat of eastern Wyoming, with a new college, a new $45 million recreation center that opened in late 2009, new Interstate 90 overpasses, and 17 mi of new roadways built in town in 2008. Travelers will find new hotels, restaurants, shopping malls, and residential areas south of Interstate 90 on State Highway 59/South Douglas Highway. Heading north on the same route takes motorists directly downtown.

9

VISITOR INFORMATION

Gillette Convention and Visitor's Bureau (✉ *1810 S. Douglas Hwy.* ☎ *307/686–0040 or 800/544–6136* ⊕ *www.2chambers.com/gillette1.htm*).

EXPLORING

Anything from a rodeo or crafts show to a concert or melodrama could be going on at the **Cam-Plex,** Gillette's multiuse facility. There's something scheduled almost every day; call or check the Web site for details. ✉ *1635 Reata Dr.* ☎ *307/682–0552, 307/682–8802 for tickets* ⊕ *www. cam-plex.com* ⊙ *Check Web site for schedule.*

You can fish, boat, swim, and camp at **Keyhole State Park.** Bird-watching is a favorite activity here, as up to 225 species can be seen on the grounds. ✉ *353 McKean Rd.* ☎ *307/756–3596, 307/756–9529 marina information* ⊕ *wyoparks.state.wy.us/index.asp* ☞ *$2 resident vehicle, $4 nonresident vehicle; camping $6 resident vehicle, $12 nonresident vehicle.*

Local artifacts, including bits, brands, and rifles, make up the collection at the Campbell County–run **Rockpile Museum.** The museum's name comes from its location next to a natural rock-pile formation that served as a landmark for pioneers and cattle drives. ✉ *900 W. 2nd St.* ☎ *307/682–5723* ⊕ *www.rockpilemuseum.com* ☞ *Free* ⊙ *Mon.– Sat. 9–5.*

At the **Eagle Butte Coal Mine,** 5 mi north of Gillette, shovels and haul trucks dwarf anything you're likely to see in a science-fiction movie. There's a surprising amount of wildlife, from falcons to deer to bobcats, dwelling in and around the huge pits. You can register for the summer tours of the mine at the Gillette Visitors Center. ✉ *Gillette Visitors Center, Flying J Travel Plaza, 1810 S. Douglas Hwy. 59* ☎ *307/686–0040 or 800/544–6136* ☞ *Free* ⊙ *Tours June–Aug., daily 9 AM and 11 AM.*

OFF THE BEATEN PATH

Thunder Basin National Grasslands. A vast 890-square-mi area that stretches from the edge of the Black Hills almost to the center of Wyoming, Thunder Basin truly is the outback of America. Except for a handful of tiny towns, deserted highways, and coal mines, it is entirely undeveloped. Farmers from the east settled this area at the end of the 19th century, hoping to raise crops in the semiarid soil. Experienced only with the more humid conditions east of the Rockies, the farmers failed, and the region deteriorated into a dust bowl. Most of the land has reverted to its natural state, creating millions of acres of grasslands filled with wildlife. Among the many species is one of the largest herds of pronghorn in the world (numbering approximately 26,000), prairie dogs, and burrowing owls that live in abandoned prairie-dog holes. Highway 116, Highway 59, and Highway 450 provide the best access; a few interior dirt roads are navigable only in dry weather. The grasslands, though, are most impressive away from the highways. Take a hike to get a real sense of the vast emptiness of this land. Stop by the District Forest Service Office in Douglas for maps, directions, and tips. ✉ *2250 E. Richards St. Douglas* ☎ *307/358–4690* ⊕ *www.fs.fed.us/r2/mbr/* ☞ *Free* ⊙ *Daily 24 hrs; district office open weekdays 8–4.*

WHERE TO EAT

$$$$
CONTEMPORARY
★

✕ The Chophouse. In the middle of a ranching town in the middle of ranching country, it's no surprise that more than half of this restaurant's menu is devoted to beef. Chef Ray Marini, who helped open the first American restaurant in the Soviet Union, uses only certified Angus, and only cuts that have been aged to his standards. The remainder of the menu is split between pasta and dishes made with fresh fish flown in at Marini's request. Of course, the beef dishes—including the massive 22-ounce bone-in rib eye—remain house favorites. The two dining rooms are on the ground floor of a renovated century-old hotel: one is cheerfully decorated in a Western motif, and the other is accented with dark-wood trim and artwork by Frank Sinatra, one of the owner's favorite celebrities. ✉ *113 S. Gillette Ave.* ☎ *307/682–6805* ▭ *AE, D, MC, V.*

$
CHINESE

✕ Hong Kong. Lunches here are served fast and cheap (between $5 and $6) and include more than 30 different dishes, such as Mongolian beef and cashew chicken. They're popular with the business crowd, so you might want to avoid the noon lunch rush. ✉ *1612 W. 2nd St.* ☎ *307/682–5829* ▭ *AE, D, MC, V.*

WHERE TO STAY

$–$$

▦ Best Western Tower West Lodge. Shades of beige and teal decorate the large, comfortable rooms of this hotel on the west side of town. Among the public spaces are an outdoor courtyard and a lobby with leather couches and chairs grouped around the fireplace. **Pros:** close to a variety of restaurants and easy interstate access. **Cons:** located a fair distance from the downtown area. ✉ *109 N. U.S. 14/16* ☎ *307/686–2210* ⊕ *www.bestwestern.com* ↪ *189 rooms* ₺ *In-hotel: restaurant, bar, pool, gym, Wi-Fi* ▭ *AE, D, DC, MC, V.*

$$–$$$

▦ Clarion Western Plaza. Travelers with a yen for exercise appreciate the gym and a pool of lap-swimming proportions at this motel with everything under one roof. Rooms are decorated in burnt red and cream colors. **Pros:** visitors can grab a cup of coffee at the Mountain Mudd Espresso shop, on-site, or take a dip in the mineral pool. **Cons:** the location provides little variety for nearby restaurants except fast food. ✉ *2009 S. Douglas Hwy.* ☎ *307/686–3000 or 800/424–6423* ⊕ *www. gilletteclarion.com* ↪ *159 rooms, 14 suites* ₺ *In-room: refrigerator (some). In-hotel: restaurant, pool, gym, Wi-Fi* ▭ *AE, D, MC, V.*

DEVILS TOWER NATIONAL MONUMENT

★ *65 mi northeast of Gillette via I–90 and U.S. 14.*

GETTING HERE AND AROUND

Located in extreme northeast Wyoming, America's first national monument can be accessed from several routes. Traveling from the west on Interstate 90, motorists may take U.S. 14 E at Moorcroft 25 mi, then Route 24 6 mi north to Devils Tower. After visiting the monument, travelers may then head south on Route 24, returning to U.S. 14 E to Sundance and I–90. Alternatively, after leaving the monument, stay on Route 24 for a scenic drive through Hulett to the small town of

Aladdin and its quirky General Store, and then return south to I–90 via Route 111.

EXPLORING

As you drive east from Gillette, the highways begin to rise into the forested slopes of the Black Hills. A detour north will take you to Devils Tower, a rocky, grooved butte that juts upward 1,280 feet above the plain of the Belle Fourche River. Native American legend has it that the tower was corrugated by the claws of a bear trying to reach some children on top, and some tribes still revere the site, which they call Bear Lodge. Geologists attribute the butte's strange existence to ancient volcanic activity. Rock climbers say it's one of the best crack-climbing areas on the continent. The tower was a tourist magnet long before a spaceship landed here in the movie *Close Encounters of the Third Kind*. Teddy Roosevelt made it the nation's first national monument in 1906, and it has attracted a steadily increasing throng of visitors ever since—up to nearly half a million people a year.

When you visit Devils Tower, take some time to stop at the **visitor center,** a few miles beyond the park entrance. Exhibits here explain the geology, history, and cultural significance of the monument, and a bookstore carries a wide selection of materials relating to the park. Park rangers can provide updated information on hiking and climbing conditions. ⊠ *Hwy. 110* ☎ *307/467–5283* ⊕ *www.nps.gov/deto/* ⊠ *Cars and motorcycles $10; bicycles and pedestrians $5* ⊙ *Butte daily 24 hrs; visitor center May–Nov., daily 9–5.*

SPORTS AND THE OUTDOORS

HIKING Aside from affording excellent views of Devils Tower and the surrounding countryside, the hiking trails here are a good way to view some of the geology and wildlife of the Black Hills region. The terrain that surrounds the butte is relatively flat, so the popular **Tower Trail,** a paved 1.3-mi path that circles the monument, is far from strenuous. It's the most popular trail in the park, though, so if you're looking for more isolation, try the 1.5-mi **Joyner Ridge Trail** or the 3-mi **Red Beds Trail.** They're a bit more demanding, but the views from the top of Joyner Ridge and the banks of the Belle Fourche River are more than adequate rewards. Both the Tower and Red Beds trails start at the visitor center; Joyner Ridge Trail begins about a mile's drive north from there.

ROCK Climbing is the premier sporting activity at Devils Tower. Acclaimed
CLIMBING as one of the best crack-climbing areas in North America, the monument has attracted both beginners and experts for more than a century. There are few restrictions when it comes to ascending the granite cone. Although climbing is technically allowed all year, there is generally a voluntary moratorium in June to allow for peaceful religious rites performed by local Native American tribes. Additionally, the west face of the formation is closed intermittently in the summer to protect the prairie falcons that nest there.

Before ascending Devils Tower you should sign in at the **visitor center** (⊠ *Hwy. 110* ☎ *307/467–5283*) and discuss conditions with park officials. You can obtain a list of park-licensed guides here; courses are offered at all skill levels and sometimes include excursions into the

Rockies or South Dakota. Some tour operators continue to guide climbs during the voluntary ban in June.

CAMPING

🛖 **Belle Fourche Campground.** Tucked away in a bend of the Belle Fourche River, this campground is small and spartan, but it is the only place in the park where camping is allowed. ♿ *Flush toilets, drinking water, picnic tables* 🔄 *47 sites* ✉ *Hwy. 110* ☎ *307/467–5283* 🖨 *307/467–5350* 🌐 *www.nps.gov/deto/* ♿ *Reservations not accepted* ➖ *No credit cards* ☽ *Apr.–Nov.*

🛖 **Devils Tower KOA.** Less than a mile from Devils Tower, this campground literally lies in the shadow of the famous stone monolith. The view of the sheer granite walls above red river bluffs is one of the property's greatest assets. Another is the bordering Belle Fourche River, which nurtures several stalwart cottonwood and ash trees that provide at least some areas with shade. Weather permitting, the campground stages a nightly outdoor showing of *Close Encounters of the Third Kind.* ♿ *Flush toilets, full hookups, partial hookups (electric and water), drinking water, guest laundry, showers, picnic tables, public telephone, general store, play area, swimming (pool)* 🔄 *25 full hookups, 99 tent sites; 11 cabins, 1 apartment* ✉ *60 Hwy. 110* ☎ *307/467–5395 or 800/562–5785* 🌐 *www.devilstowerkoa.com* ➖ *D, MC, V* ☽ *May–Sept.*

SHOPPING

At **Devils Tower Trading Post** (✉ *57 Hwy. 110* ☎ *307/467–5295*), at the entrance to Devils Tower National Monument, you can purchase informative books, Western art, buffalo hides, clothing, knickknacks, and souvenirs. A giant Harley-Davidson flag (supposedly the world's largest) flies over the store, so it's no wonder that bikers overrun the place during the massive Sturgis Motorcycle Rally the first week of August. The old-fashioned ice-cream parlor, which also serves a mean sarsaparilla, is a real treat in the heat of summer.

SUNDANCE

31 mi southeast of Devils Tower National Monument via U.S. 14.

A combination of traditional reverence and an infamous outlaw's date with destiny put Sundance on Wyoming's map, and continues to draw visitors today. Native American tribes such as the Crow, Cheyenne, and Lakota consider Sundance Mountain and the Bear Lodge Mountains to be sacred. Before whites arrived in the 1870s the Native Americans congregated nearby each June for their Sun Dance, an important ceremonial gathering. The event gave its name to this small town, which in turn gave its name to the outlaw Harry Longabaugh, the Sundance Kid, who spent time in the local jail for stealing a horse. Ranch country and the western Black Hills surround the town.

GETTING HERE AND AROUND

This is a classic small Western town where you'll be tabbed as an outsider if you don't return a "hello" from a passerby on the street. To reach the downtown area, exit Interstate 90 on U.S. 14/E Cleveland Street or Route 585.

EXPLORING

★ Thousands of buffalo bones are piled atop each other at the **Vore Buffalo Jump,** where Native Americans forced buffalos to plunge to their deaths in the era when hunting was done with spears rather than fast horses and guns. ⊠ *Frontage Rd.* ☎ *307/283–1000* ⊕ *www.sundancewyoming. com/vore.htm* ⊠ *Free* ⊙ *Daily.*

Projects by local young people are displayed at the **Crook County Fair and Rodeo** during the first week in August, from cooking and clothing to livestock projects. There also are live music shows, basketball tournaments, a Dutch-oven cook-off, pig wrestling, a micro-brewing contest, a car show and shine, and a ranch rodeo with sheepdog trials and team roping events. ⊠ *Fairgrounds Loop Rd.* ☎ *307/283–2644* ⊕ *www.crookcofair.com* ⊠ *Free.*

WHERE TO EAT

$$ ✕ **Aro Restaurant and Lounge.** This large family diner in downtown Sun-
AMERICAN dance has a cowboys-and-Indians theme and an extensive, well-priced menu. Standards include burgers, prime rib, Southwestern smothered burritos, Reuben sandwiches, and a huge Devils Tower brownie sundae dessert. Locals love this place, so it can be busy. ⊠ *203 Cleveland St.* ☎ *307/283–2000* ⊟ *D, MC, V.*

$ ✕ **Country Cottage.** This one-stop shop in the center of town sells flow-
AMERICAN ers, gifts, and simple meals, including submarine sandwiches. There's a seating area for 40, with oak floors, booths, and small tables. ⊠ *423 Cleveland St.* ☎ *307/283–2450* ⊟ *AE, D, MC, V.*

¢ ✕ **Higbee's Cafe.** This is a classic old-time café with red Naugahyde
AMERICAN booths, great food, and cheap prices, serving breakfast all day. Try the Devils Tower breakfast with biscuits smothered in sausage gravy, with sausage or ham, and an egg. ⊠ *101 N. 3rd St.* ☎ *307/283–2165* ⊟ *MC, V.*

WHERE TO STAY

¢–$$ ⊡ **Bear Lodge Motel.** A cozy lobby, a stone fireplace, and wildlife mounts on the walls distinguish this downtown motel. Hardwood furniture and patterned bedspreads add a slightly Western touch to the spacious, simple bedrooms. DVDs and players are available for use at no charge. **Pros:** downtown location; close to two restaurants. **Cons:** slightly outdated appearance. ⊠ *218 Cleveland St.* ☎ *307/283–1611* 🖷 *307/283–2537* ⊕ *www.bearlodgemotel.com* ⟿ *33 rooms* ⚙ *In-room: refrigerator. In-hotel: laundry facilities, Wi-Fi* ⊟ *AE, D, DC, MC, V.*

¢–$$$ ⊡ **Best Western Inn at Sundance.** Brown carpeting and red drapes decorate the spacious rooms of this hotel. With its inlaid cedar accents and comfortable deck chairs, the room housing the indoor pool is surprisingly stylish for a chain hotel. **Pros:** contemporary furnishings; quiet location. **Cons:** at the edge of town. ⊠ *2719 Cleveland St.* ☎ *307/283–2800 or 800/238–0965* 🖷 *307/283–2727* ⊕ *www.blackhillslodging.com* ⟿ *44* *rooms* ⚭ *In-hotel: pool, laundry facilities, Wi-Fi, some pets allowed* 🖃 *AE, D, MC, V* ⚭⦿⎸ *CP.*

$ 🖵 **Rodeway Inn.** Clean but basic rooms, friendly service, and a comfortable poolside area make this one-story ranch-style motor inn a nice place to stay. It's convenient to I–90 and across the street from area restaurants. Pros: relatively new furniture and carpeting in rooms. Cons: rooms all open to the outside; small lobby. ⊠ *26 Hwy. 585* ☎ *307/283–3737* 📠 *307/283–3738* ⊕ *www.choicehotels.com* ⇆ *42 rooms* ⚭ *In-room: refrigerator (some). In-hotel: pool, laundry facilities, some pets allowed* 🖃 *AE, D, MC, V* ⚭⦿⎸ *CP.*

CAMPING ⚠ **Mountain View RV Park.** Clean and new, this contemporary RV park offers large pull-through sites ideal for the big rigs. ⚭ *Flush toilets, drinking water, guest laundry, picnic tables, swimming (pool), Wi-Fi* ⇆ *33 RV sites, 25 tent sites; 2 cabins* ⊠ *117 Government Valley Rd.* ☎ *307/283–2270 or 800/792–8439* ⊕ *www.mtviewcampground.com* 🖃 *D, MC, V* ⊗ *Apr.–Oct.*

THE NORTH PLATTE RIVER VALLEY

Sweeping down from the Colorado Rockies into the very center of Wyoming, the North Platte River was a key waterway for emigrants because its valley was one of the few places where wagons could safely cross the mountains. A deep pioneer legacy survives here, where several trails converged along the Platte and Sweetwater rivers and snaked through South Pass. Some of the travelers put down roots, and the North Platte River valley remains one of Wyoming's important agricultural areas.

Much of this area is cattle country, for one simple reason: it's flat and dry. On some of the westernmost ranges of short grassland before the Rockies thrust up from the plains, the land is relatively treeless. The human presence consists largely of fences, livestock, a few small cow towns, and the bustling Western city of Casper. Today a hefty share of central Wyoming's wealth derives from its deposits of oil, uranium, and bentonite.

9

CASPER

115 mi south of Buffalo via I–25; 180 mi north of Cheyenne via I–25.

Several excellent museums in Casper illuminate central Wyoming's pioneer and natural history. The state's second-largest city, it's also one of the oldest. Some of the first white people to venture across Wyoming spent the winter here in 1811, on their way east from Fort Astoria in Oregon. Although they didn't stay, they helped to forge several pioneer trails that crossed the North Platte River near present-day Casper. A permanent settlement eventually arose, and was named for Lieutenant Caspar Collins; the spelling error occurred early on, and it stuck. The town has grown largely as a result of oil and gas exploration, and sheep and cattle ranchers run their stock on lands all around the city.

GETTING HERE AND AROUND
A car is your best bet for transportation.

VISITOR INFORMATION
Casper Convention and Visitors Bureau (⊠ *992 N. Poplar St., Casper*
☎ *307/234–5362 or 800/852–1889* ⊕ *www.casperwyoming.info*).

EXPLORING

Ⓒ   Five major immigrant trails passed near or through Casper between
Fodor's Choice   1843 and 1870. The best-known are the Oregon Trail and the Mormon
★   Trail, both of which crossed the North Platte River in the vicinity of
today's Casper. The **National Historic Trails Interpretive Center** examines the
early history of the trails and the military's role in central Wyoming.
Projected onto a series of screens 11 feet high and 55 feet wide, a film
shows Wyoming trail sites and scenes of wagon travelers. You can climb
into a wagon to see what it was like to cross the river, or learn about
Mormon pioneers who traveled west with handcarts in 1856. ⊠ *1501
N. Poplar* ☎ *307/261–7700* ⊜ *$6* ⊙ *Apr.–Oct., daily 8–7; Nov.–Mar.,
Tues.–Sat. 9–4:30.*

The **Fort Caspar Historic Site** re-creates the post at Platte Bridge, which
became Fort Caspar after the July 1865 battle that claimed the lives of
several soldiers, including Lieutenant Caspar Collins. A post depicts
life at a frontier station in the 1860s, and sometimes soldier reenac-
tors go about their tasks. Museum exhibits show the migration trails.
⊠ *4001 Fort Caspar Rd.* ☎ *307/235–8462* ⊕ *www.fortcasparwyoming.
com* ⊜ *May–Sept. $3, Oct.–Apr. $1.50* ⊙ *June–Aug., daily 8–7; May
and Sept., daily 8–5; Oct.–Apr., museum Tues.–Sat. 8–5 (fort buildings closed).*

Ⓒ   The **Casper Planetarium** has multimedia programs on astronomy. There
are also interactive exhibits in the lobby and a gift shop. Public programs, which last an hour, are scheduled regularly in the summer. ⊠ *904
N. Poplar St.* ☎ *307/577–0310* ⊕ *www.natronaschools.org/school.
php?id=112* ⊜ *$2.50* ⊙ *Lobby exhibits weekdays 8:30–5. Public pro-
grams June–Aug., Tues.–Sat. 7 PM–8 PM; Sept.–June, Sat. 7 PM–8 PM;
call for group rates.*

The **Werner Wildlife Museum,** near the Casper College campus, has displays of birds and animals from Wyoming and around the world. ⊠ *405
E. 15th St.* ☎ *307/268–2676, 307/235–2108 for tours* ⊕ *www.casper-
college.edu/community/campus/Werner/index.html* ⊜ *Free* ⊙ *Weekdays 10–4.*

Ⓒ   Casper College's **Tate Earth Science Center and Geological Museum** displays
fossils, rocks, jade, and the fossilized remains of a brontosaurus, plus
other dinosaur bones. ⊠ *125 College Dr.* ☎ *307/268–3068* ⊕ *www.
caspercollege.edu/tate/index.html* ⊜ *Free* ⊙ *Weekdays 9–5, Sat. 10–4.*

Ⓒ   A showcase for regional artists and mostly modern artwork, the **Nico-**
★   **laysen Art Museum and Discovery Center** also exhibits works by national
artists. The building's early-20th-century redbrick exterior and contemporary interior are an odd combination, but this makes the museum all
the more interesting. There are hands-on activities, classes, and children's programs, plus a research library and a Discovery Center. ⊠ *400
E. Collins Dr.* ☎ *307/235–5247* ⊕ *www.thenic.org* ⊜ *$5* ⊙ *Tues.–Sat.
10–5, Sun. noon–4.*

SPORTS AND THE OUTDOORS

With thousands of acres of empty grassland and towering mountains only miles away, the landscape around Casper is full of possibilities for enjoying the outdoors. Casper Mountain rises up 8,000 feet no more than 20 minutes from downtown, providing prime skiing and hiking trails.

Edness Kimball Wilkins State Park (⊠ *I–25, 6 mi east of Casper* ☎ *307/577–5150*) is a day-use area with picnicking, swimming, fishing, and a 3-mi walking path.

HIKING Much of Casper Mountain is taken up by private land, but there are some public trails, including mountain-bike routes and the Braille Trail, a simple hike with plaques (in Braille) that describe the views and ecology of the mountain. The trails can get a little crowded in the summer. Contact the **Casper Convention and Visitors Bureau** (⊠ *992 N. Poplar St.* ☎ *307/234–5362 or 800/852–1889* ⊕ *www.casperwyoming.info*) for more information.

The **Platte River Parkway** hiking trail runs adjacent to the North Platte River in downtown Casper. Access points are at Amoco Park at 1st and Poplar streets, or at Crosswinds Park, on North Poplar Street near the Casper Events Center.

SKIING Perched on Casper Mountain a few miles outside of town is **Hogadon Ski Area** (⊠ *Casper Mountain Rd.* ☎ *307/235–8499*), with a vertical drop of 600 feet. Less than a quarter of the runs are rated for beginners; the rest are evenly divided between intermediate and expert trails. Also here is a separate snowboard terrain park and a modest lodge. **Mountain Sports** (⊠ *543 S. Center* ☎ *307/266–1136*) provides more than just ski and snowboard sales. It also runs Wyomaps, which sells personal Global Positioning System products and provides custom mapping services.

WHERE TO EAT

$$ ✕**El Jarro.** Usually crowded and always noisy, this place serves hearty
MEXICAN portions of Mexican cuisine. The beef fajitas are a favorite, second only to the fine margaritas, which come in glasses the size of bowls. The place is decorated with bright colors, which only seem to encourage the generally rowdy bunch at the bar. ⊠ *500 W. F St.* ☎ *307/577–0538* ▤ *AE, MC, V.*

$$ ✕**Poor Boys Steakhouse.** Reminiscent of a frontier mining camp or West-
STEAKHOUSE ern town, this steak house has blue-and-white-check tablecloths and chair backs, quick service, and large portions of steak, seafood, and chicken. Salad comes in a bucket and is served with fresh, hot bread. Try the Moonshine Mama—grilled chicken breast smothered in mushrooms and Monterey Jack and cheddar cheeses—or enjoy a tantalizingly tender filet mignon with shrimp. For dessert try the Dutch apple pie or Ashley's Avalanche—a huge plate of ice cream, a white-chocolate brownie, cherry-pie filling, chocolate sauce, and whipped cream. ⊠ *739 N. Center St.* ☎ *307/237–8325* ⊕ *www.poorboyssteakhouse.com* ▤ *AE, D, DC, MC, V.*

$$ ✕**Sanford's Grub and Pub.** This lively spot decorated with 20th-century
AMERICAN memorabilia may be a brewery, but children are welcome here in the heart of downtown. The extensive menu includes pastas, pizzas, and

9

calzones. If you're a vegetarian, this is your best bet in Casper for its variety of meatless dishes. ⊠ *241 S. Center St.* ☎ *307/234–4555* ⊟ *AE, D, DC, MC, V.*

WHERE TO STAY

$$ ⊞ **Best Western Ramkota Hotel.** This full-service location, off I–25, has everything under one roof, from dining options to business services. Muted blues, greens, and mauves decorate the large, contemporary rooms, some of which have whirlpool tubs. **Pros:** neighboring Castaway Bay Water Park is popular with kids. **Cons:** typical chain hotel; no pets allowed. ⊠ *800 N. Poplar St.* ☎ *307/266–6000* ⊕ *www.bestwestern-wyoming.com* ⌔ *229 rooms* ⚲ *In-room: Wi-Fi. In-hotel: restaurant, bar, pool* ⊟ *AE, D, DC, MC, V.*

$$ ⊞ **Hampton Inn.** The rooms in this clean and very quiet lodging have coffeemakers, large cable TVs, white fluffy comforters, and easy chairs with ottomans. The location is right by the mountains and down the street from the Casper Events Center. You can also make use of the business center, fitness center, and continental breakfast. **Pros:** recently built structure; Cloud Nine beds give rooms a cozy feel. **Cons:** doesn't allow pets. ⊠ *1100 N. Poplar Rd.* ☎ *307/235–6668* ⊕ *www.hampton-inn.com* ⌔ *100 rooms* ⚲ *In-room: refrigerator (some). In-hotel: pool, laundry facilities, Wi-Fi* ⊟ *AE, D, DC, MC, V* ⊚⍥ *CP.*

$–$$ ⊞ **Parkway Plaza.** With a large convention center, the Parkway is one of Casper's busiest motels. The rooms are quiet and large, with double vanities, one inside the bathroom and one outside. Furnishings are contemporary in the rooms but Western in the public areas. The pool has wading and diving sections. Attached to the hotel is Old Town, a small amusement park with an arcade, a miniature-golf course, and a NASCAR-sanctioned go-kart track. **Pros:** with the attached amusement park there is plenty for the kids. **Cons:** this is a winding maze of a hotel. ⊠ *123 W. E St.* ☎ *307/235–1777 or 800/270–7829* 🖷 *307/235–8068* ⊕ *www.parkwayplaza.net* ⌔ *285 rooms* ⚲ *In-hotel: restaurant, bar, pool, gym, laundry facilities, Wi-Fi* ⊟ *AE, D, MC, V.*

THE ARTS

Both the Casper Symphony Orchestra and the Casper College Theater Department perform at the 465-seat **Gertrude Krampert Theater** (⊠ *Casper College, 125 College Dr.* ☎ *307/268–2500*). **Stage III Community Theater** (⊠ *904 N. Center St.* ☎ *307/234–0946*) presents plays and other dramatic performances at various times.

SHOPPING

The largest shopping center in a 175-mi radius, the **Eastridge Mall** (⊠ *601 S.E. Wyoming Blvd.* ☎ *307/265–9392*), anchored by such standbys as Sears, JCPenney, Target, and Macy's, is popular and important to locals.

Southern Wyoming

WITH CHEYENNE AND LARAMIE

WORD OF MOUTH

In Cheyenne, there is a museum that covers the history of rodeo and the west. It's a lot of fun.

—rockinrobin

Fort Laramie is very interesting; it's not too far off of I–25. I would stay on I–25 for most of the trip because towns in Wyoming are few and far between. Some are an hour apart, and make sure you keep your gas tank filled up! It's a pretty drive.

—tgbwc

Updated
by Shauna
Stephenson

A journey across southern Wyoming takes you through a wonderfully diverse landscape, from the wheat fields of the southeast to the mountains of the Snowy Range to the stark and sometimes hauntingly beautiful Red Desert, where wild horses still roam freely.

Cheyenne, the largest city in Wyoming and the state capital, is the cornerstone community at the eastern edge of the state and host to the annual Cheyenne Frontier Days rodeo. Evanston, a town settled by railroad workers in 1869, anchors the western edge of the state. In between are the cities of Laramie, Rock Springs, and Green River, all of which owe their origin to the construction of the Union Pacific Railroad.

Several smaller communities with unique museums, access to diverse recreational opportunities, and one-of-a-kind personalities lure travelers away from I–80, the main route through the region. Medicine Bow has a rich cowboy heritage portrayed in Owen Wister's 1902 Western novel *The Virginian*. Saratoga has a resort flavor and some of the best dining and lodging of any small town in the state. Encampment and Baggs are little, slow-paced, historically rich towns. In these and other towns across the region you can travel back in time by attending recreations of mountain-man rendezvous, cowboy gatherings, and other historical events.

Once covered by an ocean and now rich in fossils, southwest Wyoming's Red Desert, or Little Colorado Desert, draws people in search of solitude (there's plenty of it), pioneer trails (more miles of 19th-century overland emigrant trails than anywhere else in the country), and recreation ranging from wildlife-watching to fishing and boating on Flaming Gorge Reservoir, south of the town of Green River. The region is rich in history as well: here John Wesley Powell began his 1869 and 1871 expeditions down the Green River, and Jim Bridger and Louis Vasquez constructed the trading post of Fort Bridger, now a state historic site. And all across the region, evidence remains of the Union Pacific Railroad, which spawned growth here in the 1860s as workers laid the iron rails spanning the continent.

ORIENTATION AND PLANNING

GETTING ORIENTED

I–80 is the major artery through this region, running from Cheyenne at the southeast corner of the state west to Evanston in the southwest corner of the state.

Once you explore this region, it becomes apparent why Wyoming has earned the nickname the "Cowboy State." The plains remain a prime grazing spot for wild horses, cattle, and sheep. As you drive west, the plains give way to the snowcapped mountains of the appropriately named Snowy Range. After a few more hours driving west you'll reach the Red Desert, with unique rock formations and herds of wild horses and pronghorn.

PLANNING

WHEN TO GO

The best time to visit southern Wyoming is in summer or fall, when most lodging properties and attractions are open (some smaller museums, sights, and inns close between Labor Day and Memorial Day). Summer is the season for most local community celebrations, including the region's longest-running and biggest event, Cheyenne Frontier Days, held the last full week in July.

Some areas, particularly around Laramie, Centennial, Saratoga, and Encampment, are great for winter sports, including cross-country skiing, snowmobiling, and ice fishing. Bear in mind that in parts of southern Wyoming it can—and often does—snow every month of the year, so even if you're visiting in July, bring some warm clothes, such as a heavy jacket and sweater.

PLANNING YOUR TIME

All across southern Wyoming you can immerse yourself in cowboy and Old West heritage. Some of your driving can take you along pioneer emigrant trails; you can hike or ride horses on other segments. A good place to start your explorations is at one of the two major frontier-era forts, Fort Laramie (northeast of Cheyenne) and Fort Bridger (in the southwest), that served emigrants heading to Oregon, California, and Utah. From Fort Laramie, drive to Cheyenne, where you can see one of America's most complete horse-drawn wagon collections. Continue west to learn about territorial and frontier justice at the historic prisons in Laramie and Rawlins. For a rare treat, spend some time visiting the region's small museums, which preserve evocative relics of the past. Start with the Grand Encampment Museum, Medicine Bow Museum, Little Snake River Valley Museum (in Baggs), and Carbon County Museum (in Rawlins), and then head west to tour the Sweetwater County Historical Center in Green River and Ulrich's Fossil Museum west of Kemmerer.

10

If you like to spend time in the outdoors, by all means take the scenic routes. From Cheyenne, follow Highway 210, which provides access to Curt Gowdy State Park. Traveling west of Laramie, head into the Snowy Range and Sierra Madre Mountains by taking Highway 130, which links to Saratoga by way of Centennial, or take Highway 230 to Encampment and then travel over Battle Highway (Highway 70) to Baggs. The mountain country of the Snowy Range and Sierra Madres provides plenty of opportunity for hiking, horseback riding, mountain biking, fishing, and camping. There are hundreds of thousands of acres to explore on trails ranging from wheelchair-accessible paths to incredibly difficult tracks for experienced backcountry travelers only. The action continues in winter, when snowmobilers ride free-style across open country (rather than on trails), cross-country skiers glide through white landscapes, and snowshoers explore hushed forests. The lakes

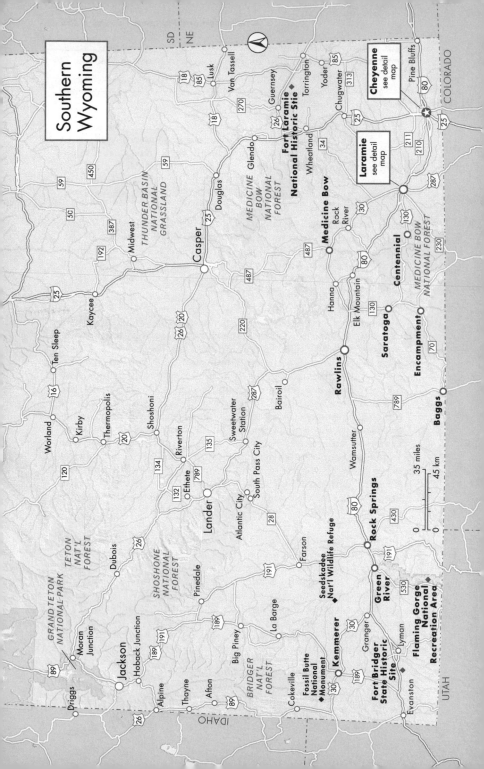

that attract anglers during summer are equally busy in winter, when ice fishing rules.

For a firsthand Western experience, stay at one of the guest ranches near Cheyenne, Laramie, or Saratoga, where you can take part in cowboy activities and ride horses. Wild horses range freely in southwest Wyoming's Red Desert, even though the area is being heavily developed for energy production. You can spot the magnificent creatures west of Baggs and north and south of Rock Springs.

GETTING HERE AND AROUND

AIR TRAVEL

Cheyenne, Laramie, and Rock Springs' Sweetwater County are the commercial airports in the area, and they all have service to and from Denver only. Many visitors to southeastern Wyoming fly into Denver International Airport and drive the 90 mi north to Cheyenne.

TOP REASONS TO GO
■ The Cheyenne Botanic Gardens are a great place to lose yourself in the scenery.
■ Cheyenne Frontier Days is the perfect place to experience the Wild West.
■ The hot springs at the Saratoga Inn Resort are havens of relaxation.
■ Bear River State Park has miles of trails with stunning views to the south.
■ With hundreds of aspen trees, Battle Highway in the fall is an explosion of color.

Airport Information Cheyenne Airport (✉ *200 E. 8th Ave., Cheyenne* ☎ *307/634-7071* ⊕ *www.cheyenneairport.com*). **Laramie Airport** (✉ *3 mi west of Laramie off Hwy. 130* ☎ *307/742-4165* ⊕ *www.laramieairport.com*). **Sweetwater County Airport** (✉ *382 Hwy. 370, Rock Springs* ☎ *307/352-6880* ⊕ *www.rockspringsairport.com*).

BUS TRAVEL

Greyhound Lines connects Cheyenne, Evanston, Laramie, Rawlins, and Rock Springs to Denver and Salt Lake City.

Bus Information Greyhound Lines (☎ *800/454-2487* ⊕ *www.greyhound. com* ✉ *5401 Walker Rd., Cheyenne* ☎ *307/635-1327* ✉ *106 N. 3rd St., Evanston* ☎ *307/789-1803* ✉ *1300 S. 3rd St., Laramie* ☎ *307/742-5188* ✉ *102 W. Cedar St., Rawlins* ☎ *307/324-4196* ✉ *1695 Sunset Dr., Suite 114, Rock Springs* ☎ *307/362-2931*).

10

CAR TRAVEL

A car is essential for exploring southern Wyoming. I–80 is the major route through the region, bisecting it from east to west. In places it runs parallel to U.S. 30. Other major access roads include U.S. 287, connecting Laramie and Medicine Bow; Highway 130, serving Centennial and Saratoga; Highway 230, running through Encampment; and Highway 70, connecting Encampment and Baggs.

Although distances between towns can be long, gasoline and other automobile services are available in each community and at various points roughly 20 to 40 mi apart along I–80. When traveling here in winter, be prepared for whiteouts and road closings (sometimes for hours, occasionally for more than a day). Always carry a blanket and warm clothing when driving in winter, along with a safety kit that includes snack food and water. Cell-phone service is getting better but is still sporadic in areas where mountains might interfere with cell towers.

Note that the Snowy Range Pass section of Highway 130, between Centennial and Saratoga, and the Battle Highway section of Highway 70, west of Encampment, close during cold weather, generally from mid-October until Memorial Day.

Contact the Wyoming Department of Transportation for information on road conditions.

Information **Wyoming Department of Transportation** (☎ *307/777–4484, 307/772–0824 from outside Wyoming for road conditions, 888/996–7623 from within Wyoming for road conditions, or 511 from a cell phone ⊕ www.wyoroad. info/).* **Wyoming Highway Patrol** (☎ *307/777–4301, 800/442–9090 for emergencies, #4357 (#HELP) from a cell phone for emergencies ⊕ whp.state.wy.us/index.htm).*

RESTAURANTS

Almost anywhere you dine in southern Wyoming, beef plays a prominent role on the menu; prime rib and steak are often specialties. Standard fare at many small-town restaurants includes burgers and sandwiches, and several eateries serve outstanding Mexican dishes. The pickings can be a bit slim for vegetarians, although most menus have at least one vegetable pasta dish or meatless entrée. Jeans and a T-shirt are acceptable attire for most places (even if the folks at the next table happen to be dressed up). Cowboy hats are always welcome.

HOTELS

Because I–80 traverses this region, there are countless chain motels, but many other interesting accommodations are available. Southern Wyoming has a large number of independent lodging properties ranging from bed-and-breakfasts to lodges to historic hotels. Dude ranches are a unique lodging experience that let you sample a taste of wrangling life, and you can even stay in a remote mountain cabin in the heart of the national forest.

WHAT IT COSTS					
	¢	$	$$	$$$	$$$$
Restaurants	under $8	$8–$12	$13–$20	$21–$30	over $30
Hotels	under $70	$70–$100	$101–$150	$151–$200	over $200

Restaurant prices are for a main course at dinner, excluding sales tax of 4%–7%. Hotel prices are for two people in a standard double room in high season, excluding service charges and 5%–10% tax.

CAMPING

Just about every community in the region has private campgrounds and RV parks. The Wyoming Campground Association can provide information on these campgrounds.

You can also camp on public lands managed by the U.S. Forest Service and local Bureaus of Land Management; these camping opportunities range from dispersed camping with no facilities to campgrounds with water, fire pits, and picnic tables. Some of the best camping spots are in the Medicine Bow–Routt National Forest near the communities of Centennial, Saratoga, Encampment, and Baggs. Camping near lakes and reservoirs is possible west of Cheyenne at Curt Gowdy State Park and south of Green River at Flaming Gorge National Recreation Area.

Information Kemmerer District Bureau of Land Management (☎ *307/828–4500* ⊕ *www.wy.blm.gov/kfo/info.htm*). **Rawlins District Bureau of Land Management** (☎ *307/328–4200* ⊕ *www.blm.gov/wy/st/en/field_offices/Rawlins. htm/*). **Rock Springs District Bureau of Land Management** (☎ *307/352–0256* ⊕ *www.blm.gov/wy/st/en/field offices/Rock_Springs htm/*). **U.S. Forest Service** (☎ *303/275–5350* ⊕ *www.fs.fed.us/r2*). **Wyoming Campground Association** (☎ *307/684–5722* ⊕ *www.campwyoming.org/*).

CHEYENNE

Cheyenne is Wyoming's largest city, but at just over 50,000 people it is not a place where you'll have to fight traffic or wait in lines—except, perhaps, during the last nine days in July, when the annual Cheyenne Frontier Days makes the city positively boom. Throughout the year it offers a decent variety of shopping, plus attractions ranging from art galleries to museums to parks.

Born in 1867 as the Union Pacific Railroad inched its way across the plains, Cheyenne began as a rowdy camp for railroad gangs, cowboys, prospectors heading for the Black Hills, and soldiers. It more than lived up to its nickname: "Hell on Wheels." But unlike some renegade railroad tent cities, which disappeared as the railroad tracks pushed farther west, Cheyenne established itself as a permanent city, becoming the territorial capital in 1868. Its wild beginnings gave way to the late 19th century to respectability with the coming of the enormously wealthy cattle barons, many of them English. They sipped brandy at the Cheyenne Club and hired hard cases such as Tom Horn (1860–1903) to take care of their competitors—which in many cases meant killing rustlers—on the open range.

Cheyenne became the state capital in 1890, at a time when the rule of the cattle barons was beginning to weaken after harsh winter storms in the late 1880s and financial downturns in the national economy. But Cheyenne's link to ranching didn't fade, and the community launched its first Cheyenne Frontier Days in 1897, an event that continues to this day. During the late July celebration—the world's largest outdoor rodeo extravaganza—the town is up to its neck in bucking broncs and bulls and joyful bluster. The parades, pageantry, and parties require the endurance of a cattle hand on a weeklong drive.

GETTING HERE AND AROUND

As with much of Wyoming, a car will be your primary mode of transportation here. Although the city has a public bus system, it can be difficult to navigate and is rarely used by tourists.

10

A GOOD TOUR OF CHEYENNE

Park your car at the **Old West Museum** ❶, within Frontier Park; this museum houses displays on the history of the region, plus the largest collection of horse-drawn vehicles anywhere in Wyoming. After you tour the museum, cross the street for a stroll through the **Cheyenne Botanic Gardens** ❷.

Head south on Carey Avenue; make a left on 24th Street to reach the **Wyoming State Capitol** ❸. Park along the street or turn right onto

Central Avenue to look for parking. Take a self-guided tour of the capitol building, and note the statue out front of Esther Hobart Morris, who helped make Wyoming the first state to grant women the right to vote. Cross Central Avenue to the **Wyoming State Museum** ❹, housing artifacts from across the state.

TIMING
You could visit all of the sights within the city in a day. Several sights close on Sunday.

I–25 runs north–south through the city; I–80 runs east–west. Central Avenue and Warren Avenue are quick north–south routes; the former goes north one way and the latter runs south one way. Several major roads can get you across town fairly easily, including 16th Street (U.S. 30), which gives you easy access to downtown. Most places of interest are in the downtown area. Most shopping is also downtown or along Dell Range Boulevard on the north side of town. Note that there are a few one-way streets in the downtown area.

TOURS
The Cheyenne Trolley takes a $10, 1½-hour tour of the historic downtown area and Frances E. Warren Air Force Base. Included in the price is admission to the Old West Museum, Nelson Museum, and Depot Museum. The trolley runs from mid-May to mid-September, Monday–Saturday at 10 and 1:30, Sunday at 11:30. Tickets are sold at the Cheyenne Area Convention and Visitors Bureau on weekdays and at the Wrangler shop, at the intersection of 16th and Capitol streets, on weekends. For a self-guided walking tour of the downtown and Capitol area, contact the Cheyenne Area Convention and Visitors Bureau.

VISITOR INFORMATION
Cheyenne Area Convention and Visitors Bureau (⊠ *One Depot Square, 121 W. 15th St., Suite 212, Cheyenne* ☎ *307/778–3133 or 800/426–5009* ⊕ *www. cheyenne.org*).

EXPLORING CHEYENNE

Numbers correspond to points of interest on the Cheyenne map.

TOP ATTRACTIONS

❷ **Cheyenne Botanic Gardens.** A vegetable garden, roses and other flowers, cacti, and both perennial and annual plants bloom within the greenhouse conservatory and on the grounds here. Be sure to visit the Paul Smith Children's Village across the parking lot from the conservatory. ⊠ *710 S. Lions Park Dr.* ☎ *307/637–6458* ⊕ *www.botanic.org/*

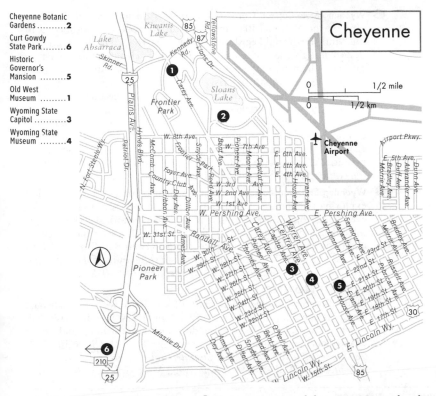

Cheyenne

🖾 *Donations accepted* ☾ *Conservatory weekdays 8–4:30, weekends 11–3:30; grounds stay open dawn–dusk.*

❻ Curt Gowdy State Park. You can fish, boat, hike, and picnic at this park named for Wyoming's most famous sportscaster, who got his start at local radio stations in the 1940s. The park, which is 24 mi west of the city, is popular with hikers, mountain bikers, and equestrians. There are almost 30 mi of hiking and biking trails. 🖾 *1319 Hyndslodge Rd., off Hwy. 210 (Happy Jack Rd.)* 🕾 *307/632–7946* ⊕ *wyoparks.state.wy.us/index.asp* 🖾 *Daily use $4 resident vehicles, $6 nonresident vehicles; camping $10 residents, $17 nonresidents* ☾ *Daily 24 hrs; entrance fee station, 7 AM–11 PM.*

❶ Old West Museum. This museum within Frontier Park houses some 60,000 artifacts—including more than 150 carriages, the largest collection of horse-drawn vehicles in the state—relating to rodeos, ranching, and Cheyenne Frontier Days. Guided tours are geared to children. During Frontier Days the museum hosts the Governor's Invitational Western Art Show and Sale, which exhibits works by top Western wildlife and landscape artists from across the country. The museum also features an interactive learning center for children. 🖾 *4610 N. Carey Ave.* 🕾 *307/778–7290* ⊕ *www.oldwestmuseum.org* 🖾 *$7* ☾ *Weekdays 9–5, weekends 10–5, with extended hrs during Frontier Days, in late July.*

FodorsChoice
★

10

❸ Wyoming State Capitol. Construction on this Corinthian-style building, now on the National Register of Historic Places, was authorized by the Ninth Territorial Legislative Assembly in 1886. The dome, covered in 24-karat gold leaf and visible from all roads leading into the city, is 50 feet in diameter at the base and 146 feet high. Standing in front is a statue of Esther Hobart Morris, a proponent of women's suffrage. One of Wyoming's nicknames is the "Equality State" because of its early advocacy of women's rights. Thanks to Wyoming's informal ways, it's not unusual to find the governor wandering the halls of the capitol. You can take a self-guided tour of state offices and the Senate and House chambers. Guided tours are also provided by appointment when time permits. ⊠ *Capitol Ave.* ☎ *307/777–7220* ⊕ *ai.state.wy.us/capitoltour/ index.htm* ⊠ *Free* ⊙ *Weekdays 8–5.*

❹ Wyoming State Museum. Several permanent exhibits are dedicated to
ℭ exploring the heritage, culture, and landscape of Wyoming, covering everything from natural resources to wildlife to historical events. There's a hands-on exhibit geared to children, and the museum hosts several additional temporary exhibits each year. ⊠ *Barrett Building, 2301 Central Ave.* ☎ *307/777–7022* ⊕ *wyomuseum.state.wy.us* ⊠ *Free* ⊙ *May– Oct., Mon.–Sat. 9–4:30; Nov.–Apr., weekdays 9–4:30, Sat. 10–2.*

WORTH NOTING

❺ Historic Governor's Mansion. Between 1905 and 1976 (when the state built a new residence for the governor), 19 Wyoming first families made their home in this Colonial Revival building. Period furnishings and ornate chandeliers remain in nearly every room. ⊠ *300 E. 21st St.* ☎ *307/777– 7878* ⊕ http://*wyoparks.state.wy.us/Site/SiteInfo.asp?siteID=18* ⊠ *Free* ⊙ *Sept.–May, Wed.–Sat. 9–5; June–Aug., Mon.–Sat. 9–5, Sun. 1–5.*

WHERE TO EAT

$$$ ✗**The Albany.** Historic photographs of early Cheyenne set the tone for
AMERICAN this downtown icon, a place that seems as old as the city itself (the structure was built circa 1900). It's a bit dark, and the booths are a bit shabby, but the American food is solid. Now if only you could get the walls to tell their stories. No doubt they've heard it all, as many of the movers and shakers in Cheyenne's past (and a few in its present) have eaten here. The menu lists hot and cold sandwiches, salads, and burgers, plus prime rib, steak, pork, lamb, and seafood. ⊠ *1506 Capitol Ave.* ☎ *307/638–3507* ▭ *AE, D, DC, MC, V* ⊕ *www.albany-cheyenne.com.*

$$$ ✗**Little Bear Steakhouse.** Locals rave about this classic American steak
STEAK house decorated with a Western theme. The seafood selections are
★ diverse and well prepared. Try the New York strip steak or the rib eye; salmon is fixed in several ways. ⊠ *1700 Little Bear Rd.* ☎ *307/634– 3684* ▭ *AE, D, DC, MC, V* ⊕ *www.littlebearinn.com.*

$$ ✗**Los Amigos.** Mexican sombreros, serapes, and artwork on the walls
MEXICAN complement the south-of-the-border food at this local favorite south of downtown. Deep-fried tacos and green chili are popular items, and the portions are big. ⊠ *620 Central Ave.* ☎ *307/638–8591* ▭ *AE, D, MC, V* ⊙ *Closed Sun. and Mon.* ⊕ *www.losamigoscheyenne.com.*

$ **✗ Shadows.** This downtown spot in the historic Union Pacific Railroad
AMERICAN Depot has its own brewery. The bar looks out on the trains that still pass
through Cheyenne. Eat sandwiches, stone-oven pizzas, pasta, fresh fish,
or steak in the bar or the adjacent restaurant. ⊠ *115 W. 15th St., Suite
1* ☎ *307/634–7625* ⊟ *AE, D, MC, V* ⊕ *www.shadowspub.com.*

$$ **✗ Texas Roadhouse.** Close to the Dell Range Boulevard shopping dis-
STEAK trict, this steak house also serves chicken, pork, and pasta. Favorite
menu items include the chicken with portobello mushroom and the
barbecue ribs. The Western atmosphere includes buckets of peanuts;
when you eat the nuts, throw the shells on the hardwood floor just
like cowboys did in the 1800s. You can wet your whistle at the bar.
⊠ *1931 Bluegrass Circle* ☎ *307/638–1234* ⊟ *AE, D, MC, V* ⊕ *www.*
texasroadhouse.com.

WHERE TO STAY

$$ **Holiday Inn.** Perched high atop a hill, this large hotel is a reliable
stop for weary travelers. The lobby has modern furniture and a cozy
fireplace; rooms are furnished with attractive upholstery and down
comforters. Stop by Sandalwoods for a meal ($$) or the Fireside Lounge
for a drink. **Pros:** right off the interstate for easy access; cozy accommo-
dations. **Cons:** not within walking distance of downtown area. ⊠ *204
W. Fox Farm* ☎ *307/638–4466* ⊕ *www.holidayinn.com/cheyennewy*
↪ *244 rooms* ⬧ *In-room: refrigerator, Wi-Fi. In-hotel: restaurant, room
service, bar, pool, gym, laundry service, Wi-Fi, parking (free)* ⊟ AE,
DC, MC, V.

$$–$$$$ **Little America Hotel and Resort.** An executive golf course and driving
Fodor'sChoice range are the highlights of this resort at the intersection of I–80 and
★ I–25. Most guest rooms are spread among several buildings clustered
around the swimming pool, and some are attached to the common
public areas via a glassed-in breezeway. On the 80-acre property are
30,000 square feet of newly renovated meeting space, making it the
largest conference center in Wyoming. Grab a cup of coffee, mocha, or a
sandwich to go at Carol's Cafe (¢), or dine at the luxuriously decorated
Hathaway's restaurant ($$$), which serves breakfast, lunch, and din-
ner (the Sunday brunch is a highlight). On the menu you will find sea-
food, steak, and prime rib. **Pros:** newly remodeled rooms and 37-inch
high-definition televisions. **Cons:** golf course is only 9 holes. ⊠ *2800
W. Lincolnway* ☎ *307/775–8400 or 800/445–6945* ☎ *307/775–8425*
⊕ *www.littleamerica.com* ↪ *188 rooms* ⬧ *In-room: refrigerator, Wi-Fi.
In-hotel: restaurant, room service, bar, golf course, pool, gym, laundry
facilities, laundry service* ⊟ *AE, D, DC, MC, V.*

$$–$$$ **Nagle Warren Mansion.** This delightful Victorian mansion B&B, built
Fodor'sChoice in 1888, has gorgeous woodwork, ornate staircases, and period fur-
★ niture and wallpaper. Antiques furnish the lavish rooms, which are
named for figures associated with the mansion's history; some rooms
have gas fireplaces. Close to downtown, the B&B is near restaurants
and within walking distance of shops. **Pros:** elegant, historic surround-
ings with many services such as English high tea and concierge. **Cons:**
high demand for lodging here requires that you plan ahead for accom-
modations. ⊠ *222 E. 17th St.* ☎ *307/637–3333 or 800/811–2610*

10

CLOSE UP

Cheyenne Frontier Days

One of the premier events in the Cowboy State is Cheyenne Frontier Days, held the last full week of July every year since 1897. The event started as a rodeo for ranch-riding cowboys who liked to show off their skills; now it consumes all of Cheyenne for nine days, when 250,000 to 300,000 people come into town.

Parades, carnivals, and concerts fill the streets and exhibition grounds, but rodeo remains the heart of Frontier Days, drawing the best cowboys and cowgirls each year. There is no rodeo quite like this one, known by the nickname "Daddy of 'Em All."

BY THE NUMBERS

Cheyenne Frontier Days includes nine afternoon rodeos; nine nighttime concerts; eight days of Native American dancing (Saturday–Saturday); four parades (Saturday, Tuesday, Thursday, and Saturday); three pancake breakfasts (Monday, Wednesday, and Friday); one U.S. Air Force air show (Wednesday); and one art show (all month).

THE RODEOS

Dozens of the top Professional Rodeo Cowboys Association contenders come to Cheyenne to face off in bull riding, calf roping, saddle or bareback bronc riding, and steer wrestling. Women compete in barrel racing; and trick riders and rodeo clowns break up the action. In one of the most exciting events, three-man teams catch a wild horse and saddle it, and then one team member rides the horse around a track in a bronc-busting rendition of the Kentucky Derby. Frontier Days wraps up with the final rodeo, in which the top contestants from a week's worth of rodeos compete head-to-head.

EXTRACURRICULARS

Each night, concerts showcase top country entertainers such as Kenny Chesney, Toby Keith, and Tim McGraw (be sure to buy tickets in advance). Members of the Northern Arapaho and Eastern Shoshone tribes from the Wind River Reservation perform dances at a temporary Native American village where they also drum, sing, and share their culture. The parades show off a huge collection of horse-drawn vehicles, and the free pancake breakfasts feed as many as 12,000 people in two hours. Crowds descend on the midway for carnival rides and games.

BOOTS AND BOOKS

Of course, there's plenty of shopping: at the Western wear and gear trade show you can buy everything from boots and belts to home furnishings and Western art. And you can pick up regional titles at book signings by members of the Western Writers of America.

PLAN AHEAD

Cheyenne Frontier Days entertains both kids and adults, in large numbers. It not only takes over Cheyenne but fills lodgings in nearby Laramie, Wheatland, Torrington, and even cities in northern Colorado. If you plan to attend, make your reservations early—some hotels book a year out.

For further information and to book rodeo and concert tickets, contact **Cheyenne Frontier Days** (✉ Box 2477, Cheyenne 82003 ☎ 307/778–7222 locally, 800/227–6336 elsewhere ⊕ www.cfdrodeo.com). The Web site is a useful resource: you can buy tickets online, see a schedule of activities, and order a brochure, all well in advance of the event itself.

🕮 *307/638–6839* ⊕ *www.naglewarrenmansion.com* ➹ *12 rooms* ⚤ *In-room: no a/c, Wi-Fi. In-hotel: gym* ☰ *AE, MC, V* ⦿*ĺ BP.*

CAMPING   🛆 **Curt Gowdy State Park.** In rolling country with pine forest and a profusion of wildflowers during spring and summer, Curt Gowdy is a good camping spot 24 mi west of the city. The park has picnic sites and areas for swimming, boating, and fishing. The campsites can be used for tents or trailers. *⚤ Flush toilets, pit toilets, dump station, drinking water, fire pits, picnic tables, public telephone, play area, swimming (lake)* ➹ *150 sites* ⊠ *1319 Hyndslodge Rd., off Hwy. 210* 🕮🕮 *307/632–7946* ⊕ *wyoparks.state.wy.us/index.asp* ☰ *No credit cards.*

🛆 **Terry Bison Ranch.** In addition to being a full-service campground and RV park with a restaurant and occasional entertainment, this is a working bison ranch, with nearly 2,500 head on the property. *⚤ Flush toilets, full hookups, drinking water, guest laundry* ➹ *86 full hookups, 100 tent sites; 7 cabins, 13 bunkhouse rooms* ⊠ *I–25 Service Rd. near the Colorado state line* 🕮 *307/634–4171* 🕮 *307/634–9746* ⊕ *www. terrybisonranch.com* ☰ *D, DC, MC, V.*

🛆 **Wyoming Campground and Mobile Home Park.** Two of the attractions at this campground are a swimming pool and Internet service. It's on the south side of Cheyenne. *⚤ Flush toilets, full hookups, partial hookups (electric), dump station, drinking water, guest laundry, showers, picnic tables, electricity, public telephone, play area, swimming (pool), Internet* ➹ *50 full hookups, 50 RV sites, 100 tent sites* ⊠ *I–80, Exit 377* 🕮🕮 *307/547–2244* ☰ *AE, D, DC, MC, V* ☺ *May–Oct.*

NIGHTLIFE AND THE ARTS

The dance floor and rock and roll beckon at **The Crown Bar** (⊠ *222 W. Lincolnway* 🕮 *307/778–9202*). You'll find live country and western plus rock and roll Tuesday through Saturday, dancing, and drinks at **The Outlaw** (⊠ *312 S. Greeley Hwy.* 🕮 *307/635–7552*).

Go see what's playing at the historic **Lincoln Movie Palace** (⊠ *1615 Central Ave.* 🕮 *307/637–7469* ⊕ *www.wyomovies.com* ➹ *$3*)

A wide variety of cultural events, including concerts, theater productions, dance recitals, and performances by the Cheyenne Symphony Orchestra take place at **Cheyenne Civic Center** (⊠ *2101 O'Neil Ave.* 🕮 *877/691–2787* or *307/637–6363* ⊕ *www.cheyenneciviccenter.org*). Original oil paintings, sculpture, and other art are sold at **Manitou Gallery** (⊠ *1715 Carey Ave.* 🕮 *307/635–0019*).

SHOPPING

For the best women's Western-style clothing in the city, ranging from belts, pants, shirts, and skirts to leather jackets, visit **Just Dandy** (⊠ *212 W. 17th St.* 🕮 *307/635–2565*). **Wrangler** (⊠ *1518 Capitol Ave.* 🕮 *307/634–3048*) stocks a full line of traditional Western clothing, ranging from Wrangler and Rocky Mountain jeans to Panhandle Slim shirts, Resistol hats, and Laredo boots. There are sizes and styles for the entire family. Handcrafted furniture, artwork, and Western home items are available at **Wyoming Home** (⊠ *210 W. Lincolnway* 🕮 *307/638–2222*).

10

SIDE TRIP TO FORT LARAMIE NATIONAL HISTORIC SITE

    ↺   *105 mi north of Cheyenne via Hwys. 25 and 26.*

Fodor's Choice
★
Fort Laramie is one of the most important historic sites in Wyoming, in part because its original buildings are extremely well preserved, but also because it played a role in several significant periods in Western history. Near the confluence of the Laramie and North Platte rivers, the fort began as a trading post in 1834, and it was an important provisioning point for travelers on the Oregon Trail in 1843, the Mormon Trail in 1847, and the California Trail in 1849, when it also became a military site. In 1851 the first treaty between the U.S. government and the Northern Plains Indians was negotiated near the fort, and in 1868 a second Fort Laramie Treaty led to the end of the First Sioux War, also known as Red Cloud's War. Costumed interpreters reenact scenes of military life and talk about the fur trade, overland migration, and relations between settlers and Native Americans. ⊠ *Goshen County Rd. 270, 3 mi west of town of Fort Laramie* ☎ *307/837–2221* ⊕ *www.nps. gov/fola* ⊠ *$3* ⊙ *Site daily dawn–dusk; visitor center Sept.–May, daily 8–4, June–Aug., daily 8–7.*

EN ROUTE
Although I–80 connects Cheyenne and Laramie more quickly, the drive between the two cities on **Happy Jack Road** (Highway 210) is very scenic, particularly in spring and early summer, when wildflowers are in full bloom. The road winds over the high plains, past Curt Gowdy State Park, and provides access to the Vedauwoo Recreation Area before linking back to I–80, 7 mi east of Laramie at the **Lincoln Monument.** At this state rest area you can obtain information about the region and view a larger-than-life sculpture of the 16th president.

The **Vedauwoo Recreation Area,** in the Medicine Bow–Routt National Forest, is a particularly unusual area and a great place for a picnic. Springing out of high plains and open meadows are glacial remnants in the form of huge granite boulders piled skyward with reckless abandon. These one-of-a-kind rock formations, dreamscapes of gray stone, are great for hiking, climbing, and photography. There's also camping here. ⊠ *31 mi west of Cheyenne off I–80 or Hwy. 210* ☎ *307/745–2300* ⊕ *www.fs.fed.us/r2/mbr* ⊠ *Free, camping $10* ⊙ *Daily 24 hrs.*

LARAMIE

The historic downtown of Laramie, nestled in a valley between the Medicine Bow Mountains and the Laramie Range, has several quaint buildings, some of which date back to 1868, the year after the railroad arrived and the city was established. For a time it was a tough "end-of-the-rail" town. Vigilantes took care of lawbreakers, hanging them from convenient telegraph poles. Then in 1872 the city constructed the Wyoming Territorial Prison on the bank of the Little Laramie River. One of its most famous inmates was Butch Cassidy. The prison has since closed, and things have calmed down in this city of approximately 30,000. It's now the center of open-plains ranching country and the site of the University of Wyoming, Wyoming's only state university.

GETTING HERE AND AROUND

I–80 skirts the south and then west sides of town; U.S. 287 (3rd Street within the city) bisects Laramie from north to south. Grand Avenue, which borders the University of Wyoming, is the primary east–west route through Laramie.

TOURS

You can get brochures from the Laramie Chamber of Commerce, on South 3rd Street, for a self-guided tour of the late-19th-century Victorian architecture. Also available are the "Architectural Walking Tour" brochure, which focuses on the historic residences in the downtown area, and the "Laramie Antique Trail" guide, with locations of antiques shops in and around downtown.

VISITOR INFORMATION

Albany County Tourism Board (✉ *210 E. Custer St., Laramie* ☎ *307/745–4195 or 800/445–5303* ⊕ *www.laramie-tourism.org*). **Laramie Chamber of Commerce** (✉ *800 S. 3rd St. Laramie* ☎ *307/745–7339 or 866/876–1012* ⊕ *www.laramie.org*).

EXPLORING

Numbers correspond to points of interest on the Laramie map.

TOP ATTRACTIONS

⑤ American Heritage Center. The center houses more than 10,000 photographs, rare books, collections of papers, and memorabilia related to such subjects as American and Western history, the petroleum industry, conservation movements, transportation, and the performing arts. Permanent and temporary art displays also fill the museum space. ✉ *2111 Willet Dr.* ☎ *307/766–4114* ⊕ *ahc.uwyo.edu* ⛱ *Free* ☉ *Mon. 8* AM–9 PM*, Tues.–Fri. 8–5.*

② Laramie Plains Museum. Edward Ivinson, a businessman and philanthropist and one of Laramie's first settlers, built the mansion that houses this museum in 1892; it's now on the National Register of Historic Places. Inside is a growing collection of historical artifacts from the Laramie plains area. ✉ *603 Ivinson Ave.* ☎ *307/742–4448* ⊕ *www.laramiemuseum.org* ⛱ *$10* ☉ *Mid-June–mid-Aug., Tues.–Sat. 9–5:30, Sun. 1–4; mid-Aug.–Dec. and Mar.–mid-June, Tues.–Sat. 12:30–5:30.*

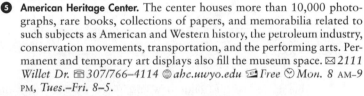

❸ Wyoming Children's Museum and Nature Center. Here children are encouraged to explore, make noise, experiment, play, imagine, discover, and invent. The hands-on exhibits emphasize wildlife, nature, and some local history. Live animals include Hissy, a great horned owl. The museum is on the edge of Labonte Park, which has playground equipment and plenty of grassy space in which children can burn off some energy. ✉ *968 N. 9th St.* ☎ *307/745–6332* ⊕ *www-lib.uwyo.edu/temp/wyshs/mus-wychildrens.htm* ⛱ *$3* ☉ *Tues.–Sat. 10–2.*

❶ Wyoming Territorial Prison State Historic Site. Perhaps because of the bedlam of the early days, Laramie became the site of the Wyoming Territorial Prison in 1872. Until 1903 it was the region's federal and state penal facility, locking down Butch Cassidy and other infamous frontier outlaws. Today the restored prison is a state historic site that brings to

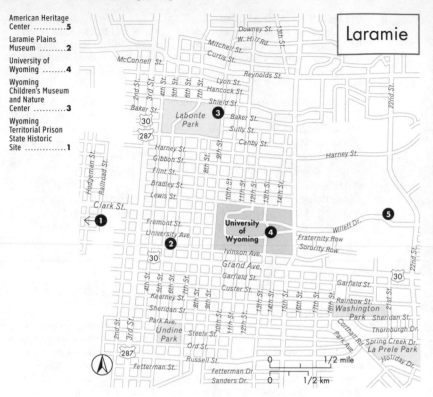

Laramie

life the legends of frontier law and justice. ⊠ *975 Snowy Range Rd.* ☎ *307/745–6161* ⊿ *$5* ⊙ *May–Oct., daily 9–6.*

WORTH NOTING

4 **University of Wyoming.** In addition to having several museums and attrac-
Ⓒ tions, the university hosts year-round events—from concerts to football
games. You can join a tour or just pick up information on the university
at the **UW Visitor Center** (⊠ *14th and Ivinson Sts.* ☎ *307/766–4075*).
The **Anthropology Museum** (☎ *307/766–5136*) houses numerous Native
American exhibits. Among the artworks displayed in the **Art Museum**
(☎ *307/766–6622*) are paintings, sculpture, photography, and folk art
from America, Europe, Africa, and Asia. Kids especially enjoy looking
at the butterflies, mosquitoes, and other crawling and flying critters at
the **Insect Museum** (☎ *307/766–3114*). You can learn about the stars
and watch laser shows at the university's **planetarium** (☎ *307/766–
6514*). The **Rocky Mountain Herbarium** (☎ *307/766–2236*) focuses
on Rocky Mountain plants, but also includes other examples of flora
from the northern hemisphere. Call individual museums for opening
times and fees (most of them are free). ⊠ *13th St. and Ivinson Ave.*
⊕ *www.uwyo.edu.*

SPORTS AND THE OUTDOORS

BICYCLING

Mountain-biking trails are scattered throughout the Medicine Bow–Routt National Forest and the Happy Jack recreation area, east of Laramie. For information, trail maps, and rentals, see Carl Gose at the **Pedal House** (✉ *207 S. 1st St.* 🌐 *www.pedalhouse.com* ☎ *307/742–5533*).

CROSS-COUNTRY SKIING

The Medicine Bow–Routt National Forest and the Happy Jack recreation area have numerous cross-country trails. For information and rentals, contact **Cross Country Connection** (✉ *117 Grand Ave.* ☎ *307/721–2851*).

WHERE TO EAT AND STAY

$$ AMERICAN Fodor's Choice ★ **Altitude Chophouse and Brewery.** A favorite of locals, this restaurant offers tasty handcrafted ales and fine cuisine. The decor is mountain themed, with a beautiful bar. The menu features American classics with surprising twists, artfully presented. Try the cedar-plank salmon, rib eye, or stromboli. Beer connoisseurs should check out the best-selling tumblewheat, a light-flavored American wheat brew. ✉ *320 S. 2nd St.* ☎ *307/721–4031* ▭ *AE, D, MC, V* 🌐 *www.altitudechophouse.com.*

$$$ AMERICAN **The Cav at Fort Sanders.** It's the food, not the look of the place, that attracts people to this restaurant on the plains, 1 mi south of Laramie on U.S. 287. The restaurant serves all prime beef, and menu highlights include prime rib, steak, fresh fish, and lobster. There's brunch on Sunday. The lounge features mounts from local game animals. ✉ *4425 S. 3rd St.* ☎ *307/745–5551* ▭ *AE, DC, MC, V* ⊗ *No lunch* 🌐 *www.cavalrymansupperclub.com.*

¢ **Howard Johnson Inn.** At this white-brick motel the lobby and halls are rustic Western knotty pine, and the rooms are basic, with contemporary furnishings. The property includes a convenience store, a restaurant, and a liquor store. It's on the western edge of town, at the Snowy Range Road exit off I–80. **Pros:** close to the interstate. **Cons:** no pets allowed. ✉ *1555 Snowy Range Rd., Exit 311 off I–80, Box 580* ☎ *307/742–8371* 🖷 *307/742–0884* *112 rooms* *In-hotel: restaurant, bar, pool, Wi-Fi* ▭ *AE, D, DC, MC, V.*

$$ **Laramie Comfort Inn.** On busy Grand Avenue, this Comfort Inn is close to restaurants and fast-food chains, as well as War Memorial Stadium at the University of Wyoming. **Pros:** many rooms have been recently remodeled; close to the stadium and conference center. **Cons:** rooms fill up fast on game weekends. ✉ *3420 Grand Ave.* ☎ *307/721–8856* 🖷 *307/721–5166* 🌐 *www.choicehotels.com/hotel/wy408* *55 rooms, 3 suites, 1 efficiency apartment* *In-hotel: pool, gym, Wi-Fi* ▭ *AE, D, DC, MC, V* 🍽 *CP.*

CAMPING **Laramie KOA.** This campground on the west side of town has lots of grassy space and some trees. For an extra fee you can have satellite TV for your RV. Wi-Fi is also available at no extra charge. There are one- and two-bedroom cabins, and the rec center has a pool table, arcade games, and a laundry room. *Flush toilets, full hookups, drinking water, picnic tables, general store, play area* *116 full hookups, 30 tent*

10

sites; 8 cabins ⊠ 1271 W. Baker St., I–80 at Curtis St. exit ☎ 307/742–6553 🖷 307/742–5039 ⊕ www.koa.com 🖃 D, DC, MC, V.

🔺 **Libby Creek Pine.** Wake up to the sound of Libby Creek as it rushes past your campsite. This campground is small and shady and tucked away from the main road. All sites are first-come, first-served. 🔥 *Vault toilet, fire grates, , picnic tables* 🤿 *6 sites* ⊠ *32 mi west of Laramie on Hwy. 130 to Libby Recreation Area, then ½ mi on Forest Rd. 351* ☎ *307/745–2300 or 877/444–6777* 🖃 No credit cards ☉ May–Oct.

🔺 **Sugarloaf Campground.** At 10,700 feet, this is the highest campground in Wyoming. Don't be surprised if you get snowed on in July. With stunning views of the mountains, getting a site here can be difficult, so plan accordingly. Heavy winter snows have prevented this area from opening until well into the summer, if at all, in some years. 🔥 *Vault toilet, fire grates, picnic tables* 🤿 *16 sites* ⊠ *40 mi west of Laramie on Hwy. 130 and then 1 mi north on Forest Service Rd. 346* ☎ *307/745–2300 or 877/444–6777* ⊕ www.reserveusa.com 🖃 No credit cards ☉ July–Sept.

NIGHTLIFE

On weekends you can kick up your heels to live country-and-western music at the **Buckhorn** (⊠ *114 Ivinson Ave.* ☎ *307/742–3554*), or listen to a DJ upstairs at the Parlour Bar Wednesday–Saturday. Take a spin around the dance floor at the **Cowboy Saloon** (⊠ *108 S. 2nd St.* ☎ *307/742–7788*) on weekends. On Thursday September through May the place hops with college kids who aren't old enough to be in the bar at other times; no alcohol is served then, but they usually have live music, dance contests, and other events. Stop by the **Library Sports Grill and Brewery** (⊠ *1622 Grand Ave.* ☎ *307/745–0500*) for beers brewed on-site. College students gather and shoot pool at **Mingles** (⊠ *3206 Grand Ave.* ☎ *307/721–2005*).

SHOPPING

Laramie's most interesting shopping is found in a shopping district called **Landmark Square** along Ivinson and Grand avenues. Stores here sell artwork, clothing, and handcrafted items.

IN AND AROUND THE SNOWY RANGE

Mountain lakes and streams, aspens and pines, camping areas, and trails for hiking, cross-country skiing, and snowmobiling draw outdoor enthusiasts to the Snowy Range, which encompasses portions of both the Laramie and Brush Creek districts of Medicine Bow–Routt National Forest. The Snowy Range Pass, a stretch of Highway 130 running west from Centennial toward Saratoga, climbs as high as 10,847 feet; driving through the pass, which is open only in summer, takes you past stunning views of the surrounding peaks, including 12,013-foot Medicine Bow Peak. The high elevation means snow caps the mountain peaks in the range year-round.

MEDICINE BOW

60 mi northwest of Laramie via U.S. 30.

When novelist Owen Wister (1860–1938) first visited Medicine Bow—the town he would immortalize in his 1902 classic Western tale *The Virginian*—he noted that the community looked "as if strewn there by the wind." Today the town still looks somewhat windblown, although the small business district is anchored by the Virginian Hotel, built in the early 1900s and named in honor of the book. This is a community of 320 struggling for survival, with an economy based on the vagaries of agriculture and mining. Although the town sits at the intersection of U.S. 30 (Lincoln Highway) and Wyoming Route 487, you'll seldom encounter much traffic here, except during the fall hunting season (the area is particularly noted for its antelope hunting) and when there are football or basketball games at the University of Wyoming. On those days, expect a crowd on the road and fans talking of sports at the Virginian Hotel.

EXPLORING

You can learn about the history of this small town at the **Medicine Bow Museum,** housed in an old railroad depot built in 1913. Owen Wister's summer cabin was relocated to the premises and stands next door. ⊠ *405 Lincoln Pl.* ☎ *307/379-2383* ⊕ *www.medicinebow.org* 🖼 *Free* ⊗ *Memorial Day–Sept., weekdays 10–5 and by appointment.*

WHERE TO STAY

¢–$ 🏨 **Virginian Hotel.** Inspired by the Owen Wister novel *The Virginian,* this sandstone hotel was built in 1909 and has been operating nearly continuously ever since. Claw-foot tubs, tulip-shape lights, and brass beds with comforters fill the Victorian-style rooms. The rooms in the main hotel don't have TVs, phones, or radios (most don't even have electrical outlets), but the atmosphere more than makes up for the lack of amenities. In the main hotel only the suites have private bathrooms; rooms in the Bunkhouse Motel annex have TVs and bathrooms. The dining room ($$–$$$), with antique oak furniture and 19th-century photographs, serves American fare such as steak and chicken. **Pros:** perfect for the history buff. **Cons:** local train tracks create a racket. ⊠ *404 Lincoln Hwy., Box 127,* ☎ *307/379-2377* 🛏 *36 rooms, 4 suites in hotel; 12 rooms in Bunkhouse Motel* ♿ *In-room: no a/c, no phone (some), no TV (some). In-hotel: restaurant, bar* ▤ *MC, V.*

10

CENTENNIAL

30 mi west of Laramie via Hwy. 130; 90 mi south of Medicine Bow via U.S. 30 and Hwy. 130.

Snuggled up against the mountains of the Snowy Range, Centennial lies at the head of the glacial Centennial Valley. As the community closest to the Snowy Range, the town makes a good base from which to take part in numerous recreational activities, including hiking, cross-country skiing, snowmobiling, and downhill skiing. This small town has a few hardy year-round residents, and many more people who summer in the area.

VISITOR INFORMATION

Centennial Visitor's Center (⊠ *Hwy. 130, 1 mi west of Centennial* ☎ *307/742–6023*).

EXPLORING

The former Centennial Railroad Depot now houses the **Nici Self Museum**, at the eastern edge of town. The museum displays ranching, farming, and mining equipment, plus artifacts typical of what you'd find in a pioneer home; there's also an outdoor-equipment exhibit. ⊠ *2734 Hwy. 130* ☎ *307/742–7763* ✍ *Donations accepted* ☉ *Mid-June–Labor Day, Fri.–Mon. noon–4; Sept., weekends noon–4.*

You can hike, picnic, fish, ski, snowmobile, or take photographs in the 400,000 acres of **Medicine Bow–Routt National Forest, Laramie District** (⊠ *Laramie office: 2468 Jackson St., Laramie* ☎ *307/745–2300, 877/444–6777 for camping* ⊕ *www.fs.fed.us/r2/mbr/*), and that is the short list. The Laramie District has 20 developed campgrounds, although some are closed for tree removal; dispersed camping is also allowed. Lodgings such as cabins, forest guard stations, and even a fire lookout tower high in the Snowy Range are available for rent in summer.

SPORTS AND THE OUTDOORS

CROSS-COUN-
TRY SKIING

The same trails that serve hikers in summer cater to cross-country skiers in winter in the Lower Snowy Range trail system. You can access several trails on Highway 130 west of Centennial in the Medicine Bow–Routt National Forest, including the Corner Mountain Trail (3 mi west of Centennial), Little Laramie Trail (5 mi west of Centennial), and the Green Rock Trail (9 mi west of Centennial). There is also a cross-country-skiing trail system at Snowy Range Ski and Recreation Area. Many of the trails are interconnected, so you can combine short trails for a longer ski trip.

HIKING

Dozens of miles of hiking trails slice through the Medicine Bow–Routt National Forest west of town. Major trailheads are on Highway 130, including trailheads for the 7-mi Corner Mountain Trail (3 mi west of Centennial), 7-mi Little Laramie Trail (5 mi west of Centennial), and 9-mi Medicine Bow Peak Trail (9 mi west of Centennial). The easy 1-mi Centennial Trail takes off from the Centennial Visitor Center at the forest boundary. More difficult is the 4½-mi Barber Lake Trail, which starts at Barber Lake and incorporates ski trails and old forest roads. Most hikers follow this trail downhill one way, and instead of doubling back use two vehicles to shuttle between Barber Lake and the Corner Mountain trailhead (the Barber Lake Trail hooks up with part of the Corner Mountain trail).

Trail maps and information are available at the Centennial Visitor's Center.

SKIING AND
SNOW-
BOARDING

Downhill skiing and snowboarding are available 7 mi west of Centennial at the **Snowy Range Ski and Recreation Area** (⊠ *6416 Mountain Mist Ct.* ☎ *307/745–5750 or 307/721–1114* ⊕ *www.snowyrange.com*). There are slopes for beginners and experienced skiers, plus some cross-country-skiing trails.

WHERE TO STAY

¢–$$ 🏨 **Old Corral Hotel & Steak House.** A crowd of Western carved-wood characters greets you on the front lawn of this log restaurant and hotel. Walking into the steak house ($$–$$$$), with its woodstove and ranch decorations, is like stepping into the Old West. Hand-hewn pine beds and dressers decorate the hotel rooms, and you have access to a deck with picnic tables and a hot tub, a pool room, and a TV room with videos. The lower level of the on-site gift shop sells T-shirts and Christmas decorations; upstairs there are antique replicas, including Native American pipes and outlaw paraphernalia. **Pros:** just down the road from the Snowy Mountains; perfect location for snowmobilers. **Cons:** hotel closings vary by season. ✉ *2750 Hwy. 130* ☎ *307/745–5918* 🖷 *307/742–6846* ⊕ *www.oldcorral.com* ⤴ *35 rooms* ♿ *In-room: no a/c, Internet. In-hotel: restaurant, some pets allowed* ⊟ *D, MC, V* ✆ *Closed mid-Oct.–mid-Dec. and mid-Apr.–mid-May.*

$$–$$$ 🏨 **Vee Bar Guest Ranch.** Along the Centennial Valley's Little Laramie River, 21 mi west of Laramie and 9 mi east of Centennial, this family-operated guest ranch builds its summer activity program around horseback riding. Other activities include fishing, hiking, river tubing, mountain biking, and trap shooting. Lodging is in nine individual cabins and four lodge suites. You can buy an all-inclusive week or stay as a nightly B&B guest; October through May, only the B&B plan is offered. B&B guests, and those not staying at the ranch, may eat in the dining room ($$$–$$$$) by reservation only. **Pros:** beautiful scenery and plenty to keep you busy. **Cons:** a short jaunt from downtown. ✉ *38 Vee Bar Ranch Rd., Laramie* ☎ *307/745–7036 or 800/483–3227* 🖷 *307/745–7433* ⊕ *www.veebar.com* ⤴ *9 cabins, 4 lodge rooms* ♿ *In-room: no a/c, no TV, refrigerator, Wi-Fi. In-hotel: laundry facilities* ⊟ *AE, D, MC, V* ℗ *FAP.*

$$–$$$$ 🏨 **Winter Creek Condos and Cabins.** Just outside town in a forest of pine and aspen, these cabins afford views of the Centennial Valley. The cabins sleep 6 to 10 people and have full kitchens and outdoor gas grills; there's a two-night minimum stay. A common area has a basketball court, playground, picnic area, and horseshoe-pitching area. Condos have satellite television. ✉ *75 Rainbow Valley Rd., Box 135* ☎ *307/721–9859* ⊕ *www.wintercreekcondos.com* ⤴ *7 units* ♿ *In-room: no a/c, no phone, kitchen, no TV (some)* ⊟ *MC, V.*

CAMPING In addition to the campgrounds listed here, there are several others in both the Laramie and Brush Creek districts of the **Medicine Bow–Routt National Forest** (☎ *877/444–6777 or 307/745–2300 Laramie District, 307/326–5258 Brush Creek District* ⊕ *www.fs.fed.us/r2/mbr/*).

🏕 **Brooklyn Lake.** On the east side of Snowy Range Pass, at an elevation of 10,500 feet, this small campground sits beside Brooklyn Lake and is surrounded by pine forest. You can fish in the lake and use nonmotorized boats. All campsites have views of the lake. ♿ *Pit toilets, fire pits, picnic tables* ⤴ *19 sites* ✉ *Hwy. 130, 7 mi west of Centennial on Hwy. 130, then 2 mi east on Brooklyn Lake Rd./Forest Rd. 317* ☎ *307/745–2300* ⊕ *www.fs.fed.us/r2/mbr/* ⊟ *No credit cards* ✆ *July–Sept.*

🏕 **Nash Fork.** Pine trees surround this simple campground at an elevation of 10,200 feet. Each site can accommodate an RV or a tent, but there are no hookups. ⚅ *Pit toilets, drinking water, fire grates, fire pits, picnic tables* ⊅ *27 sites* ⊠ *Hwy. 130, 8 mi west of Centennial* ☎ *307/745–2300* ⊕ *www.fs.fed.us/r2/mbr/* ⚄ *Reservations not accepted* ▭ *No credit cards* ⊙ *July–Sept.*

⚈ **Ryan Park.** During World War II this was the site of a camp for German prisoners, and you can still see some of the building foundations. The campground on the east side of Snowy Range Pass lies at an elevation of 8,000 feet. It has access to stream fishing as well as to hiking on forest trails and two-track roads. Just west of the small community of Ryan Park, it is 20 mi southeast of Saratoga. Check with the Brush Creek/Hayden district (307/326–5258) for closures because of tree removal. ⚅ *Pit toilets, drinking water, fire pits, picnic tables* ⊅ *48 sites* ⊠ *Hwy. 130, 20 mi southeast of Saratoga* ☎ *877/444–6777* ⊕ *www. reserveusa.com* ▭ *No credit cards* ⊙ *June–Oct.*

EN ROUTE

Highway 130 between Centennial and Saratoga is known as the **Snowy Range Scenic Byway.** This paved road, which is in excellent condition, crosses through the Medicine Bow–Routt National Forest, providing views of 12,013-foot Medicine Bow Peak and access to hiking trails, 10 campgrounds (6 right near the road), picnic areas, and 100 alpine lakes and streams. Gravel roads lead off the route into the national forest. Maps are available from the **Centennial Visitor's Center** (⊠ *Hwy. 130, 1 mi west of Centennial* ☎ *307/742–6023*).

At the top of the 10,847-foot Snowy Range Pass, about 10 mi west of Centennial, take a short walk to the Libby Flats Observation Site for views of the Snowy Range and, on clear days, Rocky Mountain National Park to the southwest in Colorado. Lake Marie, a jewel of a mountain lake at an elevation of approximately 10,000 feet, is also here. On the Saratoga side of the mountain the road passes through pine forest and descends to the North Platte River valley, with cattle ranches on both sides of the highway. Note that there is ongoing construction near the junction of Highways 130 and 230, 8 mi south of Saratoga. Also, the byway is impassable in winter and therefore is closed between approximately mid-October and Memorial Day.

SARATOGA

49 mi west of Centennial via Hwy. 130, Memorial Day–early Oct.; rest of year, 140 mi west of Centennial via Hwy. 130 east to Laramie, Hwy. 230 west to Encampment, and Hwy. 130 north or east to Laramie, I–80 west to Hwy. 130 and then south.

Tucked away in a valley formed by the Snowy Range and Sierra Madre mountains, Saratoga is a rarely visited treasure. Fine shopping and dining happily combine with elegant lodging facilities and a landscape that's ideal for outdoor activities. This is a good spot for river floating and blue-ribbon fishing: the North Platte River bisects the region, and there are several lakes and streams nearby in the Medicine Bow–Routt National Forest. You can also cross-country ski and snowmobile in the area. The town first went by the name Warm Springs, but in an attempt to add an air of sophistication to the place, townsfolk changed the name to Saratoga (after Saratoga Springs, New York) in 1884.

VISITOR INFORMATION

Saratoga–Platte Valley Chamber of Commerce (✉ *210 W. Elm St.* ⌂ *Box 1095, Saratoga 82331* ☎ *307/326–8855* ⊕ *www.saratogachamber.info*).

EXPLORING

★ Hot mineral waters flow freely through the **Hobo Pool Hot Springs,** and the adjacent swimming pool is heated by the springs. People have been coming here to soak for generations, including Native Americans, who considered the area neutral territory. Hardy folk can do as the Native Americans did and first soak in the hot water, then jump into the adjacent icy waters of the North Platte River. ✉ *201 S. River St.* ☎ *307/326–8335 or 800/22--3547* ☜ *Free* ۞ *Hot springs daily 24 hrs; pool Memorial Day–Labor Day, daily 9–8 (sometimes closed for lessons).*

The former Union Pacific Railroad depot houses the **Saratoga Historical and Cultural Association Museum,** with displays of local artifacts related to the history and geology of the area. Outdoor exhibits include a sheep wagon and a smithy. A nearby gazebo is used for occasional musical and historical programs in summer. ✉ *104 Constitution Ave.* ☎ *307/326–5511* ⊕ *www.saratoga-museum.com* ☜ *Donations accepted* ۞ *Memorial Day–Labor Day, Tues.–Sat. 1–4.*

SPORTS AND THE OUTDOORS

CANOEING **Stoney Creek Outfitters** (✉ *216 E. Walnut St.* ☎ *307/326–8750* ⊕ *www.*
& RAFTING *fishstoneycreek.com*) offers guided canoe and raft expeditions on the
★ North Platte River, plus canoe and drift-boat rentals.

FISHING Brook trout are abundant in the lakes and streams of Medicine Bow–Routt National Forest, and you will also find rainbow, golden, cut-throat, and brown trout, as well as splake. You can also drop a fly in the North Platte River. **Stoney Creek Outfitters** (✉ *216 E. Walnut St.* ☎ *307/326–8750* ⊕ *www.fishstoneycreek.com*) rents tackle and runs fishing trips on the Upper North Platte.

WHERE TO EAT AND STAY

$$ ✗ **Lazy River Cantina.** Mexican music and sombreros greet you at this
MEXICAN downtown restaurant, which also includes a bar and lounge where locals and visitors take their shot at darts. The entrées include tacos, enchiladas, burritos, and chimichangas, served in one of two small rooms. You can sit in a booth and watch folks and traffic on busy Bridge Avenue. ✉ *110 E. Bridge Ave.* ☎ *307/326–8472* ▤ *MC, V* ۞ *Closed Tues.*

$ 🛏 **Riviera Lodge.** Locally owned and simplistic in nature, the Riviera is right on the slow-moving Encampment River, a haven for trout and waterfowl. Rooms are decorated in a Western theme. An empty lobby and one of the owner's pets usually greet you as you enter. Out back you will find a large grassy area, making the property one of the few pet-friendly places in Saratoga. Anglers will appreciate the location, as it is within walking distance from local fly shops. **Pros:** only two blocks from downtown; remodeled in 2009; some budget rooms available. **Cons:** relatively few amenities. ✉ *104 E. Saratoga St.* ☎ *307/326–5651 or 866/326–5651* ⊕ *www.therivieralodge.com* ⇆ *40 rooms* ⚴ *In-room: no a/c (some), refrigerator, Wi-Fi. In-hotel: some pets allowed* ▤ *AE, D, MC, V.*

10

$$–$$$ ⬚ **Saratoga Resort and Spa.** With leather couches in the common areas,
Fodor's Choice   pole-frame beds, and Western art, this inn is as nice as any place in Wyo-
★   ming. Some rooms are in the main lodge, which has a double fireplace
lounge that opens both to the central sitting room and the back porch;
other rooms are in separate buildings surrounding a large expanse of
lawn and a hot-mineral-water swimming pool. There are five outdoor
hot tubs filled with mineral water, three of them covered with tepees, a
9-hole public golf course, and tennis courts. The Silver Saddle Restau-
rant ($$$) serves steak, pasta, and seafood in a quiet, cozy setting with
a fireplace to warm you in fall or winter. **Pros:** attractive Western decor;
high-quality spa. **Cons:** reaching here can be difficult in winter. ⬚ *601
E. Pic-Pike Rd., Box 869* ☎ *307/326–5261* ⬚ *307/326–5234* ⊕ *www.
saratogainn.com* ⬚ *50 rooms* ⬚ *In-hotel: restaurant, room service, bar,
golf course, pool, spa* ⊟ *AE, DC, MC, V.*

¢–$$ ⬚ **Wolf Hotel.** This downtown 1893 hotel on the National Register of
Fodor's Choice   Historic Places is well maintained by its proud owners. Although some
★   of the guest rooms are small, all of them have simple Victorian charm.
(Note that the rooms are on the second and third floors, and there is no
elevator; there also is no way to control the heat in individual rooms.)
The fine restaurant ($$), bar, and lounge also have Victorian furnish-
ings, including dark-green wallpaper, antique oak tables, crystal chan-
deliers, and lacy drapes. Prime rib and steaks are the specialties, and
seafood and lamb are also on the menu. Dinner reservations are strongly
recommended. **Pros:** beautiful and historic at a great price. **Cons:** lack
of elevator; no pets allowed. ⬚ *101 E. Bridge Ave.* ☎ *307/326–5525*
⊕ *www.wolfhotel.com* ⬚ *10 rooms* ⬚ *In-room: no a/c, no TV (some).
In-hotel: restaurant, bar* ⊟ *AE, MC, V.*

ENCAMPMENT

18 mi south of Saratoga via Hwys. 130 and 230.

This is the gateway community to the Continental Divide National
Scenic Trail, accessed at Battle Pass, 15 mi west on Highway 70. When
completed, this trail will run from Canada all the way south to Mex-
ico along the Continental Divide. Encampment is also a good place
to launch trips into four nearby wilderness areas in the Hayden Dis-
trict of Medicine Bow–Routt National Forest—Platte River, Savage
Run, Encampment River, and Huston Park—where you can go hik-
ing, fishing, mountain biking, snowmobiling, and cross-country skiing.
Although recreation is a quickly emerging industry, there's still a lot
of quiet mountain country to explore, and it's not yet crowded in this
town of 400 residents.

EXPLORING

☉   The modern interpretive center at the **Grand Encampment Museum** holds
Fodor's Choice   exhibits on the history of the Grand Encampment copper district and
★   logging and mining. A pioneer town of original buildings includes the
Lake Creek stage station, the Big Creek tie-hack cabin, the Peryam
homestead, the Slash Ridge fire tower, a blacksmith shop, a transporta-
tion barn, and a two-story outhouse. Among the other relics are three
original towers from a 16-mi-long aerial tramway built in 1903 to

transport copper ore from mines in the Sierra Madres. You can take guided tours, and there's also a research area. A living-history day, with music, costumes, and events, takes place the third weekend in July. ⊠ *807 Barnett Ave.* ☎ *307/327–5308* ⊕ *www.grandencampment-museum.org* 📖 *Donations accepted* ☉ *Memorial Day–Labor Day, Mon.–Sat. 10–5, Sun. 1–5; Sept., Sat. 10–5, Sun. 1–5.*

Ⓒ The ranching and cowboy lifestyle is the focus of the three-day **Grand Encampment Cowboy Gathering** (⊠ *807 Barnett Ave.* ☎ *307/326–8855*), held in mid-July. Cowboy musicians and poets perform during afternoon and evening concerts, and there's a stick-horse rodeo for children. Events take place at the Grand Encampment Museum and other venues around town.

The **Medicine Bow–Routt National Forest, Hayden District** covers 586,000 acres, including the Continental Divide National Scenic Trail and the Encampment River, Huston Park, Savage Run, and Platte River wilderness areas. The local Forest Service office (⊠ *204 W. 9th St.* ☎ *307/326–5258* ⊕ *www.fs.fed.us/r2/mbr*) can provide information on hiking, fishing, camping, cross-country skiing, and snowmobiling trails.

SPORTS AND THE OUTDOORS

CROSS-COUN-TRY SKIING A network of cross-country trails in Medicine Bow–Routt National Forest, the **Bottle Creek Ski Trails** (⊠ *Hwy. 70, 6 mi southwest of Encampment* ☎ *307/327–5720*) include several backcountry trails suitable only for expert skiers. There are also easier routes for skiers of all levels. Some trails double as snowmobile trails. All of them are free.For ski rentals and sales as well as trail information, go to the **Trading Post** (⊠ *Junction of Hwys. 70 and 230* ☎ *307/327–5720*).

HIKING There are extensive trails in the Sierra Madre range west of Encampment, ranging from developed paths around Bottle Creek to wilderness trails through Huston Park and along the Encampment River. For hiking information, contact the Forest Service office of the **Medicine Bow–Routt National Forest, Hayden District** (⊠ *204 W. 9th St.* ☎ *307/326–5258*).

HORSEBACK RIDING Rick Stevens of **Horseback Adventures** (☎ *307/326–5569*) can lead a trail ride geared to your riding level. You can choose between rides in the Snowy Range, Sierra Madres, or desert country throughout Carbon County. Rides rage in length from half-day to overnight pack trips.

WHERE TO EAT AND STAY

$$ AMERICAN ✕ **Bear Trap Cafe.** People come for the large portions of hearty but basic food at this log building with the look and feel of a Western hunting lodge. The menu is strong on burgers, steaks, fish, and chicken. ⊠ *120 E. Riverside Ave., 2 mi northeast of Encampment, Riverside* ☎ *307/327–5277* ▭ *MC, V.*

$$ AMERICAN ✕ **Pine Lodge Restaurant.** Regular offerings here include homemade pizza, burgers, and sandwiches; on some evenings there is Mexican food or prime rib. The bar is in a separate room. ⊠ *518 McCaffrey Ave.* ☎ *307/327–5203* ▭ *MC, V.*

$–$$$ ⊡ **Cottonwood Cabins.** In the quiet little town of Riverside, just across the street from the town park, these cabins have wood furniture, country quilts, outdoor grills, picnic tables, and full kitchens. **Pros:** close to outdoor recreation. **Cons:** open only through the summer. ⊠ *411 1st St.,*

10

Riverside ☎ 307/327–5151 🖥 307/327–5151 ➽ *3 cabins* ⚘ *In-room: no a/c, no phone, kitchen.* ☰ *D, MC, V* ☺ *Closed Sept.–May.*

$–$$
Fodor'sChoice
★

⊡ **Spirit West River Lodge.** Beside the Encampment River, this massive log structure has walls of lichen-covered rocks and large windows overlooking the water and surrounding scenery. Stained glass and Western artwork—most of it by owner R. G. Finney, who is known for his wildlife bronzes and paintings—fill the lodge. His wife Lynn, who serves the full breakfast, is a Senior Olympic gold medalist in cycling and a native of the area. She can direct you to the best cycling routes and cross-country-skiing trails. The lodge has a mile of private-access fishing on the Encampment River, and each room has a private entrance off a deck overlooking the river. The three-bedroom guesthouse has a full kitchen and private access, as well as river frontage. Some units have television and full kitchens. **Pros:** quiet, secluded location. **Cons:** a short jaunt from downtown. ⊠ *¼ mi east of Riverside on Hwy. 230, Box 605* ☎ *307/326–5753, 888/289–8321 for reservations* ⊕ *www. spiritwestriverlodge.com* ➽ *6 rooms* ⚘ *In-room: no a/c, no TV (some), kitchen (some)* ☰ *MC, V* ⑩⎮ *BP.*

CAMPING
★

⛺ **Hog Park.** In the Sierra Madres west of Encampment, this large campground sits beside a high mountain lake at 8,400 feet; some of the campsites have views of the water. You can use motorized boats and other watercraft on the lake. Hiking, horseback riding, and mountain-biking roads and trails abound, and there is a boat dock here as well. ⚘ *Pit toilets, drinking water, fire pits, picnic tables* ➽ *50 sites* ⊠ *20 mi southwest of Encampment; 5 mi west on Hwy. 70, then 15 mi southwest on Forest Rd. 550* ☎ *307/326–5258* ⊕ *www.fs.fed.us/r2/mbr/* ⚘ *Reservations not accepted* ☰ *No credit cards* ☺ *Mid-June–Sept.*

⛺ **Lazy Acres Campground.** The Encampment River runs past this small campground with plenty of big cottonwood trees for shade. There are pull-through RV sites, tent sites, one small cabin (you provide bedding, stove, and cooking utensils), and four no-frills motel rooms, which have cable television and Wi-Fi. ⚘ *Flush toilets, full hookups, dump station, guest laundry, showers* ➽ *17 full hookups, 14 partial hookups, 2 tent sites; 1 camping cabin, 4 motel rooms* ⊠ *110 Fields Ave., Riverside* ☎ *307/327–5968* ⊕ *www.lazyacreswyo.com* ☰ *MC, V* ☺ *May 15–Oct.*

⛺ **Six Mile Gap.** There are only nine sites at this campground on a hillside above the North Platte River. Some are pull-through camper sites and others are walk-in tent sites. Trails follow the river, which you can cross during low water to reach the Platte River Wilderness Area. ⚘ *Pit toilets, drinking water, fire pits, picnic tables* ➽ *9 sites* ⊠ *Hwy. 230, 26 mi east of Encampment, then 2 mi east on Forest Rd. 492* ☎ *307/326–5258* ⊕ *www.fs.fed.us/r2/mbr/* ⚘ *Reservations not accepted* ☰ *No credit cards* ☺ *May–Oct.*

⌐ EN ROUTE
As you make your way west to Baggs over the **Battle Highway** (Highway 70), you'll cross the Continental Divide and the Rocky Mountains. This route takes you through the mining country that was developed during the 1897–1908 copper-mining boom in the Sierra Madres; interpretive signs along the way point out historic sites. In 1879, Thomas Edison was fishing near Battle Pass with a bamboo rod when he began to

ponder the idea of a filament, which led to his invention of the incandescent lightbulb. Note that this section of the highway closes to car travel in winter, though it stays open for snowmobiles.

BAGGS

60 mi west of Encampment via Hwy. 70.

Settled by cattle and sheep ranchers, the Little Snake River valley—and its largest community, Baggs—is still ranch country. Two emigrant trails passed nearby: the south branch of the Cherokee Trail (circa 1849–50) crosses near the community, and the Overland Trail (1862–65) lies farther to the north. Notorious outlaw Butch Cassidy frequented the area, often hiding out here after pulling off a train or bank robbery. To the west of Baggs, large herds of wild horses range freely on public lands. The town is on the southern edge of what is now a major oil, gas, and coal-bed methane field, so large numbers of equipment trucks, big water trucks, and field workers ply the roads. Motels and restaurants stay busy.

EXPLORING

Ranch paraphernalia, handmade quilts, a doll collection, and the original 1870s-era cabin of mountain man James Baker are exhibited at the **Little Snake River Valley Museum** ⊠ *No. 2 N. Savery Rd.* ☎ *307/383–7262* ⊕ *www.littlesnakerivermuseum.com* ☜ *Donations accepted* ☉ *Memorial Day–late Oct., daily 11–5.*

WHERE TO EAT AND STAY

$ ✕ **El Rio.** Mexican food is the specialty in this small restaurant. Burri-
AMERICAN tos, fajitas, and red and green chili are local favorites. The menu also includes hamburgers, chicken strips, and a steak-and-shrimp meal. ⊠ *20 N. Penland St.* ☎ *307/383–7515* ▤ *MC, DC, V.*

¢ ☷ **Drifter's Inn.** Drifter's has no-frills motel rooms adjacent to a restaurant ($$) and lounge. Menu items range from burgers and steaks to chicken and fish. Friday nights there's prime rib, and Saturday nights are reserved for steak and shrimp. Pros: the attached restaurant is regularly open, unlike many other eateries in Baggs. Cons: this is pretty much the only game in town. ⊠ *210 Penland St.* ☎ *307/383–2015* ☐ *307/383–6282* ➦ *52 rooms* ☒ *In-hotel: restaurant, bar, some pets allowed* ▤ *AE, D, MC, V.*

10

RAWLINS

70 mi northeast of Baggs via Hwy. 789 and I-80.

The northern gateway to the Medicine Bow–Routt National Forest, Rawlins stands at the junction of U.S. 287 and I-80. Started as one of the Union Pacific's hell-on-wheels towns, this was an important transportation center as early as 1868, when miners heading for the goldfields at South Pass to the north rode the rails to Rawlins or points nearby, then went overland to the gold diggings. The town became a large sheep-raising center at the turn of the 20th century. Kingpins in the sheep industry, such as George Ferris and Robert Deal, also backed the development of the Grand Encampment Copper Mining District in the Sierra Madres after miner Ed Haggarty discovered copper there in 1897.

Declines in sheep raising, long Rawlins's mainstay industry, have hurt the community economically, as have downturns in regional mineral production. But the city of 10,000 is still home to many railroad workers and employees of the Wyoming State Penitentiary outside of town. In summer there are weekly free concerts in the park.

VISITOR INFORMATION
Carbon County Visitor's Council (⌂ *Box 1017, Rawlins 82301* ☎ *800/228–3547* ⊕ *www.wyomingcarboncounty.com*).

EXPLORING
About 70 mi north of Rawlins via U.S. 287 and Highway 220 are several sights of interest that are grouped together: Independence Rock State Historic Site, Devil's Gate, and Handcart Ranch.

You can fish, boat, and water-ski on the Seminoe Reservoir, the primary attraction within **Seminoe State Park.** This is also a popular spot for camping and picnicking. It's on a Bureau of Land Management backcountry byway, Carbon County Road 351, which links Sinclair with Alcova. ☎ *307/320–3013* ⊕ *wyoparks.state.wy.us/site/siteinfo. asp?siteID=11* ▨ *$4 resident vehicle, $6 nonresident vehicle; $10 resident camping, $17 nonresident camping* ⊙ *Daily 24 hrs.*

Cold steel and concrete, the Death House, and the Yard are all part of the tour of the **Wyoming Frontier Prison,** which served as the state's penitentiary from 1901 until 1981. There are occasional midnight tours, and there's a Halloween tour. ▨ *500 W. Walnut St.* ☎ *307/324–4422* ▨ *$7* ⊙ *Memorial Day–Labor Day, daily 8–5:30, call for limited hrs; rest of yr by appointment.*

WHERE TO EAT

$$ ✕ **Cappy's.** The chicken-fried steak, T-bone steak, and enchiladas are
AMERICAN   all equally good at this family-owned restaurant on the west side of the city. The dining room has a homey feel, and sunlight streams in the big banks of windows, giving the space a bright, clean feel. ▨ *2351 W. Spruce St.* ☎ *307/324–4847* ▤ *AE, D, MC, V.*

$$ ✕ **Sanfords Grub & Pub.** This downtown restaurant looks like an antiques
AMERICAN   store packed with road signs, memorabilia from the 1960s and later, and other vintage decorations. The huge menu includes beef, chicken, pasta, sandwiches, and salads, but specializes in sandwiches, many of which include a small slab of cream cheese. The restaurant is also known for its wide selection of beers, both domestic and imported. Keep an eye out for semi-local brews from Jackson or Fort Collins, Colorado, as they can be difficult to find outside the Rocky Mountain West. ▨ *401 Cedar St.* ☎ *307/324–2921* ▤ *AE, D, DC, MC, V.*

$ ✕ **Su Casa.** One of Wyoming's best Mexican menus is here, 6 mi east of
MEXICAN   Rawlins in Sinclair. The menu includes shrimp, beef, and chicken fajitas,
★   green chili, enchiladas, and Navajo tacos. Try the chiles rellenos (fried cheese-stuffed peppers) or shredded beef enchiladas. Takeout is available. ▨ *705 E. Lincoln Ave., Sinclair* ☎ *307/328–1745* ▤ *MC, V.*

Wyoming's Cowboy Symbol

Ask any old-timer in Cheyenne, Laramie, Lander, or Pinedale who the cowboy is on the Wyoming license plate's bucking-horse symbol, and you'll probably get four different answers. Artist Allen True, who designed the symbol, once said he had no particular rider in mind, but that hasn't stopped Wyoming residents from attributing the rider to regional favorites. Several well-known cowboys are often mentioned, including Stub Farlow of Lander and Guy Holt of Cheyenne (who later ranched near Pinedale).

True was not the first person to create this bucking-horse design, however. The symbol evolved over a number of years, beginning with a 1903 photograph by Professor B.C. Buffum of cowboy Guy Holt riding Steamboat, one of five horses recognized as the most difficult bucking horses of all time. In 1921 the University of Wyoming used that photograph as a model for the bucking-horse-and-cowboy logo on its sports uniforms.

But by that time there was already another Wyoming bucking-horse symbol. During World War I George Ostrom, a member of the Wyoming National Guard serving in Germany, had a bucking-horse-and-rider design painted on a brass drum. His 148th Field Artillery unit soon adopted the logo for its vehicles as well, and it became known as the Bucking Bronco Regiment from Wyoming. And which horse was the symbol modeled after? In the case of the Wyoming National Guard logo, the horse was Ostrom's own mount, Red Wing.

Using Allen True's design, the state of Wyoming first put the bucking bronco on its license plate in 1936, and the well-known, trademarked symbol has been there ever since.

WHERE TO STAY

$–$$ **Best Western Cottontree Inn.** This is Rawlins's finest motel, with spacious guest rooms decorated in greens and mauves. The inviting public areas with easy chairs are great for relaxing. There are regular water aerobics classes at the indoor pool. **Pros:** welcoming atmosphere; pool is open until 11 PM. **Cons:** location leaves a bit to be desired. ✉ *23rd and W. Spruce Sts., Box 387* ☎ *307/324–2737* ☎ *307/324–5011* ⊕ *www.cottontree.net* ↘ *122 rooms* ☊ *In-room: refrigerator, Wi-Fi. In-hotel: bar, pool, Wi-Fi, parking (free), some pets allowed* ═ *AE, D, DC, MC, V.*

$$–$$$ **Quality Inn.** This motel on the east side of town near the 287 bypass has just about everything you could ask for under one roof, from a game room to business services to a barbershop. It's convenient to shops and a grocery store; a free pass gives you full gym access at the Rawlins Recreation Center. Fat Boys Bar & Grill ($$) serves sandwiches, steak, meat loaf, pot roast, and shepherd's pie. **Pros:** easy interstate access; provides most amenities you could need. **Cons:** pool is closed once cold weather sets in. ✉ *1801 E. Cedar St.* ☎ *307/324–2783* ☎ *307/328–1011* ⊕ *www.choicehotels.com* ↘ *131 rooms* ☊ *In-room: refrigerator, Wi-Fi. In-hotel: restaurant, bar, pool, laundry service, parking (free), some pets allowed* ═ *AE, D, DC, MC, V.*

10

CAMPING   **RV World Campground.** There are pull-through RV sites and tent sites at this campground on the west side of Rawlins. ♿ *Flush toilets, full hookups, dump station, drinking water, guest laundry, showers, picnic tables* ➡ *90 hookups, 7 tent sites* ✉ *3101 Wagon Circle Rd.* ☏ *307/328–1091* ▭ *AE, D, MC, V* ☺ *Year-round.*

Western Hills Campground. There are pull-through RV sites, grassy tent sites, and an 18-hole miniature golf course at this year-round campground on the west side of Rawlins. Barbecue, play horseshoes, or browse the gift shop. You have access to immediate phone hookup, a TV area, and a public computer. ♿ *Flush toilets, full hookups, drinking water, guest laundry, showers, fire pits, picnic tables, play area, Wi-Fi* ➡ *115 full hookups, 80 tent sites, log cabins* ✉ *2500 Wagon Circle Rd.* ☏ *307/324–2592, 888/568–3040 for reservations* ▭ *MC, V.*

SOUTHWEST WYOMING

Known as the Red Desert or the Little Colorado Desert, this is a unique area of Wyoming, with a combination of badlands, desert, and mountains. Although it may appear to be desolate, there's a wealth of wildlife in this region, including the largest free-ranging herd of pronghorn in the world (numbering around 50,000) and one of the largest herds of wild horses (numbering in the hundreds) in the United States. Southwest Wyoming is known for its mineral resources and for the dinosaur fossils that have been found here.

GREEN RIVER

120 mi west of Rawlins via I–80.

A town of more than 13,000, Green River attracts those who want to explore the waterways of the Green River drainage in the nearby Flaming Gorge National Recreation Area. Of all the towns along the Union Pacific Railroad, this is the only one that predated the arrival of the rails in the late 1860s. It began as a Pony Express and stage station on the Overland Trail. In 1869 and again in 1871, explorer John Wesley Powell (1834–1902) launched expeditions down the Green and Colorado rivers from nearby sites.

VISITOR INFORMATION
Green River Chamber of Commerce (✉ *1155 W. Flaming Gorge Way, Green River* ☏ *307/875–5711 or 800/354–6743* ⊕ *www.grchamber.com*).

EXPLORING
A golf tournament, parade, arts festival in the park, and concerts are all part of **Flaming Gorge Days** (☏ *800/354–6743* ⊕ *www.flaminggorgedays. com*), a two-day celebration held each June in Green River. Tickets can be purchased for individual events, and concert tickets start at $25.

OFF THE BEATEN PATH   **Seedskadee National Wildlife Refuge.** Prairie and peregrine falcons, Canada geese, and various species of hawks and owls inhabit this 25,000-acre refuge. Trumpeter swans also occasionally use the area. Within or near the refuge there are homestead and ranch sites, Oregon Trail crossings, and ferries that cross the Green River, as well as the spot where Jim Bridger and Henry Fraeb built a trading post in 1839. Visitor information and restrooms are available during daylight hours. ⊠ *37 mi north of Green River on Hwy. 372* ☏ *307/875–2187* ⊕ *www.fws. gov/seedskadee* ▣ *Free.*

SPORTS AND THE OUTDOORS

A stroll on the paved path by the Green River takes you along the route that John Wesley Powell followed on his expedition down the waterway in 1869. Along the way you can visit Expedition Island, the Green Belt Nature Area, and the Scotts Bottom Nature Area. Access **Expedition Island** off 2nd Street, southwest of the railroad yard in Green River; wild birds, squirrels, and rabbits inhabit the grassy, tree-shaded island. Downstream from Expedition Island on the south bank of the river is the **Green Belt Nature Area**, with interpretive signs, nature paths, and numerous birds, including waterfowl. Farther south is **Scotts Bottom Nature Area**, where you'll find more interpretive signs related to the wildlife that lives in this riparian habitat.

WHERE TO EAT

$$
MEXICAN
★

✕ **Don Pedro's Family Restaurant.** Heaping plates of sizzling fajitas, enchiladas, burritos, and other traditional Mexican fare are served in a two-room restaurant where serapes, Mexican sombreros, and cactus provide decoration. ⊠ *520 Wilkes, Suite 10* ☏ *307/875–7324* ▭ *AE, D, MC, V.*

$$
AMERICAN

✕ **Krazy Moose.** Moose-theme decor abounds in this American steak house. Locals favor the chicken-fried steaks, which are handmade and enormous in size. The menu also includes such choices as sandwiches, burgers, and steaks. ⊠ *211 E. Flaming Gorge Way* ☏ *307/875–5124* ▭ *AE, DC, MC, V.*

$
AMERICAN

✕ **Penny's Diner.** The name pretty much says it all—a 1950s-style 24-hour diner with a bright shiny look, reminiscent of a railcar, and flashing neon lights. Try a burger, fries, and a milk shake. The diner is part of the Oak Tree Inn. ⊠ *1172 W. Flaming Gorge Way* ☏ *307/875–3500* ▭ *AE, D, DC, MC, V.*

WHERE TO STAY

$–$$

🏨 **Little America.** This one-stop facility stands alone in the Red Desert, and it can be a real haven if the weather becomes inclement. The hotel, founded in 1934, is the original of the small chain. The rooms are large and comfortable, with mauve-and-green comforters and lots of floral pillows; a small number of them have only showers, and no bathtubs, in the bathrooms. A full-service fuel station and a convenience store are also on the premises. **Pros:** newly remodeled; all rooms have 37-inch flat-screen TVs. **Cons:** closest town is 20 mi away. ⊠ *I–80, 20 mi west of Green River, Box 1, Little America* ☏ *307/875–2400 or 800/634–2401* 🖷 *307/872–2666* ⊕ *www.littleamerica.com/wyoming* 📼 *140 rooms* ⌂ *In-room: refrigerator (some), Internet. In-hotel: restaurant, bar, pool, gym, laundry facilities* ▭ *AE, D, DC, MC, V.*

$

🏨 **Oak Tree Inn.** This two-story inn in four buildings on the west side of town is 20 mi from Flaming Gorge and has views of unique rock outcroppings above the city. Contemporary furnishings fill the rooms, which are decorated in shades of mauve and green. **Pros:** pretty location.

10

Cons: no elevator. ✉ *1170 W. Flaming Gorge Way,* ☎ *307/875–3500* 🖷 *307/875–4889* ⟿ *192 rooms* ⚭ *In-room: refrigerator. In-hotel: restaurant, laundry facilities, Wi-Fi, some pets allowed* ⊟ *AE, D, DC, MC, V.*

FLAMING GORGE NATIONAL RECREATION AREA

20 mi south of Green River via Hwy. 530 or Hwy. 191.

The Flaming Gorge Reservoir of the Flaming Gorge National Recreation Area is formed by Green River water held back by Flaming Gorge Dam. Here you can boat and fish, as well as watch for wildlife. The area is as rich in history as it is spectacularly beautiful. Mountain men such as Jim Bridger and outlaws such as Butch Cassidy found haven here, and in 1869, on his first exploration down the Green River, John Wesley Powell named many local landmarks: Flaming Gorge, Horseshoe Canyon, Red Canyon, and the Gates of Lodore. The recreation area straddles the border between Wyoming and Utah; most of the park's visitor services are in Utah. There are marinas, campgrounds, places to rent horses and snowmobiles, and trails for mountain bikes, as well as lodging and food. The Ashley National Forest administers the area. ☎ *435/784–3445, 800/752–8525 for information on reservoir elevations and river flows, 877/833–6777 TDD, 877/444–6777 for campground reservations* ⊕ *www.fs.fed.us* ⊠ *Free, but $2 daily recreation pass to use the boat ramp* ⊘ *Daily 24 hrs.*

SPORTS AND THE OUTDOORS

BOATING **Buckboard Marina** (✉ *Hwy. 530, 25 mi south of Green River* ☎ *307/875–6927*) provides full marina services, including boat rentals, a marina store, and an RV park.

CAMPING

🏕 **Buckboard Crossing.** The campsites at this campground on the west side of Flaming Gorge can be used for tents or RVs, though only a few sites have electrical hookups for RVs. There's a boat dock here. ⚭ *Flush toilets, dump station, drinking water, showers, fire pits, picnic tables, general store* ⟿ *66 sites* ✉ *23 mi southwest of Green River on Hwy. 530, then 2 mi east on Forest Rd. 009* ☎ *435/784–3445 for information, 307/875–6927, 877/444–6777 for reservations* ⊕ *www.reserveusa. com* ⊟ *AE, D, MC, V* ⊘ *Mid-May–mid-Sept.*

🏕 **Firehole Canyon.** Located in the Flaming Gorge National Recreation Area, this campground has great canyon views. You can pitch a tent or park an RV on the campsites here, but there are no hookups for RVs. There's a beach area nearby, plus a boat ramp. ⚭ *Flush toilets, drinking water, showers, fire pits, picnic tables* ⟿ *40 sites* ✉ *13 mi south of Green River on Hwy. 191, then 10 mi west on Forest Rd. 106* ☎ *435/889–3000 for information, 877/444–6777 for reservations* ⊕ *www.reserveusa.com* ⊟ *AE, D, MC, V* ⊘ *Mid-May–mid-Sept.*

FORT BRIDGER STATE HISTORIC SITE

🕐 *51 mi west of Green River via I–80.*

★ Started in 1843 as a trading post by mountain man Jim Bridger and his partner Louis Vasquez, Fort Bridger was under the control of Mormons by 1853 after they either purchased the fort or forced the original owners to leave—historians aren't sure which. As the U.S. Army approached during a conflict known as the Mormon War of 1857, the Mormons deserted the area and burned the original Bridger post. Fort Bridger then served as a frontier military post until it was abandoned in 1890. Many of the military-era buildings remain, and the Bridger post has been rebuilt and is staffed by a mountain man and woman. You can attend interpretive programs and living-history demonstrations during the summer, and the museum has exhibits about the fort's history. The largest mountain-man rendezvous in the intermountain West occurs annually at Fort Bridger over Labor Day weekend, attracting hundreds of buckskinners and Native Americans plus thousands of visitors. ⊠ *Exit 34 off I–80* ☎ *307/782–3842* ⊕ *http://wyoparks.state. wy.us/Site/SiteInfo.asp?siteID=14* ⊠ *$2–$4* ⊙ *Grounds daily 8:30– dusk. Museum May–Oct., weekdays 9–4:30, weekends or by appointment when staff is available.*

CAMPING

🏕 **Fort Bridger RV Camp.** There's plenty of grass for tents and room for RVs as well at this campground near Fort Bridger. ♿ *Flush toilets, full hookups, drinking water, guest laundry, showers, picnic tables* 🔌 *38 full hookups* ⊠ *Corner of 64 Groshon Rd. and S. Main St.* ☎ *307/782–3150* ⊟ *No credit cards* ⊙ *Apr. 15–Oct. 15.*

SHOPPING

★ The fort's re-created **Bridger/Vazquez Trading Post** sells goods typical of the 1840s, when the post was first established, including trade beads, clothing, and leather items. It's open May–September, daily 9–4:30.

KEMMERER

34 mi north of Fort Bridger via Hwy. 412, 35 mi north of Evanston via Hwy. 189.

This small city serves as a gateway to Fossil Butte National Monument. Probably the most important person in Kemmerer's history was James Cash Penney, who in 1902 started the Golden Rule chain of stores here. He later used the name J. C. Penney Company, which by 1929 had 1,395 outlets. Penney revolutionized merchandising in western Wyoming. Before the opening of Penney's stores, the coal-mining industry dominated the region, and miners were used to working for the company and purchasing their supplies at the company store—which often charged whatever it wanted, managing to keep employees in debt. But when Penney opened his Golden Rule, he set one price for each item and stuck to it. Later he developed a catalog, selling to people unable to get to town easily.

10

VISITOR INFORMATION

Kemmerer Chamber of Commerce (✉ *800 Pine Ave., Kemmerer* ☎ *307/877–9761* ⊕ *www.kemmererchamber.com/*).

EXPLORING

A unique concentration of creatures is embedded in the natural limestone outcrop at **Fossil Butte National Monument,** indicating clearly that this area was an inland sea more than 50 million years ago. Many of the fossils—which include fish, insects, and plants—are remarkably clear and detailed. Pronghorn, coyotes, prairie dogs, and other mammals find shelter within the 8,198-acre park, along with numerous birds, such as eagles and falcons. You can hike the fossil trails and unwind at the picnic area. A visitor center here houses an information desk and exhibits of fossils found in the area, including a 13-foot crocodile. ✉ *15 mi west of Kemmerer via U.S. 30* ☎ *307/877–4455* ⊕ *www.nps.gov/fobu* ▣ *Free* ☉ *Park daily 24 hrs. Visitor center June–Aug., daily 8–7; Sept.–May, daily 8–4:30.*

The **Fossil Country Frontier Museum,** housed in a former church, has fossils and displays related to early settlement in the area. ✉ *400 Pine Ave.* ☎ *307/877–6551* ▣ *Free* ☉ *June–Aug., Mon.–Sat. 9–5; Sept.–May, Mon.–Sat. 10–4.*

At **Ulrich's Fossil Gallery** you can view fossils from around the world and even buy some specimens, particularly fish fossils. Ulrich's also runs fossil-digging excursions at private quarries; call for more information. ✉ *U.S. 30* ☎ *307/877–6466* ▣ *Gallery free, fossil-digging excursions $85. Reservations required* ⊕ *www.ulrichsfossilgallery.com* ☉ *Daily 8–6; fossil digs June–Sept., daily at 9.*

WHERE TO EAT AND STAY

$ ✕ **Busy Bee.** This local favorite on the main street of town serves hearty
AMERICAN homemade fare such as chicken-fried steak, chicken dinners, hamburgers, and omelets. The theme is cows: cow pictures and ceramic heifers dot the walls and counters. ✉ *919 Pine St.* ☎ *307/877–6820* ▤ *No credit cards.*

¢ ▦ **Energy Inn.** Southwestern colors decorate the basic rooms, and you have access to a fax machine and a microwave in the lobby. A few miles south of Kemmerer in Diamondville, the motel caters to energy-industry workers; 10 ground-floor kitchenette units are for extended stays. **Pros:** wallet-friendly price. **Cons:** accommodations are a bit shabby, and it can be difficult to get a room with the influx of energy workers. ✉ *3 U.S. 189 and Hwy. 30, Diamondville* ☎ *307/877–6901* ⊕ *www.energyinn.net* ⇆ *31 rooms, 10 kitchenette units* ⌂ *In-room: kitchen (some), refrigerator, Wi-Fi.* ▤ *AE, D, DC, MC, V.*

SHOPPING

To understand Kemmerer's roots, stop at the **JC Penney store** (✉ *722 JC Penney Dr.* ☎ *307/877–3164*), which is where James Cash Penney began his merchandising career. This small retail establishment, known as the "mother store," sells clothing.

The South Dakota Black Hills

WORD OF MOUTH

"Early in the morning we headed to Mt. Rushmore, driving along the winding, scenic Iron Mountain Road in Custer State Park. I highly recommend this approach to the park. There are a couple tunnels which frame the monument as you drive from this direction."

—texasbookworm

By T. D. Griffith It's been called "an emerald isle in a sea of prairie." With alpine meadows, thick forests, and creek-carved canyons, the Black Hills region more closely resembles Big Horn and Yellowstone country than it does South Dakota's typical flat farmland.

The Black Hills rise up from the western South Dakota plains just over the Wyoming state line and about 150 mi east of the Big Horn range of the Rocky Mountains. They aren't as high—Harney Peak, their tallest summit, measures 7,242 feet—and they cover a territory only 50 mi wide and 120 mi long, but these ponderosa-covered mountains have a majesty all their own.

The region is anchored by Rapid City; with 62,715 residents, it's the largest city for 350 mi in any direction. Perhaps better known, however, are the region's 19th-century frontier towns, including Spearfish, Lead, and Deadwood. The Black Hills also can claim one of the highest concentrations of public parks, monuments, and memorials in the world. Among the more famous are Badlands National Park, Jewel Cave National Monument, and Mount Rushmore National Memorial, whose giant stone carvings of four U.S. presidents have retained their stern grandeur for more than 60 years.

As in neighboring Wyoming and Montana, outdoor recreation reigns supreme in the Black Hills. Whatever your pleasure—hiking, mountain biking, rock climbing, horseback riding, fishing, boating, skiing, snowmobiling, cross-country skiing—you can do it here, before a backdrop of stunning countryside.

ORIENTATION AND PLANNING

GETTING ORIENTED

The 2 million acres of the Black Hills are about evenly split between private property and the Black Hills National Forest. Fortunately for visitors, the national forest is one of the most developed in the United States. Roads are numerous and generally well maintained, and navigation is easy. Towns with services are plentiful (compared with the Wyoming plains to the west), so you needn't worry about how much gas you've got in your tank or where you'll find a place to stay at night. Rapid City, the largest community in the region, is the most popular base for exploring the Black Hills. The northern towns of Deadwood and Spearfish have almost as many services, with less traffic and fewer tourists.

PLANNING

WHEN TO GO

Weather forecasters hate the Black Hills. Snow can fall in the upper elevations every month of the year, and temperatures in January occasionally register above 60°F. However, anomalies like these rarely last more than a day or two. For the most part, expect the thermometer to range between 80°F and 100°F in summer, and know that winter temperatures can plunge below 10°F. Most visitors come in the warmer months, June to September, which is an optimal time for outdoor activities. Thanks to an average annual snowfall of 150 inches, more wintersports enthusiasts are beginning to discover the area's many skiing and snowmobiling opportunities. Nevertheless, the colder months are the least crowded in the Black Hills.

The shoulder seasons are increasingly popular times to visit, a trend that should continue as the baby boomers begin to retire. Spring in the Black Hills is generally snowy and rainy, but autumn is the perfect time to visit. The days are pleasantly warm, the nights are cool, and if you arrive before mid-October you'll be treated to an incredible display of fall colors. Your only competition for space will be small groups of sportsmen and the occasional photographer out capturing images of colorful leaves.

PLANNING YOUR TIME

Every small town in the Black Hills has something to offer—a fact that you may find surprising. This region has the highest concentration of parks, monuments, and memorials in the United States, qualifying the Black Hills and badlands as more than just a stopover on the way to and from the huge national parks of western Montana and Wyoming. If you have the time, your must-see list should include Rapid City, Mount Rushmore, the Crazy Horse Memorial, Deadwood, and Custer State Park. You can see the highlights of southwestern South Dakota in 24 or 48 hours—but if you spend five days or more here, you will be amply rewarded.

You might consider a top-down approach, first exploring the Northern Hills around Deadwood. The historic sites, scenery, and casinos will keep you busy, but don't be afraid to explore the hidden treasures of the outlying towns: the new Tri-State Museum in Belle Fourche, the High Plains Western Heritage Center in Spearfish, and the Homestake Visitor Center in Lead are all worth seeing. Afterward, you can move into the central Black Hills, spending some time in Rapid City to shop, check out the Journey Museum, and sample the local cuisine. Rapid City is also a good base for a day trip to nearby Mount Rushmore and Hill City, a tiny town with a vibrant art-gallery district and its own winery and vintage steam train. When you've covered the central region, shift down to the southern hills and visit Wind Cave National Park (which we cover in the next chapter), Crazy Horse Memorial, Jewel Cave National Monument, the Mammoth Site, and the historic towns of Custer and Hot Springs—where naturally warm water still bubbles up from the earth. You can approach Badlands National Park to the

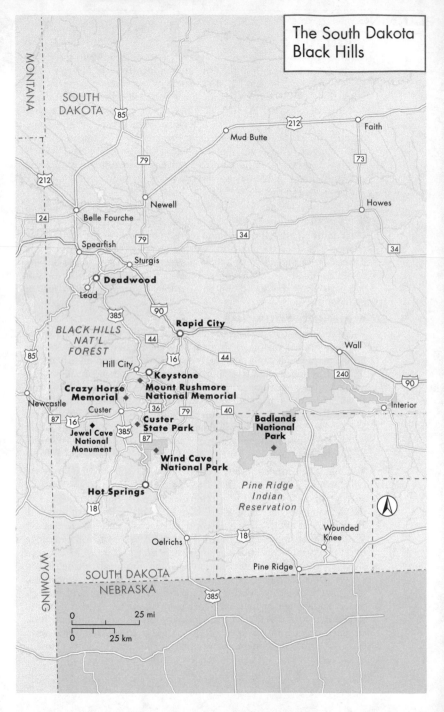

The South Dakota
Black Hills

east as a separate region if you have the time, or you might simply make it a day trip.

Spending a day in each subregion will allow you to explore most of the key attractions in the Black Hills. If you have time to spare, you will probably want to add the central and northern Black Hills,

TOP REASONS TO GO

■ The majesty of Mount Rushmore

■ Custer State Park

■ Crazy Horse Memorial

■ Deadwood

11

which are relatively unpopulated and offer exceptional natural wonders such as Spearfish Canyon.

GETTING HERE AND AROUND

AIR TRAVEL

Although there are several landing strips and municipal airports in the Black Hills, the only airport with commercial service is in Rapid City. Rapid City Regional Airport, one of the fastest-growing airports in the United States, is 11 mi east of town on Highway 44.

Delta Air provides a connection to Rapid City from Salt Lake City, Northwest has service from Minneapolis, United flies from Denver and Chicago, Frontier also has flights from Denver, and Allegiant Air has weekly service from Las Vegas and Phoenix.

Airlines Allegiant Air (☎ 800/432–3810 ⊕ www.allegiantair.com). **Delta Air** (☎ 800/221–1212 ⊕ www.delta.com). **Frontier Airlines** (☎ 800/432–1359 ⊕ www.frontierairlines.com). **Northwest Airlines** (☎ 800/225–2525 ⊕ www. nwa.com). **United Airlines** (☎ 800/241–6522 ⊕ www.ual.com).

Airport Information Rapid City Regional Airport (✉ 4550 Terminal Rd., Rapid City ☎ 605/393–9924 ⊕ www.rapairport.org).

BUS TRAVEL

Greyhound Lines provides national service out of Rapid City. Jefferson Lines serves Wall and Rapid City, with connections to most midwestern and southern cities. Powder River Transportation connects Rapid City with the smaller towns in eastern and northern Wyoming. Gray Line of the Black Hills provides charter service and tours within the Black Hills region.

Information Gray Line of the Black Hills (☎ 605/342–4461 ⊕ www.black-hillsgrayline.com). **Greyhound Lines** (☎ 307/634–7744 or 800/231–2222 ⊕ www.greyhound.com). **Jefferson Lines** (☎ 888/864–2832 ⊕ www.jefferson-lines.com). **Powder River Transportation** (☎ 307/682–0960).

CAR TRAVEL

Unless you come to the Black Hills on an escorted package tour, a car is essential. I–90 cuts directly through South Dakota from west to east, connecting the northern towns of Spearfish, Sturgis, and Deadwood (which lies about 14 mi off the interstate) with Rapid City. From there the interstate turns straight east, passing Wall and Badlands National Park on its way to Sioux Falls.

Minor highways of importance include U.S. 385, which connects the interior of the Black Hills from south to north, and U.S. 16, which winds south of Rapid City toward the Mount Rushmore and Crazy Horse memorials. Highway 44 is an alternate route between the Black Hills and the Badlands. Within the Black Hills, seven highway tunnels have limited clearance; they are marked on state maps and in the state's tourism booklet.

Snowplows work hard to keep the roads clear in winter, but you may have trouble getting around immediately after a major snowstorm, especially in upper elevations. Unlike the Rockies, where even higher elevations make some major roads impassable in winter, the only Black Hills roads that close permanently in the snowy months are minor dirt or gravel Forest Service roads.

Contact the South Dakota State Highway Patrol for information on road conditions.

Information **South Dakota State Highway Patrol** (☎ 511 ⊕ *hp.state.sd.us*).

RESTAURANTS

Like neighboring Wyoming, the Black Hills are not known for culinary diversity, and no matter where you go in this part of the world, beef is king. Nevertheless, thanks to a growing population and increasing numbers of visitors, the area is beginning to see more dining options. Rapid City and Spearfish have an abundance of national chain restaurants, and both communities have local eateries that specialize in continental, contemporary, Native American, and traditional American cooking. Although dining in Deadwood's casinos usually involves an all-you-can-eat buffet, the tiny town also claims some of the best-ranked restaurants in South Dakota. Don't be afraid to try wild game dishes: buffalo, pheasant, and elk are relatively common ingredients in the Black Hills.

HOTELS

New chain hotels with modern amenities are plentiful in the Black Hills, but when booking accommodations consider a stay at one of the area's historic properties. From grand brick downtown hotels to intimate Queen Anne homes converted to bed-and-breakfasts, historic lodgings are easy to locate. Many have been carefully restored to their late-19th-century grandeur, down to antique Victorian furnishings and authentic Western art. Other distinctive lodging choices include the region's mountain lodges and forest retreats. Usually built along creeks or near major trails, these isolated accommodations often attract outdoor enthusiasts.

WHAT IT COSTS				
¢	$	$$	$$$	$$$$
Restaurants	under $8	$8–$12	$13–$20	$21–$30	over $30
Hotels	under $70	$70–$100	$101–$150	$151–$200	over $200

Restaurant prices are for a main course at dinner, excluding sales tax of 4%–7%. Hotel prices are for two people in a standard double room in high season, excluding service charges and 5%–10% tax.

CAMPING

Camping is one of this region's strengths. There are countless campgrounds in the Black Hills and the Badlands. Most of the public land within the national forests and parks is open for camping, provided that you don't light any fires. Keep in mind when selecting your campsite that although the Black Hills don't have any native bears, there is a significant population of mountain lions.

VISITOR INFORMATION

Numerous publications, ranging from small booklets to thick magazines, provide information—and lots of advertising—to visitors headed to the Black Hills. You can pick up many of these at hotels and restaurants, usually for free.

Information **Black Hills, Badlands and Lakes Association** (✉ *1851 Discovery Circle, Rapid City* ☎ *605/355–3600* ⊕ *www.blackhillsbadlands.com*).

DEADWOOD

Fodor's Choice ★ *42 mi northwest of Rapid City via I–90 and U.S. 14A.*

Its brick-paved streets plied by old-time trolleys, illuminated by period lighting, and lined with original Victorian architecture, Deadwood today owes much of its historical character to casinos. In 1989 South Dakota voters approved limited-stakes gaming for the town, on the condition that a portion of revenues be devoted to historic preservation. Since then more than $200 million has been dedicated to restoring and preserving this once infamous gold-mining boomtown, which has earned recognition as a National Historic Landmark. Small gaming halls, good restaurants, and hotels occupy virtually every storefront on Main Street, just as they did back in Deadwood's late-19th-century heyday. You can walk in the footsteps of legendary lawman Wild Bill Hickok, cigar-smoking Poker Alice Tubbs, and the fabled Calamity Jane, who swore she could outdrink, outspit, and outswear any man—and usually did.

Several of the storefronts on **Main Street** belong to souvenir shops that typically peddle rubber tomahawks and plastic pistols to tourists. Some of the more upscale stores carry high-quality Western wear, Black Hills–gold jewelry, and fine art. Ice-cream parlors are never hard to find during summer.

GETTING HERE AND AROUND

Because most of Deadwood was laid out before the advent of automobiles, the city today is entirely walkable. Strung in a roughly straight line along the bottom of a gulch, the main points of interest are difficult to miss. The best strategy is to park in one of the lots on Main or Sherman streets and begin your pedestrian adventure from there.

The narrow confines of Deadwood Gulch can make parking a problem. Especially during busy weekends, a spot can be hard to find. Be patient, check the city lots (there is a parking ramp off Main Street), and have your quarters ready for the parking meters that can gulp them as fast as the slot machines.

VISITOR INFORMATION
Deadwood Area Chamber of Commerce & Visitor Bureau (⊠ 735 Main St.,
Deadwood ☎ 605/578-1876 or 800/999-1876 ⊕ www.deadwood.com).

EXPLORING DEADWOOD

A tour of the restored **Adams House** includes an explanation of the trag-
edies and triumphs of two of the community's founding families (the
Franklins and the Adamses) who lived here. The 1892 Queen Anne–style
mansion was closed in the mid-1930s and sat empty for more than 50
years, preserving the original furniture and decor that you see today.
⊠ 22 Van Buren Ave. ☎ 605/578-3724 ⊕ www.adamsmuseumand-
house.org ⊠ $5 ۞ May–Sept., daily 9–5; Oct.–Apr., Tues.–Sat. 10–4.

The **Adams Museum,** between the massive stone-block post office and the
old railroad depot, houses three floors of displays, including the first
locomotive used in the area, photographs of the town's early days, and
a reproduction of the largest gold nugget (7¾ troy ounces) ever discovered in the Black Hills. ⊠ 54 Sherman St. ☎ 605/578-1714 ⊕ www.
adamsmuseumandhouse.org ⊠ Donations accepted ۞ May 1–Sept. 30,
daily 9–5; Oct. 1–Apr. 30, Tues.–Sat. 10–4.

ٍ At **Broken Boot Gold Mine** you can pan for gold, and even if you don't
find any, you'll leave with a souvenir stock certificate. ⊠ U.S. 14A
☎ 605/578-1876 ⊕ www.brokenbootgoldmine.com ⊠ Tour $5, gold
panning $7 ۞ May–Aug., daily 8–5:30; Sept., daily 9–4:30.

The annual Days of '76 Rodeo—five days of parades, gallantry, horsemanship, and the best of the Old West, held at the end of July—pays
homage to Deadwood's storied past. The **Days of '76 Museum** began
almost by accident as the horse-drawn carriages and stagecoaches used
in the event's parade became an attraction in their own right. Over the
years, cowboy memorabilia, photographs, and historical clothing have
been added to the collection, and construction of a new $6 million
museum began in late 2009. For updates on progress, visit the museum
Web site. ⊠ 17 Crescent St. ☎ 605/578-2872 ⊕ www.daysof76.com/
museum ⊠ Donations accepted ۞ Mid-Apr.–mid-Oct., daily 9–5.

Mount Moriah Cemetery, also known as Boot Hill, is the final resting
place of Wild Bill Hickok, Calamity Jane, and other notable Deadwood residents. The aging landmark was revitalized by extensive res-
toration work in 2003, including the addition of a visitor center that
houses a leather Bible, a stained-glass window, and pulpit chairs from
the first and second Methodist churches of Deadwood, which were
destroyed in 1885 and 2003, respectively. From the top of the cemetery
you'll have the best panoramic view of the town. ⊠ Top of Lincoln St.
☎ 605/722-0837 ⊠ $1 ۞ Memorial Day–Labor Day, daily 7 AM–8 PM;
Labor Day–end of Sept., daily 9–5.

A heroic-scale bronze sculpture of three Native Americans on horseback driving 14 bison off a cliff is the centerpiece of **Tatanka: Story of the
Bison,** on a ridge above Deadwood. The attraction, owned by Dances
with Wolves star Kevin Costner, also includes an interpretive center
in which exhibits explain Plains Indian life circa 1840. ⊠ U.S. 85, 1

mi north of downtown ☎ *605/584–5678* ⊕ *www.storyofthebison.com* 🖼 *$7.50* ⊙ *Mid-May–Sept., daily 9–5.*

OFF THE
BEATEN
PATH

🔥 **High Plains Western Heritage Center.** Founded to honor the pioneers and Native Americans of a region now covered by five states—the Dakotas, Wyoming, Montana,

> **DEADWOOD JAM**
>
> In September Deadwood is host to the Black Hills' premier music event showcasing the top in country, rock, and blues (☎ 800/999–1876 ⊕ www.deadwoodjam.com).

and Nebraska—the center features artifacts such as a Deadwood–Spearfish stagecoach. Outdoor exhibits include a sod home, a log cabin, a one-room schoolhouse, and in summer, an entire farm set up with antique equipment. Often on the calendar are cowboy poetry, live music, festivals, reenactments, and historical talks. ⊠ *825 Heritage Dr., Spearfish* ☎ *605/642–9378* ⊕ *www.westernheritagecenter. com* 🖼 *$7* ⊙ *Daily 9–5.*

SPORTS AND THE OUTDOORS

Deadwood makes a good base for a winter sports vacation in the Black Hills, particularly if you like snowmobiling and cross-country skiing. The surrounding Northern Hills are especially popular, both for their stunning scenery and heavy snows. The rocky peaks and deep canyons are most dramatic here, and the snowfall is the heaviest. In some years the area around Deadwood sees as much as 180 inches of the white stuff, although the yearly average hovers around 150 inches. The climate here is more variable than in the Rockies, so snow doesn't blanket the region all winter. Warm spells of 50°F, 60°F, or even 70°F weather often hit the region for a week or so after big snowfalls, quickly melting the fresh powder. Before you make firm plans, be sure to check weather reports.

The community of **Sturgis** becomes South Dakota's largest city during the first week of August each year, when more than half a million motorcyclists invade for the **Sturgis Motorcycle Rally** (⊠ *13 mi east of Deadwood on U.S. 14* ☎ *605/720–0800* ⊕ *www.sturgismotorcyclerally.com*). Begun in 1940 by a handful of bike owners, the event has grown into one of the largest gatherings of Harley-Davidson owners in the world. Motorcycle shows, concerts, motorcycle tours, and national racing events are just some of the activities that fill this 10-day festival. Most hotels within a 100-mi radius of the town are totally booked for the festival up to a year in advance.

HIKING AND BICYCLING

Beginning in Deadwood and running the length of the Black Hills from north to south, the **Mickelson Trail** (⊕ *www.mickelsontrail.com*) incorporates more than 100 converted railroad bridges and four tunnels in its 109-mi-long course. Although the grade seldom exceeds 4%, parts of the trail are strenuous. A $2 day pass lets you hike or bike on the trail ($10 for an annual pass); passes are available at self-service stations along the trail, some state park offices, and through the South

Dakota Game, Fish and Parks Web site (⊕ *www.sdgfp.info/Index.htm*).
A portion of the trail is open for snowmobiling in winter.

SKIING

Heavy snowfalls and lovely views make the Black Hills prime cross-country skiing territory. Many trails are open to snowmobilers as well as skiers, but most skiers stick to the quieter trails that are closed to motorized traffic. Many of these trails run along the rim or at the bottom of narrow canyons and gulches, affording outstanding views of some spectacular country. Depending on the freeze-thaw cycle, you may catch a glimpse of frozen waterfalls, particularly in Spearfish Canyon.

Although the Black Hills don't have the massive peaks that give Colorado, Wyoming, and Montana some of the best downhill skiing in the world, a couple of rocky slopes in the Northern Hills are both steep enough and snowy enough to support modest ski resorts, with respectable intermediate-level runs.

The groomed **Big Hill Trails** (✉ *7 mi south of Spearfish on Tinton Rd., 15 mi west of Deadwood* ☎ *605/673–9200*) travel all around Spearfish Canyon. The trees here are gorgeous, ranging from the ubiquitous ponderosa and Black Hills spruce to quaking aspen and paperbark birch. The towering canyon walls, abundant wildlife, and stark contrast between the evergreens and the bare trees make this a particularly outstanding trail.

Mystic Miner Ski Resort at Deer Mountain (✉ *11187 Deer Mountain Rd., 3 mi south of Lead on U.S. 85* ☎ *605/584–3230 or 888/410–3337* ⊕ *www.skimystic.com*) has a massive beginner's area, tubing, snowboarding, sleigh rides, and the only night skiing in the Black Hills.

Perched on the sides of a 7,076-foot mountain, **Terry Peak Ski Area** (✉ *2 mi south of Lead on U.S. 85* ☎ *800/456–0524* ⊕ *www.terrypeak.com*) claims the Black Hills' second-highest mountain summit. The runs are challenging for novice and intermediate skiers and should keep the experts entertained. From the top, on a clear day, you can see into Wyoming, Montana, and North Dakota.

SNOWMOBILING

Trade and travel magazines consistently rank the Black Hills among the top snowmobiling destinations in the country for two simple reasons: dramatic scenery and an abundance of snow. You'll find both throughout the area, but especially in the Northern Hills.

Trailshead Lodge (✉ *21 mi southwest of Deadwood on U.S. 85* ☎ *605/584–3464* ⊕ *www.trailsheadlodge.com*), near the Wyoming border, has a small restaurant, a bar, gas, a repair shop, and dozens of brand-new snowmobiles for rent by the day. In summer (or during warm spells in winter when the snow melts) the lodge caters to bicyclists, horseback riders, hunters, and hikers.

WHERE TO EAT

$$ ✕**Deadwood Social Club.** On the second floor of historic Saloon No. 10,
ITALIAN this warm restaurant surrounds you with wood and old-time photo-
Fodor'sChoice graphs of Deadwood's past. Light jazz and blues play over the sound
★ system. The decor is Western, but the food is northern Italian, a com-
bination that keeps patrons coming back. The menu stretches from
wild-mushroom pasta-and-seafood nest with basil cream to chicken
piccata (sautéed and served with a lemon and parsley sauce) and melt-
in-your-mouth Black Angus rib eyes. The wine list had nearly 200
selections at last count. Reservations are a good idea. ⊠ *657 Main St.*
☎ *605/578–1533* ▤ *AE, MC, V.*

$$$ ✕**Deadwood Thymes Bistro.** Across from the historic courthouse, away
CONTINENTAL from the Main Street casinos, this bistro has a quieter, more intimate
★ feel than other town restaurants—and the food is among the best. The
menu changes frequently, but expect dishes like brioche French toast,
salmon quiche, Parisian grilled ham and Swiss, Thai burrito with peanut sauce, and lamb chops marinated in white wine and mustard and
served with parsley-gin sauce. The wine list features imports, and desserts are incredible. You might find raspberry cheesecake or chocolate angel food cake with a whiskey-bourbon sauce. ⊠ *87 Sherman St.*
☎ *605/578–7566* ▤ *MC, V.*

$$$ ✕**Jakes.** This restaurant, owned by actor Kevin Costner, is among South
ECLECTIC Dakota's classiest dining experiences. Cherrywood pillars inlaid with
★ etched-glass lights, white-brick fireplaces, and a pianist add to the ele-
gance of the atrium dining room. Among the menu's eclectic offerings
are buffalo roulade, Cajun seafood tortellini, filet mignon, and fresh
fish. ⊠ *677 Main St.* ☎ *605/578–1555* ⌔ *Reservations essential* ▤ *AE,*
D, MC, V.

¢ ✕**Moonshine Gulch Saloon.** Although it's 25 mi south of Deadwood in the
AMERICAN middle of a very empty section of the forest, the ghost town of Rochford
is worth visiting. Once the site of a prosperous gold camp, the town
now has about 15 residents and even fewer buildings. The saloon (near
the Rochford Mall, the self-proclaimed "Small of America," and one-
room Rochford University) stays quite busy in the summer despite its
remote location. After you order your sarsaparilla soda and hamburger,
look up to admire the collection of baseball caps, currency, and busi-
ness cards on the ceiling. ⊠ *Rochford Rd., Rochford* ☎ *605/584–2743*
▤ *MC, V.*

WHERE TO STAY

$–$$$ ☷ **Bullock Hotel.** A casino occupies the main floor of this meticulously
restored, pink granite hotel, which was built by Deadwood's first sher-
iff, Seth Bullock, in 1895. Rooms are furnished in Victorian style with
reproductions of the original furniture. You can order a steak or ham-
burger at the casual downstairs restaurant ($$). **Pros:** centrally located
with on-site parking; staff is friendly and attentive; on-site ghost tour is
fun and unique. **Cons:** front desk not in the most accessible of locations
because of the era in which the hotel was built; slot machines command-
ing the front lobby can be disconcerting in such a finely restored hotel.

✉ *633 Main St.* ☎ *605/578–1745 or 800/336–1876* 🖷 *605/578–1382* ⊕ *www.historicbullock.com* ⬦ *29 rooms, 7 suites* ⚿ *In-hotel: restaurant, room service, bar* ▭ *AE, D, MC, V.*

$$–$$$$ ⊡ **Franklin Hotel.** Built in 1903, this imposing hotel has housed many
Fodor's Choice famous guests, including John Wayne, Teddy Roosevelt, and Babe Ruth.
★ It still has its original banisters, ceilings, and fireplace. The guest rooms
are Victorian-style, with reproduction furniture, lace on hardwood
tables, and flowery bedspreads. A bar on the second floor spills out onto
the veranda above the white-columned hotel entrance, affording a great
view down Main Street. The hotel had a major face-lift in 2006, which
included an expanded casino and conference room. **Pros:** renovations
offer guests one of the nicest casinos in town; great views of the historic
town. **Cons:** parking is often a hike from the hotel with no valet service;
more room renovations are pending. ✉ *700 Main St.* ☎ *605/578–2241
or 800/688–1876* 🖷 *605/578–3452* ⊕ *www.silveradoffranklin.com*
⬦ *81 rooms* ⚿ *In-hotel: room service, bar* ▭ *AE, D, MC, V.*

$–$$$$ ⊡ **The Lodge at Deadwood.** Opened in the fall of 2009, this $47 million
upscale resort, casino, and convention center commands a perch high
above Deadwood with spectacular views. You can enjoy 140 rooms and
suites, gaming, a first-class restaurant, year-round indoor water park,
and sports bar, and the convention center can accommodate groups up
to 1,000. **Pros:** great location; all the virtues of a new facility. **Cons:**
short on genuine Old West charm. ✉ *100 Pine Crest La., U.S. Hwy.
85* ☎ *605/584–48001* ⊕ *www.deadwoodlodge.com* ⬦ *140 rooms, 14
suites* ⚿ *In-room: refrigerators, Wi-Fi. In-hotel: restaurant, room service, bar, pool, gym, laundry facilities* ▭ *AE, D, MC, V.*

$$$ ⊡ **Spearfish Canyon Lodge.** About midway between Spearfish and Dead-
★ wood, near the bottom of Spearfish Canyon, this lodge-style hotel com-
mands some of the best views in the Black Hills. Limestone cliffs rise
nearly 1,000 feet in all directions. The rush of Spearfish Falls is only a
¼-mi hike away, and the gentle flow of Roughlock Falls is a mile-long
hike through pine, oak, and aspen from the lodge's front door. Rooms
are furnished in natural woods, and fabrics are dark maroon and green.
Pros: scenery unmatched by any hotel in the area; a mile from one of
the most breathtaking waterfalls in the region; on snowmobile trail
that offers riders more than 300 mi of groomed trails. **Cons:** secluded—
nearly 15 mi from the closest amenities; winding approach road can be
dangerous during the winter months. ✉ *10619 Roughlock Falls Rd.,
Lead* ☎ *877/975–6343 or 605/584–3435* 🖷 *605/584–3990* ⊕ *www.
spfcanyon.com* ⬦ *54 rooms* ⚿ *In-room: Internet. In-hotel: restaurant,
room service, bar, laundry facilities* ▭ *AE, D, MC, V.*

CAMPING ⚠ **Whistler Gulch Campground.** Situated in a canyon overlooking the town
of Deadwood, this well-developed campground—and its modern log
lounge—has a spectacular view and friendly owners. **Pros:** tucked in a
quiet canyon; clean pool and restrooms; wildlife. **Cons:** up a hill; walk
to restaurants (but trolley will take you downtown). ✉ *235 Cliff St.,
U.S. 85 S, Deadwood* ☎ *605/578–2092 or 800/704–7139* ⬦ *160 sites
(110 with full hookups); 3 cabins* ⚿ *Flush toilets, full hookups, guest*

laundry, showers, fire grates, picnic tables, electricity, public telephone, general store, swimming (pool) ⊙ May–mid-Oct.

NIGHTLIFE

There are more than 80 gaming establishments in Deadwood, most of them small and personal. They generally serve other functions as well—as restaurants, saloons, and gift shops—and usually have only a few blackjack and poker tables and slot machines.

Expect a family crowd during the day and a rowdier bunch at night at the **Bodega and Big Al's Buffalo Steakhouse Stockade** (⊠ *658 Main St.* ☎ *605/578–1300*). Most evenings you can listen to live country or rock music; the entertainment moves outdoors in summer, when bands play in the stockade section. The Bodega has a rough past; from the 1890s until 1980, the upper floors were used as a brothel. The rooms now sit empty, although the secret buzzers and discreet back doors were removed only in the 1990s. It doesn't offer live music, but the casino **Midnight Star** (⊠ *677 Main St.* ☎ *605/578–1555*) is owned by actor Kevin Costner and decorated throughout with props and costumes from his movies. The bar on the first floor is named for and modeled after the bar in the film *Silverado*, in which Costner starred. Wood accents, stained glass, and plush carpeting give the structure an elegant Victorian look.

★ Billing itself as "the only museum in the world with a bar," the **Old Style Saloon No. 10** (⊠ *657 Main St.* ☎ *605/578–3346*) is littered with thousands of artifacts, from vintage photos and antique lighting to a stuffed two-headed calf and the chair in which Wild Bill Hickok was supposedly shot. A reenactment of his murder takes place four times daily in the summer. At night come for some of the region's best bands, lively blackjack tables, and quiet bartenders who cater to noisy customers. The **Silverado** (⊠ *709 Main St.* ☎ *605/578–1366 or 800/584–7005*), sprawling over half a city block at the top of Main Street, is among Deadwood's largest gaming establishments. Although the wood paneling and brass accents around the bars recall Deadwood's Wild West past, the red carpets, velvet ropes, and bow tie–clad staff give the place modern polish. The prime rib–and-crab buffet on Friday and Saturday nights attracts regulars from more than 100 mi away.

EN ROUTE The easiest way to get from Deadwood to Rapid City and the central Black Hills is east through Boulder Canyon on U.S. 14A, which joins I–90 in Sturgis. However, it's worth looping north and taking the long way around on **Spearfish Canyon Scenic Byway,** a 20-mi route past 1,000-foot limestone cliffs and some of the most breathtaking scenery in the region. Cascading waterfalls quench the thirst of quaking aspen, gnarled oaks, sweet-smelling spruce, and the ubiquitous ponderosa pine, which grow right off the edges of rocky precipices. The canyon is home to deer, mountain goats, porcupines, and bobcats. Near its middle is the old sawmill town of Savoy, a jumping-off point for scenic hikes to Spearfish Falls and Roughlock Falls, which have handicapped-accessible trails affording views of the cascading waters. The canyon opens onto the small city of Spearfish, home to several restaurants, hotels, and Black Hills State University.

RAPID CITY

42 mi southeast of Deadwood via U.S. 14A and I–90.

The central Black Hills, one of the most developed and best-traveled parts of the region, is anchored by Rapid City (population 62,715). The largest population center in a 350-mi radius, it's the cultural, educational, medical, and economic hub of a vast region. Most of the numerous shops, hotels, and restaurants in the city cater specifically to tourists, including a steady flow of international visitors; some signage displays information in multiple languages and includes metric measurements. Locals refer to Rapid City as West River, meaning "west of the Missouri." Cowboy boots are common here, and business leaders often travel by pickup truck or four-wheel-drive vehicle. At the same time, the city supports a convention center and a modern, acoustically advanced performance hall.

GETTING HERE AND AROUND

With life-size bronze sculptures by local artists on virtually every street corner downtown and a greenway with hiking and biking trails through the heart of town, Rapid City is a good place to get out of your car and stroll around. A four-lane highway, U.S. 16, links the city to Mount Rushmore National Memorial.

VISITOR INFORMATION

Rapid City Chamber of Commerce and Convention & Visitors Bureau
(✉ *Civic Center, 444 N. Mt. Rushmore Rd., Box 747, Rapid City* ☎ *605/343–1744 or 800/487–3223* ⊕ *www.visitrapidcity.com*).

EXPLORING RAPID CITY

★ The interactive exhibits at the **Journey Museum** explore the history of the Black Hills from the age of the dinosaurs to the days of the pioneers. The complex combines the collections of the **Sioux Indian Museum,** the **Minnilusa Pioneer Museum,** the **Museum of Geology,** the **State Archaeological Research Center,** and a private collection of Native American artifacts into a sweeping pageant of the history and evolution of the Black Hills. A favorite among visitors is the tepee in the Sioux Indian Museum; you have to crouch down and peer inside to watch a holographic Lakota woman talk about the history and legends of her people. ✉ *222 New York St.* ☎ *605/394–6923* ⊕ *www.journeymuseum.org* 💷 *$7* ☉ *Memorial Day–Labor Day, daily 9–6; Labor Day–Memorial Day, Mon.–Sat. 10–5, Sun. 1–5.*

The **South Dakota Air & Space Museum** has a model of a Stealth bomber that's 60% actual size. Also here are General Dwight D. Eisenhower's Mitchell B-25 bomber and more than two dozen other planes, as well as a once-operational missile silo. The museum is open year-round, but tours are not available in winter. ✉ *2890 Davis Dr.* ☎ *605/385–5188*

⊕ *www.sdairandspacemuseum.com* ✉ *Free, tour $5* ☉ *June–Labor Day, daily 8:30–6; Labor Day–June, daily 8:30–4:30.*

Although they were released in the early 1990s, the films *Dances with Wolves* and *Thunderheart* continue to generate interest and business in the Black Hills. The **Ft. Hays** *Dances with Wolves* **Movie Set** displays photos and shows a video taken during the making of the film. A chuck-wagon dinner show ($15) is offered Memorial Day through Labor Day. ⊠ *Ft. Hays Dr. and U.S. 16* ☎ *888/394–9653* ⊕ *www.rushmoretours. com/forthays.html* ✉ *Free* ☉ *Mid-May–mid-Sept., daily 7:30* AM*–8* PM.

⟳ On the west side of Rapid City is **Storybook Island,** a park on the banks of Rapid Creek that lets children romp through scenes from fairy tales and nursery rhymes. A children's theater troupe, sponsored by the Black Hills Community Theater, performs regular shows on a modest outdoor stage here and hosts workshops and acting programs. ⊠ *1301 Sheridan Lake Rd.* ☎ *605/342–6357* ⊕ *www.storybookisland.org* ✉ *Donations accepted* ☉ *May–Sept., daily 9–7.*

⟳ **Reptile Gardens.** On the bottom of a valley between Rapid City and ★ Mount Rushmore is western South Dakota's answer to a zoo. In addition to the world's largest private reptile collection, the site also has a raptor rehabilitation center. No visit is complete without watching some alligator wrestling or letting the kids check out the giant tortoises. ⊠ *8955 S. U.S. 16* ☎ *605/342–5873* ⊕ *www.reptilegardens.com* ✉ *$14* ☉ *Memorial Day–Labor Day, daily 8–7; Labor Day–Oct. 3 and Apr. 1–Memorial Day, daily 9–4; special Jingle in the Jungle mid-Dec.–late Dec., Mon.–Thurs. 10–5, Fri.–Sun. 10–7.*

⟳ **Bear Country U.S.A.** Encounter black bears and wolves at this drive-through wildlife park. There's also a walk-through wildlife center. ⊠ *13820 S. U.S. 16* ☎ *605/343–2290* ⊕ *www.bearcountryusa.com* ✉ *$15* ☉ *May–Nov., daily 8–7.*

Black Hills Caverns. Frost crystal, amethyst, logomites, calcite crystals, and other specimens fill this cave, first discovered by pioneers in the late 1800s. Half-hour and hour tours are available. ⊠ *2600 Cavern Rd.* ☎ *605/343–0542* ⊕ *www.blackhillscaverns.com* ✉ *$9.75 per hr, $7.50 per ½ hr* ☉ *May–mid-June and mid-Aug.–Sept., daily 8:30–6:30; mid-June–mid-Aug., daily 8–7.*

Museum of Geology. This South Dakota School of Mines and Technology museum hosts a fine collection of fossilized bones from giant dinosaurs. It also contains extensive collections of agates, fossilized cycads, rocks, gems, and minerals. ⊠ *501 E. St. Joseph St., O'Harra Memorial Building* ☎ *605/394–2467 or 800/544–8162* ✉ *Free* ☉ *Memorial Day–Labor Day, Mon.–Sat. 8–6, Sun. noon–6; Labor Day–Memorial Day, weekdays 8–5, Sat. 9–4, Sun. 1–4.*

SPORTS AND THE OUTDOORS

The Black Hills are filled with tiny mountain creeks—especially on the wetter western and northern slopes—that are ideal for fly-fishing. Rapid Creek, which flows down from the Central Hills into Pactola Reservoir and finally into Rapid City, is a favorite fishing venue for the city's anglers, both because of its regularly stocked population of trout and for its easy accessibility (don't be surprised to see someone standing in the creek casting a line as you drive through the center of town on Highway 44). Also popular are nearby Spearfish, Whitewood, Spring, and French creeks, all within an hour's drive of Rapid City.

Although they'll take you on a guided fly-fishing trip any time of the year, the folks at **Dakota Angler and Outfitter** (⌂ *513 7th St.* ☎ *605/341–2450*) recommend fishing between April and October. The guides lead individuals and groups on half- and full-day excursions, and they cater to all skill levels.

WHERE TO EAT

$$

ITALIAN

★

✕ **Botticelli Ristorante Italiano.** With a wide selection of delectable veal and chicken dishes as well as creamy pastas, this Italian eatery provides a welcome respite from Midwestern meat and potatoes. The artwork and traditional Italian music in the background give the place a European atmosphere. ⌂ *523 Main St.* ☎ *605/348–0089* ▭ *AE, MC, V.*

$$

AMERICAN

✕ **Firehouse Brewing Company.** Brass fixtures and fire-fighting equipment ornament the state's first brewpub, located in a 1915 firehouse. The five house-brewed beers are the highlight here, and the menu includes such hearty pub dishes as pastas, salads, and gumbo. Thursday night buffalo prime rib is the specialty. Kids' menus are available. ⌂ *610 Main St.* ☎ *605/348–1915* ⊕ *www.firehousebrewing.com* ⚎ *Reservations not accepted* ▭ *AE, D, MC, V* ☺ *No lunch Sun.*

$$

AMERICAN

✕ **Fireside Inn Restaurant & Lounge.** One of the two dining rooms here has tables arranged around a slate fireplace; you can also dine on an outdoor deck, weather permitting. The menu offers more than 50 entrées, including prime rib, seafood, and Italian dishes. Try the bean soup. ⌂ *Hwy. 44, 6½ mi west of town* ☎ *605/342–3900* ▭ *AE, D, MC, V.*

$$

AMERICAN–
CASUAL

✕ **Flying T Chuckwagon.** Ranch-style meals of barbecue beef, grilled chicken, potatoes, and baked beans are served on tin plates in this converted barn. Dinner is at 6:30, followed by a Western show with music and cowboy comedy. The fixed price includes dinner and the show. In summer it's a good idea to buy tickets in advance. ⌂ *U.S. 16, 6 mi south of town* ☎ *605/342–1905 or 888/256–1905* ⊕ *www.flyingt. com* ▭ *MC, V* ☺ *Closed mid-Sept.–mid-May. No lunch.*

$

CHINESE

✕ **Golden Phoenix.** Great food, low prices, convenient parking, and relaxed, friendly, and quick service make this one of South Dakota's best Chinese restaurants. The chef-owner, who often socializes with the locals who frequent his establishment, spices up traditional dishes from all over China with cooking elements from his native Taiwan. Try the Mongolian beef, sesame chicken, or Hunan shrimp. Local businesspeople crowd in for the daily lunch specials. ⌂ *2421 W. Main St.* ☎ *605/348–4195* ▭ *AE, D, MC, V.*

$$

ECLECTIC

✕ **Minerva's.** A pub and poolroom complement this spacious restaurant, next to hotels and the city's largest shopping mall. Specialties include linguine Minerva (chicken breast served on linguine with pesto, vegetables, pine nuts, and a cream sauce), rotisserie chicken, and a scrumptious rib eye with grilled onions and new potatoes. ⊠ *2111 N. LaCrosse St.* ☎ *605/394–9505* ▭ *AE, D, MC, V.*

WHERE TO STAY

$$–$$$$
★
🏨 **Audrie's Bed & Breakfast.** This secluded, romantic B&B, set in a thick woods 7 mi west of Rapid City, is filled with Victorian antiques. Suites, cottages, and creek-side cabins sleeping two come with Old World furnishings, fireplaces, private baths, hot tubs, and big-screen TVs. Bicycles and fishing poles can be obtained free from the office. **Pros:** great antiques, great treats, and great isolation. **Cons:** pricy for a B&B; tough to get a unit because of popularity; no restaurant within walking distance; no credit cards. ⊠ *23029 Thunderhead Falls Rd.* ☎ *605/342–7788* ⊕ *www.audriesbb.com* ⌁ *2 suites, 7 cottages and cabins* ♿ *In-hotel: bicycles, no kids under 21* ▭ *No credit cards* �🍴 *BP.*

$–$$
AMERICAN
🏨 **Radisson Hotel Rapid City/Mount Rushmore.** Murals of the surrounding landscape and a large Mount Rushmore mosaic in the marble floor distinguish the lobby of this nine-floor hotel in the heart of downtown Rapid City. Rooms are decorated with contemporary furnishings and earth tones, and feature Sleep Number beds, whose firmness level can be adjusted by users. The popular accommodation stands between Interstate 90 and U.S. 16, the highway that leads into the southern Black Hills and Mount Rushmore. **Pros:** centrally located downtown; Sleep Number beds; one of the premier fine-dining restaurants in the area; very clean rooms. **Cons:** rooms on the "bar side" can be noisy during busy nights; on-site parking can be crowded because of the popularity of its restaurant, Enigma. ⊠ *445 Mt. Rushmore Rd.* ☎ *605/348–8300* 🖷 *605/348–3833* ⊕ *www.radisson.com/rapidcitysd* ⌁ *176 rooms, 5 suites* ♿ *In-room:refrigerators (some). In-hotel: pool, gym, Wi-Fi* ▭ *AE, D, MC, V.*

CAMPING
🛎
🏕 **Whispering Pines Campground and Lodging.** Block party–style cookouts are followed by movies every night here as long as the weather is good. Located 16 mi west of Rapid City in Black Hills National Forest, the campground lies exactly midway between Deadwood (22 mi to the north) and Mount Rushmore (22 mi to the south). In addition to RV and tent sites, cabins are available at a reasonable price. ♿ *Flush toilets, full hookups, partial hookups (electric and water), dump station, drinking water, guest laundry, showers, fire pits, picnic tables, food service, electricity, public telephone, general store, play area, swimming (lake)* ⌁ *26 full hookups, 2 partial hookups, 45 tent sites; 5 cabins.* ⊠ *22700 Silver City Rd.* ☎ *605/341–3667* 🖷 *605/341–3667* ⊕ *www.blackhills-campresort.com* ▭ *D, MC, V* 🕙 *May–Sept.*

THE ARTS

The **Dahl Arts Center** (⊠ *713 7th St.* ☎ *605/394–4101* ⊕ *www.thedahl. org*), greatly renovated and expanded in 2009 after a major fund-raising campaign, is made up of three galleries, a children's interactive gallery, a 250-seat flexible event center, children's and adult art classrooms, conference and meeting space, and the Cyclorama, a 180-foot oil-on-canvas mural depicting U.S. economic history from the colonization by the Europeans to the 1970s. Once a popular art form, the mural with special narration and lighting is one of only three left in the country.

The technically and architecturally advanced **Rushmore Plaza Civic Center Fine Arts Theater** (✉ *444 Mt. Rushmore Rd. N* ☎ *800/468–6463*) hosts about a half-dozen touring Broadway shows in winter, and a brand-new ice arena. It's also the venue for the Vucurevich Speaker Series, a program that has attracted prominent names such as the humorist Dave Barry, the late astronomer Carl Sagan, and former Secretary of State Colin Powell.

SHOPPING

One of the world's top collections of Plains Indian artwork and crafts makes **Prairie Edge Trading Company and Galleries** (✉ *6th and Main Sts.* ☎ *605/342–3086 or 800/541–2388* ⊕ *www.prairieedge.com*) seem more like a museum than a store and gallery. With a collection ranging from books and CDs to artifact reproductions and artwork representing the Lakota, Crow, Cheyenne, Shoshone, Arapaho, and Assinniboine tribes of the Great Plains, Prairie Edge is one of the crown jewels of downtown Rapid City.

MOUNT RUSHMORE NATIONAL MEMORIAL

Fodor's Choice *24 mi southwest of Rapid City via U.S. 16 and U.S. 16A.*

★ At Mount Rushmore, one of the nation's most famous sights, 60-foot-high likenesses of Presidents George Washington, Thomas Jefferson, Abraham Lincoln, and Theodore Roosevelt grace a massive granite cliff, which, at an elevation of 5,725 feet, towers over the surrounding countryside and faces the sun most of the day. The memorial is equally spectacular at night in June through mid-September, when a special lighting ceremony dramatically illuminates the carving.

GETTING HERE AND AROUND
Access is well marked off of U.S. 16. With its southeasterly exposure, Mount Rushmore is best viewed in the morning light. Early risers also get to have breakfast with the presidents while encountering fewer people than crowds that flock to the memorial later in the day, as well as to the night lighting ceremony, the busiest interpretive program in the National Parks system.

**EN
ROUTE**
The fastest way to get from Mount Rushmore to Crazy Horse Memorial and the southern Black Hills is along Highway 244 west and U.S. 16/U.S. 385 south. This route, like all of the drives in the Black Hills, is full of beautiful mountain views, but the **Peter Norbeck National Scenic Byway** is an even more stunning, though much longer, route. Take

U.S. 16A south into Custer State Park, where buffalo, bighorn sheep, elk, antelope, and burros roam free, then drive north on Highway 87 through the Needles, towering granite spires that rise above the forest. A short drive off the highway reaches 7,242-foot Harney Peak, the highest point in North America east of the Rockies. Highway 87 finally brings you to U.S. 16/U.S. 385, where you head south to the Crazy Horse Memorial. Because the scenic byway is a challenging drive (with one-lane tunnels and switchbacks) and because you'll likely want to stop a few times to admire the scenery, plan on spending two to three hours on this drive. Note that stretches of U.S. 16A and Highway 87 may close in winter.

WHERE TO EAT

¢–$ ✕ **Buffalo Dining Room.** The only restaurant within the bounds of the
AMERICAN memorial affords commanding views of Mount Rushmore and the surrounding ponderosa pine forest, and exceptional food at a reasonable price. The menu includes New England pot roast, buffalo stew, and homemade rhubarb pie. It's open for breakfast, lunch, and dinner. ⊠ *Beginning of Ave. of Flags* ☎ *605/574–2515* ⊟ *AE, D, MC, V* ⊗ *No dinner mid-Oct.–early Mar.*

SHOPPING

The **Mount Rushmore Bookstore** (⊠ *Lincoln Borglum Museum, end of Ave. of Flags* ☎ *800/699–3142*) carries a selection of books, CDs, and videos on the memorial, its history, and the entire Black Hills region. There are also some titles on geology and Native American history. The **Mount Rushmore Gift Shop** (⊠ *Beginning of Ave. of Flags* ☎ *605/574–2515*), across from the Buffalo Dining Room, sells any number of souvenirs, from shot glasses and magnets to T-shirts and baseball caps. You can also buy Black Hills–gold jewelry and Native American art.

KEYSTONE

2 mi northwest of Mount Rushmore National Memorial via Hwy. 244 and U.S. 16.

Founded in the 1880s by prospectors searching the central Black Hills for gold deposits, this small town now serves the millions of visitors who pass through each year on their way to Mount Rushmore, 2 mi away. The touristy town has some 700 hotel rooms—more than twice the number of permanent residents. Its 19th-century buildings house dozens of gift shops, restaurants, and attractions that range from wax museums and miniature-golf courses to alpine slides and helicopter rides.

EXPLORING KEYSTONE

Stalagmites, stalactites, flowstone, ribbons, columns, helicites, and the "Big Room" are all part of the worthwhile tour into **Beautiful Rushmore Cave.** In 1876 miners found the opening to the cave while digging a flume into the mountainside to carry water to the gold mines below.

CLOSE UP

America's Shrine of Democracy

Like most impressive undertakings, Mount Rushmore's path to realization was one of personalities and perseverance.

When Gutzon Borglum, a talented and patriotic sculptor, was invited to create a giant monument to Confederate soldiers in Georgia in 1915, he jumped at the chance. The son of Danish immigrants, Borglum was raised in California and trained in art in Paris, even studying under Auguste Rodin, who influenced his style. Georgia's Stone Mountain project was to be massive in scope—encompassing the rock face of an entire peak—and would give Borglum the opportunity to exercise his artistic vision on a grand scale.

But the relationship between the project backers and Borglum went sour, causing the sculptor to destroy his models and flee the state as a fugitive. Fortunately, state officials in South Dakota had a vision for another mountain memorial, and Borglum was eager to jump on board. His passion and flamboyant personality were well matched to the project, which involved carving legends of the Wild West on a gigantic scale. In time, Borglum persuaded local officials to think larger, and the idea of carving a monument to U.S. presidents on a mountainside was born.

Borglum began carving Mount Rushmore in 1927 with the help of some 400 assistants. In consultation with U.S. Senator Peter Norbeck and State Historian Doane Robinson, Borglum chose the four presidents to signify the birth, growth, preservation, and development of the nation. In 6½ years of carving over a 14-year period, the sculptor and his crew drilled and dynamited a masterpiece,

the largest work of art on Earth. Borglum died in March 1941, leaving his son, Lincoln, to complete the work only a few months later.

Follow the Presidential Trail through the forest to gain excellent views of the colossal sculpture, or stroll the Avenue of Flags for a different perspective. Also on-site are an impressive museum, an indoor theater where films are shown, an outdoor amphitheater for live performances, and concession facilities. The nightly ranger program and lighting of the memorial is reportedly the most popular interpretive program in the whole national parks system.

The **Mount Rushmore Information Center,** between the park entrance and the Avenue of Flags, has a small exhibit with photographs of the presidents' faces as they were being carved. There's also an information desk here, staffed by rangers who can answer questions about the memorial or the surrounding Black Hills. A nearly identical building across from the information center houses restrooms, telephones, and soda machines. ⊠ *Beginning of Ave. of Flags* ☎ *605/574–3198* ⊕ *www. nps.gov/moru* ⊠ *Free; parking $10* ⊗ *May–Sept., daily 8 AM–10 PM; Oct.– Apr., daily 8–5.*

MOUNT RUSHMORE ATTRACTIONS

Avenue of Flags. Running from the entrance of the memorial to the museum and amphitheater at the base of the mountain, the avenue represents each state, commonwealth, district, and territory of the United States.

Lincoln Borglum Museum. This giant granite-and-glass structure underneath the viewing platform has permanent exhibits on the carving of the mountain, its history, and its significance. There also are temporary exhibits, a bookstore, and an orientation film. Admission is free, and it is open year-round.

Presidential Trail. This easy hike along a boardwalk and down some stairs leads to the very base of the mountain. Although the trail is thickly forested, you'll have more than ample opportunity to look straight up the noses of the four giant heads. The trail is open year-round, so long as snow and ice don't present a safety hazard.

Sculptor's Studio. Built in 1939 as Gutzon Borglum's on-site workshop, it displays tools used by the mountain carvers, a 1:12-scale model of the memorial, and a model depicting the unfinished Hall of Records. Admission is free. Open May–September.

The cave was opened to the public in 1927, just before the carving of Mount Rushmore began. ⊠ *Rte. 40, Keystone* ☎ *605/255–4384 or 605/255–4634* ⊕ *www.beautifulrushmorecave.com* ⊠ *$8.50* ☉ *June–Aug., daily 8–8; Sept. and Oct., daily 9–5.*

☾ At **Big Thunder Gold Mine** you can take a guided tour through the underground mine, get some free gold ore samples, and do a little panning yourself. ⊠ *Rte. 40, Keystone* ☎ *605/666–4847 or 800/314–3917* ⊕ *www.bigthundermine.com* ⊠ *$8* ☉ *May–mid-Oct., daily 8–8.*

WHERE TO EAT AND STAY

$$$ ✕ **Creekside Dining.** Dine on very good American cuisine at this casual
AMERICAN Keystone restaurant with a patio view of Mount Rushmore. Chef Bear's finest dishes are the hearty platters of prime rib, buffalo, lamb, chicken, and fish. Desserts, which include bread pudding, crème brûlée, and peach cobbler, are also excellent. A kids' menu is available. ⊠ *610 U.S. 16A, Keystone* ☎ *605/666–4904* ☰ *MC, V* ☉ *Closed Nov.–May.*

$–$$ ⊞ **Best Western Four Presidents.** In the shadow of Mount Rushmore in downtown Keystone, the hotel lies within walking distance of the town's major attractions, including several restaurants. Short pack tours into the hills by horseback can be arranged next door. **Pros:** great location near Mount Rushmore; great food; hotel overall is spotless. **Cons:** on the edge of town, away from most activities. ⊠ *24075 U.S. 16A* ☎ *605/666–4472* ☎ *605/666–4574* ⊕ *www.bestwestern.com* ◫ *45 rooms, 5 suites* ♿ *In-hotel: room service, pool, gym, laundry facilities* ☰ *AE, D, MC, V* ☉ *All but 3 rooms closed Nov.–Apr.* ⦿ *CP.*

$–$$$ ⊞ **Coyote Blues Village B&B.** This European-style lodge on 30 Black Hills
★ acres (12 mi north of Hill City) displays an unusual mix of antique furnishings and contemporary art. Swiss "no need for lunch" breakfasts include a variety of breads. Some rooms have a private deck with a hot tub. A creek runs through the property. **Pros:** probably the only touch of Europe in Black Hills; tucked away miles from highway with no neighbors; exceptional food. **Cons:** no walking distance to other restaurants. ⊠ *23165 Horseman's Ranch Rd., Rapid City* ☎ *605/574–4477 or 888/253–4477* ☎ *605/574–2101* ⊕ *www.coyotebluesvillage.com* ◫ *10 rooms* ♿ *In-room: refrigerator. In-hotel: gym* ☰ *AE, D, MC, V.*

$$$ ⊞ **K Bar S Lodge.** Set on 31 acres of lush green forest on the Norbeck Wildlife preserve, the K Bar S Lodge is an ideal location for a weekend getaway or a destination business conference (groups up to 200 can easily be accommodated). Be sure to request one of the rooms with a private deck, which offer picture-perfect views of Mount Rushmore. **Pros:** premier lodging in the Black Hills; can see Mount Rushmore off room balconies; staff extremely personable. **Cons:** can be crowded during special events—be sure to ask when booking. ⊠ *434 Old Hill City Rd.* ⌖ *Box 208, Keystone 57751* ☎ *605/666–4545 or 866/522–7724* ☎ *605/666–4202* ⊕ *www.kbarslodge.com* ◫ *64 rooms* ♿ *In-hotel: laundry facilities, Internet terminal* ☰ *AE, D, MC, V.*

$$ ⌂ **Mount Rushmore KOA–Palmer Gulch Lodge.** This huge commercial
☾ campground on Route 244 west of Mount Rushmore offers shuttles
★ to the mountain, bus tours, horse rides, and car rentals. There are also

large furnished cabins and primitive camping cabins, as well as a new lodge shadowed by the massive granite ramparts of Harney Peak. With its pools, waterslide, outdoor activities, and kids' programs, this is a great place for families, and parents will appreciate the three hot tubs. A shuttle takes you to Mount Rushmore and Crazy Horse for a nominal charge. **Pros:** idyllic setting; lots to do; many lodging options; great staff. **Cons:** large and busy; not for the wilderness camper. ⊠ *12620 Hwy. 244, Hill City* ☎ *605/574–2525* ⊕ *www.palmergulch.com* ↔ *500 sites (130 with full hookups, 192 with partial hookups); 85 cabins* ⚭ *no a/c (some), no phone (some), Kitchen (some), Wi-Fi, restaurant, pool, some pets allowed, flush toilets, full hookups, partial hookups (electric and water), dump station, drinking water, guest laundry, showers, fire grates, picnic tables, electricity, play area* ☉ *May–Oct.*

CRAZY HORSE MEMORIAL

Fodor's Choice ★ *15 mi southwest of Mount Rushmore National Memorial via Hwy. 244 and U.S. 16.*

Designed to be the world's largest sculpture (641 feet long by 563 feet high), this tribute to Crazy Horse, the legendary Lakota leader who defeated General Custer at Little Bighorn, is a work in progress. So far the warrior's head has been carved out of the mountain, and the head of his horse is starting to emerge; when work is under way, you can expect to witness frequent blasting. Self-taught sculptor Korczak Ziolkowski conceived this memorial to Native American heritage in 1948, and after his death in 1982 his family took on the project. The completion date is unknown, since activity is limited by weather and funding. Near the work site stands a vast orientation center, the Indian Museum of North America, Ziolkowski's studio/home and workshop, indoor and outdoor sculpture galleries, and a restaurant. ⊠ *Ave. of the Chiefs* ☎ *605/673–4681* ⚭ *Free* ☉ *May–Sept., daily 8 AM–9 PM; Oct.– Apr., daily 8–4:30.*

EXPLORING THE CRAZY HORSE MEMORIAL

Indian Museum of North America. When Ziolkowski agreed to carve Crazy Horse at the invitation of a Lakota elder, he determined that he wouldn't stop with the mountain. He wanted an educational institution to sit at the base of the mountain, complete with a center showcasing examples of Native American culture and heritage. The construction in 1972 of the Indian Museum of North America, built from wood and stone blasted from the mountain, was the initial step in that direction. The permanent collection of paintings, clothing, photographs, and artifacts represents many of the continent's tribes. There is also a space for temporary exhibits that often showcases works by modern Native American artists. ☎ *605/673–4681* ⊕ *www.crazyhorse.org* ⚭ *$10 per adult or $24 per carload for more than 2 adults* ☉ *May–Sept., daily 8 AM– 9 PM; Oct.–Apr., daily 8–4:30.*

WHERE TO EAT AND STAY

$$ ✕ **Laughing Water Restaurant.** This airy pine restaurant with windows
NATIVE facing the mountain sculpture is noted for its fry bread and buffalo
AMERICAN burgers. There's also a soup-and-salad bar, but you'd do well to stick
to the Native American offerings; try the Indian taco or "buffaloski" (a
Polish-style sausage made with Dakota buffalo). A kids' menu is available. ⊠ *Ave. of the Chiefs* ☎ *605/673–4681* ▭ *AE, D, MC, V* ☉ *Closed
Nov.–Apr.*

$–$$$ ▦ **French Creek Ranch B&B.** Soak up views of the Needles formation while
you sit on the porch of this luxurious B&B. On a 25-acre working horse
ranch, French Creek is designed to meet the needs of the traveling horse
owner: the stable has eight wooden box stalls, each with its own run.
Horses may be boarded for an additional fee. Facilities are also available
for a horse trailer or camper hookup. The ranch is 1½ mi from Custer
State Park and is open year-round. **Pros:** privacy; away from highway
noise. **Cons:** no restaurant within walking distance. ⊠ *25042 Kemp Dr.,
Custer* ☎ *605/673–4790 or 877/673–4790* ⊕ *www.frenchcreekranch.
com* ⤳ *3 rooms* ♿ *In-hotel: restaurant, tennis court, no kids under 13*
▭ *D, MC, V* ⟡ *BP.*

CUSTER STATE PARK

Fodor's Choice *13 mi south of Mount Rushmore*
★ *National Memorial via Hwy. 244
and U.S. 16.*

Down the road less traveled, in
71,000-acre Custer State Park,
scenic backcountry is watered
by crisp, clear trout streams. Elk,
antelope, deer, mountain goats,
bighorn sheep, mountain lions,
wild turkeys, prairie dogs, and the
second-largest publicly owned herd
of bison in the world (after the one
in Yellowstone National Park) walk

> **BUFFALO ROUNDUP**
>
> In late September or early October, don't miss the nation's largest
> buffalo roundup. It's one of South
> Dakota's most exciting events.
> Cowboys and park crews saddle
> up and corral the Custer State
> Park's 1,500 head of bison so
> that they may later be vaccinated.
> ☎ *605/255-4515.*

the pristine land. Some of the most scenic drives in the country roll past
fingerlike granite spires and panoramic views. Each year at the Buffalo
Roundup and Arts Festival, thousands of spectators watch the park's
1,500 bison thunder through the hills at the start of a Western-theme
art and food expo. ⊠ *U.S. 16A, 4 mi east of Custer* ☎ *605/255–4515*
⊕ *www.sdgfp.info/parks/Regions/Custer* ▤ *$6–$28. Several options
available, including 7-day passes for individuals and cars, as well as
season passes for both* ☉ *Year-round.*

**OFF THE
BEATEN
PATH**

★ **Jewel Cave National Monument.** Even though its 145 mi of surveyed
passages make this cave the world's second largest (to Kentucky's Mammoth Cave), it isn't the size of Jewel Cave that draws visitors, it's the
rare crystalline formations that abound in the cave's vast passages.
Wander the dark passageways, and you'll be rewarded with the sight of
tiny crystal Christmas trees, hydromagnesite balloons that would pop if

you touched them, and delicate calcite deposits dubbed "cave popcorn." Year-round, you can take ranger-led tours, from a simple half-hour walk to a lantern-light or wild caving tour. Costs vary by tour and group size. ⊠ *U.S. 16, 15 mi west of Custer* ☎ *605/673–2288* ⊕ *www.nps.gov/jeca* 🖃 *$4–$27* ⊙ *Sept.–Apr., daily 8–4:30; May–Aug., daily 8–7.*

WHERE TO EAT AND STAY

$$$

AMERICAN

✕ **Blue Bell Lodge and Resort.** Feast on fresh trout or buffalo, which you can have as a steak or a stew, in this rustic log building within the boundaries of Custer State Park. There's also a kids' menu. On the property, hayrides and cookouts are part of the entertainment, and you can sign up for rides on old Native American trails with the nearby stable. ⊠ *About 6 mi south of U.S. 16A junction on Hwy. 87, in Custer State Park, Custer* ☎ *605/255–4531 or 888/875–0001* ⊕ *www.custerresorts. com* ▤ *AE, D, MC, V* ⊙ *Closed mid-Oct.–Apr.*

$$–$$$$

🏨 **State Game Lodge and Resort.** Once the Summer White House for President Coolidge, and host to President Eisenhower as well, this stately stone-and-wood lodge has refurbished, well-appointed rooms, a handicapped-accessible entrance, and isolated pine-shaded cabins, many right on the banks of a creek. The cabins are simple and spartan, the motel rooms are comfortable, and the lodge rooms are almost stately, with elegant hardwood furniture and massive stone fireplaces. The adjacent Creekside Lodge has 30 upscale units, some with balconies overlooking Coolidge Creek. You can arrange for Jeep rides into the buffalo area. The excellent, upscale Pheasant Dining Room ($$–$$$) is known for pheasant and buffalo specialties. **Pros:** a sense of history; good on-site dining; the regal feel of America's great Western lodges. **Cons:** popularity makes booking tough; small lobby can get busy; must drive to other restaurants. ⊠ *13389 U.S. Hwy. 16A. 16 mi east of Custer on U.S. 16A, Custer* ⬠ *HCR 83, Box 74, Custer 57730* ☎ *605/255–4541 or 800/658–3530* ⊕ *www.custerresorts.com* 🛏 *7 lodge rooms, 40 motel rooms, 22 cabins* & *In-room: no a/c (some), no phone (some), kitchen (some), no TV. In-hotel: restaurant, bar, some pets allowed* ▤ *AE, D, MC, V* ⊙ *Closed Nov.–Apr.*

$$–$$$$

☺

★

🏨 **Sylvan Lake Resort.** This spacious stone-and-wood lodge in Custer State Park affords fantastic views of pristine Sylvan Lake and Harney Peak beyond. The rooms in the lodge are large and modern, and there are rustic cabins, some with fireplaces, scattered along the cliff and in the forest. The Lakota Dining Room ($–$$) has an exceptional view of the lake; its lovely veranda constructed of native stone is the perfect place to sip tea and watch the sunrise or enjoy a cocktail as the sun sets on the highest peak in the Black Hills. On the menu are buffalo selections and rainbow trout. You can canoe, fish, and swim in the lake, and numerous hiking trails make this a great choice for active families. **Pros:** wonderful views in the midst of a forest; multitude of lodging options; alpine atmosphere **Cons:** winding road to get there; limited dining options; can be pricy. ⊠ *16 mi east of Custer on U.S. 16A, Hill City* ⬠ *HC 83, Box 74, Custer 57730* ☎ *605/574–2561 or 888/875–0001* 🖶 *605/574–4943* ⊕ *www.custerresorts.com* 🛏 *35 rooms, 31 cabins* & *In-hotel: restaurant* ▤ *AE, D, MC, V* ⊙ *Closed mid-Oct.–Apr.*

HOT SPRINGS

8 mi south of Wind Cave National Park via U.S. 385.

A small and historic community of about 4,000 residents, Hot Springs is the gateway to Wind Cave National Park. It's also the entry point to scores of other natural and historical sites, including Evans Plunge, a large naturally heated indoor-outdoor pool; the Mammoth Site, where more than 50 woolly and Columbian mammoths have been unearthed; and the Black Hills Wild Horse Sanctuary.

EXPLORING HOT SPRINGS

Hundreds of wild mustangs inhabit **Black Hills Wild Horse Sanctuary,** an 11,000-acre preserve of rugged canyons, forests, and grasslands along the Cheyenne River. Take a guided tour or hike, and sign up for a chuck-wagon dinner. Drive 14 mi south of Hot Springs until you see signs off Route 71. ⊠ *Rte. 71* 🕿 *605/745–5955 or 800/252–6652* ⊕ *www.wild-mustangs.com* ⊠ *$15* ☉ *Memorial Day–Labor Day, Mon.–Sat. 9:30–5; tours at 10, 1, and 3.*

During the construction of a housing development in the 1970s, earth-moving equipment uncovered the **Mammoth Site,** a sinkhole where it's believed giant mammoths came to drink, got trapped, and died. More than 50 of the fossilized woolly beasts have been unearthed since digging began, and many can still be seen in situ. You can watch the excavation in progress and take guided tours. ⊠ *U.S. 18, 15 mi south of Wind Cave National Park* 🕿 *605/745–6017 or 800/325–6991* ⊕ *www. mammothsite.com* ⊠ *$7* ☉ *Daily; hrs vary, call ahead.*

WHERE TO EAT

$$ ✕ **Branding Iron Steakhouse.** Walking distance from the Mammoth Site,
STEAK this spacious restaurant is a hit among locals and visitors. Beef is king, with great rib eyes, New York strips, and prime rib, but you'll also find chicken and seafood on the menu. ⊠ *1648 U.S. Hwy. 18 Bypass, Hot Springs* 🕿 *605/745–4545* ⊟ *D, MC, V.*

$ ✕ **Woolly's Mammoth Family Fun.** A friendly couple operates this spot
AMERICAN that caters to families, with a modestly priced menu, video arcade, simulated golf, and shooting games. The location is tucked beside the Holiday Inn Express and close to the exceptional Southern Hills Golf Course. ⊠ *1403 Hwy. 18 Bypass, Hot Springs* 🕿 *605/745–6414* ⊟ *AE, MC, V.*

Wind Cave National Park

WORD OF MOUTH

"Black Hills has so much to offer. I wouldn't miss either Wind Cave National Park or Jewell Cave; take one of the guided tours. We did Wind Cave, and the kids loved it so much that we went to Jewell Cave the next day (they're only about 45 minutes from each other)."

—dw732

WELCOME TO WIND CAVE

TOP REASONS TO GO

★ **Underground exploring:** Wind Cave offers visitors the chance to get their hands and feet dirty on a four-hour guided tour through one of American's longest and most complex caves.

★ **The call of the wild:** Wind Cave National Park boasts a wide variety of animals: bison, coyote, deer, antelope, elk, prairie dogs, and 215 species of birds, to name just a few.

★ **Education by candlelight:** Wind Cave offers numerous educational and interpretive programs, including the Candlelight Cave Tour, which allows guests to explore the cave only by candlelight.

1 The Surface. Wind Cave lies at the confluence of western mountains and central plains, which blesses the park with a unique landscape. A series of established trails weaves in and out of forested hillsides and grassy meadows, providing treks of varying difficulty.

2 The Cave. With an explored maze of caverns totaling 132 mi, Wind Cave is considered one of the longest caves in the world. Notably, scientists estimate that only 5% of the cave has been explored to date. It is also estimated that 95% of the world's boxwork formations are found in Wind Cave, which means that visitors here are treated to some of the rarest geological features on the planet.

SOUTH
DAKOTA

12

GETTING ORIENTED

Bounded by Black Hills National Forest to the west and windswept prairie to the east, Wind Cave National Park, in southwestern South Dakota, encompasses the transition between two distinct ecosystems: mountain forest and mixed-grass prairie. Abundant wildlife, including bison and elk, roam the 28,295 acres of the park's diverse terrain. Underground, a year-round 53°F temperature gives summer visitors a cool oasis—and winter visitors a warm escape.

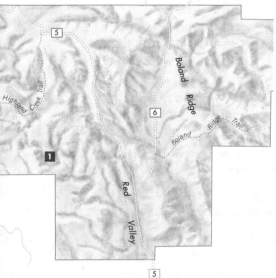

0 ⊢——⊣——⊣ 2 mi
0 ⊢——⊣——⊣ 2 km

KEY	
🏠	Ranger Station
△	Campground
🌲	Picnic Area
🍴	Restaurant
🏠	Lodge
🧗	Trailhead
🚻	Restrooms
⇉	Scenic Viewpoint
·····	Walking/Hiking Trails
······	Bicycle Path

WIND CAVE PLANNER

When to Go

The biggest crowds come to Wind Cave from June to September, but the park and surrounding Black Hills are large enough to diffuse the masses. **Neither the cave nor grounds above are ever too packed.** Park officials contend it's actually less busy during the first full week in August, when the Sturgis Motorcycle Rally brings roughly a half-million bikers to the region, clogging highways for miles around. Most hotels within a 100-mi radius are booked up to a year in advance.

The colder months are the least crowded, though you can still explore underground, thanks to the cave's constant 53°F temperature. The shoulder seasons are also unpopular, though autumn is a perfect time to visit. The days are warm, the nights are cool, and in late September/early October the park's canyons and coulees display incredible colors.

AVE. HIGH/LOW TEMPS

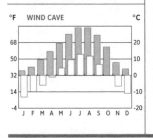

Flora and Fauna

About three-quarters of the park is grasslands. The rest is forested, mostly by the ponderosa pine. Poison ivy and poison oak are common in wetter, shadier areas, so wear long pants and boots when hiking.

The convergence of forest and prairies makes an attractive home for bison, elk, coyotes, pronghorn antelope, prairie dogs, and mule deer. Wild turkeys and squirrels are less obvious, but commonly seen by the observant hiker.

Mountain lions also live in the park; although usually shy, they will attack if surprised or threatened. Make noise while hiking to prevent chance encounters.

Bison appear docile but can be dangerous. The largest land mammal in North America, they weigh up to a ton and run at speeds in excess of 35 MPH.

Getting Here and Around

Wind Cave is 56 mi from Rapid City, via U.S. 16 and Highway 87, which runs through the park, and 73 mi southwest of Badlands National Park. The nearest commercial airport is in Rapid City. Bus lines service Rapid City and Wall. **Gray Line of the Black Hills** (☎ *605/342–4461* ⊕ *www.blackhillsgrayline.com*) offers regional tours.

U.S. 385 and Highway 87 travel the length of the park on the west side. Additionally, two unpaved roads, NPS Roads 5 and 6, traverse the northeastern part of Wind Cave. NPS Road 5 joins Highway 87 at the park's north border.

By T. D. Griffith If you don't get out of your car at Wind Cave, you haven't scratched the surface—literally. The park has more than 132 mi of underground passageways. Curious cave formations include 95% of the world's mineral boxwork, and gypsum beard so sensitive it reacts to the heat of a lamp. This underground wilderness is part of a giant limestome labyrinth beneath the Black Hills. Wind Cave ranks as fourth-longest cave in the world, but experts believe 95% of it has yet to be mapped.

12

PARK ESSENTIALS

ACCESSIBILITY
The visitor center is entirely wheelchair accessible, but only a few areas of the cave itself are navigable by those with limited mobility. Arrangements can be made in advance for a special ranger-assisted tour for a small fee.

ADMISSION FEES AND PERMITS
There's no fee to enter the park; cave tours cost $7–$23. The requisite backcountry-camping and horseback-riding permits are both free from the visitor center.

ADMISSION HOURS
The park is open year-round. It is in the mountain time zone.

ATMS/BANKS
There are no ATMs in the park. The nearest ATM and bank to the park is at the Wells Fargo Bank in Hot Springs.

CELL-PHONE RECEPTION
Cell-phone reception is hit-and-miss in the park, and western South Dakota is only serviced by Verizon Wireless and Alltel, so those with other carriers may be charged roaming fees. You won't find a public phone in the park.

PARK CONTACT INFORMATION
Wind Cave National Park ⊠ 26611 U.S. 385, Hot Springs, SD ☎ 605/745–4600 ⊕ www.nps.gov/wica.

SCENIC DRIVES

Bison Flats Drive (South Entrance). Entering the park from the south on U.S. 385 will take you past Gobbler Ridge and into the hills commonly found in the southern Black Hills region. After a couple of miles, the landscape gently levels onto the Bison Flats, one of the mixed-grass prairies on which the park prides itself. You might see a herd of grazing

WIND CAVE IN ONE DAY

Pack a picnic lunch, then head to the visitor center to purchase tickets for a morning tour of Wind Cave. Visit the exhibit rooms in the center afterward. Then drive or walk the quarter mile to the picnic area north of the visitor center. The refreshing air and deep emerald color of the pine woodlands will flavor your meal.

In the afternoon, take a leisurely drive through the parklands south of the visitor center, passing through Gobbler Pass and Bison Flats, for an archetypal view of the park and to look for wildlife. On the way back north, follow U.S. 385 east toward Wind Cave Canyon. If you enjoy bird-watching, park at a turnout and hike the 1.8-mi trail into the canyon, where you can spot swallows and great horned owls in the cliffs and woodpeckers in the trees.

Next, get back on the highway going north, take a right on Highway 87, and continue a half mile to the turnout for Centennial Trail. Hike the trail about 2 mi to the junction with Lookout Point Trail, turn right and return to Highway 87. The whole loop is about 4.75 mi. As you continue driving north to the top of Rankin Ridge, a pull-out to the right serves as the starting point for 1.25-mi Rankin Ridge Trail. It loops around the ridge, past Lookout Tower—the park's highest point—and ends up back at the pull-out. This trail is an excellent opportunity to enjoy the fresh air, open spaces, and diversity of wildlife in the park.

buffalo between here and the visitor center. You'll also catch panoramic views of the parklands, surrounding hills, and limestone bluffs.

★ **Rankin Ridge Drive (North Entrance).** Entering the park across the north border via Highway 87 is perhaps the most beautiful drive into the park. As you leave behind the grasslands and granite spires of Custer State Park and enter Wind Cave. You see the prairie, forest, and wetland habitats of the backcountry and some of the oldest rock in the Black Hills. The silvery twinkle of mica, quartz, and feldspar crystals dots Rankin Ridge east of Highway 87, and gradually gives way to limestone and sandstone formations.

WHAT TO SEE

Rankin Ridge Lookout Tower. Some of the best panoramic views of the park and surrounding hills can be seen from this 5,013-foot tower, which is typically not staffed or open to the public. Hike the 1-mi Rankin Ridge loop to get there. ⊠ *6 mi north of the visitor center on Hwy. 87.*

★ **Wind Cave.** Known to American Indians for centuries and named for the strong currents of air that alternately blow in and out of its entrance, Wind Cave was first documented by the Bingham brothers in 1881. The cave's winds are related to the difference in atmospheric pressure between the cave and the surface. When the atmospheric pressure is higher outside than inside the cave, the air blows in, and vice versa. With more than 130 mi of known passageway divided into three different levels, Wind Cave ranks the fourth longest worldwide. It's host to an incredibly diverse collection of geologic formations, including more boxwork than any other known cave, plus a series of underground lakes. The cave tours sponsored by the National Park Service allow you to see unusual and beautiful formations with names such as popcorn, frostwork, and boxwork. ⊠ *U.S. 385 to Wind Cave Visitor Center.*

VISITOR CENTER

Wind Cave Visitor Center. The park's sole visitor center is the primary place to get general information. Located on top of the cave, it has three exhibit rooms, with displays on cave exploration, the Civilian Conservation Corps, park wildlife, and resource management. ■ TIP→ There's no coffee here or elsewhere in the park, so if you need your morning caffeine fix, pick up your coffee before entering the park. ⊠ *Off U.S. 385, 3 mi north of the park's southern border* ☎ 605/745–4600 ⊕ *www.nps. gov/wica* ⊠ *Free* ⊙ *Mid-Apr.–mid-Oct., daily 8–5; mid-Oct.–early Apr., daily 8–4:30.*

SPORTS AND THE OUTDOORS

Many visitors come to Wind Cave solely to descend into the park's underground passages. While there are great ranger-led tours for casual visitors—and more daring explorations for experienced cavers—the prairie and forest above the cave shouldn't be neglected.

BIRD-WATCHING

★ **Wind Cave Canyon.** Here's one of the best birding areas in the park. The limestone walls of the canyon are ideal nesting grounds for cliff swallows and great horned owls, while the standing dead trees on the canyon floor attract red-headed and Lewis woodpeckers. As you hike down the trail, the steep-sided canyon widens to a panoramic view east across the prairies. ⊠ *About ½ mi east of the visitor center.*

Rankin Ridge. See large birds of prey here, including turkey vultures, hawks, and golden eagles. ⊠ 6 *mi north of the visitor center on Hwy. 87.*

HIKING

There are more than 30 mi of hiking trails within the boundaries of Wind Cave National Park, covering ponderosa forest and mixed-grass prairie. The landscape has changed little over the past century, so a hike through the park is as much a historical snapshot of pioneer life in the 1890s as it is exercise. Be sure to hit the Wind Cave Canyon Trail, where limestone cliffs attract birds like cliff swallows and great horned owls, and the Cold Brook Canyon Trail, a short but fun trip past a prairie-dog town to the park's edge. Besides birds and small animals such as squirrels, you're apt to see deer and pronghorn while hiking, and probably some bison.

Hiking into the wild, untouched backcountry is perfectly safe, provided you have a map (available from the visitor center) and a good sense of direction. Don't expect any developments, however; bathrooms are available only at the visitor center, and the trails are dirt or gravel. Since there are no easily accessible sources along the trails, and water from backcountry sources must be treated, pack your own.

EASY

★ **Wind Cave Canyon Trail.** This easy 1.8-mi trail follows Wind Cave Canyon to the park boundary fence. The canyon, with its steep limestone walls and dead trees, provides the best opportunity in the park for bird-watching. Be especially vigilant for cliff swallows, great horned owls, and red-headed and Lewis woodpeckers. Deer, least chipmunks, and other small animals also are attracted to the sheltered environment of the canyon. Even though you could probably do a round-trip tour of this trail in less than an hour and a half, be sure to spend more time here to observe the wildlife. This trail represents one of your best chances for seeing the park's animal inhabitants, and a little patience will almost certainly be rewarded. ⊠ *Begins on the east side of Hwy. 385, 1 mi north of the southern access road to the visitor center.*

MODERATE

Centennial Trail. Constructed to celebrate South Dakota's 100th birthday, this trail bisects the Black Hills, covering 111 mi from north to south. Designed for bikers, hikers, and horses, the trail is rugged but accommodating (note, however, that bicycling on the trail is not allowed within park boundaries). It will take you at least a half day to cover the 6 mi of this trail that traverse the park. ⊠ *Begins off Hwy. 87, 2 mi north of the visitor center.*

℃ **Cold Brook Canyon Trail.** Starting on the west side of U.S. 385, 2 mi south of the visitor center, this 1.5-mi, mildly strenuous hike runs past a former prairie-dog town, the edge of an area burned by a controlled fire in 1986, and through Cold Brook Canyon to the park boundary fence. Experienced hikers will conquer this trail and return to the trailhead in an hour or less, but more leisurely visitors will probably need more time. ⊠ *Begins on the west side of U.S. 385, 2 mi south of the visitor center.*

DIFFICULT

Boland Ridge Trail. Get away from the crowds for half a day via this strenuous, 2.5-mi round-trip hike. The panorama from the top is well worth it, especially at night. ⊠ *Trailhead off Forest Service Rd. 6, 1 mi north of the junction with Forest Service Rd. 5.*

Highland Creek Trail. This difficult, roughly 8.5-mi trail is the longest and most diverse trail within the park, traversing mixed-grass prairies, ponderosa pine forests, and the riparian habitats of Highland Creek, Beaver Creek, and Wind Cave Canyon. Even those in good shape will need a full day to cover this trail round-trip. ⊠ *Southern trailhead stems from Wind Cave Canyon trail 1 mi east of U.S. 385. Northern trailhead on Forest Service Rd. 5.*

SPELUNKING

★ You may not explore the depths of Wind Cave on your own, but you can choose from five ranger-led cave tours, available from June through August; the rest of the year, only one or two tours are available. On each tour you pass incredibly beautiful cave formations, including extremely well-developed boxwork. The least crowded times to visit in summer are mornings and weekends. The cave is 53°F year-round, so bring a sweater. Note that the uneven passages are often wet and slippery. Rangers discourage those with heart conditions and physical limitations

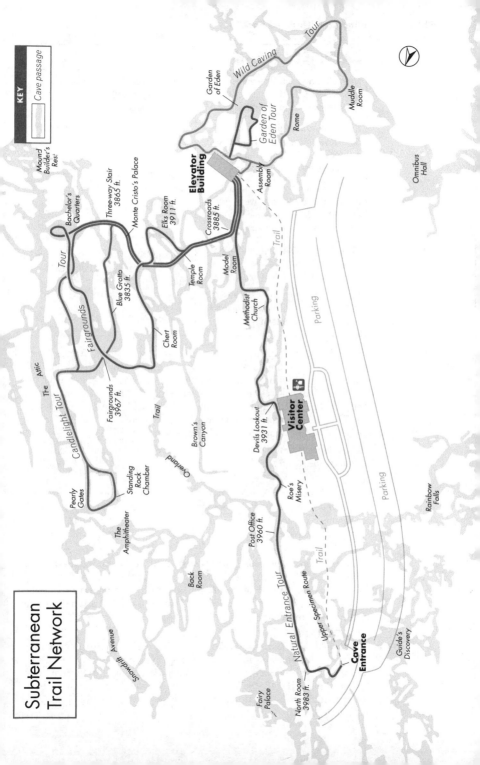

CAVEMEN SPEAK

Sound like a serious spelunker with this cavemen cheat-sheet for various *speleothems* (cave formations).

Cave balloons: Thin-walled formations resembling partially deflated balloons, usually composed of hydromagnesite.

Boxwork: Composed of interconnecting thin blades that were left in relief on cave walls when the bedrock was dissolved away.

Flowstone: Consists of thin layers of a mineral deposited on a sloping surface by flowing or seeping water.

Frostwork: Sprays of needles that radiate from a central point that are usually made of aragonite.

Gypsum beard: Composed of bundles of gypsum fibers that resemble a human beard.

Logomites: Consists of popcorn and superficially resembles a hollowed-out stalagmite.

Pool Fingers: Deposited underneath water around organic filaments.

Stalactites: Carrot-shaped formations formed from dripping water that hang down from a cave ceiling.

Stalagmites: Mineral deposits from dripping water built up on a cave floor.

from taking the organized tours. However, with some advance warning (and for a nominal fee) park rangers can arrange private, limited tours for those with physical disabilities. The park provides hard hats, knee pads, and gloves, and all cavers are required to have long pants, a long-sleeved shirt, and hiking boots or shoes with nonslip soles. If you prefer lighted passages and stairways to dark crawl spaces, a tour other than the Wild Caving Tour might appeal to you.

Tours depart from the visitor center. A schedule can be found online at ⊕ *www.nps.gov/wica*. To make a reservation, call ☎ 605/745–4600.

EASY

Garden of Eden Cave Tour. You don't need to go far to see boxwork, popcorn, and flowstone formations. Just take the relatively easy, one-hour tour, which covers about 0.25 mi and 150 stairs. It's available four times daily, June through Labor Day, and three times daily, October to early June. (It is unavailable most of September.) The cost is $7.

Natural Entrance Cave Tour. This 1¼-hour tour takes you 0.5 mi into the cave, over 300 stairs (most heading down), and out an elevator exit. Along the way are some significant boxwork deposits on the middle level. The tour costs $9 and leaves 15 times daily from June through Labor Day, and seven times daily for the rest of September.

MODERATE

★ **Candlelight Cave Tour.** Available twice daily, early June through Labor Day, this tour goes into a section of the cave with no paved walks or lighting. Everyone on the tour carries a lantern similar to those used in expeditions in the 1890s. The $9 tour lasts two hours and covers 1 mi; reservations are essential. Children younger than 8 are not admitted.

Fairgrounds Cave Tour. View examples of nearly every type of calcite formation found in the cave on this 1½-hour tour, available eight times daily, June through Labor Day. There are some 450 steps, leading up and down; the cost is $9.

DIFFICULT

Fodor'sChoice **Wild Caving Tour.** For a serious caving experience, sign up for this challenging, extraordinary, four-hour tour. After some basic training in spelunking, you crawl and climb through fissures and corridors, most lined with gypsum needles, frostwork, and boxwork. Expect to get dirty. Wear shoes with good traction, long pants, and a long-sleeve shirt. The park provides knee pads, gloves, and hard hats with headlamps. You must be at least 16 to take this tour, and 16- and 17-year-olds must show signed consent from a parent or guardian. Tours cost $23 and are available at 1 PM daily, early June through mid-August, and at 1 PM weekends mid-August through Labor Day. Reservations are essential.

EDUCATIONAL OFFERINGS

RANGER PROGRAMS

Campfire Program. A park ranger lectures for about 45 minutes on topics such as wildlife, park management, and cave history. ✉ *Elk Mountain Campground amphitheater* ✪ *June–Labor Day, nightly at 8 or 9 PM; Sept., Tues., Thurs., Sat. at 7 PM.*

Junior Ranger Program. Kids 12 and younger can earn a Junior Ranger badge by completing activities that teach them about the park's ecosystems, the cave, the animals, and protecting the environment. Pick up the Junior Ranger guidebook for $1.25 at the Wind Cave Visitor Center.

Prairie Hike. This two-hour exploration of parkland habitats begins with a short talk at the visitor center, then moves to a trailhead. ✪ *Early June–mid-Aug., daily at 9 AM.*

WHAT'S NEARBY

Hot Springs, a small and historic community of about 4,000 residents, noted for its striking sandstone structures, is the gateway to Wind Cave National Park. It is also the entry point to scores of other natural and historical sites, including Evans Plunge, a large naturally heated indoor-outdoor pool; the Mammoth Site, where more than 50 woolly and Columbian mammoths have been unearthed to date; the Black Hills Wild Horse Sanctuary, and one of the region's premier golf courses. About 30 mi north of Hot Springs, on U.S. 85, is the town of **Custer,** where George Armstrong Custer and his expedition first discovered gold in 1874, leading to the gold rush of 1875–76.

For further information about nearby towns and attractions, see chapter 11.

WHERE TO EAT AND STAY

For restaurant, hotel, and campground recommendations in the region, see chapter 11.

ABOUT THE RESTAURANTS

If you're determined to dine in Wind Cave National Park, be sure to pack your own meal, because the only dining venues inside park boundaries are the two picnic areas near the visitor center and Elk Mountain Campground. The towns beyond the park offer additional options. Deadwood claims some of the best restaurants in South Dakota. Buffalo, pheasant, and elk are relatively common ingredients in the Black Hills. No matter where you go, beef is king.

ABOUT THE HOTELS

Wind Cave claims a single campground, so you'll have to look outside park boundaries if you want to bed down in something more substantial than a tent. New chain hotels with modern amenities are plentiful in the Black Hills, but when booking accommodations consider a stay at one of the area's historic properties. From grand brick downtown hotels to intimate Queen Anne homes converted to bed-and-breakfasts, historic lodgings are easy to locate. Other distinctive lodging choices include the region's mountain lodges and forest retreats.

It may be difficult to obtain quality accommodations during summer—and downright impossible during the Sturgis Motorcycle Rally, held the first full week of August every year—so plan ahead and make reservations (three or four months out is a good rule of thumb) if you're going to travel during peak season. To find the best value, choose a hotel away from Interstate 90.

ABOUT THE CAMPGROUNDS

Camping is one of this region's strengths. While there is only one primitive campground within the park, there are countless campgrounds in the Black Hills. The public campgrounds in the national forest are accessible by road but otherwise secluded and undeveloped; private campgrounds typically have more amenities. If you're up for a more adventurous experience, most of the public land within the Black Hills is open for backcountry camping, provided that you don't light any fires and that you obtain a permit (usually free) from the appropriate park or forest headquarters. Note that the Black Hills don't have any native bears, but there is a significant population of mountain lions.

CAMPING   ⚠ **Elk Mountain Campground.** If you prefer a relatively developed camp-
$ site and relative proximity to civilization, Elk Mountain is an excellent
★   choice. You can experience the peaceful pine forests and wild creatures of the park without straying too far from the safety of the beaten path. Most of the campers who stay here pitch tents, but there are 25 pull-through sites for RVs, and sites 24 and 69 are reserved for campers with disabilities. Note that water is shut off during winter. **Pros:** generally not full; good mix of tents and RVs. **Cons:** remote; a long way to shopping or restaurants. ⊠ *½ mi north of the visitor center* ☎ *605/745–4600* ⚠ *75 sites* ⚐ *Flush toilets, running water (non-potable), fire grates, public telephone* ▭ *No credit cards* ⊙ *Apr.–late Oct.*

Badlands National Park

WORD OF MOUTH

"I recently visited Badlands National Park as part of a two-week road trip. The bold colors of the mounds and sky, as well as the interesting cloud formations, really struck me. A wind advisory was in effect and the weather was completely unpredictable. The clouds almost re-created the Badlands rock formations in the sky, and the weather allowed me to fully experience the dramatic landscape."
— Andrew Mace, Fodors.com member

WELCOME TO BADLANDS

TOP REASONS TO GO

★ **Fossils:** Since the mid-1800s, the fossil-rich Badlands area has welcomed paleontologists, research institutions, and fossil hunters who have discovered the fossil remnants of numerous species from ancient days.

★ **A world of wildlife:** Badlands National Park is home to a wide array of wildlife: antelope, deer, black-footed ferrets, prairie dogs, rabbits, coyotes, foxes, badgers.

★ **Missiles:** The Minuteman Missile Silo, located at the entrance to the park, represents the only remaining intact components of a nuclear-missile field that consisted of 150 Minuteman II missiles and 15 launch control centers, and covered over 13,500 square mi of southwestern South Dakota.

★ **Stars aplenty:** Due to its remote location and vastly open country, Badlands National Park contains some of the clearest and cleanest air in the country, which makes it perfect for viewing the night sky.

1 **North Unit.** This is the most easily accessible of the three units and attracts the most visitors. It includes the Badlands Wilderness Area.

590

Scenic

589

44

Sheep Mountain Table

Pine Ridge Indian Reservation Boundary

27

40

3
STRONGHOLD UNIT

Stronghold Table

2

Visitor Center

TO WOUNDED KNEE

2 **Palmer Creek Unit.** This is the most isolated section of the park—no recognized roads pass through its borders. You must obtain permission from private landowners to pass through their property (contact the White River Visitor Center on how to do so). If you plan on exploring here, count on spending two days—one day to hike in and one day out.

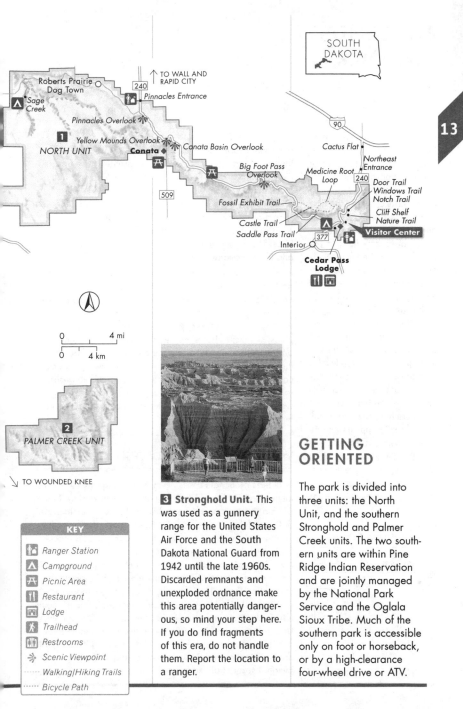

SOUTH
DAKOTA

13

TO WALL AND
RAPID CITY

240 Pinnacles Entrance

Roberts Prairie
Dog Town

Sage
Creek

Pinnacles Overlook

1 Yellow Mounds Overlook

NORTH UNIT Conata • Conata Basin Overlook

90

Cactus Flat

Northeast
Entrance

Big Foot Pass
Overlook

Medicine Root
Loop

240 Door Trail
Windows Trail
Notch Trail

Cliff Shelf
Nature Trail

509

Fossil Exhibit Trail

Castle Trail

Saddle Pass Trail

377 **Visitor Center**

Interior

**Cedar Pass
Lodge**

0   4 mi
0   4 km

2
PALMER CREEK UNIT

TO WOUNDED KNEE

KEY

🏕 Ranger Station
⛺ Campground
🪑 Picnic Area
🍴 Restaurant
🖼 Lodge
🚶 Trailhead
🚻 Restrooms
✳ Scenic Viewpoint
···· Walking/Hiking Trails
···· Bicycle Path

3 Stronghold Unit. This
was used as a gunnery
range for the United States
Air Force and the South
Dakota National Guard from
1942 until the late 1960s.
Discarded remnants and
unexploded ordnance make
this area potentially dangerous, so mind your step here.
If you do find fragments
of this era, do not handle
them. Report the location to
a ranger.

GETTING
ORIENTED

The park is divided into
three units: the North
Unit, and the southern
Stronghold and Palmer
Creek units. The two southern units are within Pine
Ridge Indian Reservation
and are jointly managed
by the National Park
Service and the Oglala
Sioux Tribe. Much of the
southern park is accessible
only on foot or horseback,
or by a high-clearance
four-wheel drive or ATV.

BADLANDS PLANNER

When to Go

Most visitors see the park between Memorial Day and Labor Day. The park's vast size and isolation prevent it from ever being too packed—though **it is usually crowded the first week of August,** when hundreds of thousands of motorcycle enthusiasts flock to the Black Hills for the annual Sturgis Motorcycle Rally. In summer temperatures typically hover around 90°F—though it can get as hot as 116°F—and sudden mid-afternoon thunderstorms are not unusual. Storms put on a spectacular show of thunder and lightning, but it rarely rains for more than 10 or 15 minutes (the average annual rainfall is 15 inches). Autumn weather is generally sunny and warm. Snow usually appears by late October. Winter can be as low as -40°F. Early spring is often wet, cold, and unpredictable. By May the weather usually stabilizes, bringing pleasant 70°F days.

AVE. HIGH/LOW TEMPS

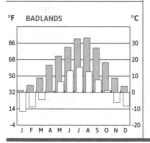

Flora and Fauna

The park's sharply defined cliffs, canyons, and mesas are near-deserts with little plant growth. Most of the park, however, is made up of mixed-grass prairies, where more than 460 species of hardy grasses and wildflowers flourish in the warmer months. Prairie coneflower, yellow plains prickly pear, pale-green yucca, buffalo grass, and sideoats grama are just a few of the plants on the badlands plateau. Trees and shrubs are rare and usually confined to dry creek beds. The most common trees are Rocky Mountain junipers and Plains cottonwoods.

It's common to see pronghorn antelope and mule deer dart across the flat plateaus; bison grazing on the buttes; prairie dogs and sharp-tailed grouse; and, soaring above, golden eagles, turkey vultures, and hawks. Also present are coyotes, swift foxes, jackrabbits, bats, gophers, porcupines, skunks, bobcats, horned lizards, bighorn sheep, and prairie rattlers. The latter are the only venomous reptiles in the park—watch for them near rocky outcroppings. Backcountry hikers might consider heavy boots and long pants reinforced with leather or canvas. Although rarely seen, weasels, mountain lions, and the endangered black-footed ferret roam the park.

Getting Here and Around

Badlands National Park is 70 mi east of Rapid City and 73 mi northeast of Wind Cave National Park in western South Dakota. It's accessed via exit 110 or 131 off Interstate 90, or Route 44 east to Route 377. Few roads, paved or otherwise, pass within the park. Badlands Loop Road (Route 240) is the most traveled and the only one that intersects I-90. It's well maintained and rarely crowded. Parts of Route 44 and Route 27 run at the fringes of the badlands, connecting the visitor centers and Rapid City. Unpaved roads should be traveled with care when wet. Sheep Mountain Table Road, the only public road into the Stronghold Unit, is impassable when wet, with deep ruts—sometimes only high-clearance vehicles can get through. Off-road driving is prohibited. There's free parking at visitor centers, overlooks, and trailheads.

By T. D. Griffith and Dustin D. Floyd

So stark and forbidding are the chiseled spires, ragged ridgelines, and deep ravines of South Dakota's badlands that Lieutenant Colonel George Custer once described them as "hell with the fires burned out." Although a bit more accessible than the depths of the underworld, the landscape is easily the strangest in the Great Plains. Ruthlessly ravaged over the ages by wind and rain, the 380 square mi of wild terrain continue to erode and evolve, sometimes visibly changing shape in a few days. Prairie creatures thrive on the untamed territory, and animal fossils are in abundance.

13

PARK ESSENTIALS

ACCESSIBILITY
Cedar Pass Lodge and the visitor centers are all fully wheelchair accessible. The Fossil Exhibit Trail and the Window Trail have reserved parking and are accessible by ramp, although they are quite steep in places. The Door, Cliff Shelf, and Prairie Wind trails are accessible by boardwalk. Cedar Pass Campground has two fully accessible sites, plus many other sites that are sculpted and easily negotiated by wheelchair users; its office and amphitheater also are accessible. The Bigfoot picnic area has reserved parking, ramps, and an accessible pit toilet. Other areas of the park can be difficult or impossible to navigate by those with limited mobility.

ADMISSION FEES AND PERMITS
The entrance fee is $7 per person or $15 per vehicle, and is good for seven days. An annual park pass is $30. A backcountry permit isn't required for hiking or camping in Badlands National Park, but it's a good idea to check in at park headquarters before setting out on a backcountry journey. Backpackers may set up camps anywhere except within a half mile of roads or trails. Open fires are prohibited.

ADMISSION HOURS
The park is open 24/7 year-round and is in the mountain time zone.

ATMS/BANKS
An ATM is located at Cedar Pass Lodge; other ATMs may be found in surrounding communities. The nearest full-service bank is in Wall.

CELL-PHONE RECEPTION
Usually near the interstate you can pick up a cell-phone signal, but within the majority of the park there is no service. You'll find pay phones at the Cedar Pass Lodge and Cedar Pass Campground.

BADLANDS IN ONE DAY

With a packed lunch and plenty of water, arrive at the park via the northeast entrance (off I-90 at exit 131) and follow Route 240 (Badlands Loop Road) southwest toward the **Ben Reifel Visitor Center.** You can pick up park maps and information here, and also pay the park entrance fee (if the booth at the entrance was closed).

Next, stop at the **Big Badlands Overlook,** just south of the northeast entrance, to get a good feel for the landscape. As you head toward the visitor center, hike any one of several trails you'll pass, or if you prefer guided walks, arrive at the visitor center in time to look at the exhibits and talk with rangers before heading down to the Fossil Exhibit Trail, where you can join the Fossil Talk at 10:30 AM (with repeats at 1:30 and 3:30 PM), usually available from early June to mid-August. Even if you miss the talk, hike this ¼-mi trail before your morning is over. The badlands are one of the richest fossil fields in the world, and along the trail are examples of six extinct creatures, now protected under clear plastic domes. After your walk, drive a couple of miles to the **Big Foot Pass Overlook,** up on the right. Here you can enjoy a packed lunch amid grassy prairies, with the rocky badland formations all around you.

After lunch, continue driving along Badlands Loop Road, stopping at the various overlooks for views and a hike or two. Near the Conata Picnic Area you'll find the **Big Pig Dig,** a fossil site that was excavated by paleontologists through the summer of 2008. When you reach the junction with **Sage Creek Rim Road,** turn left and follow it along the northern border of the 100-square-mi **Badlands Wilderness Area,** which is home to hundreds of bison. Provided the road is dry, take a side trip 5 mi down Sage Creek Rim Road to **Roberts Prairie Dog Town,** inhabited by a huge colony of the chattering critters. Children will love to watch these small rodents, which bark warning calls and dive underground if you get too close to their colony. The animals built burrow networks that once covered the Great Plains, but since European settlers established ranches in the region during the late 19th century, prairie dogs have become a far rarer sight. The park is less developed the farther you travel on Sage Creek Rim Road, allowing you to admire the sheer isolation and untouched beauty of badlands country. Hold out for a glorious sunset over the shadows of the nearby Black Hills, and keep your eyes open for animals stirring about.

PARK CONTACT INFORMATION
Badlands National Park ✑ *P.O. Box 6, Interior, SD 57750* ☎ *605/433–5361* ⊕ *www.nps.gov/badl.*

SCENIC DRIVES

For the average visitor, a casual drive is the essential means by which to see Badlands National Park. To do the scenery justice, drive slowly, and don't hesitate to get out and explore on foot when the occasion calls for it.

★ **Badlands Loop Road.** The simplest drive is on two-lane Badlands Loop Road (Route 240). The drive circles from exit 110 off Interstate 90 through the park and back to the interstate at exit 131. Start from either end and make your way around to the various overlooks along the way. Pinnacles and Yellow Mounds overlooks are outstanding places to examine the sandy pink- and brown-toned ridges and spires distinctive to the badlands. At a certain point the landscape flattens out slightly to the north, revealing spectacular views of mixed-grass prairies. The Cedar Pass area of the drive has some of the park's best trails.

13

WHAT TO SEE

HISTORIC SITES

Big Pig Dig. Until August 2008 paleontologists dug for fossils at this site named for a large fossil originally thought to be of a prehistoric pig (it actually turned out to be a small, hornless rhinoceros). Visitors will find interpretive signage detailing fossils discovered at the site. ⊠ *Conata Picnic Area, 17 mi northwest of the Ben Reifel Visitor Center.*

Stronghold Unit. With few paved roads and no campgrounds, the park's southwest section is difficult to access without a four-wheel-drive or high-clearance vehicle. However, if you're willing to trek, the unit's isolation provides a rare opportunity to explore badlands rock formations and prairies completely undisturbed. From 1942 to 1968 the U.S. Air Force and South Dakota National Guard used much of the Stronghold Unit as a gunnery range. Hundreds of fossils were destroyed by bomber pilots, who frequently targeted the large fossil remains of an elephant-size titanothere (an extinct relative of the rhinoceros), which gleamed bright white from the air. Beware of such remnants as old automobiles turned targets, unexploded bombs, shells, rockets, and other hazardous materials. If you see unexploded ordnance (UXO) while hiking in the Stronghold Unit, steer clear of it and find another route—however, note the location so you can report it to a ranger later. Within the Stronghold Unit, the **Stronghold Table**, a 3-mi-long plateau, can be reached only by crossing a narrow land bridge just wide enough to let a wagon pass. It was here, just before the Massacre at Wounded Knee in 1890, that some 600 Sioux gathered to perform one of the last known Ghost Dances, a ritual in which the Sioux wore white shirts that they believed would protect them from bullets. Permission from private landowners is required to gain access to the table; contact the White River Visitor Center for details. ⊠ *North and west of White River Visitor Center; entrance off Hwy. 27.*

SCENIC STOPS

★ **Badlands Wilderness Area.** Covering about 25% of the park, this 100-square-mi area is part of the United States' largest prairie wilderness. About two-thirds of the Sage Creek region is mixed-grass prairie, making it the ideal grazing grounds for bison, pronghorn, and many of the park's other native animals. The Hay Butte Overlook 2 mi northwest on Sage Creek Rim Road and the Pinnacles Overlook 1 mi south of the Pinnacles entrance are the best places to get an overview of the wilderness area. Feel free to park beside the road and hike your own route into the untamed, unmarked prairie—just remember that all water is unfit for drinking. ✉ *25 mi northwest of Ben Reifel Visitor Center.*

Big Badlands Overlook. From this spot just south of the park's northeast entrance, 90% of the park's 1 million annual visitors get their first views of the White River Badlands. ✉ *5 mi northeast of the Ben Reifel Visitor Center.*

Roberts Prairie Dog Town. Once a homestead, the site today contains one of the country's largest (if not the largest) colonies of black-tailed prairie dogs. ✉ *5 mi west of Badlands Loop Rd. on Sage Creek Rim Rd.*

Yellow Mounds Overlook. Contrasting sharply with the whites, grays, and browns of the badlands pinnacles, the mounds viewed from here greet you with soft yet vivid yellows, reds, and purples. ✉ *16 mi northwest of the Ben Reifel Visitor Center.*

VISITOR CENTERS

Ben Reifel Visitor Center. Open year-round, this is the park's main information hub. Stop here on your way in to pick up brochures and maps. A 22-minute video about Badlands geology and wildlife runs continually. The facility is named for a Sioux activist and the first Lakota to serve in Congress. Born on the nearby Rosebud Indian Reservation, Ben Reifel also served in the Army during World War II. ✉ *On Badlands Loop Rd., near Hwy. 377 junction, 8 mi from northeast entrance* ☎ *605/433–5361* ⊙ *June 4–Aug. 19, daily 7 AM–8 PM; Aug. 20–Sept. 9, daily 8–6; Sept. 10–June 3, daily 9–4.*

White River Visitor Center. Open only three months out of the year, this small center serves almost exclusively serious hikers and campers venturing into the Stronghold or Palmer Creek units. If you're heading into one of the southern units, stop here for maps and details about road and trail conditions. The center is located on the Pine Ridge Indian Reservation. While here, you can see fossils and Lakota artifacts, and learn about Sioux culture. ✉ *25 mi south of Hwy. 44 via Hwy. 27* ☎ *605/455–2878* ⊙ *June–Aug., daily 10–4.*

SPORTS AND THE OUTDOORS

Pure, unspoiled, empty space is the greatest asset of Badlands National Park, and it can only be experienced to its highest degree if you're on foot. Spring and autumn are the best times of the year to do wilderness exploring, since the brutal extremes of summer and winter can—and do—kill. In fact, the two biggest enemies to hikers and bicyclists in the Badlands are heat and lightning. Before you venture out, make sure you have at least one gallon of water per person per day, and be prepared to take shelter from freak thunderstorms, which often strike in the late afternoon with little warning.

AIR TOURS

OUTFIT-
TER AND
EXPEDITIONS
★

Owned and operated for 25 years by Steve Bower, **Black Hills Balloons** (☎ *605/673–2520* ⊕ *www.blackhillsballoons.com* ✉ *$245–$500*), based in Custer, provides amazing bird's-eye views of some of the Black Hills' most picturesque locations. Reservations are essential.

BICYCLING

Bicycles are permitted only on designated roads, which may be paved or unpaved. They are prohibited from closed roads, trails, and the backcountry. Flat-resistant tires are recommended.

Sheep Mountain Table Road. This 7-mi dirt road in the Stronghold Unit is ideal for mountain biking, but should be biked only when dry. The terrain is level for the first 3 mi; then it climbs the table and levels out again. At the top you can take in great views of the area. ⊠ *About 14 mi north of the White River Visitor Center.*

OUTFITTER Family-owned and -operated **Two Wheeler Dealer Cycle and Fitness** (☎ 605/343–0524 ⊕ *www.twowheelerdealer.com*), founded in 1972 and based in Rapid City, stocks more than 1,000 new bikes for sale or rent. Service is exceptional. Get trail and route information for Badlands National Park and the Black Hills at the counter.

BIRD-WATCHING

Especially around sunset, get set to watch the badlands come to life. More than 215 bird species have been recorded in the area, including herons, pelicans, cormorants, egrets, swans, geese, hawks, golden and bald eagles, falcons, vultures, cranes, doves, and cuckoos. Established roads and trails are the best places from which to watch for nesting species. The Cliff Shelf Nature Trail and the Castle Trail, which both traverse areas with surprisingly thick vegetation, are especially good locations. You may even catch sight of a rare burrowing owl at the Roberts Prairie Dog Town. Be sure to bring along a pair of binoculars.

HIKING

Fossil Exhibit Trail and Cliff Shelf Nature Trail are must-dos, but even these popular trails are primitive, so don't expect to see bathrooms or any hiking surfaces other than packed dirt and gravel. Because the weather here can be so variable, rangers suggest that you be prepared for anything. Wear sunglasses, a hat, and long pants, and have rain gear available. It's illegal to interfere with park resources, which includes everything from rocks and fossils to plants and artifacts. Stay at least 100 yards away from wildlife. Due to the dry climate, open fires are never allowed. Tell friends, relatives, and the park rangers if you're going to embark on a multiday expedition. If you have a cell phone with you, assume that it won't get a signal in the park. But most important of all, be sure to bring your own water. Sources of water in the park are few and far between, and none of them are drinkable. All water in the park is contaminated by minerals and sediment, and park authorities warn that it's untreatable. If you're backpacking into the wilderness, bring at least a gallon of water per person per day. For day hikes, rangers suggest you drink at least a quart per person per hour.

EASY

☼ **Fossil Exhibit Trail.** The trail, in place since 1964, has fossils of early
Fodor's Choice mammals displayed under glass along its ¼-mi length, which is now
★ completely wheelchair accessible. Give yourself at least an hour to fully enjoy this popular hike. ⊠ *Trail begins 5 mi northwest of the Ben Reifel Visitor Center, off Hwy. 240.*

Window Trail. This 200-yard round-trip trail ends at a natural hole, or window, in a rock wall. Looking though, you'll see more of the distinctive badlands pinnacles and spires. ⊠ *Trail begins 2 mi north of the Ben Reifel Visitor Center, off Hwy. 240.*

MODERATE

★ **Cliff Shelf Nature Trail.** This ½-mi loop winds through a wooded prairie oasis in the middle of dry, rocky ridges and climbs 200 feet to a peak above White River Valley for an incomparable view. Look for chipmunks, squirrels, and red-winged blackbirds in the wet wood, and eagles, hawks, and vultures at hilltop. Even casual hikers can complete this trail in far less than an hour, but if you want to observe the true diversity of wildlife present here, stay longer. ⊠ *Trail begins 1 mi east of the Ben Reifel Visitor Center, off Hwy. 240.*

Notch Trail. One of the park's more interesting hikes, this 1½-mi round-trip trail takes you over moderately difficult terrain and up a ladder. Winds at the notch can be fierce, but it's worth lingering for the view of the White River Valley and the Pine Ridge Indian Reservation. If you take a couple of breaks and enjoy the views, you'll probably want to plan on spending a little more than an hour on this hike. ⊠ *Trail begins 2 mi north of the Ben Reifel Visitor Center, off Hwy. 240.*

DIFFICULT

Saddle Pass Trail. This route, which connects with Castle Trail and Medicine Root Loop, is a steep, ¼-mi climb up and down the side of "The Wall," an impressive rock formation. Plan on spending about an hour on this climb. ⊠ *Trail begins 2 mi west of the Ben Reifel Visitor Center, off Hwy. 240.*

HORSEBACK RIDING

★ The park has one of the largest and most beautiful territories in the state in which to ride a horse. Riding is allowed in most of the park except for some marked trails, roads, and developed areas. The mixed-grass prairie of the Badlands Wilderness Area is especially popular with riders. However, note that the weather in the Badlands Wilderness Area can be very unpredictable. Only experienced riders or people accompanied by experienced riders should venture far from more developed areas.

There are several restrictions and regulations that you must be aware of if you plan to ride your own horse. Potable water for visitors and animals is a rarity. Riders must bring enough water for themselves and their stock. Only certified weed-free hay is approved in the park. Horses are not allowed to run free within the borders of the park. It's essential that all visitors with horses contact park officials for other restrictions that may apply.

OUTFITTER A local outfitter since 1968, **Gunsel Horse Adventures** (☎ *605/343–7608*
★ ⊕ *www.gunselhorseadventures.com* ✉ *$250 per day*) arranges pack trips into the badlands, Black Hills National Forest, and Buffalo Gap National Grassland. The four-day trips are based in one central campsite and are all-inclusive; you bring your own sleeping bag. Also available are 7- and 10-day trips. Reservations are essential.

EDUCATIONAL OFFERINGS

RANGER PROGRAMS

Evening Program. Watch a 40-minute outdoor audiovisual presentation on the wildlife, natural history, paleontology, or another aspect of the badlands. The shows typically begin around 9 PM. Check with a ranger for exact times and topics. ⊠ *Cedar Pass Campground amphitheater* ☉ *Mid-June–mid-Aug., daily usually around 9* PM.

Fossil Talk. What were the badlands like many years ago? This tour of protected fossil exhibits will inspire and answer all your questions. ⊠ *Fossil Exhibit Trail, 5 mi west of the Ben Reifel Visitor Center* ☉ *Mid-June–mid-Aug., daily at 10:30* AM, *1:30* PM, *and 3:30* PM.

Geology Walk. Learn the geologic story of the White River badlands in a 45-minute walk. The terrain can be rough in places, so be sure to wear hiking boots or sneakers. A hat is a good idea, too. ⊠ *Door and Window trails parking area, 2 mi east of the Ben Reifel Visitor Center* ☉ *Mid-June–mid-Aug., daily at 8:30* AM.

Junior Ranger Program. Children ages 7–12 may participate in this 45-minute adventure, typically a short hike, game, or other hands-on activity focused on badlands wildlife, geology, or fossils. Parents are welcome. ⊠ *Cedar Pass Campground amphitheater* ☎ *605/433–5361* ☉ *June–Aug., daily at 10:30* AM.

13

WHAT'S NEARBY

Built against a steep ridge of badland rock, **Wall** was founded in 1907 as a railroad station, and is among the closest towns to Badlands National Park, 8 mi from the Pinnacles entrance to the North Unit. Wall is home to about 850 residents and the world-famous Wall Drug Store, best known for its fabled jackalopes and free ice water. **Pine Ridge,** about 35 mi south of the Stronghold Unit, is on the cusp of Pine Ridge Indian Reservation. The town was established in 1877 as an Indian agency for Chief Red Cloud and his band of followers. With 2,800 square mi, the reservation, home, and headquarters of the Oglala Sioux, is second in size only to Arizona's Navajo Reservation.

For further information about nearby towns and attractions, see chapter 11.

WHERE TO EAT AND STAY

ABOUT THE RESTAURANTS

Dining on the prairies of South Dakota has always been a casual and family-oriented experience, and in that sense, very little has changed in the past century. Even the fare, which consists largely of steak and potatoes, has stayed consistent (in fact, in some towns, "vegetarian" can be a dirty word). But for its lack of comparative sophistication, the grub in the restaurants surrounding Badlands National Park is typically very good. You'll probably never have a better steak—beef or buffalo— outside this area. You should also try cuisine influenced by American

Indian cooking. The most popular (and best known) is the Indian taco, made from spiced meat and flat bread. In the park itself there's only one restaurant. The food is quite good, but don't hesitate to explore other options farther afield. You'll find the most choices in Wall.

ABOUT THE HOTELS

Badlands National Park is often visited by families on a vacation to see the American West, but very few opt to stay overnight here, especially when there's a profusion of accommodations in the Black Hills, situated a mere 50 mi east. As a result, there are very few lodging options in and around the park, and if you're determined to bed down within park boundaries, you have only one choice: Cedar Pass Lodge. Though rustic, it's comfortable and inexpensive. The rustic-but-comfy formula is repeated by the area's few motels, hotels, and inns. Most are chain hotels in Wall, grouped around the interstate.

ABOUT THE CAMPGROUNDS

Pitching a tent and sleeping under the stars is one of the greatest ways to fully experience the sheer isolation and unadulterated empty spaces of Badlands National Park. You'll find two relatively easy-access campgrounds within park boundaries, but only one has any sort of amenities. The second is little more than a flat patch of ground with some signs. Unless you need a flush toilet to have an enjoyable camping experience, you're just as well off hiking into the wilderness and choosing your own campsite. The additional isolation will be well worth the extra effort. You can set up camp anywhere that's at least ½ mi from a road or trail, and is not visible from any road or trail.

The handful of campgrounds located outside the park typically have more of the accoutrements of civilization. These more developed sites are more likely to attract vacationing retirees and young families, while the primitive campgrounds (and wilderness areas) seem to draw younger outdoors enthusiasts.

WHAT IT COSTS

	¢	$	$$	$$$	$$$$
Restaurants	under $8	$8–$12	$13–$20	$21–$30	over $30
Hotels	under $70	$70–$100	$101–$150	$151–$200	over $200
Campgrounds	under $10	$10–$17	$18–$35	$36–$49	over $50

Restaurant prices are per person for a main course at dinner. Hotel prices are per night for two people in a standard double room in high season, excluding taxes and service charges. Camping prices are for a standard (no hookups, pit toilets, fire grates, picnic tables) campsite per night.

WHERE TO EAT

IN THE PARK

$-$$ ╳ **Cedar Pass Lodge Restaurant.** Cool off within dark, knotty-pine walls
AMERICAN under an exposed-beam ceiling, and enjoy a hearty meal of steak, trout, or Indian tacos and fry bread. ⊠ *1 Cedar St. (Rte. 240), Inte-*

rior ☎ 605/433–5460 ⊕ *www.cedarpasslodge.com* ▭ *AE, D, MC, V* ⊗ *Closed Nov.–Mar.*

PICNIC AREAS The National Park Service provides several structured picnic areas, though you may picnic wherever your heart desires. The wind may blow hard enough to make picnicking a challenge, but the views are unrivaled. **Bigfoot Pass Overlook.** There are only a handful of tables here and no water, but the incredible view makes it a lovely spot to have lunch. Restrooms are available. ⊠ *7 mi northwest of the Ben Reifel Visitor Center on Badlands Loop Rd.*

13

Conata Picnic Area. A dozen or so covered picnic tables are scattered over this area, which rests against a badlands wall ½ mi south of Badlands Loop Road. There's no potable water, but there are bathroom facilities and you can enjoy your lunch in peaceful isolation at the threshold of the Badlands Wilderness Area. The Conata Basin area is to the east, and Sage Creek area is to the west. ⊠ *15 mi northwest of the Ben Reifel Visitor Center on Conata Rd.*

OUTSIDE THE PARK

$–$$ ✕ **Cactus Family Restaurant and Lounge.** Delicious hotcakes and pies await
AMERICAN you at this full-menu restaurant in downtown Wall. In summer you'll find a roast-beef buffet large enough for any appetite. ⊠ *519 Main St., Wall* ☎ 605/279–2561 ▭ *D, MC, V.*

¢–$$ ✕ **Elkton House Restaurant.** For a terrific hot roast-beef sandwich served
AMERICAN on white bread with gravy and mashed potatoes, make your way to this comfortable, family-friendly restaurant. The dining room is sunlit and the service is fast. ⊠ *203 South Blvd., Wall* ☎ 605/279–2152 ⊕ *www. blackhillsbadlands.com/elkton* ▭ *D, MC, V.*

¢–$ ✕ **Western Art Gallery Restaurant.** This large restaurant in the Wall Drug
AMERICAN store displays more than 200 original oil paintings, all with a Western
★ theme. Try a hot beef sandwich or a buffalo burger. The old-fashioned soda fountain has milk shakes and homemade ice cream. ⊠ *510 Main St., Wall* ☎ 605/279–2175 ⊕ *www.walldrug.com* ▭ *AE, D, MC, V.*

WHERE TO STAY

IN THE PARK

$–$$$ ⛺ **Cedar Pass Lodge.** Each small white-stucco cabin has two twin beds
★ and views of the Badlands peaks. A gallery at the lodge displays the work of local artists, and the gift shop is well stocked with local crafts, including turquoise and beadwork. There are also hiking trails on the premises. **Pros:** best star-gazing in South Dakota. **Cons:** remote location; long drive to other restaurants. ⊠ *20681 Hwy. 240., Interior* ☎ 605/433–5460 ⊕ *www.cedarpasslodge.com* ⇜ *24 cabins* ⌂ *In-room: no phone, no TV. In-hotel: restaurant, some pets allowed* ▭ *AE, D, MC, V* ⊗ *Closed Oct.–Apr.*

CAMPING ⛺ **Cedar Pass Campground.** Although it has only tent sites, this is the
$ most developed campground in the park, and it's near the Ben Reifel
★ Visitor Center, Cedar Pass Lodge, and a half-dozen hiking trails. Recently renovated to include paved interior roads, new dump station, and improved facilities. You can buy $2 bags of ice at the lodge. **Pros:** you may feel like you have the place to yourself. **Cons:** remote location;

lack of shade trees; reservations not accepted. ✉ *Hwy. 377, ¼ mi south of Badlands Loop Rd.* ☎ *605/433–5361* ⊕ *www.cedarpasslodge.com* ⚠ *96 campsites* ♻ *Flush toilets, pit toilets, dump station, drinking water, public telephone, ranger station* ⊟ *No credit cards* ⊘ *Closed mid-Oct.–mid-Apr.*

¢ ⚠ **Sage Creek Primitive Campground.** The word to remember here is primi-
(FREE) tive. If you want to get away from it all, this lovely, isolated spot sur-
rounded by nothing but fields and crickets is the right camp for you.
There are no designated campsites, and the only facilities are pit toilets
and horse hitches. **Pros:** isolated, middle of nowhere feel. **Cons:** as
primitive as it gets; long way to potable water, shopping, or restaurants.
✉ *Sage Creek Rim Rd., 25 mi west of Badlands Loop Rd.* ☎ *No phone*
⚠ *No designated sites* ♻ *Pit toilets.*

OUTSIDE THE PARK

¢ ⊡ ⚠ **Badlands Budget Host Motel.** Every room in this motel has views of
the Buffalo Gap National Grasslands, 1 mi away. You can have breakfast and dinner on the premises or walk to a nearby restaurant. Badlands
Budget also has 70 campsites ($–$$), some with full hookups. A game
room and volleyball court are on site. **Pros:** clean and comfortable; close
to the grasslands and the park. **Cons:** standard rooms with no frills.
✉ *Rte. 377, Interior* ☎ *605/433–5335 or 800/388–4643* ◀*21 rooms*
⚠ *70 campsites* ♻ *In-hotel: restaurant, pool, laundry facilities, some
pets allowed. Campground: full hookups, guest laundry, showers, play
area, fire pits, swimming (pool)* ⊟ *D, MC, V* ⊘ *Closed Oct.–Apr.*

$–$$ ⊡ **Circle View Guest Ranch.** This B&B has spectacular views and is located
♨ in the heart of the badlands. Rooms have been upgraded with queen and
king beds, private baths, a/c, and free Wi-Fi throughut. In the morning
a full ranch breakfast (generally a hearty meal of eggs, meat, potatoes,
toast, juice, and coffee) is served. A fireplace in the common area warms
up visitors on cool evenings. **Pros:** friendly people; beautiful views;
great for groups. **Cons:** small and isolated. ✉ *20055 Hwy. 44 E, Scenic*
☎ *605/433–5582* ⊕ *www.circleviewranch.com* ◀*8 rooms* ♻ *In-room:
kitchen, a/c, Wi-Fi* ⊟ *D, MC, V.*

CAMPING ⚠ **Badlands/White River KOA.** Four miles southeast of Interior, this
$$–$$$ award-winning campground's green, shady sites spread over 31 acres are
♨ pleasant and cool after a day among the dry rocks of the national park.
White River and a small creek border the property on two sides. Cabins
and cottages are also available, and you can play miniature golf and rent
bikes. The campsites have cable hookups at no extra charge. **Pros:** quiet
rural setting; lots of shade; friendly and efficient. **Cons:** remote location;
relatively large and busy. ✉ *20720 Hwy. 44, Interior* ☎ *605/433–5337*
⊕ *www.koa.com* ♻ *Flush toilets, full hookups, partial hookups (electric
and water), dump station, drinking water, showers, fire grates, picnic
tables, food service, public telephone, general store, play area, swimming (pool), Wi-Fi* ⚠ *144 sites (44 with full hookups, 38 with partial
hookups), 8 cabins* ⊟ *D, MC, V* ⊘ *Closed Oct.–mid-Apr.*

Travel Smart Montana and Wyoming

WORD OF MOUTH

"What we did, far in advance, was to contact the official state sites for each state we expected to go to—Montana, Idaho, Wyoming, South Dakota. They sent us packets that included detailed state road maps (very helpful) and other info."

—RetiredVermonter

"At Glacier National Park, I have seen it in the 80s mid-morning and then have snow showers by mid-afternoon. Moral of the story, bring layers of clothing."

—John

GETTING HERE AND AROUND

▌AIR TRAVEL

The best connections to Montana and often the shortest flights to Wyoming are through the Rockies hub cities Salt Lake City and Denver. Montana also receives transfer flights from Minneapolis, Seattle, and Phoenix. South Dakota's Black Hills may be reached via direct flight to Rapid City Regional Airport from Denver, Salt Lake City, Minneapolis, and Chicago. Once you have made your way to Denver or Salt Lake City, you will still have one or two hours of flying time to reach your final airport destination. Many of the airports in these states are served by commuter flights that have frequent stops, though generally with very short layovers. There are no direct flights from New York to the area, and most itineraries from New York take between seven and nine hours. Likewise, you cannot fly direct from Los Angeles to Montana, Wyoming, and South Dakota; it will take you four or five hours to get here from there.

At smaller airports you may need to be on hand only an hour before the flight. If you're traveling during snow season, allow extra time for the drive to the airport, as weather conditions can slow you down. If you'll be checking skis, arrive even earlier.

Airline Security Issues Transportation Security Administration (⊕ www.tsa.gov).

AIRPORTS

The major gateways are, in Montana, Missoula International Airport (MSO) and Glacier Park International Airport (GPI; in Kalispell); in Wyoming, Jackson Hole Airport (JAC), Cheyenne Regional Airport (CYS), Natrona County International Airport (CPR; in Casper), and Yellowstone Regional Airport (COD; in Cody); and in South Dakota, Rapid City Regional Airport (RAP).

Colorado Airport Information Denver International Airport (☎ 303/342–2000,

800/247–2336, or 800/688–1333 TTY ⊕ www. flydenver.com).

Montana Airport Information Glacier Park International Airport (☎ 406/257–5994 ⊕ www.glacierairport.com). **Missoula International Airport** (☎ 406/728–4381 ⊕ www. flymissoula.com).

Utah Airport Information Salt Lake City International Airport (☎ 801/575–2400 ⊕ www.slcairport.com).

Wyoming Airport Information Cheyenne Regional Airport (☎ 307/634–7071 ⊕ www. cheyenneairport.com). **Jackson Hole Airport** (☎ 307/733–7682 ⊕ www.jacksonholeairport. com). **Natrona County International Airport** (☎ 307/472–6688 ⊕ iflycasper.com). **Yellowstone Regional Airport** (☎ 307/587–5096 ⊕ www.flyyra.com).

GROUND TRANSPORTATION

All airports listed in Montana, Wyoming, and South Dakota offer shuttle services, as well as taxis and rental cars, to nearby residences and lodging properties. Thrifty travelers prefer sharing a shuttle, which can often cut costs by half, to hiring a taxi. In general, shuttles and taxis will cost less here than in urban centers. For shuttles, establish a set price with your driver before you depart from the airport to avoid any surprises, and get contact information or establish a pickup time for your return to the airport at the conclusion of your trip. Don't forget to tip—generally $1–$2 per bag.

FLIGHTS

United and Delta have the most flights to the region. Western South Dakota is served by United, Delta/Northwest, Frontier, American, and Allegiant Air.

Airline Contacts American Airlines (☎ 800/433–7300 ⊕ www.aa.com). **Continental Airlines** (☎ 800/523–3273 for U.S. and Mexico reservations, 800/231–0856 for international reservations ⊕ www.continental. com). **Delta Airlines** (☎ 800/221–1212 for

U.S. reservations, 800/241–4141 for international reservations ⊕ www.delta.com). **Frontier** (📷 800/432–1359 ⊕ www.frontierairlines.com). **Midwest Airlines** (📷 800/452–2022 ⊕ www.midwestairlines.com). **Northwest Airlines** (📷 800/225–2525 ⊕ www.nwa.com). **Southwest Airlines** (📷 800/435–9792 ⊕ www.southwest.com). **United Airlines** (📷 800/864–8331 for U.S. reservations, 800/538–2929 for international reservations ⊕ www.united.com). **USAirways** (📷 800/428–4322 for U.S. and Canada reservations, 800/622–1015 for international reservations ⊕ www.usairways.com).

∎ CAR TRAVEL

You'll seldom be bored driving through the Rockies and plains, which offer some of the most spectacular vistas and challenging driving in the world. Montana's interstate system is driver-friendly, connecting soaring summits, rivers, glacial valleys, forests, lakes, and vast stretches of prairie, all capped by that endless "Big Sky." Wyoming's interstates link classic, open-range cowboy country and mountain-range vistas with state highways headed to the geothermal wonderland of Yellowstone National Park. In Wyoming everything is separated by vast distances, so be sure to leave each major city with a full tank of gas, and be prepared to see lots of wildlife and few other people. South Dakota's Black Hills are relatively compact—about the size of Delaware—with excellent scenic highways.

Before setting out on any driving trip, it's important to make sure your vehicle is in top condition. It's best to have a complete tune-up. At the least, you should check the following: lights, including brake lights, backup lights, and emergency lights; tires, including the spare; oil; engine coolant; windshield-washer fluid; windshield-wiper blades; and brakes. For emergencies, take along flares or reflector triangles, jumper cables, an empty gas can, a fire extinguisher, a flashlight, a plastic tarp, blankets, water, and coins or a calling card for phone calls (cell phones don't always work in high mountain areas).

In the Rockies and plains, as across the nation, gasoline costs fluctuate often.

BORDER CROSSING

Driving a car across the U.S.–Canadian border is simple. Personal vehicles are allowed entry into the neighboring country, provided they are not to be left behind. Drivers must have owner registration and proof of insurance coverage handy. If the car isn't registered in your name, carry a letter from the owner that authorizes your use of the vehicle. Drivers in rental cars that are permitted to cross the border should bring along a copy of the rental contract, which should bear an endorsement saying that the vehicle is permitted to cross the border.

ROAD CONDITIONS

Roads range from multilane blacktop to barely graveled backcountry trails. Many twisting switchbacks are considerably marked with guardrails, but some primitive roads have a lane so narrow that you must back up to the edge of a steep cliff to make a turn. Scenic routes and lookout points are clearly marked, enabling you to slow down and pull over to take in the views.

Road-Condition Information Montana (📷 511 toll-free from any phone, or 800/226–7623 ⊕ www.mdt.mt.gov/travinfo/511). **Wyoming** (📷 511 toll-free from any phone, or 888/996–7623 ⊕ www.wyoroad.info). **South Dakota** (📷 511 toll-free from any phone, or 866/697–3511 ⊕ www.sddot.com).

You'll find highways and the national parks crowded in summer, and almost deserted (and occasionally impassable) in winter. You may turn right at a red light after stopping if there is no sign saying otherwise and no oncoming traffic. When in doubt, wait for the green. Follow the posted speed limit, drive defensively, and make sure your gas tank is full. In Montana, Wyoming, and South Dakota, the law requires that the driver and all passengers wear seat belts.

DRIVING IN SNOW

Highway driving through mountains and plains is safe and generally trouble-free even in cold weather. Although winter driving can present challenges, road maintenance is good and plowing is prompt. In mountain areas tire chains, studs, or snow tires are essential. If you're driving into high elevations, check the weather forecast and call for road conditions beforehand. Even main highways can close. Winter weather isn't confined to winter months in the high country, so be prepared: carry an emergency kit containing warm clothes, a flashlight, food and water, and blankets. It's also good to carry a cell phone, but be aware that the mountains, and distance from cell towers, can disrupt service. If you get stalled by deep snow, do not leave your car. Wait for help, running the engine only if needed (keep the exhaust clear, and occasionally open a window for fresh air). Assistance is never far away.

CAR RENTAL

Rates in most Montana, Wyoming, and South Dakota cities run about $50 a day and $275 to $325 a week for an economy car with air-conditioning, automatic transmission, and unlimited mileage. In resort areas such as Jackson or Kalispell, you'll usually find a variety of 4X4s and SUVs for rent, many of them with ski racks. Unless you plan to do a lot of mountain exploring, a four-wheel drive is usually needed only in winter, but if you do plan to venture onto any back roads, an SUV (about $85 a day) is the best bet because it will have higher clearance. Rates do not include tax on car rentals, which is 6% in Wyoming and 12% in South Dakota. There is no tax in Montana, but if you rent from an airport location there is an airport-concession fee.

Rental rates are similar whether at the airport or at an in-town agency. Many people fly into Salt Lake City or Denver and drive a rental car from there to cut travel costs. This makes sense if you're traveling to southern Wyoming, but if your goal is Jackson or Cody, that's a 10- to 11-hour drive from Denver. From Salt Lake City it's about a six-hour drive to Jackson and a nine-hour trip to Cody.

In the Rockies and plains you must be 21 and have a valid driver's license to rent a car. Some companies charge an additional fee for drivers ages 21 to 24, and others will not rent to anyone under age 25; most companies also require a major credit card.

Surcharges may apply if you're under 25 or if you take the car outside the area approved by the rental agency. You'll pay extra for child seats, which are compulsory for children under five (under eight in Wyoming) and cost $5 to $10 a day, and usually for additional drivers (up to $25 a day, depending on location).

▌TRAIN TRAVEL

Amtrak connects the Rockies and plains to both coasts and all major American cities. Trains run through northern Montana, with stops in Essex and Whitefish, near Glacier National Park. Connecting bus services to Yellowstone National Park are provided in the summer from Amtrak's stop in Pocatello, Idaho.

Canada's passenger service, VIA Rail Canada, stops at Jasper, near the Canadian entrance to Waterton/Glacier International Peace Park.

Information Amtrak (☎ *800/872–7245* ⊕ *www.amtrak.com*). **VIA Rail Canada** (☎ *888/842–7245* ⊕ *www.viarail.ca*).

ESSENTIALS

■ ACCOMMODATIONS

Accommodations in the Rockies and plains vary from posh resorts in ski areas such as Jackson Hole to basic chain hotels and independent motels. Dude and guest ranches often require a one-week stay, and the cost is all-inclusive. Bed-and-breakfasts can be found throughout the Rockies and plains.

The lodgings we list are the cream of the crop in each price category. We list available facilities, but we don't specify whether they cost extra. When pricing accommodations, always ask what's included and what costs extra. In almost all cases, parking is free, and only in a resort area like Jackson Hole's Teton Village will you have to pay a fee.

Most hotels and other lodgings require you to give your credit-card details before they will confirm your reservation. If you don't feel comfortable e-mailing this information, ask if you can fax it (some places even prefer faxes). However you book, get confirmation in writing and have a copy of it handy when you check in.

Be sure you understand the hotel's cancellation policy. Some places allow you to cancel without any kind of penalty—even if you prepaid to secure a discounted rate—if you cancel at least 24 hours in advance. Others require you to cancel a week in advance or penalize you the cost of one night. Small inns and B&Bs are most likely to require you to cancel far in advance. Most hotels allow children under a certain age to stay in their parents' room at no extra charge, but others charge for them as extra adults; find out the cutoff age for discounts.

■ TIP➜ Assume that hotels operate on the European Plan (EP, no meals) unless we specify that they use the Breakfast Plan (BP, with full breakfast), Continental Plan (CP, continental breakfast), Full American Plan (FAP, all meals), or Modified American Plan (MAP, breakfast and dinner), or are all-inclusive (AI, all meals and most activities).

General Information Montana Office of Tourism (✉ Department of Commerce, 301 S. Park Ave., Helena, MT ☎ 406/841–2870, 800/845-4868 ☎ TDD 406/841-2702 ⊕ www.visitmt.com). **Wyoming Travel and Tourism** (✉ 1520 Etchepare Circle, Cheyenne, WY ☎ 307/777–7777 or 800/225–5996 ⊕ www.wyomingtourism.org).

BED-AND-BREAKFASTS

Charm is the long suit of these establishments, which generally occupy a restored older building with some historical or architectural significance. They tend to be small, with fewer than 20 rooms. Breakfast is usually included in the rates.

Reservation Services Bed & Breakfast.com (☎ 512/322–2710 or 800/462–2632 ⊕ www.bedandbreakfast.com) also sends out an online newsletter. **Bed & Breakfast Inns Online** (☎ 310/280–4363 or 800/215–7365 ⊕ www.bbonline.com). **BnB Finder.com** (☎ 646/205–8016 or 888/469–6663 ⊕ www.bnbfinder.com). **Cody Lodging Co.** (✉ 1102 Beck Ave., Cody, WY ☎ 307/587–6000 or 800/587–6560 ⊕ www.codylodgingcompany.com). **Jackson Hole Central Reservations** (✉ 140 E. Broadway, Suite 24, Jackson, WY ☎ 888/838–6606 ⊕ www.jacksonholewy.com).**Black Hills Central Reservations** (✉ 68 Sherman St., Suite 206 ☎ P.O. Box 523, Deadwood, SD ☎ 866/329–7566 ⊕ www.blackhillsvacations.com).

CONDO AND CABIN RENTALS

There are rental opportunities throughout Montana and Wyoming, with the best selection in resort areas such as Big Sky and Whitefish (Big Mountain), Montana, and Jackson and Cody, Wyoming. You'll find a variety of properties ranging from one-bedroom condos to multibedroom vacation homes. The widest selection is offered by developer-owner consortiums.

Local Montana Agents Mountain Home–Montana Vacation Rentals (✉ Box 1204, Bozeman, MT 59771 ☎ 406/586–4589 or

800/550–4589 ⊕ *www.mountain-home.com).* **Resort Property Management** (✉ *3080 Pine Dr. , Big Sky, MT 59716* ☎ *406/995–4800 or 866/995–4455* 🖷 *406/993–9561* ⊕ *www. rpmbigsky.com).* **Whitefish Mountain Resort on Big Mountain** (✉ *1015 Glades Dr.* 🖶 *Box 1400 Whitefish, MT 59937* ☎ *406/862–3687 or 800/858–5439* ⊕ *www.skiwhitefish.com).*

Local Wyoming Agents Cody Area Central Reservations/Absaroka Travel (✉ *1236 Sheridan Ave., Box 984, Powell, WY* ☎ *307/754–7287 or 888/468–6996* ⊕ *www. buffalo-wy.worldweb.com).* **Cody Lodging Co.** (✉ *1102 Beck Ave., Cody, WY* ☎ *307/587–6000 or 800/587–6560* ⊕ *www.codylodgingcompany.com)* **Jackson Hole Central Reservations** (✉ *140 E. Broadway, Suite 24, Jackson, WY* ☎ *307/733–4005 or 800/443–6931* ⊕ *www.jacksonholewy.com).* **Jackson Hole Resort Lodging** (✉ *3200 McCollister Dr., Teton Village, WY* ☎ *307/733–3990 or 800/443–8613* ⊕ *www.jhrl.com).*

GUEST RANCHES

If the thought of sitting around a campfire after a hard day on the range makes your heart beat faster, consider playing dude on a guest ranch. These range from wilderness-rimmed working ranches that accept guests and encourage them to pitch in with chores and other ranch activities to luxurious resorts on the fringes of small cities, with an upscale clientele, swimming pools, tennis courts, and a lively roster of horse-related activities such as breakfast rides, moonlight rides, and all-day trail rides. Rafting, fishing, tubing, and other activities are usually available; at working ranches you may even be able to participate in a cattle roundup. In winter, cross-country skiing and snowshoeing keep you busy. Lodgings can run the gamut from charmingly rustic cabins to the kind of deluxe quarters you expect at a first-class hotel. Meals may be gourmet or plain but hearty. Many ranches offer packages as well as children's and off-season rates. The various state tourism offices also have information on dude ranches.

Information Montana Dude Ranchers' Association (✉ *Box 36, Silver Star, MT* ☎ *406/287–9878 or 888/284–4133* ⊕ *www. montanadra.com).* **Wyoming Dude Ranchers' Association** (🖶 *Box 93, Buffalo, WY 82834* ☎ *307/684–7157* ⊕ *www.wyomingdra.com).*

HOSTELS

Montana has hostels in Bozeman, East Glacier, Polebridge, and Whitefish that cater mainly to backpackers. Wyoming has a hostel in Teton Village.

Hostelling International is also an especially helpful organization for road cyclists.

Information Hostelling International—USA (🖶 *8401 Colesville Rd., Suite 600 Silver Spring, MD 20910* ☎ *301/495–1240* ⊕ *www.hiusa.org).*

HOTELS

In Montana and Wyoming most city hotels cater to business travelers, with such facilities as restaurants, cocktail lounges, swimming pools, exercise equipment, and meeting rooms. Room rates usually reflect the range of amenities offered. Most cities also have less expensive hotels that are clean and comfortable but have fewer facilities. In resort towns hotels are decidedly more deluxe, with every imaginable amenity in every imaginable price range; rural areas generally offer simple, and sometimes rustic, accommodations.

Many properties offer special weekend rates, sometimes up to 50% off regular prices. However, these deals are usually not extended during peak summer months, when hotels are normally full. The same discounts generally apply for resort-town hotels in the off-seasons.

All hotels listed have private baths unless otherwise noted.

RESORTS

Ski towns throughout the Rockies—including Big Sky and Whitefish in Montana and Jackson Hole in Wyoming—are home to dozens of resorts in all price ranges; the activities lacking in any individual property can usually be found in the town itself, in summer as well as winter. In the national parks there are both wonderfully rustic and luxurious resorts, such as Jackson Lake Lodge and Jenny Lake Lodge in Grand Teton National Park, Lake Yellowstone Hotel and the Old Faithful Snow Lodge in Yellowstone, and Many Glacier Lodge in Glacier National Park.

▮ EATING OUT

Dining in Montana and Wyoming is generally casual. Menus are becoming more varied, with such regional specialties as trout, elk, or buffalo, but you can nearly always order a hamburger or a steak. Authentic ethnic food—other than Mexican—is hard to find outside of cities. Dinner hours are from 6 PM to 9 PM. Outside the large cities and resort towns in the high seasons, many restaurants close by 9 or 10 PM. The restaurants we list are the cream of the crop in each price category.

MEALS AND MEALTIMES

You can find all types of cuisine in the major cities and resort towns, but don't forget to try native dishes such as trout, elk, and buffalo (the latter two have less fat than beef and are just as tasty); organic fruits and vegetables are also readily available. When in doubt, go for a steak, forever a Rocky Mountain and northern plains mainstay.

Rocky Mountain oysters, simply put, are bull testicles. They're generally served fried, although you can get them lots of different ways. You can find them all over the West, usually at down-home eateries, steak houses, and the like.

Unless otherwise noted, the restaurants listed in this guide are open daily for lunch and dinner.

Contacts DinnerBroker (⊕ *www.dinnerbroker. com*).**OpenTable** (⊕ *www.opentable.com*).

RESERVATIONS AND DRESS

Regardless of where you are, it's a good idea to make a reservation if you can. We mention them specifically only when reservations are essential (there's no other way you'll ever get a table) or when they are not accepted. (Large parties should always call ahead to check the reservations policy.) We mention dress only when men are required to wear a jacket or a jacket and tie.

WINES, BEER, AND SPIRITS

Microbreweries throughout the region produce a diverse selection of beers. Snake River Brewing Company in Jackson Hole, Wyoming, has won awards for its lager, pale ale, Zonker Stout, and numerous other releases. Missoula, Montana–based Big Sky Brewing Company's best seller is Moose Drool (a brown ale); the company also markets an award-winning pale ale and several other brews.

Most retail stores are open from 9 or 9:30 until 6 or 7 daily in downtown locations and until 9 or 10 in suburban shopping malls and in resort towns during high seasons. Downtown stores sometimes stay open later Thursday night. Normal banking hours are weekdays 9 to 5; some branches are also open on Saturday morning.

▮ MONEY

First-class hotel rooms in Missoula and Cheyenne cost from $85 to $225 a night; "value" hotel rooms might go for $60 to $75, and, as elsewhere in the United States, rooms in national budget chain motels go for around $60 nightly. Weekend packages, offered by most city hotels, cut prices up to 50% (but may not be available in peak winter or summer seasons). As a rule, costs outside cities are lower, except in the deluxe resorts.

In both cities and rural areas, sit-down restaurants charge between and $1 and $2 for a cup of coffee (specialty coffeehouses charge $2 to $5) and between $4 and $8 for a hamburger. A beer at a bar generally costs between $1.50 and $5, with microbrews and imports at the higher end of the range. Expect to pay double for food and drink in resort towns.

Prices throughout this guide are given for adults. Substantially reduced fees are

FOR INTERNATIONAL TRAVELERS

CAR RENTAL

When picking up a rental car, non–U.S. residents need a reservation voucher for any prepaid reservations that were made in the traveler's home country, a passport, a driver's license, and a travel policy that covers each driver. Note that in most cases, cars rented in the region are not allowed to cross into Canada.

CUSTOMS

Information **U.S. Customs and Border Protection** (P877/227–5511 wwww.cbp.gov).

ELECTRICITY

The U.S. standard is AC, 110 volts/60 cycles. Plugs have two flat pins set parallel to each other.

EMBASSIES

Contacts **Australia** (P202/797–3000 ⊕ www.austemb.org). **Canada** (☎ 202/682–1740 ⊕ www.canadianembassy.org). UK (☎ 202/588–7800 ⊕ www.britainusa.com).

For police, fire, or ambulance, dial 911 (0 in rural areas).

HOLIDAYS

New Year's Day (Jan. 1); Martin Luther King Day (3rd Mon. in Jan.); Presidents' Day (3rd Mon. in Feb.); Memorial Day (last Mon. in May); Independence Day (July 4); Labor Day (1st Mon. in Sept.); Columbus Day (2nd Mon. in Oct.); Thanksgiving Day (4th Thurs. in Nov.); Christmas Eve and Christmas Day (Dec. 24 and 25); and New Year's Eve (Dec. 31).

PASSPORTS AND VISAS

Passports are required for international travelers. Visitor visas aren't necessary for citizens of Australia, Canada, the United Kingdom, or most citizens of European Union countries coming for tourism and staying for fewer than 90 days. If you require a visa, the cost is $100, and waiting time can be substantial, depending on where you live. Apply for a visa at the U.S. consulate in your place of residence; check the U.S. State Department's special Visa Web site for further information.

Visa Information **U.S. Department of State** (⊕ travel.state.gov/visa).

PHONES

The telephone area codes are 406 for Montana, 307 for Wyoming, and 605 for South Dakota.

For international calls, dial "011" followed by the country code and the local number. For help, dial "0" and ask for an overseas operator. Most phone books list country codes and U.S. area codes. The country code for Australia is 61, for New Zealand 64, and for the United Kingdom 44. The country code for Canada is the same as the United States: 1.

CELL PHONES

The United States has several GSM (Global System for Mobile Communications) networks, so multiband mobiles from most countries (except for Japan) work here. Unfortunately, it's almost impossible to buy a pay-as-you-go mobile SIM card in the United States—which allows you to avoid roaming charges—without also buying a phone. That said, cell phones with pay-as-you-go plans are available for well under $100.

Cell phones are generally unreliable in the backcountry, especially in canyons and in remote locations far from cell towers, but coverage is improving over time.

Contacts **Verizon Wireless** (☎ 800/922–0204 ⊕ www.verizonwireless.com). **Virgin Mobile** (☎ 888/322–1122 ⊕ www.virginmobileusa.com). **Wireless from AT&T** (☎ 888/333–6651 ⊕ www.wireless.att.com/home).

almost always available for children, students, and senior citizens.

CREDIT CARDS

Throughout this guide, the following abbreviations are used: **AE**, American Express; **D**, Discover; **DC**, Diners Club; **MC**, MasterCard; and **V**, Visa.

▌PACKING

Informality reigns in the mountains and on the plains: jeans, sport shirts, and T-shirts fit in almost everywhere, for both men and women. The few restaurants and performing-arts events where dressier outfits are required, usually in resorts and larger cities, are the exception.

If you plan to spend much time outdoors, and certainly if you go in winter, choose clothing appropriate for cold and wet weather. Cotton clothing, including denim—although fine on warm, dry days—can be uncomfortable when it gets wet and when the weather's cold: a better choice is clothing made of wool or any of a number of new synthetics that provide warmth without bulk and maintain their insulating properties even when wet.

In summer you'll want shorts during the day. But because early morning and evenings can be cold, and high-mountain passes windy, pack a sweater and a light jacket, and perhaps also a wool cap and gloves. Try layering—a T-shirt under another shirt under a jacket—and peel off layers as you go. For walks and hikes, you'll need sturdy footwear. To take you into the wilds, boots should have thick soles and plenty of ankle support; if your shoes are new and you plan to spend much time on the trail, break them in at home. Bring a day pack for short hikes, along with a canteen or water bottle, and don't forget rain gear, a hat, sunscreen, and insect repellent.

In winter prepare for subzero temperatures with good boots, warm socks and liners, long johns, a well-insulated jacket, and a warm hat and gloves. Dress in lay-

ers so you can add or remove clothes as the temperatures fluctuate.

If you attend dances and other events at Native American reservations, dress conservatively—skirts or long pants for women, long pants for men—or you may be asked to leave. Be aware that you should obtain permission before you take photographs of Native Americans or their programs such as powwow dances. Generally, at a powwow the dance master will announce when it is appropriate to take photos.

When traveling to mountain areas, remember that sunglasses and a sun hat are essential at high altitudes; the thinner atmosphere requires sunscreen with a greater SPF than you might need at lower elevations.

▌PASSPORTS

Montana borders Canada, and if you plan to enter that country, you need to present a passport or a passport card (which is less expensive than a passport and can be used for ground or water—but not air—passage between the U.S. and Canada, Mexico, and Caribbean nations).

U.S. Passport Information U.S. Department of State (☎ 877/487–2778 ⊕ travel.state.gov/passport).

∎ SAFETY

Regardless of which outdoor activities you pursue or your level of skill, safety must come first. Remember: know your limits.

Many trails in the Rockies and northern plains are remote and sparsely traveled. In the high altitudes of the mountains, oxygen is scarce. Hikers, bikers, and riders should carry emergency supplies in their backpacks. Proper equipment includes a flashlight, a compass, waterproof matches, a first-aid kit, a knife, a cell phone with an extra battery (although you may have to climb atop a mountain ridge to find a signal), and a light plastic tarp for shelter. Backcountry skiers should add a repair kit, a blanket, an avalanche beacon, and a lightweight shovel to their lists. Always bring extra food and a canteen of water, as dehydration is a common occurrence at high altitudes. Never drink from streams or lakes, unless you boil the water first or purify it with tablets. Giardia, an intestinal parasite, may be present.

ALTITUDE
You may feel dizzy and weak and find yourself breathing heavily—signs that the thin mountain air isn't giving you your accustomed dose of oxygen. Take it easy and rest often for a few days until you're acclimatized. Throughout your stay drink plenty of water and watch your alcohol consumption. If you experience severe headaches and nausea, see a doctor. It is easy to go too high too fast. The remedy for altitude-related discomfort is to go down quickly into heavier air. Other altitude-related problems include dehydration and overexposure to the sun because of the thin air.

EXPOSURE
The high elevation, severe cold temperatures, and sometimes windy weather in Montana and Wyoming can often combine to create intense and dangerous outdoor conditions. In winter, exposure to wind and cold can quickly bring on hypothermia or frostbite. Protect yourself by dressing in layers, so you don't become overheated and then chilled. Any time of year, the region's clear air and high elevation make sunburn a particular risk. Always wear sunscreen, even when skies are overcast.

FLASH FLOODS
Flash floods can strike at any time and any place with little or no warning. Mountainous terrain can become dangerous when distant rains are channeled into gullies and ravines, turning a quiet streamside campsite or wash into a rampaging torrent in seconds. Similarly, desert terrain floods quickly when the land is unable to absorb heavy rain. Check weather reports before heading into the backcountry and be prepared to head for higher ground if the weather turns severe.

WILD ANIMALS
One of the most wonderful parts of the Rockies and plains is the abundant wildlife. And although a herd of grazing elk or a bighorn sheep high on a hillside is most certainly a Kodak moment, an encounter with a bear, American bison, or mountain lion is not. To avoid such a dangerous situation while hiking, make plenty of noise, keep dogs on a leash, and keep small children between adults. While camping, be sure to store all food, utensils, and clothing with food odors far away from your tent, preferably high in a tree (also far from your tent). If you do come across a bear or big cat, do not run. For bears, back away quietly; for lions, make yourself look as big as possible. In either case, be prepared to fend off the animal with loud noises, rocks, sticks, and so on. And as the saying goes, do not feed the bears—or any wild animals, whether they're dangerous or not.

When in the wilderness, give all animals their space and never attempt to feed any of them. If you want to take a photograph, use a long lens rather than a long sneak to approach closely. This is particularly important for winter visitors. Approaching an animal can cause it stress and affect its ability to survive the sometimes brutal climate. In all cases, remember that the animals have the right-of-way; this is their home, and you are the visitor.

▌ TAXES

Sales tax is 4% in Wyoming and 6% in South Dakota; Montana has no sales tax. Some areas have additional local sales and lodging taxes, which can be quite significant.

If you are crossing the border into Canada, be aware of Canada's goods and services tax (better known as the GST). This is a value-added tax of 7%, applicable on virtually every purchase except basic groceries and a small number of other items. Visitors to Canada, however, may claim a full rebate of the GST on any goods taken out of the country as well as on short-term accommodations. Rebates can be claimed either immediately on departure from Canada at participating duty-free shops or by mail within 60 days of leaving Canada. Rebate forms can be obtained from certain retailers, duty-free shops, and customs officials, or by going to the Canada Revenue Agency Web site and searching for document GST176.

Purchases made during multiple visits to Canada can be grouped together for rebate purposes. Instant cash rebates up to a maximum of $500 are provided by some duty-free shops when leaving Canada, and most provinces do not tax goods that are shipped directly by the vendor to the purchaser's home. Always save your original receipts from stores and hotels (not just credit-card receipts), and be sure the name and address of the establishment are shown on the receipt. Original receipts are not returned. To be eligible for a refund, receipts must total at least $200, and each individual receipt must show a minimum purchase of $50.

Canada Tax Refund Canada Revenue Agency (⊕ *www.cra-arc.gc.ca*).

▌ TIPPING

It is customary to tip 15% at restaurants; 20% in resort towns is increasingly the norm. For coat checks and bellhops, $1 per coat or bag is the minimum. Taxi drivers expect 10% to 15%, depending on where you are. In resort towns, ski technicians, sandwich makers, coffee baristas, and the like also appreciate tips.

TIPPING GUIDELINES FOR MONTANA AND WYOMING	
Bartender	$1 to $5 per round, depending on the number of drinks
Bellhop	$1 to $5 per bag, depending on the level of the hotel
Hotel Concierge	$5 or more, if he or she performs a service for you
Hotel Doorman	$1 to $2 for help getting a cab
Hotel Maid	$1 to $3 a day (either daily or at the end of your stay, in cash)
Hotel Room-Service Waiter	$1 to $2 per delivery, even if a service charge has been added
Porter at Airport or Train Station	$1 per bag
Skycap	$1 to $3 per bag checked
Taxi Driver	10% to 15%
Tour Guide	10% of the cost of the tour
Valet-Parking Attendant	$1 to $2, but only when you get your car
Waiter	15% to 20%, with 20% the norm at high-end restaurants; nothing additional if service is added to the bill

▌ TRIP INSURANCE

Comprehensive trip insurance is valuable if you're booking a very expensive or complicated trip (particularly to an isolated region) or if you're booking far in advance. Comprehensive policies typically cover trip cancellation and interruption, letting you cancel or cut your trip short because of illness, or, in some cases, acts of terrorism in your destination. Such policies might also cover evacuation and medical care. Some also cover you for trip delays because of bad weather or mechanical problems as well as for lost or delayed luggage.

Another type of coverage to consider is financial default—that is, when your trip is disrupted because a tour operator, airline, or cruise line goes out of business. Generally you must buy this when you book your trip or shortly thereafter, and it's available to you only if your operator isn't on a list of excluded companies.

Always read the fine print of your policy to make sure you're covered for the risks that most concern you. Compare several policies to be sure you're getting the best price and range of coverage available.

Insurance Comparison Info Insure My Trip (☎ 800/487–4722 ⊕ www.insuremytrip.com). **Square Mouth** (☎ 800/240–0369 ⊕ www. squaremouth.com).

Comprehensive Insurers Access America (☎ 800/284–8300 ⊕ www.accessamerica.com). **AIG Travel Guard** (☎ 800/826–4919 ⊕ www. travelguard.com). **CSA Travel Protection** (☎ 800/873–9855 ⊕ www.csatravelprotection. com). **Travelex Insurance** (☎ 888/228–9792 ⊕ www.travelex-insurance.com). **Travel Insured International** (☎ 800/243–3174 ⊕ www.travelinsured.com).

▮ VISITOR INFORMATION

At each visitor center and highway welcome center you can obtain maps and information; most facilities have staff on hand to answer questions. You'll also find conveniences such as phones and restrooms.

Contacts Montana Office of Tourism (✉ Department of Commerce, 301 S. Park Ave., Helena, MT ☎ 406/841–2870, 800/845–4868 ☎ TDD 406/841–2702 ⊕ www.visitmt.com). **Wyoming Travel and Tourism** (✉ 1520 Etchepare Circle, Cheyenne, WY ☎ 307/777–7777

or 800/225–5996 ☎ 307/777–2877 ⊕ www. wyomingtourism.org).

ONLINE TRAVEL TOOLS
ALL ABOUT MONTANA
The Montana Fish, Wildlife & Parks Web site has links to pages for outdoor-enthusiast information, including fishing and hunting licenses and permits, state parks and angler and hunter information, and a Montana Field Guide. The National Park Service Web site has links to information about Big Hole, Big Horn Canyon, Glacier National Park, Grant-Korhs Ranch, Little Bighorn Battlefield, the Lewis and Clark National Historic Trail, and Yellowstone National Park. *Montana Travel, or* Montana Kids.com, gives information about places that will make your family vacation kid approved. Montana Travel's Montana Big Sky Country's site has information on all the places for skiing, snowboarding, and snowmobiling, including a free winter-vacation-planning guide. Pacific Northwest Ski Areas Association provides weather conditions, information on upcoming events, snow reports, summer activities, and trip planning for Whitefish Mountain Resort and Big Mountain.

Contacts The National Park Service (⊕ www.nps.gov/state/mt). **Montana Fish, Wildlife & Parks** (⊕ fwp.mt.gov/default.html). **Montana Kids.com** (Montana Office of Tourism ⊕ montanakids.com). **Montana Travel's Montana Big Sky Country** (⊕ wintermt.com). **Pacific Northwest Ski Areas Association** (PNSAA ⊕ pnsaa.org).

ALL ABOUT WYOMING
Wyoming Travel and Tourism's Web site has informative links to Wyoming's regions, visitor services, trip planning, state parks, and more. This extensive site has a great link for planning your trip to Yellowstone, links to statewide ski and snowmobiling resorts, and tips and links to sites for outdoor enthusiasts.

Contact Wyoming Travel and Tourism (⊕ www.wyomingtourism.org).

INDEX

NOTES

ABOUT OUR WRITERS

For more decades than she cares to tally, Joyce Dalton has roamed the globe, exploring some 160 countries. Her travel articles and photos have appeared in numerous trade and consumer publications. She has contributed to several Fodor's guides and is traditional-cultures editor at www.travellady.com. She lives in Red Lodge, Montana.

Jessica Gray, a 20-year Montana resident, has explored virtually every corner of her home state. She's a regular contributor to the *Great Falls Tribune*.

For nearly a decade Amy Grisak worked on natural-history films for National Geographic television and gained extensive knowledge of Montana's wildlife. Amy and her family enjoy Montana's great outdoors year-round, and she is an avid gardener. Her writing appears in *Montana Magazine*, *Natural Home*, *Mother Earth News*, *Hobby Farms*, and the *Great Falls Tribune*.

Long-time Fodor's writer Tom Griffith, who's penned articles for such publications as *The New York Times*, the *Chicago Tribune*, *Denver Post*, and the *Houston Chronicle*, lives with his wife, Nyla, in Deadwood, S.D. He's written or co-authored more than 50 books, including *Fodor's Compass American Guides South Dakota* and *America's Shrine of Democracy*, with a foreword by President Ronald Reagan. He helped found the Mount Rushmore Preservation Fund, which raised $25 million for the mountain memorial.

Brian Kevin has covered adventure travel and the outdoors for *Outside* and Away. com, and has written about books, music, and culture for publications like *Mother Jones*, *Paste*, and *High Country News*. Author of *Fodor's Compass American Guides Yellowstone and Grand Teton*, Brian lives in Missoula, Mont., a fine basecamp for exploring the Rocky Mountain West.

Andrew McKean writes about fishing, hunting, wildlife conservation, and natural history from his home outside Glasgow, Montana. He travels the West's backcountry extensively as a field editor and contributor for several national publications. Andrew is hunting editor for *Outdoor Life* magazine and writes a weekly column on the natural history of the Northern Plains for the *Billings Gazette*. He lives on a small farm in the Milk River Valley with his wife and three children.

The experiences Ray Sikorski gained working in Yellowstone, Grand Teton, Glacier, and Denali national parks helped shape his novel *Driftwood Dan and Other Adventures*. The Bozeman-based writer's work appears in *Via*, Outside's *Go*, the *Christian Science Monitor*, and several regional publications. When not writing, Sikorski enjoys skiing, hiking, mountain biking, rock climbing, and exploring Montana's less-traveled areas.

Shauna Stephenson is the outdoors editor for the *Wyoming Tribune-Eagle* in Cheyenne. After graduating from Iowa State University, she began a career in newspapers. Covering Wyoming's outdoors has taken her to all corners of the state—making her all but useless for any sort of desk job. Most days she can be found rollicking across the wide open spaces of the high plains.